THE FACTS ON FILE DICTIONARY OF CLICHÉS

SECOND EDITION

THE FACTS ON FILE DICTIONARY OF CLICHÉS

SECOND EDITION

CHRISTINE AMMER

The Facts On File Dictionary of Clichés, Second Edition

For information contact:

Facts On File, Inc.
An imprint of Infobase Publishing
132 West 31st Street
New York NY 10001

Library of Congress Cataloging-in-Publication Data

Ammer, Christine.
The Facts On File dictionary of clichés/Christine Ammer.—2nd ed.
p. cm.
Includes index.
ISBN 0-8160-6279-X (hc: acid-free paper)
1. Clichés—Dictionaries. 2. English language—Usage—Dictionaries. I. Title: Dictionary of clichés. II. Title.
PE1689.A48 2006
423'.1—dc22 2005037999

Facts On File books are available at special discounts when purchased in bulk quantities for businesses, associations, institutions, or sales promotions. Please call our Special Sales Department in New York at (212) 967-8800 or (800) 322-8755.

You can find Facts On File on the World Wide Web at http://www.factsonfile.com

Text design by Sandra Watanabe
Cover design by Cathy Rincon

Printed in the United States of America

MP MSRF 10 9 8 7 6 5 4 3 2 1

This book is printed on acid-free paper.

Contents

In memory of Dean S. Ammer

Preface to the New Edition

While *new cliché* may seem like an oxymoron, our language is constantly changing; after all, how many folks knew about e-mail twenty years ago? And the same is true not only for individual words but also for the stock phrases we call clichés. Not only do new usages develop, but also some words and phrases die out. Thus, who today uses the phrase *corporal's guard* for a small group of some kind, or *the moving finger writes* for the passage of time? Yet both terms appeared in a dictionary of clichés published twenty years ago.

This revised and updated edition takes into account new usages and deletes some that are obsolete. I can't remember when I last heard (or saw in print) *alas and alack*, and surely *blot one's copybook* has died out along with ink-blotting and copybooks. On the other hand, I've included several hundred expressions that either qualify as clichés or are on the verge of becoming hackneyed. The business world is a rich source of new clichés, including such terms as *drum up*, *fork over*, and *go belly-up*. Another rich source is the military, which gave us *the balloon goes up*, *body count*, and *mickey mouse* and popularized *moral fiber*. Popular novels, especially mysteries and thrillers, are rife with clichés, not so much in descriptive passages as in characters' speeches. Elsewhere I've described clichés as the fast food of language, and indeed, authors of popular fiction are recording language as it is actually spoken.

Apart from these sources, I rely on the fact that new expressions, especially those used by young people, give form to the particularity of an era's attitude. A quintessential example is *whatever*, the verbal expression of what in body language is a shrug. In a *Boston Globe* column of May 10, 2005, James Carroll quoted PFC Lynndie R. England telling the judge at her court-martial that, when pressed to join in humiliating Iraqi prisoners, she said, "OK. Whatever." Not all uses of this term express such callous indifference, but it nevertheless represents a refusal of decision making, as well as a rejection of responsibility.

—Christine Ammer

Author's Note

The 4,000 or so clichés in this dictionary include some of the most commonly used verbal formulas in our language. Some of them have been so overused that they set our teeth on edge (there's one!); *have a nice day* probably fits that category. Others are useful and picturesque shorthand that simplifies communication; *an eye for an eye* is one of those. In short, not all clichés are bad, and it is not the purpose of this book to persuade speakers and writers to avoid them altogether. Rather, it is to clarify their meaning, to describe their origin, and to illustrate their use. Indeed, clichés are fine, provided that the user is aware of using them. At the very least this book helps to identify them.

For etymology, for the derivation and history of these phrases, I have relied on the standard sources used by most lexicographers. Chief among them are the early proverb collections of John Heywood, James Howell, John Ray, Erasmus, and Thomas Fuller; the record of contemporary speech made by Jonathan Swift and the dictionaries of colloquialisms by Francis Grose; and that bible of modern etymology, the *Oxford English Dictionary,* which merits one of the few acronyms used in this book, *OED.* Other modern linguists whose work has been helpful include the late Ebenezer Cobham Brewer, Eric Partridge, and John Ciardi, and the very much alive J. E. Lighter with his *Historical Dictionary of American Slang,* as well as William Safire and his many correspondents via *The New York Times.*

For quotations I have relied on similar standard sources, principally *Bartlett's Familiar Quotations* and the Oxford and Penguin dictionaries of quotations. To identify quotations from the Bible and from plays, I use the system 2:3, where 2 stands for the Bible chapter (or act of the play) and 3 for the Bible verse (or scene). Unless otherwise noted, Bible references are to the King James Version (1611).

The entries are arranged in alphabetical order, letter by letter up to the comma in the case of inversion. Thus, if a comma is part of the main term (as in *bell, book, and candle*), the entry is alphabetized as though there were no comma; if a comma is not part of the term (as in *lean over backward, to*), the alphabetization stops at the comma. Further, words in parentheses are disregarded for alphabetizing purposes; *get (something) off one's chest* is alphabetized as though it were *get off one's chest.*

Terms are listed under the initial article (*a* or *the*) only when it is an essential part of the term. For example, *the pits* is considered to begin with *t* but *a pig in a poke* is considered to begin with *p*. In phrases where a pronoun is implied, such as *lick his chops* or *take her down a peg,* I have substituted either *one(s)* or *someone;* thus it is *lick one's chops* and *take someone down a peg.* Numbers in figures, as in *A-1,* are treated as though written out (A-one). Alternate forms of a cliché are indicated by a slash, as in *make the best of it/a bad bargain.* Where there are several phrases around a central word, the term is alphabetized under that word; *to catch napping* and *to be caught napping* are found under *napping, to be caught/catch.* In cases where a reader is likely to look up an alternative word, I have supplied cross-references, which are printed in SMALL CAPITALS (for example, see also ON THE FENCE.)

Because this system is admittedly imperfect, the reader who has difficulty locating a term is advised to look in the index at the back of the book.

I am deeply indebted to the many friends and acquaintances who have lent their assistance and expertise to this project. Among those who must be singled out are the late Albert H. Morehead, who first taught me the rudiments of lexicography; and my many librarian friends, with special thanks to the reference staff of Cary Memorial Library in Lexington, Massachusetts, who unstintingly gave their precious time to help track down elusive sources. The greatest debt is owed to my late husband, Dean S. Ammer, who patiently put up with countless interruptions and supplied the best intuitive knowledge of idiomatic speech that any cliché collector could wish for. This book is vastly better owing to their help. Its errors and shortcomings are solely my own.

—Christine Ammer

a

about face, to do an To reverse a decision or change one's opinion. The term comes from the American military command to turn 180 degrees at attention, dating from the mid-nineteenth century, and by 1900 was being used figuratively. A more recent colloquial usage is *to do a 180,* but it has not yet reached cliché status.

about the size of it An approximately accurate version of a situation, event, or circumstance. It generally is used as a summing up: "That's about the size of it."

absence makes the heart grow fonder A separation enhances love. This counterpart of FAMILIARITY BREEDS CONTEMPT first appeared in an anthology of poems published in 1602 (it was the first line of an anonymous poem), but it was more or less ignored until it reappeared in 1850 as the last line of a song, "The Isle of Beauty," by T. Haynes Bayly. Within the next half-century it was used so much that by 1900 it was a threadbare cliché.

according to Hoyle On highest authority, in keeping with established rules. Edmond Hoyle, an Englishman born in 1679 and buried in 1769, wrote short treatises on five different card games (they were bound together in one volume in 1746). Within a year his name appeared on other books published by plagiarists, which also gave rules and advice for playing games. This practice has continued to the present day, and there are rule books about poker and numerous other games, all invoking the authority of Hoyle, who died long before these games were invented.

ace in the hole A hidden advantage. In stud poker the dealer gives each player a card facedown, called a "hole card"; from that point on all other cards are dealt faceup. Should the hole card be an ace, a high card, the player has an advantage unknown to his opponents. Stud poker was first introduced shortly after the Civil War and played mostly in what is now the Midwest but then was the West. In time "ace in the hole" became western slang for a hidden weapon, such as a gun carried in a shoulder holster, and by the early 1920s it was used figuratively for any hidden leverage. The related *ace up one's sleeve* comes from the practice of dishonest gamblers who would hide a winning card in just this way. See also UP ONE'S SLEEVE.

Achilles' heel A vulnerable or weak spot. The term is derived from the Greek myth of the hero Achilles, whose mother held him by the heel while dipping him into the River Styx to make him immortal. He eventually was killed by an arrow shot into his heel. The term became a literary metaphor about two centuries ago and remains current as a cliché.

acid test, the A conclusive trial to establish the truth or worth of something or someone. The term comes from a test long used to distinguish gold from copper or some other metal. Most corrosive acids do not affect gold, but a solution of nitric acid and hydrochloric acid dissolves the metal. Used literally by jewelers in the late nineteenth century, the term soon was employed figuratively, by U.S. president Woodrow Wilson among others.

across the board Affecting all classes and categories. The term, originally American, comes from horse-racing, where a bet covering all winning possibilities—win (first place), place (second place), or show (third place)—was so described. By about 1950 it was extended to other situations, principally of an economic nature, as in across-the-board wage increases (for all employees), tax reductions (for all brackets), air-fare increases, and the like.

actions speak louder than words What you do is more important than what you say. A proverb appearing in ancient Greek as well as in practically every modern language, this precise wording dates from the nineteenth century. A fifteenth-century version was "A man ought not to be deemed by his wordes, but by his workis" (*Dictes and Sayenges of the Philosophirs,* 1477).

act your age Don't be childish or act foolish. This admonition appears to date from the 1920s. "Be your age" is the caption of a 1925 *New Yorker* cartoon; "act your age" appears in a 1932 issue of *American Speech,* a journal that chronicles current usage.

add fuel to the fire/flames, to To exacerbate an already inflammatory situation, increasing anger or hostility. The Roman historian Livy used this turn of phrase (in Latin) nearly two thousand years ago, and it was repeated (in English) by numerous writers thereafter, among them John Milton (*Samson Agonistes,* 1671): "He's gone, and who knows how he may report thy words by adding fuel to the flame."

add insult to injury, to To make harm worse by adding humiliation. The phrase has been traced to a Greek fable in a bald man, trying to kill a fly on his head, misses and hits himself very hard, and the fly replies, "You wanted to kill me for merely landing on you; what will you do to yourself now that you have added insult to injury?" It has since been applied to countless situations by as many writers, and has long been a cliché.

a dog's age A long time. An American slang term dating from about 1830, this expression doesn't make a great deal of sense, since the average dog is not especially long-lived. It appeared in print in 1836: "That blamed line gale has kept me in bilboes such a dog's age" (*Knickerbocker* magazine).

a dog's life Miserable circumstances. The term has been traced to Erasmus, who pointed out the wretched subservient existence of dogs in the mid-sixteenth century, as well as to the seventeenth-century proverb, "It's a dog's life, hunger and ease." It was certainly a cliché by the time Rudyard Kipling (*A Diversity of Creatures,* 1899) wrote, "Politics are not my concern. . . . They impressed me as a dog's life without a dog's decencies." See also DIE LIKE A DOG.

afraid of one's own shadow Extremely timid, excessively fearful. In *Richard III* (c. 1513), Sir Thomas More wrote, "Who may lette her feare her owne shadowe," although a few years later Erasmus cited Plato as having said the same thing in Greek hundreds of years before. Henry David Thoreau used the phrase to describe the timidity of Concord's town selectmen in refusing to toll the parish bell at John Brown's hanging (1859), and by then it had been in use for at least two centuries.

after one's own heart Precisely to one's liking. Considered a cliché since the late nineteenth century, this phrase appears in the Old Testament's first Book of Samuel (13:14): "The Lord hath sought him a man after his own heart, and the Lord hath commanded him to be captain over his people."

against the grain, to go "There was something about Prohibition that went against the American grain," a high school history teacher once said, quite innocent of her pun on this phrase, which means contrary to expectations, custom, or common sense. The literal meaning, against the natural direction of the fibers in a piece of wood, was turned figurative by Shakespeare in *Coriolanus* ("Preoccupied with what you rather must do than what you should, made you against the grain to voice him consul"). By the time Dickens used it in *Edwin Drood* (1870) it probably was already a cliché.

age before beauty Defer to the older person. This phrase is traditionally used when inviting another individual to pass through a doorway before one. Eric Partridge described it as a mock courtesy uttered by a young woman to an older man. Currently it is used only ironically or sarcastically. According to an old story, it was said rather snidely by Clare Boothe Luce when ushering Dorothy Parker through a doorway, and Parker replied, "Pearls before swine." A related cliché is *after you, Alphonse—no, after you,*

Gaston, repeated a number of times (in Britain, *after you, Claude—no, after you, Cecil*). The American version is based on a comic strip by Frederick Burr Opper, *Alphonse and Gaston,* which was popular in the early 1900s, and pokes fun at exaggerated politeness.

ahead of the pack In advance of the rest of a group, doing better than the others. The noun *pack* has been used for a group of persons since the 1400s, although for about 400 years it had a derogatory connotation, as in "a pack of thieves." That sense is not implied in the cliché. The act of advancing beyond the others is called *breaking out of the pack.*

A related phrase is *ahead of the game,* meaning in a position of advantage, usually financial advantage. The *game* here alludes to gambling, but the term is applied to any endeavor.

aid and abet, to To assist and promote or encourage something or someone. The pairing of these nearly synonymous verbs, always in this order, comes from criminal law, where it denotes helping, facilitating and promoting the commission of a crime. The verbs themselves are quite old, *aid* dating from about 1400 and *abet* from about 1300. Although the term still is principally used in relation to criminal actions, it gradually crept into more general speech, as in "The influx of Canada geese on the golf course, aided and abetted by people feeding them . . ."

ain't it the truth That's definitely so. This slangy phrase dates from about 1900. It is often put regretfully—That's so but I wish it weren't—as in "'I'll have to lower the price if I want to sell it fast.'—'Ain't it the truth.'"

albatross around one's neck, an A burden or curse. The figurative meaning comes straight from Coleridge's *The Rime of the Ancient Mariner* (1798), a narrative poem in which a young sailor who shot an albatross, considered an extremely unlucky action, was punished by having the dead bird hung around his neck.

alive (live) and kicking (well) Very much alive and alert; still surviving. The term originated with fishmongers who thus described their wares, meaning that they were extremely fresh. By the mid-nineteenth century it was considered a cliché. A more recent version is *alive and well,* which originated as a denial to a false report of someone's death. It was given a boost by the French singer Jacques Brel, whose show and recording, translated as *Jacques Brel Is Alive and Well and Living in Paris,* became immensely popular in the 1970s.

all and sundry Everyone, both collectively and individually. The term dates from at least the fourteenth century and is tautological—that is, it needlessly repeats the same thing, just as the related *each and every* does.

all bets are off The agreement is canceled, because the relevant conditions have changed. This phrase comes from gambling, such as betting on a horse race, where it indicates that wagers are withdrawn. It is much more widely applied, as in "They say the wedding's scheduled for December, but to tell you the truth, all bets are off."

all cats are gray after dark/at night Without sufficient knowledge one cannot distinguish between alternatives. This assertion appeared in numerous proverb collections, beginning with John Heywood's of 1546, where it was put, "When all candels be out, all cats be grey." A still older version, dating back some 2,000 years and stated by the Roman writers Ovid and Plutarch as well as by later writers, had it that all women are the same in the dark, a view now disputed by all but the most hardened misogynists.

all ears, to be To pay close attention to what is said. The term may have originated in John Milton's *Comus* (1634): "I am all ear and took in strains that might create a soul under the ribs of death." It has been used again and again, by Anthony Trollope and others, to the present day.

all for naught Everything done has been in vain. Today a poetic word for "nothing," *naught* formerly meant "morally bad" or "worthless." Thus the King James version of the first Book of Kings (2:19) says, "The water is naught and the ground barren."

all hell breaks loose Chaos prevails. The expression crops up often in Elizabethan poetry (Robert Greene, Ben Jonson, William Shakespeare) and continued to be used by an amazing number of fine poets (Milton, Dryden, Swift, and Browning, among others).

all intents and purposes, for (to) In practical terms; virtually. Since *intent* and *purpose* mean the same thing, the term is a tautology. According to Eric Partridge, it has been a cliché since the mid-nineteenth century. It originated in English law in the 1500s, when it was even more long-windedly phrased, *to all intents, constructions and purposes.*

all in the/a day's work To be considered a normal part of one's job or routine. Traced back to the eighteenth century, the expression occurred with considerable frequency and was used both seriously and ironically: "As the huntsman said when the lion ate him" (Charles Kingsley, *Westward Ho!,* 1855).

all in the same boat See IN THE SAME BOAT AS.

all one's ducks in a row, get/have Be completely prepared and well organized. This colloquialism from the second half of the 1900s alludes to lining up target ducks in a shooting gallery. Sue Grafton used it in *R Is for Ricochet* (2004): "The trick is not to alert him until we have all our ducks in a row."

all other things (else) being equal Given the same circumstances. This term began as the Latin phrase *ceteris paribus;* sometimes the word *all* is omitted, and *else* is substituted for *other things.* Eric Partridge held that the Latin form was already a cliché in the eighteenth century, and the English form became one in the late nineteenth century. Thomas Babington Macaulay was among the many learned writers who used it (although slightly differently) in his *History of England* (1849–61): "All other circumstances being supposed equal . . ."

all over but the shouting, it's The outcome is certain, though it may not yet be widely known. Probably originating in the mid-nineteenth century, the phrase was first used for the outcome of sporting events, elections, and similar competitive undertakings, and still is.

all over creation Everywhere. This homespun cliché uses *creation* in the sense of everything in the world that, by implication, God created.

all present and accounted for Everyone (or everything) is here. This cliché originated in the military as a response to roll call and actually is redundant—if one is present one is also accounted for. The British version, *all present and correct,* where *correct* means "in order," makes more sense but did not cross the Atlantic.

all roads lead to Rome Any of several choices will lead to the same result. The metaphor is based on the ancient empire's system of roads, which radiated from the capital like the spokes of a wheel. As a figure of speech it appeared as early as the twelfth century. It was used by Chaucer, and occurs in numerous other languages as well.

all's fair in love and war Any tactic or strategy is permissible. The idea was expressed for centuries by numerous writers, from Chaucer (*Troilus and Criseyde*) to Maxwell Anderson (*What Price Glory?*). Modern versions sometimes add or substitute another enterprise, such as "in love and war and politics" (George Ade), or "in love and tennis (or any other competitive sport)."

all systems go Everything is ready for action. The term is relatively new, originating in the space launches of the 1960s, and became well known through widespread television coverage of these events. John Powers, the public information officer for the United States space program from 1959 to 1964, would announce, "All systems go. Everything is A-OK." The phrase soon was extended to other endeavors.

all that glitters is not gold Appearances can be deceiving. A proverbial saying since the late Middle Ages, it appears in numerous languages to this day. O. Henry wrote a story entitled "The Gold That Glittered," and two other writers observed in addition that "all isn't garbage that smells."

all things considered When everything has been taken into account. The modern sense implies a careful weighing of all circumstances involved, making this phrase a precautionary one (compare it to WHEN ALL'S SAID AND DONE). G. K. Chesterton used it as the title of a collection of his essays (1908), and it also is the name of a thoughtful but long-winded talk show on U.S. public radio. In both cases it is the idea of thoughtfulness that is stressed. In ordinary speech the phrase has been in common use for about a century.

all things to all men, to be To adapt so as to satisfy everyone. The term appears in the New Testament of the Bible, in the first book of Corinthians (9:22): "I am made all things to all men, that I might by all means save some." Today it is more often used negatively—that is, one cannot be all things to all men, although political candidates in particular continue to try. Eric Partridge believed it was a cliché by the nineteenth century.

all thumbs, to be To be clumsy. The locution was already considered proverbial in John Heywood's collection in 1546 ("When he should get ought, eche fynger is a thumbe") and has been repeated countless times since.

all-time high (low) A record achievement (or failure), never before surpassed. An Americanism from the early twentieth century, the term has been applied to matters economic (production), recreational (golf score), and numerous other areas.

all to the good Largely an advantage. The term dates from the days when *good* was an accounting term that meant profit or worth, so that "all to the good" meant net profit. By the late nineteenth century the meaning had become much more general and the phrase a cliché.

all wet, to be To be completely mistaken. The expression is American slang that became current in the first half of the twentieth century. It is not known what *wet* refers to—soaked from a rainstorm or dunking, drunk and therefore incapable of good judgment, or something else.

all wool and a yard wide Genuine, not a sham. The expression comes from the yard-goods industry, where a seller would claim that a piece of cloth was 100 percent wool and measured fully a yard, in contrast to inferior material and short measures.

almighty dollar, the The power of money; by extension, crass materialism. The term was used by Washington Irving in *The Creole Village* (1836) ("The almighty dollar, that great object of universal devotion"), perhaps echoing Ben Jonson's sentiment of two centuries earlier ("That for which all virtue now is sold, and almost every vice—almighty gold").

a long face, to wear/draw/pull To look sad or dissatisfied. A common expression in the nineteenth century, it no doubt came from the elongated look resulting from the mouth being drawn down at the corners and the eyes downcast.

along for the ride, to go/to come/just To take part but passively. The phrase, originating in the United States in the mid-twentieth century, implies some of the acquiescence of *go along with* but makes it clear that one is not IN THE DRIVER'S SEAT.

alpha and omega, the The sum of something, the beginning and the end, symbolized by the first (alpha) and last (omega) letters of the Greek alphabet. The Book of Revelation (1:8) states: "I am Alpha and Omega, the beginning and the ending, saith the Lord." The modern equivalent is *a to z*. See also FROM SOUP TO NUTS.

American dream, the The image of prosperity, achievable through hard work. A political cliché invoked by candidates, it was used by Alexis de Tocqueville in *Democracy in America* (1835) but may be even older. In 1975 psychoanalyst David Abrahansen was quoted as saying, "The American dream is in part responsible for a great deal of crime and violence, because people feel that the country owes them not only a living but a good living." A similar cliché of even less precise definition is *the American way,* evoking an image of democracy, fairness, and other desirable traits.

an apple a day (keeps the doctor away) A proverbial preventive remedy. Versions of this saying date from the seventeenth century or earlier, appearing in John Ray's proverb collection of 1670 and elsewhere. A cliché by the late nineteenth century, it gave rise to numerous humorous versions, such as "A stanza a day to keep the wolf away" by the poet Phyllis McGinley.

and then some A great deal more, more of the same. This intensifier is used in such contexts as "Their house needs new paint, a new roof, new landscaping, and then some," or "There were speeches by the president, vice-president, chief financial officer, general counsel, and then some." The phrase dates from the early 1900s.

an open book, he/she is (like an) Very obvious. See READ SOMEONE LIKE AN OPEN BOOK.

another day, another dollar Another day's work is done. The expression became current in the United States in the early twentieth century, presumably when a dollar a day was a living wage.

ants in one's pants Extremely restless, jumpy. This vivid metaphor no doubt has survived because of its rhyming character, just as alliteration enhanced its seventeenth-century forerunner, *a breeze (gadfly) in one's breech(es).* Several twentieth-century writers are credited with popularizing the phrase; among them are George Kaufman and Moss Hart, in *The Man Who Came to Dinner* (1939): "I'll get the ants out of those moonlit pants." The cliché also gave rise to the slangy adjective *antsy,* for restless or jumpy.

any port in a storm Any relief is welcome when one is in great difficulties. The phrase appears in an eighteenth-century play by James Cobb and in *Fanny Hill* (1759), by John Cleland, where it is suggested that it was already common.

A-OK Excellent. The term dates from a specific incident in 1961, when the National Aeronautics and Space Administration's Colonel "Shorty" Power misunderstood astronaut Alan Shepard's "OK" for "A-OK," indicating that his suborbital flight was going well. The term caught on, along with other space-flight terms that entered the language about the same time.

A-1 The best quality. The term originated in the 1775 edition of *Lloyd's Register of British and Foreign Shipping,* in which the state of a ship's hull was designated by a letter grade and the condition of the anchor, cables, and so forth by a number grade. This insurance rating was soon transferred to numerous other areas and has been a cliché since the late nineteenth century.

a poor thing but mine own It may not be much, but it belongs to me. The phrase misquotes Touchstone's description of Audrey in Shakespeare's *As You Like It* (5.4): "An ill-favour'd thing, sir, but mine own." It has been a cliché since the mid-nineteenth century.

apple of one's eye, the A cherished person or thing. The term comes from the ancient concept that the eye's pupil was a solid, apple-shaped body, and, being essential to sight, was precious. It appears in the Bible (Deuteronomy 32:10): "He [the Lord] kept him [Israel] as the apple of his eye."

apple-pie order Very neat. One writer speculates that the term originated in the practice of New England housewives meticulously arranging apple slices on a pie crust. However, more likely it was a British corruption of the French *nappes pliées,* neat as "folded linen," from the early seventeenth century. By the time Dickens used it in *Our Mutual Friend* (1865) it was already a cliché.

apples and oranges, like comparing Comparing two unlike objects or issues. This term, dating from the second half of the 1900s, has largely replaced *the difference between chalk and cheese,* at least in America. The latter expression of disparateness is much older, dating from the 1500s. Why apples and oranges and not some other object is unclear, especially given their similarity in that both are fruits. Nevertheless, it has caught on and is on the way to being a cliché.

après moi le déluge After I'm dead nothing will matter. This cliché, literally meaning "after me, the flood," was allegedly said in slightly different form in 1757 by Madame de Pompadour to Louis XV after Frederick the Great defeated the French and Austrians at Rossbach. (She put it *après nous le déluge,* "after us the flood.") The flood alludes to the biblical flood in which all but those on Noah's ark perished. The phrase is still always stated in French.

April showers bring May flowers Adversity is followed by good fortune. An old proverb, it was taken more literally in days gone by, and in fact it appeared in a British book of *Weather Lore* published in 1893.

apron strings, tied to (someone's) Under someone's influence. Like being UNDER SOMEONE'S THUMB, the term denotes being completely ruled by another, in this case usually a male being ruled by a woman (the traditional wearer of aprons). It probably was already a cliché by the time Thomas Babington Macaulay wrote (1849) of William of Orange, "He could not submit to be tied to the apron strings of even the best of wives." Indeed, two hundred years earlier England had a law called *apron-string tenure,* whereby a husband could hold title to property passed on by his wife's family only while his wife was alive.

armchair general A self-proclaimed military expert with little or no practical experience, who imposes his or her views on others. See also BACKSEAT DRIVER; MONDAY-MORNING QUARTERBACK.

armed to the teeth Overequipped, overprepared to do battle. The phrase was popularized through a speech by English statesman Richard Cobden in 1849, in which he held that too much of Britain's wealth was devoted to armaments. However, *to the teeth* has meant completely equipped since the fourteenth century. *Libeaus Disconus* (c. 1350) had it, "All yarmed to the teth."

as all getout To the utmost, as much as possible. This homespun cliché dates from the first half of the nineteenth century, when it was usually stated *as getout.* Mark Twain wrote, "We got to dig in like all git-out" (*Huckleberry Finn,* 1884). It remains current.

ASAP See PDQ.

as I live and breathe I am certain, I am confident. This redundant phrase—one can't be alive and not breathe—is usually stated with a sense of mild surprise. It began life as simply *as I live* in the mid-1600s and continues to be used as an intensifier—for example, "As I live and breathe, he's gone and bought another new car"—but is heard less often today.

ask a silly/stupid question (and you'll get a silly/stupid answer) A response to an unsatisfying answer or to one that is a put-down. Eric Partridge believed this nineteenth-century retort evolved from the proverb ASK ME NO QUESTIONS, I'LL TELL YOU NO LIES, but the two clichés are not identical.

ask me no questions, I'll tell you no lies If you want the truth, better not ask directly. Listed in the *Oxford Dictionary of Proverbs,* this saying recurs throughout 150 years of English literature, from Oliver Goldsmith's *She Stoops to Conquer* (1773), in which the lies are "fibs," to George Bernard Shaw's *Man and Superman* (1903).

asleep at the switch Daydreaming or forgetting to do one's job; a lapse in alertness. The term comes from American railroading, when trainmen were required to switch a train from one track to another. If they failed to do so at the right time, trains could collide.

as luck would have it As it happened, how things turned out. The phrase, with either "good" luck or "ill" luck, goes back as far as Shakespeare, who used it (as good luck) in *The Merry Wives of Windsor* (3.5), as did Thomas Shelton (as ill luck) in a translation of *Don Quixote* of the same period.

as old as Adam Extremely ancient, well known long ago. The Adam reference, of course, is to the first book of the Bible, in which Adam is the first human being created by God. The *OED* traces the expression only to 1867. Similar clichés include OLD AS THE HILLS and FROM TIME IMMEMORIAL. See also KNOW (SOMEONE) FROM ADAM.

as one man Unanimously, together. The term appears in the King James Version of the Book of Judges (20:8): "And all the people arose as one man." More recently John R. Green used it in *A Short History of the English People* (1876): "Spain rose as one man against the stranger."

ass in a sling, to have/get one's To be in deep trouble. The ass referred to is not the animal but the vulgar term for buttocks. The expression probably originated in the American South in the nineteenth century, and it is thought to refer to a kick in the buttocks so strong that the victim requires the kind of sling used to support an injured arm. The saying was common by about 1930.

as the crow flies By the most direct or shortest route. Since crows normally fly straight to their food supply, this simile came into use as the shortest distance between two points. It originated in the late eighteenth century or even earlier.

as we know it As something is currently understood or viewed. This phrase usually implies that current conditions will change, as, for example, "Nuclear warfare will mark the end of civilization as we know it." First recorded in the late 1800s, the phrase began to be widely used from the 1940s on and has reached cliché status.

as we speak, (even) At this moment, right now. An oral equivalent of AT THIS JUNCTURE. For example, "When is her plane due?—It's landing even as we speak."

at a loss, to be To be puzzled or unable to come to a decision. The English clergyman Charles Colton (c. 1780–1832) wrote, "As completely at a loss as a Dutchman without his pipe, a Frenchman without his mistress, an Italian without his fiddle, or an Englishman without his umbrella" (*Lacon,* Part 2, no. 116). One may also be at a loss *for* something, most often *at a loss for words,* meaning that one is rendered speechless.

at a snail's pace Very slowly. The slowness of snails was pointed out about 200 B.C. by the Roman poet Plautus and the term "snail's pace" in English goes back to about 1400. Relative to its size, however, a snail travels a considerable distance each day, using the undersurface of its muscular foot to propel itself.

at loggerheads, to be To disagree, dispute, or quarrel. A *logger* was a heavy wooden block, and one meaning of "loggerhead" is "blockhead," a stupid person or dolt. Possibly this meaning led to the phrase "at loggerheads," with the idea that only dolts would engage in a quarrel. Shakespeare used the word as an adjective in *The Taming of the Shrew* (4.1): "You loggerheaded and unpolish'd grooms." The full current expression appeared in the late seventeenth century.

at long last Finally, after a long delay. The expression has been traced to the sixteenth century and was usually put as "at the long last," *last* then being a noun meaning "duration." Eric Partridge cited its perhaps most famous use, the opening words of the abdication speech of King Edward VIII in 1935, when he gave up the British throne in order to marry a divorced woman. By then it had long been a cliché.

at one fell swoop A single operation, often a violent one. This term was coined by Shakespeare, who used the metaphor of a hell-kite (probably a vulture) killing chickens for the murder of Macduff's wife and children: "Oh, Hell-Kite! All? What, all my pretty chickens and their dam at one fell swoop?" (*Macbeth,* 4.3). The adjective *fell* was Old English for "fierce" or "savage."

at one's beck and call Required to tend to someone's wishes; totally under someone's control. The obsolete noun *beck,* which survives only in this cliché, meant a mute signal or gesture of command, such as a nod of the head or a pointing of the finger; the verbal form, *to beckon,* still exists, as does *call,* for a vocal summons.

at one's fingertips Ready, instantly available; at one's command. The term refers to both cognizance and competence—that is, it can mean either knowledge or the ability to carry out a task. Presumably it is based on something being as close at hand and familiar as one's own fingers. Its roots may lie in an ancient Roman proverb, "To know as well as one's fingers and toes," which in English became one's fingers' *ends* (in the proverb collections of John Heywood, John Ray, and others). Finger*tips* appears to have originated in the United States in the nineteenth century.

at one's wits' end, to be To be at a total loss, completely perplexed. "Wits" here means mental capacity or ability to think. The term was used by Chaucer (*Troilus and Criseyde*) and William Langland (*Piers Ploughman*) in the late fourteenth century and has been a cliché since the eighteenth century.

at sea, to be/all To be bewildered, to have lost one's way. Presumably it reflects the idea of literally having lost one's bearings while at sea. It was so used by Dickens and other nineteenth-century writers.

at sixes and sevens In disarray or confusion. The term comes from a game of dice in which throwing a six or seven has special significance, as it does in modern craps. There is considerable disagreement as to the precise game, or even if "six" or "seven" are not corruptions of *sinque* (five) and *sice* (six). Erasmus quoted a proverb to that effect, but, since dicing is very old indeed, the idea may be much older yet.

at swords' points Openly hostile. This term obviously refers to sword-fighting, long a thing of the past, but it has not died out. Mary McCarthy used it in her novel, *The Group* (1963): "Mrs. Hartshorn and her dead husband had had a running battle over Wilson and the League, and now Priss and Sloan were at swords' points over Roosevelt and socialized medicine." A synonymous expression it is *at daggers drawn*, first recorded in 1668 but used figuratively only from the 1800s. Robert B. Brough, *Marston Lynch, His Life and Times* (1870) had it: "Was Marston still at daggers drawn with his rich uncle?"

at the crossroads At a critical juncture or turning point. The place where two roads intersect has had special significance from ancient times. Some tribes used a crossroads as a place for religious sacrifices, and hence they came to be associated with execution. In Christian times, criminals and those who died by their own hand often were buried at a crossroads (since they could not be buried in consecrated ground). Crossroads also were a favorite spot for ambushes, highway robbery, and other nefarious deeds. The phrase "dirty work at the crossroads" crops up throughout the nineteenth century, as well as in a spate of twentieth-century murder mysteries. The idea of a figurative crossroads, a point of having to decide which road to take, is also very old. Erasmus quotes a fragment from the Greek poet Theognis's *Elegies,* dating from about 600 B.C., translated as "I stand at the crossroads."

at the drop of a hat At once, without delay. It is thought to come from the practice of dropping or waving a hat as a starting signal for a race, fight, or other event. The phrase also has come to mean "without further encouragement." The British composers Michael Flanders and Donald Swann, known for their humorous songs and revues, told their friends they could be persuaded to sing their songs "at the drop of a hat," which in the mid 1950s became the title of their first record album, followed by *At the Drop of Another Hat.* The term has been a cliché since the mid-1900s.

at this juncture/moment/point in time Now, at a particular time. Originally a journalistic locution for the simple word *now,* this verbose expression is a twentieth-century cliché. Another version, from sports, is *at this stage of the game.* Both represent an attempt to be legalistically specific. Indeed, an *Atlantic Monthly* article of January 1975 pointed out, "The phrase 'at that point in time' . . . quickly became an early trademark of the whole Watergate affair," a political scandal in which everyone tried to deny knowledge of and/or participation in various events.

avoid like the plague, to To stay away from, assiduously shun. The scourge of western Europe on numerous occasions, the plague, although poorly understood, was known to be contagious even in the time of St. Jerome (A.D. 345–420), who wrote, "Avoid, as you would the plague, a clergyman who is also a man of business."

awesome! Slang for "wonderful," "terrific," originating in the second half of the twentieth century and used widely by youngsters. It transferred the original meaning of awe-inspiring, dating from the seventeenth century. A *New Yorker* cartoon caption had it (Dec. 19, 1983): "Third grade? Third grade is awesome!"

ax to grind, an A selfish motive. Allegedly this term comes from a cautionary tale by Charles Miner, first published in 1810, about a boy persuaded to turn the grindstone for a man sharpening his ax. The work not only was difficult to do but also made him late for school. Instead of praising the youngster, the man then scolded him for truancy and told him to hurry to school. Other sources attribute it to a similar story recounted by Benjamin Franklin. Whichever its origin, the term was frequently used thereafter and apparently was a cliché by the mid-nineteenth century.

b

babe(s) in the woods Extremely naive or innocent individual(s). The term comes from a popular ballad, "The Children in the Wood" (1595), about two orphaned children. Their wicked uncle wants their inheritance and hires two men to murder them. One of the men repents and kills the other, but he abandons the children in a deep forest, where they die. The tale was kept alive by numerous writers, notably through Thomas Percy's collection, *Reliques of Ancient English Poetry* (1765).

back and fill, to To temporize or vacillate. This metaphor comes from the days of sailing ships, and refers to a mode of tacking when the tide is running with a ship and the wind against it. The sails are alternately backed and filled, so that the vessel goes first back and then forward, ultimately remaining in just about the same place.

back number Something or someone outdated. The term comes from the back issues of newspapers and other periodicals, which carry items no longer new and events no longer current. The term began to be used figuratively in the late nineteenth century in the United States.

back of one's hand, to give (someone) the To show contempt, to insult. "Here's the back of my hand to you," wrote Jonathan Swift (1738), perhaps signifying a challenging farewell. The back of the hand, of course, consists of knuckles, so the expression may once have meant a punch. Similarly, a *backhanded compliment* is actually malicious in intent.

backseat driver A passenger who gives unasked-for and usually unwanted advice to the driver of a vehicle; by extension, anyone who interferes without having real responsibility or authority. The term originated in the United States during the 1920s, when many automobiles were chauffeur-driven and their passengers sat in the backseat, often quite legitimately telling the chauffeur where to go. Today the passenger's location is irrelevant, the term being principally figurative. It has largely replaced the older ARMCHAIR GENERAL. See also MONDAY-MORNING QUARTERBACK and the very different TAKE A BACKSEAT.

back the wrong horse Make a wrong guess about a future outcome. The term comes from horse racing and is occasionally put as *bet on the wrong horse,* and has been used in this context since the late seventeenth century. It has long been applied to other situations, especially politics, where it means supporting a candidate who loses. Charles L. Graves used it in *Punch's History* (1922): "Lord Salisbury made his remarkable speech about our having backed the wrong horse, i.e. Turkey in the Crimean War."

back to square one Indication to start again from the beginning, because one has failed or has reached a dead end. The term probably came from a board game such as snakes and ladders or from a street game such as hopscotch, where an unlucky throw of dice or a marker forces the player to begin the course all over again. It was adopted by British sportscasters in the 1930s, when the printed radio program would include a numbered grid of a soccer (football) field to help listeners follow the game broadcasts.

The same sense is conveyed by *back to the drawing board,* a term originating during World War II, almost certainly from the caption of a cartoon by Peter Arno in the *New Yorker* magazine, which showed a man holding a set of blueprints and watching an airplane on the ground blow up.

A similar phrase with a slightly different sense is *back to basics*—that is, let's go back to the beginning, or return to the fundamentals of a subject, problem, or other issue. The term dates from the mid-twentieth century and probably originated in either school or laboratory, where a subject was not clearly understood or an experiment of some kind failed.

back to the salt mines It's time to return to work, implying reluctance to do so. The term refers to the Russian practice of sending prisoners to work in the salt mines of Siberia, common in both imperial and Communist times. Eric Partridge cited an authority who believes it came from a play called *Siberia,* which was popular in the 1890s.

back to the wall, with one's Hard-pressed; making a last-ditch defensive stand. The term embodies the idea that backing up against a wall prevents an attack from behind, but it also indicates that one has been forced back to this position and no further retreat is possible. Although it had been used since the sixteenth century and was already colloquial in nineteenth-century Britain, the term became famous near the end of World War I through an order to the British troops given by General Douglas Haig and reported in the London *Times* on April 13, 1918: "Every position must be held to the last man. . . . With our backs to the wall, and believing in the justice of our cause, each one of us must fight on to the end.

bad blood Anger or animosity, between individuals or groups. The blood was long regarded as the seat of human emotion, and by the sixteenth century it was particularly associated with high temper and anger. "To breed bad (or ill) blood" meant to stir up hard feelings. In the late eighteenth century both Jonathan Swift in England and Thomas Jefferson in America wrote of ill blood in this way, and a few years later the English essayist Charles Lamb wrote of bad blood.

bad hair day A day when everything seems to go wrong. The term originally meant merely that one's appearance, especially one's hair, does not look attractive. Dating from about 1980, it soon was extended to mean having a bad day. The *Denver Post* had it in 1994: "Soon you will notice how much less complaining you do, even on bad hair days."

bad penny, always turns up (comes back) like a The unwanted or worthless object or person is sure to return. A proverb in several languages besides English, this expression dates from the days when coins had intrinsic worth and a bad penny (or shilling or crown) was one that was made of inferior metal or contained less metal than it should.

bag and baggage All one's belongings, usually in the sense of departing with them. It originally was a military phrase that meant all of an army's property and was so used in the fifteenth century. To march away with bag and baggage meant that the army was leaving but was surrendering nothing to the enemy. The alliterative nature of the term has appealed to many writers, including Shakespeare. In *As You Like It* Touchstone says, "Come, shepherd, let us make an honourable retreat; though not with bag and baggage, yet with scrip and scrippage," meaning the purse and its contents (money). In time the connotation of honorable departure was dropped and the term simply described clearing out completely. "'Bag and baggage,' said she, 'I'm glad you're going,'" declared Samuel Richardson's heroine in *Pamela* (1741). See also KIT AND CABOODLE.

bag of tricks One's entire resources. It refers to the bag of the itinerant magician, which contained all the paraphernalia needed to perform his tricks. The expression dates back at least as far as one of La Fontaine's fables (1694), in which a fox carries a *sac des ruses.* It became especially common in Victorian literature.

baker's dozen Thirteen. The source of this term is a law passed by the English Parliament in 1266, which specified exactly how much a loaf of bread should weigh and imposed a heavy penalty for short weight. To protect themselves, bakers would give their customers thirteen loaves instead of twelve, and in the sixteenth century this came to be called "a baker's dozen."

bald as a coot/billiard ball Very bald indeed. The coot is a black water bird whose white bill extends up to the forehead, making it appear to be bald. Indeed, this bird was already being called a *balled cote* in the thirteenth century. The later simile, to a billiard ball, has been less recorded, but since billiards was already popular in Shakespeare's day it cannot be of very recent origin.

ballpark figure, a A roughly accurate estimate, an educated guess. Coming from baseball, this expression rests in turn on *in the ballpark,* meaning within certain limits. Although both are generally applied to numerical estimates, neither appears to have anything to do with baseball scores.

ball's in your court, the It's your turn. The expression comes from sports and became current in the United States and Canada in the mid-twentieth century. It is sometimes put as "It's your ball." David Hagberg has it in *Countdown* (1990): "'No,' the DCI agreed, 'As I said, the ball is in your court.'"

balm in Gilead Cure or solace. The expression comes from the Book of Jeremiah (8:22): "Is there no balm in Gilead; is there no physician there?" The King James version translator took as "balm" the Hebrew word *sori,* which probably meant the resin of the mastic tree; John Wycliffe translated it as "gumme" and Miles Coverdale as "triacle" (treacle). By the nineteenth century the term was used figuratively for consolation in a time of trouble, by Edgar Allan Poe (in "The Raven"), Charlotte Brontë, and others.

band-aid approach/solution A stopgap measure, a temporary expedient. This term applies the trade name for a small bandage, the Band-Aid, patented in 1924, to approaching or solving an issue in a makeshift way. It dates from the late 1960s and is approaching cliché status.

bane of one's existence, the The agent of one's ruin or misery; a THORN IN THE FLESH. The earliest meaning of the noun *bane* was "murderer" and was so used in *Beowulf* (c. A.D 800). A somewhat later meaning was "poison," which survives as part of the names of various poisonous plants, such as henbane or wolf's bane. The current sense, an agent of ruin, dates from the late 1500s. Today it is almost always used hyperbolically, as in "The new secretary loses all my messages; she's become the bane of my existence."

baptism of fire One's first encounter with a severe ordeal or painful experience. The term is believed to come from the death of martyrs, especially those who were burned at the stake. In the nineteenth century it acquired a more specific meaning in France, that is, the experience of a soldier's first battle. It was so used by Napoleon III in a letter describing his son's initiation into combat. Later it was extended to mean any initial encounter with a difficult situation—as, for example, one's first job interview.

barefaced lie/liar A shamelessly bold untruth/prevaricator. *Bare* here means bold-faced or brazen, but one writer speculates that *barefaced,* which dates from the late sixteenth century, originally meant "beardless," a condition perhaps considered audacious in all but the youngest men. In any event, by the late seventeenth century it also meant bold and became attached to *lie* in succeeding years. See also NAKED TRUTH.

bark is worse than one's bite One sounds much fiercer than one actually is. Listed in the *Oxford Dictionary of Proverbs,* this saying dates back at least to the mid-seventeenth century and is used often enough to be a cliché.

bark up the wrong tree, to To waste one's energy or efforts by pursuing the wrong scent or path. The term comes from the 1820s, when raccoon-hunting was a popular American pastime. Raccoons are nocturnal animals and generally are hunted on moonlit nights with the help of specially trained dogs. Sometimes, however, the dogs are fooled, and they crowd around a tree, barking loudly, in the mistaken belief that they have treed their quarry when it has actually taken a quite different route. "If you think to run a rig on me," wrote T. C. Haliburton (a.k.a. Sam Slick), "you have barked up the wrong tree" (*Human Nature,* 1855). The cliché became especially common in detective stories in the 1940s, owing to the obvious analogy of hunter and hunted.

basket case An individual too impaired to function. This term dates from World War I, when it denoted a soldier who had lost both arms and legs and had to be carried off the field in a basket or litter. In civilian usage the term was applied to an emotionally unstable person who is unable to cope. Today it is used still more loosely to describe an attack of nerves, as in "The mother of the bride was a basket case."

bated breath See WITH BATED BREATH.

bats in one's belfry, to have To be slightly crazy or quite eccentric. The term alludes to the bat's seemingly erratic flight in the dark, which is transferred to thoughts flying about in the head. In reality, the bat has a sophisticated sonar system whose nature came to light only recently. In flight it keeps up a constant twittering noise that bounces back from solid objects in its path. This echo enables the animal to avoid actually bumping into obstacles. Nevertheless, bats have long been associated with craziness. See also BLIND AS A BAT.

batten down the hatches, to To get ready for trouble. A nautical term dating from the early nineteenth century, it signified preparing for bad weather by fastening down the battens, strips of wood nailed to various parts of masts and spars, and fastening tarpaulins over the ship's hatchways (doorways and other openings). The term began to be used figuratively as preparing for any emergency by the late nineteenth century. See also CLEAR THE DECKS.

battle cry A slogan used in any campaign or movement. Originally used literally by soldiers or their commanders, the term was transferred to less bloody usages, such as rallying supporters in a political campaign. George Bernard Shaw played on it in *Man and Superman* (1905): "A good cry is half the battle."

battle of the bulge A jocular description of fighting middle-aged spread, named for an actual battle between the Allies and German forces during World War II. The last great German drive of the war, it began in December 1944, when Nazi troops "bulged" through the Allied lines deep into Belgium. It took a month for the Allies to drive back the German forces. The current cliché was born in the second half of the 1900s, when diet-conscious Americans deplored the seemingly inevitable advance of pounds that comes in advancing years. A *New York Times* review of the one-woman play by Eve Ensler, *The Good Body,* had it: ". . . Ms. Ensler . . . [was] soliciting the experiences of women caught up in similar battles of the bulge" (Nov. 16, 2004).

battle royal A fierce battle or free-for-all. In the seventeenth century the term signified a cockfight in which more than two birds were engaged. They would fight until there was only one survivor. By the eighteenth century the expression was a metaphor for any general fight, including a battle of wits.

be-all and end-all, the The ultimate purpose, the most important concern. An early and famous use of this term is in Shakespeare's *Macbeth* (1.6), in which the ambitious Macbeth soliloquizes about assassinating Duncan so as to become king: ". . . that but this blow [the murder] might be the be-all and the end-all here." Eric Partridge held it was a cliché by the nineteenth century, but it is heard less often today.

be all things to all men See ALL THINGS TO ALL MEN.

bean, not worth a See HILL OF BEANS.

beard the lion, to To confront a dangerous opponent; to take a risk head-on. The first Book of Samuel (17:35) tells of David, the good shepherd, who pursued a lion that had stolen a lamb and, "when he arose against me, I caught him by his beard, and smote him, and slew him." The expression often is put, "to beard the lion in his den," which in effect adds the story of the prophet Daniel, whose enemies had him thrown into a den of lions for the night (Daniel 6:16–24). Daniel survived, saying that God had sent an angel to shut the lions' mouths. In any event, the term became a Latin proverb, quoted by

Horace and Martial and in the Middle Ages by Erasmus, in which a timid hare disdainfully plucked a dead lion's beard. It began to be used figuratively by the time of Shakespeare, and was a cliché by the mid-nineteenth century.

bear the brunt, to To put up with the worst of any hardship, violence, or other misfortune. The term dates from the early fifteenth century, when *brunt* signified the main force of an enemy's assault, which was borne by the front ranks of an army aligned in the field of battle. It was used by John Lydgate in his *Chronicle of Troy* (1430) and later began to be used figuratively, as by Robert Browning in "Prospice" (1864): ". . . fare like my peers, The heroes of old, Bear the brunt . . . of pain, darkness and cold."

bear with me Be patient, make allowances, put up with me. Today used mainly as a request to hear out a long-winded story or wait for a delayed result or event, this request appeared in John Heywood's proverb collection of 1546. It may already have been considered somewhat archaic by Benjamin Franklin when he wrote, in *An Added Chapter to the Book of Genesis* (1763), "And couldst not thou . . . bear with him one night?"

beat a dead horse See DEAD HORSE.

be at a loss See AT A LOSS.

beat a (hasty/quick) retreat, to To withdraw, back down, or reverse course, usually without delay. The term comes from the military practice of sounding drums to recall troops behind the lines, or to some other position. In earlier days wind instruments, most often trumpets, were used for this purpose. Among the references to this practice is "Thai had blawen the ratret," in John Barbour's *The Bruce* (1375). Much later the expression was used figuratively to mean the same as the simple verb *to retreat,* and then, in the mid-nineteenth century, it became a cliché. A newer version is to beat a *strategic retreat,* basically a euphemism for a forced withdrawal. It came into use during World War I, as the German high command's explanation of retiring from the Somme in 1917. In the civilian vocabulary, it came to mean yielding a point or backing down from a position in an argument.

beat around/about the bush, to Indirection in word or deed; to shillyshally, to approach something in a roundabout way. This expression for overcautiousness dates from the early sixteenth century, when Robert Whytynton (*Vulgaria,* 1520) warned, "a longe betynge aboute the busshe and losse of time." Some authorities think it came from beating the bushes for game, and indeed there are numerous sayings concerning the delays caused by too much beating and not enough bird-catching, dating back even further. (See also BEAT THE BUSHES FOR.) Although the days of beaters seem remote, the phrase survives as a common cliché.

beaten track, (off) the A well-worn path, (not) the usual route or method. The origin seems obvious, since a much-used route would indeed be flattened by the tramp of many feet. The phrase began to be used figuratively, in the sense of trite or unoriginal, in the seventeenth century or before, and *off the beaten track,* in the meaning of new or unusual, is just about as old. Samuel Johnson spelled it out in 1751 when he wrote, "The imitator treads a beaten walk."

beat one's brains (out), to A more colloquial version of CUDGEL ONE'S BRAINS or RACK ONE'S BRAIN, meaning, like them, to strain to remember something or solve a difficult problem. It dates from the sixteenth century, when Christopher Marlowe wrote, "Guise beats his brains to catch us in his trap" (*The Massacre of Paris,* 1593, 1.1).

beat one's head against the wall, to See RUN ONE'S HEAD AGAINST A BRICK/STONE WALL.

beat the band See TO BEAT THE BAND.

beat the bushes for, to To seek out assiduously. The term comes from hunting, in the days when beaters were employed to flush birds out for a hunting party, and has been used in its literal sense since the fifteenth century.

beat the living daylights out of, to To punish severely, to thrash. This cliché is in effect a colorful elaboration of *to beat someone up,* an American locution dating from about 1900. The word *daylights* was a nineteenth-century American colloquialism for one's vital organs. "That'll shake the daylights out of us," wrote Emerson Bennett (*Mike Fink,* 1852). Another writer referred to "pulling out" a mule's daylights by beating it, and mystery writers of the early twentieth century sometimes had their characters "shoot the daylights" out of someone. Earlier British versions are *to beat black and blue* (Shakespeare), *beat to a jelly* (Smollett), and the equally hyperbolic *beat to a pulp.* Another American synonym is *to beat the tar out of,* which unlike the other fairly graphic equivalents is more puzzling, but has been used since about 1800.

beat to the punch/draw Move more quickly than someone to accomplish something: for example, "We headed straight for the buffet, but others beat us to the punch and got most of the lobster salad." Both versions of this cliché date from the mid-1800s and imply an aggressive move, the first alluding to fisticuffs and the second to drawing a pistol.

beautiful people, the The fashionable social set, individuals who are in vogue and widely emulated and envied. Although general use of this term began in the mid-1960s—Diana Vreeland, the editor of *Vogue* magazine, is often credited with inventing it—it appeared even earlier as the title of a William Saroyan play of 1941. It was given further currency by the Beatles song "Baby You're a Rich Man" (1967) by John Lennon and Paul McCartney, which contains the line, "How does it feel to be one of the beautiful people?" Katherine Hall Page used the phrase in her mystery *The Body in the Big Apple* (1999), with its numerous descriptions of expensive New York restaurants and elegant parties. Also see JET SET.

beauty is in the eye of the beholder What one person considers ugly may seem beautiful to another. The idea is very old and was stated in various ways from the sixteenth century on. Shakespeare's version is close to the modern: "Beauty is bought by judgement of the eye" (*Love's Labour's Lost,* 2.1). Possibly the first exact statement of the cliché in print was in Margaret Hungerford's *Molly Bawn* (1878).

beauty is (only) skin-deep A lovely appearance has no relation to more profound good qualities. "All the carnall beauty of my wife is but skin-deep," wrote Sir Thomas Overbury (c. 1613). Of course this observation was hardly new, having been made by many ancient poets long before (Vergil wrote, *O formose puer, nimium ne crede colori,* "O my pretty boy, trust not too much in your looks"). Although only skin deep, observed William Cobbett (*Advice to Young Men,* 1829), "It [beauty] is very agreeable for all that," whereas H. H. Munro (Saki) punned "I always say beauty is only sin deep" (*Reginald's Choir Treat,* 1904).

bed and board Lodging and food; by extension, the essentials one works for. Originally the term meant the full connubial rights of a wife as mistress of her household. The marriage service in the *York Manual* (c. 1403) states: "Here I take . . . to be my wedded wyfe, to hald and to have at bed and at borde, for fayrer for layther, for better for wers . . . till ded us depart."

bed of roses, a A delightful place, a very pleasant situation. The metaphor was employed by English poets from Christopher Marlowe on. Today it is often used in a negative sense—that is, some situation is *not* a bed of roses. Indeed, the metaphor lacks literal truth anyway, as garden expert Allen Lacy pointed out in a *New York Times* column of 1987: "A bed of roses isn't, considering all the fussy care they require—remove faded blossoms, minor pruning, spraying, dusting."

bee in one's bonnet, to have a To have a strange fixation about something; to have an eccentric idea or fantasy. A version of the term appears in Robert Herrick's "Mad Maid's Song" (c. 1648): ". . . the bee which bore my love away, I'll seek him in your bonnet brave." Allegedly the expression stems from the analogy of a bee buzzing inside one's hat to a peculiar idea in one's head. It has been a cliché since the eighteenth century. Lest one think it is obsolete, it appeared in a 2004 murder mystery: "By the way, what bee got into your bonnet at the meeting? Bailey had been pretty cooperative" (David Baldacci, *Hour Game).*

been there, done that I've had this experience and I'm bored with it. The implication of this relatively new and seemingly worldweary statement is, why bother to repeat something I've seen or done. However, it is also used as an expression of empathy, as in "You've offered to take care of the children for a week? Been there, done that." The phrase dates only from the early 1980s and at first referred to tourism and sightseeing, but soon was extended to just about any activity. Moreover, it became overused so quickly that it became a cliché virtually in a decade and a half. Also see SEEN ONE, SEEN THEM ALL.

beer and skittles, (life is) not all Life is not all FUN AND GAMES. Skittles, a kind of bowling game played by throwing wooden disks at pins, was very popular in Great Britain, where drinking beer remains a widespread form of recreation. Pairing the two came about quite naturally in the nineteenth century. Dickens's Sam Weller assures Mr. Pickwick, who is about to enter a debtor's prison, that the prisoners enjoy themselves there: "It's a regular holiday to them—all porter and skittles" *(Pickwick Papers).* But Dickens's contemporary Thomas Hughes observed that "Life isn't all beer and skittles" (*Tom Brown's School Days*). Essentially a British cliché, it spread to America but is heard less often today. Legendary adman David Ogilvy had it in *Confessions of an Advertising Man* (1963): "Managing an advertising agency is not all beer and skittles."

before you can say Jack Robinson At once, instantly. No one seems to be able to trace this term precisely or to discover the identity of Jack Robinson. Its earliest documented use was in 1778 in Fanny Burney's *Evelina* ("I'd do it as soon as say Jack Robinson"). It appears in Dickens's *A Christmas Carol* and Twain's *Huckleberry Finn.* According to Francis Grose's *Classical Dictionary* (1785), the original Jack Robinson was a gentleman who called on his neighbors so peremptorily that there was hardly time to announce him before he was gone.

beg, borrow, or steal Obtain in any possible way. This saying appears in Chaucer's *Canterbury Tales* (*The Tale of the Man of Law,* c. 1386): "Maugre [despite] thyn heed, thou most for indigence or stele, or begge, or borwe [borrow] thy despence [expenditure]!" In slightly different form it appears in a seventeenth-century poem with a cautionary moral that is quoted by Washington Irving ("But to beg or to borrow, or get a man's own, 'tis the very worst world that ever was known"). Almost the same wording appeared in Benjamin Franklin's *Poor Richard's Almanack* (1742).

beggar description, to Impossible to describe accurately because mere words are not enough. The phrase is Shakespeare's, who used it in referring to Cleopatra's beauty: "For her own person, it beggar'd all description" (*Antony and Cleopatra,* 2.2). It not only entered the language but was, by the late eighteenth century (according to Eric Partridge), a cliché.

beggars can't be choosers Those in need must take whatever they can get. A proverb in John Heywood's 1546 collection, this expression has been repeated ever since, with very little variation. A minor exception was Thomas Fuller's version (*Gnomologia,* 1732), "Beggars and Borrowers must be no Chusers."

beginner's luck Success from an endeavor tried for the first time. The term dates from the late 1800s and soon was used enough to become a cliché. For example, "She said she'd never made a soufflé before but it turned out perfectly. Beginner's luck, I guess."

beginning of the end, (this is) the The start of a disaster (ruin, defeat, fatal illness, or the like). The term was used by Shakespeare in *A Midsummer Night's Dream,* but without the same meaning; it appears in the tangled prologue to the play within a play (Pyramus and Thisbe) in the last act. "I see the beginning of my end" occurs in an early seventeenth-century play, *The Virgin Martyr,* by Massinger and Dekker, here meaning death. The origin of the current cliché, however, is generally acknowledged to be a statement made by Talleyrand to Napoleon after losing the battle of Leipzig (1813), "C'est le commencement de la fin." It was widely quoted thereafter, although Talleyrand may not have been the originator (he was known to borrow freely from others).

beg the question, to To assume that the very matter being questioned is true. A point of logic originally raised by Aristotle, it became a Latin proverb, *Petitio principii,* meaning "to beg the main point" (or "assume without proof"). It was most clearly defined by Thomas Reid (*Aristotle's Logic,* 1788): "Begging the question is when the thing to be proved is assumed in the premises." Since about 1990, however, it has sometimes been used differently, to mean avoiding a straight answer, as "Using a round table begs the question of who is paired with whom." An even more recent usage is as a synonym of "to raise the question," as in "King's new e-book begs the question of what constitutes a book." Because of these confusions of meaning, this cliché is best avoided in clear discourse or writing.

beg to differ, I I disagree. This polite conversational phrase uses *beg* in the sense of "ask" or "entreat," much as it is in the stock locution "I beg your pardon" for "Excuse me." This usage dates from the 1300s.

behind the eight ball In a bad situation, bad luck. The term, originating in the United States in the first half of the 1900s, comes from a form of pool in which all the balls (which are numbered) must be pocketed in a certain order. The only exception is the No. 8 ball, which is black. If another player touches the eight ball he or she is penalized. Therefore, if the eight ball is in front of the ball one is trying to pocket, one is in a difficult position.

behind the scenes In private or in secret. The term comes from the theater, where, in the seventeenth and eighteenth centuries, violent action such as a murder or execution generally took place backstage (behind the scenery). The English journalist Joseph Addison pointed out, in 1711, that this practice was followed particularly in the French theater. By the late eighteenth century the expression was used figuratively for any activity that took place out of the public eye.

behind the times Old-fashioned, outdated. From the sixteenth to eighteenth centuries this meaning was conveyed by *behindhand.* In the nineteenth century, however, it turned into the present locution, as in Dickens's *Dombey and Son* (1846): "I'm old-fashioned and behind the time."

believe it or not Appearances to the contrary, it is true. Already a common phrase by then, in December 1918, it became the title of a cartoon series originally drawn by Robert LeRoy Ripley (1893–1949). It appeared in American newspapers for many years and was continued even after Ripley's death. Each drawing represented a seemingly unbelievable but allegedly true event or phenomenon, such as a two-headed chicken or a three-legged cat.

believe one's own eyes, one cannot One finds it hard to trust one's own perception or senses. This expression of incredulity dates at least from the seventeenth century, and has been a cliché since the late nineteenth century. "Believe it tho' I saw it myself, I cannot" appeared in Bartholomew Robinson's *Latin and English Adages* (1621).

belle of the ball, the The most beautiful or most popular person present. The word *belle,* for "beautiful woman," came into English directly from French in the early seventeenth century. After balls and similar grand social occasions became relatively rare, the original meaning—the reigning beauty at a dance—was widened to include the outstanding individual (male or female) at virtually any gathering. Today the term is often used ironically, for someone who would like to be so regarded.

bellow like a (wounded) bull, to To scream in outrage. The simile is almost 2,500 years old, from the time of the Greek poet Aeschylus, who wrote, "He bellowed like a bull whose throat has just been cut." Strictly speaking this cliché is a tautology, since *to bellow* means "to roar as a bull," and has done so since the era of Middle English. Shakespeare wrote, "Jupiter became a bull and bellow'd" (*The Winter's Tale,* 4.3).

bells and whistles Extra fancy features, extravagant frills. The term dates from the second half of the 1900s, and it may allude to the features of a fairground organ. It has been applied to products, such as a computer or automobile, and also to services. A business columnist in the *New York Times,* describing Cathay Airlines's first-class amenities such as a full-size bed and an on-demand entertainment system, wrote, "So what do business travelers have to say about all the bells and whistles? Not a whole lot; their focus is on time management" (Sept. 28, 2004).

below the belt Unfair behavior. The term comes from boxing, where the Marquess of Queensberry rules, formulated in 1865, prohibit striking an opponent there. It began to be used figuratively in the late nineteenth century.

be my guest Go ahead, do or take what you asked for. This casual expression, current since about 1950, generally is a response to a request for something trivial, as in "May I see your program?—Be my guest." Eric Partridge reported that the phrase was so common by 1972 that it was used for the name of a racehorse that won quite a few races.

bend/lean over backward, to To exert oneself enormously, to go to a great deal of trouble to satisfy or please someone. Originating in the United States about 1920, this expression, with its image of straining to do a backbend, is well on its way to cliché status.

bend someone's ear, to To subject someone to a barrage of words. This somewhat slangy twentieth-century cliché comes from an older one, *to bend one's ear to someone,* meaning to listen or pay attention to someone. This usage dates from the late sixteenth century and frequently appears in poetry (for example, John Milton, "Thine ears with favor bend," 1648). Sometimes *incline* serves for *bend,* as in the *Book of Common Prayer* and in a well-known Protestant prayer response ("Hear our prayer, O Lord, incline thine ear to us," by George Whelpton, 1897).

beneath contempt Not even worthy of despising. The word "beneath" means the same as "below" or "under" but generally has been confined to poetic and archaic locutions. The pairing with "contempt" has been a cliché since the late nineteenth century.

benefit of the doubt, to give/have the To assume or treat as innocent when there is conflicting evidence. The term comes from the law in many countries, whereby a person must be assumed to be innocent of a crime unless definitely proved to be guilty; in other words, when in doubt, the verdict must be "not guilty." The expression began to be used figuratively for all kinds of situation in the nineteenth century.

bent out of shape Angry, quite upset, agitated. This likening of a distorted object to a loss of temper or composure dates from the 1960s. Earlier, the same slangy term had been used for "intoxicated," and also for "unwell." It occasionally still is. However, most often it denotes extreme anger. For example, "The bride's going to be two hours late, but don't get all bent out of shape."

be of/in two minds, to To be unable to decide, to be in doubt. This turn of phrase goes back to the early sixteenth century, although the number *two* was not fixed. Jehan Palsgrave wrote (1530), "I am of dyverse myndes," and in the eighteenth century several writers came up with as many as twenty minds. Dickens used both—"I was in twenty minds at once" (*David Copperfield*) and ". . . was in two minds about fighting or accepting a pardon" (*A Child's History of England*).

beside oneself, to be To be distraught with worry, grief, anger, happiness, or some other strong emotion. The expression appears in the King James version of the Bible (Acts 26:24): "Paul, thou art beside thyself; much learning makes thee mad." It uses the adverb *beside* in an older sense, meaning "outside of," so literally the phrase means "outside of oneself," the self in question being one's mental faculties.

beside the point Irrelevant. This expression, also put as *beside the mark* or *purpose,* dates from the sixteenth century. Thomas More wrote (1533), "He speketh al beside the purpose."

best bib and tucker, one's Dressed in one's finest clothes. A *tucker* was an ornamental piece of lace worn by women in the seventeenth and eighteenth centuries to cover the neck and shoulders. A *bib* was either a fancy frill worn at the front of a man's shirt or an actual formal shirt front. Their pairing with *best* dates from the mid-eighteenth century. The word *bib* appeared in print in America in 1795: "The old gentleman put on his best bib and band [i.e., collar]" (*The Art of Courting,* Newburyport, Massachusetts). A later locution, dating from the mid-nineteenth century, is one's

Sunday best, also known as *Sunday-go-to-meeting clothes.* It refers to an era when one's finery was reserved for church (or "prayer meeting"). These Americanisms sound archaic today. See also GUSSIED UP.

best/worst-case scenario The best or worst possible outcome for a situation. These clichés use *scenario* in the sense of an imagined situation or sequence of events, a usage that has become common since about 1960. For example, "In the best-case scenario, Dad set off the burglar alarm accidentally," or "It isn't just that the price is higher, but none are left even at that price—that's the worst-case scenario." An amusing how-to manual by David Borgenicht and Joshua Piven, *The Worst-Case Scenario Survival Handbook* (1999), probes improbable mishaps and emergencies, such as how to escape quicksand or how to land a pilotless airplane.

best foot forward See PUT ONE'S BEST FOOT FORWARD.

best-laid schemes/plans, the The most careful plans sometimes do not succeed. It was probably already a cliché by the time Robert Burns used the phrase in "To a Mouse" (1786): "The best-laid schemes o' mice an' men gang aft a-gley [go often astray]."

best of a bad bargain, to make the To try to turn adversity to good account. Already found in the proverb collection of John Ray (1670), the phrase appears and reappears to the present. By 1790 James Boswell, Samuel Johnson's biographer, refers to it as "the vulgar phrase." The related cliché, *to make the best of things,* also was current in the seventeenth century, but has been traced back much further. The Greek playwright Euripides, as quoted by Plutarch, wrote, "The man who makes the best of everything he lights upon will not fare ill." See also MAKE THE BEST OF IT. To *have the best of both worlds,* on the other hand, is to benefit from seemingly opposed circumstances, for example, living in New England but spending cold winters in Florida. "Make the best of both worlds," wrote Charles Kingsley in 1855 (*Westward Ho!*).

best of all possible worlds, the Everything is for the best. This expression of blind optimism occurs in Voltaire's *Candide* (1758), where through Dr. Pangloss the author pokes fun at the German philosopher Leibnitz. The full saying is "All is for the best in the best of all possible worlds." It has been identified with overoptimism ever since. On the other hand, *all is for the best* was already considered a profound if fatalistic truth by the Roman orator Cicero (50 B.C.), was repeated a number of times by Chaucer, and was echoed by modern sages, among them Benjamin Franklin (*Poor Richard's Almanack*). Not everyone agrees. "I hate the Pollyanna pest who says that All Is for the Best," wrote Franklin P. Adams (1924).

best thing since sliced bread See GREATEST THING SINCE SLICED BREAD.

bête noire The BANE OF ONE'S EXISTENCE; a persistent nuisance. French for "black beast," this cliché is older than the synonymous PAIN IN THE NECK and THORN IN ONE'S SIDE. It dates from the first half of the nineteenth century and became popular (in English) during the long period when French was the principal language of culture and diplomacy. It is on its way to obsolescence.

be that as it may Nevertheless. Word for word, this phrase does not really make sense—may what? one could ask—but it has been used as an equivalent to "That may be true but" since the nineteenth century. A slightly different version, *be as be may,* is found in Chaucer (*The Monk's Tale*) and persisted for four or five centuries.

bet one's bottom dollar, one can One may be very certain of something. *Bottom* here means last, or the bottom of a pile of gambling chips. An American colloquialism of the mid-nineteenth century, the phrase became a cliché in the mid-twentieth century.

better half, my My spouse, usually referring to one's wife. The term dates from the sixteenth century and originally signified a close friend or lover. Indeed, much earlier the Roman poet Horace called his friend *animae dimidium meae,* describing an intimacy in which two friends are considered the halves of one whole. The Elizabethans used it for a wife (Sir Philip Sidney in *Arcadia,* 1590) or lover (Shakespeare, Sonnet 39, c. 1600). It continued to be used seriously through the eighteenth century and then began to be used more in a jocular or ironic way, as it is today.

better late than never A time-honored rationalization for tardiness. It can be traced to Greek and Latin writers, including the historian Livy, and appears in several early English proverb collections. The full proverb is sometimes stated, "Better late than never, but better never late." There are versions in numerous other languages as well.

better mousetrap, (if one can) build a A minor but important improvement will bring fame and fortune. This idea came from a speech Ralph Waldo Emerson made in 1871 and quoted (or misquoted) by Mrs. Sarah S. B. Yule. Emerson allegedly said, "If a man can write a better book, preach a better sermon, or make a better mousetrap than his neighbor . . . the world will make a beaten path to his door."

better safe than sorry Proceed carefully so as to be sure to get there. This cautionary formula dates from the early nineteenth century, when it was phrased "better sure than sorry," and became a cliché in the mid-twentieth century. The idea, of course, is much older. Thomas Ravenscroft in 1695 wrote, "It's good to be sure."

between a rock and a hard place Faced with a choice between two unpleasant alternatives, or two evils. A newer version of BETWEEN THE DEVIL AND THE DEEP BLUE SEA and the classic BETWEEN SCYLLA AND CHARYBDIS, this expression is American in origin and dates from the early twentieth century.

between Scylla and Charybdis A choice between two evils. In Homer's *Odyssey* (c. 850 B.C.) the hero must sail a narrow passage between Scylla, a monster on a rock, and Charybdis, a fatal whirlpool. If he avoids one evil, he must run into the other. This situation was repeated figuratively by writers from Virgil to Shaw (*Pygmalion,* 1912: "It's a choice between the Skilly of the workhouse and Char Bydis of the middle class").

between the devil and the deep blue sea A choice between two evils. A term dating back to the early seventeenth century, it referred not to the devil of hellfire and brimstone but to a seam around a ship's hull near the waterline. A sailor attempting to caulk this seam in heavy seas was in danger of falling overboard and drowning. The term was used figuratively—to mean any dilemma in which one faced danger—from that time on. It became a cliché about the middle of the eighteenth century.

between you and me and the bedpost/gatepost/four walls/lamppost In strictest confidence. This elaboration of *just between you and me* is often followed by gossip about someone else. The bedpost version dates from the early nineteenth century and was used by Edward Bulwer-Lytton (*Eugene Aram,* 1832: "Between you and me and the bedpost, young master has quarrelled with old master"), Dickens, and others. The lamppost version may be a little older, but is not much heard anymore.

betwixt and between Neither here nor there, unresolved; halfway between two alternatives. *Betwixt* comes from Old English and originally meant "by two"; now considered archaic, it survives largely in this expression, which dates from the nineteenth century. An 1877 play by Besant and Rice (*Son of Vulcan,* 1.4) has it, "She's the fool and he's the knave, so it's betwix and between."

beyond the pale Unacceptable, outside the rules of society, morality, etc. The noun "pale," from the Latin *palum,* meant a stake of the kind used to make fences, or a fence made of such stakes. By extension it came to mean the limits designated by a fence, at first literally and then figuratively. In the fourteenth century *the English Pale* was a name given to the part of Ireland then under English rule and therefore within the bounds of civilization (as perceived by the English). There was a similar pale around Calais. More figuratively still, the English printer William Caxton wrote in 1483, "The abbot and 21 monks went for to dwelle in deserte for to kepe more straytelye the profession of theyr pale." Three centuries later and three thousand miles away, Thomas Jefferson referred to "within the pale of their own laws."

bid adieu Say good-bye. This formulaic farewell uses the French *adieu,* meaning "to God," and has done so since Chaucer's time. It is now considered rather formal, although it also is used humorously. In fact, humorist Charles Farrar Browne, under the pen name Artemus Ward, joked about it back in 1862: "I now bid you a welcome adoo" (*Artemus Ward: His Book. The Shakers*).

bide one's time, to To wait for the right moment to speak or take action. The verb *to bide,* meaning "to wait for" since about the year 950, survives today only in this cliché. Frederick W. Robertson used the expression in a sermon (1853): "They bide their time and suddenly represent themselves."

big as a house Physically large, overweight, said of a person in an unflattering way, as in "I saw Marion the other day and she's gotten as big as a house." Why a house should have been chosen as a simile for a large person is not clear, but it has been so used for a very long time.

big cheese, the The boss, an important person; also, a self-important person. This term is a slangy Americanism dating from the late nineteenth century, and its etymology is disputed. Some believe it comes from the Persian or Urdu word *chiz* or *cheez* for "thing"; others believe it is simply a play on the English word *chief.* There are several synonymous usages, among them *big gun*, *big shot,* and *big wheel.* The first dates from the 1830s. An 1834 citation has it, "The big guns of the nation are there [in Washington]." The last two expressions both date from the 1930s.

big deal An important matter; also, so what, who cares. The differentiation between these two phrases depends on the speaker's tone. An example of the first sense might be, "A first helicopter ride for a five-year-old is a big deal." The second sense appears in, "So she got her first choice of colleges—well, big deal!" This sense can also be conveyed by *no big deal.* All three usages date from about 1940.

big fish in a small pond An individual who is important or prominent only in a small group. This cliché, of American provenance, is used both disparagingly ("He's the firm's general counsel, but since there are only three employees he's just a big fish in a small pond") and more positively ("She didn't get accepted to the university, but it's better to be a big fish in a small pond than a small fish in a big pond").

bigger bang for the buck More for one's money. The term was invented in 1954 by U.S. defense secretary Charles E. Wilson, who was advocating better use of defense appropriations, relying principally on nuclear deterrents; "bang" refers to a nuclear explosion. Later it was extended to numerous civilian contexts calling for better value. It echoes an older advertising slogan for a soft drink, "More bounce to the ounce."

bigger they come See THE BIGGER THEY COME.

big picture, the See THE BIG PICTURE.

big-ticket item, a An expensive purchase; a large outlay. *Ticket* refers either to the price tag or to the banking term meaning a preliminary record of a transaction before it is posted in a permanent book of account. The term originated in the United States about 1940 and is a borderline cliché.

bird in the hand, a What one already has is better than what one might possibly get. The complete saying, "A bird in the hand is worth two in the bush," is an ancient Greek proverb, quoted in several of Aesop's fables. It was repeated by the Romans and appeared in English in the fifteenth century. There are numerous versions in other languages. See also POSSESSION IS NINE POINTS OF THE LAW.

bird's-eye view, a An overall view, the large picture. The term dates from about 1600 and not only means "panoramic" but also may imply a somewhat superficial picture. Thus a "bird's-eye view" of music history, for example, may try to cover five hundred years of musical composition in a one-semester course. A 1989 *New York Times* headline, "Human-Eye View," announcing a special tour of a natural history museum's ornithology collection, gave this cliché a new twist.

birds of a feather Individuals of similar taste, background, or other characteristics in common. The term is a shortening of the proverb, "Birds of a feather flock together," an observation made more than two thousand years ago by Ben Sira in the apocryphal book of Ecclesiasticus. The sentiment was transferred to human beings and repeated by numerous English writers from Shakespeare's time on.

bite off more than one can chew, to To take on more than one can accomplish; also, to be too greedy or too ambitious. Versions of this cliché, warning against taking on too much, date from the Middle Ages and appear in ancient Chinese writings as well. A lighthearted more recent example is Ogden Nash's (from "Prayer at the End of a Rope," 1939): "Let me not bite more off the cob than I have teeth to chew; please let me finish just one job before the next is due."

bite someone's head off, to To respond angrily to a moderate or harmless request or remark. It appears to have replaced two earlier versions, to bite someone's *nose* off, which dates back to the sixteenth century ("She would . . . bite off a man's nose with an answere," Thomas Nashe, 1599), and to *snap* someone's head off, current in the eighteenth and nineteenth centuries.

bite the bullet, to To brace oneself against pain or a difficult experience. This expression is believed to come from the days when those wounded in battle had to be treated without anesthesia and were made to bite on a lead bullet to brace themselves against the pain of surgery. Certainly this was the meaning in Rudyard Kipling's *The Light That Failed* (1891): "Bite on the bullet, old man, and don't let them think you're afraid." However, some authorities suggest that the term comes from the practice of gunners biting off the end of a paper-tube cartridge in order to expose the powder to the spark. In times of anesthesia and more sophisticated weaponry, biting the bullet became entirely figurative, as when P. G. Wodehouse wrote, "Brace up and bite the bullet. I'm afraid I have bad news" (*The Inimitable Jeeves,* 1923).

bite the dust, to To be defeated or killed. The term became popular from American western films, in which cowboys and/or Indians frequently "bit the dust"—that is, were shot or shoved off their horses to the dusty ground. It became current in the late 1930s. However, the term occurs even earlier in William Cullen Bryant's translation (1870) of Homer's *Iliad* ("his fellow warriors . . . fall round him to the earth and bite the dust") and it also is found in translations of Virgil's *Aeneid.*

bite the hand that feeds you, to To show ingratitude; to turn against those who have helped you. The metaphor of a dog biting the master or mistress who fills its bowl is very old. It was especially popular in the eighteenth century; for example, the Irish statesman Edmund Burke wrote, "And having looked to Government for bread, on the very first scarcity they will turn and bite the hand that fed them" (1790). Two centuries later, a physicist who insisted on anonymity said, "Nobel laureates don't want to bite the hand that feeds them" and hence are reluctant to criticize the award system (*New York Times,* Oct. 17, 1989).

bite your tongue Hope that what you just said doesn't come true. This imperative is a translation of the Yiddish saying, *Bays dir di tsung,* and is used in informal conversation. For example, "You think it'll rain on their outdoor ceremony? Bite your tongue!" A much older but related phrase is *to bite one's tongue,* meaning to remain silent when provoked—literally, to hold it between one's teeth so as to suppress speaking. Shakespeare had it in *Henry VI, Part 2* (1.1): "So Yorke must sit, and fret, and bite his tongue." See also HOLD ONE'S TONGUE.

bitter end, (fight) to the The last extremity, the conclusion of a tough battle or other difficult situation. The term comes from seamanship, where "the bitter end" is that part of the chain or anchor cable that is secured inside the vessel and is seldom used. It is so described in Captain Smith's *Seaman's Grammar* of 1627: "A bitter is but the turne of a Cable about the bitts, and veare it out by little and little. And the Bitter's end is that part of the Cable doth stay within board." It was sometimes spelled *better;* Daniel Defoe, in *Robinson Crusoe* (1719), described a terrible storm, saying, "We rode with two anchors ahead, and the cables veered out to the better end." A much earlier version is found in Chaucer's *The Squire's Tale:* "They demen gladly to the badder ende" (translated by the Reverend Walter W. Skeat as "worse end").

bitter pill (to swallow) Something that is painful or hard to accept, as in "Being fired from one's first job is a bitter pill to swallow." The term *bitter pill* has been used figuratively for an unpleasant situation or fact since the sixteenth century. Horace Walpole had the precise locution: "It was a bitter pill for the King to swallow" (*Last Journals,* 1779). On the other hand, the more philosophical view that bad-tasting medicine may be beneficial has existed alongside the cliché. "Bitter pills may have blessed effects" was recorded in James Kelly's *Scottish Proverbs* (1721), and Thomas Fuller put it as "wholesome effects" in *Gnomologia* (1732).

black as night/pitch/the ace of spades Very dark indeed. To these overused similes one can add ink (Spenser, Shakespeare), the crow or raven (Petronius, Chaucer), soot (John Ray's proverbs, 1678), ebony (Shakespeare), and coal (Chaucer). The comparison to night (and also midnight) was more common in the nineteenth century, although Milton also used it (*Paradise Lost*), whereas *black as pitch* dates from Homer's time (*Iliad*).

black book, (put) in one's Out of favor, disgraced. The term comes from actual listings of those to be censured or punished by the authorities, which date from the fifteenth century. The agents of Henry VIII, for example, compiled a black book of English monasteries listed as "sinful." An eighteenth-century history of Oxford University also describes a proctor's black book which, if one was listed in it, proscribed proceeding to a university degree. Today, however, one's *little black book* may signify a personal address book, listing the telephone numbers of friends, especially those of the opposite sex.

black sheep A deviant or eccentric; the least successful, least admirable member of a group. Black sheep were long considered less valuable than white ones because their wool could not readily be dyed. Several sixteenth-century writers wrote of the black sheep as a dangerous ("perilous") animal, among them John Lyly. In the eighteenth century, the application to the human deviant became common. Sir Walter Scott wrote, "The curates know best the black sheep of the flock" (1816), and "the black sheep of the family" was an increasingly common way of singling out the odd member.

blaze a trail, to To find a new path or begin a new enterprise. The term comes from the practice of marking a forest trail by making blazes, that is, spots or marks on trees made by notching or chipping away pieces of the bark. The term was first used in eighteenth-century America by scouts who marked new trails for the soldiers behind them, and was used figuratively from the late nineteenth century on.

bleeding heart An excessively sympathetic or tender-hearted individual. The adjective *bleeding* has been used figuratively for full of anguish from pity or compassion since the late 1500s. Edmund Spenser so used it in *The Faerie Queene:* "These bleeding words she gan to say." The cliché is much newer, dating from the first half of the twentieth century. I. T. Ross had it in *Murder out of School* (1960), "A lot of bleeding-hearts got the idea they knew about everything."

bleed someone white, to To extort money, to take someone's last penny. The term dates from the seventeenth century. One writer claims it was coined by gamblers; once a victim had been made to PAY THROUGH THE NOSE (lost all one's blood through one's nose), one was bled white. More likely the saying relates to the fact that money was considered the lifeblood of trade and commerce.

blessed event The birth of a baby. This cloyingly sentimental cliché, dating from about 1920, may well be dying out. It uses *blessed* in the sense of "happy," not in the ironic sense of "cursed" or "damned" (as in "Every blessed piece of today's mail is a bill").

blessing in disguise, a Good luck coming out of bad; a misfortune unexpectedly turning into a good thing. "E'en crosses from his sov'reign hand are blessings in disguise," wrote the eighteenth-century poet James Hervey, "cross" here meaning "a cross to bear," or burden. The phrase has been a cliché for about a century.

blind alley, (up) a A dead end, either literally (a street or passage with only one entrance) or figuratively (a situation without hope of progress). The term dates from the sixteenth century.

blind as a bat/beetle/mole Totally blind, or, figuratively, unseeing. None of these animals is, by the way, truly blind. The bat flies about in the dark in seemingly erratic paths (see BATS IN ONE'S BELFRY), and the beetle and mole burrow through the ground. Nevertheless, these similes are quite old and have become clichés. The bat analogy dates from the sixteenth century at least (John Harvey); the mole and beetle similes come from Roman times and were cited in translations by Erasmus.

blind leading the blind, the Those who try to teach or guide others, even though they know no more than their pupils. The phrase comes from the Bible, presented as one of Jesus's teachings in the books of Matthew (15:14) and Luke (6:39). It is quoted by numerous writers thereafter and is a proverb in John Heywood's collection in 1546: "Where the blynd leadth the blynd, both fall in the dike."

blithering idiot A senseless babbler. This term owes its origin to the Scots dialect verb *to blether,* meaning to talk nonsense, with *blither* being a variant spelling. Combining it with "idiot" began in the late 1800s. It appeared in the British humor magazine *Punch* in 1889: "I'll state pretty clearly that his son is a blithering idiot."

blood from a stone/turnip, one can't get This is a hopeless source of help (money, comfort, and so forth). Both stone and turnip date from the nineteenth century, and other versions exist in numerous languages. Dickens used the stone analogy a number of times, in *David Copperfield, Our Mutual Friend,* and other works, and health-food trends notwithstanding, it is more common today than turnip. However, Clive Cussler had the latter in *Sahara* (1992): "'You can't squeeze blood out of a turnip,' said Giordino. 'It's a miracle we made it this far.'"

blood is thicker than water Family ties mean more than friendship. The term is based on the idea that water evaporates without leaving a mark, whereas blood leaves a stain. It dates from the Middle Ages and appears figuratively—that is, implying the importance of a blood relationship over all others—in John Ray's proverb collection of 1670, as well as in numerous later writings.

blood, sweat, and tears Hard work; enormous effort. The phrase is associated with one of the twentieth century's finest speakers, Winston Churchill, who on becoming Britain's prime minister in 1940 said, "I have nothing to offer but blood, toil, sweat and tears" (today the "toil" is often dropped when quoting him). The phrase was not original with Churchill. In 1611 John Donne wrote (*First Anniversary*), ". . . 'tis in vaine to dew, or mollifie it [this world] with thy teares, or sweat, or blood." Among others who used similar phrases were Byron, Browning, and Gladstone.

bloody but unbowed Wounded or scarred, but not defeated. The term, expressing fierce defiance, comes from the Victorian poet William Ernest Henley's most famous work, "Invictus:" "Under the bludgeonings of chance my head is bloody, but unbowed."

blow away Kill; also, surprise, impress, overwhelm. The first usage dates from the Vietnam War but it is the second, from the 1970s, that is more current today. The CBS television show *This Morning* had it on March 20, 1990: "We were just talking about how blown away we were by [violinist] Joshua Bell." It is on its way to becoming a cliché. See also BLOW ONE'S MIND.

blow by blow Described in minute detail. The term is American and comes from sportscasting, specifically the radio broadcaster's description of a prizefight ("A left to the body, a right to the chin," and so on). It dates from the first half of the twentieth century and soon was transferred to similarly explicit accounts of other events, private or public.

blow hot and cold, to To vacillate, to be indecisive. The expression comes from Aesop's fable about a satyr and a traveler eating together on a cold day. The traveler blew on his hands to warm them and on his soup to cool it. Observing this, the satyr threw him out because he blew hot and cold with the same breath. The term then came to mean hypocrisy ("These men can blow hot and cold out of the same mouth to serve severall purposes," wrote William Chillingworth about the Protestant religion in 1638). However, it also was used to describe simple indecision ("It is said of old, soon hot, soon cold, and so is a woman," in Thomas Percy's 1765 collection, *Reliques of Ancient English Poetry*).

blow off steam, to To let out one's frustration or anger, usually by shouting. The term comes from the early days of railroading, when locomotives had no safety valves. When the steam pressure built up, the engineer would pull a lever that would blow off steam and prevent an explosion. It was transferred to human wrath in the early nineteenth century. "The widow . . . sat . . . fuming and blowing off her steam," wrote Frederick Marryat (*The Dog-Fiend,* 1837). See also LET OFF STEAM.

blow one's mind, to To shock or surprise or astonish one; also, to lose one's mind, to go crazy. This slangy phrase dates from the mid-1960s, when hippie culture and anti-establishment feelings were at their height, and when it also meant to have a drug-induced experience. By 2000 the most common usage involved amazement, as in "He managed to juggle eight oranges at a time—it blew my mind." See also BLOW AWAY.

blow one's own horn/trumpet, to To brag about one's own accomplishments or ability, to promote oneself. The term originated in Roman times, and was translated into English early on. "I will sound the trumpet of mine own merits," wrote Abraham Fleming in 1576. It was a cliché by the mid-nineteenth century, according to Eric Partridge, and gave rise to one of W. S. Gilbert's numerous puns ("The fellow is blowing his own strumpet," he said of a manager who was bragging about his actress-mistress).

blow one's top/stack/fuse, to To lose one's temper. The first two terms allude to clearing the stack of a ship by blowing air through it; the last refers to the sudden power stoppage when a fuse blows. All are slang from the first half of the twentieth century. Jane Smiley wrote in *Horse Heaven* (2000), "'It's kind of fun in a way. At least I get to blow my stack a lot and they don't mind. Blowing your stack is the way they do things here.'"

blow out of the water Defeat completely, ruin. This term comes from naval warfare; an early citation (1860) defines it as blowing a craft out of the water with broadsides. A century later it was used figuratively, as in "These bad reviews will blow our show out of the water in no time." See also BOWL OVER.

blow sky-high, to To refute completely, to explode a thesis or idea. While this expression has a modern sound, it is not so very new. Andrew Jackson, in a letter of 1845, wrote, "Put your veto on them both, or you and your Secretary will be blown sky-high."

blow the whistle (on) (someone), to To give away, to betray. This expression originally (late nineteenth century) meant ending something suddenly, as though by the blast of a whistle, but by the 1930s it had its present meaning. "Now that the whistle had been blown on his speech," wrote P. G. Wodehouse in 1934 (*Right Ho, Jeeves*).

blow(n) to smithereens Smash, destroy. Again, *blow* here means "explode," and *smithereens* probably means "little smithers," a dialect word thought to mean "bits" or "pieces." The term was appealing enough to be used often from the early nineteenth century on, even by that great wordsmith James Joyce ("Crew and cargo in smithereens," in *Ulysses,* 1922).

blue blood Of high or noble birth. The term is a translation of the Spanish *sangre azul,* which was applied to Spain's pure-blooded aristocrats, meaning those whose ancestors had not intermarried with the Moors. Consequently they were fairly light-skinned and their veins showed bluer through the skin than those in Spaniards of mixed blood. The expression was used in England from the early nineteenth century, and was, like so many, satirized by W. S. Gilbert (*Iolanthe,* 1882, where Lord Tolloller is complaining that the fair maid Phyllis is not impressed by his title): "Blue blood! blue blood! When virtuous love is sought thy power is naught, though dating from the Flood, blue blood!"

blue funk, to be in a In a sad or dejected mood. One writer suggests that the term may come from the Walloon *in de fonk zum,* which means "to be in the smoke," but this etymology has not been verified. Eric Partridge believed *funk* came from the Flemish *fonck,* for "perturbation" or "disturbance," and indeed, to be *in a funk* at first meant to be very nervous or terrified (early eighteenth century). Somehow it got changed, perhaps owing to the addition of *blue,* with its colloquial meaning of "sad." A more recent variant is *a deep funk,* said, for example, of a deep decline in the stock market: "The market's fallen into a deep funk."

blue in the face, to be/until one is To have made a great effort. The literal significance of being blue in the face is lack of oxygen, and indeed, this expression sometimes indicates that one has talked until one is breathless. But it also has been extended to other kinds of effort, as in "I tried to open that sardine can until I was blue in the face." It was current in the mid-nineteenth century, when Anthony Trollope wrote, "You may talk to her till you're both blue in the face" (*The Small House at Allington,* 1864).

body count The number of casualties from a given operation. Originating during the Vietnam War, where it denoted the number of troops killed, it later was extended to casualties of disasters such as fires and earthquakes.

body language Gestures, posture, and other movements made by a person that unconsciously convey his or her feelings or attitude. The term dates from about 1960 and, some authorities believe, originated as a translation of the French *langage corporel.* Tennis commentators on television often point to a player's body language, usually inferring a discouraged or negative attitude. The term is also used for performers (actors, singers) who consciously use gesture and movement for their presentations.

boil down to, to To simplify or abridge; to lead to the crux of the matter. This figure of speech transfers the sense of a liquid being reduced and concentrated by the process of boiling to other processes or endeavors. It dates from the late nineteenth century.

bold as brass Shameless, impudent. This simile probably has the same source as *brazen,* which can mean either "made of brass" or "shameless," "too bold." The latter is older, dating at least from Shakespeare's time ("What a brazen-faced varlet art thou!" *King Lear,* 2.2). The present cliché dates from the late seventeenth or early eighteenth century, although *brass* alone in the sense of "shameless" is older (sixteenth century). "Can any face of brass hold longer out?" wrote Shakespeare in *Love's Labour's Lost* (5.2), and Thomas Fuller (*The Profane State,* 1642) wrote still more explicitly, "His face is of brasse, which may be said either ever or never to blush."

bold-faced lie See BAREFACED LIE.

bolt from the blue, a A sudden, unexpected event, usually of a catastrophic nature. The term refers to a bolt of lightning or thunder that comes from a blue (cloudless) sky and hence is not anticipated. Although "blue" was a poetic allusion to the sky by 1700, the precise expression dates from the early nineteenth century. It appears in Thomas Carlyle's description of chaotic events of the French Revolution: "Arrestment, sudden really as a bolt out of the blue, has hit strange victims" (1837).

bone dry Very thirsty; extremely dry. The simile *dry as bone,* referring to the bones of a dead creature, dates from the sixteenth century and has survived to the present day, while others of the same period (dry as a sieve, dry as a chip, dry as a red herring) have long since died out. See also DRY AS DUST.

bone of contention, the The central point of a dispute. The phrase alludes to two dogs fighting over a single bone, and originally was a bone of *dissension* ("This became a bone of dissension between these deere friends," William Lambarde, 1576). The current cliché dates from the early eighteenth century, although the metaphor of dogs fighting over a bone had been transferred to human quarrels long before ("The devil hath cast a bone to set stryfe between you," John Heywood's *Proverbs,* 1562).

boon companion A favorite friend, a convivial associate. Now on its way to obsolescence, the adjective "boon" comes from the French *bon,* for "good," and has meant "jolly" since the twelfth century. As for the pairing with "companion," several sources cite the Roman epigrammist Martial, who wrote *nulli tefacias nimis sodalem,* which has been translated as "to no man make yourself a boon companion." The association with drinking was made explicit by John Arbuthnot (*The History of John Bull,* 1712): "A boon companion, loving his bottle and his diversion."

boonies, the The provinces, a remote rural area. This slangy term is an abbreviation of *boondocks,* which comes from the Tagalog word *bundok,* for "hill" or "mountain." It was coined by U.S. Marines fighting against Filipino guerrillas after the Spanish-American War (1899–1902) for the rough hill country there. Later American troops in the Philippines during World War II shortened it, and after the war it began to be used more widely as an equivalent for another such term, *the sticks,* which dates from the early 1900s. W. C. Handy used it in *Father of the Blues* (1957), "I continued playing for dances, touring on the road and through the sticks."

boot is on the other foot See SHOE IS ON THE OTHER FOOT.

bore to death/tears, to To be extremely tedious or dull. The literature abounds with epigrams concerning bores. Both of these clichés for being exceedingly boring allegedly date from the nineteenth century and are much duller than, for example, "Society is now one polished horde, formed of two mighty tribes, the Bores and Bored" (Byron, *Don Juan*), or "Bore, n. A person who talks when you wish him to listen" (Ambrose Bierce, *The Devil's Dictionary*).

born and bred Describing a native, a person born and raised in the same place. The alliterative appeal of this phrase no doubt led to its overuse. Joseph Addison paired the two early on (*The Spectator,* 1711): "Being bred to no business and born to no estate." The precise locution appears in Fanny Kemble's travel book (1863), "Born and bred in America."

born, not made Describing an innate ability or talent. The original phrase was a translation of the Latin *Orator fit, Poeta nascitur* (Orators are made, Poets are born), quoted by Sir Philip Sidney in his *Apologie for Poetrie* (c. 1521). Later it was extended to include other occupations. Harriet Beecher Stowe (*Uncle Tom's Cabin,* 1851) provided an interesting twist on it when she had Topsy say, "I 'spect I growed. Don't think nobody never made me."

born with a silver spoon Born rich, or lucky, or both. Several writers believe this phrase comes from the custom of godparents giving their godchild a silver spoon, and only the wealthy could afford this gift. However, the spoon here may simply be symbolic of wealth, and indeed, other locutions, such as "He was borne with a penny in 's mouth" (John Clarke, *Parœmiologia Anglo-Latina,* 1639), also occurred. The silver spoon was cited in Peter Motteux's translation of *Don Quixote* (1712), as well as in two proverb collections of the same period.

born yesterday, not (I wasn't) Not naive; more experienced than one might think. Already a popular saying by the early nineteenth century, it appeared on both sides of the Atlantic. "I warn't born yesterday," said Thomas Haliburton's Sam Slick in one of his *Wise Saws* (1843). Approximately a century later Garson Kanin used the phrase for the title of a Broadway play that became extremely popular, as did the later (1950) film version. In both, actress Judy Holliday played the quintessential dumb blonde who, despite seeming unsophistication, is graced with enormous good sense.

borrowed time, on An unexpected extension of time. It often refers to someone terminally ill or in great danger but surviving longer than was anticipated, on time that is in effect borrowed from Death. The term dates from the late 1800s. Raymond Chandler used it in *The Big Sleep* (1930): "Brody was living on borrowed time." James Patterson also had it, referring to the 48-hour deadline for a threatened bombing attack: "We were definitely operating on borrowed time" (*London Bridges,* 2004).

bosom buddy/friend An intimate friend. This turn of phrase for denoting a very dear associate is found in both the Old and New Testaments. Nathan says it "lay in his bosom and was unto him as a daughter" (2 Samuel 12:3), and in the Gospel of St. John, John, often called the "beloved disciple," is described as the bosom friend of Jesus. In his "Ode to Autumn" John Keats wrote, "Season of mists and mellow fruitfulness, close bosom-friend of the maturing sun." By this time "bosom friend" was also a euphemism for body lice, and Jonathan Swift's *Polite Conversation* (1738) includes the pun, "I'm afraid your Bosom Friends are become your Backbiters." The alliterative *bosom buddy* is of later provenance; the word "buddy," for comrade or chum, dates from the mid-nineteenth century and originated in America. See also BOON COMPANION.

bottle up feelings, to To hold one's emotions under tight control. This metaphor for containing oneself dates from the mid-nineteenth century, although by the early 1600s the term "bottling up" had been transferred to containing things other than liquid in bottles (for example, "Vapours bottl'd up in cloudes," T. Scott, 1622).

bottomless pit, the Hell; also, something or someone that uses up all one's energy or resources. The expression appears several times in the Bible, most notably in the Book of Revelation ("and to him was given the key of the bottomless pit," 9:1; "And I saw an angel come down from heaven, having the key of the bottomless pit," 20:1). In the eighteenth century the term was humorously used for the English statesman William Pitt the younger (1759–1806), who was very thin, and it still is jocularly used for a seemingly insatiable individual of huge appetite.

bottom line The ultimate result; the most important element. The term comes from accounting, where the bottom line of a financial statement shows the earnings figures. In the mid-twentieth century the term began to be transferred to the outcome of any kind of undertaking, and soon afterward it was extended to mean the crux of any problem or the consequences of any issue. It is well on its way to becoming a cliché.

bottom of it, at the/get to the To discover the origin of a problem, or the fundamental truth of an issue or event. The word "bottom" has been used in this way (to mean ultimate cause) since the sixteenth century. Shakespeare used it numerous times, as in "Is there no pity . . . that sees into the bottom of my grief?" (*Romeo and Juliet,* 3.5). Several early proverbs also refer to "bottom" in this way: "If thou canst not see the bottom, wade not"; and "He brought the bottome of the bag cleane out" (John Heywood, 1546). The pioneer anthropologist James Burnett, Lord Monboddo, wrote in 1773 (*Of the Origin and Progress of Language*), "In order to get to the bottom of this question."

bottom of the barrel, scrape the Obtain the last dregs, the least desirable remains. The sediment of wine was likened to the lowest, most despicable elements of society nearly two thousand years ago by Cicero. The metaphor remains current.

bound and determined Firmly resolved, as in "She was bound and determined to pay off the mortgage this year." This cliché is a redundancy, since both participles here mean "fixed" or "resolute," but they serve for emphasis.

bounden duty A firm obligation. The adjective *bounden,* which survives only in this cliché, means being indebted to someone. The term dates from the early 1500s and appears in the Book of Common Prayer: "We beseech Thee to accept this our bounden duty and service."

bow and scrape, to To behave obsequiously, to show too much deference. The term literally means to bow one's head and draw back one foot, which then scrapes the ground. A cliché since the mid-nineteenth century, it is becoming as obsolete as the custom of bowing has, at least in the Western world.

bowl over Overwhelm, astonish, surprise. This term originated in the mid-1800s in the game of cricket, where it signifies knocking all the bails off the wicket. It has been used figuratively since the twentieth century, as in "I was just bowled over when I learned he'd gotten the million-dollar grant." See also BLOW OUT OF THE WATER.

boys will be boys Children can be expected to act childishly. As might be expected, the observation is far from new. A Latin proverb held, *Pueri sunt pueri, pueri puerilia tractant,* translated variously as "Children/boys are boys and do childish things." The emphasis on boys in the English language probably reflects the sexist view that boys are essentially more mischievous and active than girls. The statement appears with increasing frequency in nineteenth-century literature (Bulwer-Lytton, Thackeray, Mark Twain, Shaw, et al.), when it already must have been a cliché.

boy toy An attractive younger man who is linked with an older woman, for social activities, sexual favors, or the like. In effect he is the counterpart of a SUGAR DADDY. This slangy term dates from about 1980 and may be used disparagingly or admiringly, depending on the context. A headline in the magazine *Maxim* ran "Be Her Boy Toy: Younger Guys and Older Women" (June 2004). The term, which is on its way to becoming a cliché, may also be applied to a homosexual relationship, that is, a younger man kept by an older man. It is also put as toy boy.

brass hat See TOP BRASS.

brass tacks See GET DOWN TO BRASS TACKS.

brave new world, a A bleak and dismal future. The term comes from Shakespeare's *The Tempest,* in which Miranda says despairingly, "O brave new world, that has such people in't" (5.1). British novelist Aldous Huxley borrowed it for the title of his 1932 novel, in which human beings are grown in the laboratory and designed to perform particular jobs in society.

brave the elements, to To go outdoors in bad weather. To face wind and rain with courage today seems rather an overstatement, but this archaic-sounding locution was common in the nineteenth century. "Brave you storm with firm endeavor, let your vain repinings go," wrote the poet George Cooper (1838–1927).

brazen it out, to To face a difficult situation boldly or impudently. The verb (and adjective) "brazen" both mean "brass" (see also BOLD AS BRASS). Classical mythology distinguished four ages of mankind—the Golden, Silver, Bronze, and Iron ages (described by Ovid)—and Thomas Heywood, a playwright (1572–1650), termed the third the *Brazen Age,* a period of war and violence. During the mid-sixteenth century the verb "to brazen" meant to act boldly. The precise modern expression was used by John Arbuthnot ("He would talk saucily, lye, and brazen it out") in *The History of John Bull* (1712).

bread and circuses Crowd-pleasers, events of popular appeal. The term dates from the Roman poet Juvenal's *Satires,* in which he said, *Duas tantum res anxius optat, Panem et Circenses* (Two things only the people earnestly desire, bread and [the games of the] circuses). Although this expression has survived long enough into modern times to become a cliché, it appears to be dying out. However, in the 1990s a very successful Massachusetts chain of health-food stores called itself the Bread & Circus Wholefood Supermarkets.

break a leg Good luck. There is some dispute as to when and where this seemingly nasty advice originated. It may be a translation of the German *Hals* *und Beinbruch* (Break your neck and leg), which allegedly originated among World War I aviators jocularly wishing each other well. In any event, it became widespread in the theater, both in Germany and later in the United States, and then came into more general use. It still is most often addressed to performers of some kind.

break ground, to To begin a new project; to be innovative. The term dates from the sixteenth century, when it meant literally to break up land with a plow, and began to be used figuratively by the late seventeenth century, by the poet John Dryden and others. In 1830, when De Quincey described Jeremy Bentham as "one of those who first broke ground as a pioneer . . . in Natural Philosophy," the expression was well on its way to clichédom.

break it (to someone) gently, to To reveal bad news in a calm, soothing fashion. "With a design to break the matter gently to his partners," wrote John Arbuthnot in 1712. In time the verb *to break* in the sense of "to tell" incorporated the idea of "gently," making the cliché a tautology.

break/bust one's ass Exert oneself to the utmost degree; work very hard. This rather vulgar usage dates from the first half of the 1900s. Norman Mailer had it in his war novel, *The Naked and the Dead* (1948): "What're we breakin' our asses for? Let's take it easy." Sometimes "butt" is substituted for "ass." See also WORK ONE'S TAIL OFF.

break one's neck, to To hurry as fast as one can, to proceed with reckless speed. The same idea is conveyed by *breakneck pace,* the word *breakneck* dating from the sixteenth century. At that time, however, to break someone's neck also meant to overpower or overwhelm them. This was Sir Geoffrey Fenton's meaning when he wrote, "To breake the necke of the wicked purposes and plots of the French" (*The History of Guicciardini,* 1579).

break someone's heart, to To make someone very unhappy, to cause great grief. The expression goes back at least to Chaucer's time, and is echoed by poets in just about every era. "But break, my heart, for I must hold my tongue," says Hamlet (1.2). Today the cliché is sometimes spoken ironically: "You break my heart," meaning "I really don't feel sorry for you."

break the bank, to To ruin financially, to exhaust (one's) resources. The term comes from gambling, where it means someone has won more than the banker (house) can pay. It was so used by Thackeray ("He had seen his friend . . . break the bank three nights running," *Pendennis,* 1850). Today as a negative it is sometimes used ironically, as in "I guess another ice cream cone won't break the bank."

break the ice, to To prepare the way; to overcome initial stiffness or reserve in a social setting. The expression comes from clearing the ice from the sea so that ships could pass, and indeed the special vessels still used for this purpose are called "icebreakers." By the sixteenth century, however, the term was used figuratively, as it is today, and was listed in Erasmus's collection of adages (1508). Shakespeare and many others have used it, and there are similar phrases in numerous languages.

breath of fresh air, (like) a Refreshing and new. Formerly expressed as (like) a breath of *heaven* or *spring,* this term became current in the mid-nineteenth century. "Her arrival on the scene was like a breath of fresh air," wrote W. Somerset Maugham (*Cakes and Ale,* 1930).

bright and early First thing in the morning. Edward Young (1683–1765), in his long poem "Night Thoughts," wrote, "Early, bright, transient, chaste as morning dew she sparkled." The precise expression, however, seems to come from nineteenth-century America, where it appears in writings of Washington Irving and others.

bright as a button/new penny Of quick intelligence. The expression links the sparkle of a good mind with the shininess of a brass button or new coin. The adjective *bright* has been used in the sense of "quick-witted" and "intelligent" since about 1700.

bright-eyed and bushy-tailed Lively and perky, energetic and enthusiastic. The expression is American in origin and undoubtedly comes from anthropomorphizing the squirrel, with its beady eyes and upright bushy tail. It dates from about 1930.

bright young thing An attractive, frivolous young woman. This term may have been coined by British novelist Barbara Cartland to describe the flappers of the 1920s Jazz Age and their hedonistic life style. It is heard less often in America.

bring down the house, to To cause an uproar of applause and cheers. The term comes from the mid-eighteenth-century theater and seems a little strange, in that a cheering audience will often rise to its feet. However, in its entirety the term later became "Don't clap so hard; you'll bring the house down (it's a very old house)," and was a time-honored remark used by music-hall comedians when the audience greeted a joke with silence.

bring home the bacon, to To succeed, to come back with something of value. The term most likely comes from the sport of catching a greased pig, popular at county fairs, where the winner was awarded the pig. However,

Dr. Ebenezer Cobham Brewer believed it might come from a much older practice, instituted as far back as the early twelfth century and revived by Robert Fitzwalter in 1244. This baron willed that a side of bacon be given to any married person who would travel to Dunmow, kneel on two sharp stones at the church door, and swear that for at least a year and a day there had been no fighting in his marriage and no wish to be unmarried.

brown as a berry The color brown; today, suntanned. This simile dates from the time of Chaucer, who used it in the Prologue to his *Canterbury Tales* ("His palfrey [horse] was as broune as is a berye") and in *The Coke's Tale.* It is particularly odd that the comparison should survive for more than six centuries because few, if any, natural berries are brown.

brownie points, win Earn credits to one's good standing, advancement, or the like. The term comes from the system of awards used by the junior division of the Girl Scouts of America, called the Brownies. In the mid-twentieth century it began to be applied figuratively to good deeds or worthy accomplishments in any area.

brute force Savage, senseless violence; also, sheer strength. The word "brute" came from the Latin *brutus,* which meant heavy, stupid, and unreasoning. The original meaning survives more in this cliché, dating from the eighteenth century, than in the modern English noun "brute," which means simply an animal or a cruel person. Brute force is strength applied without thought as, for example, in forcing a lock. Eric Partridge's compilation of catchphrases records one spelling this out: "brute force and ignorance," current in Great Britain in the 1970s.

bug/bugger off Leave, get out of here. The American usage is mainly the first, the British the second. Both are slang and rude, especially given another meaning of "bugger" (sodomize), and both have been in use since at least 1900. James Joyce wrote, "Here, bugger off, Harry. There's the cops" (*Ulysses,* 1922).

bull in a china chop, (like a) Clumsy, roughly awkward. There are numerous theories concerning the origin of this expression, which probably was not an actual break-in by a bull. One of Aesop's fables concerns an ass in a potter's shop, and Charles Funk long ago suggested that a nineteenth-century British cartoonist used this idea in caricaturing John Bull (symbol for England) and his awkward dealings with the China trade. The earliest use of the precise expression found so far is in Frederick Marryat's novel *Jacob Faithful* (1834).

bully for you/him/her/them Good for you/him/her/them. This term uses the adjective "bully" in the sense of "fine" or "excellent," a largely British usage.

It became popular in the United States during the Civil War but is heard less often today and may be heading toward obsolescence. Tristan Jones had it in *Ice* (1977), "Bully for him. Was there free booze?"

bum's rush, to give/get the To throw someone (be thrown) out. The term, American and dating from the 1920s, comes from the practice of bartenders and bouncers throwing out customers who are drunk and unruly, unlikely to pay their bills, or otherwise considered a disturbance. The expression may also be related to another meaning of *bum*—backside—in that such evictions are often physical and may indeed involve a kick in the pants, or worse. In 1925 Liam O'Flaherty wrote (in *The Informer*), "They might give him 'the bum's rush,' breaking his neck silently."

bum steer Bad advice. This slangy term uses *bum* in the sense of incorrect or erroneous, a usage dating from the 1890s or earlier. Former New York governor Mario Cuomo in his 1968 book, *Thieves,* wrote, "I guess I gave you a bum steer on him."

burden of proof, the The obligation to support a contention by presenting adequate evidence. The term is a translation of the Latin *onus probandi* and was used in English courts of law from the late sixteenth century on. Transferred to any situation in which there was an obligation to prove something, it became a cliché in the nineteenth century. Attorney-novelist Scott Turow used it as the title for a popular novel involving a suicide and lawsuit (1990).

burning desire An ardent wish; excited passion. This figurative use of *burning* dates back at least to 1700. Sir Richard Steele wrote in *The Tatler* (1709) of "a burning Desire to join that glorious Company."

burning question, the A pressing, urgent, or crucial issue. The term comes from the nineteenth century and relates particularly to the discussion of important public issues. There are versions in French and German, but in English one of the best-known examples is Benjamin Disraeli's use of it—"the burning question of the day"—in a speech in the House of Commons in 1873.

burn one's bridges/boats, to To commit oneself to an irreversible course of action, without possibility of backing down. The expression comes from ancient military history, when soldiers crossing a river literally burned the bridge or boats they had used in order to cut off the possibility of retreat. A cliché by the nineteenth century, the expression has invited a number of humorous twists, such as "Never burn your bridges till you come to them" (Stanley Walker, 1941). See also CROSS THE RUBICON.

burn one's fingers, to To hurt or harm oneself. Some writers believe this term comes from the old story about a monkey who persuades a cat to pull its chestnuts out of the fire (see CAT'S PAW). Others believe it comes from an old English proverb stated by James Howell in 1659 as, "Burn not thy fingers to snuff another man's candle," and by Samuel Palmer in 1810, "The busiebody burns his own fingers." The connotation of interfering in someone else's affairs has vanished, and the modern cliché means simply to get hurt by performing any hazardous or foolhardy action.

burn the candle at both ends, to (you can't) To exhaust one's energies or resources; to stay up late playing and rise early to work hard all day. This expression came into English in the seventeenth century from French (*brusler la chandelle par les deux bouts*) via Randle Cotgrave's *Dictionary* (1611), which defined it as dissipating one's material wealth. It soon acquired a more general meaning ("He consuming just like a candle on both ends, betwixt wine and women," Richard Flecknoe, 1658) and appeared regularly enough so that Eric Partridge believed it was a cliché by the mid-eighteenth century. Though clichés usually are not the province of fine poetry, Edna St. Vincent Millay's "First Fig" (1920) used this one: "My candle burns at both ends; It will not last the night; But ah, my foes, and oh, my friends—It gives a lovely light."

burn the midnight oil, to To stay up late, studying or working. This expression, which may well be as old as the first oil lamp, appeared in English in the mid-seventeenth century. It has been traced to a poem by Francis Quarles ("Emblems," 1635): "Wee spend our midday sweat, or midnight oyle; wee tyre the night in thought; the day in toyle." A more recent example is found in David Baldacci's *Hour Game* (2004): "You don't want to burn the midnight oil too much; it's bad for your complexion."

bury/hide one's head in the sand, to To ignore danger, unpleasantness, or the like by pretending not to see it. The term comes from the practice of ostriches, who spend a good deal of time burrowing headfirst in the sand. Most of the time they are eating, for these large, flightless birds consume sand and gravel, which are used in their gizzards to help digest food. However, it was long thought that they put their heads down in the mistaken belief that they then cannot be seen, and from the early seventeenth century on this mythical self-delusion was transferred to human beings who are avoiding unpleasantness.

bury the hatchet, to To make peace or call a truce. Some North American Indian tribes declared peace by burying a tomahawk, a custom described by Samuel Sewell in 1680 and referred to again in subsequent accounts of the American colonies. The term appears in Longfellow's famous poem, "Hiawatha," and by the end of the nineteenth century was a cliché for peacemaking on both sides of the Atlantic.

business as usual Proceeding as though things were normal when they actually are not. Presumably this expression came from the practice of posting a notice in an establishment announcing that its operations were continuing despite construction, fire, or some other hampering circumstance. From the time Winston Churchill said, in a speech in November 1914, "The maxim of the British people is 'Business as usual,' " the expression was a slogan for the remainder of World War I. It later came to be used as a criticism—as, for example, when a public policy is continued even though it is no longer desirable or appropriate—and for blind complacency.

busman's holiday, a Free time spent doing the same as one does during working hours. Allegedly the expression comes from the days of horse-drawn buses, when a driver spent his time off traveling about on a bus driven by a friend. It dates from the late nineteenth century.

busy as a beaver/bee Extremely industrious. The proverbial comparison to bees dates from Chaucer's time. The one to beavers is newer, going back only to the seventeenth century; it also is put as *works like a beaver* and EAGER BEAVER. Among more recent proverbial comparisons for being busy, which liken it more to nervous overactivity than ambitiousness, is *busy as a one-armed paperhanger,* an Americanism dating from about 1910.

butter wouldn't melt (in his/her mouth), looks as if Suspiciously coy or demure, too good to be true. This expression dates from the early sixteenth century and was already a proverb in John Heywood's 1546 collection. It recurs again and again (Swift, Dickens, Thackeray, Shaw) and has been a cliché for at least a century.

button your lip Keep quiet. A twentieth-century Americanism, this expression had been current long enough by 1940 for Raymond Chandler to make a play on it: "Somebody ought to sew buttons on his face" (*Farewell, My Lovely*).

buy the farm Die, be killed. This term dates from about 1950, and alludes to military pilots on training flights over rural areas of the United States. Occasionally a pilot would crash and damage a farmer's land; the farmer then would sue the government for an amount large enough to pay off the mortgage. Since such a crash was nearly always fatal, the pilot was said to buy the farm with his life. An older equivalent is *buy it,* which since World War I has meant to be killed and also, since the 1930s, to be charged for damaging something.

by a hair/whisker Very narrowly, by a very small distance or amount. For example, "He missed sideswiping that car by a hair," or "That ball was in, but just by a whisker." Both versions of this cliché allude to the fineness of a single hair. The first, also put as *by a hairbreadth,* dates from the fourteenth century, whereas the second originated in early twentieth-century America.

by all manner of means In every possible way. The phrase *all manner of* has meant "all sorts of" since the 1700s, so basically this redundant-sounding cliché would mean "by all sorts of methods." However, the same sense could be achieved in "by all means"—that is, "by all methods."

by and large Generally speaking, on the whole. The expression comes from seamanship. When a vessel is close-hauled (sails as close as possible to the wind), "by and large" instructs the helmsman to sail slightly off the wind, making it easier to steer. Because this instruction is rather vague, the term eventually came to mean "in general."

by dint of By means of. The meaning of *dint,* originally a stroke or blow, gradually changed to signify the force or power behind the stroke. Shakespeare so used it in *Julius Caesar* (3.2): "O! now you weep, and I perceive you feel the dint of pity." Today "dint" survives only in the cliché, which is always followed by an explanatory object such as "hard work," "convincing argument," or some other forceful explanation.

by hook or by crook By any possible means. There is some disagreement as to the origin of this expression, which used to mean specifically *by fair means or foul*—that is, legal or illegal (crooked). One writer suggests it may come from the medieval custom authorizing one to help oneself to as much firewood as could be reached by a shepherd's crook and cut down with a billhook. Others believe it simply uses rhyming words for "direct" (reachable with a long hook) and "indirect" (roundabout). In any event, it dates back to the time of the English theologian John Wycliffe, who used it in his *Controversial Tracts* (c. 1380).

by leaps and bounds To make very rapid progress. Since the verb "to bound" means to move by leaps (jumps), the term is tautological. Nevertheless Coleridge (1772–1834) used it in his analysis of poetic meter (*Metrical Feet*): "With a leap and a bound the swift Anapaests throng."

by the book Very correctly, in strict accordance with the rules. *Book* in this expression is a set of established rules or, originally, of moral or religious precepts. Edgar Allan Poe was writing of the card game whist when he said, "To have a retentive memory, and to proceed 'by the book,' are points commonly regarded as the sum total of good playing" ("The Murders in the Rue Morgue," 1841). A somewhat newer synonym is *to play by the rules.*

by the by/bye By the way, incidentally, as in "By the by, I saw your brother there as well." The second *by* or *bye* in this archaic-sounding cliché originally denoted a side path, whence the current sense of "in passing."

by the numbers In a prescribed, routine fashion. The term originated during the Civil War, when recruits were taught to load and fire using a number of numerical steps. For example, nine distinct operations were involved in loading a Springfield rifle. The term was revived during World War II for training certain basic operations, such as putting on a gas mask (at the count of one, unfasten the carrier, at two, remove the mask, and so on). After the war the expression was used figuratively in civilian contexts, as in, "In checking out a reserved library book she did it by the numbers — looking it up in the computer, checking the patron's card, etc." See also BY THE BOOK.

by the same token In the same manner; moreover, for the same reason. A "token" is a sign or symbol of something, a meaning dating from the fifteenth century, and until 1600 or so "by the same token" meant "on the same grounds," or "for the same reason." After 1600, however, it came to mean "the proof of this being," that is, introducing a corroborating fact or circumstance. Thus Dickens wrote in 1857, "Others caused large Fires to be made . . .; by the same token that two or three were pleased to set their houses on Fire and so effectually sweetened them by burning them down to the Ground."

by the seat of one's pants By using intuition or improvising. The term comes from World War II, when aviators used it to describe flying when instruments did not work or visibility was poor. After the war it quickly came into more general use, as in "Use a score? No, I just conducted the overture by the seat of my pants."

by the skin of one's teeth Just barely. The term comes from the Book of Job (19:20), in which Job tells Bildad of his troubles. He says, "My bone cleaveth to my skin and to my flesh, and I am escaped with the skin of my teeth," meaning that hardly anything is left of his body. The expression still is used almost exclusively to mean a narrow escape. However, Thornton Wilder used it as the title of a play, *The Skin of Our Teeth,* an allegory of how mankind survives that won the Pulitzer Prize for drama in 1943.

by the sweat of one's brow By hard work. The expression appears to be based on God's punishment of Adam for eating the forbidden fruit in the Garden of Eden. Not only was Adam expelled, but thereafter he would have to work for a living. The Book of Genesis (3:9) has it, "In the sweat of thy face shalt thou eat bread." John Donne later (1624) spelled it out: "It was part of Adam's punishment, In the sweat of thy browes thou shalt eat thy bread."

C

cabin fever Restlessness, irritability or depression resulting from prolonged confinement, as during severe winter weather. This term comes from the American West of the late 1800s, when it literally meant being stuck inside a remote cabin, a situation that could lead to fights, divorce, and occasionally even murder. It is used somewhat more loosely now.

calculated risk An action taken even though it might fail, because not taking it might be more dangerous. The term comes from World War II, where it was applied to the chances of losing bombers, personnel and equipment, weighed against the benefits of hurting the enemy. It soon was transferred to other situations. For example, "'You don't know a thing about him.' – 'It's a calculated risk'" (Robert A. Heinlin, *Double Star*, 1956), or "We took the calculated risk of . . . using inanimate mother surrogates rather than real mothers" (*Science,* Aug. 21, 1959).

call a spade a spade, to To speak frankly and bluntly, to be quite explicit. The term dates from the sixteenth century, but may go back even to Greek and Roman times. One translation of Cicero's *Ad Familiares* reads, "Here is your Stoic disquisition . . . 'the wise man will call a spade a spade.'" There are numerous repetitions throughout the 1500s, such as John Taverner's ("Whiche call . . . a mattok nothing els but a mattok, and a spade a spade," *Garden of Wysdome,* 1539), and later uses by Ben Jonson, Robert Burton, Jonathan Swift, Charles Dickens, and Mark Twain, among others. A cliché since the nineteenth century, it acquired a more sinister meaning when *spade* became an offensive slang word for a black person.

call in question, to To challenge or cast doubt on the truth of something. Since the simple verb "to question" suffices, this wordier version, a translation of the Latin *in dubium vocare* used in legal language, is unnecessary. It has been used since the sixteenth century, by John Lyly in *Euphues* ("That I should call in question the demeanour call it a day, to of all"), by Shakespeare in *As You Like It* (5.2), and many others.

call it a day, to To stop work for the time being. The phrase implies that a full day's work has been done, whether or not the clock so indicates. Indeed, J. C. Neal in *Charcoal Sketches* (1838) spelled this out: "I've a great mind to knock off and call it half a day."

call it quits, to To stop doing something, either permanently or temporarily. *Quits* here has the meaning of acquittal or discharge, that is, release from obligation; the implication is that one has done enough and so has discharged one's obligation. American in origin, the expression appears in a letter of Jack London's (1898): "Tomorrow I would cut my throat and call quits with the whole cursed business."

call of nature Euphemism for a need to use a toilet. The term dates from the mid-1700s. It appeared in *Tailor and Cutter* (Oct. 14, 1852): "The calls of nature are permitted and Clerical Staff may use the garden below the second gate." Much more recently, a *New York Times* restaurant review by Frank Bruni told patrons, "Be sure to head downstairs to the bathrooms, even if nature doesn't call" and goes on to describe their attractive appearance (Jan. 26, 2005). A similar euphemism, used mostly by women, is to *powder one's nose.* Another euphemistic cliché for a restroom is *little boys' room,* used by men no matter what their age.

call someone's bluff, to To uncover a deception, or challenge someone to carry out a threat or prove a dubious point. The term comes from poker, where the players bet as to who has the best poker hand of them all. *To bluff* is to bet on a hand one does not believe is the best; *to call* means to match a bet, that is, bet an equivalent amount. When the cards are uncovered, whoever has the best hand wins the entire pot (all the money the players have put up). The term is American in origin and dates, like American poker, from the early 1800s. It was being transferred to other pursuits by the late nineteenth century; "Where shall we be when that bluff is called," reads an entry in the *Congressional Record* (March 1896).

call the shots Be in charge, make all major decisions. This colloquialism, dating from the mid-1900s, probably alludes to target practice. David Baldacci used it in *Hour Game* (2004): "Okay, I was right; the feds call the shots and take the glory." See also RUN THE SHOW.

calm before the storm, the A sense of foreboding, during a particularly serene period, that violence is on its way. "Fair weather brings on cloudy weather" is an ancient Greek proverb. Numerous writers from approximately 1200 on also are recorded as saying that calm will come *after* a storm. Transferring fair and foul weather to human affairs, particularly to good fortune and adversity, and to peace and war, are also very old. "It is a common fault of men not to reckon on storms in fair weather," wrote Machiavelli in *The Prince* (1513). In modern times the phrase frequently has been applied to an uneasy peacetime, when war seemed imminent. It was so used in the late 1930s, when it was already a cliché.

camel through a needle's eye, a An impossibility. The whole phrase, which comes from the Gospels of St. Matthew (19:24) and St. Mark (10:25), states that it is easier for a camel to go through the eye of a needle than for a rich man to enter into the Kingdom of God. Variants appear in both Jewish religious writings and in the Islamic Koran. The thought is repeated by Shakespeare in *Richard II* (5.5): "It is as hard to come as for a camel to thread the postern of a small needle's eye."

camp follower One who follows a group without being part of it. The practice originated with the families of recruits, prostitutes, and traveling merchants, who would settle near a military encampment. Later it was extended to others who benefited from military installations. The term itself may come from a letter written by the duke of Wellington in 1810. In mid-twentieth-century America the camp followers of rock musicians and other entertainers, mostly young women who followed their idols on tour, acquired the name *groupie,* which then was extended to any ardent fan.

cannot See entries beginning with CAN'T; also YOU CAN'T.

can of worms, it's a/like opening a Introducing a complicated problem or unsolvable dilemma. The metaphor alludes to the live bait of fishermen. In a jar or other container, they form an inextricable tangle, wriggling and entwining themselves with one another. The term is American in origin, dating from the mid-twentieth century.

can't call one's soul one's own To be very much in debt or bondage to another; to have lost one's independence. This turn of phrase dates from the sixteenth century and has been repeated ever since. In Dickens's *The Old Curiosity Shop* (1841, Chapter 4), "She daren't call her soul her own" is said of Mrs. Quilp, wife of the tyrannical dwarf, Daniel.

can't complain Pretty good, in response to "How are things going?" This very modern-sounding phrase, which means one has nothing genuine to complain about (or at least will not admit it), comes from mid-nineteenth-century Britain. Eric Partridge cites an early example, R. S. Surtees's *Hawbuck Grange* (1847), in which one character observes that time is passing lightly over another, who replies, "Middling—can't complain." Today it is a frequent response to inquiries about a business. See also FAIR TO MIDDLING.

can't fight City Hall, one/you/they An ordinary person cannot overcome bureaucracy. The term is American in origin, for it is mainly in the United States that the seat of a city government is called City Hall (and has been since the late seventeenth century). The idea of combating the city bureaucracy is believed to date from the nineteenth century, when Tammany Hall was a powerful political machine that controlled the New York Democratic Party and, in effect, the city government.

can't hit the broad side of a barn Describing a person with very poor aim. The term is thought to have originated in the mid-nineteenth century in the military. It was often repeated in the early twentieth century, when it was applied to untalented baseball pitchers who could not throw the ball over the plate with any consistency. The "broad side" in this expression also suggests the old naval meaning of *broadside,* that is, a simultaneous discharge of all the guns on one side of a warship. However, there are numerous variants (the *inside* of a barn, the *right* side of a barn *with a shotgun,* and so on) that suggest the term may also have been rural in origin.

can't hold a candle to See HOLD A CANDLE TO.

can't make a silk purse out of a sow's ear One cannot turn something inherently inferior into something of value. This proverbial metaphor dates from about 1500, and with some slight variation ("silk" is sometimes "velvet") makes its way from proverb collections (by Howell, Ray, Dykes, et al.) into literature (Samuel Richardson, Laurence Sterne, Jonathan Swift, Charles Lamb, Robert Browning, George Bernard Shaw, and Clifford Odets, among others).

can't see beyond the end of one's nose Shortsighted, unable to grasp anything but the immediate problem or events. The term was a sixteenth-century French proverb cited by several English writers. It later appeared in one of La Fontaine's fables, *The Fox and the Goat,* and in a couplet in Alexander Pope's *Essay on Man* (1734): "Onward still he goes, Yet ne'er looks forward further than his nose."

can't see the forest/wood(s) for the trees Focusing on small details makes one overlook the large picture. John Heywood's proverb collection in 1546 has it, "Ye cannot see the wood for the trees." A modern twist was provided by C. S. Lewis in a critique of William Golding's novel, *The Inheritors:* "All those little details you only notice in real life if you've got a high temperature. You couldn't see the wood for the leaves."

captive audience An audience that cannot escape a particular presentation—a speech, play, sermon, or the like. For example, "The preacher always makes his sermon twice as long on big holidays—he knows he's got a captive audience." This phrase originated in the United States about 1900.

cardinal sin A major transgression. It is interesting that this phrase should have become a modern cliché, in that "cardinal" appeared in a much earlier medieval concept of the *cardinal virtues* (justice, prudence, temperance, and fortitude, on which all other virtues depend). Their counterpart in evil was known as the *seven deadly sins,* described by Chaucer (among others) in *The Persones [Parson's] Tale:* "Of the roote of thise seyene sinnes thanne is Pryde, the general rote of alle harmes; for of this rote springen certein braunches, as Ire, Envye, Accidie or Slewthe, Avarice or Coveitise (to commune understondinge), Glotonye, and Lecherys"—that is, pride, anger, envy, sloth, avarice, gluttony, and lechery. By Shakespeare's time the term had less specific meaning; in *Henry VIII* (3.1) Queen Katharine chides Wolsey and Campeius, "Holy men I thought ye . . . but cardinal sins and hollow hearts I fear ye."

cards on the table, to lay/put one's To be completely candid, to hide nothing. The term comes from numerous card games in which the players must at some point turn their cards faceup and show their hands. The expression was transferred to a more general meaning in the late sixteenth century.

carrot and the stick, the Reward and punishment. The term alludes to dangling a carrot in front of a horse or donkey to get it to move, and threatening or beating it with a stick. An essay about philosopher John Stuart Mill explains that for Mill's father, "Praise and blame . . . were to man what carrots or sticks are to a horse or an ass . . . It was this carrot and stick discipline to which Mr. John Mill was subjected." The term dates from the late 1800s.

cart before the horse, don't put/set the Don't reverse the natural order of things. This expression no doubt dates from the time when horses first were used to draw wheeled vehicles, and began to be transferred to other affairs almost immediately. Cicero accused Homer of doing so, complaining that the Greek poet stated the moral of a story before telling the story. From the 1500s on, numerous English writers—Sir Thomas More, William Shakespeare, Charles Kingsley, to mention just a few—used this turn of phrase, which also appears in Greek, Latin, French, German, and Italian. In English it was a cliché by the 1700s.

carte blanche Complete freedom, unlimited power. The term is French for "blank paper," used in the same sense as "blank check" — that is, anything may be filled in. In the 1600s it was used in the military for unconditional surrender. After World War I it was broadened to civilian contexts, such as "He's the best mechanic we have; the boss gave him carte blanche to handle all the repairs."

cash in one's chips, to See CHIPS ARE DOWN.

cash on the barrelhead Money paid immediately for a purchase, as in "I'll give you $50 for that bike, cash on the barrelhead." Why hard cash should be equivalent to putting money on the flat head of a barrel is unclear. In nineteenth-century America *barrel* was slang for money, especially for a slush fund provided for a political candidate, and a *barrel of money* signified a huge fortune. However, these usages are only loosely related to the cliché, which itself may be dying out.

cast a pall upon, to To spread gloom. A pall was a cloth or cloak thrown over a coffin. By the eighteenth century the term had been transferred to spiritual darkness ("By this dark Pall thrown o'er the silent world," Edward Young, *Night Thoughts,* 1742).

cast aspersions, to To make a derogatory or highly critical remark, either fairly or, more often, unfairly. An older meaning of the verb "to asperse" is to sprinkle or scatter, and "aspersion" itself once meant a shower or spray. The full phrase is newer, but we find the same meaning in Sheridan's play, *The Rivals* (1775), in which Mrs. Malaprop complains bitterly of "an attack upon my language! . . . an aspersion upon my parts of speech" (3:3).

cast in stone See IN STONE.

cast of thousands A great many individuals, a large crowd. This term originated in Hollywood, in advertisements for epic-scale films such as *Ben-Hur* (1926), which had an enormous cast. Legendary producer Samuel Goldwyn, during the filming of *The Last Supper,* allegedly had this exchange: "'Why only twelve [disciples]?'—'That's the original number.'—'Well, go out and get thousands.'"

cast one's bread upon the waters, to To invest one's time, money, or effort without expecting an immediate return or reward. The term comes from the Book of Ecclesiastes (11:1)—"Cast thy bread upon the waters: for thou shalt find it after many days"—urging the congregation to give generously, for one day they would indeed be rewarded. A more modern example is, "Cast your bread upon the waters and it will come back to you—buttered" (Elbert Hubbard, *Book of Epigrams,* 1911).

cast pearls before swine, to To offer something of value to those who cannot or will not appreciate it. The saying comes from Jesus' teachings as recorded in the Gospel of St. Matthew (7:6): "Give not that which is holy unto the dogs, neither cast ye your pearls before swine, lest they trample them under their feet." It was a well-known saying by Shakespeare's time ("Pearl enough for a swine," *Love's Labour's Lost,* 4.2) and a cliché long before Dickens wrote, "Oh, I do a thankless thing, and cast pearls before swine!" (*Dombey and Son,* 1848).

cast/throw the first stone, to To be quick to attack someone or something. The term comes from Jesus' defense of an adulteress against vindictive Pharisees and scribes, who quoted the law of Moses and said she must be stoned. Jesus told them, "He that is without sin among you, let him first cast a stone at her" (Gospel of St. John, 8:7). The implication that the attacker is equally vulnerable was continued in the modern-day cliché, and spelled out even more in the old proverb, PEOPLE WHO LIVE IN GLASS HOUSES SHOULD NOT THROW STONES.

cat and mouse, game of/to play Toying with a helpless opponent or victim. The cat, ready to pounce, was recorded by Jonathan Swift ("She watches him as a cat would watch a mouse"). The cat-mouse analogy most often has been applied to authorities who may do as they wish with those in their power.

catbird seat, (sitting) in the Being in a position of advantage or superiority. The term originated in the American South, where the catbird is quite common. It is thought to allude to the bird's habit of singing from a very high perch in trees. It came into common usage in the 1940s when Mississippi-born sportscaster Red Barber would use it, for example, for a pitcher who was almost certain to strike out all the batters. Barber said he himself first heard the term in a poker game where he had bluffed all but one player into dropping out, but the remaining player, who had said from the start that he was sitting in the catbird seat, proved to have an ace and an ace in the hole. James Thurber used the expression as the title of a short story about a mild-mannered accountant who was so irritated by a colleague using this and other terms that he planned to murder her.

catch as catch can By any method that can be used; without any specific plan or order. Variants of this term go back as far as the fourteenth century ("Was none in sight but cacche who that cacche might," John Gower, c. 1394) and appeared in John Heywood's 1546 collection of proverbs ("Catch that catch may"). More specifically, it is the name of both a children's game and a style of wrestling (also called freestyle) in which the wrestlers may get a hold on each other anyhow and anywhere.

catch more flies with honey than vinegar, one can One can accomplish more by being nice than by being nasty. A version of this term appears in Cervantes's *Don Quixote* ("Make yourself into honey and the flies will devour you"), and a more precise version appears about 100 years later, in Thomas Fuller's *Gnomologia:* "More Flies are taken with a Drop of Honey than a Tun of Vinegar." It is a proverb in most European languages.

catch (someone) napping See NAPPING.

catch one's death (of a cold), to To become infected with a cold. This hyperbolic phrase, often used as a warning ("Wear your hat or you'll catch your death"), dates from the late 1800s.

catch (someone) red-handed, to To apprehend in the act of committing a crime. The term, which alludes to the presence of blood on the hands of a murderer, originally referred only to that crime. Later it was extended to mean the same as "to catch in the act," an English translation of the Latin *in flagrante delicto,* taken from the Roman code and long used in law. "I did but tie one fellow, who was taken red-handed," wrote Sir Walter Scott in *Ivanhoe* (1819).

catch-22 Situation in which one can't win because one is trapped by a paradox. The term was the title of a 1961 war novel by Joseph Heller. It refers to an Air Force rule whereby a pilot is considered insane if he continues to fly combat missions without asking for relief, but if he asks for relief he is considered sane enough to continue flying. The term was further popularized by a motion picture and today is used to describe common dilemmas in civilian life. Opera singer Renée Fleming described it well: "For potential engagements, the catch-22 was that it was very hard to get an audition if you didn't have a manager, and it was almost impossible to get a manager unless you'd won an audition" (*The Inner Voice,* 2004). See also DAMNED IF YOU DO, DAMNED IF YOU DON'T.

catch (someone) with his pants down, to To embarrass someone, to surprise someone when he is at a disadvantage. The term is American and there are several theories about its origin. One holds that it comes from a husband catching another man with his wife. Another claims it refers to an enemy catching a soldier relieving himself.

cat got your tongue, has the Why are you silent? According to Eric Partridge, this term dates from the mid-nineteenth century in both England and the United States and was one of several phrases used in addressing a child who, after getting into trouble, refused to answer questions. The literal meaning is quite far-fetched, so it obviously comes from the grown-up's invention of some bizarre circumstance that prevents the child from speaking. There is an analogous French idiom, "I throw [or give] my tongue to the cat," meaning "I give up; I have nothing to say."

cat on a hot tin roof, like a Skittish, nervous, ill at ease. A similar analogy—"like a cat on a hot bake-stone"—appeared in John Ray's *Proverbs* of 1678. It was later replaced by "like a cat on hot bricks," still used in the mid-twentieth century, but Tennessee Williams preferred the more picturesque "hot tin roof" for the title of his 1955 play, *Cat on a Hot Tin Roof.*

cat's paw, (be made) a A dupe, a sucker who does another person's dirty work. The term comes from an ancient tale about a monkey who wanted to get some roasted chestnuts out of the fire and, not wanting to burn his own fingers, got his friend the cat to use his paws for this purpose. There are numerous versions of the story in various languages; often it is a dog that is made the dupe, but in English it is the cat's paw that has stuck over the years. Also see PULL THE CHESTNUTS.

cat that swallowed the canary, (look) like the Look both smug and guilty. The analogy dates back to the mid-nineteenth century and was used by many writers, especially mystery writers (Dashiel Hammett among them), in the first half of the twentieth century.

caught napping See NAPPING.

chalk and cheese, the difference between/no more alike than See APPLES AND ORANGES.

chalk it up to, to To credit or ascribe something. The term comes from the practice of keeping accounts by writing them down with chalk on a slate. It was long used in shops, restaurants, and bars, and later also to keep score in games and sports. The figurative use, as in "chalk it up to experience," dates from the nineteenth century.

champ at the bit, to To express impatience at delay, to be eager to get going. *To champ* has meant to bite, chew, or grind upon since the sixteenth century, although its precise origin is uncertain. The analogy of the cliché is to a racehorse chewing on the bit at the start of a race, anxious to be off. The term was still being used literally in the nineteenth century ("The very horses champed at their bits," *Sketch Book,* Washington Irving, 1820) but began to be used figuratively by 1900.

change of heart, a Revising one's opinion, intentions, or feelings. Although the idea is much older, the precise expression dates from the early nineteenth century and was a cliché by 1900 or so. Groucho Marx poked fun at it in the motion picture *Duck Soup* (1933); when Mrs. Teasdale says, "He's had a change of heart," Groucho, playing the role of Firefly, replies, "A lot of good that'll do him. He's still got the same face."

change of scene, a New surroundings, referring to a trip or vacation, new employment, or similar event. The term comes from the theater, where changing the scenery has been important since Shakespeare's time. The figurative use of "scene" dates at least from the seventeenth century. "Through all the changing scenes of life," wrote Nicholas Brady and Nahum Tate in their *New Versions of the Psalms* (1696).

change one's stripes/spots, cannot One cannot alter one's essential nature. The cliché refers to the tiger, who obviously cannot change its stripes. This in turn is an alteration of a much older saying, an ancient Greek proverb also found in the Bible ("Can the Ethiopian change his skin, or the leopard his spots?" Jeremiah 13:23). The phrase appears in numerous places until the end of the seventeenth century.

change one's tune, to To reverse one's views, change one's mind, switch sides in a controversy. The analogy is very old; John Gower wrote, c. 1394, "Now schalt thou singe an other song," and the actual phrase, "change your tune," appears in a ballad about Robin Hood (one of the Child ballads) from about 1600. And a character in Samuel Beckett's novel, *The Unnameable* (1953), says, "I have my faults, but changing my tune is not one of them."

chapter and verse, cite/give Back up a statement or belief by citing the precise authority on which it is based. The chapter and verse refer to the Bible, which was long considered the ultimate authority, and was (and is) frequently quoted by the clergy with precise attribution to the exact chapter and verse. The figurative use, referring to any established set of rules, dates from the seventeenth century and was long very common, but is heard less often today.

charity begins at home One should take care of oneself and one's family before worrying about others. This proverb is a version of Paul's advice to Timothy in the New Testament (Timothy 5:4), which in the King James version was translated as "But if any widow have children or nephews, let them learn first to shew piety at home, and to requite their parents." The fourteenth-century English churchman John Wycliffe wrote, c. 1380, "Charity schuld bigyne at hem-self," which soon became "at home," not just in English but in numerous other languages. Later theologians suggested that charity should begin but not end at home, yet even in the twentieth century it continued to be pointed out that it often does ("Charity begins at home and usually stays there," H. B. Thompson, *Body, Boots and Britches,* 1940).

charmed life, to bear (lead) a To be extremely lucky, to emerge from danger unscathed. The term probably was invented by Shakespeare, for whom *charmed* had the significance of "magical." Thus Macbeth proclaims he is magically protected against death ("I bear a charmed life, which must not yield to one of woman born," 5.7) but is nevertheless slain by Macduff, who "was from his mother's womb untimely ripped." The expression was transferred to less combative affairs and said of anyone who escaped unfortunate consequences. It was a cliché by the mid-nineteenth century.

chasing rainbows Pursuing illusionary goals, trying to achieve impossible things. The term comes from the old tale about finding a crock of gold if one digs at the end of the rainbow, where it touches earth. The idea of chasing rainbows as equivalent to a fruitless quest was expressed in the nineteenth century; those who did so were called "rainbow chasers." A popular song, "I'm Always Chasing Rainbows," with words by Joseph McCarthy and music by Harry Carroll (based on Chopin's C-sharp minor Fantasy Impromptu), was published in 1918. It was used in several motion pictures, among them *Ziegfeld Girl,* with Judy Garland, and was revived with considerable success in 1946.

check is in the mail, the A delaying tactic. Originally addressed to creditors to assure them their money was on the way, even if it was not, the term dates from the second half of the 1900s. *Publishers Weekly* (Jan. 31, 2005) used it in a headline for a piece about a wholesaler's cash problems: "Is Baker & Taylor's Check in the Mail?"

check out, to To die. This slangy phrase transfers other kinds of departure to leaving this life, as in "He's had several heart attacks and could check out any day." It dates from the 1920s. *To check something/someone out,* on the other hand, meaning to investigate something or someone, as in "Let's check out this new restaurant," dates from the 1940s.

cheek by jowl Close, intimate, side by side. The term is a very old one, dating back to the sixteenth century (when it apparently replaced the still older *cheek by cheek:* "I'll go with thee, cheek by jowl," wrote Shakespeare in *A Midsummer Night's Dream,* 3.2). Eric Partridge deemed it a cliché by the mid-eighteenth century.

chew the cud, to To ruminate, to deliberate over something. For more than four centuries, to chew on something has meant to think it over. Likening human chewing to that of cows and other ruminants, which bring up food in a cud that is chewed and swallowed again, goes back even further. John Wycliffe's translation of the Book of Hosea (1382) reads, "Thei chewiden cud upon shete, and wyne, and departiden fro me" (7:14); the King James Version (1611) differs ("They assemble themselves for corn and wine, and they rebel against me"). Nevertheless, half a century before that translation was published, chewing the cud in the sense of deep thinking had made its way into a book of homilies (1547).

chew the fat/rag, to To converse, or to chatter in informal fashion. In Great Britain chewing the rag originally (late nineteenth century) was a colloquial term for complaining or grumbling, although one source holds it was an army term for persisting in an argument. Another source reports that the rag in question was a piece of cloth used when soldiers ran out of tobacco. Chewing the fat, more common in America, may have meant chewing on salt pork or fatback when supplies were low. Today both are colloquial clichés that simply mean talking in a relaxed manner.

chickens come home to roost, one's One's sins or mistakes always catch up with one. The idea of retribution is, of course, very old, recorded in ancient Greek and Roman writings. Virgil's *Aeneid,* for example, has it, "Now do thy sinful deeds come home to thee." This particular turn of phrase, however, appears to have been invented by the English poet Robert Southey, who wrote it as a motto in *The Curse of Kehama* (1809): "Curses are like young chickens; they always come home to roost."

chief cook and bottle washer Individual who has most of the many and quite varied responsibilities in an enterprise. This slangy Americanism originated in the first half of the 1800s. Alluding to kitchen duties, the term is used far more broadly, as in "Mr. Miller described himself as the 'president, chief cook and bottle washer' of his company" (*New York Times,* Nov. 7, 1992).

child's play, easy as/that's Extremely simple, easily accomplished. The earliest use of this simile appears in Chaucer's *The Merchant's Tale:* "I warne yow wel, it is no childes pley to take a wyf with-outen avysement." It was probably a cliché by the time Thomas Carlyle wrote, "The craftsman finds it no child's-play" (*Chartism,* 1839).

chilled to the bone Very cold indeed. This hyperbole for feeling cold replaces the older idea of one's blood freezing. Thus Shakespeare wrote of Pericles, after he was shipwrecked, "A man throng'd up with chill; my veins are cold" (*Pericles,* 2.1). This thought persisted well into the nineteenth century, appearing in poems by Tennyson ("Till her blood was frozen slowly," in "The Lady of Shalott") and Lawrence Binyon ("In the terrible hour of the dawn, when the veins are cold," in *Edith Cavell*).

chill out Take it easy, calm down. This slangy imperative is relatively new, dating only from about 1980, but has caught on enough to approach cliché status. It alludes to being "cool," that is, clever and laid back.

Chinaman's chance, he hasn't a/not a No chance whatever. The term dates from the latter half of the nineteenth century, when Chinese immigrants came to California to help build railroads. Their presence was sharply opposed because they would work for far less than white workers. "We are ruined by cheap labor," wrote Bret Harte in his poem "Plain Language from Truthful James." According to some authorities, the term applied to those Chinese who tried to supplement their earnings by working claims and streams abandoned by gold prospectors, a virtually hopeless undertaking. Others, poet John Ciardi among them, believe it derives from the way they were regarded as virtually subhuman and had no legal recourse if, for example, they were robbed, attacked, or otherwise abused. It largely replaced the older *not a dog's chance,* at least in America, but is now considered offensive. Also see FAT CHANCE; SNOWBALL'S CHANCE.

Chinese fire drill A state of utter confusion. This cliché dates from about 1940 and today is considered quite offensive, disparaging the Chinese as disorganized. Nevertheless, it has not yet died out.

chink in one's armor, a A vulnerable spot, a weakness. The term alludes to the medieval knight's armor made of mail—interlinked rings of metal jointed at various points. When a crack, or chink, developed between the links or joints, he was less protected against a spear or arrow. The noun "chink" has been used figuratively for such a fissure since the 1600s, and the current term came soon afterward. See also ACHILLES' HEEL.

chip off the old block, a An individual who closely resembles a parent in abilities, behavior, or appearance, most often a son resembling his father. The analogy is to wood—that is, a chip consists of the same wood as the block from which it came—and dates back to ancient Greek times. Theocritus called it a chip-of-the-old-flint (*Idyls,* c. 270 B.C.). The wood analogy appeared in several writings of the seventeenth century, although usually as a chip *of* the old block (Robert Sanderson, William Rowley, John Milton, and others), and John Ray's 1670 proverb collection had it, "Kit after kind. A chip of the old block."

chip on one's shoulder, to have a To be quarrelsome; to carry a grievance. This turn of phrase originated in nineteenth-century America, when, according to an article in *Harper's Magazine* (1857), placing a chip on a man's shoulder and daring someone to knock it off was a provocation to fight.

chips are down, the The situation is urgent or desperate, or both. The term comes from poker, where the chips represent money being wagered. When all the bets are in, the hand is over and the cards must be turned faceup to determine who has the winning hand. From the same source come two other clichés, *to cash in one's chips,* meaning to die, since turning in one's chips for money signifies the end of the game; and *in the chips,* meaning to be rich, that is, having very many chips. All these expressions date from the late nineteenth and early twentieth centuries.

choice between (of) two evils, a Two unpleasant alternatives. The full expression, "choose the *lesser of two evils,*" was already a proverb listed by John Heywood in 1546 and dates, in slightly different form, from Plato's and Aristotle's times. "Of harmes two, the lesse is for to chese," wrote Chaucer in *Troilus and Criseyde.* Since it is not always possible to decide between two such alternatives, C. H. Spurgeon may offer the best advice: "Of two evils, choose neither" (*John Ploughman's Talk,* 1880).

Christmas comes but once a year Take this opportunity to enjoy yourself to the fullest. This seemingly modern cliché actually dates from the sixteenth century, when Thomas Tusser included it as one of his *Five Hundreth Pointes of Good Husbandrie* (1573): "At Christmas play and make good cheere, for Christmas comes but once a yeere."

city slicker A smart, sophisticated urbanite. This American colloquialism, dating from the 1920s, is presumably taken from the adjective "slick" in the sense of smooth and plausible. The cliché gained renewed currency with two motion pictures, *City Slickers* (1991) and its 1994 sequel. The first film, which won Jack Palance an Oscar for best supporting actor, concerns three city-dwelling friends who sign up for a two-week cattle drive.

claim to fame, one's A characteristic for which a person or thing is particularly noted. For example, describing a bridge player who won several big titles, Alan Truscott wrote, "He had three other claims to fame. His friends knew him as an extraordinary raconteur, and . . . he was addicted to opening the bidding in a three-card major suit and perpetrated outrageous psychic bids" (*New York Times,* April 13, 2000). This twentieth-century cliché undoubtedly owes its popularity to its rhyme.

clean as a hound's tooth Spotlessly clean. This proverbial simile, current from about 1900, is as puzzling as one of its fifteenth-century antecedents, "clene as a byrdes ars." The teeth of hounds are no cleaner than those of other carnivores, but therein may lie the source of the saying, that is, "clean" here may first have meant "sharp." By the 1950s, however, when it was being applied to President Dwight D. Eisenhower's administration, it meant clean in a more conventional figurative sense, that is, free of corruption.

clean as a whistle Thoroughly or neatly done; also, pure, unsoiled. The early-nineteenth-century use of this term, which appears in William Carr's *The Dialect of Craven* (1828) as a proverbial simile meaning "wholly" or "entirely," was in such guise as "Head taken off as clean as a whistle" (W. S. Mayo, *Kaloolah,* 1849). Why this should be analogous to a whistle is not certain. In the eighteenth century the simile was "clear as a whistle," presumably referring to the pure sound produced by a whistle, relatively free of overtones. From "clear" and "pure" to "clean" is not so very far. Another theory holds that "whistle" came from "whittle"—that is, clean as wood is after being whittled—but this analogy seems less likely.

clean bill of health, to have a/be given a To have passed a rigorous inspection. The term comes from the nineteenth-century practice of issuing an actual bill of health, a document signed by the authorities and given to the ship's master, stating that no infectious diseases existed in the port of embarkation. If there was some kind of epidemic, the ship received a *foul* bill of health. Before long the term was transferred to the assurance that an individual or group or organization was found, after investigation, to be morally sound.

cleanliness is next to godliness Physical cleanliness betokens spiritual purity. The idea is an ancient one, found in both Babylonian and Hebrew religious tracts. The precise phrase first appears in a sermon by John Wesley in 1778, which puts it in quotation marks but does not reveal the source. It is much quoted thereafter, by Dickens and Shaw ("Cleanliness which comes next to godliness, if not before it," *Man and Superman,* 1903), among others.

clean slate, have a/start with a A fresh chance after past debts or offenses have been canceled or forgiven. A nineteenth-century term, it comes from the schoolroom and tavern, where slate blackboards and chalk were used for exercises and totting up bills (see also CHALK IT UP TO). Mistakes and debts so recorded could literally be erased. It may have been a translation of the earlier Latin *tabula rasa* ("scraped tablet"), on which anything could be inscribed. By the second half of the nineteenth century the term was transferred to mean making any kind of fresh start. Another version of the term is *to wipe the slate clean* (so as to obtain a clean slate). As Rudyard Kipling wrote about *The Absent-Minded Beggar* (1900), "He's out on active service, wiping something off a slate."

clean sweep, (make) a Get rid of anything or anyone old, extraneous, unwanted. The term often refers to new officeholders who are extremely zealous about making a completely new start. It probably came from the much older locution, "New broom sweeps clean," quoted in John Heywood's proverb collection of 1546 and repeated often over the years, but now virtually obsolete.

clear as a bell Describing a tone free from harshness, rasping, or hoarseness, pure as the sound of a bell. The simile was already current in the seventeenth century; it appeared in John Ray's proverb collection of 1670. Today it is often used figuratively to describe something that is readily understood. See also LOUD AND CLEAR.

clear as mud Murky, obscure, anything but clear. This jocular cliché, spoken ironically to indicate that something is unclear, dates from the early nineteenth century. It appears in R. H. Barham's *Ingoldsby Legends* (1842) and is still frequently heard.

clear conscience, to have a To feel free from blame, obligation, or a similar burden because one is guiltless (or so believes). The sixteenth-century writer John Lyly used the term several times in his *Euphues* (1580)—"a cleere conscience is a sure card"—and the same phrase turned up in James Howell's proverb collection of 1659. Nearly a century later Benjamin Franklin wrote, "Keep Conscience clear, then never fear" (*Poor Richard's Almanack,* 1749).

clear the air, to To remove confusion or controversy. The analogy to stormy weather was made as long ago as the fourteenth century, although at first the term meant to free something from clouds or other obscuring elements. In time it came to mean getting rid of the sultry oppressiveness common before a storm, which then was transferred to the removal of misunderstanding or ambiguity. Thus a British reporter wrote, "His explicit . . . reply to Parnell's speech . . . cleared the air" (*Manchester Examiner,* 1885).

clear the decks, to To prepare for action. This term comes from naval warfare. In the times of wooden sailing ships, a crew prepared for battle by fastening down or removing all loose objects on the decks, lest they get in the way or cause an injury. By the eighteenth century the term was being used to mean getting ready for any major undertaking by getting small details out of the way. See also BATTEN DOWN THE HATCHES.

cliff-hanger A situation whose outcome is in extremely suspenseful doubt until the last moment. The term comes from serialized adventure films popular in the United States in the 1920s and 1930s, in which, at the end of each installment, the hero or heroine is left in a very dangerous situation, sometimes literally dangling from a cliff. The rationale, of course, was to entice the audience to return for the next installment in order to see what happened. By the 1940s the term was being transferred to other suspenseful states of affairs—for example, "the election was a cliff-hanger."

climb the wall(s), to To be driven to action out of restlessness or frustration. In the Book of Joel (2:7) the writer says, "They shall climb the wall like men of war," and, in fact, until relatively recent times cities and towns were surrounded by defensive walls, which protected them against their enemies. The fierceness of attackers who climbed such walls survives in the sense of frenzy suggested by the modern cliché. See also DRIVE (SOMEONE) UP THE WALL.

clinging vine An extremely dependent person. Today this term is mildly pejorative—such a person is not considered particularly admirable—but earlier uses of this figure of speech carry no such criticism. Indeed, the vine in question, nearly always a woman or wife, was also praised for potential or actual fruitfulness (i.e., childbearing ability). "Thy wife shall be as a fruitful vine by the sides of thine house," says the Book of Psalms (128:3).

clip joint An establishment such as a nightclub or restaurant that habitually overcharges or cheats customers. The verb "to clip" has been a slangy synonym for "to cheat" since the 1920s. The equally slangy cliché came soon afterward. It is still a frequent usage. The television comedy *Seinfeld* had it in 1992: "What kind of clip joint are you running here?"

clip someone's wings, to To deflate a conceited person. Although at first glance this phrase might seem to have a military origin (from demoting an officer whose rank is indicated by wings), the metaphor actually comes from birds—specifically, the practice of clipping the wings of domestic fowl so they cannot fly away—and dates from ancient Roman times. "Away to prison with him, I'll clippe his winges," wrote Christopher Marlowe (*The Massacre at Paris,* 1590, 3.2).

cloak-and-dagger Describing a secret or undercover operation. The term dates from seventeenth-century Spain, and the popular swashbuckling plays of Lope de Vega and Pedro Calderón de la Barca, filled with duels, intrigue, and betrayal. They were referred to as *comedias de capa y espada,* which was variously translated as "cloak-and-sword" or "cloak-and-dagger plays." Somewhat later, in the nineteenth century, the term began to be applied to various kinds of romantic intrigue, and still later, to espionage. The idea of concealment was, of course, much older, and indeed, Chaucer wrote of "The smyler with the knyf under the cloke" (*The Knight's Tale*).

close but no cigar, (it was) Nearly successful, but not quite. This slangy Americanism dates from the first half of the twentieth century. It most likely came from the practice of giving a cigar as a prize to the winner of a contest, such as hitting the target in a carnival shooting gallery.

close call/shave, a A narrow escape, a near miss. Both phrases are originally American. The first dates from the 1880s and is thought to come from sports, where a *close call* was a decision by an umpire or referee that could have gone either way. A *close shave* is from the early nineteenth century and reflects the narrow margin between smoothly shaved skin and a nasty cut from the razor. Both were transferred to mean any narrow escape from danger. Incidentally, a *close shave* was in much earlier days equated with miserliness. Erasmus's 1523 collection of adages has it, "He shaves right to the quick," meaning he makes the barber give him a very close shave so that he will not need another for some time. Two synonymous modern clichés are *too close for comfort* and *too close to home.*

close on the heels See HEELS OF.

close quarters, at/in Crowded, in a confined space. The term comes from eighteenth-century naval warfare. Wooden barriers were placed at various points on a ship, so that when an enemy boarded, the crew could retreat behind them and fire at the enemy through loopholes. The crew then were said to be fighting in close quarters, that is, in close contact with the enemy. The term later was transferred to any close contact or crowded situation.

close ranks Unite against a common opponent, present a united front. The term originated in the 1600s in the military, where it also was put as "to close files." It alluded to the style of battle in which the troops were aligned side by side in neat rows; the order to "close ranks" meant to move the rows closer together, creating a seemingly impenetrable mass of men. The term was soon being used figuratively and became a cliché. For example, "Will the wankel [engine] be enough to sustain NSU as an independent motor company, or will NSU one day have to close ranks further with Citroen?" (*Economist,* Sept. 2, 1967).

close to the chest See PLAY ONE'S CARDS CLOSE TO ONE'S CHEST.

clothes make the man Outer appearances are very important. The thought appears in ancient Babylonian writings, and Erasmus's collection of adages (1523) refers to the fact that the statement "Clothes are the man" appeared in Homer and numerous ancient Latin sources. In sixteenth-century England it was usually put as "apparel" rather than "clothes";

Shakespeare's Polonius pontificates, "The apparel oft proclaims the man" (*Hamlet,* 1.3). It was a cliché by the nineteenth century.

clutch at straws See GRASP AT STRAWS.

coals of fire See HEAP COALS OF FIRE.

coals to Newcastle, to carry/bring To do something that is unnecessary or superfluous. The Newcastle referred to is the city of Newcastle-upon-Tyne, a seaport in northeastern England that was given a charter to mine coal by Henry III in 1239 and became a major coal center. By the seventeenth century this metaphor for bringing an unneeded thing was current, and it remained so in all English-speaking countries. There were (and are) equivalents in numerous languages. In French it is to carry water to a river.

coast is clear, the The authorities aren't looking; one can proceed without fear of getting caught. Several writers hold that this term comes from the days of piracy and smuggling, when it declared the absence of coast guards. However, one of the earliest references dates from 1530, appearing in J. Palsgrave's book about the French language: "The kynge intendeth to go to Calays, but we must first clere the costes." By the late sixteenth century the term was also being used figuratively. Eric Partridge regarded it as a cliché from the eighteenth century on.

cobbler, stick to your last Do not advise about or interfere with matters of which you know little or nothing. This turn of phrase comes from an anecdote about a painter of ancient Greece named Apelles. One day a shoemaker saw a painting of his and pointed out that the shoe in the picture was not accurately portrayed. The painter corrected that part of the picture. Then the next day the shoemaker pointed out a mistake in the painting of a leg. But the painter replied, "Shoemaker, do not go above your last." The story was repeated in various accounts and made its way into John Taverner's translation of Erasmus as "Let not the shoemaker go beyonde his shoe." Although the cobbler's day appears to be nearly over, at least in America, the cliché survives.

cock and bull story A far-fetched tale, intended to deceive. This term dates from approximately 1600, but its origin is obscure. Some say it refers to the name of an English coaching inn, a wayside stop for travelers where such tales were often spun. Others believe it alludes to a fable or folktale about a cock and a bull. By the eighteenth century the term meant a tall tale.

cock of the walk The leader in a group, especially one who is quite conceited about the position. The term comes from animal husbandry, where an enclosure for domestic fowl was called a *walk,* and in that area they would fight for supremacy until only one remained—the supreme leader, or cock of the walk. The strutting pride of roosters had been transferred to bossy, conceited human beings for much longer, but the precise term *cock of the walk* in this sense dates only from the early nineteenth century.

coin a phrase, to To fashion an expression. This term, dating from the 1940s, is often used ironically to apologize for using a cliché, as in "He acts like the cock of the walk, to coin a phrase." Of course it can also be used straightforwardly and refer to inventing an expression, a usage dating from the late 1500s.

cold blood, in Calculatedly ruthless. This expression comes from the days when it was commonly believed that blood rules the temper and was boiling hot when one was excited and ice-cold when one was calm. The French call it *sang-froid,* a term taken over in English with the same meaning. Thus Byron wrote of Don Juan, "Cross-legg'd with great sang-froid among the scorching ruins he sat smoking." In more recent times Truman Capote used the term as the title of a detailed account (1965) of a deliberate act of murder.

cold comfort That's little or no consolation. "Colde watz his cumfort," reads a poem of unknown authorship written about 1325. The alliterative phrase appealed to Shakespeare, who used it a number of times (in *King John, The Tempest, The Taming of the Shrew*). It acquired cliché status by about 1800. Stella Gibbons used it in the title of her humorous book *Cold Comfort Farm* (1932).

cold enough to freeze the balls off a brass monkey Frigid, extremely cold. This term, already known by 1835, comes from naval warfare, in the days when cannonballs were stacked in pyramid form on brass trays called "monkeys." In cold weather the metal would contract and the balls fall off. For a similar hyperbole, see CHILLED TO THE BONE.

cold feet, to get/have To be timid; to back off from some undertaking. This expression appears to date from the nineteenth century, at least in its present meaning. In the early seventeenth century it was an Italian proverb that meant to have no money; it was so used by Ben Jonson in his play *Volpone.* The source of the more recent meaning is obscure. Some believe it comes from soldiers retreating in battle because their feet are frozen. Another source cites a German novel of 1862 in which a card player withdraws from a game because, he claims, his feet are cold.

cold fish, a A person who is unfeeling, or at least shows no emotion. "Cooler than a fish on a cake of ice," P. G. Wodehouse put it (*Money in the Bank,* 1942). He was scarcely the first. Shakespeare wrote, "It was thought she was a woman and was turned into a cold fish" (Autolycus telling of a ballad against the hard hearts of maids, *The Winter's Tale,* 4.4). See also COLD HEART.

cold hands, warm heart Undemonstrativeness need not signify lack of feeling. In the singular the term appears in a collection of sayings published by Vincent Lean in 1902 ("A cold hand and a warm heart"). A similar idea is behind Alan S. Blinder's book on economic policymaking, *Hard Heads, Soft Hearts* (1987), which claims it is not only possible but necessary to have an economic policy that is both rational and efficient (hardheaded) and socially compassionate (softhearted).

cold heart, a A dispassionate, unaffectionate individual. This term already meant lack of love in Shakespeare's time. In his *Antony and Cleopatra* (3:13) Antony asks the queen if she now prefers Caesar to him, saying, "Cold-hearted toward me?" and she, denying it, replies, "Ah! dear, if I be so, from my cold heart let heaven engender hail, and poison it in the source; and the first drop in my neck."

cold shoulder, to give/show the To snub someone; to assume a distant manner, or show indifference. The term dates from the early nineteenth century and was frequently used by Sir Walter Scott. It is believed to come from the custom of serving hot meat to welcome guests, and of serving a cold shoulder of mutton or beef, considered a much inferior dish, when they had outstayed their welcome.

cold turkey Abrupt withdrawal from any habitual activity. This term, which came into use in the early twentieth century primarily for withdrawal from some addictive substance (drug or alcohol), soon was transferred to quitting other habits and activities. Its ultimate origin is unclear. It may have come from TO TALK TURKEY, which was sometimes put as "to talk cold turkey," both meaning to speak in an unvarnished way about an unpleasant matter.

cold water, to pour/throw To discourage, to dampen pleasure or enthusiasm. The analogy dates back at least to Roman times, when Plautus used it (*Aquam frigidam suffundunt,* "They pour cold water on us"), and also appears in William Scarborough's collection of Chinese proverbs (1875).

color of your money, let's see the Back up your claim with hard evidence. A twentieth-century Americanism, according to Eric Partridge, it originated in gambling or betting, as a challenge or to make sure that the bettor actually had enough cash to cover a bet. One writer holds that it was already common in eighteenth-century England, but his citation is not verifiable. In any event, it is unlikely that the actual hue of the money was in doubt, unless the questioner felt it might be counterfeit. More likely "color" was used figuratively for something readily identifiable.

come See under COMES.

come again? What did you say? Did I hear you correctly? This phrase, dating from about 1900, usually implies surprise or disbelief, as in "'Her science teacher doesn't believe in evolution.' 'Come again? That can't be true.'"

come apart at the seams, to To become disordered; to go to pieces. This graphic analogy to a garment becoming, as it were, unsewn, is American and dates from the mid-twentieth century. "In a few instances when I thought that I would come apart at the seams . . . I managed to make the director listen" (Josef von Sternberg, *Fun in a Chinese Laundry,* 1965, an account of making a movie).

comeback, to make/stage a To return to one's former standing, after a withdrawal or a lapse in popularity or ability. This term originated in America about 1900 or so. "With a little effort you could still stage a comeback," wrote F. Scott Fitzgerald in *This Side of Paradise* (1920).

come clean, to To tell the whole truth, to confess. A slangy Americanism dating from the early twentieth century, it most often appeared in crime novels and pertained to confessing guilt. Listed in a collection of argot published in 1919, the term became a cliché through its overuse in murder mysteries. P. G. Wodehouse played on it in *Sam the Sudden* (1925): "You'd best come clean, Soapy, and have a showdown."

come down on, to See LIKE A TON OF BRICKS.

come full circle See FULL CIRCLE.

come hell or high water No matter what happens; COME WHAT MAY. The origin of this expression has been lost. One authority claims it is a variation of BETWEEN THE DEVIL AND THE DEEP BLUE SEA, "hell" and "high water" representing similar great obstacles. It appears to have originated shortly after 1900. In 1939, at the outbreak of World War II, A. Keith wrote about imperialism, "Let empires be built—come hell or high water, they build 'em."

come-hither look A seductive or flirtatious glance, a come-on. This cliché represents one of the few surviving uses of the adverb *hither,* for "to this place" or "here," which was commonplace in Shakespeare's day ("Come hither, come hither, come hither" is in the song "Under the Greenwood Tree," *As You Like It,* 2.5). The cliché dates from the first half of the 1900s and was frequently applied to film stars in romantic movies, in an era when a blunter sexual approach was frowned on.

come in from the cold Return to safety and acceptance. This phrase became popular following the publication of John Le Carré's bestselling espionage novel, *The Spy Who Came in from the Cold* (1963) and the motion picture based on it (1965).

come off it Quit pretending or acting foolish or lying. Originally American slang dating from about 1900, it may, as one writer suggests, be related to coming down from a high perch or position of lofty pompousness (see ON ONE'S HIGH HORSE). W. Somerset Maugham, a master of realistic dialogue, wrote, "Come off it, Roy . . . I'm too old a bird to be caught with chaff" (*Cakes and Ale,* 1930).

come on board Join an organization or other kind of group. This transfer from the nautical meaning of getting on a ship or boat dates from the twentieth century. It is often expressed as a hearty invitation to join a business organization, as in "The personnel officer was very impressed with you, so we hope you'll come on board."

come out of one's shell, to To overcome one's shyness or inhibitions. Ebenezer Brewer believed this saying alludes to the tortoise, which hides from danger by retreating under its shell. It might equally well allude to a newly hatched bird. "The shell must break before the bird can fly," wrote Tennyson (*The Ancient Sage,* 1885).

come out of the closet Reveal one's homosexuality. This term began to be widely used in the second half of the 1900s and also has been shortened to *come out.* It refers to the older usage, *closet homosexual,* that is, one who is well concealed. It is occasionally used in a nonsexual sense, as in "Cathy's come out of the closet about her peanut-butter binges."

comes with the territory Is part of specific conditions or circumstances. For example, "You may not like dealing with difficult customers, but it comes with the territory." The term, which originally alluded to traveling salesmen who had to accept whatever they found in their assigned region, or "territory," soon came to be extended to other areas. It dates from the second half of the twentieth century.

come to a grinding/screeching halt Stop suddenly. Referring to the noise made by gears or brakes during a sudden stop, these phrases date from the second half of the 1900s. The *National Observer* of December 4, 1976, had: "A lot of that stuff is going to come to a screeching halt quickly, and we're not going to do the screeching." It is also put as *grind to a halt.*

come to a head, to To reach a climax or culminating point. The analogy is to an ulcer or boil that has ripened to the point of suppuration, that is, bursting. Indeed, such sores were said to "come to a head" as early as the early seventeenth century. By then the term had long since been transferred to other matters (the *OED* lists the earliest figurative use of it from 1340). In 1596 Edmund Spenser, describing the state of Ireland, wrote, "to keep them [i.e., these affairs] from growing to such a head."

come to blows, to To begin fighting, usually physically. "Their controversie must either come to blowes or be undecided," wrote Thomas Hobbes in *The Leviathan* (1651). It also was sometimes put as "fall to blows," as in Shakespeare's *Henry VI, Part 2,* 2.3.

come to grief, to To fail or to falter; to experience a misfortune. A common locution in the early nineteenth century, it rapidly reached cliché status. "We were nearly coming to grief," wrote Thackeray (*The Newcomes,* 1854).

come to pass, to To happen. Probably the most famous occurrence of this phrase is at the beginning of the Christmas story as related in the Gospel of St. Luke (2:1): "And it came to pass in those days, that there went out a decree from Caesar Augustus." Eric Partridge said it was already a cliché by about 1700, but this archaic turn of phrase has survived nevertheless.

come to the same thing, to To make no difference. "It all comes to the same thing at the end," wrote Robert Browning ("Any Wife to Her Husband," 1842), the words of a dying wife concerning the likelihood that her widowed husband will remarry. It also has been put as *amount to* or *add up to* the same thing.

come up smelling like roses, to To emerge untarnished from a sordid situation. A fuller version of this saying is given by Eric Partridge: "could fall into the shit and come up smelling of roses." American in origin, it dates from the early twentieth century. It is sometimes shortened to "come up like roses," as in, "It's the second spring of George Bush's 'Don't worry, be happy' presidency, and everything continues to come up roses for the politician who two years ago was a symbol of hopelessness" (Mary McGrory, *Boston Globe,* 1990).

come what may Whatever should happen, as in "Come what may, he'll get to the wedding on time." This cliché originated in the 1500s as "Come what will" and is known in numerous languages.

compare notes, to To exchange opinions, impressions, or information. The original meaning referred to written notes, but the phrase soon included verbal exchanges as well. It was known by at least 1700. In 1712 Richard Steele wrote (in the *Spectator*), "They meet and compare notes upon your carriage."

comparisons are odious To draw an analogy is offensive; one cannot compare apples and oranges fairly. This term was already so well known in Shakespeare's time that he was able to make a pun—more accurately a malapropism—on it and be sure it would be perfectly understood ("Comparisons are odorous," says Dogberry in *Much Ado about Nothing,* 3.5). The earliest reference recorded is from about 1430, and there are equivalents in French, Italian, and numerous other languages.

conk out, to Fall asleep or lose consciousness. This colloquialism was coined by aviators during World War I. It was thought to be imitative of the noise an engine makes just before it breaks down completely. The term is still used for mechanical failures, but by the mid-1900s it was being applied to human beings. Thus, Maurice Herzog had it in *Annapurna* (1952): "I told Lionel that rather than conk out next day on the slope, it seemed far better for me to go down."

conspicuous by one's (its) absence Noticeable by the very fact of not being there. The idea was expressed very early on by the Roman historian Tacitus, in recording the absence of Junia's brother, Brutus, and her husband, Cassius, at her funeral procession. The phrase became popular in the nineteenth century, and continued to be applied often to political matters, such as the absence of certain provisions in a law, or the absence of political leaders on certain important occasions.

conspicuous consumption Showing off one's material wealth. The term was coined by the American economist Thorstein Veblen in *The Theory of the Leisure Class* (1899), where he roundly criticized the well-to-do (leisure class) for preying on the rest of society and then flaunting their acquisitions. The term, always used as critically as by its author, has become a cliché.

conspiracy of silence An agreement, either tacit or explicit, to disclose nothing about an individual or situation. The term nearly always refers to disclosing something unfavorable, or even criminal. For example, physicians often have been accused of protecting an incompetent member of their profession by keeping quiet. Dating from the late nineteenth century, the term at first was used by individuals complaining of lack of attention. The poet Lewis Morris reportedly complained to Oscar Wilde that a conspiracy of silence prevented his works from being reviewed and asked what he should do, whereupon Wilde replied, "Join it."

conventional wisdom, the What the majority believe and act upon. The term was coined by the American economist John Kenneth Galbraith in *The Affluent Society* (1958), in which he so described economic views that are familiar, predictable, and therefore generally accepted. It was soon transferred to other areas in which public opinion plays an important role in influencing events. It has just about replaced the now virtually obsolete cliché, *climate of opinion.*

cook someone's goose, to To ruin someone's undertaking or plan. There are numerous colorful theories about the origin of this term. According to one, the inhabitants of a besieged town in the sixteenth century hung out a goose to show their attackers they were not starving; the enraged enemies then set fire to the town and thus cooked the goose. According to another, the term comes from the fable about the goose that laid golden eggs, which, when the farmer killed it to obtain the gold inside, left him with nothing but a goose to cook. The earliest written records of the term date from the mid-nineteenth century, one being in a street ballad opposing the Pope's appointment of a particular cardinal ("If they'll come here we'll cook their goose, the Pope and Cardinal Wiseman," 1851).

cook the books Falsely adjust the accounts. The verb "to cook" has meant to manipulate ever since the 1600s and continued to be used, especially with reference to changing figures, to the present day. The current phrase popularized the concept, its rhyme more attractive than simply "cook the accounts," and it has largely replaced other versions since the second half of the 1900s. The 1986 film *Legal Eagles* had it ("The three partners were cookin' the books"), as did a *New York Times* editorial about the Environmental Protection Agency: "The agency was thus ordered to cook the books, deliberately underestimating the reductions that would be possible under alternative approaches . . ." (March 21, 2005).

cool! Stylish, fashionable, clever. This slangy term expressing admiration dates from the early 1900s as an adjective and was popularized by black jazz musicians from the late 1940s. As an interjection it was then taken up by teenagers and then by the general population. Describing the plan for an assassination, a character in James Patterson's *London Bridges* (2004) exclaimed, "Not only is this smart, it is cool as hell."

cool as a cucumber Perfectly composed, self-possessed. The cool temperature of cucumbers apparently was observed long ago, and indeed one modern writer quotes recent evidence that the inside of a field cucumber on a warm day is 20 degrees cooler than the air. Beaumont and Fletcher described "young maids . . . as cold as cucumbers" (*Cupid's Revenge,* 1615, 1.1), and in 1732 John Gay, in a *New Song on New Similies,* wrote, "I . . . cool as a cucumber could see the rest of womankind." A more recent version with essentially the same meaning is *cool, calm, and collected,* which likewise owes its popularity to its alliterative appeal. The earliest (and only partial) reference cited by the *OED* is Sir J. Hannen's in an 1885 law journal: "A calm and collected and rational mind."

cool it, to To calm down. This slangy Americanism emerged about 1950 and caught on rapidly. It is thought to come from the usage of "cool" to mean calm and unflustered. In 1953 E. Gilbert wrote, "Cool it, girl. Nobody's interested" (*Hot and Cool*). Related expressions from the same period are *to keep one's cool,* meaning to remain calm, and the antonym *to lose/blow one's cool,* for losing one's composure.

cool one's heels, to To be kept waiting. Presumably this saying comes from the fact that one's feet become warm in the act of walking and cool off when one sits or stands still in the act of waiting. It dates from the early seventeenth century and was common enough by the 1630s to appear in several sources (William Rowley, Thomas Dekker). A century later Henry Fielding wrote, "In this parlour Amelia cooled her heels, as the phrase is, near a quarter of an hour" (*Amelia,* 1752).

coon's age, a A long time. An American expression from the first half of the nineteenth century, it is based on the mistaken idea that raccoons (or "coons") are long-lived. They are not, but their fur, widely used from colonial times, is sturdy and long-lasting. An early example appears in black dialect in *Southern Sketches* (1860): "This child haint had much money in a coon's age."

corridors of power The highest echelons of government bureaucracy. This term was coined in the 1956 novel *Homecomings* by C. P. Snow, who later used it as the title of another novel, *Corridors of Power* (1964). By that time Snow realized it had become a cliché, but said, "If a man hasn't the right to his own cliché, who has?" (quoted by William Safire, *New York Times,* May 14, 2000). However, it is heard less often today.

cost an arm and a leg/a pretty penny, to Excessively expensive, exorbitant. The first phrase is American in origin and dates from the mid-twentieth century. The source is obvious: giving up an arm and a leg to buy something is clearly too costly. The use of "pretty" to mean considerable in amount was originally British and is now archaic except in a few well-worn phrases like this one, a cliché since the late nineteenth century. It was common throughout the eighteenth century, and crossed the Atlantic as well ("The captain might still make a pretty penny," Bret Harte, *Maruja,* 1885). A similar term was a *fine penny,* now obsolete.

couch potato A physically lazy individual who prefers watching television to other leisure activities. This slangy expression, alluding to an inert object (*potato*) sitting on a sofa, was invented in the 1970s and quickly gained currency. It also has been suggested that the term is a play on *boob tube* (slang for television set), since a potato is a tuber. With the proliferation of remote-control devices, the dedicated television addict did not even need to get up to change programs or adjust the volume. The cliché is occasionally used more broadly as well, for anyone who is basically indolent.

couldn't care less, he/I/she It doesn't matter one bit; describing total indifference. The term originated in Great Britain, probably in the late 1930s, and was very popular by the 1940s. It not only expressed bored indifference but, during World War II, bravado. An informal history of civilian ferry pilots during the war by Anthony Phelps was entitled *I Couldn't Care Less* (1946). In the mid-1960s the term was unaccountably changed by some Americans to *I could care less,* possibly influenced by the locution *I should care,* also meaning "I don't care." It, too, is now a cliché. Another variation recorded by Eric Partridge was *I couldn't care fewer,* which, however, was short-lived.

counting your chickens See DON'T COUNT YOUR CHICKENS.

count noses, to To determine the number of persons present. The term may come from horse dealers, who count their stock by the nose (whereas cattle dealers count by the "head"). However, it has been around a long time, since the seventeenth century, when it was sometimes put as "to tell noses." In 1711 the earl of Shaftesbury, a moral philosopher who studied with John Locke, wrote, "Some modern zealots appear to have no better knowledge of truth, nor better manner of judging it, than by counting noses" (*Characteristics of Men, Manners, Opinions, Times*).

count one's blessings Appreciate what one has, or one's good fortune. This Pollyanna-like phrase is often used to help avoid worrying about what one lacks or one's bad luck. (*Pollyanna,* a children's book from the early 1900s by Eleanor H. Porter, is the story of an orphan girl who remains resolutely cheerful and sweet-tempered in the face of considerable adversity.) A modern version of the cliché is THINK POSITIVE.

country cousin A visiting unsophisticated relative or friend whose naiveté or rough manners embarrass the host. Such a person became a stock figure of fun in Restoration comedies (of the late seventeenth and early eighteenth centuries). The precise term was current by the second half of the eighteenth century and a cliché by the mid-nineteenth century. Anthony Trollope's son's reminiscences (Thomas Adolphus Trollope, *What I Remember,* 1887) included, "One of the sights of London for country cousins was to see the mails starting." The term is heard less often today.

coup de grace Finishing stroke. The phrase is French for "blow of mercy," a death blow administered to end a wounded person's suffering. It probably originated in dueling or other sword fighting and had been adopted into English by about 1700 and was already being used figuratively for the finishing stroke for any kind of enterprise. For example, "He carefully placed the figures of bride and groom on top of the cake, the coup de grace for an artistic creation."

courage of one's convictions, to have the To act in accordance with one's beliefs. The term may have originated in France since at first it was stated as the courage of his opinions (*le courage de son opinion*); it so appears in John Morley's biography of *Diderot* (1878). A 1989 political cartoonist put an amusing twist on it in criticizing President George H.W. Bush's changing stand on abortion: "It's nice to see he has the courage of his elections" (Wasserman, *Boston Globe,* Nov. 9, 1989). See also PUT ONE'S MONEY WHERE ONE'S MOUTH IS.

cover one's/your ass (CYA) Protect oneself in case of failure, avoid being blamed for something. This rather rude expression dates from the 1950s and may have originated in the military. It has since been used in many different contexts. For example, the *McLaughlin Group,* a television panel, used the acronymic form: "Is he a hero . . . [or] a CYA practitioner?" (July 26, 1987).

cover the waterfront, to To include or comprise everything about something, to leave nothing out. Why this American colloquialism should use "waterfront" to mean everything about some subject is a mystery: for example, "This American history course begins with Columbus and ends with the last election—it really covers the waterfront."

crack down on, to To take strong measures against someone or something, as in "The police are cracking down on drug dealers." This colloquialism first appeared in the 1930s and caught on quickly, especially with reference to repression by authority figures.

crack of dawn, (at) the Early in the morning. The origin of this expression is uncertain. One writer suggests that "crack" is derived from the ancient meaning of a sudden loud noise (since the word comes from Old English *cracian,* "to resound"), because the sun comes up suddenly. Rudyard Kipling used similar imagery in his poem "Mandalay," where "the dawn comes up like thunder outer China 'crost the Bay." On the other hand, "crack" may refer to a small space or opening—that is, the wedge of light that appears as the sun rises over the horizon. Whichever, the phrase originated in America in the late nineteenth century. It may already have been a cliché when W. Somerset Maugham wrote (*Catalina,* 1948), "He had slipped away at the crack of dawn."

crack the code, to To solve a difficult problem or mystery. The term is derived from deciphering coded intelligence during wartime and became current during World War II, when cryptography, used by armies at least since Napoleon's day, reached new heights of sophistication. After the war it began to be transferred to other areas, such as solving a difficult scientific problem (cracking the genetic code, for example). See also TOUGH NUT TO CRACK.

cramp someone's style, to To restrict someone's natural actions; to prevent someone from doing his or her best. This seemingly up-to-date locution was first used by Charles Lamb in 1819. He was alluding to writer's cramp, which constricted the natural flow of one's pen. Figuratively the term came into use in the early twentieth century. W. Somerset Maugham used it in his early spy novel, *Ashenden or: The British Agent* (1927): "I can't help thinking it would cramp your style."

crazy as a coot/loon Lunatic behavior. The simile to the water bird dates from the sixteenth century, when John Skelton (*Phyllyp Sparowe,* 1529) wrote, "the mad coote, with a balde face to toote." It is not known whether the craziness refers to the bird's strange behavior in winter, when flocks of coots on a frozen pond sometimes fly wildly at one another, or to the senile behavior of the very old. (See also BALD AS A COOT.) A related ornithological simile is *crazy as a loon,* probably derived from the weird loud cry of this bird. However, *loony* for "crazy" comes not from the bird but from *lunatic,* in turn related to the ancient belief that the phases of the moon (Latin *luna*) influence human behavior.

crazy like a fox Seemingly silly but actually very crafty. The title of a book (1944) by the great American humorist S. J. Perelman, this ungrammatical term came to be applied more widely soon afterward and is a borderline cliché.

crazy mixed-up kid A psychologically troubled youth. This term was born about 1940 and soon was extended to describe a merely eccentric person, and not necessarily young. It also is used jestingly, but may be dying out.

cream of the crop, the The very best of all. Cream is, of course, the richest part of milk and rises to the top. It was transferred to mean the best of any collective entity by the seventeenth century. John Ray, for example, included "That's the cream of the jest" in his collection of English proverbs (1678). The exact locution involving the best of the *crop* was no doubt adopted for its alliterative appeal. The French version, *la crème de la crème,* literally "the cream of the cream," meaning the best of the best, was well known in English by 1800 or so and also is considered a cliché. It gained new impetus in Muriel Spark's novel *The Prime of Miss Jean Brodie,* first made into a play, then a motion picture (1969), in which the schoolteacher-heroine assures her students that they will, under her tutelage, become the *crème de la crème.*

creature comforts Life's material amenities. The term dates from the seventeenth century; it appears in Thomas Brooks's *Collected Works* (1670), and again in Matthew Henry's 1710 *Commentaries on the Psalms* ("They have . . . the sweetest relish of their creature comforts").

credibility gap Lack of belief in a statement or policy. This phrase came into being in 1965 during the Vietnam War, when the American public became aware of differences between what the government said and what actually happened. After the war it was extended to discrepancies between the words and actions of both individuals and corporations. Some believe this term was spawned by the *missile gap* invoked during the 1960 presidential campaign, when John F. Kennedy charged that U.S. missile production was lagging behind the Soviet Union's. Soon after the election the charge was dismissed as false. Since then, according to William Safire, "missile gap" has been used to mean exaggerated and misleading claims.

crème de la crème See CREAM OF THE CROP.

cricket See NOT CRICKET.

cried all the way to the bank, he/she Exulted in a sizable monetary gain from something that either had been criticized for lacking merit or simply had not been expected to yield much. This expression, always used ironically, originated in the United States about 1960. The popular pianist Liberace, criticized by serious musicians for his flashy, sentimental style, is said to have so replied to a detractor (as reported in his autobiography, published in 1973). A kindred expression, *laughed all the way to the bank,* is occasionally substituted.

crocodile tears, crying/to cry Pretended grief; hypocritical sorrow. The term comes from an ancient myth that a crocodile weeps while eating its prey. It was quoted by the English traveler Sir John Mandeville in 1400 but was already current far earlier, in Roman times. Indeed, the writer Spartianus, in his *Lives of the Emperors* (c. A.D. 300), said that the Emperor Caracalla shed crocodile tears at the death of some of his enemies. The term was picked up by Shakespeare, Sir Francis Bacon, and numerous other writers, and was a cliché by the time Tennyson wrote, "Crocodiles wept tears for thee" ("A Dirge," 1830).

cross as a bear Irascible, peevish, vexed, cantankerous. This simile dates from the late eighteenth century and has survived as a cliché on both sides of the Atlantic even though the adjective *cross* for "angry" is heard less frequently in America. Why a bear should be considered particularly prone to anger is not entirely clear, and indeed, over the years writers have amplified the description somewhat—for example, "cross as a bear with a sore head," "mad as a beaten bear," "grumbled like a bear with a sore ear."

cross my heart (and point to God/hope to die) What I'm saying is really true. Originally a solemn oath for veracity, this phrase became a schoolyard assertion. The first version was traditionally accompanied by crossing one's arms over the chest and then raising the right arm. The cliché dates from the second half of the 1800s. A twentieth-century synonym is *Scout's honor!,* alluding to the promise of honesty taken by Boy (and Girl) Scouts. It dates from about 1900. J. A. Jance had it in her mystery novel, *Devil's Claw* (2000), "Joanna was shocked. 'You didn't tell her that!'—Now it was Butch's turn to grin. 'I did,' he said. 'Scout's honor.'" And Jan Burke even combined the two: "'Swear you'll keep me posted on your progress?'—'Girl Scout's honor. Or may I simply cross my heart?'" (*Remember Me, Irene,* 1996). Also see HONEST TO GOODNESS.

cross that bridge when you come to it Hold off making a decision until it is necessary; don't anticipate trouble until it actually occurs. "Don't cross the bridge till you come to it, is a proverb old and of excellent wit," said Henry Wadsworth Longfellow (*The Golden Legend,* 1851), and eighty years later that witty playwright Noël Coward said, "I don't believe in crying over my bridge before I've eaten it" (*Private Lives,* 1930). The ultimate origins of the term have been lost.

cross the Rubicon, to To take an irrevocable step. The term dates from 49 B.C., when Julius Caesar crossed this river between Italy and Cisalpine

Gaul, thereby invading Italy and disobeying Pompey and the Roman Senate. The Senate, he had learned, intended to disband his army, whereupon Caesar joined his advance guard on the Rubicon's banks and told them, "We may still draw back, but once across that little bridge we will have to fight it out." The term has been a cliché since about 1700.

cross to bear, a/one's A burden of misfortune, guilt, or other suffering. The term comes from the story of Jesus's crucifixion, in which a passerby named Simon the Cyrene was stopped and told to carry the cross to be so used to Calvary, the place of execution (Matthew 27:32; Mark 15:21; Luke 23:26; the last Gospel account, John 19:17, has Jesus carrying his own cross). From this, carrying a cross came to symbolize Jesus' suffering, and by extension, the suffering of all human beings. Today the term is frequently used more lightly, as for example, "The Dallas Cowboys, who are mired in a slump this season, are her cross to bear" (Robin Finn, *New York Times,* writing about the tennis player and Cowboys fan Martina Navratilova, Nov. 13, 1989).

crown of glory A triumphant victory; a splendid achievement. The term appears in the King James Version of the Bible, in 1 Peter (5:4), which says that good behavior will be rewarded, when the Shepherd shall appear, with "a crown of glory that fadeth not away." A hymn (1820) by Thomas Kelly repeats this thought and also relates it to Jesus' crown of thorns: "The Head that once was crowned with thorns is crowned with glory now." On the other hand, in ancient Greek and Roman times, a victorious military hero was rewarded with a crown of laurels, so the term may allude to temporal rather than spiritual reward.

crux of the matter, the The essential, pivotal point of an issue. The word "crux" came into English from Latin unchanged except in meaning; in Latin *crux* means "cross," specifically the kind used in crucifixions and other executions. The English word "crux," on the other hand, also signifies a difficulty or puzzle. This meaning, some writers believe, stems from the crossing of the two lines that make up a cross, which is also called a knot or node, whence the transfer to a "knotty problem." Songwriter John Lennon, of Beatles fame, punned on the cliché in *The Fingeltoad Resort:* "That seems to be the crutch of the matter."

cry See CRIED; CRYING.

crying over spilled milk, it's no good/use Don't regret what's done and can't be helped. That milk once spilled cannot be recovered must have been observed from the first day milk was put into a container. "No weeping for shed milk" appears in two seventeenth-century proverb collections

(James Howell, 1659; John Ray, 1678), and the idea is still so well known that the mere words "spilled milk" convey the entire cliché.

cry one's eyes out, to To weep or mourn excessively. This hyperbole—how could weeping actually cause eyes to fall out?—dates back at least to the early eighteenth century. It appears in Colley Cibber's 1705 play, *The Careless Husband* (1.1), "I could cry my eyes out," and also in Jonathan Swift's *Polite Conversation* (1738). In the nineteenth century it was sometimes altered to *crying one's heart out,* especially in popular romantic novels such as Margaret Oliphant's *Joyce* (1888).

crystal ball, look into one's See into the future. The fortune-teller's crystal ball probably predates the term's appearance in print by a good many years. An early instance is in Robert Browning's *Men and Women* (1855): "The sights in a magic crystal ball."

crystal clear Transparently obvious. This simile (clear as crystal) dates from biblical times. In the Book of Revelation the writer describes the great city of Jerusalem as "having the glory of God; and her light was like unto a stone most precious, even like a jasper stone, clear as crystal" (21:11). The term appealed to numerous medieval poets and crops up in their ballads. By the time Dickens (in *Edwin Drood,* 1870) and Arthur Conan Doyle (in *The Resident Patient,* 1893) used it, it was a cliché.

cry wolf, to To give a false alarm. The term comes from an ancient tale about a shepherd lad watching his flock on a far-off hillside. Lonely and fearful, he called for help by crying out, "Wolf!" After people had responded to his cries several times and found no wolf had threatened him, they refused to come to his aid when a wolf finally did attack his sheep. It soon was transferred to all such false alarms, and was already a cliché by the time R. D. Blackmore wrote about the French invasion, "The cry of wolf grows stale at last, and then the real danger comes" (*Springhaven,* 1887).

cudgel one's brains, to To think hard; to make a vigorous attempt to solve or answer some question, or to remember something. The verb "to cudgel" means to beat with a cudgel (a short thick stick). Possibly the allusion here is to thrashing a schoolboy for failing to answer promptly or correctly. The word "cudgel" is hardly ever heard anymore except in this context, which dates from before 1600. Shakespeare had a clown say to another who was puzzling over a riddle, "Cudgel thy brains no more about it, for your dull ass will not mend his pace with beating" (*Hamlet,* 5.1). See also BEAT ONE'S BRAINS; RACK ONE'S BRAIN.

cup of tea See NOT ONE'S CUP OF TEA.

curry favor, to To flatter insincerely in order to get ahead. The term, which has been known since the sixteenth century, comes from a fourteenth-century satirical romance about a horse named Fauvel. This horse was a symbol of cunning bestiality, and to curry (groom) it meant that one was enlisting its services of duplicity and other nasty traits. The English version of Fauvel at first was *favel,* which by the sixteenth century had been corrupted into "favor."

customer is always right, the A commercial paean to the buyer. This phrase was introduced in the 1930s by H. Gordon Selfridge, an American who founded Selfridge's, a large department store in Great Britain. A highly successful salesman who personally oversaw his retail operation, he insisted that his staff always defer to customers, whether they were right or wrong. The refrain was taken up by other businesses and has survived.

cut and dried Commonplace, routine, hackneyed; settled beforehand. The term dates from the early eighteenth century, and there is some disagreement as to its origin. Most authorities believe it referred to timber, which customarily is cut to standard sizes and dried before it is used. One writer, however, believes it refers to the wares of English herbalists, which were cut and then dried before being sold. Jonathan Swift used the phrase figuratively for boring speech (*Betty the Grisette,* 1730): "Set of phrases, cut and dry, evermore thy tongue supply."

cut and run, to To make a hasty departure. The term comes from the nautical practice of cutting a ship's anchor cable to let it run before the wind, usually done only as an emergency measure. It was defined in *Rigging and Seamanship* (1794) as "to cut the cable and make sail instantly without waiting to weigh anchor." It soon was used figuratively, as in Dickens's *Great Expectations* (1861): "I'd give a shilling if they had cut and run."

cut a (wide) swath, to To make a showy display, to attract attention. The term originated in America and comes from mowing, a "swath" being the amount cut by one big sweep of the scythe. It was transferred to human showoffs by the mid-nineteenth century. "How he was a strutting up the side-walk—didn't he cut a swath!" wrote Ann S. Stephens in *High Life in New York* (1843). It is heard less often today, but has not quite died out.

cut corners, to To do a hasty, slipshod job; also, to act illegally. The term comes from using a direct route that omits corners or from moving very fast and rounding turns very closely. It dates from about the middle of the nineteenth century. Mark Twain used it in *Innocents Abroad* (1869): "He cuts a corner so closely now and then . . . that I feel myself 'scooching.'"

cute as a button Daintily attractive. The word "cute" dates from the seventeenth century. It was originally an abbreviation of *acute* and had the same meaning: clever, shrewd, ingenious. In America, however, it came to be applied to attractive persons or things, those with an appearance of dainty charm rather than outright beauty. A button is small and round; so are some cute objects. For some reason this simile took hold in the early twentieth century. The synonym *cute as a bug's ear* similarly alludes to something very small—and in fact nonexistent (bugs don't have ears).

cut from whole cloth See OUT OF WHOLE CLOTH.

cut no ice, to To have no influence, to make no impression. An Americanism dating from the late nineteenth century, it may come from skating, that is, the image of a poor skater who cannot cut figures in the ice. Or it may come from an icebreaker that cannot break up ice floes as it should. Still another source suggests it comes from the prerefrigeration practice of cutting ice from ponds in winter and storing it for use in summer.

cut off at the pass, to To stop or intercept. This expression comes from chase sequences in western movies of the 1930s and 1940s, in which pursuers (usually the "good" cowboys) would try to intercept their quarry (the outlaws) at a mountain pass. It gradually was extended to other endeavors. According to *Brewer's Dictionary of Twentieth-Century Phrase and Fable,* in 1973 President Richard Nixon used the term on the Watergate tapes, saying that the charge of obstructing justice might be cut off at the pass.

cut off one's nose to spite one's face, to To act out of pique in a way that injures oneself more than anyone else. The term appears about 1200 as a Latin proverb recorded by Peter of Blois. It was repeated in the mid-seventeenth century by Gedéon Tallemant des Réaux in recounting the history of France: "Henry IV understood very well that to destroy Paris would be, as they say, to cut off his nose to spite his face."

cut off one's right arm See GIVE ONE'S RIGHT ARM.

cut off with(out) a shilling/cent Disinherited. To write a will leaving someone just one shilling is equivalent to being left nothing; without a shilling, of course, explicitly means left nothing. The former is not just an insult. English law at one time required that some bequest be made so as to show that the disinheritance was intentional, and not an oversight. In

America, "cent" was sometimes substituted for "shilling." A cliché since about 1800, the term is now dying out.

cut of his/her jib, I don't like the I don't like his/her general appearance or manner. The jib is a triangular foresail, and in the days of sailing ships sailors often would recognize the nationality of a particular vessel by the precise shape of its jib. By 1800 or so the term had been transferred to human beings. In 1823 Robert Southey wrote, in a letter, that the likability of some individuals "depends something upon the cut of their jib."

cut one's teeth on, to To begin one's education or career with; to mature. The analogy is to the emergence ("cutting" through the gums) of a baby's teeth, which occurs during the first year of life. The earliest uses of this term involved not just plain teeth but *eyeteeth;* to cut one's eyeteeth meant to gain experience. "There is no dealing with him without having one's eyeteeth," one J. J. Morier wrote in 1730. The eyeteeth, or upper canines, came to be so called because their nerves pass close to the eyes. By 1770 a book of American proverbs included "have his eyeteeth," meaning to be mature, which probably came from the fact that the upper canines do not emerge until several other baby teeth have been cut. (See also GIVE ONE'S EYETEETH.) By 1860 the "eye" portion had been dropped and Charles Reade wrote, in his novel *The Cloister and the Hearth,* "He and I were born the same year, but he cut his teeth long before me."

cut out for, to be To be suited for or capable of some activity or position. The term comes from tailoring, where cloth is cut out (into pieces) to make a specific garment. It was used figuratively by 1700. An early appearance occurs in Gilbert Burnet's *History of My Own Times* (c. 1715): "He was not cut out for a Court."

cut someone some slack, to To give someone more time or more of a chance, to ease up on someone. This term, dating from the mid-1900s, alludes to a slackening of tautness in a rope or sail. Sandra Brown had it in *Alibi* (1999), "'Don't lean on him yet; let's cut him some slack for now.'"

cut the Gordian knot, to To get out of trouble by taking a single decisive step. According to legend, Gordius, a peasant who became king of Phrygia, dedicated his wagon to the god Jupiter and tied the yoke to a tree with such a difficult knot that no one could unfasten it. Alexander the Great was told that whoever could untie the wagon would rule all Asia, whereupon he simply cut the knot with his sword. Many writers have alluded to this myth, among them Shakespeare ("Turn him to any cause of policy, the Gordian Knot of it he will unloose"), in *Henry V* (1.1). It has been a cliché since about 1800 but is seldom heard today.

cut the ground from under, to To foil or thwart someone, to trip someone up. The idea of *leaving someone no ground to stand upon* in an argument was expressed in the late sixteenth century by several writers; occasionally "grass" was substituted for "ground." James Howell's French proverb collection of 1659 included *Couper l'herbe sous les pieds,* "To cut the grass under one's feet." Anthony Trollope used the expression in several of his books, including *The Warden* (1869): "The ground was cut from under her."

cut the mustard, to To do a good job; to come up to a required standard; to succeed. It often is put negatively, as someone cannot cut the mustard, that is, is *not* performing adequately. The term is American slang, and its origin is disputed. According to one authority, "mustard" used to signify the best or main attraction in a show, probably because this condiment enhances the flavor of other foods. It was this sense that O. Henry apparently intended when he wrote, "I'm not headlined in the bills, but I'm the mustard in the salad dressing, just the same" (*Cabbages and Kings*), and later (1904), "I . . . found a proposition that exactly cut the mustard." Another etymologist believes it comes from the military term, to PASS MUSTER. A third theory is that it comes from the preparation of the condiment, which involves adding vinegar to ground-up mustard seed; the vinegar is said to "cut" the bitter taste.

cutting edge, at/on the In the forefront of new developments. The analogy is to the sharp edge of a knife or other tool, which is in front during the act of cutting. The term came into use in the field of scientific and technologic research about 1950 and soon was extended to practically any area of endeavor. For example, in a radio interview on November 14, 1989, Craig Wich, the director of Opera Lab, explained that his organization's approach to integrating movement, emotion, and singing was at the cutting edge of a new approach to opera (Boston, WCRB). A similar metaphor widely used is *the leading edge.* Dating from the 1870s and at first describing only the forward edge of a ruddler or propeller blade that cuts the water, it was later expanded to mean any device or system that extends an aircraft's speed, altitude, and range, and eventually transferred to the vanguard of anything—"the leading edge of technology," for example.

cut to the chase Get on with it, get to the point. This phrase, often an imperative, comes from the film industry of the 1920s, where it means to edit ("cut") film so as to get to an exciting chase sequence, an intrinsic part of many early movies. It gradually became more general in meaning, as in "She went on and on about her vacation, until I told her to cut to the chase and tell us where she stayed."

cut to the quick To be deeply wounded; to have one's feelings hurt. The noun "quick" means the living, as well as the most vital and important part;

today it also means the very sensitive flesh between the fingernails and skin. To be *touched to the quick,* meaning to be deeply affected, has been used since the sixteenth century; it appears in John Heywood's *Proverbs* and in several places in Shakespeare's plays (*Hamlet, The Comedy of Errors,* and others). Another version is *stung to the quick,* as in "The last appellation stung her to the quick" (Henry Fielding, *Joseph Andrews,* 1742). "Cut to the quick" is a still later wording and has been a cliché since about 1850. See also QUICK AND THE DEAD.

d

damned if I/you/they do, damned if I/you don't Acting or not acting are equally harmful, an insoluble dilemma. This expression dates from the first half of the 1900s, and thus is older than the synonymous CATCH-22. For example, "If I tell Harry I'm going to John's party and he's not invited, both he and John will be furious—I'm damned if I do and damned if I don't."

damn sight, a A great deal. The noun "sight" has been so used since the first half of the 1800s, and the intensifier "damn" had been added by about 1930. Roy Campbell had it in *The Georgiad* (1931): "He could be heterosexual with either, too—A damn sight more than you or I could do!"

damn with faint praise, to To compliment so slightly that it amounts to no compliment at all, or even the reverse, a condemnation. The Roman writer Favorinus said, about A.D. 110, that it is more shameful to be praised faintly and coldly than to be censured violently. The practice was taken up early on, especially by literary critics. The classic quotation is from Alexander Pope's *Epistle to Dr. Arbuthnot* (1733). In poking fun at the critic Joseph Addison, here called Atticus, Pope said he would "Damn with faint praise, assent with civil leer, and, without sneering, teach the rest to sneer." See also LEFT-HANDED COMPLIMENT.

dance attendance on, to To obey someone's slightest whim or wish, to act as someone's obsequious flunky. The term comes from the ancient custom of having the bride dance with every wedding guest, whether she wanted to or not. It has been used since the early sixteenth century, first in the sense of waiting for someone to grant an audience, as by John Skelton (*Why Come Ye Not to Court?* 1522), "And syr ye must daunce attendance . . . for my Lord's Grace hath now no time nor space to speke with you as yet." By Shakespeare's time it had been extended to being at someone's beck and call ("To dance attendance on their lordships' pleasures," *Henry VIII,* 5.2). It was a cliché by about 1700.

darken my door (again), don't/never Go away and don't come back. This expression, today indelibly affixed to Victorian melodrama in which a young woman is thrown out of the parental home for marrying, not marrying, or some other sinful deed, actually dates back much further. The darkening involved is that of one's shadow across the *threshold,* a word occasionally substituted for "door." Jonathan Swift used the term in *Polite Conversation* in 1738: "I never darkened his door in my life." It has been a cliché since the nineteenth century, but may be dying out.

dark horse, a An unexpected potential winner. The term dates from the nineteenth century and comes from racing, where a horse is termed "dark" when its ancestry and history are unknown. It was so used by Benjamin Disraeli in his novel, *The Young Duke* (1831), but the precise origin is obscure. Some think it comes from the owner's dyeing a horse's hair to disguise it and so get better odds; others cite the practice of a particular American horse trader who made his fast black stallion look like an ordinary saddle horse, rode into town, set up a race, and consistently came out a winner. The term was soon transferred to political candidates on both sides of the Atlantic. The first American presidential dark horse was James Polk, who won the 1844 Democratic nomination only on the eighth ballot and went on to become president.

dawn on (someone), to To perceive or understand for the first time. See LIGHT DAWNED.

day in, day out All day and every day, regularly, constantly. The expression was so defined in a dialect book by W. Carr in 1828 and was widely used by the end of the century. It was a cliché by the time C. Day Lewis used it in describing his school days in his autobiography, *The Buried Day* (1960): "One boy . . . was kicked around, jeered at or ostracised, day in day out for several years."

day of reckoning The time when one is called to account. The idea no doubt comes from the biblical Day of Judgment, when Jesus is supposed to return to earth for God's final sentence on mankind. The day of reckoning came to have a somewhat more benign meaning, referring to paying one's debts, or accounting for one's actions. The expression became common in the nineteenth century. "There will be a day of reckoning sooner or later," wrote Dickens (*Nicholas Nickleby,* 1838).

days are numbered, one's/his/its One's life or usefulness is about to end. Perhaps the earliest instance of this expression is in the Book of Daniel, in which Daniel reads King Belshazzar's fate in the writing on the wall: "God hath numbered thy kingdom and finished it" (Daniel 5:26). Another early version appears in a collection of Chinese proverbs made by William Scarborough (1875): "Man's days are numbered." See also NUMBER'S UP.

dead and gone Permanently absent. While this expression seems tautological as uttered by Ophelia, driven mad by terrible events ("He is dead and gone, lady, he is dead and gone; at his head a grass-green turf; at his heels a stone," she sings to the queen in *Hamlet,* 4.5), it has another implication as well. "Not dead but gone before," wrote Matthew Henry in his biblical commentary (1710)—that is, going on to a presumably glorious afterlife. Nevertheless, the sense of "gone forever" prevailed. The phrase was probably a cliché by the time Dickens wrote, "When she was dead and gone, perhaps they would be sorry" (*Barnaby Rudge,* 1840).

dead as a doornail Dead, unresponsive, defunct. This simile dates from the fourteenth century and the source of it has been lost. A doornail was either a heavy-headed nail for studding an outer door or the knob on which a door knocker strikes. One plausible explanation for the analogy to death is that it alluded to costly metal nails (rather than cheap wooden pegs), which were clinched and hence "dead" (could not be re-used). The expression was used in a fourteenth-century poem of unknown authorship, *William of Palerne,* and was still current when Dickens wrote *A Christmas Carol* (1843). There have been numerous similar proverbial comparisons—dead as a mackerel, dead as mutton, dead as a herring, dead as a stone—but this one, with its alliterative lilt, has survived longest.

dead duck, a A has-been or a loser. The term dates from the second half of the nineteenth century and may have been derived from LAME DUCK. At first it denoted a person whose political influence had declined. Later it simply came to mean someone who has no hope of winning, or who has already lost.

dead from the neck up Extremely stupid. This slangy metaphor was first recorded in 1911. John Dos Passos used it in *Forty-second Parallel* (1930): "Most of the inhabitants are dead from the neck up."

dead heat, in a Tied for first place. The term comes from horse-racing, in which "heat" used to mean simply a race (today its meaning is a bit more specific). It was in use by the late eighteenth century ("The whole race was run head and head, terminating in a dead heat," *Sporting Magazine,* 1796). It later was applied to any contest in which there was a tie.

dead horse, to beat/flog a To pursue a futile goal or belabor a point to no end. That this sort of behavior makes no sense was pointed out by the Roman playwright Plautus in 195 B.C. The analogy certainly seems ludicrous; what coachman or driver would actually take a whip to a dead animal? The figurative meaning has been applied for centuries as well; often it is used in politics, concerning an issue that is of little interest to voters. However, some writers, John Ciardi among them, cite a quite different source for the cliché. In the late eighteenth century British merchant seamen often were paid in advance, at the time they were hired. Many would spend this sum, called a *dead horse,* before the ship sailed. They then could draw no more pay until they had worked off the amount of the advance, or until "the dead horse was flogged."

dead in the water A failure. The analogy here is to a dead fish floating. The cliché dates from the second half of the 1900s and is most often applied to a struggling business that is about to fail completely.

dead of night/winter, the The time of most intense stillness, darkness, or cold. This usage dates from the sixteenth century. Shakespeare had it in *Twelfth Night* (1.5), "Even in the dead of night," and Washington Irving used the alternate phrase in *Salmagundi* (1807–08), "In the dead of winter, when nature is without charm."

dead on one's feet Extremely tired. This graphic hyperbole, with its use of "dead" in the meaning of "utterly fatigued," is probably related to *dead tired,* where "dead" means "very" or "absolutely." This locution has been traced to Irish speech and appears in such clichés as *dead wrong* for "completely mistaken," *dead right* for "absolutely correct," *dead certain* for "totally sure," and others. "Dead on one's feet" became common in the mid-twentieth century. John Braine used it in *Life at the Top* (1962): "Honestly, I'm dead on my feet."

dead ringer A person or object that exactly resembles another, an exact counterpart in appearance. The usage of "ringer" for look-alike has been around since the late 1800s, when it was used for a horse that was fraudulently substituted for another in a race. It also was applied to the person who made such a substitution, but this usage has died out. However, in 1891 the term was made more emphatic with the addition of "dead," here used in the sense of "exact," as it is in DEAD HEAT for an exact tie.

dead set against Unutterably opposed. This Americanism probably comes from industry, where a machine is said to be *dead set* when it is fastened so that it cannot be made to move. The transfer to firm resolve or hostility against some person, course of action, and so on, was made by the early nineteenth century. "A dead set is to be made from various quarters against the abominable innovation of publishing Divisions by authority" (General P. Thompson, 1836).

dead to rights Absolutely without doubt; also, red-handed, in the act of doing something. The term originated in the United States in the mid-nineteenth century and was used mostly with reference to criminal activity.

George Washington Marsell defined it in his *Vocabulum or The Rogue's Lexicon* (1859): "Dead to rights [means] positively guilty and no way of getting clear." It is heard less often today.

dead to the world Asleep or unconscious, and hence oblivious to one's surroundings. That deep sleep resembles death was noted in biblical times, but the precise expression does not surface in print until 1899 or so ("Our host is dead to the world," George Ade, *Doc' Horne*).

dead weight An oppressive burden or heavy responsibility. The physical attributes of such a weight were noted early on, but the figurative use of the expression dates from the early eighteenth century. The English philosopher Lord Shaftesbury (the third Earl) wrote (1711), "Pedantry and Bigotry are millstones able to sink the best Book, which carries the least part of their dead weight."

dead wrong See DEAD ON ONE'S FEET.

deaf as a post Unable to hear or to listen. The simile dates from the sixteenth century, when J. Palsgrave wrote (*Acolastus,* 1540), "He wotteth ful lyttel how deffe an eare I intended to gyue him . . . he were as good to tell his tale to a poste." It caught on and has survived to the present, outliving such similes as *deaf as an adder* (first recorded in the Book of Psalms, 58:4–5), *deaf as a beetle,* and *deaf as a white cat.* See also FALL ON DEAF EARS; TURN A BLIND EYE/DEAF EAR.

dear John A letter or other notification calling off a romantic relationship. The term was born during World War II, when a serviceman stationed overseas received a letter from his girlfriend or wife ending their relationship. After the war it was extended to both genders and used quite loosely, sometimes even for other kinds of rejection.

death and taxes, (certain as) Absolutely inevitable. This ironic phrase was coined by Benjamin Franklin in a letter to Jean Baptiste Le Roy in 1789: "But in this world nothing can be said to be certain, except death and taxes." It has been repeated ever since.

death's door, at/near Moribund, dangerously ill. Presumably this metaphor originated in the idea that death was a state of being one could enter, that is, an afterlife. It was used by Miles Coverdale (an early translator of the Bible) in *A Spyrytuall Pearle* (1550), "To bring unto death's door," and was repeated by Shakespeare and eventually, in more secular context, by later writers. Eric Partridge deemed it a cliché by about 1850.

death wish A desire, either conscious or, most often, unconscious, to die or to ruin oneself. The term dates from the late 1800s and originally was a translation from the German psychological term, *Todeswunsch.* By the 1930s it was being used figuratively, as in a 1947 article in the *Partisan Review*: "Even in America the death-wish of the business community appears to go beyond the normal limits of political incompetence and geographical security."

December, May and A marriage between a young and a much older individual. This disparity was called *January and May* by Chaucer, January standing for the hoary frosts of old age and May for the young breath of spring. In Chaucer's *The Merchant's Tale* the young girl, May, marries January, a baron aged sixty. This fourteenth-century idea was transformed into December and May by the early 1600s (although January and May survived as well). December, of course, is not only cold but also comes at the end of the calendar year and so may provide a better analogy for late in life. "You doe wrong to Time, enforcing May to embrace December," wrote Thomas Dekker (*The Seven Deadly Sinnes of London,* 1606).

deep pockets Seemingly unlimited funds, a source of great wealth. Alluding to figurative pockets filled with money, the term dates from the second half of the 1900s. For example, "Lacking a large endowment, the college relied on alumni with deep pockets." See also FAT CAT.

deep-six, to To abandon, reject, or otherwise get rid of. This slangy term dates from the mid-1900s and originated in the navy, where it meant throwing something or someone overboard. The "six" refers to the six-foot nautical fathom, the standard unit of measurement for sea depth. It soon was adopted into civilian language, as in an editorial about Massachusetts Governor Mitt Romney's chances for national office: "I'd deep-six the joke [he tells] about the wily old farmer who pretends he's feeding an alligator in order to scare some naked coeds out of a swimming hole" (Scot Lehigh, *Boston Globe,* March 11, 2005).

den of thieves, a A group of individuals or a place strongly suspected of underhanded dealings. This term appears in the Bible (Matthew 21:13) when Jesus, driving the moneychangers from the Temple, said, "My house shall be called the house of prayer; but ye have made it a den of thieves." Daniel Defoe used the term in *Robinson Crusoe,* published in 1719, and by the late eighteenth century it was well known enough to be listed with other collective terms such as "House of Commons" in William Cobbett's *English Grammar* in a discussion of syntax relating to pronouns.

desperate straits A very difficult situation. The noun "strait," usually in the plural (straits), has been used since the 1600s to mean a dilemma of some kind. One of the earliest pairings with "desperate" was in Harriet Martineau's *The History of England during the Thirty Years' Peace* (1849): "Never were Whig rulers reduced to more desperate straits." Today the term is used both seriously and ironically, as in "We're in desperate straits today—the newspaper never arrived."

devil's advocate, (to play) To take a position against something that many others support, either for the sake of argument or to examine its validity. The term is a translation of the Latin *advocatus diaboli,* an official appointed by the Roman Catholic Church to argue against a proposed canonization. By the 1700s it was extended to broader use. R. Buchanan used it in *The Heir of Linne* (1887), "Even the Socialist party regarded him as a devil's advocate, and washed their hands of him." More recently, David Baldacci had it in *Hour Game* (2004), "'Didn't you try your best to convince me he was innocent?' . . . 'Just playing devil's advocate.'"

devil take the hindmost, the Too bad for whoever or whatever is last or left behind. The term comes, it is thought, from children's games like tag, in which the person left behind is the loser. By the sixteenth century it had been transferred to out-and-out selfishness ("Every one for him selfe, and the divel for all," John Florio, *First Fruites,* 1578). Beaumont and Fletcher wrote, "What if . . . they run all away, and cry the Devil take the hindmost?" (*Philaster,* 1608, 5.1).

devil to pay, the Serious trouble, a mess. The expression originally referred to making a bargain with the devil, and the payment that eventually would be exacted. It first appeared in print about 1400: "Be it wer be at tome for ay, than her to serve the devil to pay" (*Reliquiare Antiquae*). This Faustian type of trouble was later lightened to mean any kind of problem (Jonathan Swift, *Journal to Stella,* 1711: "The Earl of Strafford is to go soon to Holland . . . and then there will be the devil and all to pay"). In the nineteenth century the expression was expanded to "the devil to pay and no pitch hot." This form referred to "paying," or caulking, a seam around a ship's hull very near the waterline; it was called "the devil" because it was so difficult to reach. (See also BETWEEN THE DEVIL AND THE DEEP BLUE SEA.) Sir Walter Scott used it in *The Pirate* (1821): "If they hurt but one hair of Cleveland's head, there will be the devil to pay and no pitch hot."

devil you know is better than the devil you don't know, the A familiar misfortune is preferable to a totally unexpected one. This adage first appeared in John Taverner's *Proverbs of Erasmus* (1539), and Anthony

Trollope referred to it as "an old proverb" in *Barchester Towers* (1857). It may be dying out.

diamond in the rough, a An individual of intrinsic merit but uncultivated manners. The simile comes from mining, where the uncut, unpolished diamond resembles a hunk of worthless rock but may, after processing, be both beautiful and very valuable. John Fletcher's 1624 play, *A Wife for a Month,* has it, "She is very honest, and will be hard to cut as a rough diamond" (4.2).

dictates of conscience The guiding principles of what one believes is right. The word "dictate" has been so used, for the authoritative words of law, scripture, and the like, since the late sixteenth century. In 1656 Archbishop John Bramhall wrote, "Contrarie to the dictate of his conscience."

die in harness, to To keep on working to the end. The analogy of a draft horse working until it drops dates from Shakespeare's time (or earlier). "At least we'll die with harness on our back," says Macbeth before his fateful battle with Macduff (*Macbeth,* 5.5). Such a death, incidentally, is considered desirable and admirable. "It is a man dying with his harness on that angels love to escort upward," said the American preacher Henry Ward Beecher (*Proverbs from Plymouth Pulpit,* 1887). Precisely the same is meant by to *die with one's boots on,* although more likely this expression comes from the battlefield (soldiers dying on active duty).

die is cast, the A final decision has been made; there is no turning back. The term comes from Julius Caesar's invasion of Italy in 49 B.C. (see CROSS THE RUBICON). According to Suetonius's account, Caesar said *Jacta alea est* (The dice have been thrown), which has been repeated through the ages whenever a figurative player must abide by the result of a throw of the dice. It was a cliché by the time George Meredith wrote, "The die is cast—I cannot go back" (*The Egoist,* 1879).

die like a dog, to To meet a miserable end. Actually, to lead *a dog's life* is no better, a fact pointed out about the same time that "die like a dog" first surfaced in print. "He lyved like a lyon and dyed like a dogge," wrote John Rastell (*The Pastyme of People,* 1529). In ancient Greek times dying like a dog was even worse because it signified being left unburied, a fate regarded with dread. See also A DOG'S LIFE.

die with one's boots on See DIE IN HARNESS.

difference between chalk and cheese See APPLES AND ORANGES.

different strokes for different folks See NO ACCOUNTING FOR TASTES.

dime a dozen, a Readily available, so cheap as to be without value. The dime being an American coin, declared the ten-cent piece by the Continental Congress in 1786 (the word comes from the French *dime,* for "tithe," or one-tenth), this expression is obviously American in origin and probably owes its long life to alliterative appeal. Inflation has further degraded the meaning. Early in the twentieth century a dime could buy a paperback book (*dime novel*) or a cup of coffee and a doughnut; "Brother, can you spare a dime?" was the universal cry for a handout during the Great Depression of the 1930s.

dire straits, in In an awful situation, terrible circumstances. The adjective "dire," which dates from the mid-1500s, is rarely heard today except in this cliché and one other phrase, *dire necessity,* which uses it more or less hyperbolically (as, for example, in Elizabeth Barrett Browning's 1836 letter, "The dire necessity of having every window in the house open . . ."). In contrast, the cliché describes a genuine difficulty or danger, as in "The stock-market crash left him in dire straits financially."

dirt cheap Very inexpensive. The idea of something being as cheap as dirt dates back at least to Roman times. Petronius's *Satyricon* (A.D. 60) says, "In those days food could be had for dirt" (*Illo tempore annoma pro luto erat*). It may already have been a cliché by the time Dickens used it in *Oliver Twist* (1838): "I sold myself . . . cheap, dirt cheap!"

dirty mind, a Prurient, describing someone who thinks of or sees the obscene or indecent aspects of something. The adjective "dirty" has been used in this sense since the 1500s, but the phrase dates only from the 1900s. Stephen Price played on it in *Just for the Record* (1961): "He had a real porny [pornographic] article . . . not just dirty, mind you, but Art."

dirty tricks Covert, deceitful, and damaging policies and actions. The term dates from the later 1600s and was long used simply to describe a nasty action, as in "When no one was looking Jim grabbed the last decent sleeping bag; that was a dirty trick." However, it acquired a new meaning during the 1960s when it was applied to the activities of the Central Intelligence Agency (CIA), which was even called "Department of Dirty Tricks" for some of its propaganda and secret interventions in other countries' affairs. In the 1970s it began to be applied to the unethical and even illegal tactics of political campaigns, such as smearing an opponent with false accusations, illicitly using campaign funds, and the like.

dismal science, the Economics. The term is Thomas Carlyle's, and he first used it in *On the Nigger Question* (1849), writing: "The social science—not a 'gay science' but a rueful—which finds the secret of this Universe in 'supply and demand' . . . what we might call, by way of eminence, the dismal science." He repeated it the following year in a pamphlet, and it gradually caught on, becoming particularly popular among students struggling with the subject's complexities.

divide and conquer/rule/govern, to To win by getting one's opponents to fight among themselves. This strategy not only was discovered to be effective in wartime by the most ancient of adversaries, but was also applied to less concrete affairs by Jesus: "Every kingdom divided against itself is brought to desolation; and every city or house divided against itself shall not stand" (Matthew 12:25). The exact term is a translation of a Roman maxim, *divide et impera* (divide and rule).

DOA Acronym for "dead on arrival," also written D.O.A. The term, dating from the mid-1900s, originally denoted a victim arriving at a hospital or clinic already deceased. Thus T. Flint put it in *Emergency Treatment* (1958), "Cases in which a spark of life is detected should not be classified as 'D.O.A.'" Although still used in this sense, more recently the phrase has been extended to other situations. On February 7, 2005, on the PBS news program *Lehrer Report,* one of the commentators described a provision in President Bush's new budget as "dead on arrival," suggesting that it would never be passed by Congress.

do a number on, to To ruin, cheat, or trick someone. This slangy phrase dates from the late 1960s and originated in black English. For example, "That boss of yours really did a number on you; you'll never get promoted."

do a power of good, to To effect a great improvement. This somewhat unsophisticated turn of phrase uses "power" in the sense of "much" or "a great deal." For example, "Those vitamins will do her a power of good."

do as I say, not as I do Follow my advice but not my example. Although the idea is undoubtedly older, this specific phrase first appeared in print in 1654: "Preachers say, do as I say, not as I do" (John Selden, *Table-Talk: Preaching*). Parents have been saying it to children ever since.

does See entries beginning with DO; DON'T.

dog days The hottest days of summer. This cliché is a literal translation from the Latin *caniculares dies.* The ancient Romans ascribed the apex of summer heat to the ascendancy of the dog star, or Sirius. The brightest star in the heavens, it is located in the constellation Canis Major, meaning "big dog." Although modern meteorologists may scoff, the term has survived for nearly two thousand years.

dog eat dog Ruthless competition. Although this saying dates from the sixteenth century, it was at first put very reluctantly, because a much older observation has it that dog does *not* eat dog (a Latin proverb). Thus Thomas Fuller (*Gnomologia,* 1732) pointed out that "dogs are hard drove, when they eat dogs." The transfer to human affairs had it otherwise, however. "Dog won't eat dog, but men will eat each other up like cannibals," wrote C. H. Spurgeon (*John Ploughman,* 1869).

dog in the manger A person who takes or keeps something wanted by another out of sheer meanness. The expression comes from one of Aesop's fables about a snarling dog who prevents the horses from eating their fodder even though the dog himself does not want it. It was probably a cliché by the time Frederick Marryat wrote (*Japhet,* 1836), "What a dog in the manger you must be—you can't marry them both."

dog's age See A DOG'S AGE.

dog's chance, not a See CHINAMAN'S CHANCE.

dog's life See A DOG'S LIFE.

dollars to doughnuts Absolutely, certainly. This expression is most often preceded by the verb "to bet" and indeed comes from wagering. If someone is willing to bet dollars against doughnuts, he or she is absolutely sure of winning, the pastries being considered worthless compared to hard cash. The term began to be employed in the late 1800s. F. W. Bronson used it in *Nice People Don't Kill* (1940), "You can bet a dollar to a doughnut." Alliteration no doubt helped it to survive.

done deal, a An irreversible agreement, a final decision or compact. This relatively new synonym for the long-used FAIT ACCOMPLI dates only from the late 1970s, but according to William Safire, it had a near predecessor in *a done thing.* The latter surfaced about 1700, and Dickens used it: "It was a done thing between him and Scrooge's nephew" (*A Christmas Carol,* 1843). The current cliché is also often used in the negative (*not a done deal*), as in "We can interview another architect; it's not a done deal, you know."

donkey's years A long time. The origin here is disputed. Some say it is a rhyming term for donkey's *ears,* which are quite long, and possibly also a punning allusion to the Cockney pronunciation of "years" as "ears"; others believe it alludes to donkeys being quite long-lived. The expression dates only from the late nineteenth century. Edward Lucas used it in *The Vermilion Box* (1916): "Now for my first bath for what the men call 'donkey's years,' meaning years and years."

don't ask You don't want to hear bad news, a long story, or something unpleasant or embarrassing. This slangy phrase, used since the 1960s and only in conversation, may be a response to a direct question, such as "How did you do on the exam?" or used to impart information, as in "Ask me how much we have left in the bank."—"How much?"—"Don't ask." It differs from *don't ask me,* said with the emphasis on *me,* which is a casual and somewhat impolite reply that means "I don't know" (as in "'When does the restaurant open?'—'Don't ask me.'" A newer variation is *don't ask, don't tell*, which in the early 1990s began to designate a policy on homosexuality adopted by the U.S. military in 1994. Under this policy, personnel are not asked about their sexual orientation, and homosexuals are allowed to serve provided they do not openly reveal their orientation. This usage quickly spread to other contexts, as in "Our veterinarian has a "'don't ask, don't tell'" policy about what happens to pets who must be put away."

don't call us, we'll call you We'll let you know when a decision—probably an unfavorable one—has been made. This formulaic brush-off dates from the mid-1940s and probably comes from the theater, ending an audition for a part. It was soon broadened to many areas where a candidate is rejected (for a job, political office, athletic team, and so on). A newer version of the theatrical rejection is *Thank you very much*, said without a hint of the gratitude implied by the words. It, too, may become a cliché.

don't change/swap horses in midstream Don't change methods or leaders in the middle of a crisis. Although originating a quarter of a century earlier, the expression became famous through its use by President Lincoln in 1864 when he learned that his renomination for a second term was being backed by the National Union League. Several versions of his speech were recorded, some having it *change* and others *swap.*

don't count your chickens before they hatch Don't spend or try to profit from something not yet earned. This expression comes from Aesop's fable about a milkmaid carrying a full pail on her head who daydreams about selling the milk for eggs that will hatch into chickens and make her so rich she will toss her head at offers of marriage; but she prematurely tosses her head and spills the milk. It was, like so many Greek fables, translated into modern European languages and passed on. The expression was in use figuratively by the sixteenth century and appeared in proverb collections soon afterward.

don't cry over spilled milk See CRYING OVER SPILLED MILK.

don't give/care a rap for Worthless to me; without any interest. The "rap" in question was a base halfpenny that was worth only half a farthing and was circulating in Ireland in the early eighteenth century because small coins at that time were very scarce. Jonathan Swift described it in *Drapier's Letters* (1724): "Copper halfpence or farthings . . . have been for some time very scarce and many counterfeits passed about under the name of raps." Consequently the name was adopted for anything of little value and was so used by the early nineteenth century. W. H. Ainsworth wrote (*Rookwood,* 1834), "For the mare-with-three-legs [i.e., the gallows] I care not a rap."

don't hold your breath See WITH BATED BREATH.

don't know from Adam See KNOW FROM ADAM.

don't let the grass grow under your feet Act with dispatch; don't delay. This expression dates from the sixteenth century. It appeared in print in 1607 in Edward Topsell's natural history, *Foure-Footed Beasts* ("The hare . . . leaps away again, and letteth no grass grow under his feet").

don't look a gift horse in the mouth Accept a gift in good faith. This saying, which dates from St. Jerome's biblical commentary (c. A.D. 420) on St. Paul's Epistle to the Ephesians, is based on the fact that a horse's age is revealed by its teeth. Looking inside a horse's mouth therefore will tell you if someone is passing off an old nag for a spry colt. The same expression is found in French, Italian, Portuguese, and other languages.

don't take any wooden nickels Protect yourself (against fraud, loss, and so on). This warning against counterfeit coins dates from about 1900 and is distinctly American in origin, the nickel being a U.S. or Canadian five-cent coin. Why a *wooden* coin was selected is not known. Presumably making coins of wood would always have been more expensive than the intrinsic value of metal coins. Several writers suggest it replaced *don't take any wooden nutmegs,* a now obsolete saying dating from colonial times when sharp traders sold wooden nutmegs mixed in with the real spice. In print the expression is found in Ring Lardner's story, *The Real Dope* (1919), "In the mean wile—until we meet again—don't take no wood nickles [*sic*] and don't get impatient and be a good girlie."

doom and gloom See GLOOM AND DOOM.

do one's heart good, to To cheer or be cheered up, to make someone feel good, to gratify. A cliché since the nineteenth century, it was known in the sixteenth century, and appeared in Shakespeare's *A Midsummer Night's Dream* (1.2): "I will roare that I will doe any man's heart good to heare me." See also WARM THE COCKLES OF ONE'S HEART.

do one's own thing, to To find self-expression or self-fulfillment in some activity. Although this term is very old indeed—numerous references can be found in Chaucer, as in *The Merchant's Tale* ("where as they doon hir thynges")—it became hackneyed during the 1960s. Rebelling against the establishment, the unconventional "dropped out" of society and joined communes where they would "do their own thing." One might wonder how many of them were familiar with Ralph Waldo Emerson's essay, *Self-Reliance* (1841), in which he said, "I have difficulty to detect the precise man you are. . . . But do your own thing and I shall know you."

do or die, to To make a last-ditch effort. This extreme measure was first recorded in print in the seventeenth century. An early use occurs in John Fletcher's play *The Island Princess* (1621), where a character says, "Do or die" (2.4). Before long it came to be used figuratively, although it reverted to literal use (and changed form) in Tennyson's "The Charge of the Light Brigade" (1854): "Theirs not to reason why, Theirs but to do and die. Into the valley of Death Rode the six hundred."

do's and don'ts Rules about what one should and shouldn't do or say in certain situations. One of the earliest uses of this term appeared in 1902 as the title of a book, *Golf Do's and Don'ts.* It rapidly spread into numerous other contexts, as in "Her big sister was about to tell her the do's and don'ts of a first date." It has been a cliché for some decades.

dose of one's own medicine See OWN MEDICINE.

do someone proud, to To make much of, to extend lavish hospitality. This turn of phrase dates from the nineteenth century. "You've done yourselves proud," wrote Mark Twain in *Innocents at Home* (1872).

do tell Is that really so? This phrase, expressing either disbelief or sarcasm, has been around since the early nineteenth century. John Neal used it in *The Down-Easters* (1833), "George Middleton, hey?—do tell!—is that his name?"

do the honors, to To render courtesies to guests; to act as a host, making introductions, carving the turkey, and the like. This expression was being used by 1700. It appears in Alexander Pope's *Imitations of Horace* (1737): "Then hire a Slave, or (if you will), a Lord, to do the Honours, and to give the Word."

do the trick Accomplish something, succeed. Dating from the early nineteenth century, this cliché uses "trick" in the sense of an accomplishment. For example, "Add some pepper to the sauce and that should do the trick." The synonymous *turn the trick,* dating from the same period, is heard less often today. "A couple of college products turned the trick for the Whalers," wrote a sports columnist (*Springfield Daily News,* April 22, 1976). *To turn a trick,* on the other hand, uses "trick" in the slangy sense of a prostitute's customer and means to engage in a sexual act with such an individual. Also see THAT DOES IT.

dot the i's and cross the t's, to To be precise and meticulous. The source of this expression, it is alleged, is the possibility of confusing these letters if they are carelessly penned, and presumably it began as an admonition to schoolchildren and/or scribes. It was soon transferred to other affairs, and has been a cliché since the late nineteenth century.

double-edged sword An argument, compliment, or other statement that cuts either way, that is, has a double meaning. "'Your Delphic sword,' the panther then replied, 'is double-edged and cuts on either side,'" wrote John Dryden (*The Hind and the Panther,* 1686). See also LEFT-HANDED COMPLIMENT.

doubting Thomas A person who habitually questions every issue. The term alludes to Jesus's disciple Thomas, who refused to believe in the resurrection until he had solid evidence of it (recounted in the Book of John, 20:24–25). The term has been applied to similarly doubtful individuals ever since, although the exact wording dates only from the late 1800s. W. C. Wyckoff used it: "Doubting Thomases, who will only believe what they see, must wait awhile" (*Harper's Magazine,* June 1883).

do unto others The so-called *golden rule,* that is, behave toward others as you would have them behave toward you; also, the converse, do *not* do to others what you would not like done to yourself. The sources for this statement are manifold: Confucius, Aristotle, the New Testament, the Koran, the Talmud. It continued to turn up in such sources as *McGuffey's Reader* (1837): "You know, my child, the Bible says that you must always do to other people, as you wish to have them do to you." George Bernard Shaw, never one to be put off by age-old precepts, quipped, "Do not do unto others as you would they should unto you. Their tastes may not be the same" (*Maxims for Revolutionists,* 1902).

down and dirty Unfair, vicious; also, coarse, explicit about unpleasant matters. The first usage of this colloquialism dates from the mid-1900s, as in "The neighbors were furious about the new ordinance and waged a real down and dirty fight." The second surfaced a decade or two later, as in the film entitled

Down and Dirty (1976), a black comedy about a depraved family whose interests include adultery, murder, revenge, and incest.

down and out At the end of one's resources, destitute. The term is believed to be an American colloquialism that comes from boxing, where a fighter who is knocked down and stays down for a given time is judged the loser of the bout. O. Henry transferred it to a more general sort of loser in *No Story* (1909): "I'm the janitor and corresponding secretary of the Down-and-Out Club." The English writer George Orwell used it as a title, *Down and Out in Paris and London* (1933), for a book about his experiences of poverty in those cities. The actor Orson Welles quipped, "When you are down and out something always turns up—and it is usually the noses of your friends" (*New York Times,* April 1, 1962).

down at the heels Needy and therefore shabby. The expression alludes to the worn-out heels of shoes needing repair, and also to holes in one's socks. Indeed, one of the earliest references in print is to the latter: "Go with their hose out at heles" (Thomas Wilson, *The Arte of Rhetorique,* 1588). The expression was common by 1700 and well worn enough to be a cliché by 1800.

down in the dumps, to be To be sad or dispirited. The "dumps" referred to are not the modern rubbish heap but a heavy, oppressive mental haze or dullness (from the Dutch words *domp* and German *dumpf*). The expression was used several times by Shakespeare (*Titus Andronicus* 1.1; *The Taming of the Shrew* 2.1; *Much Ado about Nothing* 2.3) and was well known as "in the dumps" until the eighteenth century. See also DOWN IN THE MOUTH.

down in the mouth Sad, unhappy. The term refers to a mournful facial expression, with the corners of the mouth drawn down. Known by the mid-seventeenth century, it appears in print in Bishop Joseph Hall's *Cases of Conscience* (1649): "The Roman Orator was down in the mouth, finding himselfs thus cheated by the moneychanger." Occasionally it appeared with *at* instead of *in* ("He'll never more be down-at-mouth," Dante Gabriel Rossetti, *Dante and His Circle,* 1850), a usage that is now obsolete. See also DOWN IN THE DUMPS.

down memory lane Looking back on the past. Often put in a nostalgic way, this term may have originated as the title of a popular song of 1924, "Memory Lane," words by Bud de Sylva, and music by Larry Spier and Con Conrad. It was revived in the film *In Society* (1944), starring Abbott and Costello. That is where former movie actor, President Ronald Reagan, may have picked it up; he then used it in his 1984 speech accepting the Republican nomination, "Well, let's take them [his opponents] on a little stroll down memory lane."

down on one's luck Short of cash or credit. A nineteenth-century description of financial embarrassment, usually of a temporary nature, this term implies, with *down,* that the person so described at one time had more resources. Thus Thackeray wrote, "The Chevalier was. . . . to use his own picturesque expression, 'down on his luck'" (*Pendennis,* 1849).

down the drain Wasted resources. The term, alluding to water flowing down a drain, was transferred to expending effort or funds on a useless enterprise. "Well, fancy giving money to the Government! Might as well have put it down the drain," wrote Sir Alan Patrick Herbert (1890–1971) in *Too Much.* To *go down the drain* means to become worthless. It was so used by W. Somerset Maugham (*The Breadwinner,* 1930): "All his savings are gone down the drain."

down the hatch Drink it down, a toast for drinkers. The allusion is to the naval hatch, an opening in a ship's deck through which cargo, passengers, or crew can pass. The transfer to the human mouth or throat was made long before this slangy expression came into use. John Heywood's 1546 proverb collection included, "It is good to haue a hatche before the durre," meaning it is good to have some impediment to speaking before one opens one's mouth, so as to have time to reflect. The metaphor also appears in Stephen Gosson's *The Schoole of Abuse* (1579): "I wish that every rebuker shoulde place a hatch before the door." The drinker's meaning, however, is a twentieth-century expression, first appearing in print in the early 1930s, as in Malcolm Lowry's *Ultramarine* (1933): "Well, let's shoot a few whiskies down the hatch."

down the road In the future, as in "He'd love to buy another store, but that's down the road a ways," or "Her doctoral degree is about three years down the road." This colloquialism dates from the second half of the 1900s.

down-to-earth Practical, forthright, realistic. It is the opposite of having one's HEAD IN THE CLOUDS. The adjectival use of this term dates from the first half of the twentieth century. The *OED* quotes a book review that appeared in the *Canadian Forum* in 1932: "This book is full of such 'down to earth' observations."

down to the wire At the very last minute; at the end. The term, an Americanism dating from the late nineteenth century, alludes to the practice of stretching a wire across and above the track at the start and finish of a racecourse. Here "down to" actually means the same as "up to," that is, all the way to the finishing line. It began to be transferred to occasions other than horse races about 1900, and appears in print in *Down the Line* (1901) by H. McHugh (pseudonym for George Vere Hobart): "Swift often told himself he could . . . beat him down to the wire."

dragon lady A fierce and formidable woman. The term comes from a popular comic strip of the 1930s, "Terry and the Pirates," which featured such a woman. In the mid-eighteenth century the word *dragon* alone was used to describe a fierce and violent person of either sex, although by the mid-1800s it was so used only for a woman. Possibly this was the original source for the comic-strip dragon lady.

draw a bead on (someone), to To take careful verbal aim at a person. An Americanism dating from about 1830, the term comes from aiming a revolver or rifle, on which the "bead" was a small knob on the foresight. It was being used figuratively by about 1930.

draw a blank, to To be unable to remember or to find something. The term refers to a losing ticket in a lottery, which has no number printed on it—that is, it is blank. It first appeared in print in the early nineteenth century.

draw a veil over, to To conceal; to say no more about something. A cliché from the mid-nineteenth century, this analogy to hiding one's face behind a veil is often used to gloss over the details of an embarrassing situation. Daniel Defoe, long known as a historian before he turned his hand to fiction, wrote in *The True-born Englishman* (1701), "Satyr, be kind! and draw a silent Veil! Thy native England's vices to conceal."

draw/pull in one's horns, to To retreat, to back down. This expression, which dates back at least to the mid-fourteenth century, refers to the practice of snails, which can withdraw the soft, projecting parts of their body inside their shell when they feel threatened. The snail has no genuine horns. Rather, the front end of its muscular foot has sensory tentacles that look a little like horns, whence the expression. About 1350 an unknown chronicler wrote about Richard the Lionhearted in a particular campaign, "They . . . gunne to drawen in their hornes as a snayle among the thornes." It has been a cliché since about 1800.

draw the line at, to To set a specific limit, particularly on one's behavior. This expression, heard in such contexts as "He drew the line at outright cheating," comes from drawing some sort of boundary, but no one is quite certain as to what kind. Some speculate it comes from the early game of court tennis, in which the court had no specific dimensions and the players had to draw their own lines. Others believe it signified a line cut by a plow across a field to designate the property boundary. The term was used figuratively from the late eighteenth century on and was probably a cliché by the time W. S. Gilbert wrote, "I attach but little value to rank or wealth, but the line must be drawn somewhere" (*H.M.S. Pinafore,* Act I).

dream on See IN YOUR DREAMS.

dream team An outstanding combination of individuals or factors that promises huge success. This term originated in the second half of the twentieth century in sports, where it signified a team made up of the best players. It soon was transferred to other venues, as in the *New York Times* headline for a story about wealthy lawyer Johnnie L. Cochran (Sept. 3, 2000), "Finding a 'Dream Team' for his Finances." It is well on its way to clichédom.

dressed to kill/to the nines Very fashionably attired. The first expression is a nineteenth-century Americanism. It appears in print in E. G. Paige's *Dow's Patent Sermons,* c. 1849 ("A gentleman tiptoeing along Broadway, with a lady wiggle-waggling by his side, and both dressed to kill"). The precise analogy is no longer known. "Kill" may allude to the idea of making a conquest, or perhaps it is an extension of something "done to death"—that is, overdone. *Dressed to the nines,* also put as dressed *up* to the nines, is British in origin and literally means elaborately dressed to perfection. The "nines" were singled out to signify "superlative" in numerous other contexts from the late eighteenth century on, but no one is quite sure why. Some say it is because nine, as the highest single-digit number, symbolizes the best. Today, however, it is the numeral ten that signifies the best (as, for example, in Olympics judging). Other writers suggest that *nines* is a corruption of "to then eyne"—that is, to the eyes—but this interpretation doesn't make much sense either. Describing an old department store holding its final sale before closing and lavishly decorated for Christmas, Mary Cantwell observed that "the corpse was dressed to the nines" (*New York Times,* Dec. 1989).

dribs and drabs Small quantities. This phrase, dating from the early nineteenth century, consists of nouns that rarely appear elsewhere. *Drib,* originating in the early 1700s, probably alludes to "dribble" or "trickle"; *drab* has meant a petty sum of money since the early 1800s.

drink like a fish, to To drink a great deal, usually meaning alcoholic beverages. The simile comes from the fish's breathing apparatus, which causes it to be openmouthed much of the time, so that it looks as if it were constantly drinking. The expression is quite old, appearing in print in the mid-seventeenth century, and has outlived drinking like frogs, like elephants, and like knights templar, as well as the medieval proverb, *to drink like a pope.* The newer synonym *to drink under the table* calls up an image of inebriated persons rolling under the table.

drive a hard bargain, to To exact as much as possible from a transaction. *Drive* in this expression is in the sense of vigorously carrying through something. It was so used as long ago as the sixteenth century, when Sir Philip Sidney wrote, "There never was a better bargain driven" (*My True Love Hath My Heart,* 1583). *Hard,* in the sense of "unyielding," is coupled with *bargain* even earlier, in a translation from the Greek of Suidas (*Lexicon,* c. A.D. 950): "A hard bargainer never gets good meat."

drive (someone) to drink, to To annoy someone to distraction. A twentieth-century Americanism, this expression implies that alcohol-induced oblivion is the only form of escape from the pest in question. W. C. Fields turned it around in his quip, "I was in love with a beautiful blonde once—she drove me to drink—'tis the one thing I'm indebted to her for" (quoted in *Whole Grains,* by A. Spiegelman and B. Schneider). See also DRIVE UP THE WALL.

drive (someone) up the wall, to To harry someone to the point of mad desperation. The image here is forcing a person to escape a pest by literally climbing up and over a wall. An earlier version was *to drive to the wall,* the wall being as far as one could go to escape. It dates from the sixteenth century. "I am in this matter euen at the harde walle, and se not how to go further," wrote Sir Thomas More (1557). The current cliché dates from the twentieth century, and probably comes from the behavior of an addict deprived of drugs or alcohol who actually tries to climb the walls of a room or cell in desperation (see also DRIVE TO DRINK). However, it is most often used to express exasperation at being "driven crazy": "'Mad as a hatter,' said Gillian Soames complacently. 'Stark raving bonkers. Up the wall. Round the twist'" (Robert Barnard, *Death and the Chaste Apprentice,* 1989).

drop a bombshell, to To announce sensational news. This metaphor dates from World War I and likens the devastation caused by falling bombs to the shock of suddenly receiving unexpected tidings. "The letters do not drop any historical bombshells," wrote a *Manchester Guardian* reviewer in 1928. See also BOLT FROM THE BLUE.

drop dead I hate you, you are contemptible. This rude imperative dates from the early 1900s. An early example appeared in John O'Hara's novel *Appointment in Samarra* (1934): "'Let's put snow on his face.' 'Oh, drop dead.'" Interestingly enough, in the second half of the 1900s the term, now hyphenated *drop-dead,* began to be used as an adjective or adverb meaning "very" or "exceedingly" and usually in a positive context. It was frequently paired, especially in the phrase *drop-dead gorgeous.* For example, "She arrived at the screening in furs and diamonds, looking drop-dead gorgeous."

drop in the bucket A negligible amount, something that makes little difference. This expression is found in the King James version of the Bible: "Behold, the nations are as a drop of a bucket and are counted as the small dust of the balance" (Isaiah 40:15).

drop like a hot potato, to To abandon as quickly as possible; to ditch. The simile is based on the fact that potatoes, which hold a fair amount of water, retain heat very well, as anyone who has so burned his or her fingers will testify. The figurative hot potato is likely to be an embarrassing subject or ticklish problem. The term originated as a colloquialism in the early nineteenth century. It probably was a cliché by the time W. Somerset Maugham wrote, "She dropped him, but not like a hot brick or a hot potato," meaning that she let him down gently (*Cakes and Ale,* 1930).

drop like flies, to To collapse rapidly, referring to a group rather than an individual. Although this term calls to mind flies that are hit with a spray of insecticide and is, in fact, used for human beings subjected to gunfire or an epidemic of disease, *like flies* has meant in large numbers or quantities since Shakespeare's time. "The common people swarm like summer flies" wrote the bard (*Henry VI, Part 2* 6.8).

drop of a hat See AT THE DROP OF A HAT.

drowned rat, like a/wet as a Thoroughly soaked and utterly bedraggled. Despite their frequent presence in sewers and similar wet places, rats do not like water, a fact observed for many centuries ("It rained by the bucket and they came home wet as drowned rats," Petronius, *Satyricon,* c. A.D. 60). See also SOAKED TO THE SKIN.

drug on the market An overabundant commodity or service for which there is little or no demand. This expression clearly predates modern times, since drugs on the market, both illegal and legal, now are very profitable indeed. The English clergyman Thomas Fuller (*The History of the Worthies of England,* 1662) wrote, "He made such a vent for Welsh cottons, that what he found drugs at home, he left dainties beyond the sea." The *OED* suggests that "drug" here has some different meaning but does not come up with a convincing explanation. Another writer suggests it may come from the French *drogue,* for "rubbish," which makes more sense.

drum (something) into one's head, to To force an idea on someone by means of persistent repetition. This expression, used since the early nineteenth century, alludes to performing drumbeats over and over. John Stuart Mill used it in his *Political Economy* (1848): "This doctrine has been . . . tolerably effectively drummed into the public mind."

drum up To gather, to summon. Alluding to summoning recruits by beating a drum, this term has been used figuratively since the 1600s. It is often used in a business sense, as it was by Thomas Gray in a letter of 1849: "I will then drum up subscribers for Fendler." An antonym is *to drum out*, meaning to dismiss or oust. In the military this, too, was signaled by beating a drum. This came to mean being fired from a job but is not heard as often today.

drunk as a lord/skunk Extremely intoxicated. The first expression, known since the seventeenth century and considered a proverb by 1651 ("The proverb goes 'As drunk as a lord,'" John Evelyn, *A Character of England*), is based on the idea that the aristocracy could and did indulge in drunkenness more than commoners did, presumably because they could afford to. The more recent *drunk as a skunk,* American in origin, undoubtedly became popular on account of its rhyme; it dates from the early 1900s. Both clichés have survived the demise of numerous other similes, among them drunk as an ape (from Chaucer's time), tinker, fish, goat, owl, emperor, piper, fiddler (because he was plied with alcohol at wakes, fairs, and similar feasts), swine or pig, devil, beggar, blazes, David's sow (based on an ancient anecdote explained in Francis Grose's *Classical Dictionary,* and current from the seventeenth century), and others. See also DRINK LIKE A FISH; TIGHT AS A TICK.

dry as dust Dull, boring, desiccated. The simile itself dates from about 1500 and has been a cliché since the eighteenth century. Nevertheless, William Wordsworth deigned to use it in "The Excursion": "The good die first, and they whose hearts are dry as summer dust burn to the socket."

dry behind the ears, not (yet) See WET BEHIND THE EARS.

duck soup, like Extremely simple, easily accomplished. This American colloquialism dates from about 1910, and its origin is no longer known. It gained currency after it became the title of one of the Marx Brothers' zaniest motion pictures (1933).

dull as dishwater Flat, boring. This expression began life in the eighteenth century as *dull as ditchwater,* alluding to the muddy color of the water in roadside gullies. "He'd be sharper than a serpent's tooth, if he wasn't as dull as ditchwater," says Dickens's Fanny Cleaver (*Oliver Twist*). This version survived on both sides of the Atlantic well into the twentieth century. Either through careless pronunciation or through similar analogy it occasionally became dishwater—water in which dishes had been washed and which consequently was dingy and grayish.

dumb down, to To simplify or otherwise revise in order to appeal to someone of less education, taste, or intelligence. This slangy expression dates from the first half of the 1900s. *Publishers Weekly* used it in a review of *The Business of Books* by André Schiffrin: ". . . the attempt to appeal to the lowest common denominator of taste, which has, he says, led network television and movies in such depressing directions, has dumbed down publishing to an alarming degree" (Aug. 21, 2000).

Dutch courage Boldness induced by drinking. The term alludes to the reputation of the Dutch as heavy drinkers, which in the case of the whiskey-loving British is a case of the POT CALLING THE KETTLE BLACK. The idea dates back at least to the seventeenth century, when Edmund Waller wrote, "The Dutch their wine, and all their brandy lose, disarm'd of that from which their courage grows" (*Instructions to a Painter,* 1665). Sir Walter Scott used the term several times, but it may be dying out.

Dutch treat A meal or entertainment in which the participants all pay their own way. It is an American term dating from the late nineteenth century and may be derived, one writer suggests, from the thrift observed in Dutch immigrants. However, there was an earlier term, *Dutch feast,* defined by Francis Grose (*A Classical Dictionary of the Vulgar Tongue,* 1785) as an occasion when the host gets drunk before his guests (see also DUTCH COURAGE). A more recent version of Dutch treat is *going Dutch,* which has the identical meaning.

Dutch uncle, talk (to one) like a A person who reproves or criticizes someone severely. Dating from the early nineteenth century, the term appeared in print in Joseph C. Neal's *Charcoal Sketches* (1837). The precise origin is not known, but it is probably safe to presume that the Dutch were considered a stern, sober people, admirably suited to giving someone a talking-to in no uncertain terms.

duty bound, to be To be firmly obligated. This term is derived from *bounden duty,* which dates from the 1500s and was actually redundant, since from the 1400s *bound* also meant "under obligations." Nevertheless, it appears in the Communion Service of the Book of Common Prayer (1559): "We beseech thee to accept this our bounden duty and service." It also retains this form three centuries later: "It was his bounden duty to accept the office" (Harriet Martineau, *The Manchester Strike,* 1833). At some point this locution was grammatically changed to the present participial usage, as in "I'm duty bound to report this violation to the dean."

dyed in the wool Thoroughgoing, complete. The term, which dates from at least the sixteenth century, alludes to cloth made from wool that was dyed while raw (before it was spun) instead of being dyed piece by piece. The color therefore was "true" throughout, and this concept was transferred to other kinds of genuineness. "In half an hour he can come out an original democrat, dyed in the wool," said Daniel Webster in a speech (Feb. 10, 1830). It has been a cliché since the early 1900s.

dying day, to one's For the rest of one's life. The English poet George Sandys used the expression as long ago as 1599: "To have a sight of her sometime before their dying-dayes." The cliché usually appears in a somewhat melodramatic or hyperbolic context, such as "I'll never forget this garden, not to my dying day."

e

eager beaver An overzealous or extremely ambitious individual. The beaver has been known as an especially hard worker since at least the seventeenth century, on a par with BUSY AS A BEE. It was only in the twentieth century that this not-quite-rhyming expression gained currency. It was widely used for overzealous recruits during World War II who chronically disobeyed the unwritten rule, Never volunteer, and rapidly became a cliché.

eagle-eyed Keen-sighted, either literally or figuratively. Like all birds of prey, eagles of necessity have excellent eyesight, which they need to spot their food supply. Their perspicacity has been transferred to human beings since Roman times. Horace pointed out (*Satires,* 35 B.C.) that those who are eagle-eyed in spotting others' faults are blind to their own. "Faith, being eagle-eyed, can . . . see the majestie of God," wrote Bishop William Barlow in 1601. Later the term was often put as *having an eagle eye.*

early bird catches the worm, the Those who get there first have the best chance of success. This stricture appeared in William Camden's book of proverbs (1605) and has remained part of the work ethic ever since.

earth move, to feel the To have an extremely good sexual experience. This hyperbole first appeared in Ernest Hemingway's *For Whom the Bell Tolls* (1940), "But did thee feel the earth move?" It has been repeated, usually in humorous fashion, ever since.

ear to the ground, to have/keep an To be well informed. The allusion here, one writer conjectures, is to the days of cowboys and Indians, when one literally put one's ear to the ground in order to hear the sound of horses miles away. An Americanism dating from the late nineteenth century, the term was a cliché by the time Stanley Walker poked fun at it (and two others) in *The Uncanny Knacks of Mr. Doherty* (1941): "He had his ear to the ground and his eye on the ball while they were sitting on the fence."

easier said than done Describing something that is more readily talked about than accomplished. This expression dates back as far as the fifteenth century, when it appeared in several sources, including the Vulgate (Latin) Bible. It was sometimes put as *sooner* or *better* said than done; the latter appears in John Heywood's 1546 collection of English proverbs.

easy as pie Not difficult; requiring little or no effort or expertise. The analogy no doubt is to eating pie rather than making it, which requires both effort and expertise. An American term dating from the early twentieth century, it became a cliché relatively recently. See also DUCK SOUP; EASY AS ROLLING OFF A LOG.

easy as rolling off a log Not difficult; requiring little or no effort. One writer claims that this term, which is American, dates from colonial times, but the earliest written records date from the 1830s. Mark Twain used it in *A Connecticut Yankee in King Arthur's Court* (1889): "I could do it as easy as rolling off a log." The analogy, no doubt, is to remain standing on a log floating downstream, which is no easy feat. Indeed, it is sometimes put as *easy as falling off a log.* See also DUCK SOUP; EASY AS PIE.

easy come, easy go What is readily achieved or gained is also readily lost. This principle was noted hundreds of years ago by the Chinese sage Chuang-tsze ("Quickly come and quickly go," c. 400 B.C.) and appears several times in Chaucer's writings—for example, "As lightly as it comth, so wol we spende" (*The Pardoner's Tale*). "Light come, light go" is also in John Heywood's 1546 proverb collection. *Easy* was substituted for *lightly* and *quickly* in the nineteenth century.

easy street, on Very well off, financially secure. This phrase uses *easy* in the sense of "in comfortable circumstances," a usage dating from about 1700. The phrase itself came into use about two hundred years later.

eat crow/humble pie/dirt, to To acknowledge an embarrassing error and humiliatingly abase oneself. All these expressions date from the early nineteenth century, *eating crow* from America and *eating humble pie* and *dirt* from Britain. The origin of the first is not known, although it is generally acknowledged that the meat of a crow tastes terrible. A story cited by Charles Funk and published in the *Atlanta Constitution* in 1888 claims that toward the end of the War of 1812, during a temporary truce, an American went hunting and by accident crossed behind the British lines, where he shot a crow. He was caught by an unarmed British officer who, by complimenting him on his fine shooting, persuaded him to hand over his gun. The officer then pointed the gun and said that as punishment for trespassing the American must take a bite out of the crow. The American obeyed, but when the officer returned his gun, he took his revenge and made the Briton eat the rest of the bird.

The source of *humble pie* is less far-fetched; it is a corruption of (or pun on) *umble-pie,* "umbles" being dialect for the heart, liver, and entrails of the deer, which were fed to the hunt's beaters and other servants while the lord and his guests ate the choice venison. This explanation appeared in 1830 in *Vocabulary of East Anglia* by Robert Forby.

The analogy to eating dirt is self-evident. It appeared in Frederick W. Farrar's *Julian Home* (1859): "He made up for the dirt they had been eating by the splendour of his entertainment."

eat like a bird/horse, to To eat very little/very much. The first comes from the misconception that birds don't eat much, and indeed, they seem to peck away at tiny bits of seed and other food. In fact, however, they do eat quite a bit relative to their size, some birds actually consuming their weight in food each day. In print the term appeared only in the twentieth century, as in Barnaby Ross's *The Tragedy of X: Drury Lane's Mystery* (1930): "She ate like a bird, slept little." To "eat like a horse," based on the idea that horses eat a great deal, dates from the eighteenth century.

eat one's cake and have it, too, to To have it both ways; to spend something and still possess it. This metaphor was already a proverb in the sixteenth century, included in John Heywood's collection of 1546 (as "You cannot eat your cake and have your cake") and has reappeared with great regularity ever since, probably because, as A. C. Benson wrote (*From a College Window,* 1907), "There still remains the intensely human instinct . . . the desire to eat one's cake and also to have it."

eat one's hat, to To declare one's readiness to consume one's headgear if a statement should prove false, an event should not occur, and so on. The likelihood of actually doing so is presumably very remote, which is the very analogy being drawn (to a statement's being false, an event not occurring, and so on). The expression appeared in Dickens's *Pickwick Papers* (1836), in the words of one clerical gentleman, "Well if I knew as little of life as that, I'd eat my hat and swallow the buckle whole."

eat one's heart out, to To worry excessively. "Eating our hearts for weariness and sorrow" appeared in Homer's *Odyssey* (c. 850 B.C.). Presumably here, as in later usage, eating one's heart is analogous to consuming one's inmost self with worry or anxiety. Later English writers, including John Lyly and Sir Francis Bacon, ascribed the saying to the Greek philosopher Pythagoras, who also used it ("Eat not thy heart," *Praecentum,* c. 525 B.C.). A modern slangy variant invoking a different feeling is the spoken imperative *eat your heart out,* meaning "doesn't that make you jealous." A translation from the Yiddish *es dir oys s'harts,* it originated in America in the 1960s and was popularized by the television show *Laugh-In.*

eat one's words, to To be forced to retract a statement, usually in a humiliating way. The term first appeared in a sixteenth-century tract by John Calvin on Psalm 62: "God eateth not his word when he hath once spoken." In 1618 Sir Walter Raleigh wrote in his memoirs, "Nay wee'le make you confesse . . . and eat your own words," and in 1670 the expression appeared in John Ray's collection of English proverbs.

eat out of someone's hand, to To be quite submissive. This expression, referring to a tame animal eating from a person's hand, dates from the early twentieth century. "He's like that," wrote Joseph Conrad (*Victory,* 1915), "sometimes that familiar you might think he would eat out of your hand."

eat someone out of house and home, to To consume a great deal. This expression is at least two thousand years old. It appeared in the Alexandrian philosopher Philo's *De Agricultura* (c. A.D. 40) as well as in numerous English writings, before Shakespeare used it for Mistress Quickly's description of the gluttonous Falstaff: "He hath eaten me out of house and home" (*Henry IV, Part 2,* 2.1).

egg in your beer, what do you want? Why are you complaining? What special advantage do you think you're entitled to? This American slang expression dates from the first half of the twentieth century and became popular in the armed forces during World War II, in reply to any kind of griping. The actual addition of an egg to a glass of beer is presumably viewed as some kind of enrichment; one writer suggests it was regarded as an aphrodisiac, enhancing potency. The traditional English wassail bowl contains porter, eggs, and sherry, and Thomas Hardy (in *The Three Strangers,* 1883) gives a recipe for mead that includes egg white, but few if any other recipes call for such a combination, and probably they have nothing to do with this cliché anyway.

egg on one's face, to have/wipe off the To have made a fool of oneself. An Americanism of the mid-twentieth century, this self-evident metaphor for having made a mess of oneself soon crossed the Atlantic. (John Ciardi, however, speculates it may derive from an entertainer's being pelted with garbage, including raw eggs, by a dissatisfied audience.) The other version, to *wipe* the egg off one's face, means the same thing, implying that one has made an embarrassing error (not that one is correcting it). See also LAY AN EGG.

ego trip A display of self-importance, a vehicle for self-satisfaction: for example, "These annual art shows of hers are simply an ego trip; she has no talent whatsoever." This pejorative term dates from the second half of the 1900s. It brands someone as an egotist, which Ambrose Bierce defined as "A person of low taste, more interested in himself than in me" (*The Devil's Dictionary,* 1911).

eighth wonder A marvel; an astonishing or surprising thing or event. This expression, often used sarcastically, implies that something is (or is scarcely) worthy of being classed with the so-called seven wonders of the ancient world: the Pyramids of Egypt, Hanging Gardens of Babylon, Tomb of Mausolus, Temple of Diana at Ephesus, Colossus of Rhodes, statue of Jupiter by Phidias, and the Pharos of Alexandria. The English novelist Maria Edgeworth wrote in a letter in 1831, "A spoiled child of 30 whose mother and father . . . think him the 8th wonder of the world." See also NINE-DAY WONDER.

elbow grease, to use To apply physical effort. It has been said that this expression, dating from the seventeenth century, originally referred to a joke played on a new apprentice, who was sent out to a shop to purchase "elbow grease." Originally meaning simply to use one's arm vigorously in scrubbing or polishing, it soon was transferred to other kinds of effort as well. "Forethought is the elbow-grease which a novelist—or poet, or dramatist—requires," said Anthony Trollope (*Thackeray,* 1874).

elbow room Enough space. This metaphor for having enough space to extend one's elbows has been used since the sixteenth century. "Now my soul hath elbow-room," wrote Shakespeare (*King John,* 5.7).

elevator doesn't go to the top floor, the Describing someone who is simple-minded, not very intelligent. The top floor in this slangy insult denotes the brain. One synonym is a *few/two/three bricks shy of a load,* indicating a person is short of intelligence. Another is *not playing with a full deck,* which refers to the card game of poker. Yet another is *having only one oar in the water* (or *not having both oars in the water*). All these slangy expressions date from the second half of the twentieth century. For example, "But now this new opportunity had presented itself, and . . . how could he really lose? Okay, she probably wasn't playing with a full deck, but he didn't figure her for any more gun wielding" (David Baldacci, *Hour Game,* 2004).

eleventh hour, at the Just in time; at the last possible moment. This expression occurs in the biblical parable of the laborers (Matthew 20:1–16), in which those workers hired at the eleventh hour of a twelve-hour day received as much pay as those who began work in the first hour. Eric Partridge claimed that the current cliché does not allude to this story but offered no alternative source. The American poet Forceythe Willson (1837–67) wrote, "And I heard a Bugle sounding, as from some celestial Tower; and the same mysterious voice said: 'It is the Eleventh Hour!'" ("The Old Sergeant"). The armistice ending World War I came into force at 11 A.M. on November 11, 1918, at the eleventh hour of the eleventh day of the eleventh month.

eloquent silence, an Speechlessness that speaks louder than speech. "Often there is eloquence in a silent look," wrote the Roman poet Ovid in his *Artis*

Amatoriae (The Art of Love), a three-volume how-to text for lovers (c. 1 B.C.). Cicero, Tasso, and La Rochefoucauld were among the many who echoed the sentiment, although not all in the service of love. In English, the playwright William Congreve said (*Old Batchelour,* 1693, 2:9), "Even silence may be eloquent in love." It was already a cliché by the time Thomas Carlyle (*On Heroes and Hero-Worship,* 1840) wrote, "Silence is more eloquent than words." A newer synonym, dating from the second half of the 1900s and rapidly becoming a cliché, is *deafening silence.* It is used especially to refer to a refusal to reply or to make a comment. The *Times* had it on Aug. 28, 1985: "Conservative and Labour MPS [Members of Parliament] have complained of a 'deafening silence' over the affair." See also ACTIONS SPEAK LOUDER THAN WORDS.

embarrassment of riches, an Too much of a good thing, an overabundance. The term is a direct translation from the French, where it first appeared as the title of a comedy by the Abbé Léonor d'Allainval, *L'embarras des richesses* (1726), translated into English by John Ozell and opening in London in 1738.

empty calories Food that has little or no nutritional value but adds to one's caloric intake. This expression was born in the diet-conscious era of the late twentieth century and applied to, for example, liquor, soft drinks, snack foods, and desserts, as in, "She loads up on empty calories like potato chips." It is on its way to clichédom.

end game The concluding stage of some process. The term originated about 1880 in the game of chess, where it means the late stage of a game when most of the pieces have been removed from the board. It began to be used figuratively in the mid-1900s, as in, "We hope this diplomatic end game will result in a peace treaty."

end of one's rope/tether, at the/come to the To have exhausted one's resources or abilities. The term alludes to a tethered (roped) animal that can graze only as far as the length of the rope permits. "Being run to the end of his Rope, as one that had no more Excuses to make," wrote Sir John Chardin in 1686 (*The Coronation of Solyman the Third*). "I am at the end of my tether" was close to being a cliché by the time Royall Tyler used the line in his comedy *The Contrast* (first U.S. production in 1787).

end of the world, it's not/wouldn't be the It's not that disastrous a calamity. This hyperbole of reassurance dates from the late nineteenth century. George Bernard Shaw used it in *Major Barbara* (1907): "Nothing's going to happen to you . . . it wouldn't be the end of the world if anything did."

end run An evasive maneuver, a diversion. The term, dating from about 1900, is a transfer from football, where it denotes a running play in which the ball carrier runs around the defensive end. It soon was transferred to other contexts. An editorial in the *Boston Globe* about allowing drilling for oil in the Arctic National Wildlife Refuge had it: ". . . they now plan to include drilling in the budget bill, which cannot be filibustered. Senators should see this gimmick for the procedural end run it is, and reject it." (Jan. 31, 2005).

ends of the earth, (from) the The remotest parts of the globe. The phrase first appeared in the Bible: "All the ends of the earth have seen the salvation of our God" (Psalms 98:3). This turn of phrase is based on the idea of a flat earth, which actually has "ends." Nevertheless, it survived the general acknowledgment that the globe is spherical and was a cliché by the late nineteenth century.

enough is enough That is sufficient, no more is needed or wanted. "There is now enough" appeared in the works of numerous Roman writers (Horace, Martial, Plautus, and others), and "Enough is enough" was already a proverb by the time John Heywood amassed his 1546 collection. Versions in other European languages—Italian, French, Dutch—append the notion that not only is enough sufficient, but that too much is bad. In any event, the expression was well on its way to being a cliché by the time Robert Southey wrote (*The Doctor,* 1834), "As for money, enough is enough; no man can enjoy more." Wallis Warfield, Duchess of Windsor (1896–1986) reportedly disagreed, saying, "You can never be too rich or too thin" (attributed). A much more recent synonym is the interjection *enough already,* a translation of the Yiddish *genug shoyn.*

enough rope, to give (someone) To allow someone to continue behaving badly until he or she reaps the consequences. The rope in question alludes to enough rope to hang oneself, which is how the phrase is often completed. It was well enough known by the mid-seventeenth century to appear in four slightly different forms in John Ray's *English Proverbs* (1678), the most common being "Give him rope enough and he'll hang himself."

enough said No further amplification is needed. Although Plautus's *Dixi satis* (in *Rudens,* c. 200 B.C.) has been so translated, the expression in English became current only in the nineteenth century, on both sides of the Atlantic. It was well known enough in America to acquire what Eric Partridge called a "comic perversion," that is, the variant *nuff said,* which the *OED* editors traced back as far as 1840 in a U.S. newspaper. Its most emphatic use appeared in Gertrude Stein's poem, *Enough Said* (1935), which in its entirety consists of this expression repeated five times.

enter the lists, to To engage in combat, rivalry, or competition. The term comes from medieval jousting tournaments, in which the *list* or *lists* was the barrier around the arena for such a contest. It was used figuratively already by Shakespeare ("Now is she in the very lists of love," *Venus and*

Adonis, 1592). In 1647 Nathaniel Bacon used the full expression, "The King, loth to enter the List with the Clergy about too many matters" (*Historical Discourse of the Uniformity of the Government of England*). The term is similar to the slightly newer *eager for the fray* or *enter the fray,* "fray" being a battle, skirmish, or other fight, usually of a noisy nature. The first originated as a direct quotation from Colley Cibber's version of Shakespeare's *Richard III* (5.3): "My soul's in arms, and eager for the fray." However, all these expressions appear to be dying out.

esprit de corps A sense of unity, pride, or common purpose among the members of a group. The term came directly from French into English in the late eighteenth century and often was misspelled, as by Jane Austen in *Mansfield Park* ("I honour your esprit du [*sic*] corps"). It continued to be used because, as Sir Frank Adcock put it, it describes "that typically English characteristic for which there is no English name" (1930). An American equivalent from the sports world is *team spirit.*

eternal triangle, the A threesome of lovers, either two men involved with or vying for one woman or two women and one man. "Eternal" here simply means that this situation has occurred over and over through the ages. The term has been traced to a book review appearing in the *London Daily Chronicle* in 1907, describing a novel that "deals with the eternal triangle, which, in this case, consists of two men and one woman."

et tu, Brute! You, my so-called friend, are also betraying me. This expression is generally credited to Shakespeare, who used the exact Latin locution (literally, "and you, Brutus") in *Julius Caesar* (3.1) in 1599. However, Shakespeare actually was loosely quoting the real Julius Caesar, who reportedly said, "You too, my child?" when Marcus Brutus stabbed him in 44 B.C. Caesar made this dying remark in Greek (according to Suetonius's account). Incidentally, "Brute" did not signify "brute" in the sense of animal; it simply is the proper Latin case for this name. A more recent version, *with friends like that/you, who needs enemies,* became current in America in the 1960s. It usually is a response to a far less dire betrayal—a tactless remark by a friend, for example.

every cloud has a silver lining The worst situation has some element of hope or some redeeming quality. John Milton appears to have been the originator of this metaphor, in *Comus* (1634): "A sable cloud turns forth its silver lining on the night." It was adopted by numerous later writers and so was already a cliché by the time it appeared in the popular World War I song, "Keep the Home Fires Burning" (Ivor Novello and Lena Guilhert, 1915): "There's a silver lining through the dark clouds shining." Noël Coward played on it in a song of the 1930s: "Every silver lining has its cloud."

every dog will have his day Even the lowliest will eventually have their revenge. Erasmus traced this metaphor to a Macedonian proverb about the death of Euripides in 406 B.C. While on a visit to the king of Macedonia, the Greek playwright was attacked and killed by dogs that a rival had set upon him. John Heywood included it in his 1546 proverb collection ("As euery man saith, a dog hatha daie"), and George Bernard Shaw used it as well ("Every dog has his day, and I have had mine," *Caesar and Cleopatra,* 1897).

every little bit helps Any tiny contribution to a cause, collection, or undertaking can be useful. This expression began life, according to the *Oxford Dictionary of Proverbs,* as "Everything helps, quoth the wren when she pissed into the sea," dated 1590. Another version, "Every little helps," appeared in print in 1791 (in O'Keeffe's play, *Wild Oats,* 5.3, "Here—it's not much! But every little helps"). "Bit" appears to have been added in America in the early twentieth century. A. W. Upfield used it in *The Man of Two Tribes* (1956): "Every little bit helps."

every man for himself Everyone looks out for his or her best interest. Originally this phrase expressed approval. It appeared in Chaucer's *The Knight's Tale* ("Ech man for him-self, ther is non other"), implying that if one did not look out for oneself no one else would. It was included in John Heywood's 1546 proverb collection ("Praie and shifts eche one for himselfs, as he can, every man for himselfs, and God for us all"). This latter turn of phrase (with "God for all") occurs with minor variations in numerous languages, including French, German, Dutch, Italian, and Spanish. Slightly later versions changed God to the devil (see also DEVIL TAKE THE HINDMOST)—in print by 1574—and it is probably from this locution that the modern meaning of the cliché, describing not-so-admirable selfishness, is derived.

every man/everyone has his price No one is immune to bribery or corruption. This expression has been traced to a speech given by Sir Robert Walpole in 1734, as reported in William Coxe's *Memoirs* of the British statesman (1798). Walpole was castigating corrupt members of Parliament, whom he called pretended patriots and said, "All those men have their price." However, another source printed in 1734 refers to the same expression as "an old maxim." Whatever the ultimate origin, this cynical view of politicians has survived and has long been applied to anyone, male or female, whose influence or loyalty could be bought.

every man Jack/mother's son Everyone without exception. The first term has been traced to Dickens's *Barnaby Rudge* (1841) and has remained largely British. The second is considerably older, appearing in the Middle English legend of *Kyng Alisaunder* (c. 1300)—"Mekely ilka modir sound"—as well as in Sir Thomas Malory's *Morte d'Arthur* (1485) and Shakespeare's *A*

Midsummer Night's Dream (1596)—"That would hang us, every mother's son." It was surely a cliché by the time Gilbert and Sullivan had the Dragoons sing, "The soldiers of our Queen are linked in friendly tether, Upon the battle scene they fight the foe together, There every mother's son prepared to fight and fall is; the enemy of one the enemy of all is" (*Patience,* 1881).

everything but the kitchen sink Virtually everything, implying things inappropriate as well as fitting. This term is thought to have originated in the early twentieth century and became very common after World War II. "[We] military services . . . are such perfectionists that we want everything but the kitchen sink in a weapon" (*Wall Street Journal,* 1958).

everything in its place/season See PLACE FOR EVERYTHING.

everything is copacetic Things are fine, everything is going well. The adjective *copacetic,* for excellent, dates from the early 1900s (the *OED*'s earliest citation is from 1919), but its origin has been lost.

every Tom, Dick, and Harry Everyone, including those of low social status; the common herd. Although this term dates, in slightly different form, from Shakespeare's time (he used Tom, Dick, and Francis in *Henry IV,* Part 1, [2.4]), the names that survived into clichédom come from the early nineteenth century, when they were quite popular. One of the earliest references in print is from the *Farmer's Almanack* of 1815, although there it may have literally meant three specific individuals ("He hired Tom, Dick, and Harry, and at it they all went"). John Adams used it (1818) in its present meaning: "Tom, Dick, and Harry were not to censure them"—in other words, not just anybody had the right to censure them.

every which way In all directions, as in "The wind scattered the newspapers every which way." An Americanism dating from the 1920s or earlier, it sometimes was put as "every which a ways." Mark Twain used it in *Roughing It* (1872): "He . . . wound on rope all over and about it and under it every which way."

evil eye, the The power of being able to inflict harm at a glance. This age-old superstition—the Roman poet Vergil speaks of it bewitching lambs—is in modern times expressed figuratively and sometimes ironically. Edward Bulwer-Lytton used it in *The Last Days of Pompeii* (1834): "'He certainly possesses the gift of the evil eye,' said Clodius of Arbaces the Egyptian." As for a modern jocular example: "Where house plants are concerned, I seem to have the evil eye."

ex cathedra With authority like that of the Pope. The expression, Latin words meaning "from the chair," literally refers to the doctrine of papal infallibility, whereby the Pope, in statements on faith and morals, cannot be wrong. It began to be used figuratively in the early nineteenth century. "He was a great lover of form, more especially when he could dictate it ex cathedra" (Sir Walter Scott, *Rob Roy,* 1818).

exception proves the rule, the Although something may not conform to it, the general rule is still valid. This term originated in the 1500s and is considered a proverb. Playwright Thomas Heywood used it in *The Rape of Lucrece* (1608), "If the general rule have no exceptions, thou wilt have an empty consistory." However, in the 1800s several scholars maintained that "proves" in this phrase actually means "tests" (and not "verifies"). Whichever is intended, the phrase is still used, as in "Jane was the only woman who opposed this measure; well, the exception proves the rule."

excuse my French See PARDON MY FRENCH.

explore every avenue, to To investigate every conceivable possibility. Synonymous with LEAVE NO STONE UNTURNED, this expression dates from the early twentieth century. "He explores every avenue which may lead . . . to view his life in its new meaning" (*The Saturday Review,* 1926).

eye for an eye, an Revenge or retribution, repayment in kind. This term comes from Mosaic law as expressed in the books of Exodus and Deuteronomy (19:21): "Thine eye shall not pity, but life shall for life, eye for eye, tooth for tooth, hand for hand, foot for foot." The sentiment and wording were repeated in the Book of Leviticus (24:20) but countermanded in the Gospel of St. Matthew (5:38–39), which tells us instead to TURN THE OTHER CHEEK.

eye for/to the main chance, to have an To look out for one's own best interest or for the opportunity that will be most profitable. The term is thought to come either from betting in cockfights (*main* being an obsolete word for cockfight) or from a game of chance called hazard, in which the *main* signified the number (anywhere from 5 to 9) called by the caster before the dice were thrown and *chance* signified the second throw of the dice, which determined the total. In any event, the expression dates from the sixteenth century, was recorded by John Lyly and Shakespeare, among others, and appeared in John Ray's *English Proverbs* of 1670.

eye of a needle See CAMEL THROUGH A NEEDLE'S EYE.

eyes in the back of one's head, to have To be exceptionally alert. This expression dates from Roman times, appearing in Plautus's play *Aulularia* (c. 210 B.C.) and cited by Erasmus in his collection of adages. Put slightly differently, it appeared in John Still's play *Gammer Gurton's Needle* (c. 1565): "Take heed of Sim Glovers wife, she hath an eie behind her!" (2.2).

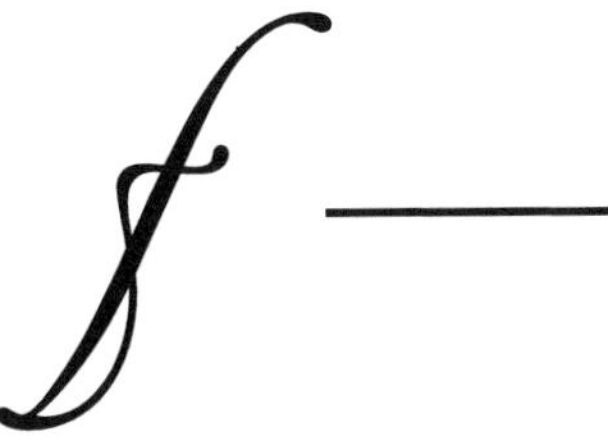

face that launched a thousand ships, the An exceptionally beautiful woman; or, ironically, someone lacking in beauty. The phrase comes from Christopher Marlowe's play *Doctor Faustus* (c. 1588), and describes Helen, wife of King Menelaus of Greece, whose legendary beauty led to her abduction by Paris, which set off the Trojan War. "Was this the face that launched a thousand ships, And burnt the topless towers of Ilium?" wrote Marlowe.

face the music, to To meet the consequences of one's bad behavior, mistakes, and the like; to confront difficulties bravely. This term, American in origin, is believed to come from the theater and refers to the orchestra in the pit, which an actor must face along with a perhaps hostile audience. Another writer suggests it comes from the armed services, where a soldier's dismissal in disgrace might be accompanied by the band's playing the "Rogue's March." An 1871 book of American sayings quotes James Fenimore Cooper discussing, about 1851, Rabelais's "unpleasant quarter [of an hour]," when the French writer found he could not pay his bill and turned on the innkeeper with an accusation of treason, which so frightened him that he let Rabelais leave without paying. Cooper said that "our more picturesque people" called this facing the music. A less picturesque synonym is *to face up to something.*

fact of the matter, the The truth. This rather empty phrase, for which plain and simple "fact" would do just as well, is somewhat newer than its turnaround companion, *as a matter of fact,* which means "in truth" and, as Eric Partridge pointed out years ago, often precedes a lie. Both have been clichés since the nineteenth century. Two closely related locutions are *the truth of the matter* and *if truth be known,* which generally precede an emphatic statement of how the speaker sees a situation. On the other hand, *matter-of-fact* used as an adjective has a quite different meaning, that is, straightforward and commonplace, and *a matter of fact* without *as* has meant, since the sixteenth century, something of an actually factual nature.

fair and square Just and unequivocal. This expression, recorded since the early seventeenth century, owes its appeal to its rhyme and has survived despite its tautology ("square" here means the same as "fair," surviving in such phrases as "a square deal"). "You are fair and square in all your dealings," wrote William Wycherley (*The Gentleman Dancing Master,* 1673).

fair game A legitimate object of attack, pursuit, or mockery. The analogy, of course, is to hunting, and the term has been used figuratively since the early nineteenth century. "They were indeed fair game for the laughers," wrote Thomas Macaulay in his essay on Milton (1825).

fair-haired boy The current favorite, the individual singled out for special treatment. This male counterpart of "gentlemen prefer blondes" comes from the late nineteenth century. "The old crowd of Fair-haired Correspondent Boys who hung to the ear of President Roosevelt" appeared in the *Saturday Evening Post* in 1909.

fair sex, the Females in general. This cliché, which is rapidly dying out, is a direct translation of the French *le beau sexe,* a phrase popularized by the English journalists Joseph Addison and Richard Steele ("That sex which is therefore called fair," *The Spectator,* 1712). It was already a cliché by the time Arthur Conan Doyle (*The Second Stain,* 1905) put it in Sherlock Holmes's mouth: "Now Watson, the fair sex is your department."

fair shake, a An equitable opportunity or treatment. An Americanism dating from the early nineteenth century, the term probably alludes to the shaking of dice, but was soon transferred. An 1830 issue of the *Central Watchtower and Farmer's Journal,* a Kentucky publication, had it, "Any way that will be a fair shake."

fair to middling So-so, moderately good, a reply to "How are you?" Since "fair" and "middling" here mean the same thing—that is, pretty good or mediocre—the expression is basically jocular. It originated in the mid-nineteenth century, probably in America. An early citation in the *OED* is from Artemus Ward's *His Travels* ("The men are fair to middling," 1865). See also CAN'T COMPLAIN.

fair-weather friend A friend who is faithful in good times but fails you in time of trouble. It is the opposite of a FRIEND IN NEED IS A FRIEND INDEED. The transfer of "fair weather" to "good times" presumably occurred long before, but the adjectival application to a friend of dubious loyalty did not take place until the early eighteenth century.

fait accompli, a A deed or action already completed. The term is French for "accomplished action" and was adopted into English in the early nineteenth century. The French critic Nicolas Boileau, exponent of the classical style, may have been one of the first to popularize the term in French, in his treatise *L'Art poétique* (1674), expounding the classic unities of drama: "*Qu'en un lieu, qu'en un jour, un seul fait accompli tienne jusqu'à la fin le théâtre rempli*" (One place, one time, one single action will keep the audience in the theater to the end).

fall by the wayside, to To drop out, fail to finish. The term comes from the Bible, specifically Jesus's parable of the sower as related in the Gospel of Matthew, Chapter 13: "Behold, a sower went forth to sow and when he sowed, some seeds fell by the wayside, and the fowls came and devoured them up." The seeds then are likened to the word of God, and the fowls to the wicked who "snatch up" the word from those who do not understand it. Subsequently, persons who strayed from the STRAIGHT AND NARROW were said to fall by the wayside. Jonathan Swift included it in his *Polite Conversation* (1738), "If you fall by the way, don't stay to get up again."

fall for something/someone, to To be taken in or deceived; or to be captivated by or enamored of. Originating in American slang in the late nineteenth century, the expression was adopted on both sides of the Atlantic. The two meanings are differentiated by the context. The first sense is meant in "The mayor fell for it" (R. L. McCardell, *Conversations with a Chorus Girl,* 1903), and the second in "I fell for her the first time I seen her" (*Saturday Evening Post,* 1914).

fall from grace, to To lapse into sin; to lose favor. The term comes from the Bible, in which St. Paul says that those who lose faith in God are "fallen from grace" (Galatians 5:4). "Grace" here, and in subsequent ecclesiastical writings, means God's grace, which is necessary to be saved from eternal damnation. However, the expression later was transferred to any kind of temporal decline or disgrace.

fall on deaf ears, to To be disregarded. The expression most often refers to something a person does not wish to hear, such as a reproach or advice, and therefore he or she reacts as though physically unable to hear it. The term dates from the fifteenth century and has been a cliché since the nineteenth century.

fall on one's feet, to To make a lucky recovery from potential disaster. The term alludes to the cat, which has a remarkable ability to land on its paws after falling or being tossed from a height. The analogy was made long ago, appearing in John Ray's proverb collection of 1678 ("He's like a cat; fling him which way you will he'll light on 's legs") and was certainly a cliché by the time William Roughead wrote (*Malice Domestic,* 1929), "That lady had indeed, as the phrase is, fallen on her feet."

fall short (of), to To fail to attain a certain standard; to be insufficient. The expression comes from archery, horseshoes, and other activities in which a missile may fall to the ground before reaching the desired goal, or mark (it is sometimes put as *falling short of the mark*). The essayist William Hazlitt wrote, "Cavanagh's blows were not undecided and ineffectual—lumbering like Mr. Wordsworth's epic poetry, nor wavering like Mr. Coleridge's lyric prose, nor short of the mark like Mr. Brougham's speeches" (*Table Talk,* 1821–22).

false colors See SAIL UNDER FALSE COLORS.

familiarity breeds contempt Overexposure to or knowing something or someone too thoroughly can turn liking into hostility. The idea behind this expression dates from ancient times—the Roman writer Publilius Syrus used it about 43 B.C.—and approximately twelve hundred years later Pope Innocent III repeated it, also in Latin. The first record of it in English appeared in Nicholas Udall's translation of Erasmus's sayings (1548): "Familiaritye bringeth contempt." Later writers often stated it with humor or irony, notably Mark Twain in his unpublished diaries (*Notebooks,* c. 1900): "Familiarity breeds contempt—and children."

famous last words A satirical rejoinder to what the speaker considers a fatuous remark or easily refuted statement. The expression alludes to the so-called famous last words of history—for example, "this is the war to end all wars," or "it [meaning some calamity] could never happen here." Its exact origin is not known, but Eric Partridge believed it began in the armed services during World War II, first in Britain. After the war it crossed the Atlantic. It now is applied to just about any situation, even as a self-deprecating comment on one's own remark ("That's the last time I strike out—famous last words").

fan the flames, to To exacerbate an already inflammable situation, or to revive a flagging situation. The fact that wind stirs up a fire has, of course, been known since ancient times, but the precise metaphor here, with its alliterative lilt, is considerably newer. Dickens used it in *The Old Curiosity Shop* (1840): "Fan the sinking flame of hilarity with the wing of friendship."

far and away Beyond comparison, surpassing by a wide margin. This tautological phrase ("far" and "away" here both mean a considerable distance) dates from the mid-nineteenth century. Anthony Trollope wrote, "He was far and away the cleverest of his party" (*The Duke's Children,* 1880).

far and wide To great lengths and distances; affecting many individuals or many localities. This term is one of the oldest English ones in this book: It appears in an Old English work dating from about the year 900, "He . . . ferde [fared] . . . feorr and wide." Shakespeare also used it in *Romeo and Juliet* (4:2): "I stretch it out for that word 'broad'; which added to the goose, proves thee far and wide a broad goose."

far be it for/from me to . . . A disclaimer, often quite false. This expression, which basically means "I would not dream of doing/saying [something] when in truth I really would," dates from the fourteenth century and has been a cliché for at least two hundred years. The earliest record is in John Wycliffe's translation of Genesis (44:17): "Josephe answerede, Fer be it fro me, that Y thus do"; the King James Version has it "God forbid that I should do so."

far cry, a A long way, literally or figuratively. This expression is believed to have its source in measuring one's distance from an enemy in terms of shouting. Sir Walter Scott indicated (*The Legend of Montrose,* 1819) that it was a proverbial expression of the Campbell clan, which meant that their ancient hereditary domains lay beyond the reach of invaders. However, the term was already being used figuratively by then.

far out Excellent; also, daringly unusual. This slangy expression originated in jazz about 1950, where it was used for particularly avant-garde performances. Almost immediately it was extended to mean outstanding. It is used both as an adjective ("this performance is far out") and as an interjection ("This is great—far out!"). Its overuse soon made it a cliché.

fast and furious Rapid and intense. This alliterative phrase dates from the eighteenth century. It appeared in Robert Burns's poem "Tam o' Shanter" (1793): "The mirth and fun grew fast and furious." It often is applied to extreme gaiety.

fast and loose See PLAY FAST AND LOOSE.

fast lane/track, in/on the An exciting, competitive, high-pressure activity or life-style. Alluding to the express lane of highways and (originally) railroad lines, this metaphor originated about the middle of the twentieth century and may refer not only to hectic high-pressure activity but also to rapid advancement. Richard M. Nixon used it in 1965: "New York . . . is a place where you can't slow down—a fast track" (*New York Times Magazine*).

fast one See PULL A FAST ONE.

fatal attraction An affinity for something or someone inherently harmful. This twentieth-century term appears in such locutions as, "Even after the deaths of hundreds of climbers, Mt. Everest continues to exert a fatal attraction for many mountaineers." It was used as the title of a 1987 motion picture about a happily married man who has a weekend affair with a beautiful woman; she turns out to be psychotic and tries to destroy his and his family's life.

fat cat A wealthy individual. This rhyming term, originating in America about 1920, once had a more specific meaning, that is, a rich individual who made large contributions to a political party or campaign. Later it was extended to any wealthy person, as well as an individual who has become lazy or smug as the result of material assets. Thus, an article in the *Saturday Review of Literature* in 1949, "Hollywood celebrities, literary fat cats." See also DEEP POCKETS.

fat chance Practically no chance at all. Although *fat* in this context means "good," the term is always used ironically to mean hardly any opportunity. A slangy Americanism of the twentieth century, it was used by P. G. Wodehouse in *Laughing Gas:* "A fat chance, of course. I should have known his psychology better." For synonyms, see CHINAMAN'S CHANCE; SNOWBALL'S CHANCE.

fat city Prosperous circumstances. This slangy Americanism originated about the middle of the twentieth century and is on its way to becoming a cliché. "This last jump in the Dow average has put Mr. Welch in fat city" (*Boston Globe,* 1987).

fate worse than death, a Seduction or rape of a woman. This term, originating about the mid-seventeenth century, became a cliché in the late nineteenth century, when it also began to be used in a jocular fashion for sexual relations among willing partners. E. R. Burroughs, however, still meant it seriously: "The ape . . . bearing Jane Porter away toward a fate a thousand times worse than death" (*Tarzan,* 1917).

fat is in the fire, the It's too late for a rescue; a crisis is imminent. This expression already appeared in John Heywood's proverb collection of 1546 in its present form and has continued to be used with great regularity to the present day. A long-lived cliché that is by no means obsolete, it refers, of course, to the way a fire flares up when grease is spilled into it, an idea soon transferred to the more general sense that damage has been done.

feast one's eyes on, to To enjoy the sight of something or someone. Shakespeare's Sonnet 47, "With my love's picture then my eye doth feast," is one of the early sources of this metaphor. It may have been a cliché by the time George Meredith used it in *The Adventures of Harry Richmond* (1871): "The princess . . . let her eyes feast incessantly on a laughing sea."

feast or famine Either an overabundance or a shortage. This expression originated as *either feast or fast,* which is how it appeared in Thomas Fuller's *Gnomologia* (1732) and still survived in 1912 ("Dock labour has been graphically described as 'either a feast or a fast,'" *London Daily Telegraph*). In America, *famine* was substituted sometime during the twentieth century. The term is still frequently applied to alternating overabundance and shortages of work, as is often the case for freelancers, seasonal laborers, and the like.

feather in one's cap, a A special honor or achievement. This term comes from the custom of numerous peoples—American Indian tribes, Turks, Himalayan peoples, among others—of placing a feather in a soldier's cap for every enemy he kills. The term began to be used figuratively by the early seventeenth century and was a cliché by the time Laurence Sterne wrote, "The feather put into his cap of having been abroad" (*Tristram Shandy,* 1761–67).

feather one's nest, to To enrich oneself, to provide well for oneself. Alluding to the practice of birds making a soft nest for their eggs and young, this expression originated in the sixteenth century. It appeared in the 1553 play *Respublica* (1:1) by an unknown author, as well as in several other works of the period. It was a cliché by the eighteenth century.

fed to the gills Thoroughly disgusted. This American version of the earlier British *fed to the (back) teeth* and *fed (up) to the eyelids* is based on the slang meaning of *gills* for the human mouth.

feeling is mutual See THE FEELING IS MUTUAL.

feel it in one's bones, to To anticipate something; to have a premonition or warning of a coming event. The expression appeared in Shakespeare's *Timon of Athens,* in which the Third Lord responds to the statement that Timon is mad, "I feel 't upon my bones" (3.6). The saying, which has been a cliché for a hundred years or so, most likely alludes to the alleged ability of those with old bone fractures and/or arthritis to forecast a change in weather (usually rain) based on their aching bones.

feel one's oats, to To act frisky or lively. This saying, with its analogy to a horse that is lively after being fed, is American in origin and dates from the early nineteenth century. It appeared in print in Amos Lawrence's *Extracts from Diary and Correspondence* (1833): "We both 'feel our oats' and our youth."

feel someone's pain, to To empathize completely with someone. This hyperbolic idea is often asserted hypocritically, or by someone who is actually causing the pain. Thus, "I feel your pain" can be a politician's response to a constituent who is complaining about the minimum wage, even though he actually voted against its being increased. This expression needs to be differentiated from *feeling no pain,* a slangy phrase from the mid-twentieth century describing someone who is intoxicated, and from *I feel for you but I can't quite reach you,* a slangy response expressing lack of sympathy for someone's hard-luck story.

feet of clay, to have A failing or fault in one who is held in high regard. The term comes from the Bible's Book of Daniel (2:33), in which the prophet interprets King Nebuchadnezzar's dream of an image of gold, silver, and brass, but "his feet part of iron and part of clay." These feet were what made the image vulnerable and, according to Daniel, predicted the breakup of the empire.

femme fatale An attractive woman who is, for one reason or another, dangerous. French for "fatal woman," the term has been used in English since about 1900, and today it is often used more ironically than seriously. Michael Arlen used it in *The Green Hat* (1924): "So you heard about it from that femme fatale, did you?" Much more recently Richard Dyer used it in the sense of "very glamorous" in describing the singer who played the leading role in the opera *Carmen*: "She's physically and vocally limber, and revels in her femme-fatale look" (*Boston Globe,* March 24, 2005).

few and far between Seldom; at wide intervals. This expression is a quotation from Thomas Campbell's poem "The Pleasures of Hope" (1799): "What though my winged hours of bliss have been, like angel-visits, few and far between?" At first it was largely applied to rare pleasures, but later it was extended to any rare occurrence.

few bricks shy of a load See ELEVATOR DOESN'T GO TO THE TOP FLOOR.

fickle fortune Capricious fate. The alliteration of this phrase has long appealed to writers, and the idea behind it is even older. The expression appeared in the sixteenth century, in Shakespeare's *Romeo and Juliet* (3.5)—"O fortune, fortune! all men call thee fickle"—and elsewhere. Benjamin Franklin also used it: "Fortune is as fickle as she's fair" (*Poor Richard's Almanack,* 1749).

Laugh-In, a popular television show of the 1960s and 1970s, used a similar expression, *the fickle finger of fate,* in a mock talent contest ("Who knows when the fickle finger of fate may beckon you to stardom?"), and issued a mock prize to the winner, the Flying Fickle Finger of Fate Award. According to Eric Partridge, "f——d by the fickle finger of fate" was Canadian armed forces slang in the 1930s for being fouled up in some way, and this probably was the source of the *Laugh-In* usage. See also WHEEL OF FORTUNE.

fiddle while Rome burns, to To busy oneself with trivial matters during a crisis. The expression comes from the legend that during the burning of Rome (A.D. 64), the Emperor Nero played his lyre while watching the spectacle from a high tower. Indeed, the historian Suetonius alleged that Nero had ordered the fire set in order to see how Troy had looked when it burned. The expression was probably already a cliché by the time Charles Kingsley wrote in *Westward Ho!* (1855), "It is fiddling while Rome burns to spend more pages over . . . Rose Saltenere, while the destinies of Europe are hanging on the marriage between Elizabeth and Anjou."

field day, to have a To take part in an enjoyable, exciting occasion or pursuit. The expression dates from the mid-1700s and originally meant a special day set aside for troop maneuvers and exercises, as it still does in military circles. Early in the 1800s it began to be transferred to civilian occasions, at first involving groups of people (such as a school outing), and later to any pleasant experience, as in "Mike's having a field day with his new camera."

fifth wheel An unneeded extra, a superfluous person or thing. This expression was already listed as a proverb in the sixteenth century in a French collection; in its complete form it pointed out that the fifth wheel on a wagon does nothing but impede it (C. B. Bouelles, *Proverbia Vulgaria,* 1531). Thomas Dekker repeated it in a play (*Match Me in London,* 1631, Act I), again in fairly literal fashion: "Thou tyest but wings to a swift gray hounds heele, and addest to a running charriot a fift Wheele." But it also was being used figuratively during this period, and has continued to be ever since.

fig, not care/give/worth a See NOT CARE/GIVE A FIG.

fight fire with fire Counter an evil or adversity with equal force. The Greek philosopher Plato counseled just the opposite—don't add fire to fire—and was quoted by numerous subsequent writers, from Plutarch to Erasmus. Nevertheless, the idea that fire is put out by fire prevailed. "The only way I know how to fight fire is with fire," wrote Stewart Sterling (*Down among the Dead Men,* 1943).

fighting chance, a A possibility of success through great effort. An Americanism dating from the late nineteenth century, this phrase has been used in a large variety of contexts. For example, "Free school breakfasts and lunches will give these inner-city children a fighting chance of graduating," or "Hunting with a bow and arrow gives the deer a fighting chance."

fighting mad Infuriated. This colloquial expression of American origin dates from the late nineteenth century. William James used it in a letter of 1896: "If any other country's ruler had expressed himself with equal moral ponderosity, wouldn't the population have gone twice as fighting-mad as ours?"

fight tooth and nail See TOOTH AND NAIL.

figment of the imagination, a An imaginary occurrence; a pipe dream. This expression is tautological, since *figment* means a product of fictitious invention. Nevertheless, it has been used since the mid-nineteenth century. It appeared in Charlotte Brontë's *Jane Eyre* (1847): "The long dishevelled hair, the swelled black face, the exaggerated stature, were figments of imagination."

filled to the brim As full of something as possible. The transfer from a container filled to the very top to other matters took place in the sixteenth century, so by 1601 Shakespeare wrote, "He will fill thy wishes to the brimme" (*Antony and Cleopatra,*" 3.13). W. S. Gilbert used the term to describe the three little maids in *The Mikado* (1885): "Filled to the brim with girlish glee."

fill the bill, to To satisfy the requirements, to suit a purpose. This term originally came from the nineteenth-century American stage, where the posters announcing a program would list the star attractions and then add lesser-known entertainers to complete the show (or fill out the bill). By mid-century the term had been transferred to other areas, where it acquired a more primary sense of providing what was needed. Thus a political article in *Harper's Magazine* in 1890 included the comment. "They filled the bill according to their lights."

filthy lucre Money acquired by dishonorable means. The term comes from St. Paul's Epistle to Titus (1:11), in which he criticizes those who teach things which they ought not "for filthy lucre's sake." Later the term came to be used ironically for money in general, even if it had been honestly earned. Perhaps scruples have changed, for the term is heard less often today.

finders, keepers Those who obtain something simply by discovering it are entitled to keep it. There are several versions of this expression, all of them referring to the law that a person who finds something, even if it is someone else's property, may keep it for himself or herself. The earliest references are in writings of the Roman playwright Plautus and date from approximately 200 B.C. Two millennia later, D. M. Moir (*Mansie Wauch,* 1824) referred to "the auld Scotch proverb of 'he that finds, keeps, and he that loses seeks.'" Charles Reade also called it a proverb: "Losers seekers, finders keepers" (*It Is Never Too Late to Mend,* 1856). The modern schoolyard version is "Finders keepers, losers weepers." Legal implications aside, the poetic rhythm of this expression no doubt helps account for its long life.

find it in one's heart, (not) to To be inclined to do something; or to be unwilling to do something. This expression implies that a person is doing considerable soul-searching concerning an action, and as a cliché it may be obsolescent. It first appeared in the sixteenth century, in Sir Thomas More's *Utopia:* "They cannot find in their hearts to love the author thereof." It also appears in the King James Bible (1611) in the second Book of Samuel (7:27): "Therefore hath thy servant found in his heart to pray this prayer unto thee."

fine and dandy Excellent. This redundant American colloquialism—*fine* and *dandy* both mean excellent—today is most often used ironically, for a circumstance that is far from excellent. Originally, however, in the early 1900s, it was stated straightforwardly, as in "'Has she recovered from her fall?' 'Yes, she's fine and dandy now.'"

fine fettle, in In excellent condition. This expression comes from the old dialect verb "to fettle," which meant to put right. It was first put as "in good fettle," and was so used throughout the nineteenth century. Alliteration has helped it to survive.

fine-tooth comb, to go over with a To search for or investigate with scrupulous care. Although combs have been known since the time of ancient Egypt, and presumably some had finer teeth than others, the term "fine-tooth comb" dates only from the first half of the nineteenth century. The transfer of combing out nits to other kinds of search or investigation took place only in the late nineteenth century.

finger in every pie, to have a To be involved in numerous activities, usually in the sense of meddling. This metaphor from finger-licking in the kitchen dates from the sixteenth century. Shakespeare used it in *Henry VIII* (1.1), where the Duke of Buckingham complains of Cardinal Wolsey, "No man's pie is freed from his ambitious finger."

finger itches to, one's/my I am (one is) extremely eager to do something. The use of "itch" for "desire" is almost as old as the desire to scratch something that itches. "Our fingers wyll itch at hym," wrote John Stubbs (*The Discoverie of a Gaping Gulf,* 1579), and soon afterward Shakespeare wrote, "If I see a word out, my finger itches to make one" (*The Merry Wives of Windsor,* 1601, 2.3). Considerably later came Charles Kingsley with his "The men's fingers are itching for a fight" (*Hypatia,* 1853), which subsequently was shortened to *itching for a fight.* See also ITCHY PALM.

finishing touch(es) The final stroke(s) that ensure completion or perfection. The term is derived from painting, that is, the last stroke of the artist's brush, and was soon transferred to any creative effort, ranging from cake-baking to assembling a costume. Its earliest appearance in print dates from the mid-eighteenth century, and Eric Partridge concluded it became a cliché within a hundred years.

fire away Go ahead; say what you must say; ask what you will. This expression, referring to a gun loaded to the muzzle, dates from the early days of firearms and was transferred to other proceedings by the eighteenth century, as in "Mr. Burney fired away in a voluntary [on the organ]" (Frederick Marryat, *Poor Jack,* 1775).

fire on all cylinders Go all out. The term comes from automobiles, where it means all of a car's cylinders have been ignited and the engine is fully powered. It has been used figuratively since the second half of the 1900s, as in "That was a great speech; he was really firing on all cylinders." See also PULL OUT ALL THE STOPS.

first and foremost Most notable, most important. This tautological expression—*first* and *foremost* mean just about the same thing—has survived since the fifteenth century, when it was recorded in a work by William Caxton (1483). Deemed a cliché by the mid-nineteenth century, it is still popular with lecturers and others who like to enumerate the various points of their argument or elements of a list.

first blush, at Without prior knowledge; at first glance. The earliest use of this expression dates from the sixteenth century, when *blush* meant not a reddening of the cheeks with embarrassment but "glimpse." Thus, "Able at the first blushe to discearne truth from falsehood," wrote Philip Stubbes (*The Anatomie of Abuses,* 2:7) in 1583.

first come, first served The prompt get first choice. This idea was stated by Chaucer (c. 1386) in *The Wife of Bath's Tale,* "Whoso first cometh to the mill, first grist," and was cited as a proverb by Erasmus. An early reference with the exact modern wording dates from about 1545, in Henry Brinklow's *Complaynt of Roderick Mors.* See also EARLY BIRD CATCHES THE WORM.

first magnitude/order/water, of the The best; of the highest quality. *Magnitude* refers to the grading of the brightness of stars, the first being the brightest. It has been transferred to other matters since at least the seventeenth century. "Thou liar of the first magnitude," wrote William Congreve in 1695 (*Love for Love,* 2.2). *Water* refers to a system for grading diamonds for their color or luster (the latter being akin to the shininess of water), the best quality again being termed the first. This grading system is no longer used, but the transfer to other matters has survived since the early nineteenth century. Sir Walter Scott's journal has, "He was a . . . swindler of the first water

(1826). *Order,* which here refers to rank, is probably more often heard today than either of the others. It dates from the nineteenth century. The *OED* cites "A diplomatist of the first order," appearing in a journal of 1895. A synonymous term, *first rate,* originated from the time the Royal Navy's warships were rated on a scale of one to six, based on their size and the weight of the weapons they carried. By the 1700s this term, along with *second-rate, third-rate,* and so on, was later transferred to general use, most often as a hyphenated adjective. For example, "He's definitely a second-rate poet, nowhere near as good as his father."

first things first The most important task should have priority. The implication of this expression, which dates from the nineteenth century, is that there may well be no time to do more than the most important thing. Or, as Shirley Conran put it (in *Superwoman,* 1975), "First things first, second things never."

fish or cut bait Get on with what you're doing or quit and give someone else a chance; stop putting it off. This metaphor, alluding to a fisherman who ties up the use of a boat or rod when he could at least be preparing bait for others to use, originated in nineteenth-century politics. It appeared in the *Congressional Record* in 1876, when Congressman Joseph P. Cannon, telling the Democrats to vote on a bill that would legalize the silver dollar, said, "I want you gentlemen on the other side of the House to 'fish or cut bait.'" A ruder twentieth-century American version is *shit or get off the pot.*

fish out of water, a A person who is out of his or her element. It presumably was observed in ancient times that fish cannot survive long out of water, because their gills cannot take oxygen from the air if they are dry. St. Athanasius is credited as the first to transfer this idea to human beings out of their usual environment, sometime before A.D. 373. The simile reappears in numerous fourteenth-century writings, by John Wycliffe, Geoffrey Chaucer, and others, and survives as a cliché to the present day.

fish story, a A tall tale. This term alludes to the tendency of sports fishermen (and women) to exaggerate the size of their catch, and originated in America in the early nineteenth century. It may have been invented by the journalist who described an event he termed "a fish story," the appearance of shoals of whitefish in such large numbers that they choked a channel and prevented a steamboat from passing (*St. Louis Enquirer,* Dec. 8, 1819).

fish to fry, to have better/bigger/other To have other, more important matters to attend to. Referring to fish cookery, this term dates from the seventeenth century. "I fear he has other fish to fry," wrote John Evelyn in his *Memoirs* (1660). Actually, this term also appeared in an early translation of Rabelais's *Pantagruel* (1552) by Motteux, but it did not seem to catch on until later.

fit as a fiddle In excellent health, in good working order. The proverbial likening of human good health to a fiddle dates from 1600 or earlier, but there is no completely convincing explanation of the analogy. It appeared in print in the early seventeenth century and was in John Ray's proverb collection of 1678. *Fit* in those days meant "appropriate," as "fitting" still does, but why a fiddle should be considered especially appropriate is unknown. It was only in the nineteenth century that the meaning of physical fitness was attached to the expression, where it remains today.

fit like a glove, to To suit or conform extremely well. The analogy dates back at least to the eighteenth century. Tobias Smollett used it in *Humphry Clinker* (1771): "The boots . . . fitted me like a glove." See also TO A T.

fits and starts, by In bursts of activity, spasmodically. The *fits* portion of this expression dates from the sixteenth century, and the pairing with *starts* came soon afterward, in the early seventeenth century. "Thou hast these things only by fits and starts," wrote Robert Sanderson in one of his *Sermons* (1620). John Ray's proverb collection of 1670 put it slightly differently: "By fits and girds, as an ague takes a goose."

fit to be tied Extremely angry, enough so to suggest that physical restraint might be indicated to prevent major damage. This expression originated in the late nineteenth century. James Joyce used it in *Ulysses* (1922), "I was fit to be tied," one of the more understandable expressions of feeling in that difficult book.

flash in the pan A brief triumph, or a promising start followed by a failure. This expression comes from the seventeenth-century flintlock musket, which had a depression in the lockpan to hold the priming powder. When all went well, the flash of the priming powder ignited the charge in the bore and fired the weapon. Sometimes, however, it failed, and there was only a flash in the pan.

flat as a pancake Exceedingly flat, sometimes excessively so. This simile has been around since the sixteenth century, appearing in Nicholas Udall's translation of Erasmus (1542) and Henry Porter's play *The Two Angrie Women of Abington* (1599, 2.3). Morever, it survived and replaced the equally old *flat as a flounder* and is still frequently used today, often in deprecating fashion to describe a woman's lack of mammary endowment.

flat-footed, to be caught/catch To surprise/be surprised; to be caught unprepared. This antonym to being ON ONE'S TOES is believed by some to come from baseball terminology (it was so defined in the linguistics journal *American Speech* in 1912). However, other authorities believe it comes from horse-racing, where it is said of a horse whose jockey is unprepared to start a race.

flat out Thoroughly, outright; also, using all one's resources, at full speed. An early recorded use of this adverbial phrase in 1932 (according to the *OED*) was in connection with automobile racing—that is, "driving flat out," meaning as fast as possible. Presumably it alluded to a straight and level run of track, allowing full speed. This sense was soon transferred in such locutions as "They worked flat out to get the job done in time." In succeeding decades the expression began to be used adjectivally in the sense of outright, as in "His last book was a flat-out failure" or "That's a flat-out lie."

flattery will get you nowhere Appealing to my vanity will not advance your cause. Although this idea is very old, the expression dates only from the mid-twentieth century and originated in the United States. Aristophanes (c. 388 B.C.), Cato (c. 175 B.C.), and Cicero (c. 45 B.C.) are but three of the ancients who warned against flattery. The current cliché appears in Ellery Queen's *A Fine and Private Place* (1971; cited by Partridge), "'Flattery will get you nowhere, Queen,' the murderer said." It is sometimes used ironically, in response to an insulting remark, and there is also a humorous variation, *flattery will get you everywhere* (a retort to a compliment).

flea in one's ear, to have a To be upset or annoyed by a rebuke or a rejection. This term dates back at least to the fifteenth century in English, and may be older yet in French. It appeared in John Heywood's 1546 proverb collection and has continued to be used ever since.

flesh and blood, I'm only/one's own I'm only human; members of my family. The pairing of *flesh* and *blood* dates back very far. In English it appears in the Bible (Matthew 16:17; Ephesians 6:12), Shakespeare's *Julius Caesar* (3.1: "and men are flesh and blood, and apprehensive"), and numerous other writings, mostly in the meaning of being only human (Thomas Hood, "The Song of the Shirt": "Oh God! that bread should be so dear and flesh and blood so cheap!").

The other sense, of blood relations, appeared in a 1300 manuscript ("He . . . es your aun fless and blod"), and numerous other early sources, as well as in Shakespeare's *The Merchant of Venice* (where Gobbo says to his son, "If thou be Launcelot, thou art mine own flesh and blood," 2.2).

flight of fancy An imaginative but impractical idea. This cliché uses *flight* in the sense of a soaring imagination, a usage first recorded in 1668. Given this sense, *fancy,* meaning imagination, makes the phrase somewhat redundant, and it is not clear exactly when it was added. Oliver Goldsmith had the idea, if not the exact wording, in his poem "The Traveller" (1764): "To men of other minds my fancy flies."

flip one's lid, to To lose one's temper, or to become very excited. An American slang expression dating from the twentieth century, it implies the metaphor of a pot boiling over and pushing off its cover. It appeared in 1951 in the *New York Times Book Review:* "The funniest book of the lot is enough to make a reader 'flip' or 'flip his lid.'" The closely related *flip one's wig* needs no explanation.

flog a dead horse See DEAD HORSE.

flotsam and jetsam Odds and ends; trash. These words for a ship's wreckage and cargo floating at sea (*flotsam,* from the Old French *floter,* to float) and goods thrown overboard to lighten a ship (*jetsam,* from the French *jeter,* to throw) date from the early sixteenth century. Only in the nineteenth century were they used figuratively, for odds and ends of things as well as for human vagrants. Several twentieth-century humorists punned on them, including the poet Ogden Nash (*No Doctors Today, Thank You,* 1942): "Does anybody want any flotsam? I've gotsam. Does anybody want any jetsam? I'll getsam."

flower children Hippies of the 1960s, so named because they frequently wore or carried flowers as symbols of love and peace. Their antimaterialistic, antiwar philosophy was characterized as *flower power,* whose motto was "Make love, not war." Overused for several decades, these terms now may be dying out.

flower of youth, the The best or finest time of life, at the peak of good looks, good health, and vigor. "He hath the flower of youth, wherein is the fulness of strength," wrote Homer in the *Iliad* (c. 850 B.C.). Shakespeare used similar language, but not the precise wording of the cliché. But John Dryden did, in *Alexander's Feast* (1697), describing the lovely Thais "in flow'r of youth and beauty's pride."

flower power See FLOWER CHILDREN.

fly-by-night An unreliable or irresponsible individual, particularly one not to be trusted in business dealings. Originating in the late eighteenth century to describe a person who evades creditors by sneaking away at night, this expression is now used both as a noun and as an adjective. However, according to Francis Grose's *Dictionary of the Vulgar Tongue* (1796), the term was also once a derogatory name for an old woman accused of being a witch (flying at night). Much later it became British slang for a prostitute (who worked mostly at night), and by extension, a prostitute's vagina.

flying blind Proceeding by guesswork, groping one's way. The term originated during World War I and alluded to poor visibility. Later it was extended to other enterprises, as in, "My predecessor quit without leaving any instructions, so for this first department meeting I'm flying blind." See also BY THE SEAT OF ONE'S PANTS.

flying colors, come off with To succeed; to win. This term, which alludes to the victorious battleship sailing with flags high, dates from the late seventeenth century. "It may . . . bring a man off with flying colours," wrote philosopher John Locke (*A Letter Concerning Toleration,* 1692).

fly in the face of, to To challenge, to take on despite overwhelming odds. This expression, which often adds something that one flies in the face of—danger, Providence, or the like—may well come from the barnyard, alluding to an angry hen flying in the face of another, larger animal, or to falconry, where an irritated hawk might fly into its master's face. It appeared in print in the sixteenth century and was well on its way to being a cliché by the time Henry Fielding wrote, "This was flying in Mr. Alworthy's face" (*Tom Jones,* 1749).

fly in the ointment A trifling annoyance that spoils one's enjoyment. This term comes from the Bible (Ecclesiastes 10:1): "Dead flies cause the ointment of the apothecary to send forth a stinking savor; so doth a little folly him that is in reputation for wisdom and honor." It has been so used ever since.

fly off the handle, to To lose one's temper. The analogy here is to a loosened hammer head that comes off after it has struck a blow. The term is American in origin and dates from the early nineteenth century. "He flies right off the handle for nothing," wrote Thomas Haliburton (*Sam Slick in England,* 1843).

fly the coop, to To escape. This expression, with its analogy to barnyard fowl escaping from a chicken coop or other enclosure, is American in origin and dates from about 1900. "On the third day I flew the coop," wrote O. Henry (*The Enchanted Profile,* 1909). More recently Harry Kemelman used it in *Saturday the Rabbi Went Hungry* (1966): "This man ran off . . . flew the coop, beat it."

foam at the mouth, to To express fury, to rage uncontrollably. Dogs afflicted with rabies foam at the mouth, their saliva forming a frothy substance, and also behave crazily. The analogy to extreme human anger was drawn as far back as the fifteenth century, and has been a cliché since the mid-nineteenth century. Washington Irving used the expression in *Salmagundi* (1807–08): "I expected every moment to see them fall down in convulsions and foam at the mouth." Isaac Disraeli (father of Benjamin) used it more figuratively still in a piece of literary criticism: "A tedious invective, foaming at the mouth of its text with quotations and authorities" (*Curiosities of Literature,* 1817).

fold our tents, (let us) Quietly depart, go home. This term comes from Longfellow's poem "The Day Is Done" (1844): "And the night shall be filled with music, And the cares, that infest the day, Shall fold their tents, like the Arabs, And as silently steal away." Today it is often used jocularly, as in "Come on, it's after eleven. Time to fold our tents."

follow in the footsteps of, to To succeed someone; to accept someone as an exemplary master or guide. This same idea was expressed in the Bible, in the first Book of Peter (2:21), "Because Christ also suffered for us, leaving us an example, that ye should follow his steps," as well as in the Christmas carol, "Good King Wenceslas," by John Mason Neale (1818–66), "Mark my footsteps, good my page, tread thou in them boldly." A more sinister meaning also exists, namely in guerrilla warfare, where troops march single file, each stepping into the footprints of the one before, with the last warrior obliterating all the prints. This practice was used by American Indians in the French and Indian wars of the eighteenth century and consequently was called *Indian file.* See also HARD ACT TO FOLLOW.

follow one's nose, to To go straight ahead. This expression dates from the fifteenth century or even earlier. "Right forth on thy nose. Recta via encode," wrote John Stanbridge in a collection of common expressions dated 1510. In the nineteenth century the retort "Follow your nose," in answer to someone asking directions, was a rather less polite way of saying the same thing.

follow suit, to To imitate someone; to follow someone's example. The expression comes from card games such as whist or bridge, in which one must play a card of the same suit as that which was led. The practice was literally spelled out in Cotton's *Complete Gamester* (1680), but had obviously been transferred by the time Herman Melville used the expression (*Moby-Dick,* 1851): "I quickly followed suit and descending into the bar-room accosted the grinning landlord."

food for thought Something to ponder. This metaphor, which implies that the mind can chew or digest an idea, dates from the early nineteenth century, although words to that effect were cited by Erasmus in his *Adagia* of the sixteenth century ("Nor try to put courteous conversation into the minds of impudent men, for speech is the food of thought"). The modern cliché was used by Mark Twain (*A Connecticut Yankee in King Arthur's Court,* 1889): "There was food for thought there."

food for worms Dead and buried. This expression dates back to the thirteenth century, or perhaps even earlier. "Ne schalt tu beon wurmes fode?" wrote the unknown author of the Middle English *Ancren Riwle* about 1220. Shakespeare picked it up in *Henry IV, Part 1* (5.4), when the mortally wounded Hotspur says of himself, "No, Percy, thou art dust, and food for—" and dies, so Prince Henry completes it, "For worms, brave Percy."

fool's paradise, a Bliss based on illusion, ignorance, or misunderstanding. The expression dates from the fifteenth century, when it appeared in print in William Paston's letters (1462: "I wold not be in a folis paradyce"). It recurs again and again, in numerous sixteenth-century sources (including Pettie, Lyly, and Shakespeare), and was certainly a cliché by the time George Bernard Shaw wrote, "Beguiling tedious hours with romances and fairy tales and fools' paradises" (*Misalliance,* 1910).

foot-in-mouth disease The knack of always saying the wrong thing. The expression is both a verbal play on the foot-and-mouth disease that affects livestock and on the expression "to put one's foot in one's mouth," meaning to make a verbal blunder. The latter dates from the late nineteenth or early twentieth century (see also PUT ONE'S FOOT IN IT). The current cliché is much newer, dating from the mid-twentieth century.

footloose and fancy-free Unattached, especially in the sense of romantic involvement. The word *footloose,* meaning free to go anywhere, originated in the late seventeenth century. *Fancy-free,* meaning not in love (fancy once meant "in love"), dates from the sixteenth century. It was used by Shakespeare in *A Midsummer Night's Dream* (2.2), where Oberon tells Puck, "But I might see young Cupid's fiery shaft quench'd in the chaste beams of the watery moon, and the imperial votaress passed on, in maiden-meditation, fancy-free."

for all intents and purposes See ALL INTENTS AND PURPOSES, FOR (TO).

for a song, to go/to buy/to sell Something sold or bought for a trifling sum, by implication for far less than its worth. The expression is believed to come from the pennies given to itinerant songsters performing outside inns and public houses (bars), as well as the very small amount required to buy sheet music. The expression dates from the sixteenth century. Shakespeare used it in *All's Well That Ends Well* ("I know a man . . . sold a goodly manor for a song" [3.2]). It was a cliché by the time Byron wrote, "The cost would be a trifle—an 'old song'" (*Don Juan,* 1824).

for auld lang syne/for old times' sake In memory of the good old days; for nostalgic reasons. This expression today is invariably associated with the song Robert Burns allegedly took down from an old man's singing in 1788. Presumably it began its life with an emphasis on remembering "auld acquaintance"—that is, old friends—which appeared about 1670 in a ballad by Francis Semphill and repeated a phrase that was already proverbial. The anglicized version, *for old times' sake,* probably dates from the same period. Eric Partridge deemed both to be clichés by the mid-nineteenth century.

for better or for worse In whatever circumstances, good or bad. The term became famous through its presence in the marriage service of the Book of Common Prayer (1549), where bride and bridegroom each must pledge to hold by the other "for better, for worse, for richer, for poorer, in sickness or in health." This expression was derived from the still older *Sarum Manual* (c. 1500), which in turn may have taken it from John Gower's *Confessio Amantis* (c. 1390), "For bet, for wers, for oght, for noght." Today it is used quite loosely, as in "For better or for worse, I've made a down payment on the condo."

forbidden fruit An unlawful pleasure, usually one that is stolen; especially, illicit love. The expression alludes to the story of Eve in the Book of Genesis (2:17–3:6), in which she caused herself and Adam to be expelled from the Garden of Eden because she ate the forbidden fruit of the tree of knowledge. "Forbidden fruit is sweet" subsequently became a proverb, quoted in numerous early English sources, and was applied to any illicit pleasure.

for crying out loud An exclamation of anger or frustration. This euphemism for "for Christ's sake" is of American origin and dates back to about 1900. One writer suggests it was coined by the cartoonist Thomas Aloysius Dorgan (1877–1929), who signed his work as TAD and is credited with inventing the name "hot dog."

foregone conclusion, a A result that is already known and therefore is taken for granted. The term comes from Shakespeare's *Othello* (3.3), in which, after hearing Iago's lie about Cassio talking in his sleep of his love affair with Desdemona, Othello says this "dream" is a "foregone conclusion"—that is, it clearly denotes that his wife has been unfaithful to him with Cassio (as Iago intended him to believe all along). Some four centuries later the term is still around: "But it could be argued that it was a surprise so many Spaniards were prepared to take part in a vote which was a foregone conclusion" (*Economist*, Feb. 26, 2005).

forewarned is forearmed Advance knowledge enables advance preparation. The term originated as a Latin proverb, *Praemonitus, praemunitus,* which was adopted into English by the early sixteenth century. Two sources from c. 1530 put it similarly: "He that is warned is half armed." Shakespeare used a version in *Henry VI, Part 3* (4.1): "I will arm me, being thus forewarn'd." It was soon extended to nonmilitary applications, such as a hostess preparing for expected guests.

forget it Overlook it, disregard it. This colloquial imperative, dating from about 1900, is used in several ways. It can mean the same as "don't mention it" or "you're welcome," as in, "'Thanks for picking me up.' 'Forget it, it was no trouble.'" It also can mean "it won't happen" or "it's impossible," as in "Find a parking space near the theater? Forget it!" These same meanings can be conveyed by *forget about it,* which, however, also may mean not to recall something and is not a cliché.

forgive and forget Both pardon and dismiss someone's mistake, rudeness, or other transgression. This expression has been an English proverb since at least the thirteenth century. William Langland in *Piers Ploughman* held it up as a form of Christian charity to be practiced by all: "So will Cryst of his curteisye, and men crye hym mercy, bothe forgive and forgeter." It appears in John Heywood's 1546 collection of proverbs and was used by Shakespeare in at least four of his plays, including *King Lear* (4.7): "Pray you now, forget and forgive; I am old and foolish." It remains current to the present day.

for good measure In excess of what is really needed; as an extra. This more recent cliché for BAKER'S DOZEN similarly alludes to the excess yardage or poundage given by a generous seller, although it is not always kindly used (for example, "And I'll give you a kick for good measure").

for heaven's/Pete's/pity's sake An expression of surprise, emphasis, exasperation, outrage, and so forth. These all are euphemisms for "for God's sake," which in some circles is considered blasphemous. "For heaven's sake" dates at least from the nineteenth century. "For Pete's sake" appeared in *Dialect Notes* in 1924. "For pity's sake" dates from the sixteenth century; Michael Drayton used it in one of his *Idea* sonnets of 1593: "Rebate thy spleen, if but for pities sake!" See also FOR THE LOVE OF MIKE/PETE/GOD.

fork over, to To pay up, to hand over. This slangy term probably comes from the verb "to fork," underground slang for picking someone's pocket using only two fingers (resembling a two-tined fork). Dating from the first half of the 1800s, the term occasionally alluded to turning over something other than money, but it is the monetary version that survived. It also is put as an imperative, "Fork it over!" According to an article in *Fortune* by Rob Norton, it is one of the many clichés particularly favored by business journalists (Jan. 13, 1997).

forlorn hope An undertaking with little chance of success; a lost cause. This expression, while seemingly quite straightforward in English, actually came from a Dutch term of the late sixteenth century, *verloren hoop,* which meant "a lost troop of soldiers," that is, an expendable squad. The British mistook *hoop* for *hope* and changed the meaning to a desperate undertaking, which has persisted since the seventeenth century.

for love or money See NOT FOR LOVE OR MONEY.

for my/one's money In my (one's) opinion or choice. This seemingly modern colloquialism actually dates from the mid-sixteenth century. Shakespeare had it in *Much Ado about Nothing* (2.3), "Well, a horn for my money when all's done." It is still current.

for old times' sake See FOR AULD LANG SYNE.

for sure Certainly, without doubt; also, I agree. This seemingly modern phrase dates from the late 1500s, at least in the first sense. John Milton used it in *Paradise Regained* (1671), "Now, now, for sure deliverance is at hand." The second sense is somewhat more recent, and is often put as *that's for sure.* C. Bonington had it in *Annapurna South Face* (1971), "We can't do it in the next two days.—That's for sure."

for the birds, it's/that's It's useless, worthless; not to be taken seriously. This slangy Americanism dates from the first half of the twentieth century and crossed the Atlantic after World War II. One writer suggests it alludes to droppings left by the horses of horse-drawn carriages, from which small birds would extract the seeds. If this source is correct, the expression is a euphemism for "horseshit."

for the life of me I cannot/could not do something even to save my own life. The expression dates at least from the early eighteenth century and is generally used hyperbolically, that is, one's life is not actually at stake. An early version appeared in Oliver Goldsmith's *The Vicar of Wakefield* (1766): "Nor could I for my life see how the creation of the world had anything to do with what I was talking about."

for the love of Mike/Pete/God An expression of exasperation, surprise, or the like. Pete and Mike both are euphemisms for God, which is considered blasphemous by some. They date from the early 1900s. See also FOR

HEAVEN'S/PETE'S/PITY'S SAKE. James Joyce used one in *Ulysses* (1922), "For the love of Mike, listen to him."

for the record For publication; for public knowledge. Originating in the twentieth century, this expression appeared in Arthur Clarke's science-fiction novel, *Prelude to Space* (1953): "For the record, you can be one of our legal advisers." See also OFF THE RECORD.

for the umpteenth time An uncountable or indefinitely large number of times. The word *umpteen* is an American coinage that was believed, by John Ciardi and several other writers, to have come from nineteenth-century Morse code. In an early version of the code, *M,* pronounced "umpty," meant "many," probably based on M, the Roman numeral for one thousand. To this was added "teen," for "ten," presumably now meaning tens of thousands or, simply, a very large number. The expression "for the umpteenth time," usually pronounced with some exasperation, means in effect that one has said or done something time and again and is thoroughly tired of the repetition.

fortunes of war The results of combat or other competition (see also WIN SOME, LOSE SOME). This expression, at first meaning simply that the issue of battle is uncertain (as Cicero put it in *Pro Milone,* 52 B.C.), dates from the fifteenth century, when William Caxton used it in his version of one of Aesop's fables ("fortune of warre"). Later it was transferred to other undertakings in which the outcome is not a certainty.

forty winks A short nap. A *wink* has meant a sleep since the fourteenth century, when William Langland wrote "Thenne Wakede I of my wink" (*Piers Ploughman,* 1377). There is an apocryphal story about the origin of forty winks, stemming from an article in *Punch* (1872), the English humor magazine, about the long and tedious articles of faith required for Church of England clergy ("If a man, after reading through the thirty-nine Articles, were to take forty winks . . ."). However appealing this source, the term had appeared in print nearly a half-century earlier (in Pierce Egan's *Tom and Jerry,* 1828), and its true origin has apparently been lost.

for what it's worth For whatever value or merit it seems to have (to you). This expression, which normally precedes the expression of one's opinion on a controversial topic, implies that the listener may not think much of it, but there it is, anyway. "The fact is so peculiar that I insert it here for what it may be worth," wrote Frank Harris in his autobiography, *My Life and Loves* (1922), long banned in America and England.

four corners of the earth, the The farthest ends of the world. This expression is believed to come from a passage in the Bible: "And gather together the dispersed of Judah from the four corners of the earth" (Isaiah 11:12). At that time and for many years thereafter the expression meant the entire world—that is, from all parts of the world. John Dryden switched it somewhat in *To the Memory of Mrs. Killigrew:* "When rattling bones together fly from the four corners of the sky." In 1965 scientists actually designated four particular areas as the "corners" of the earth. Each of them is several thousand square miles in area, 120 feet higher than the geodetic mean, and has a gravitational pull measurably stronger than surrounding areas. They are located in Ireland, southeast of the Cape of Good Hope, west of the Peru coast, and between New Guinea and Japan.

fraught with danger/peril Very risky indeed. *Fraught with* means "full of" and is rarely used today except in the sense of something undesirable. The expression, a cliché since the nineteenth century, first appeared in print in 1576 as "fraught with difficulties"; the precise cliché was first cited by the *OED* as appearing in 1864 in H. Ainsworth's *Tower of London:* "This measure . . . is fraught with danger."

free and easy Without ceremony; casual; informal. This expression, an older equivalent of today's slangy *hanging loose,* acquired a new meaning as a noun in the nineteenth century, when for a time a "free-and-easy" was a saloon or a house of ill fame. "He would have a song about it, and sing it at the 'free and easies,'" wrote J. C. Neal in his *Charcoal Sketches* (1837). This meaning did not survive, however, while the eighteenth-century sense of casualness did.

free as a bird Totally at liberty. Being able to fly about at will has long seemed to be the epitome of freedom. The simile here dates back at least to the seventeenth century, when "as free as a bird in ayre" appeared in the *Somers Tracts* (1635).

free lunch A gift or benefit for which no return is expected. This expression, dating from the early 1800s, alludes to the practice of taverns offering free food to their customers to induce them to buy more drinks. In today's bars such offerings amount to little more than a bowl of peanuts or pretzels, if that, and indeed, figuratively the term is often used in a negative context—for example, "He'll hardly offer you a job if you don't contribute to his party; there's no free lunch in political campaigns." The economist Milton Friedman went even further, declaring "There's no such thing as a free lunch" (attributed).

fresh as a daisy Vigorous, well rested, full of energy. This simile has survived the much older *fresh as a rose,* used by Chaucer and seldom heard today. It dates from the late eighteenth or early nineteenth century. Dickens used it to perfection in *The Cricket on the Hearth* (1845): "She presently came bouncing back—the saying is as fresh as any daisy; *I* say fresher." The daisy's name comes from the Old English *daeges eage,* meaning "day's eye," which refers to the flower's yellow disk. Like many flowers, daisies close their petals in the evening, concealing the disk, and reopen them in the morning; possibly the simile alludes to this characteristic.

fresh out of Recently or completely depleted. This American colloquialism from the late 1800s is generally used for a supply of something, as in "Sorry, we're fresh out of that brand of cereal."

friend in need is a friend indeed, a A dependable friend. This expression is thought to come from a Latin proverb stated by Ennius in *Hecuba* (c. 180 B.C.), quoted by Cicero and Erasmus and literally translated as "The certain friend is discerned in uncertain circumstances." It had been quoted many times—by William Caxton, John Heywood, and others—by the time Shakespeare used it in *The Passionate Pilgrim* (1599): "He that is thy friend indeed, he will help thee in thy need."

friends in high places Individuals who can help someone by virtue of their power or authority. This expression began life as a *friend (friends) at court.* One of its earliest appearances was in a translation of the medieval *Roman de la Rose* by, possibly, Chaucer: "For freend in court ay better is than peny in purs, certis" (c. 1365). It made its way into several proverb collections. After the decline of monarchies, beginning about 1800, the same idea began to be expressed slightly differently: "You must remember that I was once a minister. . . . I still have good friends in high places" (Wilbur Smith, *A Time to Die,* 1989).

fritter away Gradually waste or wear down. This seemingly rustic expression was used by Alexander Pope in *The Dunciad* (1728), in which he lampooned all his literary enemies: "How prologues into prefaces decay, And these to notes are fritter'd quite away."

from A to Z See ALPHA AND OMEGA.

from bad to worse A downhill course; matters are deteriorating. This expression is very old indeed. "He . . . fell from euyll [evil] to worse, and from worse, to worste of all," wrote Hugh Latimer in a sermon in 1549. Thirty years later, Edmund Spenser (*The Shepheardes Calender,* 1579) put it more poetically: "From good to badd, and from badde to worse, from worse unto that is worst of all." See also IF WORST COMES TO WORST.

from day one Since long ago; also, from the beginning. This twentieth-century locution continues to be used in both senses. The former appears in,

"The weather forecasts have been wrong from day one." Dermot Healy had the latter sense in *Goat's Song* (1994): "From day one I was hung up on my son." See also SINCE THE BEGINNING OF TIME.

from head/top to heels/toe/foot One's entire body; totally. The earliest of these slightly varied expressions is *from head to foot,* which Homer used in the *Iliad,* Aristophanes in *Plutus,* Plautus in several plays, and many others after them. Shakespeare used *from top to toe* in *Hamlet* (1.2). The alliterative *head to heels,* dating from about 1400, was favored by the English poet William Cowper (*Anti-Thelypthora,* 1781): "So polished and compact from head to heel." See also STEM TO STERN.

from hell Terrible, obnoxious, the worst of its kind. This phrase, put as "——from hell," may be applied to individuals ("the mother-in-law from hell"), events ("the walking tour from hell"), a time period ("the summer from hell")—in short, to just about anything. It dates from the second half of the 1900s and is rapidly becoming a cliché.

from pillar to post From one place or thing to another; hither and yon. This expression, which originally (fifteenth century) was *from post to pillar,* is believed by some to come from the old game of court tennis and to allude to the banging about of balls in a sport that had much looser rules than present-day lawn tennis. Another theory is that the term originally meant from whipping-post to pillory (punishment to hanging), which would better account for the original order. It first appeared in John Lydgate's *The Assembly of Gods* (c. 1420). Dickens (*Bleak House,* 1853) used both the old and the new versions: "So badgered, and worried, and tortured, by being knocked about from post to pillar, and from pillar to post."

from soup to nuts From the beginning to the end; the whole thing. The analogy to a complete meal of numerous courses dates back many years. John Heywood's proverb collection of 1546 has it "from potage to cheese," and John Clarke's 1639 collection, "from th'egges to th'apples." The precise locution of *soup to nuts* appears to be American and dates only from the early twentieth century. A very similar cliché, *from start to finish,* comes from sports, particularly rowing races. The earliest example in print, according to the *OED,* dates from a sports publication of 1868. This cliché is more common in Britain, where *finish* is used as a noun more often than it is in America. See also ALPHA AND OMEGA; FROM THE WORD GO.

from the bottom of one's heart Fervently, sincerely, without reservation. This expression has been traced to Vergil's *Aeneid* and resurfaces in the Book of Common Prayer (1545): "Be content to forgive from the bottom of the heart all that the other hath trespassed against him." It has been a cliché since the mid-nineteenth century.

from the horse's mouth, straight From the best authority. The analogy here is to examining a horse's teeth, which reveal its age with some accuracy. Although this fact has been known for centuries (and indeed gave rise to the adage, DON'T LOOK A GIFT HORSE IN THE MOUTH, dating from the fifth century), the expression dates only from the 1920s. "I have it straight from the mouth of a horse," wrote Christopher Morley (*Kitty Foyle,* 1939).

from the sublime to the ridiculous From outstanding to measly, famous to infamous, wonderful to silly. This expression appears to have been coined in America by Thomas Paine in his *The Age of Reason* (1794). The full quotation is, "The sublime and the ridiculous are often so nearly related that it is difficult to class them separately. One step above the sublime makes the ridiculous, and one step above the ridiculous makes the sublime again." The expression was rephrased in French by the encyclopedist Jean-François Marmontel and then repeated by Napoleon, who used it to describe the retreat of his army from Moscow.

from the word go From the very beginning. *Go* here is the indication that it is time to begin a race. This seemingly modern colloquialism originated in nineteenth-century America. Davy Crockett used it in *Narrative of the Life of Davy Crockett* (1834): "I was plaguy well pleased with her from the word go." A newer equivalent is *from the get-go,* which originated in black English in the 1960s and is on its way to clichédom.

from time immemorial Since ancient times; prior to anyone's recall. According to Ebenezer Brewer, this term comes from English law, where it meant beyond legal memory—that is, before the reign of Richard I (1189–99), fixed by the Statute of Westminster (1275) as the legal limit for bringing certain kinds of legal action (similar to the present-day statute of limitations). Later it came to mean simply a very long time ago. Thus Oliver Goldsmith wrote (*The Bee,* 1759), "This deformity . . . it had been the custom, time immemorial, to look upon as the greatest ornament of the human visage." Exactly the same is meant by *time out of mind,* which dates from the fifteenth century, when it appeared in print in *Rolls of Parliament.* Both terms have been clichés since about 1800. See also SINCE THE BEGINNING OF TIME.

front burner, on a/the A position of high priority. This relatively new term, from the 1960s, alludes to a cook's putting food that needs the most attention on the front burners of the stove. It was soon being used figuratively, as in "Put this editorial on a front burner; it's going into the next issue." For the converse, see PUT ON HOLD.

front runner Someone who is expected to win. The term comes from horse racing and began to be used figuratively in the first half of the 1900s. Its most prominent context is political, referring to a candidate who leads his or her opponents in an election, but it also occurs in other kinds of contest. Thus Wilbur Smith used it in *Gold Mine* (1970): "He had joined C.R.C. a mere twelve years previously and now he was the front runner."

frosting/icing on the cake, the An extra advantage or additional benefit. This term refers to the sweet creamy topping of a cake and has been transferred since the mid-1900s. A book review in *The Listener* used it: "All this theology is icing on the cake" (April 3, 1969; cited by the *OED*).

full circle, come/go The cycle is completed. This expression, probably originated by Shakespeare in *King Lear* ("The wheel is come full circle," 5.3), has been used ever since to describe a situation in which events run their course and things end much as they began.

full-court press, a A vigorous attack. This expression comes from a basketball tactic in which the defense exerts pressure on their opponents along the full length of the court, trying to interfere with their dribbling and passing in order to get back the ball. It began to be used figuratively in the late 1970s, particularly in politics. During the Persian Gulf War the (George H. W.) Bush administration used it to signify a major offensive.

fullness of time, in the At the appropriate or destined time. The expression occurs in the Bible (Galatians 4:4): "But when the fulness of the time was come, God sent forth his Son." It continued to be used, usually in a literary or somewhat pompous context, as in a 1751 sermon: "Which in the fullness of time should be made manifest."

full of beans Lively, high-spirited. The earliest appearance of this expression is in Robert Smith Surtees's *Handley Cross* (1843), a continuation of the adventures of a sporting grocer, John Jorrocks ("Ounds, 'osses and men are in a glorious state of excitement! Full o' beans and benevolence!"). A slang dictionary of 1874 defined the term to mean arrogant and offensive concerning one's newfound prosperity (nouveau riche snobbery) and held that it came from stable slang. It was so used for a time in the late nineteenth century, but then was superseded by the earlier (and present) meaning, which survives in the cliché.

full of piss and vinegar Very energetic, quite aggressive. This rather impolite cliché (*piss,* for urine, used to be quite acceptable language but no longer is) dates from the mid-1900s. Mickey Spillane used it in *Death Dealers* (1966), "You were young and fast and strong. Full of piss and vinegar."

full speed/steam ahead! Proceed with all possible rapidity and power. Both versions refer to the steam engine in ships and locomotives, as does *with a full head of steam.* "Full steam" meant a boiler that had developed maximum pressure. The terms became popular through an order attributed to David Glasgow Farragut at the Battle of Mobile Bay (Aug. 5, 1864): "Damn the torpedoes! Full steam ahead!" (Torpedoes in those days referred to mines.) They were transferred to nonmilitary enterprises soon afterward, but ironically one of them resurfaced in literal fashion more than a century later. In 1989 environmental activists from the Greenpeace movement sailed out among U.S. Navy boats that were testing torpedoes off the coast of Florida in order to impede what they perceived as a hazard to the surrounding ecology. The Greenpeace order of the day was, again, "Damn the torpedoes! Full speed ahead," and the navy, either unwittingly or on purpose, collided with the Greenpeace vessel, which was severely damaged.

fun and games Sheer pleasure and amusement. This modern equivalent of BREAD AND CIRCUSES and BEER AND SKITTLES is, like them, often used ironically or with a negative (life is *not* all fun and games). It dates from the early twentieth century. "We've had lots of fun and games since I last saw you" appeared in H. C. McNeile's popular detective novel *Bull-Dog Drummond* (1920).

funny money Peculiar currency, either because it is counterfeit or because it comes from dubious sources. This expression originated in the United States in the 1930s and became popular after World War II, when American tourists began to use it for any foreign currency as well. It is somewhat derogatory, implying that foreign money is not as "real" or has less worth than domestic currency.

G

game is not worth the candle, the The undertaking does not warrant the time, effort, or expense involved. This expression originally was a translation of the French essayist Montaigne's statement, "Le jeu ne vault pas la chandelle" (1580), and found its way into John Ray's proverb collection of 1678. In the days of candlelight illumination, it literally meant that the card game being played was not worth the cost of the candles used to light the proceedings. It soon was transferred to any undertaking and so persisted through the centuries.

garden path, to lead up/down the To deceive, to trick. This expression, often put simply as "up the garden," originated early in the twentieth century and tends to suggest a romantic or seductive enticement. Often found in popular novels of the 1930s and 1940s, it is less frequently heard today. See also PRIMROSE PATH.

gentleman and a scholar, a Well behaved and well educated. This term dates from the days when only well-born boys and men (or those who entered a religious order) received any education at all. Its earliest appearance in print was in George Peele's *Merrie Conceited Jests* of 1607 ("He goes directly to the Mayor, tels him he was a Scholler and a Gentleman"). It probably was close to being a cliché by the time Robert Burns used it jokingly in his *The Twa Dogs* (1786): "His locked, letter'd braw brass collar shew'd him the gentleman an' scholar."

get a grip Get hold of yourself, calm down. This imperative had several earlier meanings; one, dating from the 1940s in the military, was to put effort into what one was doing. Another, in college slang a few decades later, was to pay attention. The current meaning, however, is the one that has survived. In a *Boston Globe* editorial (Oct. 31, 2004) describing former New York City mayor Ed Koch's complaint that the Democratic National Convention in Boston "had no excitement," the writer said, "Get a grip, Ed. It was only our first one. Beginner's luck." The usage is the converse of *to lose one's grip,* to lose composure, first recorded in 1875 and cited by the *OED.* See also GET A HANDLE ON SOMETHING.

get a handle on something, to To succeed in dealing with a difficult problem. Dating from the mid-twentieth century, this slangy Americanism alludes to coping with a cumbersome object by attaching a handle to it.

However, "handle" has been used both figuratively and literally in several ways for many years. "Most things have two Handles; and a wise Man takes hold of the best," wrote Thomas Fuller in *Gnomologia* (1732). Further, "handle" has been a colloquialism for a title, and by extension a name, since about 1800. The current saying, on its way to becoming a cliché, thus can allude either to getting a secure hold on a slippery problem, or to identifying it correctly by naming it. A synonym for the former sense is *get a grip on something,* meaning to take a firm hold on it. See also GET A GRIP.

get a kick out of (something/someone), to To derive pleasurable excitement from. This twentieth-century American expression achieved immortality in Cole Porter's song, "I Get a Kick out of You" (from *Anything Goes,* 1934).

get a life Find some interests, social life, or concerns of one's own. This slangy term is quite new, dating only from about 1980, but has quickly caught on. It is often put as a disdainful imperative, as in "Don't just sit around complaining—get a life!"

get a load of something/someone Look at/listen to that. This slangy verbal phrase dates from the 1920s. It is often put as an imperative to call attention to something or someone, as in "Get a load of this!" (Edmund Wilson, *The Twenties,* 1929). It is also put straightforwardly, as in "Just wait till Jane gets a load of your new car."

get a rise out of someone, to To provoke to action or to anger. This term probably comes from fishing, in which the angler drops a fly in a likely spot and lets it float, hoping that the fish will rise to the bait. It was transferred to figurative use—that is, getting someone to lose his or her temper—early in the nineteenth century. Thackeray wrote, "Oh, but it was a rare rise we got out of them chaps" (*Catherine,* 1840).

get away from it all Escape one's responsibilities, problems, or work. This phrase, enlarging on the much older *to get away* (from c. 1300), dates only from the twentieth century. It generally denotes a temporary respite rather than a permanent escape, as in "I'm going off for a long weekend—I need to get away from it all."

get away with, to To escape the usual penalty. This Americanism originated in the second half of the nineteenth century and at one point also meant to get the better of someone. It was still considered slangy when it appeared in the *Congressional Record* in 1892: "[They] will have to be content with the pitiful $240,000 that they have already 'got away with.'"

get cracking/rolling Begin, get busy, hurry up. The first of these colloquialisms originated in Great Britain in the 1930s and appears to have crossed the Atlantic during World War II. It uses *crack* in the sense of "move fast," a usage dating from the late nineteenth century, and is often put as an imperative, as in "Now get cracking before it starts to rain." The synonymous *get rolling,* dating from the first half of the 1900s, alludes to setting wheels in motion. It, too, may be used as an imperative, but is more often heard in such locutions as "Jake said it's time to get rolling on the contracts."

get down to brass tacks, to/let's To arrive at the heart of the matter. Some think this late nineteenth-century term comes from Cockney rhyming slang for *hard facts.* Another possible and perhaps more likely source is the American general store, where a countertop was marked with brass tacks at one-yard intervals for measuring cloth, and "getting to brass tacks" meant measuring precisely. Still another theory is that in upholstered furniture, brass tacks were used to secure the undermost cloth, and to reupholster properly one had to strip the furniture to that layer. A mid-twentieth-century American synonym is to *get down to the nitty-gritty,* alluding to the detailed (nitty) and perhaps unpleasant (gritty) facts of the case. It was borrowed from black English, where it signified the anus and alluded to picking body lice (nits) from that body part. This association had been largely forgotten by the time the term was popularized by the 1964 hit song "The Nitty Gritty" by Shirley Ellis.

get in/into one's hair, to To annoy someone more or less persistently. The allusion here may well be to head lice but is not known for certain. Presumably it was already in common use by the time Mark Twain wrote, "You'll have one of these . . . old professors in your hair" (*A Tramp Abroad,* 1880).

get in on the ground floor, to To take part in an enterprise from the start and thereby gain some advantage. The term is used especially often with regard to new investments and probably originated in the financial world of late nineteenth-century America.

get into hot water, to To get in trouble, or into an embarrassing situation. Presumably the allusion here is to water hot enough to burn one. Although Lord Malmesbury wrote in a letter in 1765, "We are kept, to use the modern phrase, in hot water," the term had appeared in print more than two centuries earlier. In the sixteenth and seventeenth centuries it was put as "to cost hot water." It was probably already a cliché by the time it appeared in Richard H. Dana's *Two Years Before the Mast* (1840): "He was always getting into hot water."

get into/in the act, to To thrust oneself into another's conversation, performance, undertaking, or the like. The term comes from the theater and is analogous to another theatrical cliché, STEAL SOMEONE'S THUNDER. The American comedian Jimmy Durante popularized it from the 1930s on with his frequent complaint that "Everybody wants to get into the act" (cited by Eric Partridge in his compendium of catchphrases). It no doubt originated years earlier in vaudeville.

get into the swing of (things), to To become active; to take lively part in. This expression appears to be a nineteenth-century change on being IN FULL SWING (already very active in something), dating from the sixteenth century. An early use cited by the *OED* is by Thomas Huxley in 1864: "I shall soon get into swing."

get lost Go away, leave me alone. This rude, slangy imperative dates from the first half of the 1900s. It seems to be replacing the somewhat earlier *scram,* with the same meaning, heard less often today. P. G. Wodehouse had it in *Company for Henry* (1967), "Can I have a word with you? In private . . . Get lost, young Jane."

get off my back Stop nagging or pestering me. This slangy expression has been popular since the late 1930s, and its precise origin has been lost. It may have come from the older saying, to *have a monkey on one's back,* which once meant to be angry or annoyed but since about 1930 has meant to be addicted to drugs. More likely "get off my back" alludes simply to a burden. As governor of California (1966–74), Ronald Reagan frequently used the term, saying we need to "get government off our backs."

get (something) off one's chest, to To unburden oneself of a secret, criticism, worry, or the like. The London *Daily Chronicle* of 1902 is cited by the *OED:* "To deliver a message to the world or to express the individual personality—to 'get it off your chest' is the horrid vulgar phrase."

get off one's duff Get moving, become active. This slangy idiom uses *duff* in the sense of buttocks, a usage dating from about 1840 and at that time considered impolite. It no longer is, at least not in America, and if anything this cliché is a euphemism for still ruder synonyms, such as *get off one's butt* or *get off one's ass.*

get one's act together Get organized, behave effectively. This slangy expression, dating from about 1960, alludes to show business. It does so even more explicitly in "I'm getting my act together and taking it on the road" (*New York Times,* June 15, 1980).

get one's comeuppance Get one's JUST DESERTS, get the retaliation one deserves. This term dates from the mid-1800s and features virtually the only use of the noun *comeuppance.* William Dean Howells used it in *The Rise of Silas Lapham* (1884): "Rogers is a rascal . . . but I guess he'll find he's got his comeuppance."

get one's feet wet, to To venture into new territory. The allusion here is to the timid swimmer who is wary of getting into the water at all. Although this particular expression dates only from the early twentieth century, a similar idea was expressed more than four hundred years earlier by John Lyly in *Euphues and his England* (1580): "I resemble those that hauing once wet their feete, care not hoe deepe they wade"; in other words, once having gotten up one's nerve to try something new, one is more willing to plunge in all the way. In *The Glorious Fault* (1960) Leonard Mosley combined two metaphors: "In parliamentary life, he [Curzon] was to be one who stayed to get his feet wet before deciding that a ship was sinking."

get one's money's worth, to To obtain full value for something. This term actually dates back as far as the fourteenth century, and from that time on there are numerous appearances in print citing the legal exchange of "money or money-worth"—that is, payment is to be made in cash or its equivalent worth. It is spelled out in Shakespeare's *Love's Labour's Lost* (2.1), in which the King of Navarre explains that, in surety of the hundred thousand crowns still owing, "one part of Aquitaine is bound to us, although not valued to the money's worth." The precise modern wording dates from the nineteenth century. The English scholar Benjamin Jowett wrote (1875), "I give my pupils their money's worth."

get one's teeth into (something), to To come to grips with something; to work energetically at something. Though the image of sinking one's teeth into something is surely much older, the expression appears to come from the early twentieth century. In Dorothy Sayers's wonderful mystery *Gaudy Night* (1935), one of the women says, "If one could work here . . . getting one's teeth into something dull and durable."

get real Be realistic, see things as they are. This slangy imperative from the second half of the twentieth century is often used to disabuse someone of a mistaken or fanciful notion. For example, "Win a new car by filling out those forms? Get real!"

get rolling See GET CRACKING.

get someone's back up, to To make someone angry. The expression alludes to the behavior of the domestic cat, which arches its back when it is attacked by a dog or is otherwise annoyed. This term began in the early eighteenth century as to *put* or *set* up the back. By 1864 it was, "He goes his own way . . . if you put his back up" (*Sunday Magazine*). See also GET SOMEONE'S DANDER UP.

get someone's dander up, to To make someone very angry. The origin of this term is disputed. Most likely "dander" comes from the Dutch *donder,* for "thunder," but there are numerous other theories. The earliest reference in print dates from 1830, in Seba Smith's *Letters of Major Jack Downing:* "When a Quaker gets his dander up it's like a Northwester." Also see GET SOMEONE'S BACK UP.

get someone's goat, to To annoy someone, to make a person lose his or her temper. This term is definitely American in origin, but its precise provenance has been lost. H. L. Mencken was told that it came from the practice of putting a goat inside a skittish racehorse's stall in order to calm it down. Removing the goat shortly before the race would upset the horse and reduce its chances of winning, a ruse supposedly planned by a gambler who had bet on the horse's losing. This explanation seems more far-fetched than a possible connection of the term with the verb "to goad." In any event, it came into use about 1900.

get the lead out of one's feet Get going, stop delaying. Lead being a heavy material, the source of this expression, usually an imperative ("Get the lead out of your feet!"), seems fairly clear. There are numerous variants for "feet," mostly less polite (pants, britches, ass, butt), and *shake* is sometimes substituted for "get." It is also sometimes shortened to simply *get the lead out.* The term originated in America in the first half of the twentieth century and became widely used in the armed services during World War II.

get to first base, to To succeed in the initial phase of an undertaking. This phrase, derived from baseball, was transferred to other enterprises by the late nineteenth century. In the mid-twentieth century it acquired another more specific meaning as well: to reach the first stage of petting, which is kissing.

get to the bottom of See BOTTOM OF IT.

get to the point, to To speak plainly; to address the main issue. This expression, which in British parlance is usually phrased *come to the point,* dates from Chaucer's time. Chaucer himself wrote in the "Prologue" to *The Canterbury Tales,* "This is the poynt, to speken short and pleyn."

get under someone's skin, to To annoy someone. This expression no doubt alludes to the irritation caused by burrowing insects, which can cause intense itching. Cole Porter, however, used the expression quite differently in his song, "I've Got You under My Skin" (from *Born to Dance,* 1936), which describes a romantic addiction to a person rather than an insect infestation or a persistent annoyance.

get up and go Vital energy, enthusiasm. The *Random House Unabridged Dictionary* (1987) hyphenates this term and lists it as a noun, originating in the United States in the early years of this century. However, it has numerous precedents, the most common of which was *get up and get,* still used in some parts of the United States (President Lyndon Johnson's wife, Lady Bird, was quoted as saying it in the early 1960s). The *OED* gives a 1907 use of the current cliché: "I wish . . . folk here had a little git-up-and-go to them" (N. Munro, *Daft Days*).

get up on the wrong side of bed See GOT UP ON THE WRONG SIDE OF BED.

get wind of something, to To acquire knowledge; to hear a rumor. This expression transfers the ability of many animals to detect the approach of others from their scent carried by the wind. Originating about 1800, the term appeared in print in B. H. Malkin's translation of *Gil Blas* (1809): "The corregidor . . . got wind of our correspondence."

ghost of a chance See NOT A GHOST OF A CHANCE.

gift of gab Fluency of speech; also, a tendency to boast. *Gab,* both the noun meaning "speech" and the verb meaning "to chatter," is believed to have come from the Gaelic dialect word *gob,* for "mouth." Indeed it so appeared in Samuel Colvil's *Whiggs Supplication* (1695): "There was a man called Job . . . He had a good gift of the Gob." During the next century it became *gab,* as in William Godwin's *Caleb Williams* (1794): "He knew well enough that he had the gift of the gab." Later "the" was dropped.

gild the lily, to To add excessive ornament; to pile excess on excess. This term is a condensation of Shakespeare's statement in *King John* (4.2), "To gild refined gold, to paint the lily . . . is wasteful and ridiculous excess." Earlier (sixteenth-century) versions of this idea cited whitening ivory with ink (Erasmus, *Adagia*) and painting fine marble (George Pettie, *Petite Pallace*). Byron quoted Shakespeare correctly ("But Shakespeare also says, 'tis very silly to gild refined gold, or paint the lily"), in *Don Juan* (1818), but sometime during the succeeding years it became the cliché we now know.

gird (up) one's loins, to To prepare for action (hard work, a journey, warfare). The term comes from the Bible, both Old and New Testaments, and uses *gird* in the sense of "encircle with a belt or band." The ancient Jews wore loose clothing and put on a girdle, or belt, only when they went to work or set out to travel. Thus, "He girded up his loins, and ran" appears in I Kings (18:76), and "Gird up now thy loins like a man" in Job (in several passages). It had already become figurative in the New Testament, where 1 Peter has it, "Gird up the loins of your mind, be sober" (1:13).

girl/man Friday Trusted assistant. This term comes from Daniel Defoe's *Robinson Crusoe* (1719), in which Crusoe found a young savage on a Friday, and this man became his faithful servant and companion on the desert island. "I take my man Friday with me," said Crusoe. Some mid-twentieth-century advertising pundit invented "girl Friday"—or gal Friday—to describe the female clerk-of-all-work, presumably on the assumption that it lent some glamour to a low-level, poorly paid position. It caught on mainly through being used as the title of a 1940 motion picture starring Cary Grant and Rosalind Russell, *His Girl Friday*. In the 1970s, when affirmative action came to the American labor market, the term fell into disrepute.

give a bad name to, to To speak ill of someone or something in order to give it a bad reputation. This term comes from the proverb, "Give a dog an ill name and hang him," quoted in James Kelly's collection of Scottish proverbs (1721). It has been a cliché since about 1800.

give and take Mutual concessions; a fair exchange. Used as a noun, this expression dates from the eighteenth century. (The verbal form, *to give and take,* dates from the early 1500s.) One writer believes the phrase originated in British racing and denoted a prize for a race in which larger horses carried more weight and smaller ones less than the standard. "Give and take is fair in all nations," wrote Fannie Burney in *Evelina* (1778), echoed in T. C. Haliburton's *Wise Saws* (1843): "Give and take, live and let live, that's the word." See also LIVE AND LET LIVE.

give (someone) an inch and they'll take a mile Yield only a little and you'll be taken advantage of. This expression began life as a proverb, "Give him an inch and he'll take an ell," cited in Heywood's 1546 collection. Around the turn of the twentieth century *mile* entered the picture, as in W. D. Steele's *The Man Who Saw Through Heaven* (1927): "Give these old fellows an inch and they'll take a mile."

give a wide berth to, to To avoid. This term, which in the eighteenth century literally meant to give a ship plenty of room to swing at anchor, was transferred to other objects of avoidance and soon became a cliché. "I recommend you to keep a wide berth of me, sir," wrote Thackeray (*The Newcomes,* 1854).

give it one's best shot, to To try one's hardest; to expend optimum effort. Originally a military term, *best shot* in the sixteenth century denoted the soldiers who could most accurately shoot the enemy, according to William Safire. However, the word *shot* also had meant an attempt or a try from the mid-eighteenth century on, casting some doubt on this and other etymologies, which trace the term to billiards and boxing. In any event, in the twentieth century it became commonly used in politics ("The candidate was willing to give it her best shot"), as well as in other contexts. David Baldacci had it in *Hour Game* (2004): "'If you can wake them up....'— 'We'll give it our best shot,' said King."

give me a break That's preposterous, you can't expect me to believe that. This exasperated reply to a statement, usually made half-jokingly, dates from the second half of the 1900s. For example, "She's planning a luncheon at the Ritz? Give me a break!" This expression is not the same as to *give someone a break,* meaning to give someone an opportunity or special consideration, which dates from about 1900.

give no quarter See GRANT NO QUARTER.

give one's eyeteeth for, to To yearn for; to go to any lengths to obtain. The eyeteeth, the upper canines, have been so called since the sixteenth century, presumably because their nerves are quite close to the eyes and a toothache in those teeth is felt as pain in that area. Since they are extremely useful for biting and chewing, giving up one's eyeteeth entails a considerable sacrifice. However, this hyperbole most likely began life as to *give one's eyes,* a greater sacrifice still. Anthony Trollope used it in *Barchester Towers* (1857): "Bertie would give his eyes to go with you." Substituting eyeteeth, it is a safe guess, simply made the expression more colorful rather than affecting the underlying meaning in any way. It appeared in W. Somerset Maugham's *Cakes and Ale* (1930): "He'd give his eyeteeth to have written a book half as good." See also CUT ONE'S TEETH ON; GIVE ONE'S RIGHT ARM.

give one's right arm, to To go to any lengths. Also put as *cut off one's right arm for,* this term expresses a major sacrifice for all but the lefthanded, perhaps even more so than to GIVE ONE'S EYETEETH. An Americanism from the twentieth century, it presumably was well known by the time Robert G. Dean used it in *Layoff* (1942): "He'd cut off his right arm for her, as the saying goes."

give pause to, to To stop temporarily; to hesitate; to hold back in order to reflect. This term, too, comes from Shakespeare, from Hamlet's famous soliloquy on death (3.1), "For in that sleep of death what dreams may come

. . . must give us pause." Eric Partridge said it has been a cliché since the mid-nineteenth century.

give short shrift See SHORT SHRIFT.

give someone his/her head, to Allow someone to achieve an end in his or her own way. The term comes from horseback riding, where since the sixteenth century a horse has been said to be given its head when the rider loosens the reins and lets it go where it will. It had been transferred to human beings by about 1700, as it was in Richard Steele's play *The Tender Husband* (1703, 1.1): "What a fool I have been to give him his head so long."

give someone the ax, to To fire someone from his or her job. See also SACK.

give the devil his due Even the bad may deserve some credit. This expression dates from the sixteenth century and was in print by 1589, in *Pappe with an Hatchet,* possibly by John Lyly ("Giue them their due though they were diuels"). Shakespeare used it in several plays, as did John Fletcher, John Dryden, and others. It was a cliché by the time Mark Twain wrote "We must give even Satan his due" (*A Connecticut Yankee in King Arthur's Court,* 1889).

give the lie to, to To refute, to prove false; also, to accuse of lying. This expression dates from the sixteenth century. Sir Walter Raleigh used it in his poem "The Lie," in which he tells his soul to survive his body: "Go, since I needs must die, and give the world the lie." It is less often heard today.

give (someone/something) the once-over, to To make a quick assessment or examination. An Americanism dating from the early twentieth century, *once-over* was defined in *Dialect Notes* in 1915 as "a glance." In Elizabeth Bowen's novel *The Death of the Heart* (1938), "Daphne gave the rest of the cakes a rather scornful once-over."

give the shirt off one's back, to To give one's all; the ultimate in generosity. This hyperbole appeared in Tobias Smollett's novel of 1771, *Humphry Clinker,* and has been employed ever since. Elinor Wylie used it in her ironic poem "Portrait in Black Paint": "She'd give the shirt from off her back except that she doesn't wear a shirt."

give (someone) the time of day, not to/won't To refuse to pay someone the slightest attention. The analogy here is to refusing to answer even the simple question "What time is it?" The expression dates from the mid-twentieth century.

Norman Mailer used it in *Advertisements for Myself* (1959): "You don't even give me the time of day. You're the coldest man I've ever known."

give up the ghost, to To die. This expression, common throughout English literature but now dying out, first appears in the Bible, in the Book of Job (14:10), "Man dieth, and wasteth away: yea, man giveth up the ghost." The ghost here is the soul, thought to be separated from the body upon death.

glass ceiling An invisible barrier to promotion. This term was born in the women's movement of the 1970s, when it became clear that in many organizations and businesses discrimination barred women and minorities from advancing beyond a certain point. It is well on its way to clichédom.

gloom and doom Utter pessimism, expecting the worst. This rhyming phrase, which is sometimes reversed to *doom and gloom,* dates from the mid-1900s but became widely used only from the 1980s on. Nigel Rees cites an early use in the musical comedy *Finian's Rainbow* (1947), in which a pessimistic leprechaun sings, "I told you that gold could only bring you doom and gloom, gloom and doom." More recently, Clive Cussler wrote, "Pitt stared at Gunn, mildly surprised that the second-in-command was prey to his own thoughts of doom and gloom" (*Sahara,* 1992).

glutton for punishment, a A masochist, a person who seeks out odious or onerous tasks, or habitually takes on more than is reasonable. The earliest version of this term was a *glutton for work* and dates from the latter part of the nineteenth century. It was used by Kipling in his story *A Day's Work* (1895): "He's honest, and a glutton for work." Whether work is viewed as punishment or not is clearly up to the viewer. The *OED,* which cites a *glutton for punishment* only in 1971, makes no such judgment.

gnash one's teeth, to To express one's anger or frustration. This term, dating from the late sixteenth century, is redundant, since *to gnash* means "to strike the teeth together." Today the verb is practically always figurative (no one actually strikes the teeth together) and is never heard except in this cliché. The King James Bible of 1611 has it: "But the children of the kingdom shall be cast out into outer darkness; there shall be weeping and gnashing of teeth" (Matthew 8:12).

go ape, to To act frenzied with delight, fury, or some other strong emotion. Why such behavior should be described as apelike is not known. The slangy term dates from about 1950 and is used in such contexts as "The audience went ape over the new jazz combo," or "The school board goes ape over the very mention of budget cuts." A related and possibly derivative cliché is *to go bananas,* with roughly the same meaning. It dates from the

1960s. The National Public Radio show *All Things Considered* had it: "When you mention the word 'nuclear,' people start to go bananas" (April 13, 1983). See also GO BALLISTIC.

go around in circles, to To keep trying but get absolutely nowhere. The idea behind this expression dates back to the time when it was first observed that persons who are lost tend to wander in circles and hence cannot ever reach their desired destination. Plato used the term figuratively (*Charmides*) for an argument that leads nowhere: "You drag me round and round in a circle." See also RUN AROUND IN CIRCLES.

go ballistic, to To become irrationally angry and out of control. This slangy expression originally referred to a guided missile that went out of control. It began to be used to describe human anger in the 1980s and quickly caught on. The *New Republic* used it on November 6, 1989: "He would go ballistic over the idea of reopening the capital gains tax break for real estate." It is well on its way to being a cliché.

go bananas See GO APE.

go belly-up Die; also, go bankrupt or otherwise fail. This slangy Americanism, which dates from the second half of the 1800s, initially referred to dead fish, which float in precisely that fashion. The transfer to humans as well as to inanimate objects, such as a business, took place in the early 1900s. It continues to be used in both senses, as in, "If those instruments fail, the astronauts will go bellyup" (that is, die), or as John Dos Passos put it in *Chronicle* (1920), "Labor's belly up completely—The only hope is the I.W.W. [union]."

go by the board, to To be lost or abandoned. The term originally referred to falling or being thrown overboard (from a ship), without hope of recovery. The "board" was the ship's side. This meaning dates from the seventeenth century, but by the mid-1800s the term had long since been transferred to anything lost. Longfellow still echoed the older meaning in his poem "The Wreck of the Hesperus" (1856): "Her rattling shrouds, all sheathed in ice, With the masts went by the board."

go climb a tree/fly a kite Go away and stop annoying me. There are many other versions of these colloquial imperatives, from *go chase yourself,* dating from about 1900, to *go jump in the lake, sit on a tack,* or *soak your head,* also of twentieth-century provenance. All could be classed as clichés. See also GO TO THE DEVIL.

God/heaven forbid Let it not happen, or let it not be true. This invocation of the almighty is very old indeed—it dates from the thirteenth century—but, belief in God and heaven no longer being universal, it is no longer used literally. Thus, in such uses as "God forbid that their plane crashes" or "'Is Dad going hunting next weekend?' 'Heaven forbid, Mom's baby is due then,'" no one is calling for a deity's intervention. Also see PERISH THE THOUGHT.

go downhill Deteriorate, decline. Although it would seem that going down a hill is easier than going up, downhill has meant a decline since the 1500s, although Daniel Defoe also used it in the sense of easy ("a very short cut, and all down hill," *Robinson Crusoe,* 1719). An 1856 history of England had the sense of declining: "The monks had traveled swiftly on the downhill road of human corruption."

God's country A beautiful rural area; also, the back country or provinces, the sticks. This expression, alluding at first to an area considered especially favored by God, originated in the United States during the Civil War. A Union soldier who was imprisoned in the South so referred to the North: "If I could only get out of that horrible den, into God's country once more" (R. H. Kellogg, *Rebel Prisons,* 1865).

God's gift to the world Something or someone particularly propitious or welcome or marvelous. This expression, dating from the first half of the twentieth century, is nearly always used ironically or sarcastically of a person who either is very conceited or is regarded as anything but God-given. Thus Ellery Queen's mystery *The Four of Hearts* (1938) has a chapter entitled "God's Gift to Hollywood," and fellow mystery writer Margery Allingham wrote, "Amanda was God's own gift to anyone in a hole" (*The Traitor's Purse,* 1941).

goes without saying, it/that It/that is a matter of course, so generally accepted that it need not be stated at all. This expression, which often is followed by exactly what supposedly need not be said, is a translation of the French proverb *Cela va sans dire,* which at first was directly adopted into English and later was translated (in the last half of the nineteenth century). "It goes without saying that the books are not ordinary ones," appeared in an issue of a literary journal in 1897.

go figure It's puzzling; I can't explain this contradiction or anomaly, but perhaps you can. William Safire believes this imperative came from the Yiddish *gey rekhn,* meaning "go reckon," or "go figure it out." More idiomatic English would have it as "go and figure," but the conjunction was dropped. However, it may also be a version of the American *you figure it* (with the emphasis on "you"), a phrase Eric Partridge said dates from the 1920s. Whatever the source, the brief phrase expresses a wealth of feeling.

go for broke Risk everything; SHOOT THE WORKS. Most authorities believe this term comes from gambling, in which one may stake one's resources for "all or nothing," and probably originated in the nineteenth century. Eric Partridge claimed a more recent origin, sometime during World War II. However, *broke* has meant "bankrupt" or "without funds" since the late seventeenth century.

go for it Try your hardest; aim to win. This slangy imperative appears to have originated in college sports events in the second half of the twentieth century and was soon transferred to all kinds of enterprise. President Ronald Reagan used it in the mid-1980s to exhort Congress to pass tax reform. A more specifically athletic event gave rise to the related *go for the gold,* an Olympic slogan of 1980 urging athletes to aim for the gold (highest) medal. That may be dying out, but the slightly older term is fast becoming a cliché.

go haywire, to To run amok; to become hopelessly entangled or to break down. There are two theories as to the origin of this term, which is originally American. One holds that it came from the practice of using old baling wire to make repairs, a makeshift solution at best. The other, upheld by H. L. Mencken, says it refers to the difficulty of handling coils of wire used for bundling hay, which readily become entangled.

go hog wild, to To go berserk; to go crazy with excitement. An Americanism dating from about 1905, this expression is a mysterious metaphor. Possibly it refers to the manic struggles of animals being taken away for slaughter, or perhaps it once meant unseemly enthusiasm, hogs being associated mostly with negative characteristics.

golden oldie A recording, film, or other entertainment item that was once very popular and is still admired. This slangy term was born in the 1960s and originally applied to phonograph records but soon was broadened. For example, "I always do my aerobics workouts to tapes of golden oldies."

golden parachute An employment agreement that gives generous benefits to its high-ranking executives if they are dismissed owing to a company merger or takeover. This term, dating from about 1980, may have been based on the older *golden handshake,* which offers an employee generous benefits or a bonus in exchange for early retirement. It dates from the mid-1900s, when a dwindling school population prompted many localities to offer such an incentive to teachers. In contrast, *golden handcuffs* are a financial incentive to keep an employee from leaving a company. Stock options that can be exercised only far in the future are a popular form of golden handcuffs. This term dates from about 1970.

gone to pot Ruined, destroyed. This seemingly modern slang expression dates from the sixteenth century. John Heywood's 1546 proverb collection includes "The weaker goeth to the potte," referring to being cut into pieces like stew meat for the pot, and Sir John Harington's translation of *Orlando Furioso* (1591) has "If any more we take the field, our side goes to the pot."

good as gold Singularly well-behaved or authentic. This proverbial comparison has an ancient ring to it, but it dates only from the nineteenth century. Dickens used it several times (in *The Old Curiosity Shop* and *A Christmas Carol*) as did W. S. Gilbert in *Patience* (1881): "Gentle Jane was good as gold, She always did as she was told."

good, bad, or indifferent However something or someone may be, take it/him/her as they come. The phrase appears in Laurence Sterne's *Tristram Shandy* (1760–67) and is spelled out in Joel Barlow's poem, "Hasty-Pudding" (1792): "E'en Hasty Pudding, purest of all food, May still be bad, indifferent, or good."

good egg, a An agreeable, trustworthy person. This slangy expression has outlived *bad egg,* which it actually implied in the sixteenth century. "Neither good egge nor good bird," went the saying, meaning the young (egg) would not turn into praiseworthy adults (bird). In the nineteenth century this continued to be spelled out: "A bad egg [is] a fellow who has not proved to be as good as his promise" (*The Athenaeum,* 1864). The favorable aspect of *good egg* dates from the early twentieth century. Rudyard Kipling used it in *Traffics and Discoveries* (1904): "'Good egg!' quoth Moorshed."

good graces, to be/get in one's To insinuate oneself into favor, to ingratiate oneself. "Good graces" has meant the condition or act of being favored since the fifteenth century and appears throughout English literature. The seventeenth-century diarist John Evelyn wrote (*Memoirs,* 1675), "A sprightly young lady much in the good graces of the family."

good grief An expression of surprise, dismay, alarm or other emotion, usually negative. The term, a euphemism for "good God," dates from the early 1900s. It appeared frequently in Charles M. Schulz's comic strip, *Peanuts,* where various characters would use it in addressing the hapless hero, "Good Grief! Charlie Brown!"

good head on one's shoulders, to have a To be intelligent or shrewd. This term began life in the sixteenth century as having an *old head on young shoulders,* meaning a young person who has an old person's wisdom. Sometime in the course of time "old" was clarified into "good," although in the nineteenth century it was also put as simply having a head on one's shoulders.

good old days, the The past viewed with nostalgia. "Last year was always better," recorded Erasmus in his *Adagia* (quoting Diogenianus, from his *Adagia* of c. A.D. 125). The human propensity to view the past as superior to the present has often been pointed out by philosophers since ancient times, and the validity of this view has just as often been called into question. Consequently, the current cliché is often used ironically or sarcastically. Its counterpart, dating from about 1930, is *the bad old days,* signifying a less sentimental view of the past.

good riddance (to bad rubbish) I'm glad something/someone is gone. This rather rude and modern-sounding interjection actually dates from the late eighteenth century, when it was first put as "happy riddance." It remains current.

good Samaritan A selfless helper of anyone in distress. The term comes from the biblical story (Luke 10:30–35) told by Jesus. He compared the treatment accorded to a man, robbed and left half dead, by a priest, a Levite, and a Samaritan. The first two passed him by, but the Samaritan took him to an inn and cared for him. Although the term "good Samaritan" does not appear in any of the translations of this parable, it somehow evolved over the years.

good scout, a An amiable person. This slangy expression originated in America, probably in the late nineteenth century. It appeared in Meredith Nicholson's *Hoosier Chronicle* of 1912: "Dad's a good old scout."

good-time Charlie A very sociable, gregarious fellow. The term dates from the first half of the twentieth century and the original Charlie, if ever there was one, has been forgotten. The *Atlantic* used it ironically in November 1969: "A royal-style good-time Charlie . . . akin to Edward VII."

goody-two-shoes A self-righteous, smugly virtuous person. The term comes from the title and main character of a nursery tale, *The History of Goody Two-Shoes* (1765), believed to have been written by Oliver Goldsmith. She owned but a single shoe, and when she was given a pair of shoes she was so delighted that she showed them to everyone, saying, "Two shoes." Today the term is often shortened to *goody-goody,* as in "She's a real goody-goody, always playing up to her boss."

go off at half-cock/half-cocked, to To act prematurely. The term comes from about 1700, when the hammer of a firearm could be set halfway between the firing and retracted positions. This setting was supposedly secure, but occasionally it slipped and the gun would go off unexpectedly. The term soon was transferred to other occasions when something was done prematurely, especially in the United States. The *OED* cites an appearance in the 1833 *Debates of Congress:* "The gentleman from Maryland has gone off half-cocked."

go off one's chump/head/rocker, to To go crazy; to become insane. The oldest of these three expressions is "off his head," which was current although slangy by the time Thomas Hood wrote *The Turtles* (1844), "He was 'off his head.'" The word *chump* became British slang for "head" in the late nineteenth century; subsequently, "off his chump" was used several times by Shaw, in *Pygmalion* and *Heartbreak House. Off one's rocker* comes from the same period, but its origin is more puzzling. One writer suggests it may indirectly allude to the elderly, associated with both rocking chairs and diminished mental capacity. Yet another variant is *to go off one's trolley,* which alludes to a motorman getting off a streetcar to reposition the trolley wheel on the overhead wire that carried electric current to the car's motor. To be disconnected from this power source came to mean becoming crazy, a usage dating from the late 1890s. With the demise of streetcars in many American cities, this expression is heard less often today.

go overboard, to To go to extremes; to overreact, especially in favor of something or someone. This expression, which conjures up the extreme act of jumping or falling off a ship, dates from the first half of the twentieth century. For a time it signified living beyond one's means, but that meaning is no longer current. John P. Marquand used the term in its contemporary sense (*Melville Goodwin,* 1951): "Did you ever hear about General Goodwin going overboard over an American girl in Paris?"

Gordian knot See CUT THE GORDIAN KNOT.

gory details, the Unpleasant particulars. The word *gore,* from Old English and German words meaning blood that had been shed and clotted, came to denote, by extension, murder, bloodshed, and other kinds of violence. It was so used by Dickens in *Barnaby Rudge* (1841), "Something will come of this. I hope it mayn't be human gore." Literally, therefore, *gory details* means "bloody details," but despite violence being by no means obsolete, the term has been transferred to mean the unpleasant particulars of just about anything, ranging from a business transaction to a divorce. It is also used ironically for any details, whether pleasant or not.

go scot-free, to To be let off without penalty or punishment. This expression has nothing to do with Scotland, but rather with the early meaning of *scot,* that is, a tax assessment. Thus *scot-free* meant not having to make such a payment, and later was extended to mean being exempted from other kinds of obligation, including punishment. The earliest use of the term dates from the Magna Carta of 1215. Later it was transferred to non-legal issues, as in Samuel Richardson's novel *Pamela* (1740): "She should not, for all the trouble she has cost you, go away scot-free."

go south Fail, go bankrupt, decline. This colloquialism probably alludes to two-dimensional maps where north is up (at the top) and south is down. Another theory is that in some Native Americans' (Sioux) belief system the term means "to die." From the first half of the twentieth century on, however, it became particularly common among business writers. For example, "Dorothea's become involved in some questionable real estate ventures that went south very recently" (David Baldacci, *Hour Game*, 2004). See also GO BELLY-UP.

gospel truth Something that may safely be believed. This term dates from the Middle Ages, when Christianity was almost universally accepted in Western civilization. Thus Chaucer used "gospel" in numerous places to mean incontrovertible truth. The word "gospel" is actually a corruption of the Old English *godspel,* meaning "good tidings," and was used to signify the glad tidings preached by Jesus, the life of Jesus as told in the New Testament (whose first four books are generally referred to as the Gospels), and the religious doctrine set forth there. Thus *gospel truth* literally means something as true as what is contained in the Gospels, which once were believed to be literally true, and the term has survived universal belief in that faith by a good many years.

go the extra mile Make a special effort to accomplish something, go beyond the norm. This twentieth-century expression may be used to exhort someone to greater effort, as in "The coach wants us to go the extra mile in this game," or simply to describe additional effort. A 1957 song combines it with several other clichés: "Working like a beaver, Always with a smile, Ready to take the rough and smooth, To go the extra mile" ("All We Ask Is Kindness," by Joyce Grenfell).

go through the roof, to To rise unexpectedly high; also, to lose one's temper. Both meanings date from the mid-twentieth century, the first slightly antedating the second. In 1946 Eric Hodgins in his popular novel *Mr. Blandings Builds His Dream House* wrote "The Knapp sales curves were going through the roof." For losing one's temper, this cliché, becoming common in the 1950s, is a synonym of HIT THE CEILING.

go to hell in a handbasket, to To deteriorate rapidly. This expression, originating in America in the early twentieth century, owes its appeal to alliteration. It also makes sense: something carried in a handbasket is light and easily conveyed, whence the phrase can mean going to ruin easily and rapidly. However, more likely it is simply an alliterative elaboration of *gone to hell,* which has meant ruined or destroyed since the early nineteenth century. The cliché tends to be applied to large generalities, as in "The economy is about to go to hell in a handbasket." See also GO TO THE DEVIL; GO(ING) TO THE DOGS.

go to one's head, to To be unduly influenced by praise or success. This expression, which likens the effect of praise to that of alcoholic beverages, dates from the twentieth century. The *OED* cites its appearance in Agatha Christie's *Ten Little Niggers* (published in the United States as *And Then There Were None,* 1939): "He's played God Almighty for a good many months. . . . That must go to a man's head eventually."

go to pot See GONE TO POT.

go to seed See RUN TO SEED.

go to the devil/hell Go away and don't come back. These two imperatives date from the Middle Ages, when most of the Western world believed that unrepentant sinners were, after death, condemned to eternal punishment in a place called hell presided over by an evil spirit called the devil. *Go to the devil* appears in several parts of Chaucer's *Canterbury Tales,* and *go to hell* in numerous later writings. Also see GO TO HELL IN A HANDBASKET.

go(ing) to the dogs To be ruined. This expression, which has meant to come to a bad end since the seventeenth century, assumes that dogs are inferior creatures, as so many other sayings do (A DOG'S LIFE, DIE LIKE A DOG, SICK AS A DOG, and so on). It was already a cliché by the time Shaw wrote, "The country is going to the dogs" (*Augustus Does His Bit,* 1917).

go to the well too often Keep calling on the same resource after it has been exhausted. This expression is a modern version of an ancient proverb, appearing in various ways and numerous languages from the fourteenth century on. Thomas Fuller (*Gnomologia,* 1732) put it, "The pitcher that often goes to the well comes home broken at last."

go(ing) to town To do something successfully and/or with great enthusiasm. A nineteenth-century Americanism, this expression probably originally alluded to the special treat of a trip to town for rural folks. "Chocolate creams are one of the things I am fondest of. I was feeling low and I went to town," said a character in Erle Stanley Gardner's *The Case of the Silent Partner,* indicating he had eaten a great many of them.

got up on the wrong side of bed In a moody, grumpy state of mind. This expression dates from ancient times, when it was believed to be extremely bad luck to put the left foot down first. Supposedly Augustus Caesar, the Roman emperor, was exceedingly superstitious about this practice. It was still regarded as a bad omen in the seventeenth century, when the expression appeared in several plays (William Congreve's *Love for Love;* Ben Jonson's *Tale of a Tub;* Aphra Behn's *Town-Fop:* "Sure I rose the wrong way today. I have such damned ill luck"). By the nineteenth century, however, it specifically became a sign of churlishness and ill temper. "Thou art angry this morning . . . hath risen from thy wrong side, I think," wrote Sir Walter Scott (*Redgauntlet,* 1824).

go while the going is good Get away while you can; make progress while conditions are favorable. This turn of phrase, a twentieth-century Americanism, appears in several popular novels of the first half of the century, among them John O'Hara's *Appointment in Samarra* (1934), as well as in a letter of H. L. Mencken's of 1916: "You would be a maniac not to go out for all that money while the going is good."

go whole hog See WHOLE HOG.

go with the flow Go along with the crowd, be amenable to what others are doing. The "flow" in this late-twentieth-century colloquialism alludes to the ebb and flow of tides. The phrase, which undoubtedly owes its popularity to the rhyme, describes a laid-back demeanor, as in "I don't care which restaurant they pick; I'll just go with the flow."

granddaddy of them all The first, oldest, or greatest example of something. This colloquialism dates from about 1900 and is never applied to a person. For example, "That was the granddaddy of all hurricanes, according to the weather forecaster." The Persian Gulf War of 1991 gave rise to a similar locution, *the mother of all . . . ,* meaning the greatest or best of something and based on a translation from Arabic. It was first applied by Iraqi leader Saddam Hussein to a major battle ("the mother of all battles"). At this writing it has not yet supplanted *granddaddy,* but possibly one day it will.

grandstand play An ostentatious action; behavior designed to attract maximum attention. The term comes from nineteenth-century American baseball, where certain players deliberately sought the attention and favor of the spectators in the grandstands. It appeared in one of W. K. Post's *Harvard Stories* of 1893: "They all hold on to something. . . . To faint or fall over would be a grand-stand play."

grand tour, the A thorough inspection of any building, facility, business enterprise, or the like. The term comes from the custom, begun in the seventeenth century, of sending the son of a well-to-do family on an extended tour of the European Continent for the purpose of completing his education. Later the custom was extended to daughters as well. In time the term was transferred to other kinds of tour.

grant no quarter Show no mercy. This term comes from the ancient practice of sparing the life of an enemy who has come into one's power, which was described as giving or *granting quarter.* Granting *no* quarter meant they were killed. The meaning of "quarter" has been disputed. The most likely explanation lies in "quarters" in the sense of "barracks," a use of the word since the late sixteenth century. To *grant no quarter* thus meant to provide no housing for prisoners, who of course would not need it if they were dead. Wrote Nathan Bailey in 1725 (trans. *Erasmus' Colloquies*), "It is grown into a proverb, I'll give you no more quarter than a dog does a wolf."

grasp at straws, to To make a hopeless effort to save oneself. The term comes from the ancient image of a drowning man clutching at insubstantial reeds in an attempt to save himself, and it often was put as to *catch* or *clutch at straws.* It appeared in print as early as the seventeenth century and soon was regarded as a proverb. Indeed, Samuel Richardson so identifies it in *Clarissa* (1748): "A drowning man will catch at a straw, the proverb well says."

grass is always greener (on the other side of the fence), the What one doesn't have always looks more appealing than what one has. A proverb first cited in Erasmus's *Adagia* (1545), this maxim remains true and the phrase remains current.

grass roots The fundamental level of anything; specifically, the rank and file of the electorate. Both usages date from about 1900, but the more common one today is the political one. Thus a candidate might concentrate on appealing to the grass roots of his or her constituency, or be said to be running a grass roots campaign.

gravy train, the Easy money; the good life, obtained with little effort. This American slang term became current during the financial boom of the 1920s. It originated in railroad slang, where "gravy train" meant a run on which there was good pay and little work. (*Gravy* itself became slang for easy money, or an illicit profit obtained through graft, in the early 1900s.) "There was a moment . . . when the whole Jocelyn sideshow seemed to be boarding the gravy train . . . on to fatter triumphs" (Mary McCarthy, *The Groves of Academe,* 1953).

gray eminence The power behind the throne; a person who wields considerable power but secretly or surreptitiously. The term is a translation from the French of *L'Eminence grise,* a name given to François Leclerc du Tremblay (1577–1638), also called Père Joseph, a Capuchin monk who was the trusted behind-the-scenes adviser of Cardinal Richelieu. The term came into English in the early 1940s when Aldous Huxley wrote a book about him entitled *Grey Eminence* (1941). See also POWER BEHIND THE THRONE.

grease someone's palm/fist, to To bribe someone; also, to give a gratuity. This term has been around since the sixteenth century, and apparently a version of it was known even in Roman times, when Pliny the Younger called it *unguentarium,* translated as "ointment money" (*Epistles,* c. A.D. 98). "Wyth golde and grotes they grese my hande," wrote John Skelton (*Magnyfycence,* c. 1529).

greater love hath no man A supreme sacrifice; the ultimate demonstration of friendship or goodwill. The term comes from the Bible: "Greater love hath no man than this, that a man lay down his life for his friends" (John 15:13). Detective-story aficionado Anthony Boucher (*The Case of the Seven Sneezes,* 1942) made an amusing play on it: "Greater love hath no man than this, that he should lay down his checkbook for his life."

greatest thing since sliced bread, the A useful new invention. Originating in the mid-twentieth century, probably in the armed forces, this expression also can be used sarcastically; indeed, not everyone regards packaged presliced bread as a taste treat, although it is undoubtedly a convenience. In Britain it is also put as *best thing since sliced bread.* Rona Jaffe used the term in *The Fame Game* (1969): "You're the greatest thing since sliced bread." Numerous variants have arisen, such as the greatest thing since the hamburger, chewing gum, and indoor plumbing, but none became as common as *sliced bread.*

great guns, going Proceeding vigorously. This term comes from British naval slang of the late eighteenth century, when *blowing great guns* signified a violent wind or storm. Another meaning for *great guns,* important persons, persisted throughout the nineteenth century, whereas in America the term was also an expletive for astonishment, comparable to "By George!" or "Great Scott!" It is the naval meaning that was transferred into the slangy cliché, however.

great unwashed, the The working classes. The term showed up in print in the early nineteenth century in Theodore Hook's *The Parson's Daughter* (1833), where it appears in quotation marks. Exactly who first coined the phrase is not known, but in Britain it was used to describe the rabble of the

French Revolution who rose up against the privileged classes. Although Eric Partridge said that its snobbishness had made it obsolescent by the 1940s, it is still used ironically.

Greeks bearing gifts, beware of/like Do not trust enemies who pretend to be friends. The term refers to the treachery of the Greeks during the Trojan Wars, when they entered the city of Troy bearing the "gift" of a large wooden horse that was actually filled with soldiers who then burned down the city.

Greek to me, it's/that's (all) It is completely unintelligible; I don't understand. This term, used by generations of schoolchildren, was coined by Shakespeare in *Julius Caesar* (1.2), where the conspirator Casca says of Cicero's speech, "For mine own part, it was Greek to me." In the play Cicero actually spoke in Greek, in order to prevent some people from understanding, but the term soon was transferred to anything unintelligible and has been so used ever since.

green around the gills Looking ill; sick to one's stomach. A green complexion has signified illness since about 1300, and "rosy about the gills" has meant being in good health since the late seventeenth century. Sir Francis Bacon used *red* about the gills to signify anger (1626), whereas in the nineteenth century *white* and *yellow* about the gills meant looking ill. However, *green* won out and survives in the present-day cliché.

green-eyed monster/green with envy Jealousy. The green-eyed monster comes straight from Shakespeare's *Othello* (3.3), where the villain Iago tells Othello, "O! beware, my lord, of jealousy; it is the green-ey'd monster which doth mock the meat it feeds on." The poet's allusion is to the green-eyed cat family who tease their prey, seeming to love and hate them at the same time. However, a greenish complexion also was associated with jealousy, and elsewhere Shakespeare wrote "Troubled with the green sickness" (*Antony and Cleopatra,* 3.2). Jealousy and envy are not precisely synonyms; the first is a feeling of resentment against someone who enjoys success or an advantage, or who is a rival; the second is more a feeling of covetousness with regard to someone's possessions or advantages. Nevertheless the color green came to symbolize envy as well, although somewhat later.

green light, get/give the Permission to proceed. The term alludes to the green of traffic lights, signifying "go ahead," which began to be used on railroads in the nineteenth century. Terence Rattigan in his play *French without Tears* (1937) wrote, "We had a bottle of wine and got pretty gay, and all the time she was giving me the old green light" (3.1).

grim reaper, the Death. This expression is actually a combination of the older *grim death,* which dates from about 1600, and the artistic depiction of death with a scythe, which began somewhat later. The first appeared in a play by Philip Massinger (1583–1640), *The Roman Actor,* and also in John Milton's *Paradise Lost* ("Before mine eyes in opposition sits Grim Death, my son and foe"). The second appeared in a song from "Des Knaben Wunderhorn" and in Longfellow's poem, "The Reaper and the Flowers" ("There is a Reaper whose name is Death, and, with his sickle keen"), as well as in earlier but more obscure sources.

grin and bear it Put up with adversity with good humor. This expression originated as *grin and abide.* It so appears in Erasmus Darwin's *Zoonomia* (1794), "We have a proverb where no help could be had in pain, 'to grin and abide,'" so it presumably was a well-known saying by then. A few years earlier W. Hickey wrote in his *Memoirs* (1775), "I recommend you to grin and bear it (an expression used by sailors after a long continuance of bad weather)." It has been a cliché for about a hundred years, well known enough for poet Sam Walter Foss (1858–1911) to pun on it in his *The Firm of Grin and Barrett* ("Never yet has any panic scared the firm of Grin and Barrett").

grind to a halt, to See COME TO A GRINDING HALT.

grin like a Cheshire cat To smile broadly. The origin of this expression, which was well known in the eighteenth century, has been lost. Most explanations involve the traditional Cheshire County cheese, sold in the shape of a wheel and, perhaps, once so molded that it resembled a cat's grinning face. Another theory holds that it refers to a Cheshire forest ranger named Caterling who frightened off poachers with his fierce grin. At any rate, the term has been appearing in print since the late 1700s in the works of such writers as William Thackeray and Charles Lamb, as well as in the work of its most famous exponent, Lewis Carroll.

grist for the mill, that's That's something useful, of which advantage can be taken. This metaphor refers to *grist,* the amount of grain to be ground at one time. It has been used figuratively since the sixteenth century. Arthur Golding, translator of Calvin's theological writings, wrote, "There is no lykelihoode that those thinges will bring gryst to the mill" (1583). It was surely a cliché by the time Dickens wrote, "Meantime the fools bring grist to my mill, so let them live out their day" (*Nicholas Nickleby,* 1838).

grit one's teeth, to To summon up strength to bear pain, misfortune, or some other unpleasant matter, or determination for a difficult task. The idea of *setting* one's teeth goes back to the ancient Greeks and Romans. Menander wrote, "Set your teeth and endure" (*The Girl from Samos,* c. 300 B.C.). "Gritting the teeth" describes both setting or clamping them together and grinding them with the effort. In 1797 Thomas Jefferson described his colleague, "Mr. Adams . . . gritting his teeth, said . . ."

groves of academe An institution of higher education (college or university), or those associated with it. This term refers to an actual place in ancient Greece, the Grove of Academus, an olive grove outside Athens presented by the Spartans to the Athenian hero Achilles, who had helped to rescue Helen. About 387 B.C. Plato had a house and garden adjoining this place, where he would meet with his students, and his school of philosophy came to be called, after it, Academia. Years later, the Roman poet Horace referred to it (*Epistles,* 20 B.C.): "To seek for truth in the groves of Academe"; and John Milton also referred to it in *Paradise Regained* (1671). Today the term is often used ironically, as by Mary McCarthy, who made it the title of her satirical novel *The Groves of Academe* (1953).

grow like Topsy Grow very quickly. This phrase alludes to the little African-American slave girl in Harriet Beecher Stowe's *Uncle Tom's Cabin* (1851), who when asked where she came from, replied, "I 'spect I growed. Don't think nobody never made me."

guiding light A mentor or an exemplary principle. Presumably this expression refers to the light of a lantern or beacon guiding someone through the dark. The earliest transference of this idea was religious, "light" referring to God or the church. Thus the American Transcendentalist Theodore Parker wrote, "We look to Thee; Thy truth is still the Light which guides the nations, groping on their way." Sometime in the latter part of the nineteenth century the term began to be used for secular mentors of various kinds.

gung-ho Very enthusiastic, dedicated to the task at hand; also, overzealous. The term, also spelled gung ho, comes from a Chinese phrase meaning "work together," adopted as the name for small producer cooperatives organized in the late 1930s to help the Chinese economy during the Chinese-Japanese war. The term was then adopted by Marine Lieutenant Evans F. Carlson for his battalion of volunteers, Carlson's Raiders, formed just after Pearl Harbor. In 1943 a war movie dramatizing one of the Raiders' early victories was entitled *Gung Ho!* and the term caught on. In the military, however, it also came to be applied to an offensively ardent follower of rules and regulations. Richard Martin Stern had an early civilian usage, "In those days he was very gung ho for National Socialism" (*The Kesssler Legacy,* 1968).

gussied up, to get (all) To be dressed or to dress in one's best clothes. This Americanism from the first half of the twentieth century is of uncertain origin. One theory is that it comes from *gusset,* a triangular piece of material put into a garment so that it fits better; this word in turn comes from the French *gousset* and dates from the Middle Ages, when such pieces were put into mail armor so that the knight it enclosed could move better. Because gussets might be considered a bit of fancy dressmaking, the theory holds, one's best clothes would have more of them than everyday attire.

h

hail fellow well met On easy, congenial terms; also, superficial friendliness. This expression, which has a quintessentially Victorian ring, actually dates from the sixteenth century. Presumably it began as a greeting, but by 1550 it was being used figuratively and so appeared in Thomas Becon's *New Catechisme* ("They would be 'hail fellow well met' with him").

hair of the dog A small amount of what made one ill might be used as a remedy; recipe for curing a hangover. This expression appeared in John Heywood's *Proverbs* of 1546 ("I pray thee let me and my fellow have a haire of the dog that bit us last night") and alludes to the even older folk remedy of treating a dog bite by placing the burnt hair of a dog on the wound. Although having a drink is a dubious cure for the aftereffects of alcoholic overindulgence, the expression is still used, and occasionally is transferred to other matters.

hair shirt A self-imposed punishment or penance. The term comes from the medieval practice of doing penance by wearing a shirt made of coarse haircloth (made from horsehair and wool), mentioned from the thirteenth century on in numerous sources, including Chaucer's *Canterbury Tales* (*The Second Nun's Tale*). It also appears in a couplet by Alexander Pope (1737), "No prelate's lawns with hair-shirt lin'd is half so incoherent as my mind." See also SACKCLOTH AND ASHES.

hale and hearty Healthy and vigorous. This term, which dates from the mid-nineteenth century, is redundant, since *hale* and *hearty* both mean "healthy." It survived, no doubt, because of its pleasing alliteration. Thomas Hardy used it in *The Dynasts* (1903): "We be the King's men, hale and hearty."

half a loaf is better than none Something is better than nothing, even if it is not all you wanted. This expression was already a proverb in John Heywood's 1546 collection. G. K. Chesterton repeated it in his essay, *What's Wrong with the World:* "Compromise used to mean that half a loaf was better than no bread. Among modern statesmen it really seems to mean that half a loaf is better than a whole loaf."

half a mind See HAVE A GOOD/HALF A MIND.

half the battle A very successful start. This expression is part of an older proverb, "The first blow is half the battle," which dates from the eighteenth century. In Oliver Goldsmith's comedy, *She Stoops to Conquer* (1773), two men wish to make a good impression on their host's daughter. One says, "I have been thinking, George, of changing our travelling dresses," and the other replies, "You're right: the first blow is half the battle. I intend opening the campaign with the white and gold [waistcoat]." During the nineteenth century the first half of the expression was dropped, and with overuse the term became a cliché.

hammer and tongs, go at it Engage with great vigor in work, a contest, a fight, or some other undertaking. This metaphor from the blacksmith's tools—the hammer used to shape hot metal taken from the fire with tongs—replaced an earlier metaphor from the same source, "between the hammer and the anvil," with a meaning similar to that of BETWEEN A ROCK AND A HARD PLACE. The current expression was in print by 1708 and has been a cliché since the mid-nineteenth century.

hand in glove On very intimate terms; allies. This metaphor for a close fit (as glove fits hand) was already a proverb in John Ray's 1678 collection, although it originally was put as hand *and* glove. "Connected as the hand and glove is, madam, poetry and love," wrote David Lloyd (*Epistle to a Friend,* c. 1792).

hand over fist Moving quickly. This term comes from sailing and began life as *hand over hand,* which is how sailors climbed a rope. In nineteenth-century America it was changed to *hand over fist* and was transferred to any enterprise in which rapid, easy progress is being made. Thus Seba Smith wrote, "They clawed the money off of his table hand over fist" (*Major Downing,* 1833).

hands are tied, my/one's Not free to act. This metaphor became common after the mid-seventeenth century. An early appearance in print was in clergyman Thomas Fuller's *The Holy State and the Profane State* (1642): "When God intends a Nation shall be beaten, He ties their hands behind them."

hands down Easily, without effort. The term comes from racing, where a jockey may drop his hands and relax his hold on the reins when he is sure to win the race. Dating from the mid-nineteenth century, the term still is used with regard to various kinds of competition, as in, "She won the nomination hands down."

handsome is as handsome does Actions, not appearances, are what count. This proverb was already an "ancient adage" in 1580 (Anthony

Monday, *Sunday Examples*) when it was put as "goodly is he that goodly dooth"; it appeared in modern form in John Ray's proverbs of 1670 and has been repeated over and over by numerous writers.

hand that rocks the cradle, the A mother is a powerful influence, a thought derived from this phrase's completion: "is the hand that rules the world." It comes from a poem by William Ross Wallace, "The Hand that Rules the World" (1865), and has been quoted ever since. A British schoolmistress's change on it makes for a humorous mixed metaphor: "The hand that rocks the cradle kicked the bucket." A more sinister interpretation is given in the 1992 motion picture *The Hand That Rocks the Cradle,* about a demented nanny seeking revenge for the death of her husband.

hand to mouth, exist/live from Living with a minimum of sustenance or support. This term, which dates from about 1500, implies that one has so little to live on that whatever comes to hand is consumed. "I subsist, as the poor are vulgarly said to do, from hand to mouth," wrote the poet William Cowper (1790).

handwriting on the wall See WRITING ON THE WALL.

hang by a thread, to To be in a precarious situation. This expression comes from the story of Damocles, a servile courtier to Dionysius I of Syracuse. Tired of hearing Damocles praise him to the skies, Dionysius invited him to a magnificent banquet. Seated there, Damocles looked up and saw a naked sword suspended over his head by a single hair, whereby the king intended to show his servant the insecurity of his position. By the sixteenth century the story had been converted into a proverb, "It hangs by a hair," listed in Erasmus's *Adagia* (1523), and in the course of time *hair* was changed to *thread.*

hanged for a sheep (as well) as a lamb, (might) as well be One might as well commit a great crime as a small one, since the punishment would be the same; also, do not stop at half-measures, but enjoy something to the fullest. This term comes from the times when both sheep and lamb were considered so valuable that the theft of either was punishable by death. "As good be hanged for an old sheep as a young lamb" appeared in both John Ray's *English Proverbs* (1678) and James Kelly's *Scottish Proverbs* (1721), and has persisted to the present day. See also IN FOR A PENNY, IN FOR A POUND.

hanging fire Delayed; undecided. This term comes from the seventeenth-century flintlock musket. Frequently an attempt to fire it would end with a flash in the lockpan, a depression that held the priming powder, which would fail to explode the main charge. Thus the gun was left hanging fire, that is, slow to fire a charge. See also FLASH IN THE PAN.

hang in the balance A state of doubt or suspense regarding the outcome of something. The balance referred to is the old weighing device in which an object to be weighed is put in one pan and weights of known quantity are added one by one to the other pan, until the two are balanced. The unknown weight here is fate—that is, the outcome. The expression dates at least from the fifteenth century; it appeared in John Lydgate's translation of the *Fall of Princes* (1430) and has been used ever since.

hang in there Keep at it, persevere. An American slang expression dating from the first half of the 1900s, this imperative is believed to have originated in sports, where it is often shouted as an encouragement to a competitor or team. However, it also is used as a simple verb meaning the same thing, as in, "He has managed to hang in even though he does not have tenure."

hang loose Relax, take it easy. This expression dates from the mid-1900s and became very popular during the hippie era of the 1960s. R. S. Parker had it in *Effective Decisions* (1977), "It is a popular philosophy today to 'hang loose, trust your feelings, do what you really want to do.'"

hang out one's shingle, to To open an office, especially a professional practice. This term comes from nineteenth-century America, when lawyers, doctors, and various business concerns often used actual shingles for signboards. Van Wyck Brooks, in *The World of Washington Irving* (1944), wrote, "Catlin hung out his shingle as a portrait-painter."

happy as a clam (at high tide) Delighted with one's lot. An American expression dating from the early nineteenth century, it comes from clamming, which involves digging clams out of the sand at low tide. At high tide it is difficult, if not impossible, to dig for clams. Safety thus is the obvious reason for the mollusk's carefree state of mind.

happy hunting ground Heaven; a place of abundance, replete with what one wants. The idea comes from the beliefs of Native American tribes that after death they will go to a paradise with an abundance of game and therefore always enough to eat. The term appears in the works of James Fenimore Cooper and other writers on Indian subjects. As Cooper wrote in *The Pathfinder* (1840), "'Do the dead of the savages ever walk?' demanded Cap. 'Ay, and run, too, in their happy hunting grounds.'" Later the term became a euphemism for death, and still later it was transferred to any place of abundant treasures.

hard/tough act to follow An outstanding person or performance. The term comes from American vaudeville around the turn of the twentieth century and originally referred to a particularly good act that might make the one following it look mediocre by comparison. In time it was applied to any particularly successful enterprise or admirable individual.

hard and fast Describing a strict rule that cannot be altered under any circumstances. This term originally described a ship that was out of the water, either because it had run aground or because it was in dry dock, and hence could not move. In the mid-nineteenth century the term was transferred to inalterable courses of action or precepts. The *OED* lists an early figurative use in two different speeches given in the House of Commons in 1867: "The House has . . . determined to have no hard and fast line."

hard as nails Unyielding, tough, usually describing a person. This simile, which replaced the earlier *hard as flint* or *stone* (dating from Chaucer's time), seems to allude to a nail's ability to withstand the blows of a hammer. Shaw used it in at least three of his plays (*You Never Can Tell, Heartbreak House, Man and Superman*) to describe an unsentimental character.

hard nut to crack See TOUGH NUT TO CRACK.

hard/tough sledding A difficult route, difficult progress. Dating from the first half of the nineteenth century, this term alludes to the usual ease with which a sled travels toward some goal. The antonyms *easy* or *smooth sledding* date from the late nineteenth century.

hard way See THE HARD WAY.

hatchet man A person who performs nasty tasks for his or her superior, such as firing subordinates, attacking the character of a political opponent, spreading rumors about a competitor, or the like. The term, so used since the 1940s, was applied particularly in politics and journalism, and the work so performed was also called a *hatchet job.* The magazine *Newsweek* had it on July 27, 1968: "He'll be the hatchet man . . . just like Nixon was in 1952." It also is used in other contexts, for example, "This critic did a real hatchet job on her concert." A related term is *character assassination*, dating from about 1950, but it is no longer heard as often.

hat in hand, to go/with To behave submissively or obsequiously; to plead for something (pardon, a favor, and the like). The term alludes to the old custom of removing one's hat as a sign of respect. "A man's hat in his hand never did him any harm," wrote Samuel Palmer (*Moral Essays on*

Proverbs, 1710). The custom of wearing and doffing a hat has become far less common, so the term is dying out, but it is still used in diplomatic circles.

hat in the ring, to put/throw one's To enter a contest; to become a candidate in an election. This expression comes from boxing, where in the early nineteenth century the practice of throwing one's hat into the ring indicated a challenge. "Throw in his hat, and with a spring get gallantly within the ring," wrote John Hamilton Reynolds (*The Fancy,* 1820). Later the term was transferred to other kinds of challenge, particularly political ones. It was so used by Theodore Roosevelt in 1912, when he told a journalist, "My hat's in the ring," indicating his candidacy.

haul/rake over the coals, to To administer a severe reprimand. The term alludes to the medieval practice of pulling an alleged heretic over the coals of a slow fire, which is described in numerous sixteenth-century church chronicles. By the early nineteenth century the term had been transferred to more benign kinds of punishment, often signifying only a severe scolding, as in Byron's poem "Beppo" (1818): "They'd haul o'er the coals."

have a bone to pick, to To have a point to argue, an unpleasant issue to discuss, or a complaint. This term, which alludes both to a dog worrying a bone and to two dogs fighting over a single bone, dates from the early sixteenth century. "I will add this, which may be a bone for you to pick on," wrote James Calfhill (*Answer to Martiall,* 1565)—that is, an issue to worry to death. "There is a bone for the gastronomers to pick," Sir Walter Scott was quoted as saying about 1830, denoting something for more than one person to argue about.

have a conniption fit, to Display hysteria; an extreme emotional upset. This term dates from the early 1800s. Seba Smith had it in *Major T. Downing* (1860), "And Keziah fell down in a conniption fit." The phrase has a rustic sound and is heard less often today.

have a good/half a mind to, to To be strongly inclined toward; to be somewhat inclined toward. The first term began life back in the fifteenth century as having a *great* mind to do something, as in "I have a great mynd to be a lecherous man" (John Bale, *Kyng Johan,* c. 1550). In 1674 Lord Clarendon wrote in *History of the Rebellion,* "The duke of Lorrayne had a very good mind to get a footing in Ireland." The second phrase, which implies indecision—half of one's mind inclines one way and the other half the other way—was known by 1700 or so and appeared more and more often in the nineteenth century. "She had half a mind to reply," wrote Edward Bulwer-Lytton (*My Novel,* 1853).

have a nice day A cordial good-bye to you. This intrusive imperative became extremely common after 1950 among U.S. truckers who used it on their citizens-band radios. In Britain it often is put as *have a fine day* or *have a good day.* The latter, which may have its origin in the Middle English *have good day* (c. 1200) and was frequently used by Chaucer, apparently died out for some centuries and then was revived. It is often heard in America and occasionally is altered to *have a good one.* Since the late 1960s these phrases have become ubiquitous. They often are used ironically, either knowingly or unconsciously. Following a precipitous drop in the New York Stock Market in October 1987, the telephone clerks employed by Pacific Brokerage continued to report to the company's clients, as they always had, "This is Pacific Brokerage Calling. You just sold 30,000 shares of Widget Manufacturing at $1. Have a nice day." Conceivably this message might have driven the investor who bought Widget at 32 straight out of the nearest window. Or take the insurance agent who said, "I'm sorry to hear about your husband's death. Have a nice day." By about 2000, however, *have a nice/good day* had largely become a synonym of "good-bye," and was taken no more literally than the "God be with you" that was the original source of that word. A related term increasingly heard in restaurants is *Have a nice meal,* which similarly induces teeth-gnashing irritation when voiced by a particularly incompetent waiter.

have another guess coming, to To be wrong or mistaken. This phrase also implies that though one is wrong, one has a chance to reconsider and correct one's error. It dates from the first half of the 1900s. C. Day Lewis used it in *Child of Misfortune* (1939): "If you think that's your doing, you've got another guess coming."

have at one's fingertips See AT ONE'S FINGERTIPS.

have it in for, to To hold a grudge against. The *it* in this expression presumably means bad things in store. The term became especially common in popular novels of the first half of the twentieth century. "I have had it in for that dog since the second Sunday," wrote P. G. Wodehouse (*Meet Mr. Mulliner,* 1927).

have one's cake and eat it too See EAT ONE'S CAKE.

have one's ear to the ground See EAR TO THE GROUND.

have one's hands full, to To be completely occupied or very busy, to have more than enough to do. This expression dates from the fifteenth century or earlier. It appears in Thomas Malory's *Morte d'Arthur:* "Ye shalle have bothe your handes ful of me." See also PLATE, TO HAVE A LOT/ENOUGH ON ONE'S.

have one's say See under SPEAK ONE'S MIND.

have one's wits about one, to To be wide awake and alert. *Wits* in the plural has long meant keen mental faculties. Ben Jonson so used it in *The Alchemist* (1612): "They live by their wits." About the same time, the expression of having one's wits about one—in effect, ready to serve one—came into use. It appeared in James Mabbe's 1622 translation of *Guzman de Alfarache* ("I had my wits about me") and has been used ever since. To *live by one's wits,* on the other hand, also implies managing by means of clever expediency rather than honest work.

have one's work cut out (for one) See WORK CUT OUT FOR ONE.

have other fish to fry See FISH TO FRY.

head and shoulders above, to be To be considerably superior. This expression, which likens superiority to physical stature (a tall person's head and shoulders obviously are higher than a short person's), appeared in the 1864 edition of Noah Webster's *American Dictionary.* However, it was used in a different sense earlier, that is, the forceful pushing ahead of something or someone. "Any, whom necessity thrusts out by head and shoulders," wrote Nathaniel Ward (*The Simple Cobbler of Agawam in America,* 1647).

head in the clouds, to have one's Daydreaming, absentminded. *In the clouds* has been used figuratively to mean obscure or fanciful since the mid-seventeenth century. It was not until relatively recent times that a vague, dreamy person was said to have his or her head in the clouds. See also ON CLOUD NINE.

head over heels (in love), to be/fall So completely that one is upside down. This expression began life as *heels over head,* a far more logical description of being turned upside down, and appeared in print in a collection of *Early English Alliterative Poems* dating from c. 1350. Four hundred years later an unknown poet turned the saying around: "He gave [him] such an involuntary kick in the face as drove him head over heels" (*The Contemplative Man,* 1771). This corruption stuck, but the principal sense in which the term is now used dates only from the nineteenth century. An early appearance in print is in David Crockett's *Narrative of the Life of David Crockett* (1834): "I soon found myself head over heels in love with this girl."

hear a pin drop, one/you could Complete silence. This hyperbole dates from the early nineteenth century. An early appearance in print is in

Susan Ferrier's *The Inheritance* (1824): "You might have heard a pin drop in the house while that was going on." Although pins are a far less common household item than they once were, the expression survives.

heart in one's mouth, to have one's To be frightened or extremely apprehensive. This term has nothing to do with EAT ONE'S HEART OUT but rather alludes to the heart-pounding and choking feeling of sudden fear. It was already used by Homer in the *Iliad* (c. 850 B.C.), "My heart leaps to my mouth," and appeared in English in Nicholas Udall's translation of Erasmus (1548): "Hauyng their herte at their verai mouth for feare." Mark Twain put it more colorfully: "My heart flew into my mouth so suddenly that if I hadn't clapped my teeth together I should have lost it" (*Life on the Mississippi,* 1874).

heart in the right place, to have one's To mean well; to have good intentions. This term dates only from about 1800 but quickly gained currency. Among the many writers who used it were Benjamin Disraeli (in his novel *Infernal Marriage,* 1834) and Helen MacInnes (in her thriller *Above Suspicion,* 1941).

heart of gold, (to have) a A singularly kind person. This term dates from the sixteenth century and was already well known by the time Shakespeare wrote *Henry V* (1599), in which Pistol describes his master: "The king's a bawcock, and a heart of gold" (4.1). (A *bawcock,* in Elizabethan jargon, was a fine fellow; the term comes from the French *beau coq,* "fine bird.")

heart of stone, to have a To be an unfeeling, pitiless person. This term dates from the time of Homer: "Thy heart is even harder than stone" appears in his *Odyssey* (c. 850 B.C.). Several centuries later it turns up in the Bible, in the Book of Job (41:24): "His heart is as firm as a stone; yea, as hard as a piece of the nether millstone."

heart's content, to one's To one's complete satisfaction. Shakespeare was particularly fond of this expression, using it in several plays (*Henry VI, Part 2*; *The Merchant of Venice*).

heart-to-heart talk, a A confidential, intimate conversation. This expression, which implies that two persons are opening their hearts to each other, in fact often refers to a conversation in which one is warning or reproaching the other. The term dates from about 1900 and was sometimes abbreviated, as in S. E. White's *Rules of the Game* (1910): "Let's have a heart-to-heart, and find out how we stand."

heavens to Betsy An expression of astonishment. This version of FOR HEAVEN'S SAKE, which Charles E. Funk liked well enough to use as the title of one of his books, comes from nineteenth-century America and first appeared in print in 1892. It may be dying out.

heavy heart, a Unhappiness. This expression comes from the Bible. The Book of Proverbs (12:25) states, "Heaviness in the heart of man maketh it stoop." It remains current.

heavy hitter A person who gets results. This American colloquialism probably alludes to baseball's best hitter, the player who gets a home run when the bases are loaded. *Heavy* has been used for "important" and "influential" since the mid-1800s. Its pairing with *hitter* and transfer to business and politics occurred about a century later. For example, "The heaviest hitters in the magazine industry are reputedly losing their collective grip (*Publishers Weekly,* Aug. 10, 1990).

heels of, at/on the Close behind; closely following. Although these two clichés are very similar, they are not wholly interchangeable. To be *at* someone's heels is to be immediately behind, with the implication of chasing or otherwise harrying the person. To be *on* the heels of someone (or something) means to be following in quick succession (but not necessarily catching or overtaking). Both terms conjure up the idea of a dog being at one's heels, and both are quite old. John Gower wrote in 1390, "There bene also somme as men sale that folwen Simon ate heles." And Shakespeare wrote, "One woe doth tread upon another's heel, so fast they follow" (*Hamlet,* 4.7).

hell freezes over See TILL HELL FREEZES OVER.

hell has no fury like a woman scorned Beware the anger of a woman rejected in love. The term is an adaptation of the closing lines from William Congreve's play *The Mourning Bride* (1697): "Heav'n has no rage, like love to hatred turn'd, nor Hell a fury like a woman scorn'd." Neither the idea nor the expression was original. At least three seventeenth-century plays had similar lines, including Colley Cibber's "No fiend in hell can match the fury of a disappointed woman—scorned, slighted" (*Love's Last Shift,* 1696), and the idea had been expressed by the Roman writers Propertius and Juvenal, by Chaucer, and by numerous others.

hell is paved with good intentions, the road/way to Meaning well is not the same as doing well and may even make matters worse. Allegedly this phrase was first uttered by St. Bernard of Clairvaux (c. 1150) but was not attributed to him until early in the seventeenth century. By 1678 it was part of John Ray's proverb collection, as "Hell is full of good meanings and wishes, but heaven is full of good works." Dickens was one of the many writers who have referred to it; in *Our Mutual Friend* (1865) he wrote, "You recollect what pavement is said to be made of good intentions. It is made of bad intentions, too."

hello? Did you hear me? Do you really mean that? This slangy term is not the conventional greeting, but pronounced with strong stress on the second syllable (hel-LO?), it acquired this new meaning in the late 1900s. For example, "You mean you've never heard of America Online? Hello?" It is on its way to clichédom.

hell on wheels Tough, wild, mean. This expression dates from the mid-1800s, especially during the 1860s construction of the Union Pacific Railroad. As the track was extended into virtual wilderness, freight cars moving forward as track was laid transported a town. It consisted of tents occupied by the construction workers, liquor dealers, gamblers, prostitutes, and other camp followers of a rough and unsavory nature. Hence the town was called "hell on wheels." Later the term was adapted for any individual or organization considered very aggressive, as in "On Monday mornings my boss is hell on wheels." It also has been used admiringly, as in "Don't underestimate her; she's hell on wheels for getting things done."

hell or high water See COME HELL OR HIGH WATER.

hell's bells An interjection or mild expletive expressing surprise or annoyance. Dating from the first half of the nineteenth century, this expression undoubtedly owes its longevity to its rhyme. John Dos Passos used it in *Manhattan Transfer* (1925), "But hell's bells, what's the use when this goddam war takes the whole front page?"

hell to pay, there'll be The consequences will be terrible; there'll be a heavy penalty. Originating about 1800, this term once meant discord or severe trouble. The *OED* quotes a letter by Lord Paget (1807): "There has been hell to pay between the Dukes of York and Cumberland."

hem and haw, to To avoid giving a definite answer. This expression is imitative of the sounds made in clearing the throat or making a slight noise to attract attention, signify agreement, or express doubt. Its use to express indecision began in the early eighteenth century. Jonathan Swift's poem "My Lady's Lamentation" (1728) had one version: "He haws and he hums. At last out it comes." Much later Bliss Carman defined it poetically: "Hem and Haw were the sons of sin, created to shally and shirk; Hem lay 'round and Haw looked on while God did all the work" ("Hem and Haw," 1896).

here, there, and everywhere All over the place. This expression began in the thirteenth century as *here and there,* which we still use to describe something that is present but in no specific location. Christopher Marlowe appears to have been the first to use the longer form, in *Doctor Faustus* (c. 1588): "If you turne me into any thing, let it be in the likelinesse of a little pretie frisking flea, that I may be here and there and euery where." See also HITHER AND THITHER.

here today and gone tomorrow Describing an ephemeral phenomenon, a passing fancy, a fad. Originally this expression referred to the relatively brief span of a human life. It was recorded by numerous writers and was included in James Kelly's *Scottish Proverbs* of 1721. By the nineteenth century it had become a less serious thought. T. C. Haliburton (Sam Slick) included it in *Wise Saws* (1843): "I am a bird of passage—here today and gone tomorrow."

hide nor hair See NEITHER HIDE NOR HAIR.

hide one's head in the sand See BURY ONE'S HEAD IN THE SAND.

hide one's light under a bushel, to To conceal one's talents; to be extremely modest. The term comes from the Bible (Matthew 5:15): "Neither do men light a candle, and put it under a bushel, but on a candlestick." The bushel in question was not presumably the unit of weight so called but the container that would hold it—in other words, a bushel basket. Although modesty is generally considered a desirable trait, those who have used this expression over the centuries do not necessarily extol or even recommend it.

high and dry Stranded. Originally this expression alluded quite literally to a ship that had run aground or was in dry dock. By the late nineteenth century it had begun to be used figuratively. See also OUT ON A LIMB. John Galsworthy still was referring to the nautical source in *Castles in Spain* (1927): "A true work of art remains beautiful and living, though an ebb tide of fashion may leave it for the moment high and dry."

high and mighty Arrogant, conceited. Although originally used to describe either spiritual or temporal rulers, this term soon came to mean individuals who used their position of real or imagined power to act haughtily. Thus, while fifteenth- and sixteenth-century sources might address a ruler as "Right heigh and mighty Prince" (as in Hall's *Chronicle of Edward IV,* 1548), a century later Richard Whitlock (*Zoötamia,* 1654) would write of "their high and mighty word, Experience." It was a cliché by the time

Thackeray wrote, "Some of these bankers are as high and mighty as the oldest families" (*The Newcomes,* 1855).

high dudgeon See IN HIGH DUDGEON.

high horse See ON ONE'S HIGH HORSE.

high off the hog, to eat/live To live well; to prosper. This term comes from the practice of the choicest cuts for ham and bacon being taken from high up on the pig's side. It originated in the American South in the nineteenth century and became extremely common in the mid-twentieth century. It is sometimes put as eating *high on the hog.*

high society Prominent in fashionable society, implying wealth and position. The term dates from the first half of the 1900s and was used as the title of a popular film of 1956, starring Grace Kelly (in her last acting role), Bing Crosby, Frank Sinatra, Louis Armstrong, and others, and featuring some songs by Cole Porter. See also UPPER CRUST.

high-water mark The acme of achievement. The term alludes to the mark left when a body of water reaches its highest level, as in a flood. By the early nineteenth century it had been transferred to the peak of other events or accomplishments, as in Ralph Waldo Emerson's statement in 1856, about William Wordsworth: "'The Ode on Immortality' is the high-water mark which the intellect has reached in this age."

highway robbery So expensive that it is considered extortion. This expression simply transfers the literal meaning—armed robbery of travelers on an open road—to the more or less legitimate charging of exorbitant prices. As J. B. Priestley put it in *It's An Old Country* (1967), "Nothing on the wine list under two-pound-ten. Highway robbery by candlelight."

hill of beans, doesn't amount to a/not worth a Trivial, worthless. Beans apparently have been considered of little value since the thirteenth century. Chaucer, in *Troilus and Criseyde* (c. 1380), wrote, "Swich [such] arguments ne been nat worth a bene." The *hill* part of the expression refers to a common method of planting beans. Instead of arranging the seeds in a row, they can be planted in small clumps of four or five seeds in a little mound or hill of soil. This practice is followed principally in American home gardens (rather than by commercial growers), and indeed the expression "hill of beans" originated in America in the nineteenth century.

hit below the belt See BELOW THE BELT.

hitch one's wagon to a star, to To aim high. This metaphor was coined by Ralph Waldo Emerson, who in 1870 wrote, "Hitch your wagon to a star. Let us not fag in paltry works which serve our pot and bag alone" (*Society and Solitude: Civilization*). Ogden Nash played on this cliché in his poem "Kindly Unhitch That Star" (1940).

hither and thither/yon Here and there; from here to there. The terms, which today have a somewhat archaic or poetic ring, include words that are rarely used outside these expressions: *hither,* for here; *thither,* for there; and *yon,* for yonder. Edward Fitzgerald's translation of Omar Khayyam describes destiny (fate) playing a game of chess with human beings: "Hither and thither moves, and mates, and slays" (1859). W. Somerset Maugham used the second expression with a similar meaning: "The wan characters of Chekhov's stories drifted hither and yon at the breath of circumstances." (*Christmas Holiday,* 1939).

hit it off, to To get along well (with someone). *To hit* has long meant, in a secondary sense, to succeed, probably from a sport or game. Shakespeare used it in this way in numerous plays; for example, "Have all his ventures fail'd? What, not one hit?" appears in *The Merchant of Venice* (3.2). To "hit it off" seems to be an elaboration of the same meaning, and dates back to the eighteenth century. "How do you and the great Mrs. Montague hit it off," wrote diarist Madame d'Arblay in 1780.

hit or miss Haphazard, at random. This term almost certainly comes from shooting or throwing at some kind of target and was transferred very early on to making an attempt of any kind, knowing that one might succeed or fail. It has been so used since the sixteenth century. "But hit or miss, our project's life this shape of sense assumes," wrote Shakespeare (*Troilus and Cressida*). It later appeared in several collections of proverbs.

hit the ceiling, to To lose one's temper. The image of rising with fury seems quite natural. This expression comes from early twentieth-century America and soon crossed the Atlantic. P. G. Wodehouse used it in *Very Good, Jeeves!* (1930): "I haven't breathed a word to Angela. She'd hit the ceiling." It echoes a locution dating from the sixteenth century, to be *up in the house roof* (or *at the house-top*), meaning to be enraged. See also RAISE THE ROOF.

hit the ground running, to To seize an opportunity at the earliest possible moment. This expression, which is undoubtedly American and became a cliché in the late 1970s, is of disputed origin. According to *New York Times* columnist William Safire, some believe it originated in one of several arenas of World War II—as an instruction given to paratroopers (as to what to do when they land), or to soldiers dropped into a combat zone by helicopter, or to naval personnel landing on a beach. Another authority maintains that it comes from hoboes or other stowaways jumping off a freight train as it nears a station in order to escape capture. Still another theory traces the term to horseback riders, first in the Pony Express, when they "hit the ground running" so as to avoid delays when changing mounts, and later in rodeos, when they got up and away quickly after being thrown from a horse that might try to stomp them on the ground.

hit the hay/sack, to Go to bed, go to sleep. The first expression dates from about 1900 and presumably alludes to a hayloft as a soft bed. A sports book of 1905 held it to be baseball players' slang. The second term dates from World War II, although *sack* for "bed" originated in the U.S. Navy in the 1820s.

hit the high spots, to To do something superficially. Presumably this expression comes from sloppy cleaning or polishing, that is, attending to the raised surfaces and ignoring the rest. Used since about 1900, it is applied to any kind of haphazard performance.

hit the jackpot, to To win; to achieve a sensational success. The term comes from a form of draw poker in which a hand can be opened only if the declarer holds a pair of jacks (or higher cards). Since several rounds may be dealt before someone holds a hand good enough to open and the players must ante up (put in money) for each round, the pot, or total amount being held, called the *jackpot,* is likely to be larger than usual. Hence winning it constitutes a sizable gain, and the term, which originated in nineteenth-century America, soon was transferred to similar big winnings or successes.

hit the nail on the head, to To say or do exactly the right thing. This analogy dates from the early sixteenth century and has counterparts in numerous languages. It was a cliché by the time Henry David Thoreau used it in *A Week on the Concord and Merrimack Rivers* (1849): "He will hit the nail on the head, and we shall not know the shape of the hammer."

hit the spot, to To please or satisfy extremely well. This slangy Americanism dates from the mid-nineteenth century. It was widely popularized through a commercial jingle heard on the radio through the 1930s and 1940s: "Pepsi-Cola hits the spot, twelve full ounces, that's a lot." It remains current.

Hobson's choice A choice that represents no choice at all; an enforced decision. The term supposedly originated with the practice of a Cambridge,

England, carrier named Thomas Hobson (1544–1631), who insisted that his customers take whichever horse was nearest the stable door. If they refused that horse, he would give them no other. Whether this origin is true or not, the term was adopted and appeared in print in several mid-seventeenth-century sources. It is heard less often today.

hog wild See GO HOG WILD.

hoi polloi, the The masses. This term, which was Greek for the common people or the crowd, was used by John Dryden in his *Essay of Dramatick Poesie* (1668). "If by the people," he wrote, "you understand the multitude, the hoi polloi, 'tis no matter what they think; . . . their judgment is a mere lottery."

hoist with one's own petard Caught in one's own trap, defeated by one's own weapons. The term alludes to an ancient weapon, a thick iron canister filled with gunpowder, which was fastened to a gate or other barrier in order to breach it. It was a dangerous weapon, because the engineer who set it off could easily be blown up ("hoist") when it detonated. Shakespeare was among the first to transfer the term, in *Hamlet* (3.4): "Let it work; for 'tis the sport to have the enginer hoist with his own petar."

hold a candle to, cannot/not fit to To be vastly inferior to someone. Holding a candle for someone else was already considered a menial task in the sixteenth century. "Who that worst maie, shall holde the candell" appeared in John Heywood's 1546 collection of proverbs, and "I be not worthy to hold a candle to Aristotle," wrote Sir Edward Dering (1640). A rhyming example appears in John Byrom's poetic account, *On the Feud between Handel and Bononcini* (1773): "Others aver that he to Handel is scarcely fit to hold the candle."

hold at bay, to To keep some adverse situation from worsening; to hold off an enemy. The term comes from the Old French *tenir a bay,* which meant to hold open or in suspense, and referred to a hunted animal being cornered by its pursuers. The term was used literally by the fourteenth century, and figuratively soon thereafter. It is also phrased as *to keep at bay.*

hold no brief for, to To refuse to endorse, support, or defend. The term comes from law, where to hold a brief for someone means to act as counsel for that person and to argue in his or her favor. The negative form of the expression became extremely common in the nineteenth century. The *OED* cites R. A. Knox writing in *Spiritual Aeneid* (1918): "When I was at Balliol we used to adopt the phrase 'I hold no brief for so-and-so.'"

hold one's own, to To stand one's ground successfully against attack, competition, or some other pressure. The *own* here refers to position or advantage. In use since the sixteenth century, the expression was a cliché by the nineteenth century. It appears in a famous speech by Winston Churchill in 1942, during World War II: "Let me, however, make this clear. . . . We mean to hold our own. I have not become the King's First Minister in order to preside over the liquidation of the British Empire." An alternate synonym is *to hold one's ground.* James Patterson used it in his thriller, *London Bridges* (2004), in a response to a bomb thrown at a building: "A decision had been made not to abandon the building, to hold our ground."

hold one's tongue, to To refrain from speaking or replying. The term appears in Miles Coverdale's translation of the Gospel of Matthew (26:63), "Jesus helde his tonge," but had been used earlier by Chaucer ("Thee is bettre holde thy tonge stille, than for to speke," *Tale of Melibeus,* c. 1387). It later appeared in John Ray's 1670 collection of proverbs, and remains current.

hold(ing) the bag, to/be left Abandoned by others, left in the lurch to carry the responsibility or blame. The implication in this expression, used since the eighteenth century, is that one is left holding an empty bag while others have made off with the presumably valuable contents. The phrase has often been used in international relations—for example, by Thomas Jefferson ("She will leave Spain the bag to hold," *Writings,* 1793), and on the eve of America's entrance into World War II, by Clare Boothe (Luce) in *Europe in the Spring* (1940): "When bigger and better bags are made, America will hold them."

hold the fort, to To keep things going until further support arrives. The expression comes, as might be suspected, from a literal military order. It has been traced to one given by Gen. William Tecumseh Sherman in 1864, during the American Civil War, to Gen. John M. Corse at Allatoona. Corse was told to give up so as to avoid unnecessary bloodshed, but he refused, saying he had received an order from Sherman saying, "Hold the fort at all costs, for I am coming." Records show that the actual words had been, "Hold out, relief is coming," but *fort* is what caught on and was further popularized when it was made the refrain of a gospel song by Philip Paul Bliss.

hold water, to To bear close inspection; to be valid. This expression, used since about 1600, refers to the soundness of a container that holds water without leaking. "Let them produce a more rational account . . . that will hold water," wrote John French (*The Yorkshire Spaw,* 1626).

hold your horses Be patient. Originally this nineteenth-century Americanism directly instructed the driver to hold his team of horses, and later it became a colloquial imperative to slow down and wait.

holier than thou Sanctimonious, pretending moral superiority. This term comes from the Bible (Isaiah 65:5), where the prophet, speaking of sinners, holds that they say "Come not near me, for I am holier than thou." The term is often used as an adjective (and hyphenated: holier-than-thou) as in Sinclair Lewis's novel *Babbitt* (1922), "But I don't want you to think you can get away with any of that holier-than-thou stuff."

home away from home, a A comfortable place or dwelling where one feels quite at home. At first put as a *home from home,* this expression dates from the second half of the 1800s. In the 1920s it took its present form. The *OED* cites a lyric from Henry Kirk's *The Transport Workers Songbook* of c. 1926: "It's like a home away from home." Since then the expression has become standard usage in advertisements for hotels and other lodgings, vacation spots, and the like.

home free, to be To succeed without difficulty or obstacles, as in, "With this new spreadsheet, my tax problems are over—I'm home free." The expression comes from children's games such as "Kick the Can," where a player must reach "home" (such as a particular tree) without being tagged ("caught") by another.

home is where the heart is One's true home is where one's affections are centered. This particular expression was listed in Elbert Hubbard's *A Thousand and One Epigrams* (1914) but had been known for centuries before that. According to Burton Stevenson, several authorities attribute it to the Roman writer Pliny. See also HOME, SWEET HOME.

home, sweet home A sentimental or ironic view of home as a wonderful place. The term was the title of a song composed by Henry R. Bishop, with words by the American lyricist John Howard Payne, used in the opera *Clari, or The Maid of Milan* (1823). The song became virtually a sacred text for middle-class Victorians and achieved a fame far beyond that of the opera or its composer. The great soprano Adelina Patti used it as an audition piece, and the equally great Jenny Lind sang it in all her concerts all over the world from 1850 on. Its most famous performer, however, was the Australian soprano Dame Nellie Melba, and audiences around the world would chant "Home! Sweet Home!" to bring her back for another encore.

honest to goodness/God/Pete Truly; I swear this is true. These assertions of veracity date from about 1900. The earliest seems to have been *honest to God,* which appeared in Jack London's *Valley of the Moon* (1913). *Goodness* and *Pete* are probably euphemisms for "God," which some might have considered blasphemous. Another equivalent, now considered offensive, is *honest Injun* (or *Indian*), dating from the second half of the 1800s and popularized by Mark Twain in *The Adventures of Huckleberry Finn* and *The Adventures of Tom Sawyer.*

hook, line, and sinker Completely, totally, all of it. The expression is often phrased as to *swallow* [something] *hook, line, and sinker,* alluding to the gullibility of a fish that takes in bait so completely that it swallows the fishing hook, line, and sinker as well. The term originated in the United States in the mid-nineteenth century. In the late 1980s Len Deighton used it in the titles of a series of three espionage novels involving complicated deceit, *Spy Hook, Spy Line,* and *Spy Sinker.* See also LOCK, STOCK, AND BARREL.

hope against hope, to To keep wishing for something even though the odds are against its coming about. This term can be found in the Bible, in Paul's Epistle to the Romans (4:18): "Who against hope believed in hope, that he [Abraham] might become the father of many nations." It has been a cliché since the late nineteenth century. See also HOPE SPRINGS ETERNAL.

hope springs eternal It is human nature to keep on hoping against all odds. This particular expression was coined by the poet Alexander Pope in *An Essay on Man* (1732), "Hope springs eternal in the human breast," and very quickly became proverbial. It was quoted by Robert Burns and Charles Dickens, among many others, usually without benefit of quotation marks.

hopping mad Extremely angry. The term implies that one is enough enraged to jump up and down or to hop about; it originated in the early nineteenth century in the United States. One of Seba Smith's humorous political letters stated, "I had a long talk with the General . . . he was hopping mad" (*The Life and Writings of Major Jack Downing,* 1833).

horns of a dilemma, on the Faced with two equally undesirable alternatives. In Greek logic a *lemma* was a premise, a matter taken for granted in an argument, whereas a *dilemma* (a double lemma) was an either/or proposition. The Romans called this an *argumentum cornutum,* or "horned argument," because one could be caught on either horn. In the sixteenth century Nicholas Udall, translator of Erasmus, turned it into a horned question: "Because that to whether of both partyes a bodye shall make a direct aunswere, he shall renne on the sharpe poyncte of a horne." Soon thereafter it began to be called "the horns of a dilemma."

horse of another/different color, a A different affair altogether. This term was more or less invented by Shakespeare, who in *Twelfth Night* (2.3) wrote, "My purpose is, indeed, a horse of that colour," meaning, my aim is indeed something like that. Eventually this was changed to difference rather than likeness, as in Anthony Trollope's *Last Chronicles of Barset* (1867): "What did you think of his wife? That's a horse of another colour altogether."

horse sense Good common sense. The origin of this Americanism is a matter of dispute, since there is considerable disagreement concerning the native intelligence of horses. Some think they are rather stupid animals, although it is generally conceded that they have enough sense to return to their barn whenever they have a chance. Others believe the shrewdness denoted by *horse sense* is possessed principally by horse traders, who are well known for that quality. In any event, the term originated in the first half of the nineteenth century in the American West and was still considered relatively new in 1870, when it was defined in an issue of *The Nation,* although it had appeared in print a number of times from 1833 on. Comedian W. C. Fields supposedly said, "Horse sense is a good judgment that keeps horses from betting on people."

hot air Empty boasting, pretentious talk; also, verbal nonsense. The term presumably refers to exhaling while pontificating. Mark Twain used it in *The Gilded Age* (1873): "The most airy schemes inflated the hot air of the Capital," and indeed the term is often used with reference to politicians.

hot cakes See SELL LIKE HOT CAKES.

hot to trot Ready for action, especially for sexual activity. This somewhat vulgar slangy phrase dates from the mid-1900s. Bill Pronzini used it in a conversation between two characters about to attack a homosexual, "'You ready?' Bix giggled the way he always did . . . 'Hot to trot'" (*Nightcrawlers,* 2005). With the sexual innuendo, it appeared in a 2002 article about a sexy award-winner: "Not only is she hot to trot on a night out, she's spot on when it comes to the 'less is more' rule."

hot under the collar, to be To be upset, agitated, angry. The heat of anger has been noted since ancient times, and it often manifests itself in a flushed, warm face and neck. The precise expression here has been used since the late nineteenth century, when still high collars were in fashion for men. It was well known enough by 1907 for O. Henry to play on it: "That makes Alice warm under the lace yoke" (*The Sphinx Apple*).

house of cards A weak, insubstantial construction, plan, or organization. Building "houses" by balancing upright playing cards against one another surely dates from the earliest days of paper or cardboard playing cards, which in Europe was the late Middle Ages (earlier in China). Likening a precarious structure to a "house of cards" presumably began soon afterward. An elegant use of the metaphor came in John Milton's *Of*

Reformation Touching Church Discipline (1641): "Painted Battlements of Prelatry, which want but one puff of the King's to blow them down like a pastboard House built of Court-Cards."

how time flies See TIME FLIES.

hue and cry A public uproar or protest. This term once denoted an English system of apprehending robbers and other criminals. Neighbors and bystanders were obliged to join a "hue and cry," that is, shout and make other noise while a suspect was chased to the bounds of a manor (*hue* comes from the Old French *huer,* "to shout"). Later the term was transferred to any public outcry. John Ruskin used it ironically in *Mode Painting* (1846): "The public took up the hue and cry conscientiously enough," meaning they supported the fashionable view.

hurry up and wait Rush to an appointment or make haste in response to an order and then be required to wait for a long time. This expression became current in the armed forces during World War II and quickly moved into civilian life. Greg Rucka described it graphically in *A Gentleman's Game* (2004): "It's hurry up and wait, you knew that was the job when you signed up. Months of sitting . . . punctuated by bouts of . . . panic."

i

I can't complain See CAN'T COMPLAIN.

I could/couldn't care less See COULDN'T CARE LESS.

I don't think so I don't agree with what was just stated, either by myself or by someone else. Generally pronounced with a marked emphasis on *think,* this twentieth-century expression started out as *I don't think,* with the emphasis on *don't,* in the nineteenth century. Dickens had it in *Pickwick Papers* (1837): "'Amiably disposed . . . , 'I don't think,' resumed Mr. Weller, in a tone of moral reproof." A slangy one-word synonym used in the same way is *not,* which became very popular from the late 1980s on. It actually originated a century or so earlier; J. E. Lighter cites the *Princeton Tiger* of March 30, 1893: "An Historical Parallel—Not." It reappeared on the television show *Saturday Night Live* and in the film *Wayne's World* (1992), but may again be dying out.

if it ain't broke don't fix it See LEAVE WELL ENOUGH ALONE.

if looks could kill See LOOK DAGGERS.

if not now, when? An explanation, sometimes a bit rueful, of the reason a person is embarking on a particular enterprise, a trip, or some other, perhaps surprising undertaking. It often refers to the fact that the person feels the approach of old age and attendant infirmities, and wants to accomplish something while it is still possible. For example, "When I asked Joe just why he was booking a trekking trip to Nepal, he said, 'I'm turning 65 next year. If not now, when.'" But the expression also may simply refer to the fact that an excellent opportunity has presented itself, one to take advantage of, as in "That jeweler's going out of business and I'm buying myself a diamond ring—if not now, when?"

if push comes to shove See PUSH COMES TO SHOVE.

ifs, ands, or buts Reservations or restrictions; excuses. This expression actually mingles two older ones, *ifs and ands* with *but me no buts.* The first, dating from the sixteenth century, was more or less the equivalent of wishful thinking, and its most famous version is Charles Kingsley's rhyme of

1850: "If ifs and ans were pots and pans, there'd be no trade for tinkers." Almost as old is "but me no buts," meaning make no objections or excuses, which according to Eric Partridge was popularized by Sir Walter Scott's use of it in *The Antiquary* (1816). The current cliché is most often used as a negative imperative, as in, "I want this done by tomorrow, and no ifs, ands, or buts."

if the mountain will not come to Mohammed . . . When you can't get your own way, bow to the inevitable. The complete expression is, "If the mountain will not come to Mohammed, Mohammed must go to the mountain." This expression, with the spelling Mahomet (a slightly different transliteration from Arabic), is based on the story that Mohammed once asked for miraculous proof of his teachings and ordered Mount Safa to come to him. When the mountain did not move, he said, "God is merciful. Had it obeyed my words it would have fallen on us to our destruction." Sir Francis Bacon retold the story, saying, "If the Hil will not come to Mahomet, Mahomet will go to the Hil" (in *Of Boldnesse,* 1597). It was repeated in John Ray's *English Proverbs* (1678) and numerous sources thereafter, including Shaw's play, *The Doctor's Dilemma* (1906).

if the shoe fits, wear it If something applies to you, accept it. This expression is a version of an older term, *if the cap fits, put it on,* which originally meant a fool's cap and dates from the early eighteenth century. This version is rarely heard today. Its replacement by a shoe probably came about owing to the increased popularity of the Cinderella story, and indeed, an early appearance in print, in Clyde Fitch's play *The Climbers* (1901), states, "If the slipper fits."

if truth be told To be perfectly honest, to present all the facts of a case. James Patterson used it in his novel, *Roses Are Red* (2000): "I am a little scared, truth be told." See also FACT OF THE MATTER; TRUTH TO TELL.

if worst comes to worst If the most unfavorable or injurious circumstances should occur. This term would make more sense as *if worse comes to worst* (comparative to superlative), but it has been used in its present form since the late sixteenth century. It generally is followed by some expedient solution, as in "If worst comes to worst he'll declare bankruptcy." The Restoration dramatists had fun with it. John Dryden said (*Sir Martin Mar-All,* 1667), "If worst comes to the worst, he leaves you an honest woman," and William Congreve (*The Way of the World,* 1700) wrote, "If the worst comes to the worst, I'll turn my wife to grass."

ignorance is bliss It sometimes is better not to know one's fate, or the outcome. Although the idea was stated by the Greek playwright Sophocles (c. 409 B.C.) and quoted by Erasmus in the early sixteenth century, the precise wording of the cliché comes from the closing lines of Thomas Gray's poem, "Ode on a Distant Prospect of Eton College" (1742): "Where ignorance is bliss, 'tis folly to be wise." Both it and *blissful ignorance* became clichés in the nineteenth century, but the latter has died out.

ill wind that blows no one any good, it's/'tis an Someone or other usually benefits from a misfortune or loss. This expression appeared in John Heywood's 1546 proverb collection and several of Shakespeare's plays. Today it remains current, often shortened simply to an *ill wind.* Laurence McKinney punned on it in *People of Note* (1940), saying of the notoriously difficult oboe, "It's an ill wood wind [sic] no one blows good."

I'm from Missouri, you've got to show me I won't believe it without proof. This expression, signifying shrewd native skepticism rather than provincial stupidity, has been traced to a number of sources. The oldest source of the thought suggested to date is the Missouri Compromise of 1820, a proviso that the constitution of the then new state would not prohibit slavery, which was reached after several years of dickering. As for the wording, one writer cites a speech made by Congressman Willard D. Vandiver in 1899; another refers to a song from the same period, "I'm from Missouri and You've Got to Show Me," with lyrics by Lee Raney and music by Ned Wayburn. Thomas Oliphant, describing Senator Edward Kennedy's doubts about a Supreme Court nominee, wrote, "Kennedy has become the leading Show Me Senator" (*Boston Globe,* Sept. 29, 2005).

in a dither, all In a jittery, agitated state. This expression dates from the early 1800s, when it also was put as *of a dither.* The noun *dither* comes from the Middle English verb *didderen,* meaning "to tremble." A newer synonym is *in a tizzy,* dating from the first half of the 1900s. Its origin is not known.

in a heartbeat Extremely quickly. This hyperbolic expression—what could actually happen in the space of a single heartbeat?—dates from the late 1800s.

in a huff Angry. The verb *to huff* in the late 1500s meant to bluster, or blow out puffs of breath in anger. It thus appeared in the nursery tale of *The Three Little Pigs,* in which the wolf threatened, "I'll huff and I'll puff and I'll blow your house in" (published in J. Jacobs, *English Fairy Tales,* 1890). The noun usage with the current meaning of "angry" was first recorded in 1599 and has been so used ever since.

in a jam See IN A PINCH.

in a nutshell Concisely or compactly, usually referring to written or spoken words. The Roman writer Pliny in his *Natural History* stated that Homer's great (and very long) epic poem, the *Iliad,* was copied in such tiny handwriting that the whole text could be enclosed in a nutshell. This obvious hyperbole caught the imagination of numerous subsequent writers who referred to "the *Iliad* in a nutshell," among them Jonathan Swift and Thomas Carlyle. Later "the *Iliad*" was dropped and anything extremely compressed was described as being in a nutshell, a cliché since the mid-nineteenth century. See also IN A WORD.

in any way, shape, or form, not Not at all, in no possible manner. Also put as *in no way, shape, or form,* this emphatic and partially redundant phrase (*shape* and *form* mean the same thing) dates from the mid-1900s. It is generally a reply to a question, such as "'Are you planning another family reunion?' 'No, not in any way, shape, or form.'" Also see NO WAY.

in a pickle, to be/get In a bad situation; in trouble. Although it sounds very up to date, this expression dates from Shakespeare's time. "How camest thou in this pickle?" says Alonso to his fellow-conspirator (*The Tempest,* 5.1). The term has been so used ever since.

in a pig's eye Never! Several sources have been suggested for this Americanism from the late nineteenth century. One holds that it is rhyming slang for "when pigs fly," which of course is never. Another, more probable theory is that it is a euphemism for "in a pig's ass," which came from a bawdy song. Whatever the true origin, it has been on its way to becoming a cliché since about 1950.

in a pinch When hard-pressed. The British version of this expression, "at a pinch," dates from the fifteenth century, when William Caxton in his translation of *The Book of Faytes of Armes and of Chyualrye* (1489) wrote, "Corageously at a pynche [he] shal renne vpon hem." By the time Robert Louis Stevenson wrote *Black Arrow* (1888) it also was put as, "It yet might serve him, in a pinch." A related expression of more recent provenance is *in a jam,* which similarly implies that one is "compressed" or "squeezed," by circumstance, into a tight spot.

in a trice See IN TWO SHAKES OF A LAMB'S TAIL.

in at the death/finish Present at the end, usually meaning at someone's ruin, but sometimes only at the climax of an important event. The term comes from fox hunting, where, in the eighteenth century, it denoted the presence of hunters and hounds at the killing of a fox they had run to the ground. By 1800 the term was being transferred to other kinds of demise.

in a word Briefly, concisely. This expression, which is usually followed by a fair number of words—as in, "In a word, the bank is unable to accommodate Mr. Brown's request for a loan"—was used by Shakespeare in *Two Gentlemen of Verona* ("And in a word . . . he is compleat in feature and in mind"). It was much favored by various of Dickens's more verbose characters, such as Mr. Micawber.

in clover, to be/live To prosper. This expression, with its analogy to cattle feeding happily in a field of clover, dates from the early eighteenth century. It occasionally has been put *like pigs in clover,* and, in twentieth-century America, *rolling in clover.* All of them mean "to live well."

in for a penny, in for a pound Do not stop at half-measures; once involved, even a little, one is involved a lot. This term, which originally meant that if one owes a penny one might as well owe more, dates from the seventeenth century. Thomas Ravenscroft wrote, "Well, that, O'er shooes, o'er boots, And In for a penny, in for a Pound" (*The Canterbury Guests,* 1695, 5.1). It was quoted over and over. Dickens, always intrigued with debt, used it in at least three of his novels (*Nicholas Nickleby, Oliver Twist, The Old Curiosity Shop*). Today it is common mostly in Britain and Ireland, where the pound is a unit of currency, but it is still occasionally heard in America.

in full swing Vigorously active. Various etymologists to the contrary, this term comes from a sixteenth-century use of *swing* for the course of a career or period of time. The only modern vestige of this meaning is in the cliché, which has survived. Indeed, it was already a cliché when George Meredith wrote (*Evan Harrington,* 1861), "A barrister in full swing of practice."

in high dudgeon Angrily, resentfully, IN A HUFF. The origin of *dudgeon* has been lost and today the word is never used except with *high*—never alone and not even with *low.* In use from about 1600 on, the term was a cliché by the time explorer David Livingstone wrote "He went off in high dudgeon" (*The Zambezi and Its Tributaries,* 1865). The phrase may be dying out.

in no uncertain terms Emphatically, very clearly. This double negative appears to have become very popular about the middle of the twentieth century. Lawrence Durrell used it in *Balthazar* (1958): "I told Abdul so in no uncertain terms." A slightly slangier synonym is LOUD AND CLEAR.

in one ear and out the other Inattentive; soon forgotten. This vivid image dates from Roman times. "The things he says flow right through the ears," wrote Quintillian (*Institutionis Oratoriae,* c. A.D. 80). The sentiment was echoed by Chaucer and joined John Heywood's 1546 proverb collection

("Went in the tone eare, and out at the tother"). Thomas Hood punned on it in his "Ode to the Late Lord Mayor" (1825): "He comes in at one year, to go out by the other!"

in one's element In one's natural or most comfortable surroundings or occupation; happily situated. The Elizabethans were much concerned with the four elements—earth, water, air, and fire—and regarded these as the proper abode of both living creatures and inanimate objects. By Shakespeare's time the terms were used figuratively as well, so that he could write, "Down, thou climbing sorrow! Thy element's below" (*King Lear,* 1.4). To be out of one's element, like a FISH OUT OF WATER, was also possible. "He is as much out of his Element, as an Eel in a Sandbag," wrote Thomas Fuller (*Gnomologia,* 1732).

in one's heart of hearts In the innermost recesses of one's mind or feelings. This expression was used by Shakespeare, "In my heart's core, ay in my heart of heart" (*Hamlet,* 3.2), as well as by William Wordsworth (*Intimations of Immortality,* 1806) and Anthony Trollope (*The Last Chronicle of Barset,* 1867).

in one's right mind Sane. This expression, today usually used in a negative way—"no one in his right mind would . . ."—appears in the Bible in the Gospel of Mark (5:15), in which Jesus has helped a man who was deranged: "And they . . . see him that was possessed with the devil . . . sitting, and clothed, and in his right mind."

in over one's head, to be To be swamped (with debts, work, responsibilities, and so forth). The analogy in this expression is to being in water over one's head when one presumably is not a good swimmer. In the early seventeenth century it was put simply as *over one's head,* as in "That silly women shall be dipt over head in a Gumble-stool for scolding" (Richard Baxter describing a ducking-stool in 1653).

in point of fact In reference to a fact, in fact. This long-winded way of saying "in fact" dates from about 1700 (Swift used it in a 1711 entry of his *Journal to Stella*) and was already considered cumbersome and old-fashioned by the late nineteenth century. Nevertheless, it persists.

ins and outs, the All the intricacies or ramifications of a situation. Originally this term referred to those in favor and those out of it, and then to those in or out of political office. As Chaucer put it in *Troilus and Criseyde,* "Weep if thou wolt, for out of doute, this Diomede is inne, and thou art oute." Years later Thomas Jefferson (*Writings,* c. 1814) similarly referred to "two parties, the INS and the OUTS." Only in the nineteenth century did the term come to mean intricacies, referring to the windings and turnings of a complicated path or passage. Thomas Hood so used it in a late poem ("Laying Down the Law," 1845): "The celebrated judge, too prone to tarry, to hesitate on devious ins and outs."

in short order At once, without delay. This term uses the noun "order" in the sense of a sequence. It dates from the first half of the 1800s. *Publishers Weekly* (May 24, 1976) had it: "Linda descends on twenties London to become, in short order, a model, the toast of Lords."

inside track, the A position of special advantage. The term comes from racing, alluding to the inner or shorter track of a course, on which it is easier to win. It originated in America in the mid-nineteenth century. "It gave him the inside track, as the sporting men say, with reference to any rival" (Oliver Wendell Holmes, *Guardian Angel,* 1867).

in stitches Overcome with laughter. This expression, which in this precise form dates from about 1930, uses *stitches* in the sense of "a stitch in the side," that is, uncontrollable laughter can actually make one's sides hurt. Shakespeare used a version of it in *Twelfth Night* (3.2): "If you desire the spleen, and will laugh yourselves into stitches, follow me."

in stone, cast/carved/written Completely set, unchangeable. This phrase is often put in the negative—something is *not* cast in stone. It alludes to sculpture, where *to cast* means to pour and harden a material into a final form, and possibly also to the epitaphs engraved on gravestones. The first usage dates from the early 1500s. Most often it appears in such statements as, "Of course we can change it; this proposal is not cast in stone."

in the bag Sure to succeed. The expression alludes to the game bag in which hunters placed small game like birds and which was called simply "a bag" from about 1600 on. However, transferring this idea to a future success did not occur until the first half of the twentieth century. "Don't you worry, it's all in the bag" is a relatively early appearance in print, in Raymond Postgate's mystery, *Verdict of Twelve* (1940).

in the cards A likely or probable occurrence. The term refers to the cards of fortune-telling and began life as *on the cards.* It was well known by the time Dickens used it in several novels, as in *Bleak House* (1852): "It don't come out altogether so plain as to please me, but it's on the cards."

in the dark, to be/keep someone To be mystified or uninformed; to fail to inform someone. The figurative use of *dark* for ignorance is very old indeed. "We can't keep it dark any longer," wrote the Roman playwright

Plautus (*Aulularia,* c. 210 B.C.), and Shakespeare wrote, "Till then I'll keep him dark" (*All's Well That Ends Well,* 4.1).

in the doghouse In disgrace. The term alludes to sending a dog that misbehaves indoors to its outdoor kennel. It is of relatively recent origin, presumably from about 1900. In James Barrie's *Peter Pan* (1904) Mr. Darling mistreats the children's favorite, a dog named Nana, and in penance goes to live in the dog's house.

in the doldrums Depressed, DOWN IN THE DUMPS; stagnant, inactive. The word, whose origin is uncertain, began to be used in the early nineteenth century both for the maritime doldrums, a belt of calms and light winds north of the equator in which sailing ships often found themselves becalmed, and for a feeling of depression. Thus Frederick Marryat wrote, in *Jacob Faithful* (1835), "Come father, old Dictionary is in the doldrums; rouse him up."

in the driver's seat In control. The analogy here is obvious, but the actual expression did not become common until the nineteenth century. Lord Beaverbrook is quoted (*New Statesman,* 1963) as saying of David Lloyd George, "He did not care in which direction the car was travelling, so long as he remained in the driver's seat." See also IN THE SADDLE.

in the dumps See DOWN IN THE DUMPS.

in the groove Hits the mark; in the popular fashion. This seemingly very modern expression actually dates from the mid-nineteenth century, when it referred to running very accurately within a fixed channel, or groove. In the 1930s the term became jazz slang for performing very well and also gave rise to *groovy,* for splendid. Then it probably alluded to a phonograph needle running in the groove of a recording. In subsequent decades the term began to die out, although pop singer Madonna recorded "Get into the Groove" in the late 1980s.

in the last analysis In the end, after everything has been considered. This phrase, also put as *in the final analysis,* apparently is a translation of the French *en dernier analyse.* It was used by Edgar Allan Poe (*Chambers's Journal,* 1844): "Now this mode of reasoning . . . what in the last analysis is it?"

in the limelight In the center of public attention. The term comes from a vivid lighting device used in theaters from about 1840 on to throw a strong light on the star of a performance. Relying on the combustion of oxygen and hydrogen on a surface of lime and a lens for directing the light, it was invented in 1826 by Thomas Drummond. George Bernard Shaw, in a letter concerning a controversy about censorship (c. 1900), wrote, "Look after the limelight, and the play will look after itself."

in the long run Over a long period of time; in the end. The term refers to running a race, specifically to a runner who is passed by others at the beginning but pulls ahead at the end (analogous to the fable of the slow but steady tortoise who wins over the fast but erratic hare). Originally it also was put as *at the long run* (seventeenth century). One of economist John Maynard Keynes's most famous remarks concerning economic planning was, "In the long run we are all dead."

in the nick of time See NICK OF TIME.

in the offing In the future; likely to occur. The term was first used in the seventeenth century to describe the open sea as seen between shore and horizon. In the eighteenth century it began to be used figuratively to describe something nearby or in prospect. Thus Nancy Mitford wrote (*Love in a Cold Climate,* 1949), "That look of concentration which comes over French faces when a meal is in the offing."

in the pink In excellent condition; in good health. This term has its roots in Shakespeare's time, when *the pink* meant the embodiment of perfection. Thus, in *Romeo and Juliet,* "the very pink of courtesy" (2.4) means the ultimate in politeness. The cliché, however, dates only from about 1900 and today refers almost exclusively to good health.

in the pipeline Under way, in process or in progress. The word *pipeline* entered the language in the latter half of the nineteenth century, and by the 1920s the term was used also for a channel of supplies or information. The current cliché came into use about thirty years later. "All these reforms will take time . . . there are measures in the pipeline already," editorialized the *London Observer* in 1964.

in the saddle In a position of authority. This term dates from the seventeenth century, or perhaps even earlier. Machiavelli in his famous discourse on politics, *The Prince* (trans. 1675), wrote, "Such as by the favour of fortune . . . have got into the saddle." It was misinterpreted by one writer, R. G. White (*England Without and Within,* 1881), who said, "The phrase 'in the saddle,' as an expression of readiness for work, is a peculiarly English phrase." In fact, it has always meant a position of authority, not necessarily come by through honest toil.

in the same boat as, to be To be in similar circumstances or in the same position. This expression, which alludes to the risks shared by all those present in a small boat at sea, dates from the time of the ancient Greeks and has been used figuratively for many centuries. It often is stated as *all in the same boat,* as it was by Artemus Ward (*The Draft in Baldinsville,* 1862): "We are all in the same boat."

in the swim Actively engaged, in the thick of things. This term comes from fishing, where a large number of fish in one location was sometimes called "a swim." This term was transferred to mean the main current of affairs. It dates from the mid-nineteenth century. "He knew I was in the swim down here," wrote Arthur Conan Doyle (*The Stock-broker's Clerk,* 1893).

in this day and age Now, as opposed to the past or future. This expression, often preceded by *not,* is one of those verbal redundancies that grate on the ear. It has been used since the early twentieth century. "She knew that in this day and age a nun could be a scientist" (*Time,* 1941).

in two shakes of a lamb's tail Instantly, very quickly. Lambs surely were known to be frisky creatures long before, but this expression, often shortened to *in two shakes,* dates only from the early nineteenth century and originated in America. Mark Twain changed it in *The Adventures of Huckleberry Finn* (1884) to "three shakes of a sheep's tail," suggesting it was already very well known by the late nineteenth century. A similar cliché, *in a trice,* which came from a now obsolete word meaning to pull on a rope and alluded to a single pull, is rarely heard today but was extremely common from the eighteenth century on.

inventing the wheel See REINVENT THE WHEEL.

in vino veritas Drunks speak the truth. This Latin expression, literally "In wine [is] truth," was already used by the ancient Greeks and probably survived so long in the Latin form because Erasmus in his widely circulated *Adagia* so rendered it. There are versions in numerous languages. The cliché is heard less often nowadays, but as the study of Latin is slowly reviving it may surface more often.

in your dreams Never, no matter how much you wish for it. Often put as an interjection, this slangy term dates only from the 1980s but has quickly caught on. For example, "I just know they'll win the pennant this year.—In your dreams!" A synonymous phrase is *dream on,* used as the title of a number of popular songs dating back as far as the 1950s and a television sit-com.

in your face Rudely confrontational; an expression of extreme contempt. This impolite phrase apparently originated in basketball in the 1970s, where it would be used against one's opponents. By the 1980s it had been extended to other kinds of confrontation, where it calls up the belligerent gesture of putting one's own face close to the other person's. However, the term also is used merely to describe something that is quite obvious. It was so used in a *Boston Globe* editorial (Feb. 2, 2005) about a Harvard professor who made a career of looking into things just because they are interesting: "He said that what excites him 'are things so in your face that almost no one thinks about them.'" The equally slangy *get out of my face,* for "stop bothering me," originated in black English c. 1930.

iron hand (in a velvet glove), to rule with an To rule with absolute firmness (concealed by a mild manner). Ruling with iron was an idea expressed in the Bible, in the Book of Revelation: "And he shall rule them with a rod of iron" (2:27). *Iron hand in a velvet glove* comes from Thomas Carlyle's *Latter-Day Pamphlets* (1850) and is there ascribed to Napoleon Bonaparte: "'Iron hand in a velvet glove,' as Napoleon defined it." However, the phrase has been attributed to other rulers, too, among them Charles V. Today it is more often used for lesser authorities, such as a strict parent, but may be dying out.

irons in the fire, lots of/too many More projects than one can handle. This expression comes from the smithy and has long survived the profession of blacksmith. The smith who tries to heat too many irons at once is apt to spoil the forging of some of them. It has been used figuratively since the sixteenth century.

I should care See COULDN'T CARE LESS.

is the Pope Catholic? A positive response (yes) to what one considers a stupid question. Dating from the mid-twentieth century, this answer should be avoided in polite society.

itching for a fight See FINGER ITCHES TO.

itchy palm, to have an Corruptible, greedy, asking for a bribe. This term, like so many, was originated by Shakespeare. In *Julius Caesar* (4.3) Brutus says, "Let me tell you, Cassius, you yourself are much condemned to have an itching palm." See also GREASE SOMEONE'S PALM.

it never rains but it pours When something happens, it often happens to excess. This proverbial expression originated in 1726 from a twice-used title, *It Cannot Rain But It Pours,* an article by Jonathan Swift and Alexander Pope (in *Prose Miscellanies*) and a book by John Arbuthnot. It is not known if they happened on it by coincidence or if one copied from the other, or if the phrase was already well known. It was used by numerous writers thereafter, among them Thomas Gray, Charles Kingsley, and Anthony Trollope, and has since attained proverbial status. A play on it was made in a 1911 advertising slogan for Morton salt—"when it rains it pours"—assuring consumers that dampness would not prevent this product from flowing freely.

it's all in your mind You're imagining it, it's not real. This cliché differs from such earlier uses as *in my mind* or *to my mind,* which meant "in my opinion" from the early 1500s but are heard less often today, and *on one's mind,* meaning "occupying one's thoughts," dating from the mid-1800s. The current cliché is generally used as a denial of another's statement, as in "'I'm sure this woman doesn't like me.' 'No, it's all in your mind.'"

it's a small world One encounters familiar people or events in unexpected places. As might be expected, this expression originated only when widespread travel and the transportation facilities to make it possible became commonplace. "Not such a large world after all," wrote G. A. Sala in 1886 upon unexpectedly meeting someone in San Francisco after an interval of thirty-one years (*America Revisited*). By 1906 George Ade wrote (*In Pastures New*), "'It's a small world.' This is one of the most overworked phrases of the globe-trotter . . . most frequently by those who follow the beaten paths."

it's more fun than a barrel of monkeys Singular amusement or diversion. This American phrase has been current since about 1920 and alludes to the mischievous playfulness of the primates, perhaps as seen from their circus tricks. A watered-down version of this expression is a *barrel of laughs.*

it's not over till it's over Don't count on an outcome until the very end. Exactly where this twentieth-century adage comes from is not known, nor is the more widely quoted *it's not over till the fat lady sings.* There are various theories about the provenance of the latter. A fairly logical one is, *the opera isn't over till the fat lady sings,* which appeared in the *Washington Post* on June 13, 1978. It actually was a reply from sports editor Dan Cook to "The rodeo ain't over till the bull riders ride." Another theory is that the saying alludes to Kate Smith, a popular singer in the 1930s and 1940s with a figure as ample as her big voice. Whichever, the phrase has quickly become a cliché.

it takes all sorts Humankind is made up of many kinds of individuals, markedly different from one another. The Book of Common Prayer (1548) includes a Prayer for All Conditions of Men, which prays to God "for all sorts and conditions of men; that thou wouldest be pleased to make thy ways known unto them." This may have been the source of the next version, *It takes all sorts to make a world,* which became current in the seventeenth century. Indeed, Samuel Johnson's biographer, James Boswell, quotes philosopher John Locke as using this phrase. George Bernard Shaw was particularly fond of it. In the late nineteenth century it was shortened to *it takes all sorts* and by now is a cliché.

it takes one to know one The critic is as bad as the person being criticized. This expression, a modern version of the proverbial "set a thief to catch a thief," and "a thief knows a thief as well as a wolf knows a wolf," dates from the early twentieth century.

it takes two to tango Certain enterprises require the active cooperation of two participants. Although in Australia (according to Eric Partridge) this term referred to premarital sex from the 1930s on, in the United States it originated at least a decade earlier, soon after the Latin American tango became a popular dance, and was transferred to any kind of partnership activity. Its currency was aided by a song, "Takes Two to Tango" (1952, by Al Hoffman and Dick Manning), popularized by the singer Pearl Bailey. The phrase was repeated by President Ronald Reagan (Nov. 11, 1982) concerning the future of Soviet-American relations after the death of Leonid Brezhnev. Its ultimate origin may be in a much earlier proverb, *it always takes two to make a bargain*, appearing in John Lyly's *Euphues, the Anatomy of Wit* (1579). It is often abbreviated to *it takes two.*

it will all come out in the wash Everything will be settled satisfactorily. This term, which alludes to the removal of dirt and stains by laundering, originated in Britain in the late nineteenth century, although a version of it occurred in Cervantes's *Don Quixote* (1605): *Todo saldrá en la colada* ("All will come out in the laundry"). "It all goes into the laundry, but it never comes out in the wash," wrote Rudyard Kipling (*Stellenbosh,* 1881).

it will soon blow over It will soon be forgotten. This metaphor, referring to a gale that subsides and ceases, was transferred to human affairs, especially scandals and other items of gossip, in the eighteenth century. Gouverneur Morris used the phrase in 1794: "The affair is blown over."

ivory tower A situation or attitude remote from practical affairs. The term originated in the French critic Sainte-Beuve's description of poet Alfred de Vigny as living in an ivory tower (1837), that is, isolated from life's harsh realities. Subsequently, the term has been used to describe academics, artists, writers, or indeed anyone complacently aloof from everyday affairs. Cyril Connolly (*Enemies of Promise,* 1938) used it to disparage Walter Pater: "Pater, calling an art-for-art's sake muezzin to the faithful from the top-most turret of the ivory tower." The term is heard less often today but is by no means obsolete.

j

jack of all trades A person who is good at everything. This term dates from 1600 or before. An early appearance in print is in Geffray Mynshul's *Essayes and Characters of a Prison* (1618). Further, it was pointed out even earlier that someone good at everything is not outstanding at anything. This observation occurs in an ancient Roman proverb, but only much later was put as *jack of all trades, master of none* by Maria Edgeworth (*Popular Tales: Will,* 1800).

January and May See DECEMBER, MAY AND.

jaundiced eye, (look on) with a Seeing only the faults or bad side. This term is based on the old belief that to a person suffering from jaundice (a condition in which the skin and whites of the eyes turn yellow), everything looks yellow. John Webster put it into so many words in *The White Devil* (1.2): "They that have the yellow jaundice think all objects they look on to be yellow" (1612). The expression long survived the belief and was a cliché by 1800 or so.

Jekyll and Hyde An individual who has two completely different sides, one very good and the other evil. The term comes from Robert Louis Stevenson's, *The Strange Case of Dr. Jekyll and Mr. Hyde* (1886), in which one character can switch from the good Dr. Jekyll to the evil Mr. Hyde by taking a drug. Leslie Purnell Davies defined it in *The Shadow Before* (1971), "We are all a mixture of good and evil, Jekyll and Hyde if you like."

jet set A fashionable social group. The term, which originated in the 1950s soon after the introduction of travel by jet-propelled aircraft, caught on rapidly, probably aided by its rhyme. It was applied first to the affluent socialites who traveled around the world to fashionable resorts; later it was extended to a well-to-do social group in general, whether or not its members actually traveled frequently. It replaced the earlier *smart set,* at least in America. See also BEAUTIFUL PEOPLE.

jockey for position, to To maneuver or manipulate, to further one's own interest. The verb *to jockey* has meant to gain an advantage through adroit maneuvering from about 1700 or so. *To jockey for position* was used literally (meaning to maneuver a racehorse) in the early twentieth century and was only transferred to other endeavors about 1950. The London *Times* had it in 1955, "Lawyers jockeying for position to appear before the right judge."

Joe Six-Pack A working-class male. The *six-pack* in this somewhat derogatory name refers to a half-dozen bottles or cans of beer that are packaged together, to be bought as a unit, and supposedly a workingman's beverage of choice. *Six-pack* came into use in the early 1950s, and *Joe Six-Pack* was first recorded in 1970 and quickly proliferated. Reporter Martin F. Nolan used it in an article about Joe Moakley's political campaign against Louise Day Hicks for Congress: "Moakley plans to make Mrs. Hicks the major issue in the campaign, talking about issues in the media and shouting in Joe Six-Pack's ear to wake up and face the unsimplistic facts of life (*Boston Globe,* August 28, 1970). The *Globe* headline was "After the Soul of Joe Six-Pack." See also JOHN DOE.

John Doe The average person. This appellation actually dates from the thirteenth century, when it was used in legal documents to disguise the identity of witnesses; the tenant plaintiff was called *John Doe* and the landlord defendant *Richard Roe.* In the nineteenth century the name acquired the present meaning of ordinary person. A book, *The O'Hara Family* (1825), included "Tales, Containing . . . John Doe," and almost a century later a movie starring Gary Cooper was entitled *Meet John Doe* (1941). Similar appellations include *Joe Blow,* first recorded in 1867; *Joe Doakes,* from the 1920s; and *John Q. Public,* coined by the writer William Allen White in 1937. John Doe has outlived them all.

John Hancock One's signature. John Hancock was the first man to sign the Declaration of Independence and did so in an exceptionally large, clear hand. Indeed, he supposedly remarked, "I guess King George will be able to read that" (July 4, 1776). In the mid-nineteenth century his name was transferred to anyone's signature.

Johnny-come-lately A late arrival; a newcomer. This term originated in the early nineteenth-century British navy as Johnny Newcomer, meaning a seaman new to a ship. In the United States it was changed to *Johnny-come-lately,* first appearing in print in Charles F. Briggs's novel, *The Adventures of Harry Franco* (1839).

Johnny-on-the-spot A person who is present at a crucial time. This term comes from nineteenth-century America. An early appearance in print is in George Ade's *Artie* (1896): "I could see that a Johnny-on-the-spot . . . was trying to keep cases on her."

joker in the deck, a Any item or device, such as a clause in a contract, that unexpectedly changes the nature of something, either for better or for worse. The noun "joker" alone has been used in this way since the mid-1800s, as in "The postal rate increase had within it a joker that would hurt nonprofit organizations." Today the term, also put as *joker in the pack,* sometimes refers to a person whose behavior is unexpected on unpredictable.

jump at the chance, to To seize an opportunity. Jumping at various kinds of opportunity is recorded from the seventeenth century on, often likened to how a cock would jump at a gooseberry. Sir Walter Scott particularly liked this analogy, using it for jumping at an offer and jumping at "the ready penny."

jump down someone's throat, to To criticize, reprimand, or disagree sharply and suddenly. This vivid metaphor has been around since the late nineteenth century. Anthony Trollope used it in his *Cousin Henry* (1879): "Was she to jump down your throat when you asked her?"

jump in with both feet, to To enter wholeheartedly. This phrase is actually redundant, since to jump means to leap with the feet together as opposed to hopping on one foot. A twentieth-century Americanism, it may allude to jumping into a pool, rather than testing the water with one foot.

jump the gun, to To act prematurely or too hastily. The term comes from the starter's gun that often marks the beginning of a race, and those who "jump" the gun are starting before the gun goes off. At first this was expressed as to *beat the pistol* (c. 1900), but by 1942 the *American Thesaurus of Slang* (by Berrey and Van den Bark) defined *jump the gun* as "to make a false start." The British journal *The Economist* has been very fond of this expression since about 1950.

jump to conclusions, to To draw inferences too hastily from insufficient evidence. Also put in the singular (*to jump to a conclusion*), this cliché dates from about 1700.

just deserts Deserved reward or punishment. The word *desert* in this meaning—that is, what is deserved—is almost obsolete except in this cliché but was commonly used until about the mid-eighteenth century. "Desert and rewarde be oft tymes thinges far od" appeared in John Heywood's *Proverbs* (1546) and several later collections as well. In other words, what one deserves and the reward one receives are often quite different.

just don't/doesn't get it, you/he/she You don't (he doesn't) catch on, or really understand what's going on. This phrase gained enormous currency in the 1980s when presidential nominee Ronald Reagan used it in a televised political debate with his opponent. Thereafter it was used often, particularly where the speaker is exasperated with someone's failure to understand something. To *get it* has been a colloquialism for "to understand" since the late nineteenth century.

just folks Ordinary people; unpretentious, down-to-earth individuals. This term has been around since about 1900. Zona Gale used it in *Friendship Village* (1908): "I see 'em all comin' from the funeral . . . neighbors an' friends an' just folks." See also MAN IN THE STREET.

keep an eye on, to To keep watch over something or someone. See also EYE FOR/TO THE MAIN CHANCE; KEEP YOUR EYES . . .

keep a stiff upper lip, to Do not give way to adversity; appear to be resolute and stoical without showing your true feelings. This term comes from America in the early 1800s and presumably refers to a trembling lip, which betrays that one is about to burst into tears. The expression actually does not make much sense, since it is usually the lower lip that trembles before weeping, but certainly any tremor of the upper lip would be particularly obvious in a man wearing a mustache, in the ubiquitous fashion of the 1830s. "What's the use of boohooin'? . . . keep a stiff upper lip," appeared in John Neal's *The Down-Easters* (1833), and the expression soon crossed the Atlantic.

keep a straight face, to Do not burst out laughing; look appropriately serious. This cliché is of fairly recent vintage. Henry Miller used the term in *Plexus* (1953): "All I felt called upon to do was keep a straight face and pretend that everything was kosher."

keep at arm's length, to To avoid familiarity, to keep someone at a distance. This expression, with its inevitable image of extending one's arm to push someone away, has long been used figuratively to signify distancing oneself from a problem, group, political stand, and so forth. In the sixteenth century it was put as *at arm's end,* as Sir Philip Sidney had it in *Arcadia* (1580), but by the mid-seventeenth century it began to appear as *at arm's length.*

keep body and soul together, to To sustain life, often just barely. This term, frequently used to describe a job that pays scarcely enough to live on, rests on the idea that the soul gives life to the body, which dies when the soul is separated from it. Dating from the early eighteenth century, it became a cliché by the mid-nineteenth century or so. Writing on prostitution in the *Manchester Guardian* in 1974, Suzanne Lowry quipped, "Keeping body and soul together is never as difficult as trying to keep them separate."

keeping up with the Joneses Attempting to live in the style of one's more affluent neighbors or acquaintances. The term was coined by Arthur

R. ("Pop") Momand, a cartoonist who used it as the title for a series run in the *New York Globe* from 1913, and in other papers as well, for several decades. Momand based the series on his own experiences as a newly wed young artist living in an affluent New York suburb on a limited salary. Although he and the series are scarcely remembered, the title caught on and by mid-century was a cliché.

keep one's See KEEP YOUR . . .

keep one's ear to the ground See EAR TO THE GROUND.

keep oneself to oneself, to To be reserved and aloof, avoiding the company of others. Samuel Richardson used this phrase in *Clarissa* (1748), and it was repeated by numerous writers, some of whom pointed out that it was a quintessentially English form of behavior. "He kept, in popular parlance, himself to himself. Like many policemen, Dunday thought," wrote British novelist Robert Barnard (*Death and the Chaste Apprentice,* 1989).

keep one's fingers crossed, to To hope for success. This saying comes from an ancient superstition that making the sign of the cross will avert bad luck. Often put as *Keep your fingers crossed,* meaning "Wish me luck," it dates from the 1920s. One writer points out it may also have come from children's games in which crossing one's fingers denotes that one is "safe," as well as the gambit of telling a lie with one's fingers crossed, presumably to avoid punishment for this sinful act.

keep one's head above water, to To avoid financial ruin; also, to avoid being overwhelmed by overwork, too many commitments, or other excessive demands. This saying, with its analogy to being drowned, dates from the early eighteenth century. "I have almost drowned myself to keep his head above water," wrote John Arbuthnot in *John Bull* (1712).

keep (someone) posted, to To supply someone with up-to-date information. This term originated in the United States in the early nineteenth century and comes from accounting, where the latest figures entered into a system are said to be "posted." It originally was put as being *posted up,* as in "Mr. M. is not well posted up, or he would have said less on this subject" (*The Weekly Oregonian,* 1854).

keep the ball rolling, to To continue or sustain an activity without a letup. Some writers believe this is a metaphor from ball games, but a much earlier use referred to the sun or planets (including Earth) as a rolling ball. In any event, this term became popular in the United States during the election campaign of 1840, when the supporters of candidate William Henry

Harrison ("Tippecanoe" hero) rolled large "victory balls" in political parades and chanted, "Keep the Harrison ball rolling."

keep the faith Carry on, continue the good work. This phrase, often put as *keep the faith, baby,* became common among activists in the American civil rights struggles of the 1960s. Originally it probably alluded to maintaining one's religious beliefs, but this sense was superseded by the nonsectarian efforts to obtain equal rights for all American citizens. Subsequently, it lost both meanings and became a more neutral expression used when two friends or colleagues part. Stanley Ellin used it in *The Man from Nowhere* (1975), "I'll leave it to you, Jake.—Keep the faith, baby."

keep the wolf from the door, to To ward off starvation or insolvency. This term, based on the lupine characteristic of ravenousness, dates from the sixteenth century and was already included in John Heywood's *Proverbs* (1546). A cliché by about 1800, it is heard less often today.

keep (something) under one's hat, to To preserve secrecy. This term, with its vivid image of hiding a secret under headgear, dates from the late nineteenth century and has remained current even though hats are worn much less frequently today. A popular song of the 1920s had it: "Keep it under your hat! You must agree to do that. Promise not to breathe a word" (quoted by Eric Partridge). See also IN THE DARK.

keep your See KEEP ONE'S.

keep your chin up Don't lose courage. This term has replaced the older British *keep your pecker up,* current there since the 1840s, when *pecker* actually was defined in a dictionary as meaning "courage" or "resolution." The latter did not catch on much in America, where "pecker" is also slang for "penis," changing the meaning entirely. *Keep your chin up,* however, has been a cliché for some time; it certainly was by the time P. A. Taylor wrote, "You have to keep your chin up" (*The Six Iron Spiders,* 1942).

keep your eyes peeled/skinned Be particularly watchful; remain alert. This American expression dates from the mid-nineteenth century and presumably likens *peeled* or *skinned* to being wide open. An early reference in print occurs in J. S. Robb's *Squatter Life* (1847): "Keep your eye skinned for Injuns."

keep your nose clean Stay out of trouble. This slangy phrase began to be heard in Britain in the late nineteenth century and crossed the Atlantic soon afterward. Why cleanliness should be invoked is not known. Presumably keeping one's nose clean would be equivalent to not dirtying it by poking it into someone else's business (see POKE ONE'S NOSE INTO). Anyhow, the term was very common by the 1940s, when it appeared in such popular novels as Manning Long's *False Alarm* (1943): "Keep your nose clean and you'll keep out of trouble."

keep your powder dry Take care of yourself; be prepared. This phrase was uttered by Oliver Cromwell in 1642, when his regiment was about to attack the enemy at the battle of Edgehill. "Put your trust in God," he told his troops, "but keep your powder dry." Wet gunpowder was very difficult to ignite, and with it a soldier would in effect be unarmed. The term was transferred to other enterprises in the nineteenth century. In the twentieth century it was sometimes used jocularly to mean a woman's makeup (face powder).

keep your shirt on Remain calm and patient; don't lose your temper. Dating from the nineteenth century, this American expression refers to the practice of a man removing his shirt before a fight, lest it get torn, and at first literally meant not to rush into a fight. "Tell E. Stanton to keep his undergarmints on," wrote Artemus Ward (*In Washington,* 1863). Later it came to mean being patient as well.

kettle of fish, a fine/pretty A messy predicament. This term is believed to come from a Scottish custom of holding a riverside picnic, itself called a "kettle of fish," where freshly caught live salmon are thrown into a kettle boiling over an open fire and then are eaten out of hand, definitely a messy procedure. Sir Walter Scott described just such a picnic in *St. Ronan's Well* (1824), but the transfer to other kinds of messy predicament had already occurred in the early eighteenth century. The term appears in Henry Fielding's *Joseph Andrews* (1742) and works by Dickens, Hardy, Shaw, and many others, but it may now be dying out, at least in America.

kick ass/butt Enforce one's authority, strongly assert oneself. Both versions of this vulgar term seem to have originated in the mid-1900s in the military, where they meant to defeat overwhelmingly, and soon entered the civilian vocabulary. The latter, only slightly more polite, was used by President George H.W. Bush during the Persian Gulf War, when he referred to "kicking a little you-know-what" (cited by Paul Dickson).

kick in the (seat of the) pants, a A reproof or reprimand; also, a goad or spur to get someone moving. Both can be literal or figurative. The idea must be very old indeed, and the expression, a euphemism for a kick in the posterior, appeared in Samuel Butler's *Hudibras* (1663). A more recent term with the same meaning as the first sense is a *kick in the teeth,* used from the mid-twentieth century on.

kick over the traces, to To break loose, away from control. The traces referred to are a pair of ropes or straps attaching a harnessed horse to a wagon or other vehicle. A horse can kick over these attachments when refusing to run or pull the vehicle. The term was transferred to anyone breaking free from restraint in the latter half of the nineteenth century. It appeared in Henry Kingsley's *Ravenshoe* (1861): "I'll go about with the rogue. He is inclined to kick over the traces."

kick the bucket, to To die. This expression, which comes from eighteenth-century Britain, has several explanations. One is that the bucket referred to is the East Anglian word for a beam on which a pig is hung by its feet to be slaughtered and which it kicks against in its death struggles. Another theorizes that a person committing suicide by hanging may stand on an overturned bucket to fasten the rope and then kick it away. The term was loosely used for anyone dying by any means by 1785, when it was so defined in Francis Grose's *A Classical Dictionary of the Vulgar Tongue.*

kick up one's heels, to To enjoy oneself exuberantly; to frolic. This term, which calls to mind a prancing horse or a vigorous dancer, originally meant to be knocked down or killed. Thomas Dekker used it in this sense in his play, *The Honest Whore* (1604): "I would not for a duckat she had kickt up her heeles." The modern sense dates from the late nineteenth or early twentieth century.

kick upstairs, to To promote someone to a higher rank with less responsibility in order to get him or her out of the way. Although one may tend to associate this expression with modern business practices, it was already being used in the early nineteenth century. J. W. Croker recorded it in an 1821 diary entry: "Lord Melville informs me that he is about to be kicked upstairs (his expression) to be Secretary of State."

kid gloves, to handle/treat with To deal with very gently. This term, dating from the nineteenth century, is an elaboration of the slightly earlier term to *handle without gloves,* meaning to treat harshly. Gloves made of kidskin, from the hide of a young goat, were known from the early eighteenth century on and were considered elegant finery, whence the transfer to delicate treatment.

killing pace, a An extremely fast or hectic rate. Originally referring to the breakneck speed of a horse or human being, leading to exhaustion, this expression was by the mid-nineteenth century being transferred to any human endeavor. "You can't keep up the pace . . . it will kill you," wrote Thackeray (*Pendennis,* 1850).

kill the fatted calf, to To prepare a warm homecoming for a relative or a splendid celebration for a guest. This term alludes to the biblical parable of the prodigal son (Luke 15:30), in which one son stayed home and helped his father while the other went abroad and wasted his inheritance. When the second son returned, the father welcomed him with a fine feast, killing a fatted calf in his honor and saying that he who was "lost" has been "found." The term has signified such a welcome ever since.

kill the goose that lays the golden eggs Destroy a source of wealth through greed, neglect, or stupidity. This term refers to Aesop's fable about a farmer whose goose suddenly begins to lay eggs of gold, one at a time. Wanting to get all the eggs at once, the farmer kills the goose, only to find that he has lost the source of golden eggs. An English proverb from the fifteenth century on, it was widely applied to numerous situations in the nineteenth century. Thoreau's version was, "Every fowl lays golden eggs for him who can find them" (*Autumn,* 1860).

kill time, to To make time pass by performing some unessential activity. The term dates from the early 1700s. Leslie Stephen had it in *Hours in the Library* (1874), "Tapestry, in which ladies employed their needles by way of killing time." In a theater review in the *Boston Globe* (Feb. 1, 2005), Ed Siegel wrote, "As Josh and Sal . . . kill time in a hospital waiting room, nervous about whether a third friend is going to survive a drug overdose."

kill two birds with one stone, to To achieve two goals with a single effort. Although the idea dates from Roman times, the precise expression, however unlikely it may be as a literal reality (just try killing two birds by shooting off a single rock), dates from about 1600. Thomas Hobbes wrote, "T. H. thinks to kill two birds with one stone, and satisfy two arguments with one answer" (*Liberty,* 1656). A more feasible operation is *to kill two flies with one flap* (John Ray, *Proverbs,* 1678), but this term did not catch on.

kill with kindness, to To overwhelm with benevolence. The original saying was "to kill with kindness as fond apes do their young," conjuring up the image of a large simian crushing its baby to death with too vigorous a hug. It appeared as a proverb in the mid-sixteenth century and was quoted in numerous sources thereafter. *A Woman Kilde with Kindnesse* is the title of one of Thomas Heywood's best-known plays (1607). It was surely a cliché by the time Byron wrote (*Letters and Journals,* 1815), "Don't let them kill you with claret and kindness."

kindred spirit, a A soulmate; a person very like oneself in temperament, views, likes, and dislikes. Used since the mid-nineteenth century and sometimes put as *kindred soul,* the expression appears in one of George Eliot's letters of 1849: "You won't find any kindred spirits at Plongeon."

king is dead, long live the king, the The old has gone, replaced by the new. This phrase originated in 1461, on the death of Charles VII (*Le Roi est mort. Vive le Roi!*) and was repeated for a number of French kings, most dramatically at the death of Louis XIV. In English it dates only from the mid-1800s but was soon transferred to other events. Virginia Postrel had a version in discussing the Oscar awards of 2000 and Hollywood's search for successful formula movies: "The formula movie is dead. Long live the formula movie" (*New York Times,* March 23, 2000).

kiss and tell, to To betray an intimate secret. The term comes from Restoration England ("And if he needs must kiss and tell, I'll kick him headlong into Hell," Charles Cotton, *Burlesque,* 1675). Numerous writers since have warned against such shameful (or shameless) behavior, from William Congreve and Robert Burns to George Bernard Shaw (*Misalliance,* 1910).

kiss of death, a/the A destructive or fatal relationship or action, undertaken with seemingly good intentions. The term refers to the betrayal of Jesus by his disciple, Judas Iscariot, who pointed out Jesus to his enemies by kissing him (Matthew 26:47–49). Although the term *Judas kiss* signified such a betrayal from the sixteenth century, the current cliché dates only from about 1940 and does not necessarily signify treason or disloyalty. For example, publishing an attractive gift book too late to take advantage of Christmas sales might be said to give it the kiss of death—that is, the poor timing will result in significantly fewer copies being sold.

kiss the blarney stone, to To engage in outrageous flattery. The term comes from the fifteenth-century Blarney Castle, near Cork, Ireland, which has a triangular piece of engraved limestone embedded high on its wall. According to legend, anyone who could reach the stone and kiss it would be rewarded with acquiring the ability to cajole and flatter with great eloquence. To indulge tourists, the modern-day Irish have provided a substitute stone that is easier to reach and is, they claim, equally effective. The noun *blarney* has meant "inflated nonsense" since about 1800.

kit and caboodle, (the whole) Everything; all of it. Several writers speculate that *caboodle* comes from the Dutch *boedel,* meaning a large quantity, whereas *kit* has long meant a set of tools or equipment for a specific purpose, such as a tool kit or makeup kit. However, the *OED* maintains that *caboodle* is a corruption of *kit and boodle,* and gives quotations for *whole caboodle* (1838), *kit and cargo* (1852), *kit and boiling* (1859), and finally, *the hul kit and boodle* (1861). They all meant the same thing—"the lot."

kith and kin Friends and family. This term is very old indeed, appearing in William Langland's *Piers Ploughman* (1377), when *kith* meant "one's native land," and by extension one's countrymen, and *kin* meant, as it still does, "members of one's family." Presumably the alliteration helped it survive. It became a cliché in the nineteenth century but is much less heard now and may be obsolescent. Ogden Nash played on it in "Family Court" (1930): "One would be in less danger From the wiles of the stranger If one's own kin and kith Were more fun to be with."

knee-high to a grasshopper Small and, usually, quite young. The term, used most often to describe someone's extreme youth, originated in America about 1850, when it replaced the earlier nineteenth-century hyperboles *knee-high to a mosquito, bumble-bee,* and *splinter.* A challenge arose in *knee-high to a duck,* current from about 1900 to the 1940s, but grasshopper outstripped and survived it, too.

knight in shining armor, a A rescuer or deliverer. This term, which recalls the age of chivalry through the image of a dashing knight on horseback clad in polished armor, dates from the sixteenth century but has been in figurative use only since the mid-twentieth century. John Ciardi pointed out that the phrase has been used with two meanings: the "Mr. Right" of a young girl's dreams, rescuing her from the humdrum with the promise of romance, and in politics, the idealistic reformer. One might add a third, the *white knight* of the modern-day corporation, who rescues the company from a hostile raider and averts an unwanted takeover. Quite figuratively, the poet William Rose Benét wrote, "Like a knight in glittering armor, Laughter stood up at his side" ("The Last Ally").

knock-down drag-out fight, a A violent altercation; a free-for-all, literal or figurative. This term, which has a modern ring to it, actually dates from the 1820s and originated in America. In those days it was nearly always used with reference to westerners, at least in print. James Fenimore Cooper used it in *The Prairie* (1827): "It was thinking of what you call consequences . . . that prevented me from . . . making it a real knock-down and drag-out."

knock (someone) down with a feather, to To overcome with surprise. This hyperbole dates from the early nineteenth century. An early appearance in print is in William Cobbett's *Rural Rides* (1821): "You might have knocked me down with a feather." Today it is more often used with the conditional *could* (instead of *might*).

knock oneself out, to To make a great effort, to apply oneself to the point of exhaustion. This hyperbolic expression, alluding to knocking oneself unconscious with extreme effort, dates from about 1930. It is often put negatively, as in "Don't knock yourself out; we can finish this project tomorrow." In the mid-1900s a newer slang usage surfaced, *knock yourself out,* meaning enjoy yourself, have fun. Unlike the earlier usage, it is not yet a cliché.

knock on wood Avoid misfortune and/or hope for good luck. This magical formula, put as *touch wood* in Great Britain, is based on the superstition that touching or rapping on anything wooden will avoid a disaster, especially after one has boasted. "Touch wood, it's sure to come good," is the proverbial saying. There may have been an ancient religious significance to the gesture, perhaps from the time of the Druids, who regarded certain trees as sacred, but the precise meaning has been forgotten.

knock the spots off, to To defeat overwhelmingly or to excel. This term, which Ebenezer Brewer believed to come from target practice with playing cards, with the object of knocking out all the pips or spots from a card, dates from the mid-nineteenth century. "We did knock the spots off them that time," wrote Henry Latham (*Black and White,* 1867), meaning we beat them, and Mark Twain wrote, "He knocked the spots out any acting ever I see before" (*Huckleberry Finn,* 1884), meaning he surpassed all others. It is currently heard less often than a similar expression, to *knock someone's socks off.* A seemingly still more unlikely accomplishment, it, too, means to beat or trounce someone. Catherine Beecher used it in a letter in 1845: "You must knock the socks off those Old School folks!" More recently it has acquired another meaning, "to astonish" or "delight," as in "The special effects in that movie will knock your socks off."

know (someone) from Adam, doesn't/not to Not acquainted with someone. The *Adam* referred to in this mid-nineteenth century term is the first human being according to the Book of Genesis. One writer suggests that the inability to recognize Adam is the height of foolishness, since he had no name and wore only a fig leaf, but this point does not seem particularly relevant. The French have a similar saying that includes Eve as well (*"Je ne connais ni d'Eve ni d'Adam"*).

know like a book, to To be very familiar or knowledgeable about something or someone. Presumably this expression, which dates from the early nineteenth century, alludes to a book one has read very carefully. Also see READ SOMEONE LIKE A BOOK. A much newer synonym is *to know like the back of one's hand,* where the allusion is obvious; it dates from the mid-1900s.

know one's own mind, to To be certain of one's opinions or plans; to be self-assured. This term has been known since about 1700. Jonathan Swift included it in *Polite Conversation* (1738), "You don't know your own mind," an accusation still often voiced in just this way.

know the ropes, to To be well informed about the details of an operation, situation, or task. The term comes from the days of sailing ships, when sailors had to learn the details of the rigging in order to handle a ship's ropes. It appeared in print in Richard Dana's *Two Years Before the Mast* (1840) but was transferred to non-nautical matters by the late nineteenth century. Shaw used it and included a definition: "He knows the ropes: he knows his way about" (*Fanny's First Play,* Introduction, 1911).

know what/which side of the bread is buttered (on), to To know where one's best interests lie. This metaphor appeared in John Heywood's *Proverbs* of 1546 ("I know on which syde my bread is buttered"), and was used so often over the centuries that it was a cliché by about 1800.

know what's what, to To be cognizant of the full situation; to be familiar with all the facts. This term may have been coined by Samuel Butler (*Hudibras,* 1663): "He knew what's what, and that's as high as metaphysic wit can fly." Dickens's Sam Weller (*Pickwick Papers*) used it too: "'That 'ere young lady', replied Sam. 'She knows wot's wot, she does.'"

knuckle under, to To give in under pressure; to admit defeat. The origin of this expression is disputed. One writer claims it comes from the custom of striking the underside of a table with the knuckles when one was defeated in an argument. However, the noun *knuckle* once meant the end of any bone at the joint where it forms a protuberance, as at the knee, elbow, and finger joints. The verb *to knuckle* originally meant "to bend down" or "stoop" (probably from the joint's bending), and by extension "to comply with" or "submit to"—it was so used from the 1700s on. The first appearance in print of *knuckle under* with this same meaning was in 1882. *To knuckle down,* on the other hand, while it originally may have been synonymous with *knuckle under,* today means to apply oneself resolutely to something. This meaning was first recorded in 1864.

labor of love, a Work done for the pleasure of accomplishment or from personal interest rather than for monetary reward or from a sense of duty; this book, for example. The phrase appears in two Epistles of St. Paul in the New Testament, one to the Hebrews (6:10) and the other to the Thessalonians (1:3), both referring to the faithful who do God's work as a labor of love.

ladies'/lady's man A man who puts himself out to be attractive to women and is very attentive to them. This term dates from the eighteenth century, and presumably contrasts such a person with the STRONG SILENT TYPE known as a man's man. William Cowper used the expression in *Tiroc* (1784): "A slave at court, elsewhere a lady's man."

Lady Bountiful A woman known for her generous charity. The term is the name of a character in George Farquar's play *The Beaux's Stratagem* (1706), and in Britain it was transferred later to the lady of the manor or to the village benefactress. Still later, when such behavior sometimes was disparaged as being too patronizing, the term was not always used in complimentary fashion. Today it is nearly always used ironically.

la-la land, in Out of touch with reality. This slangy equivalent of NEVER-NEVER LAND dates from the 1980s. The *New York Times* stated (Jan. 10, 1992), "Stanford is a multicultural la-la land. . . . It's not the real world." Capitalized, *La-La Land* is a jocular nickname for Los Angeles, California, a term that also dates from the 1980s.

lame duck, a A person finishing a term of office, employment, or other engagement, and soon to be supplanted by another. This term had quite another meaning in eighteenth-century Britain. Then it denoted a stock-exchange jobber (broker) who could not pay his debts and therefore was struck from the members' list, forced to "waddle away" from the Exchange. In the nineteenth century, however, the term began to be used for any ineffectual person, on both sides of the Atlantic. Some decades thereafter it began to be used in its present meaning in the United States, that is, for government officials who have failed to be reelected but must serve out their term of office, even though their endeavors are hampered because they are about to be replaced.

land-office business, a A booming enterprise. This term dates from the 1830s and refers to local land offices of the U.S. government that registered applicants for purchasing government lands in the West. Although the government had been in the business of selling its land to settlers since Revolutionary times, from the 1820s on this business was greatly augmented and land offices saw long lines of applicants. By the mid-nineteenth century the term *land-office business* had been transferred to any fast-expanding or very profitable enterprise. Reporting on an election in 1875, the *Chicago Tribune* stated, "The taprooms adjoining the polls were all open and doing a land-office business."

land of milk and honey, the A place abounding in good things. The term comes from the Book of Exodus (3:8), where God tells Moses, "And I am come down to deliver them out of the hand of the Egyptians . . . unto a land flowing with milk and honey."

lap of luxury, the Affluent circumstances. This term, with its allusion to a traditional place of comfort and ease, the human lap, no doubt owes its popularity to its fluid alliteration. It dates from the late eighteenth century and appeared in print in 1802 in Maria Edgeworth's *Moral Tales.*

large as/larger than life, as Life-size, appearing to be real; on a grand scale. The first expression may be an English version of a much older Latin saying, *ad vivum,* or "to the life." It dates from the late eighteenth century, when it appeared in Maria Edgeworth's *Lame Jervas* (1799): "I see the puppets, the wheelbarrows, everything as large as life." In the nineteenth century a number of writers not only used the term but added to it, "and quite as natural." Among them were Cuthbert Bede (1853), Lewis Carroll (in *Through the Looking Glass,* 1871), and George Bernard Shaw (1893). A similar addition, essentially meaningless, was "and twice as natural." The second version, *larger than life,* conveys the idea of being on a grand or heroic scale. A less alliterative form, *big as life,* is sometimes used.

last but not least Last in a sequence but not least in importance. This expression dates from the sixteenth century, when it was used by John Lyly, who may have been its originator. "Of these three but one can stand me in steede, the last, but not the least" (*Euphues and His England,* 1580). Soon afterward it was used by Sir Philip Sidney, Edmund Spenser, and several times by Shakespeare (*Julius Caesar, King Lear*).

last-ditch defense/effort A desperate final measure. In military terminology of the seventeenth century the "last ditch" was the ultimate line of defense. By the eighteenth century the term was being used figuratively, as in Thomas Jefferson's description, "A government driven to the last ditch by the universal call for liberty."

last gasp, the Nearing the end; on the point of death. The gasp here literally means one's breath, but the term often is used loosely to mean either extremely tired (exhausted) or a final effort. In the first meaning the term appears in one of the Apocryphal books of the Bible (2 Maccabees 7:9) and in Shakespeare's *Henry VI, Part I* (1.2), where Joan of Arc tells Charles, "Fight till the last gasp; I will be your guard."

last laugh, to have the To win in the end, after some earlier setbacks. This term is a slightly later version of a proverb recorded by John Ray in 1678, "Better the last smile than the first laughter," which then became "He who laughs last, laughs best." The same proverb exists in French, Italian, and other languages. There have been several modern plays on it, such as H. W. Thompson's "He laughs best whose laugh lasts," and Terry Cohen's wry "He who laughs last is generally the last to get the joke."

last of the big spenders, the A tightwad. This term, often used deprecatingly of oneself, originated in the United States during the 1920s, presumably referring at first to the lavish extravagances of the boom preceding the Great Depression. During the Depression it began to be used ironically and self-deprecatingly, as it still is (for example, "I picked it up at a yard sale—I'm the last of the big spenders"). Possibly by design but more probably by coincidence, the term echoes the much older "After great getters come great spenders," which originated in the sixteenth century, and "Great spenders are bad lenders," from the seventeenth century, which became proverbial.

last straw, the The final minor irritation; one last superfluous item. This term, also put as *the straw that broke the camel's back,* appears in Dickens's *Dombey and Son* (1848). It is a version of the earlier "last feather that breaks the horse's back," found in Archbishop John Bramhall's *Works* (1677) and repeated in Fuller's *Gnomologia* (1732). Both convey a vivid image of something that would not be burdensome if there were not too much of it, but the straw version is the one that survived and became a cliché.

last word, to have the To have the final say in a decision, or the closing rejoinder in a debate. This term is very old indeed, dating from the sixteenth century. One version, by Ben Jonson in his play *A Tale of a Tub* (1633), became a proverb: "He will have the last word though he talk bilk for it.—Bilk! What's that?—Why nothing: a word signifying Nothing; and borrowed here to express nothing." More recently, the *New York Times* played on the expression in a headline over an article about lexicographers: "In Land of Lexicons, Having the Last Word." (March 19, 2005).

late bloomer A person who matures or achieves some goal more slowly than his or her peers. This cliché transfers the tendency of certain plants to bloom late in the growing season to human beings who are late to achieve their potential: for example, "He didn't marry until he was in his mid-forties, a late bloomer if there ever was one." The noun *bloomer* for a plant dates only from the first half of the eighteenth century, and the cliché from the twentieth century.

laughed all the way to the bank See CRIED ALL THE WAY TO THE BANK.

laugh one's head off See SPLIT ONE'S SIDES.

laugh or cry, don't know whether to I am amused and upset at the same time. This expression is a modern version of several much earlier sayings. Chaucer wrote, "She ys fals [is false]; and ever laughynge, with oon eye, and that other wepynge," indicating more hypocrisy rather than being torn by conflicting feelings. This version became a proverb, "Cry with one eye and laugh with the other" (in Ray's 1678 and Fuller's 1732 collections). Another version, "to laugh and cry both with a breath"—that is, to laugh and cry at the same time—was so put by Shakespeare (in *Venus and Adonis*) and also recorded in the above-named proverb collections. The modern cliché dates from the nineteenth century.

laugh out of court, to To ridicule without mercy; to treat as not worth being taken seriously. The court here referred to is a court of law, and the idea of dismissing a case as laughable is mentioned in Horace's *Satires* (35 B.C.). The modern term dates from the late nineteenth century and has lost its legal significance entirely, as in Walter de la Mare's use (*A Private View,* 1909): "Longfellow, Emerson, and hosts of lesser men be laughed out of court."

laugh out of the other side of your face/mouth, you'll/to You'll be sorry; to feel anger or annoyance or disappointment after having felt happy. This term dates from the seventeenth century and was then spelled out by Giovanni Torriano (1666): "The English say, when one has conveniently reveng'd ones self on another, now you can laugh but on one side of your mouth." Later it was sometimes put as *laughing on the wrong side of one's mouth.*

laugh up one's sleeve, to To be secretly amused. This term, originally *laughing in one's sleeve,* alludes to concealing mirth by hiding one's face in the big loose sleeves of old-time fashions. It dates from the early sixteenth century and was included in John Heywood's 1546 proverb collection. See also UP ONE'S SLEEVE.

law and order Strict enforcement of laws, especially with regard to controlling crime. This policy was first expounded by the Greek philosopher Aristotle in his *Politics:* "Law means good order." However, it also acquired a bad name among those who point to its association with infringements of civil rights in the mid-1900s. More than a century earlier Rhode Island had a restrictive property qualification for voters. A Suffrage Party was formed and led a rebellion in 1842; its opponents were called the "Law and Order" party. The term was also used in 1881 with reference to maintaining law and order in Ireland (surely a controversial issue), and became a cliché in the course of several mid-twentieth-century American political campaigns. The British journal *The Economist* commented in 1968, "Mr Nixon . . . and Mr Humphrey are both making concessions to this overriding concern about law and order." In the 1990s the term had largely lost its repressive connotation. A popular television series entitled *Law and Order* dealt with the cooperative crime-fighting efforts of police officers and lawyers.

lay an egg, to To fail, to make an embarrassing mistake. In Britain this term comes from cricket, where a player or team failing to score has, since the mid-nineteenth century, been said to get a duck's egg (meaning 0, or zero). In America the term appeared in the latter part of the nineteenth century in vaudeville and theater, similarly signifying a flop of a performance. It was transferred to other arenas by the early twentieth century, and fittingly, a headline in *Variety* (*the* American chronicle of show business at the time) read, in October 1929, "Wall Street Lays An Egg."

lay down the law, to To pontificate; to give orders or make dogmatic statements. *Lay down* here means simply to "make," and the expression today is often used ironically, since it rarely involves an actual legislator, or even an authority. It still did in 1765, however, when Blackstone's *Commentaries* stated, "We may now . . . lay down the law of redress against public oppression."

lay eyes on, to To see, to look at. This expression is first recorded in a Middle English manuscript from about 1225. Poet Andrew Marvell used it in *Mr. Smirke* (1676), "The fairest thing that ever eyes were laid on."

lay it on the line, to To speak frankly. This Americanism of the early twentieth century originally meant to hand over money (from about the 1920s). However, by mid-century it meant to speak plainly or categorically, and in the 1960s acquired still another sense, to *lay something on the line,* meaning to put that thing at risk (as in, "The Marines laid their lives on the line").

lay it on thick, to To exaggerate, especially in flattery. This term began life in Shakespeare's *As You Like It* (1.2) as *lay it on with a trowel,* which survived well into the mid-twentieth century. The trowel referred to is the tool for applying mortar or plaster, not the garden digging tool. *Thick* was inserted into the original term and *with a trowel* was eventually dropped.

lay/lie of the land, the The general state of affairs. This term, which in Britain is always put as the *lie* of the land, originated in the seventeenth century and alluded to surveying. An early appearance in print is in *A New Dictionary of the Canting Crew* (c. 1700): "How lies the land? How stands the reckoning?" In the twentieth century it came to be used figuratively for any investigation of conditions, without reference to real estate. Thus E. H. Gombrich wrote (*The Story of Art,* 1950), "To show the newcomer the lie of the land without confusing him."

lay on, Macduff Strike; attack violently. This imperative, straight from Shakespeare's *Macbeth* (5.7), consists of Macbeth's final words before he is killed by Macduff: "Before my body I throw my warlike shield. Lay on, Macduff, and damn'd be him that first cries, 'Hold, enough!'" For some reason this vivid cry caught on enough to be used in any situation calling for vigorous action, and was a cliché from about 1800 on. From the late nineteenth century on it also was often misquoted as *lead on, Macduff,* which itself became a cliché; it, however, means "Let's get going; start us off."

lay to rest Bury; also, settle something with finality. In the first sense, this expression dates from the late nineteenth century, although *rest* in the sense of death was so used from about 1400 on. It appears in an American cowboy song, "And they laid him down to rest, with a lily on his chest." In the second sense, it was earlier expressed as *set at rest* and dates from Shakespeare's day. Charles Kingsley used the present locution in *Westward Ho!* (1855): "His fears, such as they were, were laid to rest."

lazy man's load An extremely heavy burden undertaken so as to move it in one trip rather than making several trips. Always referring to moving something physically, this cliché dates from the turn of the twentieth century and may be dying out.

lead by the nose, to To dominate. Although this phrase, which alludes to an animal led by a ring passed through its nostrils, occurs in a slightly different form in the Bible (Isaiah 37:29), its first use in English appears in a translation of Lucian's *Dialogues of the Gods* (c. A.D. 170), cited by Erasmus in *Adagia.* By the sixteenth century it had been transferred to human beings. Arthur Golding's translation of Calvin's writings (1583) states it as, "Men . . . suffer themselves to be led by the nose like brute beasts."

leading edge See CUTTING EDGE.

lead on, Macduff See LAY ON, MACDUFF.

lead-pipe cinch An absolute certainty; an easy success. Unlike the meaning of this cliché, the etymology is uncertain. It originated in America in the late nineteenth century and may refer to (l) the cinch that holds a horse's saddle in place, which, if well fastened, makes it easier for the rider to win a race; or (2), more likely, to plumbing, where a lead pipe is fastened with a steel band to another pipe or fixture, making for a very secure joint. O. Henry used the term in a short story published in 1907 (*The Sphinx Apple*): "An engagement ain't always a lead-pipe cinch."

lean over backward See BEND OVER BACKWARD.

leap of faith A belief or trust in something or someone that has no basis in past experience or fact. It is often applied to technological breakthroughs, as in "It took a real leap of faith for the first astronaut to step out on the Moon." A *Boston Globe* article by Thomas Oliphant quotes Senator Edward Kennedy discussing a Supreme Court nominee: "The confirmation of nominees to our courts should not require a leap of faith. Nominees must earn their confirmation by providing us with full knowledge of the values and convictions they will bring to decisions. . . ." (Sept. 29, 2005).

least little thing, the See LITTLE THINGS.

leave in the lurch, to To abandon or desert someone in a difficult position. This seemingly slangy modern term dates from the sixteenth century and is believed to come from a French dicing game called *louche,* similar to backgammon. To incur a lurch at first meant to be left far behind, a meaning that survived in several other games, including cribbage. By the early seventeenth century, however, the expression had been transferred to any kind of abandonment, and was so used in Richard Tarton's *Jests* (1611): "Ile leave him in the lurch and shift for my selves."

leave no stone unturned, to To spare no trouble or expense; to make every possible effort. This term actually dates back to a Greek legend recounted by Euripides. One of Xerxes's generals, Mardonius, was said to have abandoned a great treasure in his tent when he was defeated in the battle of Plataea (477 B.C.). Polycrates of Thebes looked for the treasure but could not find it, and turned to the Oracle of Delphi for advice. The oracle replied, "Move every stone," which Erasmus later translated as, "Leave no stone unturned." Of the many repetitions over the centuries, one of the most amusing is Ogden Nash's, "When I throw rocks at seabirds, I leave no tern unstoned."

leave out in the cold, to To exclude. This term, evoking the image of a person who is refused admittance to a house and must remain outside in cold weather, presumably began by meaning just that, in the late nineteenth century. It soon was transferred to mean exclusion not only from shelter but from a social group, information, or the like. It had long been a cliché by the time John le Carré entitled his espionage novel, *The Spy Who Came in from the Cold* (1963), in which the main character returns from the German Democratic Republic (Communist East Germany)—figuratively out in the cold—to the West.

leave to someone's tender mercies Literally, kind usage of someone. The phrase "tender mercies" comes from the Bible's Book of Psalms (25:6), "Remember, O Lord, thy tender mercies and they loving kindnesses." Since at least 1900 or so the term has been used ironically, as in Stella Rimington's *At Risk* (2004): "'What would you have done if the guy had refused to give back the money?' 'Left him to your tender mercies,' said Liz . . . .'We don't do violence.'"

leave/let well enough alone Do not try to improve matters lest you make them worse. This idea was stated in ancient Greek times. In Aesop's fable, the fox refused the hedgehog's offer to remove its ticks, "lest by removing these, which are full, other hungry ones will come." There is a medieval French version of the saying, *Assez est bone, lessez ester* (It is good enough, let it be). An English proverb for many centuries, the phrase became the motto of Sir Robert Walpole, prime minister from 1715 to 1717 and again from 1721 to 1742. A slangy twentieth-century Americanism meaning the same thing is *if it ain't broke don't fix it.* Reporting on a meeting between West German Chancellor Helmut Kohl and President George H.W. Bush concerning the future of NATO in view of German unification, Strobe Talbott wrote, "They both believe in the old adage, 'If it ain't broke, don't fix it.' NATO has kept the peace for 40 years, and there's no reason to believe it can't do so for another 40" (*Time,* July 2, 1990). See also LET SLEEPING DOGS LIE.

left hand doesn't know what the right hand is doing, the An uncoordinated action; also, taking a stand on an issue despite one's ambivalence. This term appears in the Bible (Matthew 6:3) with a quite different meaning. Quoting Jesus's Sermon on the Mount, the Gospel writer says one should do good quietly rather than publicize one's actions: "When thou doest alms, let not thy left hand know what thy right hand doeth: that thine alms may be in secret." Over the centuries, the idea of secrecy vanished, and the term was applied first to individuals who took a stand or acted without being wholly committed to that direction, and later to organizations in which one branch or department took actions quite contrary to another's.

left-handed compliment, a An expression of praise or admiration that is actually a faintly disguised insult or reproach. The association of left-handedness with ambiguity or doubtfulness may come from the practice of the morganatic marriage ceremony (between royalty and a commoner who renounces all claim to the spouse's title and property); in it the groom gave the bride his left hand instead of the right hand used in conventional marriage ceremonies.

left to one's own devices, to be To be allowed to do as one pleases; to be left alone. The word *devices* in this meaning—projects or stratagems—survives mainly in this cliché, which dates from the late nineteenth century. It also appears in a phrase still used from the 1552 Anglican Book of Common Prayer: "We have followed too much the devices and desires of our own hearts.")

leg to stand on, doesn't have a/not a/without a To have no chance of success. This metaphor, which dates from the sixteenth century, applies the lack of physical support to an argument or hypothesis. The Elizabethan satirist Thomas Nashe (*The Unfortunate Traveller,* 1594) stated, "Faine he would have pacht out a polt-foot tale, but (God knows) it had not one true leg to stand on."

lend one's ear, to To listen, to pay attention. This locution appears in Shakespeare's *Julius Caesar* (3.2) in Mark Antony's famous speech, "Friends, Romans, countrymen, lend me your ears." It is heard less often today.

lesser of two evils See CHOICE BETWEEN TWO EVILS.

less is more Simplicity is superior to elaborate embellishment. This phrase is commonly associated with the architect Ludwig Mies van der Rohe (1886–1969), who used it referring to the desirability of less visual clutter in buildings and homes. Actually the very same words appeared a century earlier in Robert Browning's poem *Andrea del Sarto,* referring to the painter's creed: "Yet do much less, so much less . . . Well, less is more, Lucrezia; I am judged." Although both citations refer to the visual arts, the term has been extended to other contexts. For example, "Featherbrains can also count on enjoying Karen Shaw's variations on the theme of 'less is more,' in which language, numbers and symbols are all put through the mincer to convivial effect" (*New York Times,* June 20, 1980).

let bygones be bygones Don't worry about the past; FORGIVE AND FORGET. Although the idea dates from ancient times, the wording comes from the seventeenth century, when it was cited by several writers as a proverb or parable. It continued to be widely quoted (by Scott, Tennyson, and Shaw, among others). The word *bygone,* meaning "past," dates from the fourteenth century and survives principally in the cliché.

let her rip Allow an engine to go as fast as possible. An American colloquialism dating from the first half of the nineteenth century, this term presumably was first applied to locomotive or steamship engines. The American journalist

Park Benjamin recorded it about 1840: "Another phrase, which often glides in music from the lip, is one of fine significance and beauty, 'Let her rip!'"

let it all hang out Be completely candid; conceal nothing. This American slang expression became both current and overused in the 1960s. One writer suggests it may originally have referred to the penis, but it quickly was transferred to the uninhibited expression of feelings, opinions, and ideas.

let off steam, to To give vent to one's feelings, or to work off excess energy. The term comes from the safety valve in steam locomotives, which prevented steam from building up to the point of exploding. Henry James used it in a letter in 1869, "I feel an irresistible need to let off steam periodically and confide to a sympathetic ear." See also BLOW OFF STEAM.

let/take one's hair down, to To give free expression to one's private views; to behave informally. The term alludes to the long-standing practice of women wearing their long hair pinned up in a variety of styles and taking it down only in the privacy of the bedroom. At first (mid-nineteenth century) the term was to *let down the back hair;* later it was simply *hair.* P. G. Wodehouse used it in *Heavy Weather* (1933): "We can take our hair down and tell each other our right names."

let's face it Let us accept reality; let's see things as they are. The title of a 1941 Cole Porter musical, the term took hold in the next two decades and soon became a cliché.

let's get the/this show on the road Let's get going; stop delaying. Originally an Americanism from show business of about 1910, when companies presenting plays, vaudeville, and circuses toured all over the country, it came to be used more generally by 1940 or so. In Britain it rivals "Let's get on with it," a phrase popularized in a variety act of the 1930s and 1940s.

let sleeping dogs lie Don't stir up trouble; LEAVE WELL ENOUGH ALONE. Rabelais quoted this thirteenth-century proverb, as did Chaucer in *Troilus and Criseyde,* both alluding to rousing a potentially fierce watchdog.

letter perfect Correct in every detail; verbatim. The term comes from the nineteenth-century stage, in which actors were told to memorize their parts precisely to the letter of every word. It probably evolved from an earlier expression, *to the letter,* which had very much the same meaning. "I will obey you to the letter," wrote Byron (*Sardanapalus,* 1821).

let the cat out of the bag, to To give away a secret. This expression dates from an ancient practice of substituting a worthless cat for a valuable suckling pig by a dishonest tradesman in a farmer's market. When the hapless buyer got home and opened the bag, the cat was revealed. See also PIG IN A POKE.

let the chips fall where they may Whatever the consequences, do the right thing. This term alludes to woodcutting, and suggests that the cutter stick to the principal task and ignore the small pieces of wood flying about. It was used figuratively in a speech by Roscoe Conkling nominating General Ulysses S. Grant at the Republican Convention of 1880: "Hew to the line of right, let the chips fall where they may." The expression was frequently quoted thereafter and was a cliché by the mid-twentieth century.

let the grass grow under one's feet See DON'T LET THE GRASS GROW UNDER YOUR FEET.

level best, to do one's To exert oneself to the fullest. A nineteenth-century Americanism, this term has been traced to the days of the California gold rush, when miners panning for gold would shake sand and gravel until it was level and revealed the ore. It appeared in *An Arkansaw Doctor* in 1851: "We put our horses out at their level best." Mark Twain also used it, in a poem, "He Done His Level Best" (1875): "If he'd a reg'lar task to do, he never took no rest; or if 'twas off-and-on, the same, he done his level best."

lick and a promise, a A superficial cleaning; a hasty, perfunctory performance. The term, in which the promise is to do a better job sometime later, possibly alludes to the quick lick a cat might give itself. It dates from the nineteenth century. The *OED* cites W. White's *All Round the Wrekin* (1860): "We only give the cheap ones a lick and a promise."

lick one's chops, to To anticipate something with obvious pleasure. The word *chops* (or *chaps*) has meant the jaws or mouth since about 1350, usually referring to the lower jaw of animals. This meaning survives in the current cliché, as well as in musicians' slang for the embouchure of wind instruments. In jazz slang of the 1930s and 1940s, *licking one's chops* meant warming up before a performance. In jazz parlance *chops* also came to mean ability or skill, a usage from the 1960s.

lie in wait (for), to To ambush, to prepare to attack from a hiding place. This cliché, which dates from the fifteenth century, originally alluded to a physical attack. It was soon being used metaphorically, as by Jonathan Swift in *A Tale of a Tub* (1704): "A ring of disciples, who lie in wait to catch their droppings."

lie low, to To conceal oneself or one's intentions. An American colloquialism of the nineteenth century, the term calls up the image of a hunter quietly concealed in the brush, waiting for game. An early appearance is in one of Joel Chandler Harris's Uncle Remus stories: "All this while Brer Rabbit lay low."

lie through one's teeth, to To prevaricate outrageously. Versions of this seemingly modern expression appeared as long ago as the fourteenth century. William Safire cites its use in *The Romance of Sir Guy of Warwick* ("Thou lexst amidward thi teth"), as well as in a still earlier Northumbrian poem, but points out that Shakespeare preferred the throat to the teeth (*Twelfth Night,* 3.4; *Hamlet,* 2.2). Of more recent provenance is to *lie like a trooper,* dating from the late 1800s; the British version is to *swear like a trooper.* Why a trooper should have been singled out is a matter of conjecture. Presumably it alludes to the legendary lack of truthfulness in the military, especially the lower ranks, who lie to escape punishment. Originally "like a trooper" meant vigorously, or with great enthusiasm, which clearly was carried over to lying.

life in the fast lane See FAST LANE.

life is just a bowl of cherries Everything is just great. This slangy phrase, often used ironically, gained currency as the title of a song by Ray Henderson (lyrics by Lew Brown) performed by Ethel Merman in the *Scandals* of 1931. Today it is nearly always used ironically, as in the title of humorist Erma Bombeck's book: *If Life Is Just a Bowl of Cherries, What Am I Doing in the Pits?* (1978). See also THE PITS.

life of Reilly, leading/living the Living a life of luxury. There are several theories as to the precise origin of this term and the identity of Reilly (or Riley). The earliest attribution is to a comic song, "Is That Mr. Reilly?" popularized by vaudevillian Pat Rooney in America in the 1880s and describing what Reilly would do if he struck it rich. However, H. L. Mencken said it came from another source, "The Best in the House Is None Too Good for Reilly," by Lawlor and Blake, popular about 1900. Though the original Reilly is no longer known, the cliché survives.

life of the party, the A lively individual who helps make a social gathering a success. This term, dating from the first half of the nineteenth century, began as *the life* and soul *of the party,* but in time the second half was dropped.

life style Manner of living. This term, invented by psychologist Alfred Adler in 1929, has become so entrenched in the language that some dictionaries list it as one word, with or without a hyphen (lifestyle or life-style). Adler meant something quite different from the present meaning: that is, one's basic character as established in early childhood, which he believed governs one's behavior for life. Today, the term signifies a style of living that reflects one's economic or social status, values, and attitudes. It is also frequently used by health care providers to refer to a patient's diet, exercise regimen, and similar habits affecting health and well-being.

lift a finger, he/she doesn't/won't Refusing to exert oneself in the slightest. This hyperbole has an ancient ring to it, but the earliest citation in the *OED* is to David Garnett's *The Flower of the Forest* (1955): "Could anyone honestly say that we should have allowed Paris to be occupied and France defeated without lifting a finger?"

light as a feather Extremely lightweight. This simile dates from the sixteenth century, appearing in Edward Hall's *Chronicles* (1548) and many times thereafter. Indeed, it eventually gave rise to the word *featherweight,* used in boxing to describe a contender who weighs less than 126 pounds (57 kg).

light at the end of a tunnel, (see) the A solution emerges at long last. This metaphor, evoking the end of a long, dark mining or railroad tunnel, came into widespread use only in the mid-twentieth century. It was used by President John F. Kennedy in a 1962 press conference on the Vietnam War and became common throughout that conflict. However, the image was used nearly a century earlier in a letter by English novelist George Eliot, and the expression also appeared in a letter from J. Middleton Murry to his wife, Katherine Mansfield (1922): "I begin to feel that the horror may move away and that there is a big round spot of real daylight at the end of the tunnel."

light dawned, the At last one understands; one finally grasps the meaning or an idea, or the like. Strictly speaking this expression is tautological, since the noun *dawn* means the reappearance of light and the verb *to dawn* means to become light. However, when it is transferred to human perception, as it has been since about 1800, it makes sense as the beginning (*dawn*) of understanding (*light*). The British locution does not raise this problem, since it is *came the dawn.*

lighten up Don't be so serious, relax. Originally, this slangy imperative, dating from the 1940s, meant to calm down, but in succeeding decades it took on its present meaning. Tracy Kidder had it in *Among Schoolchildren* (1989): "Me and my precious schedules . . . I've got to lighten up. Chill out."

like a bat out of hell Moving very fast indeed. This expression arose in the Air Force during World War I, originally likening the flight of fighter planes to that of the only surviving flying mammal. It soon was extended to any fast movement. A synonym with a similar combative origin is *like a shot,* dating from the late 1800s and alluding to the rapidity of a gunshot.

like a bump on a log Motionless; inactive. This simile, comparing a wooden protuberance to a stolidly inactive individual, was used by Mark Twain (1863), "You have been sitting there for thirty days like a bump on a log," and was repeated by such popular writers as Kate Douglas Wiggin (in *The Birds' Christmas Carol,* 1899).

like a chicken with its head cut off, (run about) Behave distractedly and crazily. This graphic simile apparently is based on barnyard experience: the body of a decapitated chicken sometimes continues to totter about crazily for a time following the dirty deed.

like a house afire/on fire Very quickly and efficiently; very well. The simile is based on how houses made of timber or thatch burn very fast, as was the case with the log cabins of American pioneers. Washington Irving used the expression in *Knickerbocker's History of New York* (1809), "At it they went like five hundred houses on fire," and Dickens is quoted as having used it to mean very well ("I am getting on . . . like 'a house on fire'") in a letter of 1837.

like/as two peas in a pod Closely resembling each other. The similarity of peas in a single pod was observed by the ancients, and the transfer to other close resemblances took place by the sixteenth century. It has been repeated ever since.

like a ton of bricks, (come down) Very heavily, unsubtly. This expression originated in early nineteenth-century America as "a thousand of brick," presumably because bricks in such quantity were more commonly counted than weighed. "If folks is sassy, we walk right into 'em like a thousand o' brick," wrote Caroline Kirkland (*Forest Life,* 1842). Sometime in the early twentieth century it was replaced by *ton,* which has survived. Thus, *to come down on like a ton of bricks* means to reprimand or punish severely. This colloquialism dates from the first half of the 1900s. The novelist Graham Greene used it in *Brighton Rock* (1938): "If there's any fighting I shall come down like a ton of bricks on both of you."

like death warmed over/up, to feel/look To feel or look utterly exhausted or extremely ill. This comparison to one step away from death originated in the twentieth century, perhaps during World War I; it appears in a dictionary of soldiers' slang of 1939. It may be obsolescent, although a shortened form, *to feel like death,* is still current.

like gangbusters, come on/going Proceed noisily and vigorously. The term originated in the United States in the 1940s, when *Gangbusters* was the name of a popular radio program in which the police "busted" (pursued and caught) gangsters. The program was known for its sound effects, especially at the beginning, which featured police sirens, roaring motors, screeching brakes, and the like. This noisy urgency later was transferred to any enterprise.

like greased lightning Very rapid(ly). The speed of lightning had been likened to any fast action since the sixteenth century. "It must be done like lightning," wrote Ben Jonson in 1598 (*Every Man in His Humour,* 4.5). In the early nineteenth century somebody or other decided that grease would exaggerate the idea of haste even more. Some attribute it to Americans, others to Britons. An early appearance in print was in the *Boston Herald* of 1833: "He spoke as quick as 'greased lightning.'" Almost synonymous is the expression *like a blue streak,* which since about 1830 has also meant "very fast." However, it acquired another meaning when used in the context of talking. *To talk a blue streak* has meant, since the mid-1800s, to talk fast and intensely, virtually without stopping. A letter of S. Hale's (1895) stated, " I drove in . . . talking a blue streak two miles to her house." See also TALK ONE'S HEAD OFF; QUICK AS A WINK.

like it or lump it Put up with it, whether or not you like it. An Americanism dating from the early nineteenth century, John Neal used it in *The Down-Easters* (1833). It was quoted by Dickens ("If you don't like it, it's open to you to lump it," *Our Mutual Friend,* 1864) and by numerous later writers. The precise source of *lump* has been lost. One authority suggests it comes from a British dialect word meaning to look sullen; another believes it is a polite version of "stuff it (up your behind)."

like it was going out of style Describing something being done with extreme urgency, as though it was the last chance to do it. This ungrammatical expression and the synonymous *like there's no tomorrow* date only from about 1970 but are well on their way to becoming clichés. They are used in such contexts as "He's spending his trust fund like it was going out of style" or "They attacked the buffet table like there's no tomorrow." Purists frown on the conjunctive *use* of *like* (instead of *as*) but the clichés persist.

like lambs to the slaughter Helpless and unaware of danger. This figure of speech first appeared in the Old Testament's Book of Isaiah ("He is brought as a lamb to the slaughter," 53:7) and again in the Book of Jeremiah ("I was like a lamb or an ox that is brought to the slaughter," 11:19) and has been repeated ever since. In recent decades it was sometimes changed to *like pigs to the slaughter,* with essentially the same meaning.

like money in the bank A guaranteed success, a reliable asset. Dating from the 1930s, this colloquial phrase has been applied in numerous contexts. An early use appeared in the *Zanesville* [Ohio] *Times Recorder* of Jan. 3, 1939: "Money in the bank, dearie, money in the bank. That's what diamonds are" (cited by the *OED*).

like shooting fish in a barrel Extremely easy; ridiculously simple. Why anyone would want to shoot fish at all, let alone when they are inside a barrel, is not known. Clearly this is a fanciful hyperbole. It dates from the twentieth century. Gene Fowler used it in *The Great Mouthpiece* (1931), "It's like shooting fish in a barrel," and presumably it was already a well-known phrase.

like taking candy from a baby Ridiculously easy. This twentieth-century simile, also stated as *like stealing candy from a baby,* almost invariably refers to accomplishing something that is not quite legitimate.

like the wind, go/run Very swiftly. "Swifter than the winds" appears as far back as the Roman poet Virgil's *Aeneid* and is echoed by numerous later writers. Another old expression, no longer heard, is *on the wings of the wind,* which appears twice in the Book of Psalms and was repeated by many later writers.

like water off a duck's back Easily, smoothly, without ill effect. This expression, dating from the early nineteenth century, alludes to the way a duck's feathers shed water. Charles Kingsley used it in *The Water Babies* (1863), "When men are men of the world, hard words run off them like water off a duck's back."

line one's pockets, to To accept bribes, or acquire money in some other questionable way. One writer claims that this term originated when a court tailor who wanted the patronage of Beau Brummel gave him a gift of a coat lined with banknotes. However, the term *to line one's purse,* meaning to cram it full of gold or money, predates the eighteenth-century dandy by some two hundred years; Shakespeare used it in *Othello* (1.1), where Iago speaks of dishonest servants who "have lin'd their coats."

lion's share, the The greater part of something. This term comes from one Aesop's fables, in which the lion got not just the largest part of the kill acquired in hunting with an ass, fox, and wolf, but all of it, since the others were afraid to claim their share.

lips are sealed, his/my He/I will keep this secret. Although the idea of keeping one's mouth tightly shut is much older and sealing up someone else's lips dates from the late 1700s, this particular expression became current only in the early twentieth century. It was much repeated by Prime Minister Stanley Baldwin when asked about the rumored abdication of King Edward VIII, who wished to (and eventually did) marry a divorced American, Wallis Simpson. See also MUM'S THE WORD.

lip service, to give/pay An insincere expression of friendship, devotion, or support. Both the Old and New Testaments contain references to honoring God or Jesus only with one's lips (Isaiah 29:13; Matthew 15:8). The religious association is maintained in an early English reference, "Pleasing themselves in their lip-service in bearing a part in it," in the 1644 *Directory for the Publique Worship Throughout the Three Kingdoms of England, Scotland, and Ireland.*

listen up Pay attention, listen carefully. This slangy imperative probably originated in the armed forces during World War II and soon entered the civilian vocabulary. William Safire used it in a quotation, "I'm only going to say this once, so listen up" (*New York Times Magazine,* Sept. 28, 1980).

little bird told me, a I have information from a secret source. A version of this saying appears in John Heywood's 1546 proverb collection, and another a few decades later in Brian Melbancke's *Philotimus* ("I had a little bird that brought me news of it"). It is still widely used by journalists protecting their sources of information.

little learning is a dangerous thing, a Knowing a little may make one mistakenly assume that one knows everything. This expression is a direct quotation from Alexander Pope's *Essay on Criticism* (1709), which echoed a sentiment stated in the sixteenth century by the French essayist Montaigne.

little pitchers have big ears Small children may overhear what they should not. This metaphor, which likens the human ear to the pitcher's handle, was already stated in one of John Heywood's proverbs (1546): "Avoyd your children, small pitchers have wide eares." It was repeated several times by Shakespeare and was surely a cliché by the time Dickens referred to it in *Bleak House* (1853): "Charley verified the adage about little pitchers, I am sure."

little things, the The unimportant matters, the minor concerns. This term dates back to the ancient Romans, or perhaps even further. Writers have deemed *little things* either as too trivial to make a difference (Ovid: "Little things affect little minds," repeated by Disraeli and Oliver Goldsmith, among others) or as being the building blocks of important matters (Browning: "We find great things are made of little things"). A related phrase is *the least little thing,* meaning the least important matter or occurrence, as in "The least little thing will set her off in a temper tantrum."

live and learn Experience is a great teacher. This adage was already stated in the sixteenth century by George Gascoigne in his play *Glass of Government* and has been repeated many times since, in numerous languages. James Howell's *English Proverbs* (1659) expanded it a bit: "One may live and learn, and be hanged and forget all."

live and let live Live in your own way and show tolerance for the ways of others. This sentiment was quoted in the seventeenth century as a Dutch proverb (by Gerard de Malynes, in *The Ancient Law-Merchant,* 1622) and was subsequently included in English proverb collections and numerous other sources. See also GIVE AND TAKE.

live and well See ALIVE AND KICKING.

live by one's wits See HAVE ONE'S WITS ABOUT ONE.

live dangerously, to To take risks; to be daring. This advice, given by the German poet Goethe in *Faust* and by the philosopher Nietzsche in numerous writings, was much touted through the first half of the twentieth century. Today it is more often used either critically or jocularly.

live in sin, to To cohabit outside marriage. This term from the early 1800s, is used mostly jocularly today, given society's more liberal views.

live like a prince, to To live extremely well, in lavish circumstances. This simile dates from the sixteenth century and has somehow outlived the days when royalty was preeminent in wealth and position. It is still used just as Samuel Pepys did in his *Diary* in 1660: "We came to Sir W. Batten's, where he lives like a prince."

live on borrowed time, to See BORROWED TIME, ON.

living doll, a An extremely nice person, amiable and generous. Why a child's toy should be chosen for this metaphor is not known. *Doll* alone has meant a young and attractive woman since the mid-1800s, as in Frank Loesser's hit musical comedy *Guys and Dolls* (1950). However, the current usage, dating from the 1940s, is applied to individuals of either sex and any age.

living hell, a A condition or place of acute misery and distress. This expression uses *hell* in the sense of the afterworld's place of eternal torment. "Even after the divorce was final, he made her life a living hell." Also put as *hell on earth,* it appears in such contexts as "Jungle warfare is a true hell on earth."

loaded for bear Ready to fight, up in arms. This term, from the mid-nineteenth century, alludes to the heavy ammunition needed to kill such a large animal. Max Shulman used it in *Rally round the Flag Boys!* (1957), "The O'Sheel woman is coming in loaded for bear this time."

load off one's mind, a A great relief. This cliché, transferring a physical burden to mental anxiety or anguish, dates from the mid-nineteenth century.

In slightly different guise, however, Shakespeare used *load* in this figurative sense, as in "Those that wring under the load of sorrow" (*Much Ado about Nothing,* 5.1).

lo and behold What a surprise! Can you believe it! The very old word *lo,* which means "look" or "see," today survives only in this tautological imperative, which dates from the mid-nineteenth century and is nearly always used lightly. As Edward Bulwer-Lytton wrote (*Night and Morning,* cited by the *OED*), "The fair bride was skipping down the middle . . . when lo and behold! the whiskered gentleman advanced."

lock horns with, to To engage in a fight, to clash. This transfer from the battles of stags, bulls, and other beasts that use their horns to fight is surprisingly recent, dating only from the nineteenth century. W. T. Porter used it in *A Quarter Race in Kentucky* (1846): "We locked horns without a word, thar all alone, and I do think we fit [fought] an hour."

lock, stock, and barrel The whole thing; all of something. Originally this term meant all three elements of a firearm—the lock or firing mechanism, the stock or handle, and the barrel or tube. It began to be transferred to the entirety of anything in the early nineteenth century, although for a time it was also put as *stock, lock, and barrel.* See also HOOK, LINE, AND SINKER.

lock the barn/stable door after the horse has bolted/is stolen, to To take precautions after damage has been done. This proverb, found in many languages, first appeared in a French collection of c. 1190 and found its way into a Middle English manuscript, *Douce MS,* by about 1350. It has been repeated ever since. Stanley Walker poked fun at it (*The Uncanny Knacks of Mr. Doherty,* 1941): "He locked the stable door while they were putting the cart before the horse."

long and the short of it/the matter, the The essence of the matter; IN A NUTSHELL. This expression, sometimes reversed (that is, *the short and the long of something*), dates from the fourteenth century. Shakespeare preferred the reversed form (*Henry V,* 3.2; *The Merry Wives of Windsor,* 2.1), but by the end of the seventeenth century *long* nearly always preceded *short.*

long face See A LONG FACE.

long in the tooth Aging or old. This unflattering term alludes to the fact that a horse's gums recede as it gets older, and transfers the same phenomenon to humankind. The transfer understandably is not very old, since until relatively recent times adults who were old enough to experience gum recession generally had lost most or all of their teeth. It dates from the nineteenth century. Thackeray used it in *Henry Esmond* (1852): "She was lean and yellow and long in the tooth."

long shot, (not by) a (Not) a remote chance. Early firearms were notoriously inaccurate, and a shot from a distance rarely hit the target. In the late eighteenth and early nineteenth centuries a long shot meant just that, a shot fired from afar. By the late nineteenth century the term had been transferred to other improbable circumstances, such as a wild guess or, more specifically, a bet against considerable odds. From about 1865, however, it also meant far-fetched, as in this *OED* citation from *Young Gentleman's Magazine* (1873): "This did not, however, suit her long-shot tactics."

long suit, one's One's particular strength or advantage. This term comes from whist and related card games, including present-day contract bridge, in which holding a hand with numerous cards in a single suit may convey a strong advantage, particularly if that suit is the trump suit. The term began to be transferred to other enterprises about 1900.

long time no see I haven't seen you for ages, usually used as an informal greeting. This expression originated in the pidgin English used by the Chinese and Westerners dealing with them in the late nineteenth century, which gave rise to other simplified locutions such as "No can do." This particular phrase is a translation of an actual Chinese greeting, *ch'ang chih mei* (or *hao jiu mei jian*). Heard very often until the mid-twentieth century, with its provenance long forgotten, this cliché may be obsolescent.

look askance, to To view with doubt, suspicion, or mistrust. This term dates back to the sixteenth century and literally means "to look sideways," but it has had somewhat different significance over the years. Sometimes it meant to look enviously, at other times to look scornfully or contemptuously. The present meaning dates from about 1800, and Washington Irving used it in *Tales of a Traveller* (1824): "Eyeing the enemy askance from under their broad hats."

look before you leap Consider the consequences before you act. This ancient adage, like so many others, has its roots in one of Aesop's fables. The fox, unable to climb out of a well into which he fell, persuades the goat to jump in, too. He then climbs out by standing on the goat's shoulders, leaving the goat in the well. "First loke and aftirward lepe" appeared in the *Douce MS* of about 1350. Charlotte Brontë used it ironically (for her time) in *Shirley* (1849): "When you feel tempted to marry . . . look twice before you leap."

look daggers at, to To glare at someone. The term first appeared in the Greek playwright Aristophanes's *The Birds* (c. 414 B.C.) and was alluded to several times by Shakespeare. "There's daggers in men's smiles," he wrote

(*Macbeth,* 2:3). The image aptly conveys the fierceness of such a glance and appealed to numerous other writers, including Thoreau. A synonymous cliché is *if looks could kill,* which has been around since the early 1900s. Frank Harris used it in *My Life and Loves* (1922): "When they let me up I looked at Jones, and if looks could kill, he would have had short shrift."

look down one's nose at, to To regard or treat someone with disdain. One writer suggests that this term comes from a customary attitude of disapproval shown by lowering the eyelids and looking downward, thereby focusing on one's own nose. This explanation does not jibe with the body language involved in TURN UP ONE'S NOSE, yet both expressions involve contempt or disdain, and indeed, *to look down on* has meant expressing contempt from about 1700; *nose* was added about 1900. "He went in to look down his nose at them—it might give him some faint satisfaction," wrote John Galsworthy (*To Let,* 1921).

look high and low Seek everywhere, hunt for in all possible places. Oddly enough, *high and low* has a very old and quite different meaning, that is, designating people of all social conditions, high-born as well as low-born. This sense dates from about 1200; Shakespeare used it in *The Merry Wives of Windsor* (2.1): "He wooes both high and low, both rich and poor, both young and old." In the current cliché, *high and low* refers simply to location, as in "I've looked high and low for the key and can't find it anywhere."

look who's talking See POT CALLING THE KETTLE BLACK.

loose as a goose Completely relaxed. This phrase, probably aided in longevity by the rhyme, dates from the first half of the 1900s. In earlier usage it sometimes denoted promiscuity (loose morals), diarrhea (loose bowels), and so on, but since about 1950 it has mostly stuck to its present meaning. The *Los Angeles Times* (April 7, 1979) had it in this sense: "Philadelphia Phillies' manager Danny Ozark is loose as a goose despite intense pressure to win."

loose cannon, a A grave and unpredictable hazard. This term comes from the days of sailing ships, when cannon—guns for firing heavy projectiles—were mounted on deck. If during combat or a storm a cannon came loose from its mounting and rolled about the deck, it could severely damage the hull, causing the ship to sink, as well as injure the crew. In the twentieth century the expression began to be used figuratively for a person who behaves unpredictably and is potentially damaging, as in "The president's secretary was a loose cannon—she couldn't keep these matters confidential."

loose ends, to be at In an unsettled situation; unfinished; unemployed. This term refers to a rope or tether that has become unfastened, leaving one or both ends dangling. It appeared in print as long ago as 1546, when John Heywood's proverb collection stated, "Some loose or od ende in life." Similarly, to *tie up loose ends* means to settle various unsettled details.

Lord giveth and the Lord taketh away, the Good fortune may be followed by misfortune. The term alludes to the Bible's Book of Job, in which Job suffers considerable misfortune. "The Lord gave and the Lord hath taken away; blessed be the name of the Lord" (Job 1:21). Today it is generally used more lightly and without invoking the deity, as in, "After winning the prize, we just learned we have to pay tax on it — the Lord giveth and taketh away." The *New York Times* travel section, in a piece about one airline providing pillows and the other no longer doing so, played on the phrase in a headline: "Virgin Giveth, American Taketh Away" (Dec. 12, 2004). For a modern equivalent, see also WIN SOME, LOSE SOME.

lord it over, to To behave arrogantly, assuming airs of authority and self-importance; to dominate. The noun *lord* was already present in Middle English about A.D. 900. It began to be used as a verb to denote domineering in the seventeenth century, and was being used more figuratively still by the early nineteenth century, when Wordsworth wrote, "You grey towers that still rise up as if to lord it over air" (*Sonnets upon the Punishment of Death*). His contemporary across the Atlantic, Washington Irving, wrote, "The Kaatskill Mountains are seen . . . lording it over the surrounding country" (*Rip Van Winkle,* 1820).

Lord (only) knows, the Who knows? I certainly don't. The locution that only God knows the answer to something dates from the eighteenth century or earlier. (It is also put as *God knows* and *Heaven knows.*) Defoe wrote (*The True-Born Englishman,* 1701), "Great families of yesterday we show, and lords, whose parents were the Lord knows who," and a few decades later Swift wrote (*Polite Conversation,* 1738), "Lord of the Lord knows what."

lose face, to To suffer embarrassment; to be publicly humiliated. Both the concept and term are associated with Asian customs, specifically China; in fact, the term is a translation of the Chinese *tiu lien.* In English it has been used since the late nineteenth century, an early example being R. Hart's chronicle about China, *Arrangements by Which China Has Lost Face* (1876). See also SAVE FACE.

lose it, to To lose one's temper or composure, to go berserk. Dating from the second half of the 1900s, this expression is rapidly becoming a cliché. The *Washington Post* (May 29, 1983) described it, "His eruptions at umpires are genuine furies. 'When something goes against his grain . . . he just completely loses it.'"

lose one's head, to To become so agitated that one cannot act sensibly. This expression, which at one time meant literal decapitation and was used figuratively from the mid-nineteenth century on, differs from the more recent catchphrase "You'd lose your head if it wasn't screwed on," addressed to an extremely absentminded person. Thomas Macaulay's *History of England* (1855) stated, "He lost his head, almost fainted away on the floor of the House."

lose one's shirt, to To lose everything. This term alludes to betting on or investing everything one owns in some venture, but at one time it meant to become very angry (in effect the opposite of KEEP YOUR SHIRT ON). The current cliché, aided and abetted by the Great Depression, is a twentieth-century locution. "He hit the market . . . about the time the bottom dropped out of it. He lost his shirt!" (E. B. Mann, *Thirsty Range,* 1935).

lose sleep over, to To worry about. This expression, often used negatively—that is, something *not* to lose sleep over, dates from the mid-twentieth century. The novelist Norman Mailer used it in *Advertisements for Myself* (1959), "It's not the sort of thing I lose sleep over."

losing battle, (to fight) a A hopeless undertaking that is nevertheless continued. See LOST CAUSE.

lost cause, a An undertaking doomed to fail. Two early uses of this term date from the 1860s. An item in the *New York Herald* of July 2, 1868, referred to the cause of the South in the American Civil War as "a lost cause." The quotation marks appeared in the article, indicating that the writer may have been quoting a familiar phrase or perhaps Matthew Arnold's description of Oxford University as "the home of lost causes" (in *Essays in Criticism,* 1865).

lost in the shuffle Part of a large group and not standing out; lost in the crowd. The term alludes to the thorough mixing of playing cards before dealing, and was transferred to human beings about 1900. A piece by Damon Runyon in *Collier's* magazine in 1930 stated, "I find we are about lost in the shuffle of guys with little mustaches."

lot of hooey, a Complete nonsense, total rubbish. The precise origin of the slangy noun *hooey* has been lost, but its meaning dates from the early 1900s. Elmer Rice had a version of it in his Pulitzer Prize–winning play, *Street Scene* (1928): "T'hell with all that hooey." James M. Cain virtually defined it in *The Postman Always Rings Twice* (1934): "It's just a lot of hooey that this guy thought up so that he could fool the judge."

loud and clear Plainly audible and understandable; emphatically. This expression was widely used in the armed forces during World War II to acknowledge radio messages. It often was a response to "How do you read me?" the answer being "I read you loud and clear." The same pairing, however, was made by Lewis Carroll in *Through the Looking Glass* (1872), in which Humpty Dumpty recites to Alice, "I said it very loud and clear; I went and shouted in his ear. But he was very stiff and proud; He said, You needn't shout so loud." This meaning persists in the cliché—that is, I understand you perfectly well, and you need not repeat that over and over.

louse (something) up, to To ruin or botch, to blunder. Undoubtedly alluding to the unhappy condition of being "loused up," that is, infested with lice, this slangy term dates from the first half of the 1900s. At first it was used as a transitive verb, as in John O'Hara's *Appointment in Samarra,* "Lousing up your date." A decade or two later it was also being used intransitively, as in "Don't trust her with the reservations; she's sure to louse up."

love conquers all True love triumphs over adversity. This ancient adage was first stated by the Roman poet Virgil in *Ciris: "Omnia vincit amor: quid enim non vinceret ille?"* (Love conquers all: for what could Love not conquer?). It has been repeated ever since, by Chaucer and Tennyson, among others, but it may be obsolescent.

love 'em and leave 'em Seduce a woman and then abandon her. This expression, with its rakish Edwardian sound, was recorded only in 1923 in J. V. Weaver's *Finders:* "Love 'em and Leave 'em—that's me from now on." However, an earlier citation (1885) recorded in the *OED, love you and leave you,* allegedly was a common saying in Chester (England) when a visitor was departing.

love is blind Lovers cannot perceive each other's faults. By the time Shakespeare used this phrase (*Two Gentlemen of Verona*, 2.1; *Romeo and Juliet,* 2.1, 3.2; *The Merchant of Venice,* 2.6; *Henry V,* 5.2), it was already well known, havinq been stated by Plato, Plautus, and, in English in the late fourteenth century by Chaucer and John Gower.

lower the boom, to To punish severely, to take a decisive action against. This slangy expression, also sometimes used in the meaning of literally delivering a knockout punch, dates from the first half of the 1900s. It alludes to a sailboat's boom, which can swing wildly in a changing wind. For example, "The bank lowered the boom on Jim and demanded the collateral on his loan."

low man on the totem pole Last in line, lowest-ranking, least important. The humorist H. Allen Smith used this phrase as the title of a book (1941) after the radio comedian Fred Allen had used the term to describe him in an introduction to an earlier book. The position on an actual totem pole, by the way, has no such significance. Nevertheless the term caught on quickly enough to become a cliché.

low profile, keep a Avoid publicity or attention, try to be inconspicuous. The term dates from the mid-1900s. William Safire suggests it may have originated in the military, where tanks and other armored vehicles are less vulnerable when they present a low profile. Another theory is that it is a translation of the Japanese *teishisei*, for "low posture," the motto for Hayato Ikeda's cabinet of 1960–64. It is now used in a large variety of contexts, ranging from politics (as in, "Let's keep a low profile on abortion rights") to celebrities in various fields.

luck of the devil/draw/Irish Fortuitous blessings, good fortune. Good luck (and bad luck) have long been regarded superstitiously, associated with supernatural forces (the devil), a particular group (the Irish), or pure chance (the random drawing of a card or cards). The luck of the draw appears in print only in the second half of the twentieth century; the luck of the Irish is older, appearing, for example, in Lee Thayer's *The Sinister Mark* (1923).

lunatic fringe, the A minority group who have what others consider very extreme beliefs. The term was first used (and perhaps coined) by Theodore Roosevelt in *History as Literature* (1913): "There is apt to be a lunatic fringe among the votaries of any forward movement." At first used mainly for political extremists, the expression was later extended to other venues, as by Diana Ramsay in *Deadly Discretion* (1973): "Antique shops were magnets for the lunatic fringe."

lunatics have taken over the asylum, the The individuals who should be overseen or regulated are running the show. The term appears to have been first used in 1919, when the four most powerful figures in the American film industry—Charlie Chaplin, Douglas Fairbanks, Mary Pickford, and D.W. Griffith—decided to found their own distribution company, called United Artists. In response the producer Richard Rowland remarked, "The lunatics have taken over the asylum." The remark got wide publicity and entered the language, subsequently applied to many other situations of a comparable nature and becoming a cliché. In 1981 Metro-Goldwyn-Mayer absorbed United Artists but retained the name, but in 2004 Sony Corporation agreed to buy Metro-Goldwyn-Mayer, and the future of United Artists was in doubt.

m

mad as a hatter Crazy. Although many readers associate *mad hatter* with Alice's tea party in Wonderland, attended by both a March Hare and a Hatter, the term is considerably older and is thought to come from the fact that the chemicals used in making felt hats could produce the symptoms of Saint Vitus' dance or other nervous tremors. In literature, references occur in Thomas Haliburton's *The Clockmaker* (1837) and Thackeray's *Pendennis* (1850), both predating Lewis Carroll's *Alice's Adventures in Wonderland* (1865). The synonym *mad as a March hare,* incidentally, which dates from Chaucer's time, is virtually obsolete.

mad as a wet hen Extremely angry. The source of this expression is a bit puzzling, since hens, while not waterfowl, are not distressed by wetness. Conjecture has it that it comes from a farmer's tossing a bucket of water at hens and thereby causing a flapping uproar. The term appears in *Money in the Bank* (1942) by that noted purveyor of clichés, P. G. Wodehouse. A more logical variant is *mad as a hornet.* H. L. Mencken referred to it as a familiar simile in *The American Language* (1919), and it continues to be used.

made my day, that/you've/he/she That has made me very happy, restored my confidence, and otherwise gratified me. This twentieth-century expression relies on the meaning of *make* as "succeed." However, in the mouth of a tough police detective named Dirty Harry, a film role played by Clint Eastwood, the phrase was turned into "Go ahead—*make* my day," meaning "Give me a chance to get back at you." In the presidential campaign of 1988 George H.W. Bush used the phrase quite frequently, as President Ronald Reagan had before him, and it was not always clear which meaning was intended. However, the more common usage was that employed by P. G. Wodehouse in his novel, *The Luck of Bodkins* (1935), "That will be great. That will just make my day."

mad money Cash carried by a woman in case she wants to leave her escort and return home alone; also, extra spending money. The first meaning uses *mad* in the sense of angry—that is, money to be used by a woman angry at her date, either owing to his making unwanted advances, flirting with other women, or some such reason. It dates from the 1920s, when respectable women began to go out with men without benefit of a chaperone. The second meaning uses *mad* in the sense of impetuous—that is, money to be spent on an impulse purchase.

E. M. Miller used it in *Exile* (1963): "In the zip pocket under the pencil holder on his upper left arm he kept a ten-dollar bill—'mad money.'"

maid of all work The female equivalent of JACK OF ALL TRADES.

make a beeline for Go directly to. This phrase is based on the assumption that a bee will take the shortest, most direct route back to the hive, in effect a straight line. It appeared in the *Massachusetts Spy* on November 24, 1830: "The squirrel took a beeline and reached the ground six feet ahead."

make a clean breast of something, to To make a full confession. The word *breast* here is a synonym for "heart," long considered the seat of private emotion and, by extension, secrets. Shakespeare referred to cleansing one's bosom in *Macbeth* (5.3). The current cliché dates from the early eighteenth century.

make a long story short, to To get to the point. Although the idea of abbreviating an account is very old—the Roman writer Pacuvius used a similar expression about 160 B.C. (*Ut multa paucis verba unose obnuntiem*)—in English the term became current only in the nineteenth century. Thoreau played on it: "Not that the story need be long, but it will take a long while to make it short" (*Letter to Mr. B.,* 1857).

make a mountain out of a molehill, to To exaggerate trifling problems. This English equivalent of the French *faire d'une mouche un éléphant* (make an elephant out of a fly) first appeared in 1570, in John Fox's *The Book of Martyrs.* The legendary humorist Fred Allen played on it: "A vice-president in an advertising agency is a 'molehill man' who has until 5 P.M. to make a molehill into a mountain. An accomplished molehill man will often have his mountain finished before lunch" (*Treadmill to Oblivion,* 1954).

make an ass of oneself/someone, to To make an utter fool of oneself or someone else. This term has been current since Shakespeare's time, for the "ass"—along with the donkey—has been equated with stupidity and foolishness since Cicero's day. A ruder version is to make *a horse's ass* (a horse's behind) of someone.

make an honest woman of her Marry a woman who was seduced; restore virtue. Honesty and chastity have been verbally equated since the 1600s. The cliché is still used, mostly ironically or figuratively. Thus, "For an encore, Jackiw, Zander and company made an honest woman of that hoary standard, 'Meditation' from Massenet's *Thais*" (*Boston Globe*, June 15, 2001).

make a virtue of necessity, to To make the best of things. This expression dates from the time of Chaucer, who may have been its originator in

English ("Thanne is it wisdom, as it thinketh me, To maken virtu of necessitie," *The Knight's Tale*); there are still earlier versions in Latin. It has been repeated ever since.

make ends meet, to To live within one's income. Some writers claim that the ends in question are the beginning and end of the (fiscal) year, and indeed the phrase was so stated by Tobias Smollett in 1748. Earlier examples, dating from the seventeenth century, are less specific, and the word *end* could equally well denote the sum total (end result or BOTTOM LINE) of income and of expenditure. On the death of Herbert Hoover in 1964, someone recalled that he said, "About the time we can make the ends meet, somebody moves the ends."

make hay while the sun shines Take advantage of any good opportunity. This adage, dating from the early sixteenth century, alludes to the need for dry conditions in order to cut grass. R. C. Trench, the Archbishop of Canterbury, was quite specific about it (*On the Lessons in Proverbs,* 1852): "Make hay while the sun shines is truly English, and could have had its birth only under such variable skies as ours."

make head or tail of something, to be unable to To fail to understand something. This term was already used to denote total confusion by Cicero (*Nec caput nec pedes,* meaning "neither head nor feet"). Whether it refers to beginning or end, or top or bottom, or, as someone suggests, the two sides of a coin, is not known, but to make *neither head nor tail* of something has been so used ever since, in English from the seventeenth century to the present.

make headway, to To advance. This term transfers the original meaning of *headway,* the forward motion of a ship, to any kind of progress. Augustus Jessopp had it in *Arcady for Better or Worse* (1887), "Rarely, except in the open parishes, do the demagogues make headway."

make love, not war See SWORDS INTO PLOUGHSHARES.

make my day See MADE MY DAY.

make nice Be agreeable, behave well. Dating from the mid-1900s, this slangy phrase may, according to lexicographer J. E. Lighter, be imitative of baby talk. It appeared in the musical *West Side Story* (1957), "You're gonna make nice with the PRs [Puerto Ricans] from now on" and has become a cliché.

make no bones about it, to To do or say something without hesitation, formality, or evasion. This saying is so old that its original meaning has been lost. Nicholas Udall used it in *Apothegms from Erasmus* (1548): "He made no manier bones ne stickyng, but went in hande to offer up his ownly son" (he made no bones about sacrificing his only son). One writer suggests it comes from a diner who makes no fuss if he encounters bones in his food. Others relate it to dice, so called because they were originally made from bones, and suggest it meant simply throwing the dice without making any prior fuss about it.

make one's blood boil, to To enrage someone. The term *the blood boils* has meant anger since the seventeenth century. The precise cliché appears in Thomas Macaulay's *History of England* (1848): "The thought of such intervention made the blood, even of the Cavaliers, boil in their veins."

make one's hair stand on end, to To terrify. The Book of Job (4:14–15) states, "Fear came upon me . . . and the hair of my flesh stood up." The allusion here is to the goose pimples aroused by fear (or cold), the raised bumps on the skin that cause the hairs around them to stand up. Centuries later this gave rise to the adjective *hair-raising,* a synonym for terrifying.

make one's mouth water, to To make someone long for or desire something; to arouse eager anticipation. The term, which alludes to salivating in anticipation of food, transferred the phenomenon to other human desires early on. Richard Eden used the term in writing of cannibals anticipating their prey (*The Decades of the New Worlde,* 1555). By 1663, when Samuel Butler used it in *Hudibras,* the term was purely figurative, as it still is, even when it refers to food.

make or break, to To bring on either success or ruin. This term began life as the alliterative *make or mar,* which dates from the fifteenth century ("Neptunus, that dothe bothe make and marre," John Lydgate, *Assembly of Gods*). Dickens was among the first to substitute the current rhyming cliché (in *Barnaby Rudge,* 1840), which has largely replaced the older form.

make out like a bandit Operate very successfully. This slangy term refers not to an outlaw but to the *one-armed bandit* of gambling—that is, a slot machine. Since slot machines invariably win, making out like one is synonymous with success. Sometimes shortened to simply *like a bandit,* the phrase dates from the second half of the 1900s. Cartoonist Gary Trudeau used it in *Doonesbury* in 1985: "Unlike our farm belt cousins, Californians have been makin' out like bandits."

make short work of, to To dispose of something with dispatch. This term, too, is an old one, recorded as far back as 1577, when it appeared in John Grange's *The Golden Aphroditis* ("Desirous to make shorte worke thereof"). It is often used jocularly. See also SHORT SHRIFT.

make someone's day See MADE MY DAY.

make the best of it/a bad bargain, to Adapt as well as possible to ill fortune, bad circumstances, or other adversity. This advice was already being given in the sixteenth century. In the seventeenth century *game* or *market* was sometimes substituted for *bargain,* and the term was found in the proverb collections of John Kelly, John Ray, and others. See also BEST OF A BAD BARGAIN.

make the feathers/fur fly, to To shake things up and cause a commotion. Both versions of this term allude to hunting, and to what happens when dogs are set on a bird, rabbit, raccoon, or similar creature. *Flying fur* is the older image, dating at least from the seventeenth century. "I'll make the fur fly about the ears of that old cur," wrote Samuel Butler in *Hudibras* (1663). *Feathers* dates from the early nineteenth century. "He'd make the feathers fly" appeared in John Neal's *Brother Jonathan* (1825). A somewhat newer variant is *fur will fly*, meaning a violent confrontation will follow. An Americanism from the early 1800s, it is probably heard more often today than the older terms. A headline in *U.S. News and World Report* had it on January 18, 1988: "Watching the Fur Fly."

make the grade, to To reach a given standard or pass a test. This term apparently alludes to climbing a steep hill or gradient and was transferred to mean any kind of success in the first half of the twentieth century. An early appearance in print is in S. Ford's *Inez and Trilby* (1921): "Three days! I doubt if she can make the grade."

make tracks, to To leave in a hurry. This nineteenth-century American colloquialism was recorded by Thomas Chandler Haliburton (1796–1865) in his "Sam Slick" papers, which originally appeared in a Nova Scotia weekly in 1836, as well as in several earlier journals. Presumably it alludes to running away with a heavy tread, thereby leaving tracks in the dirt.

make waves, to To create a disturbance; to shake up the existing state of affairs. This twentieth-century Americanism is well on its way to clichédom. Alison Lurie used it in *Love and Friendship* (1962): "I think it will be best if she tells him herself . . . we don't want to make waves."

man after my own heart See AFTER ONE'S OWN HEART.

man Friday See GIRL/MAN FRIDAY.

man in the moon, (no more than) the A mythical figure, hence nothing, or a figment of the imagination. Mention of the man in the moon dates from the early fourteenth century. In *Troilus and Criseyde* Chaucer quotes, indirectly, a myth that a man who desecrated the Sabbath was banished to the moon. By the sixteenth century, however, this turn of phrase was linked with something so distant as to be unlikely ("as farre from her thought as the man that the rude people saie is in the moone," Edward Hall, *Chronicle of Richard III,* c. 1548).

man in the street, the The ordinary person, such as anyone might meet walking down the street. It is the views of such persons that pollsters seek in order to determine that elusive quantity, public opinion. This term dates from the early nineteenth century, when the opinions and thoughts of ordinary folk began, through elections, to influence the course of public events. Charles Fulke Greville used it sarcastically in his *Memoirs* (1831): "Knowing as 'the man in the street' (as we call him at Newmarket) always does, the greatest secrets of kings . . ." Ralph Waldo Emerson (*Worship,* 1860) also did not have a flattering view: "The man in the street does not know a star in the sky." The modern news media—both print and electronic—continue to use the general public to flesh out their reports, frequently seeking the opinion of both male and female bystanders at events of importance.

manna from heaven, like Any sudden or unexpected advantage or help. The word *manna* is used in the Bible, in Exodus (16:15), where it means a miraculous food that suddenly appears to succor the children of Israel on their journey from Egypt to the Holy Land. Exactly what it meant is no longer known, but it may have been a corruption of the Egyptian word *mennu,* the sweet, waxy exudation of the tamarisk tree. In English the term came to mean an unexpected welcome gift from heaven or some other benevolent source. It was already being used humorously in the early eighteenth century by Matthew Green (1696–1737), who wrote (in *The Spleen*), "Or to some coffee-house I stray, for news, the manna of a day."

man of few words, a A person who speaks little but to the point; also, by implication, a person of action rather than words. Although most writers trace this expression to the Old Testament ("Let thy words be few," Ecclesiastes 5:2), it is actually much older, appearing in Homer's *Iliad* ("Few were his words, but wonderfully clear"). It appeared in John Ray's 1678 proverb collection, and a version of "Few words are best" occurs in numerous other languages as well. See also STRONG SILENT TYPE.

man of the world, a An experienced, sophisticated individual. Originally (sixteenth century) this term meant simply a married man, as opposed to a "man of the church," that is, a priest, who was celibate and a man of God or the spirit. Shakespeare echoed this definition when he has Audrey reply to Touchstone's statement that they would marry tomorrow: "I do desire it . . . and I hope it is no dishonest desire to be a woman of the world" (*As You Like It,* 5.3). It is not exactly clear when the term began to denote sophistication (worldliness), but it certainly did by the time Emerson used it in *The Conduct of Life* (1860): "The finished man of the world must eat of every apple once."

man or a mouse, (are you) a Bold and brave or timid and cowardly. This alliterative comparison dates from the sixteenth century, when an unknown writer penned, "Fear not, she saith unto her spouse, a man or a mouse whether ye be" (*Scholehouse of Women,* c. 1541).

man to man Openly, frankly. This term, dating from the days when certain kinds of frankness were deemed unfit for female ears, seems archaic today, although it may survive in father-son talks. See also HEART-TO-HEART TALK.

many a slip 'twixt the cup and the lip, there's Nothing is certain until one possesses it. This old proverb is thought by many to come from the ancient Greek legend of Antaeus, helmsman of the ship *Argo.* A slave told him he would never live to taste the wine from his own vineyard. As some wine from his grapes was set before him, he sent for the slave to show him his mistake, but the slave allegedly said, "There's many a slip 'twixt the cup and the lip." Just then a messenger arrived, telling him the Calydonian boar was destroying his vineyard. Antaeus jumped up, set down his wine, and went out to kill the boar, but was himself killed by the ferocious animal. Another writer believes the phrase comes from Homer's *Odyssey,* in which Odysseus aimed an arrow at Antinous as he was about to drink some wine. The arrow hit him in the throat, and the cup fell from his hands before he could drink.

march to (the beat of) a different drummer, to To follow principles quite different from those of most others. This term, which became current in the mid-twentieth century, actually has its source in the last chapter of Thoreau's *Walden* (1854): "If a man does not keep pace with his companions, perhaps it is because he hears a different drummer." Thoreau, champion of individualism, was hailed by the antiestablishmentarians of the 1960s in particular, who picked up a version of his phrase. Quoting a business executive, Connie Bruck wrote in a 1990 *New Yorker* article, "We saw ourselves . . . as the tough guys, very smart, who were marching to our own drummer."

mark my words Listen to me because you'll see I'm right in the end. This term, found in the Coverdale translation of the Bible (1535) in the Book of Isaiah ("Pondre and merck my wordes wel," 28:23), has been used as an admonishment ever since.

marriage made in heaven, a A match decreed by destiny; a very successful pairing. Already a well-known adage by the mid-sixteenth century, this term was quoted many times over and appeared in numerous proverb collections. It was often used sarcastically but was largely confined to actual matrimony until the twentieth century, when it began to be applied to other kinds of match—as, for example, a merger of two business corporations.

matter of life and death, a An issue of vital importance. This term, used since the mid-nineteenth century, makes more sense as a matter of life *or* death, and indeed it sometimes is so used. An 1837 letter of Dickens states, "It is matter of life or death to us, to know whether you have got Ainsworth's MS yet." However, a *life-and-death matter* appears with equal frequency.

May and December See DECEMBER.

mea culpa It's my fault, my mistake. The term was taken over from Latin as far back as the 1200s and continues to be used in this way. Ian Rankin had it in *Strip Jack* (1992), "'You haven't had a proper lock fitted yet.' 'Mea culpa, Inspector. Fear not, one's on its way.'"

meal ticket A source of financial support, particularly from one of the opposite sex. This transfer from a literal ticket that entitles one to a meal in a restaurant or other facility took place around 1900. At first it was used mainly for a SUGAR DADDY, but in time it was broadened. Thus on May 22, 1949, the *New York Times* had it, "Man and Superman [the play] . . . is the title of [actor] Maurice Evans' current meal ticket."

mean streak, a A tendency toward nastiness. In effect, the phrase implies that a person is not entirely bad but is given to occasional spiteful or malicious behavior. The *Toronto Daily Star* used it on June 16, 1960: "A girl who would be attracted to Bud's mean streak and bad temper must be a little out to lunch." See also OUT TO LUNCH.

meanwhile, back at the ranch As we were saying before. This formula for a verbal flashback comes from the silent Western movies popular in the 1920s, and also the radio program *The Lone Ranger*. During the course of a battle between settlers and Indians or cowboys and outlaws, there would be a flashback to the ranch preceded by the caption (or radio message), "Meanwhile, back at the ranch." It soon was transferred to general conversation. During Lyndon Johnson's presidency (1963–69), according to William Safire, the phrase was used to refer to activities at the LBJ Ranch in Texas.

meat and drink to me, it is A source of great pleasure. This term appears in Shakespeare's *As You Like It* (5.1), in which Touchstone declares, "It is meat and drink to me to see a clown," but it appears in earlier sources as well. The phrase was hyperbole from the very start, since meat (meaning food) and drink are clearly essential to life. More straightforward is the much newer *meat and potatoes,* used from the mid-twentieth century on to signify the basics of an issue (transferring the idea that meat and potatoes are the basics of the human diet).

meat and potatoes See MEAT AND DRINK TO ME, IT IS.

meet one's match, to To encounter a person who is one's equal in ability. This term began life as *to find* one's match, a locution that dates back to the fourteenth century or earlier. "He fond his mecche," wrote Robert Manning of Brunnea (*The Story of England,* c. 1330). By the late sixteenth century the alliterative *meet* had been substituted and has survived to the present day.

meet one's Waterloo, to To experience a major defeat. Alluding to the final defeat of Napoleon at Waterloo in 1815, Wendell Phillips used the term in1859 to describe the defeat of abolitionist John Brown in organizing a slave uprising at Harpers Ferry, Virginia ("Every man meets his Waterloo at last").

memory lane, down See DOWN MEMORY LANE.

mend one's fences, to To strengthen one's position by reestablishing good relations among one's supporters. The term apparently came from a speech by Sen. John Sherman to his neighbors and friends in 1879 in Mansfield, Ohio, in which he said, "I have come home to look after my fences," presumably literally meaning the fences around his farm there. (Indeed, mending fences is a major and time-consuming chore for nearly all American farmers.) However, the newspaper reports of the speech interpreted it as a political statement that meant Sherman was really home to campaign among his constituents. The term continued to be used in this way, with *repair* and *mend* substituted for *look after.* In the twentieth century it was broadened to mean placating personal, business, or professional contacts who might have felt neglected or offended and trying to regain their support. Vice President Al Gore used it after his defeat in the 2000 presidential election, saying he planned to mend his fences.

method in one's madness, there is There is an underlying purpose in crazy behavior. Shakespeare was hardly the first person to make this observation, but his statement of it in *Hamlet* (2.2) gave rise to the modern locution ("Though this be madness, yet there is method in't"). It was probably already a cliché by the time G. K. Chesterton played on it (*The Fad of the Fisherman,* 1922): "There nearly always is method in madness. It's what drives men mad, being methodical!"

mickey mouse Trivial, unimportant, petty. The term, sometimes capitalized (Mickey Mouse), alludes to the cartoon character appearing in Walt Disney films which by the mid-1930s had become childish and silly. It acquired widespread use during World War II, when soldiers used it to describe absurd regulations and petty discipline, and thereafter was applied to almost anything. Studs Terkel used it in *American Dreams* (1979), "We got a Mickey Mouse educational system that doesn't teach us . . . how the government works."

Midas touch, the The ability to make any undertaking extremely profitable. According to legend, Midas, King of Phrygia, asked the gods that everything he touched would turn into gold. Dionysus granted his request, but when the very food Midas wished to eat turned to gold, he asked the gods to take back their gift. Dionysus then ordered Midas to bathe in the River Pactolus, thereby washing away the gift. By the seventeenth century the idea was applied figuratively to any person with a gift for making money. See also RICH AS CROESUS.

might makes right The powerful dictate justice; the strongest are always in the right. This observation was made by the Greek philosopher Plato in *The Republic* (c. 375 B.C.) and has been stated many times since, in numerous languages. Some writers applaud it, others deplore it. The poet Algernon Charles Swinburne put it ironically (*A Word for the Country,* c. 1880): "Where might is, the right is: Long purses make strong swords. Let weakness learn meekness: God save the House of Lords."

mile a minute, a Very fast. As one might guess, this term dates only from the days when this literal speed was relatively reasonable. The *OED* cites its first use in a 1957 issue of *Railway Magazine,* announcing "a new table of their mile-a-minute runs." It frequently is used figuratively, as in "He was talking a mile a minute."

milk it/something dry, to To drain something completely, to exhaust all the possibilities of something. The verb *to milk,* meaning to obtain milk from a cow, was in the early sixteenth century transferred to getting money from someone. In subsequent centuries it was expanded to stealing messages from a telephone or telegraph wire, obtaining maximum audience laughter or applause, and similar unrelated endeavors. Today it appears in such locutions as, "His thesis on Wordsworth's mentions of flowers milks the subject dry."

milk of human kindness, the Sympathy, compassion. This expression, too, comes from Shakespeare. He used it in *Macbeth* (1.5), where Lady Macbeth tells her husband, "Yet do I fear thy nature. It is too full o' th' milk of human kindness" (to act as ruthlessly as he must in order to become king). Numerous writers have used the term, often to comment on the souring or curdling of that very milk, although one writer reports of one bishop meeting another and saying, "He had often heard of the milk of human kindness, but never hitherto had he met the cow" (E. M. Sneyd-Kynnersley, *H.M.I.,* 1908).

mills of the gods grind slowly, the One's destiny or one's deserved fate may not come fast, but it will arrive eventually. The earliest instance of this expression is attributed to the third-century Greek philosopher Sextus Empiricus, who was quoting another poet when he said, "The mills of the gods grind slowly, but they grind small." Later it was put as, "God's mill grinds slow but sure" (George Herbert, *Jacula Prudentum,* 1640), and still later Longfellow, translating a German poet, said they "grind exceeding small."

millstone (around one's neck), to bear/carry a To bear a heavy burden, literal or figurative. The idea is mentioned in the Bible in the Gospel of Matthew (18:6), as a stone to be hung around the neck of an offender who will then be drowned. Even though grain continued for many centuries to be ground by using a pair of heavy circular stones, by the sixteenth century the term was also being used figuratively for an emotional or mental burden. Jeremy Bentham used it in his treatise on usury (1787): "The millstone intended for the necks of those vermin . . . the dealers in corn, was found to fall upon the heads of the consumers."

mince words, not to To speak plainly, without equivocating to avoid giving offense. This expression, also put as *not to mince matters,* dates from Shakespeare's time (he used it in *Othello* and *Antony and Cleopatra*) and in effect transfers the cutting into small pieces of some object, like meat, to moderating or softening one's language.

mind one's own business, to To refrain from meddling, to keep to one's own affairs. The wisdom of this course of action was observed in ancient times by Plato, Seneca, and others, and even found expression in the Bible (1 Thessalonians 4:11, "Do your own business"). In plain English it was expressed from the sixteenth century on. John Clarke used it in *Paroemiologia* (1639): "Mind your business." Among many later writers echoing this sentiment was Lewis Carroll, in one of his enjoyable non sequiturs (*Alice's Adventures in Wonderland,* 1865), "'If everybody minded their business,' the Duchess said in a hoarse growl, 'the world would go round a great deal faster than it does.'"

mind one's p's and q's, to To be very particular about one's words and/or behavior. The original meaning of *p* and *q* has been lost, and there are various theories, ranging from "pints and quarts" in the bartender's accounts, to children confusing the two letters in learning their alphabet, to the French dancing master's *pieds* and *queues,* figures that must be accurately performed. The term was used from the seventeenth century on but is heard less often today.

mind over matter Willpower triumphs over material or physical considerations. The idea is very old indeed, expressed by Vergil in the *Aeneid* (*Mens agitat molem,* "mind moves matter"), and, in an entire system of philosophy, by Britain's Bishop George Berkeley (1685–1753), who held that nothing in the world exists unless it is perceived by the human mind. In the twentieth century, however, the cliché is most often invoked for or by someone who is carrying on normal activities despite being physically ill or otherwise incapacitated. The humorist Jack Benny quipped, "Age is strictly a case of mind over matter. If you don't mind, it doesn't matter" (quoted in *New York Times,* Feb. 15, 1974).

mind's eye, in my In my imagination. This figure of speech dates from the early fifteenth century. Thomas Hoccleve used it in *De Regimine Principium* (1412): "Haue often him byfore your myndes ye." So did Shakespeare in Hamlet's statement to Horatio that he thinks he sees his dead father: "In my mind's eye" (*Hamlet,* 1.2).

mind the store, to To take charge in someone's absence. This phrase, dating from about 1920, originally meant literally taking over the business of a store when the owner was temporarily away. Later it was expanded to more general usage, as in "She's on sabbatical leave this semester, so Professor Jones is minding the store."

mine of information, a A good source of data. The term is sometimes used ironically: Our family privately used to describe a particular history teacher as a gold mine of misinformation (based on our children's quotations of her dicta). The word *mine* has been used figuratively to mean an abundant supply since the sixteenth century. The *OED* quotes a 1905 issue of *Athenaeum:* "Her book is a mine of valuable information."

mint condition, in Appearing to be brand-new and unused; in excellent shape. A favorite hyperbole of used-car salesmen and secondhand dealers, this term was borrowed from philatelists who so describe a new, unused stamp. It began to be transferred to other objects by the 1920s. Iris Murdoch used it in her novel *The Flight from the Enchanter* (1956): "The books were chaotic, but in mint condition."

mint of money, make a Strike it rich; earn a huge profit. The mint in question here is the place where money is manufactured under government auspices, and by extension it betokens a vast amount of cash. "Mint of money" has been so used since the sixteenth century, but the idea of "making" it dates only from the nineteenth century, when large sums began to be acquired less from inherited wealth than from business enterprise.

misery loves company Fellow sufferers make pain easier to bear. This observation dates from ancient Greek and Roman times or even earlier; Sophocles (*Oedipus at Colonnus,* c. 408 B.C.) and Seneca (c. A.D. 54) both wrote words to that effect. John Lyly's *Euphues* stated it as "In misery it is great comfort to haue a companion" (1579), but the precise wording of the modern cliché does not appear until the nineteenth century. More recently, Brian Moore quipped, "If misery loves company, then triumph demands an audience" (*An Answer from Limbo,* 1962).

miss a trick, doesn't/not to Not overlooking a single opportunity to profit. This term very likely comes from whist and related card games, in which a trick is a group of cards played and won in one round. The player who amasses the highest possible number of tricks wins the game. It began to be transferred to other activities in the mid-twentieth century. "Those boys haven't missed a trick," wrote Emma Lathen in *Murder Against the Grain* (1967).

miss is as good as a mile, a Falling short by a small amount is as bad as falling short by a great deal. This condensation of the older proverb, "An inch of a miss is as good (or bad) as a mile (or ell) of a miss," known in the sixteenth century, is believed to have originated with Sir Walter Scott, who wrote in his *Journal* (Dec. 3, 1825), "He was very near being a poet—but a miss is as good as a mile, and he always fell short of the mark."

miss one's guess, to To be mistaken, to be wrong in one's assumptions. This phrase, dating from the first half of the 1900s, is often put negatively, as in "And, when you're older, an overdose of sex appeal, or I miss my guess" (M. de la Roche, *Whiteoak Harvest,* 1936).

miss the boat/bus, to To fail to take advantage of an opportunity; to arrive too late to profit. The analogy to missing a scheduled transport is fairly obvious and has been drawn since about 1900. One of its more curious uses was in a speech by Prime Minister Neville Chamberlain commenting (April 4, 1940) on Adolf Hitler's invasion of Norway, "Hitler has missed the bus." This was odd in view of Chamberlain's own temporizing and attempts at pacification, which gave Hitler more time to embark unimpeded on his conquest of Europe.

mixed bag, a A haphazard collection of objects, people, or categories. This phrase dates from the first half of the 1900s. For example, "Representatives of the press, a mixed bag in age, but not in sex" (A. Behrend, *Samurai*

Affair, 1973), indicates journalists of many different ages but all either male or female.

mixed blessing, a A fortunate occurrence that has some unhappy elements. The *OED*'s first citation of this phrase is dated 1933, in *Discovery* (October issue): "The introduction of European influences may prove a mixed blessing."

moment of truth, the The critical instant, at which one is put to the ultimate test. The term is a translation of the Spanish *el momento de la verdad,* which signifies the time in a bullfight in which the matador is about to kill the bull. It was first described in English by Ernest Hemingway in his story *Death in the Afternoon,* and subsequently was transferred to other critical outcomes. The final calculation in making out one's income tax return, for example, could be described as one's moment of truth.

Monday-morning quarterback A person who criticizes decisions or actions after the fact, with TWENTY-TWENTY HINDSIGHT. The term originated in the 1930s when football as a spectator sport was seen mostly on weekends, and office discussions of the previous weekend's game would often be dominated by one or more "experts" who "revised" the quarterback's instructions to the team so as to achieve superior results. In print the term appeared in Barry Wood's *What Price Football* (1932), in which he applied it to sportswriters who were not content with reporting the game but felt they had to analyze it. In succeeding decades it was transferred to anyone second-guessing any past decision.

money burns a hole in one's pocket Someone can't refrain from spending whatever money he or she has. This usage is very old, appearing as early as 1557 in Sir Thomas More's *Works:* "A little wanton money . . . which burned out the bottom of his purse." The allusion is hyperbole—that is, one must remove the money before it burns a hole.

money is the root of all evil Materialism is the source of evil-doing. This term is a misquotation of a New Testament teaching: "The *love* of money is the root of all evil" (1 Timothy 6:10). Another frequently quoted version is a translation from the Latin *Radix malorum est cupiditas:* "The desire for money is the root of evil." Shaw turned it around in *Man and Superman* (1905): "Lack of money is the root of all evil." He may have been paraphrasing Samuel Butler, who said much the same thing several decades earlier (in *Erewhon,* 1872).

money talks Wealth is power. This idea is probably as old as money. It was stated by the Greek playwright Euripides in *Medea* and cited among Erasmus's *Adagia* (1523)—"Against the talking power of money eloquence is of no avail"—as well as by scores of others.

monkey business Tricks; underhanded goings-on. This term, which transfers the mischievous, sly actions of monkeys to human beings, began to be used in the 1880s. It may have been a replacement for *monkeyshines,* which originated in the United States about 1820 and meant mischievous tricks. Today we generally use "monkey business" to mean more nefarious activities.

monkey see, monkey do A comment to or about someone who is imitating another's actions. It originated in the United States in the 1920s, probably as part of a children's game, and is most often heard as a criticism or admonition.

monkey's uncle, I'll be/am a An expression of surprise or disbelief. Why that particular animal was chosen is no longer known, and indeed the cliché, which dates from the early 1900s, is heard less often today. Eric V. Lustbader used it in *White Ninja* (1990): "If this doesn't turn out to be a suicide, I am a monkey's uncle."

monkey wrench in the works, put/throw a Sabotage an operation or plan. The monkey wrench, called an "adjustable spanner" in Britain, appears to have reminded someone of a monkey's jaws, which loosely resemble the sliding jaws of this very useful tool. This name was acquired about the middle of the nineteenth century. It was not until the early twentieth century that it became associated with sabotage. This suggestion first appeared in print in 1920 in Philander Johnson's story, *Shooting Stars:* "Don't throw a monkey-wrench into the machinery!" The locution not only caught on in America but was adopted in Britain as well, although in the form of *throw a spanner in the works.*

month of Sundays, a A very long time. It is doubtful that this expression, which dates from the early nineteenth century, was ever meant literally—that is, a period of thirty Sundays (or weeks). It first appeared in print in Frederick Marryat's *Newton Forster* (1832) and was surely a cliché by the time Ogden Nash played on it in "My Dear, How Did You Ever Think up This Delicious Salad?" (1935): "The salad course nowadays seems to be a month of sundaes." The British version, *a week of Sundays,* is never heard in America.

moon (is) made of green cheese, (and) the The most ridiculous thing imaginable. This farfetched figure of speech dates from the early sixteenth century. Despite the opinion of one collector of proverbs, F. E. Hulme (*Proverb Lore,* 1902), who believed it referred to the newness ("greenness") of the moon each month, it has always been used as an example of outrageous absurdity.

moot point, a A debatable question. This term was originally exclusively a legal one, a *moot case* or *moot point* being a case for discussion in a *moot,* or meeting, of law students. By the eighteenth century, however, it was being used figuratively in a far more general way. For example, "It is a very moot point to which of those causes we may ascribe the universal dulness of the Irish," wrote Sir C. Wogan (1732–33), cited by the *OED*.

moral fiber Ethical courage. The term dates from the second half of the 1800s. It was applied to World War II pilots who snapped under the strain of combat and refused to fly, and were then accused of *lack of moral fiber*. Playwright Terrence Rattigan used it in *Flare Path* (1942): "And on my confidential report they'd put—grounded. Lack of moral fibre" (2:2).

more fun than a barrel of monkeys See IT'S MORE FUN THAN A BARREL OF MONKEYS.

more or less Approximately. This term has been around since the thirteenth century and still serves as an inexact answer. It also has been subject to numerous word plays, such as "More or less, but rather less than more" (Phoebe's comment on her betrothal to Wilfred, W. S. Gilbert, *The Yeomen of the Guard*); "A little more than kin and less than kind" (Shakespeare, *Hamlet,* 1.2); and "Less is more" (the simpler the better; Robert Browning, "Andrea del Sarto").

more power to you/him/them Good for you; good luck. This earlier version of RIGHT ON dates from the mid-nineteenth century. A variant that appeared on both sides of the Atlantic is "More power to your elbow," an encouragement to drink more, which first appeared in print in 1860 in a letter of James Russell Lowell's and was repeated by Shaw in *John Bull's Other Island*. That version is now obsolete, but the cliché survives.

more sinned against than sinning Less guilty or responsible than others who have done one wrong. This particular phrase comes from Shakespeare's *King Lear* (3.2), when Lear wanders about the heath during a terrible storm and complains of his plight. The idea, of course, is much older. Nevertheless the phrase appealed particularly to Shaw, who used it in at least two plays (*Captain Brassbound's Conversion,* 1899; *Fanny's First Play,* 1911).

more (to it) than meets the eye One is seeing only the surface or a portion of something that has a deeper or larger significance. This nineteenth-century term became a favorite British cliché, as well as the object of fun. John Galsworthy used it in *The Man of Property* (1906): "'There's more here, sir,' says the Inspector over the dead body, 'than meets the eye.'" Critic Alexander Woollcott quoted actress Tallulah Bankhead as quipping about the revival of a play by Maurice Maeterlinck, "There is less in this than meets the eye." See also TIP OF THE ICEBERG, (ONLY) THE.

more than one bargained for More than one expected from a particular situation, deal, or arrangement. The transfer of a higher than anticipated cost in a transaction to more than one expected in any situation took place in the nineteenth century. In print it appeared in Frederick Marryat's *Olla Podrida* (1840): "More wind than we bargained for."

more than one way to skin a cat, there's There are many ways to accomplish the same end. American in origin, this term is similar to the British locution, "There are more ways of killing a cat than choking it with cream," which appeared in Charles Kingsley's *Westward Ho!* (1855). Mark Twain used the current cliché, "She knew more than one way to skin a cat," in *A Connecticut Yankee in King Arthur's Court* (1889). Several writers claim the expression has nothing to do with literally skinning an animal, but rather describes a child's maneuver in getting into a sitting position on a tree branch. There is no evidence for this etymology.

more the merrier, the The larger the number of participants, the greater the fun. This thought was expressed by Cicero, but the precise phrase first appeared in English as "The mo the meryer; the fewer, the better fare" (Jehan Palsgrave, 1530) and was credited by some to have been said first by King James I of Scotland (c. 1423). John Heywood picked it up in his proverb collection of 1546, also indicating that "the fewer, the better fare," meaning with fewer people there would be more for each to eat. *Better fare* was sometimes changed to *better cheer,* presumably meaning more for each to drink.

morning after, the The generally unpleasant consequences of a previous action or activity. The term originated in the late nineteenth century and at first referred exclusively to the aftereffects of a drinking bout; it often was put as *the morning after the night before.* By the mid-twentieth century it had been extended to include the consequences of any prior action, although it retained the negative implications of a hangover. It is also used in the colloquial name for an oral contraceptive taken after intercourse has occurred, the *morning-after pill.*

most unkindest cut See UNKINDEST CUT OF ALL.

Mother Nature A personification of nature as a basic force, often a nurturing one. Dating from about 1525, this term has been used over and over ever since. Jack London had it in *Sea Wolf* (1904), describing a coming storm, "Old Mother Nature's going to getup on her hind legs for all that's in her."

mountain out of a molehill See MAKE A MOUNTAIN OUT OF A MOLEHILL.

mountain will not come to Mohammed See IF THE MOUNTAIN WILL NOT COME TO . . .

move heaven and earth, to To exert oneself to the utmost to accomplish something. This hyperbole dates from the eighteenth century and is heard somewhat less often today. It was a cliché by the time F. Anstey wrote (*Tinted Venus,* 1885), "There's the police moving heaven and earth to get you back again."

movers and shakers Individuals with the power and/or influence to effect change. At first each of these nouns alluded specifically to God, but in the nineteenth century they began to be paired and applied to human beings. The *OED* quotes A. O'Shaughnessy's *Music and Moonlight* (1874): "Yet we are the movers and shakers of the world forever, it seems."

much ado about nothing A commotion over a trifle; a TEMPEST IN A TEAPOT. It is best remembered as Shakespeare's title for a comedy, but the term was already known by the time he used it. The noun *ado,* meaning "a big fuss," survives largely in this cliché.

muddy the waters, to To confuse the issue. This analogy to stirring up the mud from the bottom of a clear pond, lake, or stream dates from the early nineteenth century. The *OED* quotes *Blackwell's Magazine* (1837): "He . . . began to muddy the water."

mum's the word Keep it a secret. This seemingly modern slang phrase was used by Shakespeare—"Seal up your lips, and give no words but—mum" (*Henry VI, Part 2,* 1.2)—as well as numerous earlier writers. The word *mum* has meant silent since about 1350 and comes from the imitative sound made when one's lips are closed (a kind of hum). The actual locution "Mum's the word" appears in print over and over from about 1700.

Murphy's law If anything can go wrong, it will. This expression appears to have originated in the mid-1900s in the U.S. Air Force. According to an article in the *San Francisco Chronicle* of March 16, 1978 (cited in the *Random House Historical Dictionary of American Slang*), during some testing at Edwards Air Force Base in 1949 Captain Ed Murphy, an engineer, was frustrated with a malfunctioning part and said about the technician responsible, "If there is any way to do things wrong, he will." Within weeks his statement was referred to as "Murphy's Law," and by about 1960 it had entered the civilian vocabulary and was attached to just about any mistake or mishap. In succeeding decades it became a cliché.

museum piece, a An old-fashioned or decrepit item or person. Basically this term is a genuine description of an item of value or rarity that was used ironically or pejoratively from about 1915 on. John Galsworthy used it in *Swan Song* (1928): "The girl and her brother had been museum pieces, two Americans without money to speak of."

musical chairs See PLAY MUSICAL CHAIRS.

mutual admiration society A shared feeling of esteem, real or pretended, between two individuals for each other. This reciprocal relationship was first so called by Thoreau in 1851 and picked up by Oliver Wendell Holmes in *The Autocrat of the Breakfast-Table* (1858). Today we often use the term sarcastically for individuals who publicly pay lavish compliments to each other but may have little respect for each other in private, or who admire each other but are not highly regarded by others.

my heart bleeds for you I don't feel sorry for you at all. Originally this term surely expressed heartfelt sympathy, but it was presumably beginning to be used ironically by Samuel Johnson in 1763, when James Boswell *(Life of Johnson)* reports him to have said, "When a butcher tells you that his heart bleeds for his country he has, in fact, no uneasy feeling."

my lips are sealed See LIPS ARE SEALED.

my name is mud See NAME IS MUD.

n

nail in one's coffin, drive/put a Perform some destructive (or self-destructive) act. The term first appeared in print in Peter Pindar's (John Wolcot's) Ode no. 15 (1789): "Care to our coffin adds a nail." It was repeated over the years, and in the early twentieth century was taken up by the Anti-Cigarette League, which announced that every cigarette smoked was a nail in one's coffin, giving rise to the colloquial name *coffin nail* for a cigarette. "Have you a coffin nail?" wrote O. Henry (*The Higher Abdication,* 1907).

nail one's colors to the mast Adopt an unyielding attitude. This nineteenth-century expression alludes to flying a flag from a ship's mast. If the flag is nailed to the mast, it cannot be hauled down. Sir Walter Scott may have been the first to put it in writing: "Stood for his country's glory fast, And nailed her colours to the mast" (*Marmion,* 1808). Although the days of flag-flying sailing ships are in the past, the expression lives on. It appeared in *Great Outdoors* (Sept. 27, 1989): "The prince neatly side-stepped nailing his colours to the mast in the national parks debate."

naked as a jaybird Nude. This expression is definitely American in origin, but the simile is as puzzling as the older British *naked as a robin.* Neither bird is very plain in appearance ("bare"). It appears in print with some frequency from the mid-twentieth century on. For example, D. Delman used it in *Sudden Death* (1972): "The corpus was as naked as a jaybird."

naked truth The plain unvarnished facts. Allegedly this term came from a fable in which Truth and Falsehood went bathing. Falsehood finished first and dressed in Truth's garments, whereupon Truth, unwilling to take Falsehood's clothes, went naked. Appealing as this tale may be, the image of unvarnished truth is not that exotic. Tennyson used it in *Idylls of the King:* "Mere white truth in simple nakedness." William Safire pointed out that in the 1970s it was a favorite term with journalists, who thus contributed to its survival.

name is mud, one's One is discredited. This term apparently originated in the British Parliament in the early nineteenth century, when it was used for any member who disgraced himself, through either a singularly bad speech or an overwhelming defeat in an election. (In the eighteenth and nineteenth centuries *mud* was slang for "a fool" or "a stupid fellow.") In time, however, the meaning became milder, simply denoting that someone had made a bad mistake.

name of the game, the The heart of the matter, the true purpose. The origin of this twentieth-century Americanism is uncertain, but Eric Partridge believed it came from sports, where either a coach or a sportswriter would say it in the sense of, "Scoring the most runs—that's the name of the game" (i.e., the ultimate goal). A popular television series entitled *The Name of the Game* (1968–71), which was developed from a 1966 film, *Fame Is the Name of the Game,* helped the expression gain currency.

napping, to be caught/catch To be surprised off guard, taken unawares. This term began life in the sixteenth century as *to be taken napping.* "Take Nappynge as Mosse toke his Meare" was the title of a 1569 ballad. The term was included in John Ray's proverb collection of 1670, in which Ray commented, "Who this Moss was is not very material to know. I suppose some such man might find his mare dead, and taking her to be only asleep, might say, 'Have I caught you napping?'" Yet Shakespeare and other sixteenth-century writers used the phrase in the modern sense of taking someone unawares; "Nay, I have ta'en you napping, gentle love," Tranio says to Bianca (*The Taming of the Shrew,* 4.2).

nature abhors a vacuum Empty spaces are usually filled. This seemingly very scientific statement actually was first made by Rabelais in *Gargantua* (1534), in Latin: *Natura abhorret vacuum;* Rabelais later repeated it in French in *Pantagruel* (1548). A century later Thomas Fuller also stated, "Queen Joan . . . (hating widowhood as much as nature doth vacuum) married James, King of Majorca."

nearest and dearest One's closest and fondest companions, friends, and/or relatives. This expression, which no doubt owes its longevity to its rhyme, is often used ironically, and has been ever since the sixteenth century. Shakespeare so used it in *Henry IV, Part 1* (3.2), when King Henry tells his son, Prince Hal, "Why, Harry, do I tell thee of my foes, which art my near'st and dearest enemy? Thou that art like enough . . . to fight against me under Percy's pay." So did Thomas Middleton in his comedy, *Anything for a Quiet Life* (5.1), produced in 1615. A contemporary context might have it, "We're having an intimate gathering—for only a hundred of our nearest and dearest."

neat as a pin Trim, orderly. This term dates from the late eighteenth century and appeared in print in several works by John Wolcot (who used the pseudonym Peter Pindar), as "neat as a new pin."

necessity is the mother of invention Urgent need prompts one to devise a new solution. Words to this effect date from the time of the ancient Greeks, but the precise phrase first occurs in William Wycherley's play *Love in a Wood* (1672, 3.3): "Necessity, mother of invention!" It is a proverb in Italian, French, German, and probably numerous other languages.

neck and neck A close competition. The term comes from horse-racing, when two horses running very close appear to be neck against neck. It began to be transferred to human affairs in the early nineteenth century. John W. Croker used it in *Croker Papers* (c. 1812): "In the House of Commons, . . . where the parties were, if I may use the expression, neck and neck."

neck of the woods, this This particular region or neighborhood. An Americanism once meaning a forest settlement, this term appeared in print in the 1850s. "She is welcome to the hospitalities of this neck of the wood," wrote Alice Cary (*Married, Not Mated,* 1856).

nectar of the gods A delicious drink. In classical mythology nectar was the life-giving drink of the gods, and ambrosia their food. The term was transferred to any delicious beverage in the sixteenth century.

needle in a haystack, (like finding) a An item that is extremely difficult, if not impossible, to find. This term dates from the sixteenth century, although "haystack" at first appeared as "meadow" (in Sir Thomas More's *Works,* 1532), "bottle of hay" (Robert Greene, 1592), or "load of hay" (John Taylor, 1619). The same metaphor exists in numerous languages.

needless to say Unnecessary to state. This phrase, which always precedes the statement of that very thing which need not be said, originated as "Nedelesse to speke" in the early sixteenth century. See also GOES WITHOUT SAYING.

need (something) like a hole in the head, to A superfluous item, something one does not want at all. A slangy Americanism of the 1940s, it is the modern equivalent of "as much need on't, as he hath of the pip [a disease], or of a cough" (John Ray, *English Proverbs,* 1678) and "as much need of it as a toad of a side pocket" (Francis Grose, *A Classical Dictionary of the Vulgar Tongue,* 1785). The 1944 collection of articles from the U.S. Army publication *Yank* had "The Partisans need chow-chow like they need a hole in the head" (*Best from Yank*).

neither fish, flesh, nor fowl Not one or the other; not fitting any category. This term dates from the sixteenth century and appeared in John Heywood's 1546 *Proverbs* as "She is nother fyshe, nor fleshe, nor good red hearyng [herring]." The analogy refers to food for monks (fish), for the people (meat), and for the poor (red herring). Shakespeare also used the term; when Falstaff insults Mistress Quickly, he says she's an otter because "She's neither fish nor flesh; a man knows not where to have her" (*Henry IV, Part 1,* 3.3).

neither here nor there Irrelevant, unimportant. This term dates from the sixteenth century, appearing in Arthur Golding's translation of Calvin (1583), "Our so dooing is neither here nor there (as they say)," as well as in Shakespeare's *The Merry Wives of Windsor, Othello,* and elsewhere.

neither hide nor hair Nothing; no part of something. The term, which dates from Chaucer's time, alludes to the fact that the outside of an animal is made up of hide and hair, which therefore constitute its entirety. The negative version, nearly always meaning that something or someone cannot be seen or found, became common in the mid-nineteenth century. "I haven't seen hide nor hair of the piece," wrote Josiah G. Holland (*The Bay-Path,* 1857).

neither rhyme nor reason No sense whatever. This term dates from the fifteenth century, when an unknown French writer wrote, *En toy ne Ryme ne Raison* ("In you neither rhyme nor reason," *Maistre Pierre Pathelin,* c. 1475). Sir Thomas More is credited with the following remark made to a friend who had put into verse a mediocre book: "Yea, marry, now it is somewhat, for now it is rhyme; whereas before it was neither rhyme nor reason." The term made it into John Ray's proverb collection of 1678 and is by no means obsolete.

ne plus ultra Ultimate perfection, the highest point to which something can be brought. The words are Latin for "nothing further" and allegedly quoted an inscription on the Pillars of Hercules, in the Strait of Gibraltar, meant to prevent ships from going any farther. The term was taken over into English in the 1600s and with overuse became a cliché. For example, "In the fascination of young Russians for Western things, jeans are the ne plus ultra of the modish. . . ." (Collin Thubron, *Among the Russians,* 1983).

nervous Nellie A person who worries unduly or is foolishly fearful. The term apparently originated in the late 1920s and referred to Secretary of State Frank B. Kellogg, who served from 1925 to 1929. It soon was picked up and used for any individual, male or female, who showed such qualities. Richard Dyer used it in a review of *Acis and Galatea,* writing: "The direction presented him [Acis] as a kind of nervous Nellie, unable to decide which shirt to wear to impress Galatea" (*Boston Globe,* Nov. 23, 2004). See also WORRY WART.

never a dull moment Something exciting is always occurring. This term, usually stated ironically when something dangerous, stressful, or otherwise unpleasant is happening, became common in the Royal Navy in the 1930s and spread from there across the Atlantic and to civilian situations.

Never-Never Land An imaginary place; a fantasy. This term was invented by James Barrie in *Peter Pan* (1904) for the place where Lost Boys and Red Indians lived. The Australians took it over and used it for the vast unsettled areas of their continent, the so-called outback. After the publication of *We of the Never Never* (1908) by Mrs. Aeneas Gunn, it referred specifically to Australia's Northern Territory. Elsewhere it continues to be used more generally.

never say die Never give up. Although the analogy is an obvious one, the phrase dates only from the mid-nineteenth century. Dickens used it in *Pickwick Papers* (1837), "Never say die—down upon your luck," and numerous writers did after him. In the twentieth century it was more often used ironically, but in the same meaning—that is, keep on trying against all odds.

new lease on life, a Renewed health and vigor; a fresh start, or opportunity for improvement. This seemingly very modern expression alluding to a new rental agreement dates from the early nineteenth century. Sir Walter Scott used it in a letter of 1809 concerning an invalid friend who appeared to be improving: "My friend has since taken out a new lease of life and . . . may . . . live as long as I shall." By the mid-nineteenth century it had been transferred to any kind of fresh start.

new wrinkle, a A happy expedient, a novel or different device. The transfer of "wrinkle" from rumpled clothing or age-lined skin took place in the 1800s, but the idea of novelty was added in the United States in the early 1900s. Jazz composer W. C. Handy used it in *Father of the Blues* (1941): "In addition to twirling their batons, they added the new wrinkle of tossing them back and forth." This cliché is particularly popular with business journalists.

next to nothing A very small amount, barely more than nothing at all. This expression uses *next to* in the sense of "almost," a usage dating from the seventeenth century, as in "She ate next to nothing," or "I earned next to nothing last year."

nick of time, (just) in the At the last minute, just in time. This term comes from a now obsolete meaning of *nick,* that is, "the critical moment." A 1577 chronicle states, "The Romane navie . . . arrived at the very pinch, or as commonly we say, in the nicke." Nearly a century later *of time* was added to clarify the issue, although *just in the nick* continued to be used for many years. It probably was a cliché by the time Sir Walter Scott wrote (*The Pirate,* 1821), "The fortunate arrival of Gordaunt, in the very nick of time."

NIMBY Acronym for "not in my backyard," voicing a strong objection to construction projects or institutions considered detrimental to one's neighborhood or locality. The term is relatively new, dating from about 1980, although the sentiment expressed is much older. A *Boston Globe* editorial on October 27, 2003, describing a compromise in proposed zoning for multifamily housing, was entitled "A Nod to NIMBY-ism."

nine-day wonder, a A short-lived sensation. This term originated in a proverb dating from Chaucer's time, "For wonder last but nine night nevere in toune." It was recorded by John Heywood in 1546: "This wonder (as wonders last) lasted nine daies." Another version is "A wonder lasts nine days, and then the puppy's eyes are open," referring to the fact that dogs are born blind, which may be the ultimate source of the analogy—that is, after nine days one's eyes are open and the so-called wonder is seen for what it really is. The term continues to appear in all kinds of context, as in, "There is great risk in becoming involved in a product that is a nine-day wonder" (T. Lundberg, *Starting in Business*, 1985, writing about skateboards—he was clearly wrong).

nip and tuck A very close contest. The ultimate source of this phrase has been lost, but it appears to have originated in nineteenth-century America. An early example is, "It will be like the old bitch and the rabbit, nip and tack [sic] every jump" (*Quarter Race in Kentucky,* 1836). It is used in the same way as NECK AND NECK.

nip in the bud, to To stop something before it can develop further. This analogy to an early spring frost that kills off flower buds dates from the sixteenth century. Sir Boyle Roche (1743–1807), a member of Parliament, was quoted in this memorable mixed metaphor: "Mr. Speaker, I smell a rat; I see him forming in the air and darkening the sky; but I'll nip him in the bud."

no accounting for tastes, there is no Each to his or her own preference. This locution for the inexplicability of likes (and dislikes) began as "there is no disputing about tastes" in the sixteenth century. It was changed to "accounting for" by the early nineteenth century. Anthony Trollope, in the last of his *Barset Chronicles* (1867), said of Major Grantly as a suitor, "There was . . . no accounting for tastes." A similar mid-twentieth-century phrase that is on its way to clichédom is *different strokes for different folks,* which originated in American regional slang. All these are synonymous with the much older proverb, *One man's meat is another's poison,* originating in Roman times and proverbial since about 1700. See also TO EACH HIS OWN.

no-brainer Something obvious, requiring little thought. Dating from about 1970, the term quickly caught on and is on its way to clichédom. The *Wash-*

ington Post had it on October 3, 1991: "The rich guy is willing . . . This is a no-brainer. Let him build it." See also ROCKET SCIENTIST, YOU DON'T HAVE TO BE A.

no can do I can't do what you ask; this cannot be done. This slangy expression is derived from the pidgin English antonym *can do,* picked up by sailors in the Far East and soon turned around. Although the earliest citation for it is dated January 4, 1906 ("No can do Johnny, no can do. . . . Him gloatee too muchee lolry," *Independent,* cited by *Random House Historical Dictionary of American Slang*), Eric Partridge believed it dates back to 1850 or even earlier. Both positive and negative versions were widely used in the military and soon spread to civilian language.

no comment I don't want to talk about it. This ambiguous reply to a question one doesn't wish to answer originated in the mid-twentieth century among politicians and diplomats responding to journalists or interviewers. It soon began to be used more widely by other public figures and is fast approaching the status of a cliché.

nodding acquaintance, a Superficial knowledge. An early nineteenth-century term, it conjures up the era when the formal bow was a normal greeting. Thomas Hughes used it in *Tom Brown at Oxford* (1861): "Many with whom he had scarcely a nodding acquaintance."

no dice Nothing doing; useless and ineffective. A twentieth-century American colloquialism, this term clearly comes from gambling, but its precise origin is obscure. Presumably it meant that without dice one couldn't have a game. It appears in print in several popular novels of the early 1940s, including A. Marshall's *Some Like It Hot* (1941), which became a very successful motion picture ("No dice. I'll get along in my own piddling fashion"). See also NO WAY.

no flies on him/her/me See THERE'S NO FLIES ON HIM/HER.

no fool like an old fool See THERE'S NO FOOL LIKE AN OLD FOOL.

no good deed goes unpunished A kindness or other positive behavior often is rewarded with opprobrium or abuse. This new, equally sarcastic take on "the way to hell is paved with good intentions" dates from the late 1900s. William Lashner used it, "But that's the way of it, Detective . . . No good deed goes unpunished."

no great shakes Nothing special; ordinary. There are several theories as to the origin of this term, which dates from the early nineteenth century. One holds that it comes from sailors shaking a cask, that is, dismantling it and picking up the staves, or shakes, which then had little value. Another believes it comes from shaking dice with only a poor result. Whichever is true, it was transferred to anything deemed mediocre by about 1800, as in, "I'm no great shakes at braggin'" (John Neal, *Brother Jonathan,* 1825).

no holds barred Without any restrictions. The term comes from wrestling, where certain holds are illegal. Its figurative use dates from the mid-1900s. For example, "No holds were barred, so to speak, for the Prince's unorthodox education" (*Times,* Nov. 28, 1958).

no laughing matter A serious issue. This term, which is always put in this negative way—one never hears of something that *is* a laughing matter—dates from the sixteenth century. Playwright Richard Brinsley Sheridan is quoted as having said (1793), "A joke in your mouth is no laughing matter."

no love lost between them, there's They hate each other. This term, which dates from the sixteenth century, used to have either of two meanings: (1) they love each other or (2) they dislike each other. The former is intended in the seventeenth-century poem, "The Children in the Wood": "No love between these two was lost, each was to the other kind" (*Reliques of Ancient English Poetry,* 1765). This meaning persisted until the eighteenth century but is now obsolete. The current cliché signifies only that two persons have *no* love for each other, as in, "There was not a great deal of love lost between Will and his half-sister" (Thackeray, *The Virginians,* 1858).

no matter how you slice it See SLICE THE PIE.

no more Mr. Nice Guy Instead of being agreeable and amiable, I (or he, or she, or they) will be tough and uncompromising. This colloquialism dates from the mid-1900s, and is a modern, far more benign substitute for GRANT NO QUARTER. It appears in numerous contexts and sometimes does not even involve a person, as in "The weatherman has stopped playing Mr. Nice Guy," which simply means he is announcing a change to bad weather. Lawrence Block used it with more dramatic meaning in *All the Flowers Are Dying* (2005): "'Get three [guns],' she said. 'One for each of us. No more Mr. Nice Guy.'"

non compos Crazy; mentally incapacitated and therefore unable to be responsible for one's speech or actions. This term is an abbreviation of the Latin *non compos mentis,* literally translated as "not master of one's mind," or "not of sound mind." It dates from the seventeenth century and today is loosely used for irrational behavior, as well as surviving in legal terminology.

no news is good news To hear nothing means that all is well. This proverbial phrase dates from the early seventeenth century. King James I is supposed to have said, in 1616, "No newis is bettir than evill newis," and the adage has been quoted again and again over the centuries, by James Howell, Charles Dickens, and Noël Coward, among others.

no-no, a A prohibition or taboo; something that is forbidden or at least discouraged. The term dates from the mid-1900s and was popularized in the late 1960s in a television show, *Rowan & Martin's Laugh-In*. Danielle and John Kinkel used it in the *Boston Globe* (Feb. 24, 2005) in a piece about the shortage of Roman Catholic priests: "First, everyone knows that ordaining women is a papal no-no and will not be acted upon in the near future."

nook and cranny, every Every place, all over. This expression combines *nook,* which has meant an out-of-the-way corner since the fourteenth century, and *cranny,* meaning a crack or crevice since the fifteenth century. Frederick Marryat used it in *Japhet in Search of a Father* (1836): "After examining every nook and cranny they could think of."

no pain, no gain See NOTHING VENTURED, NOTHING GAINED.

no picnic No easy task; not an enjoyable experience. This term began to be used frequently in the late nineteenth century. Rudyard Kipling used it several times, as in *Wee Willie Winkie* (1888): "T'ain't no bloomin' picnic in those parts, I can tell you."

no problem That's fine; you're welcome; I'd be glad to help. This conventional reply expressing acquiescence and other positive feelings originated in America in the mid-twentieth century. It also has taken hold in numerous parts of the non-English-speaking world; the author has heard it in France, Austria, Yugoslavia, and Singapore from individuals who otherwise knew almost no English (other than "okay"). Others report having heard it in Russia, where it is often used ironically, Kenya, and China. In Australia, however, it alternates with *no worries* (probably from the 1930s British locution, *not to worry*). The journal *American Speech* recorded "no problem" in 1963 as an equivalent of NO SWEAT. The *OED*'s citations include Martin Amis's *Rachel Papers* (1973): "He . . . gave it back to me, saying 'No problem' again through his nose." It has quickly become as ubiquitous and as divorced from the words' original meaning (i.e., "there is no difficulty") as HAVE A NICE DAY and TAKE CARE. Indeed, Pico Iyer pointed out that today "'No problem' . . . in every language means that your problems are just beginning" (*Time,* July 2, 1990).

no quarter given See GRANT NO QUARTER.

no rest for the weary (wicked) No peace and quiet for anyone; to be kept very busy. This term, dating from about 1900, today is used facetiously by or about a person who simply is kept very busy. It presumably echoes several biblical passages stating that God will take care of good people but will provide no peace for evildoers (Isaiah 48:22 and 57:21). *Wicked* is used more in Britain, *weary* in America. After a two-foot snowfall and predictions of at least another foot of snow, meteorologist Michael Henry said, "There's no rest for the weary. Just when they . . . cleaned up after the last storm, here comes another" (*Boston Globe,* March 9, 2001).

nose out of joint, to have one's/put someone's To be irritated or jealous, particularly when one is displaced or supplanted by someone else. This term appeared in print as long ago as 1581 and has continued to be used in the same sense ever since. The image is a bit puzzling, since it implies that the nose can be dislocated (it can't—it has no joint), but that has not deterred its continued use. Shaw used it in at least two plays, *Major Barbara* and *Heartbreak House:* "The new bloke has put your nose out of joint."

nose to the grindstone, have/keep one's To work hard all the time. The image, transferred from tools that must continuously be sharpened, is a vivid one and has been used since the sixteenth century. "This Text holdeth their noses to hard to the grindstone, that it clean disfigureth their faces," wrote John Faith (*A Mirrour to Knowe Thyselfe,* 1539).

no skin off my nose, it's/that's It's no affair of mine; it doesn't bother or harm me in any way. An early twentieth-century colloquialism, this expression is believed to come from boxing, where, if one is not at all involved, one is unlikely to lose skin from one's nose. "It's no skin off any nose of mine," wrote F. C. Davis (*The Graveyard Never Closes,* 1941).

no smoke, no fire See WHERE THERE'S SMOKE, THERE'S FIRE.

no sooner said than done Carried out immediately. This hyperbolic statement dates from Roman times, when it was put *Dictum factumque facit frux* (by Ennius in *Annals,* c. 180 B.C.). Erasmus in *Adagia* (1508) had *Simul et dictum et factum,* "At the same time said and done," and the precise English wording appeared about one and a half centuries later, in Head and Kirkman's *The English Rogue* (1671).

no spring chicken, (she's) No longer young. This unflattering remark has been made since the early eighteenth century and, as far as can be gathered, is applied mostly to women. Men seldom are accused of aging in just this way. In print, it appeared (without "spring") in Addison and Steele's *The Spectator* (1711) and soon after was taken up by Jonathan Swift in *Stella's Birthday* (1720): "Pursue your trade of scandal-picking, Your hints that Stella is no chicken."

no sweat No trouble, no extra effort will be required (to accomplish what you ask). This term has been around since about 1930 or even earlier and, several lexicographers (including Eric Partridge) to the contrary, is nearly always used in the sense of the perspiration that might result from overexertion (rather than that coming from anxiety or mental stress, as they suggest). It is closely related to the slightly newer NO PROBLEM but unlike it has not acquired such extended meanings as "OK?" or "You're welcome."

not! See I DON'T THINK SO.

not a ghost of a chance Not the least likelihood. This term, which uses *ghost* in the sense of an insubstantial shadow, dates from the nineteenth century. In print it appeared in Thomas Hughes's *Tom Brown's School Days* (1857): "Williams hadn't the ghost of a chance with Tom at wrestling." See also NOT A HOPE IN HELL; CHINAMAN'S CHANCE.

not a hope in hell No chance at all. This term, with such variations as not a SNOWBALL'S CHANCE IN HELL, has been used since the early twentieth century. The *OED* cites O. Onions, *Peace in Our Time* (1923), as its first appearance in print: "'I rather fancied Lovelightly.'—'Lovelightly? Not a hope in Hell!'"

not all black and white Not clearly distinguished, not all bad or good: for example, "John warned us that this controversy was not all black and white; both sides were partly in the wrong." This expression is based on the identification of black with evil or wrong, and white with good or right, which goes back at least two millennia.

not all it's cracked up to be Not as outstanding as its reputation; disappointing. This term uses the verb *to crack up* in an older meaning rarely heard today, that is, "to praise." The cliché dates from the nineteenth century. Wrote John A. Clark, "One of the lodgers . . . remarked that the Galt House was not after all just what it was cracked up to be" (*Gleanings by the Way,* 1837).

not batting an eye See WITHOUT BATTING AN EYE.

not by a long shot See LONG SHOT.

not care/give/worth a fig, to Not care at all, not give a damn. *Fig* has denoted something worthless since about 1400. Moreover, in Mediterranean countries the sign of the fig is an obscene gesture, made by clenching one's fist and pushing the thumb between the first and middle fingers. According to John Ciardi, the thumb represents the penis, the fingers the labia, and the gesture means "Fuck you." Dante so used it in the *Inferno* section of *The Divine Comedy.* Centuries later, however, the phrase's obscene provenance began to be largely ignored, and the cliché survives.

not cricket, it's/that's Unsportsmanlike, unfair, dishonorable. Eric Partridge traced this term to 1867 but believed it was not widely used until the early twentieth century. Among the early references in print is Stanley Houghton's 1914 play, *The Partners,* ". . . but it is not playing the game. In other words, Cynthia, it is not cricket." Although cricket is a sport popular exclusively in Great Britain and most of its former colonies, the term crossed the Atlantic and became a cliché in the United States as well.

not enough room to swing a cat Extremely cramped quarters. The origin of this expression is disputed. Many believe it alludes to swinging a cat-o'-nine-tails, a whip with nine lashes fastened to a handle, which was long used to punish offenders in the British military (it was formally abolished only in 1948). Others believe it refers to the Scots word *cat* for scoundrel, and thus to a criminal swinging from the gallows. Still others say it comes from the practice of swinging a live cat by its tail to serve as target practice for archers. Whatever the origin, the term was used by Smollett, Dickens, Twain, and numerous other writers.

not for all the tea in China Not at any price. Eminent lexicographers agree that this term originated in Australia in the 1890s and soon spread to the rest of the tea-drinking English-speaking world. The *OED* cites K. Tennant's *Ride on, Stranger* (1943): "I'm not going to stand in my girl's light for all the tea in China."

not for love or money Under no circumstances. The earliest reference to this expression dates from the late tenth century, and it has been increasingly repeated ever since. Maria Edgeworth had it in *Castle Rackrent* (1801): "When there was no room to be had for love or money, [many chose] to sleep in the chicken-house."

nothing doing Absolutely not. This response to a request, suggestion, or statement of something one considers untrue dates from the late 1800s. *People* used it on June 22, 1947: "It was suggested that she should come incognito. Nothing doing." Also see NOT ON YOUR LIFE, and, for a more recent expression of denial or refusal, NO WAY.

nothing new under the sun Everything has existed or happened before. This seemingly world-weary view was first stated in Ecclesiastes (1:9), appearing in John Wycliffe's 1382 translation, "No thing vndir the sunne is newe."

nothing to write home about Unremarkable and ordinary. This term became common in the late nineteenth century, probably originating among troops stationed overseas. G. D. H. Cole used it in *The Man from the River* (1928): "He was . . . bleeding a bit, but nothing to write home about." Another example is, "Ross won, Julie lost, neither of them enough to write home about" (June Drummond, *Junta,* 1989).

nothing ventured, nothing gained If you won't take a chance you can't expect to achieve anything. There are two older proverbial forms of this expression, *nothing (nought) venture, nothing (nought) have,* stated by Chaucer (c. 1374), and *nothing venture, nothing win,* stated by William Caxton about a century later. The modern form appears in Thomas Heywood's play *Captives* (1624): "I see here that nought venters, nothinge gaynes." It has been repeated in numerous languages ever since. Another, seemingly modern form is *no pain, no gain,* today frequently uttered by coaches, trainers, and physical therapists. Versions of this date from the early seventeenth century—"Pain is forgotten where gain follows" appeared in several early proverb collections—and the current rhyming cliché was proverbial by the mid-nineteenth century.

not just a pretty face Describing a person with more substance than mere physical beauty. Dating from the second half of the 1900s, the phrase was used for the title of a biography of screen actress Hedy Lamarr by Courtney Baalman (May 1999), which described her as a woman accomplished in many fields, as well as a popular song title ("She's Not Just a Pretty Face" by Shania Twain). In 2004 Democratic vice presidential candidate John Edwards, known for his good looks, was described as "not just a pretty face" by columnist Laura Lasky.

not know beans Be quite ignorant about something. This colloquialism dates from the early nineteenth century, when *beans* denoted something small or worthless. However, from the mid-1800s to the early 1900s the converse, *to know beans,* meant to be quite knowledgeable. The latter has not survived, but we still hear, for example, "Don't ask Harry's advice; he doesn't know beans about cars." A more specific and much ruder variant is *not know one's ass from one's elbow*, which dates from about 1900 and denotes general stupidity. Other versions replace "elbow" with "hole in the ground," but "elbow" is heard more often and has become a cliché. A 1963 citation has it, "These medics don't know their asses from their elbows."

not know from Adam See KNOW FROM ADAM.

not lift a finger See LIFT A FINGER.

not long for this world Expected to survive only for a short time. This expression dates from the early nineteenth century. In a letter of 1822, Byron wrote, "If it is, I cannot be long for this world."

not one's cup of tea It doesn't suit one, it isn't to one's taste. The ultimate origin of this term is not known, although it definitely is British. Tea had become an immensely popular beverage in Europe by the mid-eighteenth century, and the positive version—he or she *is* my cup of tea—was used from the late nineteenth century. The negative is slightly newer, from the 1920s. Josephine Tey used it in *The Franchise Affair* (1948): "Probably she isn't your cup of tea. You have always preferred them a little stupid, and blonde."

not on your life Under no circumstances. This expression, which means just about the same as "not if your life depended on it," dates from the late nineteenth century. It appeared in print fairly often from 1900 on, as in Jack London's *The Valley of the Moon* (1913): "'You'd vote the socialist ticket.'—'Not on your life.'" Its positive counterpart is YOU (CAN) BET YOUR LIFE.

not to See DON'T.

not to be sneezed at Not to be dismissed. This term, which presumably comes from turning up one's nose at something to express contempt, was already current in the early nineteenth century. "As I am situated, £300 or £400 a year is not to be sneezed at" (Sir Walter Scott, letter, 1813).

not to put too fine a point on it To speak bluntly. This analogy to a cutting tool was particularly favored by Dickens. He used it frequently and on occasion defined it, as in "Not to put too fine a point upon it—a favourite apology for plain-speaking with Mr. Snagsby" (*Bleak House,* 1852). It may be obsolescent in Britain and obsolete in America.

not trust someone as far as one can throw him/her He (or she) is extremely unreliable and untrustworthy. According to Eric Partridge, this seemingly modern phrase dates from about 1870, and it remains current.

not until hell freezes over See TILL HELL FREEZES OVER.

not until the cows come home Not for a long time. Presumably the time referred to is when cows return to the barn for milking. The term has been around since the late sixteenth century. Beaumont and Fletcher's play *The Scornful Lady* (1610) stated, "Kiss till the cow come home."

not what it's cracked up See NOT ALL IT'S CRACKED UP TO BE.

not worth a (tinker's) damn Worthless. The catalog of similes signifying "without worth" is seemingly endless. This one, beginning life as "a tinker's curse," then became a tinker's *dam,* a wall of dough raised around a place where a plumber is trying to repair a hole with solder. The dough holds the solder until it hardens and then is discarded. Misspelling turned it into *damn* and today "tinker" is usually omitted. (However, "damn" alone was also used in the eighteenth century.) Among the hundreds of similes denoting worthlessness that are still heard today are *not worth a bean* (see HILL OF BEANS); *not worth a fig* (also see under FIG); *not worth a button* (thirteenth century); *not worth a (brass) farthing* (seventeenth century); *not worth the paper it's written on* (usually applied to an IOU or bad check); *not worth a pin* (fifteenth century); *not worth a plugged nickel* (*plug* meant a debased coin; nineteenth century); *not worth the powder to blow it up* (nineteenth century); *not worth a rap* (a counterfeit half-penny circulating in Ireland in the early eighteenth century); *not worth a* RED CENT (the cent being the smallest American coin, red because it used to be made of pure copper; nineteenth century); *not worth a straw* (fourteenth century). See also WORTH ONE'S SALT.

no two ways about it There's no alternative, no room for disagreement. This expression became popular in America in the early 1800s, and was picked up by Dickens in his *American Notes* (1842): "They're pretty nigh full . . . and no two ways about it." It remains current.

no way Under no circumstances. This relatively new assertion of impossibility dates from the 1960s and is American in origin. Slangy in tone, it has several variations: the rhyming *no way, José* and the enumerative *in no way, shape, or form.* (See also IN ANY WAY, SHAPE, OR FORM). J. G. Vermandel used it in *Dine with the Devil* (1970): "No way can I do it any faster than that."

no-win situation, a A condition in which none can benefit or succeed; an impasse. Originating in America about 1960, presumably it originally referred to such a military situation and was soon extended to other kinds of hostile encounter. A 1962 article in *The Economist* stated, "He recommended an agreement . . . a 'no-win' approach, in fact, 'an accommodation with tyranny.'"

now or never Last chance to speak or act. This term goes back to the ancient Greeks and Romans. In English, Chaucer used it in *Troilus and Criseyde* ("Never er now? what sey ye, no?") and Shakespeare in *Henry VI, Part 2,* 3.1: "Now, York, or never, steel thy fearful thoughts."

number's up, one's/your/his Death or capture is imminent. This term seems to have its roots in the military. In the Royal Navy in the nineteenth century it was usual to say of someone who was killed or drowned, "He lost the number of his mess." The term was taken up in the U.S. Army, a dead soldier being said to have "lost his mess number." Eventually "mess" was dropped, and the current cliché was born.

nuts and bolts, the The essential components of something. This allusion to basic machine parts, dating only from the mid-twentieth century, is mildly puzzling. Why nuts and bolts rather than nuts and screws, for example, or even wheels and gears? Whatever the ultimate reason, it is these two items that caught on. T. E. Allbeury used it in *A Choice of Enemies* (1973), "That's pretty well a nuts and bolts area for us. We know it inside out."

nuttier than a fruitcake Crazy, eccentric. This term originated in America about 1920 and transfers the actual nuts in a fruitcake to the colloquial meaning of *nutty* as crazy. The term later gave rise to the usage *fruitcake* for an eccentric individual.

nut to crack See TOUGH NUT TO CRACK.

O

Occam's razor The simplest explanation of something is apt to be the correct one. This principle is named for the English scholar William of Occam (or Ockham), who lived from 1280 to 1349. A Franciscan monk, he so angered Pope John XXII through both his writings on the nature of knowledge and his defense of his order's vow of poverty that he was excommunicated. William, whom his colleagues called *Doctor Singularis et Invincibilis* ("singular and invincible doctor"), put his principle in Latin: *Entia non sunt multiplicanda praeter necessitatem,* "Entities should not be unnecessarily multiplied." In effect, he held that any unnecessary parts of a subject being analyzed should be eliminated. Obviously, this could simply be called Occam's Principle, and indeed, the *razor* did not enter into it until a French philosopher, Etienne Bonnot de Condillac, in 1746 called it *Rasoir des Nominaux,* "the razor of the nominalists," that is, cutting through complicated arguments to reach the truth. In 1836 Sir William Hamilton, lecturing on metaphysics and logic, put the two ideas together, saying, "We are therefore entitled to apply Occam's razor to this theory of causality." While some may believe that this phrase, with its ancient and rather abstruse origin, is obsolete, novelist Archer Mayor clearly disagreed, for he entitled his 1999 murder mystery *Occam's Razor.*

Ockham's razor See OCCAM'S RAZOR.

odd man out One of a group who is not selected or included, or who differs markedly from the others. At first applied only to persons, the term later was extended also to inanimate objects, as in "This checkered tablecloth is odd man out in a formal dining room."

odds and ends Fragments and remnants; a miscellaneous collection. This term may have originated as *odd ends,* meaning short leftovers from bolts of cloth. It was transferred to miscellany of other kinds by the mid-sixteenth century, and by the mid-eighteenth century it had become the modern cliché.

odor of sanctity, the A reputation for holiness. Today generally used ironically, for extreme or hypocritical piety, this term is based on the medieval notion that the dead body of a saintly person gives off a sweet smell. From this came, "He died in the odor of sanctity," meaning he died a saint, which later was extended to mean saintliness in general. G. K. Chesterton used it in his poem "A Song of Self-Esteem"—"The Faith of Tennessee has wafted o'er the sea, the odour of its sanctity—and Golly how it stank!"—in which he derided the prosecution of John Scopes in 1925 for teaching evolution in his class at the Dayton (Tennessee) High School.

off again, on again Intermittently; at intervals. Also, capricious, fickle. This nineteenth-century Americanism was originally a railroad term referring to minor mishaps, in which a train went off track and then back on again. It was reinforced by a popular song of about 1910, "Finnigin to Flannigan," by Strickland Gillilan, which went, "Bilin' down his repoort, wuz Finnigin! An' he writed this here: 'Muster Flannigan—Off agin, on agin, Gone again.—FINNIGIN.'" Today the term is frequently applied to romantic and other relationships characterized by intermittence. It is, of course, a version of *off and on,* current since the mid-nineteenth century.

off base Mistaken, incorrect, wrong. This term dates from the first half of the 1900s and alludes to baseball, where a runner whose foot is not touching a base may be put out. John Steinbeck used it in *In Dubious Battle* (1936): "If they can catch us off base, they'll bounce us."

off one's head, rocker, etc. See GO OFF ONE'S HEAD.

off the beam See ON THE BEAM.

off the beaten track See BEATEN TRACK.

off the cuff Extemporaneously, impromptu. This term allegedly comes from the practice of after-dinner speakers making notes for a speech on the cuff of their shirtsleeve at the last minute, as opposed to preparing a speech well beforehand. It originated in America in the 1930s. See also OFF THE TOP OF ONE'S HEAD.

off the deep end, to go To overreact; to let one's emotions carry one away. The "deep end" presumably means the deep water at the end of a swimming pool, which it is rash to enter unless one can swim. The term became current in the early twentieth century. "There's no reason for your going off the deep end," wrote Kathleen Knight (*Rendezvous with the Past,* 1940).

off the hook, to get/to be let To escape from some difficulty. The analogy is to throwing a fish one has caught back into the water, saving its life. The term *on the hook* goes back to the seventeenth century; the current cliché dates only from the mid-1800s. Anthony Trollope used it (*The Small*

House at Allington, 1864): "Poor Caudle . . . he's hooked, and he'll never get himself off the hook again."

off the record In confidence; unofficially. This twentieth-century expression became current in America in mid-century, used with increasing frequency by public officials giving the media information that was not for publication. Ultimately, it probably stems from an older legal term whereby a courtroom judge directs that certain evidence be struck from the court record (because it is irrelevant or improper), and at the same time instructs the jury to disregard it. See also FOR THE RECORD.

off the reservation Beyond acceptable limits. This term, which dates from about 1900, alludes to Native Americans who leave their assigned tracts of land, which could be dangerous. In politics, according to William Safire, to go off the reservation acquired a special meaning: to refuse to support a party's candidate but still remain in the party. President Harry S. Truman so used it in referring to Southern Democrats who refused to support Al Smith in the 1928 election, thereby gaining support for Herbert Hoover.

off the top of one's head Extemporaneously, impromptu; impetuously. A mid-twentieth-century Americanism, the term appeared in Harold L. Ickes's *Secret Diary* (1939): "He was impetuous and inclined to think off the top of his head at times." Author June Drummond (*Junta,* 1989) wrote: "'And then, you just acted off the top of your head.' Richard half-smiled. 'You know I have that failing.'"

off the wall Extremely unconventional, unorthodox, eccentric. This expression, which dates from about 1960, probably alludes to the erratic path of a ball bounced against a wall in a sport like squash or racquetball, as in "Answering multiple-choice questions by writing in new and different choices, that's off the wall."

of that ilk Of the same kind or class. The word *ilk* is now rarely used (except in Scotland) other than in this cliché, which is actually a twisting of the original meaning. It comes from the Old English *ilca,* meaning "the same," and is correctly used only in referring to a person whose last name is the same as that of his estate; for example, *Cawdor of that ilk* means "Cawdor of Cawdor."

of the first magnitude/order/water See FIRST MAGNITUDE.

oil on troubled waters See POUR OIL ON TROUBLED WATERS.

old as the hills, (as) Very old indeed. The term refers, presumably, to geological time, when mountains were first formed, but one writer suggests a relation to a biblical passage: "Art thou the first man that was born? or wast thou made before the hills" (Job 15:7). The expression dates from about 1800 and was used by Sir Walter Scott and Charles Dickens, among others. See also AS OLD AS ADAM; FROM TIME IMMEMORIAL.

old-boy network, the Social contacts among a group of insiders who help one another advance. The term *old boy,* originally British, refers specifically to a former pupil at one's own public school, signifying a common background (upper-class male) and therefore a mutually beneficial interest. Although the practice of fellow alumni helping one another is much older, *network* was added only in the mid-twentieth century, when the idea began to be transferred to members of a social club, professional organization, business corporation, and other groups. Long an exclusively male province, it came under vigorous attack from about 1970 on by women who maintained it gave men an unfair advantage in the workplace.

old chestnut A stale joke, anecdote, or adage. This term has a specific source, the play *The Broken Sword* by William Dimond, first produced in 1816. The principal character, a Captain Xavier, constantly repeats the same stories, one of which involves a cork tree. Pablo, another character, interrupts, saying, "Chestnut, you mean, captain. I have heard you tell the joke twenty-seven times, and I am sure it was a chestnut." The play has long since been forgotten, but the term survives, and has itself become an old chestnut.

old codger/coot/fogy Unflattering names for an elderly man. *Old codger,* dating from the mid-1700s, may imply that he is testy or crusty, whereas *old coot,* from the mid-1800s, indicates he is silly or ignorant. As for an *old fogy,* he may be hidebound in tradition. None of these is a desirable epithet, or, as Terrel Bell put it, "There's only one thing worse than an old fogy, and that's a young fogy" (commencement address at Longwood College, Virginia, June 17, 1985). A newer and decidedly vulgar synonym is *old fart,* dating from the first half of the 1900s. Phil Donahue said it of himself on his NBC television show in 1992: "I didn't always look like an old fart like this."

old college try, (give it) the Do the best you can, even if you think it's a hopeless cause. This slangy Americanism dates from the 1930s when college football films became very popular in the United States. The phrase was one of the cheers intended to urge on a team that was falling behind or facing overwhelming odds. Transferred to other endeavors, it came to be used more or less ironically.

old enough to know better Mature enough to have good judgment. This phrase, sometimes completed with *but young enough to learn,* dates from the nineteenth century. Oscar Wilde played with it in *Lady Windermere's Fan* (1892): "My experience is that as soon as people are old enough to know better, they don't know anything at all."

old guard The established, conservative members of any movement or party, who tend to resist any change. The term is a translation of *Vieille Garde* (French for "old guard"), the name given to Napoleon's Imperial Guard, who were the elite veteran regiments of his army and intensely loyal to him. It was they who made the last French charge at Waterloo. The name began to be used for American political conservatives in the early 1840s.

old hat Outmoded, old-fashioned, uninteresting. The term, it has been suggested by several writers, comes from the fact that hats go out of style long before they are actually worn out. The term began to be used figuratively during the late nineteenth century. Shaw used it in *Platform and Pulpit* (1932): "If I mention that sort of thing I am told that is old hat."

old saw A proverb, maxim, or adage. This term comes from a much older meaning for *saw,* derived from the Old English *sagu* and meaning just about the same as "saying." The "old" here is not necessarily derogatory, rather signifying "wise." Thomas Cooper in his *Thesaurus* (1565) defined a proverb as "an olde sayed sawe."

old stamping ground A favorite or habitual haunt. This Americanism dates from the eighteenth century and originally referred to a place where horses or cattle were gathered together (presumably stamping down the ground with their hooves). By the early 1800s it had been transferred to a gathering place for human beings. D. Dunklin used it in an 1821 letter: "It is unnecessary to undertake to give you any details of affairs in your old stamping ground."

old wives' tale A superstitious story. This term actually dates back to Plato, who repeated the phrase in a number of writings and was so cited by Erasmus. In English a version of it appeared in John Trevisa's translation of *Polycronicon,* "And useth telynges as olde wifes dooth" (1387), and then began to be used frequently from the sixteenth century on. "These are trifles and mere old wives' tales" wrote Christopher Marlowe in *Doctor Faustus* (c. 1589). Arnold Bennett used it as the title of a novel (1908), and this sex- and age-biased cliché persists to the present day.

on an even keel In stable condition, well balanced. The keel is a structure in the bottom of a vessel's hull, extending along its full length and forming, in effect, its backbone. A boat is said to be on an even keel when it rides flat in the water, without tilting to either side. The image was extended to human affairs in the mid-nineteenth century.

on a/the rampage Violently excited; furious. This term appears to have come from the Old Scots verb *to ramp,* meaning "to storm and rage." The current cliché was known in the mid-nineteenth century. Dickens used it in *Great Expectations* (1861), in which Joe Gargery tells the hero, "On the Rampage, Pip, and Off the Rampage, Pip; such is Life!"

on a roll Enjoying a series of successes or a run of good luck. This expression, which alludes to successful rolling of dice, dates from the second half of the 1900s. Brian Fremantle used it in *Dead Men Living* (2000), "As Charlie headed south across the river . . . he thought happily that when you're on a roll you're on a roll, and it was one of the better feelings."

on a shoestring On a strict budget; with very limited means. The source of this term is not wholly clear. One writer suggests it comes from one's resources being limited to shoelaces. In Exeter, England, there is a legend that prisoners confined in debtor's prison would lower a shoe from the window to collect money so they could get out of prison, a tale appealing to tourists but far-fetched. The likeliest explanation is the physical nature of a shoelace—that is, a very slender cord or string, which became a metaphor for slender resources stretched to their utmost. It originated (according to the *OED*) in America in the late nineteenth century. A 1904 issue of *Cosmopolitan* stated, "He speculated on a shoestring—an exceedingly small margin."

once and for all Finally and decisively. This phrase, literally meaning "this one final time which will serve forever," dates from the fifteenth century. The earliest appearance in print is in William Caxton's translation of the *Foure Sonnes of Aymon* (c. 1489): "We oughte to ask it of hym ones for all."

once bitten, twice shy One injury will make one extra cautious in the future. This proverbial saying appears to date from the mid-nineteenth century, although the idea is centuries older. William Scarborough's version of *Chinese Proverbs* (1875) stated, "Once bitten by a snake in passing by, a second time he will of grass be shy."

once in a blue moon Very rarely; once in a long while. The earliest reference to a blue moon is skeptical, as well it might be: "Yf they saye the mone is blewe, we must believe that it is true" (Roy and Barlow, *Rede Me and Be Not Wrothe,* 1528). An early reference to the moon as a time period occurred in Thomas Dekker's *A Knight's Conjuring* (1607): "She would have trickes (once in a moone) to put the divell out of his wits." The pairing of the two came only in the nineteenth century: "That indefinite period known as a 'blue moon'" (Edmund Yates, *Wrecked in Port,* 1869). Modern astronomers now say "blue moon" refers to the occurrence a fourth full moon in a season, in addition to the usual three.

on cloud nine, to be sitting To be blissfully happy. Some writers believe this expression began as being on cloud *seven,* akin to being in SEVENTH HEAVEN. Others feel *nine* has legitimacy in its own right, since it has been a mystical number since the times of the ancient Greeks. Nine is a trinity of trinities (3 x 3), and a trinity itself represents a perfect unity. In any event, the cliché dates only from the mid-twentieth century.

one fell swoop See AT ONE FELL SWOOP.

one foot in the grave On the verge of death. This graphic hyperbole was already being used in the sixteenth century, when William Painter wrote (*The Pallace of Pleasure,* 1566), "Takyng paines to visite him, who hath one of his feet alreadie within the graue, and the other stepping after with conuenient speede."

one for the road One last drink (alcoholic). Eric Partridge believed the term originated with traveling salesmen who applied it either to one last drink after a night's carousing or to one more drink before one literally set out "on the road" to see more customers. Originating early in the twentieth century, it is heard less often today, at least in America, where heavy drinking is increasingly frowned upon, especially for drivers.

one good turn deserves another I owe you for the favor you did me previously. This adage, usually said by a person returning a favor, dates as far back as c. 1400, appearing in a Latin manuscript of that period, and by the mid-sixteenth century it was part of John Heywood's proverb collection.

one-man band A person able to perform many different tasks well. The literal term applies to a musician who can play many instruments, sometimes even simultaneously. In one of his shows the composer and musical humorist Peter Schickele blew a bassoon while at the same time playing the piano with one hand or elbow. The term dates from the 1800s. The *Burlington (Iowa) Hawk-Eye* had it on July 1, 1876: "The one-man band, comprising drums, cymbals, violin, and a squeaking pipe . . . had one thing to recommend it. You can kill the drummer and thus obliterate the whole band." The term is also applied to multitalented individuals in other fields.

one man's meat is another's poison See NO ACCOUNTING FOR TASTES.

one-night stand A single performance or sexual encounter. This term comes from the days of touring theater companies, who would perform for only one night in a town that was likely to provide the audience for only one engagement. By the mid-twentieth century it had been transferred not only to other one-time performances of various kinds but also, in colloquial usage, to a single sexual encounter that was unlikely to be repeated by the same couple and therefore implied some promiscuity.

one on one A direct encounter between two persons. This expression was transferred to general use from several sports. In basketball it signifies an informal game with just two players. It also means the standard form of defense, in which one player guards one opponent. In football it similarly means a player covering (or being covered by) a single opponent. About 1960 it began to be used for nonathletic encounters, as in "Dean never liked a big party; he preferred social events where he could be one on one."

one picture is worth a thousand words A graphic illustration communicates more meaning than a verbal one. In the December 8, 1921, issue of *Printers' Ink* Fred R. Barnard wrote, "One look is worth a thousand words." Six years later (March 10, 1927) he changed it to "One picture is worth a thousand words," and, so that it would be taken seriously, said it was an ancient Chinese proverb. Since then other writers have indeed cited a Chinese proverb that holds one picture to be worth ten thousand words, but the evidence for this origin (since none cites a source) is obscure. Nevertheless, the statement became a cliché.

one swallow does not make a summer A single portent or element of something does not mean the totality is here. This ancient adage, known already in Greek times, may come from one of Aesop's fables. A swallow emerges on a warmer-than-usual winter day, and a young man, seeing it, sells his warm cloak and spends the proceeds on drink and carousing. The following week, the weather turns cold again, and he, shivering without his cloak, discovers that one swallow did not mean summer had arrived. Appearing in many proverb collections and in numerous languages, along with numerous variants (One grain does not fill a sack, one actor cannot make a play, and the like), the term was defined by George Pettie in 1576: "As one swallow does not make sommer, so one particularity concludeth no generality."

one-track mind, to have a To be focused on a single issue, action, or undertaking; to be unable to take on more than one thing at a time. This cliché refers to the single-track railway line, which allows traffic in only one direction at a time. In a 1917 speech President Woodrow Wilson said, "I have a single-track mind," one of the early figurative uses of the term.

on one's high horse, to be To put on airs; to behave arrogantly. As long ago as the fourteenth century, persons of high rank rode very tall horses, a custom that came to symbolize superiority and arrogance. By 1800 or so, to be or to get on one's high horse meant to act superior, with or without justification.

on one's last legs, to be To be extremely tired or about to collapse; near the end. Despite the implication, this term never meant that legs were in any way serial—that is, beginning with the first and ending with the last. Rather, it uses *last* meaning "near the end" (of one's energy or life). The expression was already used in the sixteenth century; it appears in the play *The Old Law* (1599) by Thomas Middleton and Philip Massinger: "My husband goes upon his last hour now—on his last legs, I am sure." In John Ray's *Proverbs* (1678) the term is defined as meaning "bankrupt," and since then it has been transferred to anything nearing its end or about to fail, as in, "This cliché may be on its last legs."

on one's toes, to be To be fully alert, ready to act. The metaphor of the dancer or runner poised on tiptoe, prepared to go, has been applied to any kind of readiness since the early twentieth century. John Dos Passos used it in *Three Soldiers* (1921): "If he just watched out and kept on his toes, he'd be sure to get it."

on pins and needles, to be To be extremely nervous or uneasy; in suspense. The image is as clear as that of a CAT ON A HOT TIN ROOF. Robert Louis Stevenson appears to have been the first to use it metaphorically, in *St. Ives* (1897): "He was plainly on pins and needles." It was a cliché by the mid-twentieth century. See also ON TENTERHOOKS.

on second thought After reconsidering. This phrase, which often precedes announcing a change of opinion or decision, has been around for centuries. Many writers have proclaimed that second thoughts are superior to first; Euripides, Cicero, Sir Francis Bacon, and John Dryden all held that "Second thoughts are best." Almost as many others have disagreed and maintained that second thoughts are markedly inferior, among them Lord Byron, Robert Fitzgerald, and the Earl of Shaftesbury (1711): "Men's first thoughts are generally better than their second."

on tenterhooks, to be In a state of painful suspense. The frame on which newly woven cloth was stretched was called a *tenter* and the hooks used to hold the cloth in place thus were *tenterhooks*. Tobias Smollett appears to have been the first to use the term metaphorically: "I left him upon the tenterhooks of impatient uncertainty" (*The Adventures of Roderick Random,* 1748). Clothmaking has changed, and "tenterhook" today survives only in the cliché.

on the ball Efficient and/or effective. This American colloquialism is believed to come from baseball, where the pitcher who puts spin or speed on the ball is apt to strike out more batters. It was being transferred to mean any kind of competence by 1912, when an article in *Collier's* stated, "He's got nothing on the ball."

on the bandwagon, to get/climb/hop To join the cause, movement, or party. The original bandwagon was a horse-drawn wagon bearing a brass band, used in a circus parade. In the second half of the nineteenth century such wagons began to be used in political campaigns as well, accompanying a candidate on speech-making tours. During William Jennings Bryan's presidential campaign of 1900 the term began to be extended to mean supporting the movement itself. It also was used in Britain: "The *Mirror* . . . does not jump on bandwagons . . . it isn't, never has been, and never will be a tin can tied to a political party's tail" (*Daily Mirror,* 1966; cited by William Safire).

on the beam On course; on the right track. This colloquialism originated about the mid-twentieth century, when aircraft began to be directed by radio beams. Its converse is *off the beam,* meaning "wrong" or "incorrect." Both expressions began to be transferred to other enterprises almost at once.

on the carpet, to be/call/put To be reproved or interrogated by one's superior. In the eighteenth century a carpet was also a table cover, and to put something on the carpet meant for it to be on the table—that is, under discussion. However, to *walk on the carpet* meant, in the early nineteenth century, to be reprimanded, as generally only employers or gentry used carpeted floors, and a servant who did so was being summoned for a reproof. By the late nineteenth century carpets were exclusively floor coverings, but still confined to the rooms of the rich, highborn, or employers. Presumably they sometimes summoned underlings for other purposes than reprimand, but only that meaning survived, as in G. H. Lorimer's 1902 letter: "The boss of the canning-room [will be] called on the carpet" (*Letters of a Self-Made Merchant to His Son*).

on the dot Exactly on time. The dot in question is the minute indication on the face of a clock or watch. The term has been around since about 1900. Rex Stout used it often to describe his compulsively punctual detective, Nero Wolfe, as in *Champagne for One* (1958): "At six, on the dot as always, Wolfe entered."

on the fast track See FAST LANE.

on the fence, to be/sit To be undecided or uncommitted. This term dates from the early nineteenth century and conjures up the image of a person who cannot or will not decide to which side of the fence to jump. At first the term was most frequently applied to politics—that is, which candidate or party one would support—and indeed it was even so defined in John Bartlett's 1859 *Dictionary of Americanisms:* "Fenceriding: The practice of 'sitting on the fence,' or remaining neutral in a political contest until it can be seen 'which way the cat is going to jump.'" Subsequently the term began to be applied to any kind of hedging.

on the fly Hurriedly, on the run. This expression originally meant "on the wing," that is, in flight, and was being used figuratively by the mid-1800s. An article in *The Nation* stated, "He may be said to have caught the Melanesian people on the fly" (Aug. 4, 1892).

on the fritz Out of commission; broken. No one really knows the origin of this term, which has been used since about 1900. Everyone agrees that Fritz was a derogatory name for a German, but how—or even if—it became equated with disrepair has been forgotten. P. G. Wodehouse used it in *Bill the Conqueror* (1924): "Everything's on the fritz nowadays."

on the go, to be To be extremely active and busy. Formerly used to mean a variety of conditions, among them intoxication and imminent catastrophe, this term acquired its present meaning in the first half of the nineteenth century. Thomas B. Aldrich used it in *Prudence Palfrey* (1874): "Ever since the day we said good-bye . . . I have been on the go."

on the hustings Campaigning for office. The noun *hustings* comes from the Old Norse *husthing,* for house assembly, which meant a council held by a king or other leader that included his immediate followers (rather than a large assembly of the people). In England *husting* became a court of law, specifically the highest court of the City of London. Eventually it was transferred, in the plural, to the platform where the city officials sat, and later still to the platform from which candidates for Parliament were nominated. From this last sense came its current meaning of the candidates' platform for campaign speeches, or simply campaigning. A synonymous phrase with a far simpler history is *on the stump.* An Americanism dating from the 1700s, it alludes to a tree stump used as a platform by a frontiersman making a speech.

on the level, to be Honest, straightforward, and sincere. An American colloquialism originating in the late nineteenth century, this term may have come from Freemasonry, in which the carpenter's level symbolizes integrity. Ngaio Marsh used it in a 1936 novel (*Death in Ecstasy*), "He's on the level all right."

on the loose Not constrained by responsibilities, free to indulge oneself. This seemingly modern slangy expression dates from the mid-1700s, when it could also mean to live by prostitution. That may or not have been intended by John Cleland when he wrote, "The giddy wildness of young girls once got upon the loose" (*Memoirs of a Woman of Pleasure,* 1749).

on the make, to be Actively seeking personal gain of some kind (financial, social, or the like); also, specifically looking for sexual conquest. An American slang expression of the second half of the nineteenth century, it refers to financial gain in Sir James Barrie's play, *What Every Woman Knows* (1918): "There are few more impressive sights in the world than a Scotsman on the make." The even slangier use for sexual conquest became popular in the 1920s and 1930s.

on the QT Clandestinely, secretly. This slangy expression, dating from the late 1800s, uses *QT* as an abbreviation for "quiet." George Moore had it in *A Mummer's Wife* (1887), "It will be possible to have one spree on the strict Q.T."

on the rocks, to be Ruined, either financially or in some other way. This term comes from a ship that has run aground on rocks and will break into pieces unless it can be hauled or floated off in time. The term began to be used as a metaphor for other disasters in the late nineteenth century. A common modern application appears in Tennessee Williams's play *Cat on a Hot Tin Roof* (1955): "When a marriage goes on the rocks, the rocks are there, right there [pointing to the bed]." A more recent meaning for *on the rocks* is for a beverage, usually containing liquor, that is served over ice cubes ("rocks").

on the ropes, to be To be on the brink of collapse or ruin. The term comes from boxing, where a fighter who is on the ropes surrounding the ring is in a defenseless position, often leaning against them to keep from falling. It began to be transferred to other catastrophic situations about 1960. A *Boston Globe* article used it in 1988: "He acknowledged that the Dukakis campaign was on the ropes."

on the same page, to be To be in complete agreement. This term, from the second half of the 1900s, alludes to reading from the same page of a book. It has largely replaced the earlier *on the same wavelength*, which alluded to the radio waves of a broadcast and dates from the first half of the 1900s. The newer version appears in David Baldacci's *Hour Game* (2004), "We need to coordinate and keep each other informed. We all need to be on the same page."

on the side of the angels, to be Supporting the good side. This expression comes from a speech by Benjamin Disraeli (1864) concerning the problems raised by Darwin's theory that mankind is descended from apes: "The question is this: Is man an ape or an angel? Now I am on the side of the angels." The phrase was later extended to mean siding with goodness and upholding the moral or spiritual view.

on the sly Secretly, furtively. This early-nineteenth-century term appeared in a letter of John Keats's (1818): "It might have been a good joke to pour on the sly bottle after bottle into a washing tub." It remains current.

on the spot Immediately, at once; also, in a very difficult situation. Both meanings are several hundred years old. "If once they get you on the spot you must be guilty of the plot," wrote Jonathan Swift in 1723 (*To Charles Ford, Esq.*), clearly meaning a bad situation. To put someone on the spot, however, appears to be an American locution of the twentieth century, and in gangster slang meant marking someone for execution. The other meaning—at once or immediately—dates from the nineteenth century. "I couldn't stand it, sir, at all, but up and kissed her on the spot," wrote poet William Pitt Palmer (1805–84) in "The Smack in School." This meaning also gave rise to JOHNNY-ON-THE-SPOT.

on the spur of the moment Spontaneously and impulsively, without deliberation. This figure of speech, which likens the right time (*the moment*) to the goading action of spur to horse, dates from the late eighteenth century. Archibald Duncan used it in *Lord Nelson's Funeral* (1806): "The contrivance of Mr. Wyatt, on the spur of the moment."

on the tip of one's tongue Ready to say something but unable to remember it precisely. This graphic image was stated early in the eighteenth century by Daniel Defoe (*Moll Flanders,* 1722): "She had arguments at the tip of her tongue." However, a similar term that is even older had quite a different meaning: *at one's tongue's end* meant that one could not keep from saying something but blurted it out. Thus, "Having always at her tongue's end that excellent proverb" (Henry Fielding, *Amelia,* 1751) meant she could not stop repeating it. This version is obsolete, but "on the tip of the tongue" has been a cliché since about 1850.

on the up and up Honest, frank, and sincere; legitimate. Literally this term makes little sense; why should "higher and higher" mean OPEN AND ABOVEBOARD? One writer speculates that something that is "up" can be clearly seen. Despite unclear analogy, the term has been around since the mid-nineteenth century, mainly in America. Dashiell Hammett used it in *Red Harvest* (1929): "He phoned . . . to find out if the check was on the up and up."

on the wagon, to be To refrain from drinking alcoholic beverages. This term began life as being *on the water wagon,* referring to the horse-drawn water cart used to spray dirt roads in order to keep down the dust. The metaphor for abstaining from liquor originated about the turn of the century. It was given a definition ("To be on the water wagon, to abstain from hard drinks") in *Dialect Notes* of 1904. B. J. Taylor used it in *Extra Dry* (1906): "It is better to have been on and off the Wagon than never to have been on at all." To resume drinking is also put as *to fall off the wagon.*

on the warpath, to be/go To be infuriated enough to seek out the person or agency responsible. This Native American term was used quite literally by James Fenimore Cooper in *The Deerslayer* (1841) to describe a character who had never engaged in battle ("He has never been on a warpath"). By the end of the nineteenth century it was loosely used to describe anyone on an angry rampage.

on thin ice, to be/skate A hazardous course of action or conversation. "In skating over thin ice our safety is in our speed," wrote Ralph Waldo Emerson in his essay *Prudence* (1841). Literally, it is possible to skate over very thin ice without breaking through if one glides quickly enough, but Emerson was already using the expression figuratively.

on top of the world, to be To feel elated; to be extremely successful. This metaphor for the peak of well-being dates from the early twentieth century. P. G. Wodehouse used it in *Very Good, Jeeves!* (1930): "If ever a bird [fellow] was sitting on top of the world, that bird was Bingo."

onward and upward Striving to advance and improve. This mid-nineteenth-century rallying cry was invoked by, among others, Frances Anne Kemble (1809–93) in her *Lines addressed to the Young Gentlemen leaving the Lenox Academy, Massachusetts:* "Fail not for sorrow, falter not for sin, but onward, upward, till the goal ye win." Today it is sometimes used ironically, as in the *New Yorker* magazine's title for comments on unwittingly amusing news: "Onward and Upward with the Arts."

open and aboveboard Honest and fair. This term comes from the rule that players, when dealing cards, must keep their hands above the board (i.e., table). Presumably when they put their hands under the table they could be changing their own cards. The expression appeared in print as early as 1608, in Joseph Hall's *Virtues and Vices:* "All his dealings are square, and aboue the board." It has been so used ever since.

open arms, with Extremely welcoming, very cordial. This term was used by Erasmus in the sixteenth century (in Latin). In English it appears from the seventeenth century on. Alexander Pope used it in his *Epistle to Arbuthnot* (1735): "With open arms received one Poet more."

open book, like an See OPEN SECRET; READ (SOMEONE) LIKE A BOOK.

opening gambit The first move in a contest, game, or competition of some kind. The term comes from chess and is actually redundant, since in that game *gambit* signifies a way of opening the game that involves sacrificing a pawn or other piece in order to gain some advantage over one's opponent. It was being used figuratively by the mid-1800s, and for some reason *opening* was added in later decades.

open question, an An issue that has not been finally settled or determined. The adjective *open* has been so used since the early nineteenth century. The term acquired a specific meaning in the British Parliament: on open questions members may vote as they wish, independent of party. David Masson used it figuratively, as it often is today: "The summary decision of what had hitherto been an open question in the Church" (*The Life of John Milton,* 1859).

open secret, an Something that is supposedly clandestine but is actually well known. This term was used as the Italian title of a play (*Il pubblico secrete*) translated by Carlo Gozzi in 1769 from a Spanish play by Calderón de la Barca, *El secreto a voces* (literally, "the noisy secret"). In English it came into general use in the nineteenth century for a secret in name only.

open sesame An effective means for achieving a desired goal. The term comes from the story about Ali Baba and the Forty Thieves (*The Arabian Nights Entertainments,* c. 1375), in which Ali Baba uses the words "Open, Sesame" to open the door of the robbers' den. By 1800 or so the words had become synonymous with any password. For example, Sir Walter Scott wrote in a letter to Lord Dalkeith (Feb. 11, 1806), "Your notoriety becomes a talisman—an 'Open Sesame' before which everything gives way."

order of the day, the The agenda; the most important activity or issue. This term originated in the seventeenth century and was used both in the military, for specific commands given to the troops for the day, and in legislative bodies for the day's agenda. By the late eighteenth century it was being used figuratively, as by George Washington, quoted as saying (1795), "Peace has been (to borrow a modern phrase) the order of the day." The poet Howard Fish put it very cynically (*The Wrongs of Man,* 1819): "The good but pine; the order of the day is—prey on others, or become a prey."

or what? Isn't that so? This rhetorical question always follows a statement and serves either to emphasize its truth or indicate that its answer is obvious. For example, "Is this fun or what?" says emphatically that this pursuit is fun. As a slangy usage, it dates from the 1960s. However, the phrase can also be the last choice among a series of options, and this usage dates from the mid-1700s. For example, a diary entry by John Adams in 1766 stated, "In what is this man conspicuous? in reasoning? imagination? in painting? in the pathetic? or what?"

other fish to fry See FISH TO FRY.

other side of the coin, the An alternative view; the opposite side. This metaphor has replaced the older *other side of the medal/shield* since about 1900. W. B. Yeats wrote, in a letter of 1904, "*Cuchullain* or *The King's Threshold* are the other side of the half-penny."

other things being equal See ALL OTHER THINGS BEING EQUAL.

out and out Thoroughly, wholly. This term preserves the old meaning of the adverb *out* as "to the conclusion" or "to an end" (from c. 1300). Chaucer used it in *Troilus and Criseyde* (c. 1374): "For out and out he is the worthiest, save only Ector."

out in left field Out of contact with reality; also, completely mistaken. The term refers to the left field of baseball, but there is some mystery as to how it acquired its current meaning. William Safire lists a number of theories, among them that in older, unsymmetrical ballparks, left field was deeper (and therefore farther from the batter) than right field; that the left fielder must play farther back when the batter is right-handed; and that at the Chicago Cubs's old ballpark, the Neuropsychiatric Institute (a mental hospital) was located just behind the left field stands (leading to the implication that anyone out in left field was crazy). None of these theories has been verified, but most likely those concerning distance are closest to the mark, since it is often put as *way out in left field.* Used from about 1950 on, the term appeared in *Publishers Weekly* (1974): "Novak's use of religious metaphor may put him in left field."

out like a light Suddenly asleep; unconscious. A mid-twentieth-century Americanism, it appeared in Billie Holiday's autobiography, *Lady Sings the Blues:* "Bobby, I just can't make it no further—and I passed out like a light."

out of a clear (blue) sky Unexpectedly, suddenly. The image of something dropping from the sky was transferred to sudden or surprising events in the late nineteenth century. "He dropped upon me suddenly out of a clear sky," wrote W. E. Norris (*Marietta's Marriage,* 1897). It also was put simply as *out of the blue,* "the blue" having signified the sky (or the sea) since the seventeenth century. Oliver Wendell Holmes wrote in a letter in 1910, "I got an encouragement out of the blue . . . in the form of an honorary degree."

out of harm's way In a safe place, away from possible accident or injury. This term dates from the mid-1600s. Richard Steele had it in *The Spectator* (1711) in what might well be hyperbolic form: "People send Children to school to keep them out of harm's way." Oddly enough the corollary, "in harm's way," never caught on.

out of kilter/whack Out of adjustment or alignment, not working properly. *Kilter* is an American variant of *kelter,* an English dialect word used since the seventeenth century to mean "in good condition." James Lowell used it in an 1862 letter, "I must rest awhile. My brain is out of kilter." The origin of the synonymous *out of whack,* dating from the late 1800s, is more mysterious. The *OED* suggests it may come from *wacky,* for "crazy," but that is by no means certain. Both terms are used to describe malfunctioning mechanisms ("This tape recorder is out of kilter and won't rewind") as well as figuratively ("He may have a conscience, but if you ask me, it's slightly out of whack").

out of sight, out of mind What is absent is soon forgotten. This phrase has been proverbial since Homer's time. The Greek poet had it in the *Odyssey* (c. 50 B.C.), and the earliest English appearance is in a 1501 translation of Thomas à Kempis's *The Imitation of Christ.* For the opposite sentiment, see ABSENCE MAKES THE HEART GROW FONDER. *Out of sight,* a twentieth-century slangy expression meaning "Wonderful!" or "Beyond belief!" may become a cliché.

out of the blue See OUT OF A CLEAR (BLUE) SKY.

out of the frying pan into the fire From bad to much worse. This cliché, a proverb in many languages, was already known in the early sixteenth century, appearing in Sir Thomas More's treatise on heresy (1528), "They lepe lyke a flounder out of the fryenge panne into the fyre." Shaw used it in one of his cynical remarks: "We shall fall out of the frying-pan of the football club into the fire of the Sunday School" (*The Revolutionist's Handbook,* 1903).

out of the mouths of babes The young and innocent are often unexpectedly wise. This term originated in the Old and New Testaments. The Book of Psalms (8:2) has God ordaining strength out of the mouths of babes and sucklings; the Gospel of Matthew (21:16) has praise emerging from the same source. Over the centuries the meaning was changed to wisdom.

out of the running Not competing; having no chance of winning. This term was transferred from racing to other endeavors in the mid-nineteenth century. Charles Kingsley used it in *Water-Babies* (1863): "Which quite put her out of the running."

out of the woods Out of trouble or danger. The image of emerging from a dangerous forest goes back at least to Roman times. The playwright Plautus used it (in *Menaechmi,* c. 200 B.C.), as did other Roman writers. In Great Britain it is usually put as *out of the wood.*

out of whole cloth A fabrication; untrue. From the mid-fifteenth century on, *whole cloth* meant a piece of cloth of full size, as opposed to one from which a portion had been cut. The term was used figuratively in various ways from the late sixteenth century on, and the current cliché came into use in the early 1800s. Lexicographer Charles Funk suggested that the turnaround came from the fact that some tailors deceived customers by using patched or pieced goods instead of a genuine full width of cloth. William Safire commented that by ironic transference the fabrication (cloth) was treated as another kind of fabrication (a lie). An early appearance in print came in Thomas Chandler Haliburton's *The Clockmaker* (1840): "All that talk about her temper was made out of whole cloth. . . . What a fib!"

out on a limb Stranded, exposed. The image of an animal crawling out on the branch of a tree and then afraid or unable to retreat was figuratively applied to other vulnerable conditions by the late nineteenth century. Marion Holbrook defined it further in *Suitable for Framing* (1941): "This is what they mean when they talk about being out on the end of a limb. Or painted into a corner." See also TWIST IN THE WIND.

out the window Discarded, gone forever. The transfer from objects thrown or dropped out of a window to ideas and other more ephemeral things took place in the seventeenth century. Dickens played with it in *Pickwick Papers:* "'I am ruminating,' said Mr. Pickwick, 'on the strange mutability of human affairs.'—'Ah, I see—in at the palace door one day, out at the window the next. Philosopher, sir?'—'An observer of human nature, sir,' said Mr. Pickwick."

out to lunch Extremely absentminded or stupid; also, crazy. The *Science Digest* of August 1955 defined this mid-twentieth-century slangy expression: "'Out to lunch' refers to someone who, in other years, just wasn't 'there'—and he is told immediately to 'Get with it.'" See also the quotation under MEAN STREAK.

over a barrel In a weak position; helpless, in someone's power. This term allegedly was derived from the practice of reviving drowning victims by positioning them headfirst over a barrel and rolling it back and forth, thereby attempting to empty the lungs of water. Happily this practice has been replaced by better methods of resuscitation, but the helpless position of the victim has survived in the current cliché. Raymond Chandler gave it a double meaning in *The Big Sleep* (1939): "We keep a file on unidentified bullets nowadays. Some day you might use that gun again. Then you'd be over a barrel."

over and above In addition to, more than. This cliché is most often used with reference to some amount, to signify more than that amount, and thus is redundant, for both words mean the same thing. However, the repetition serves as emphasis. It has been around since the early 1500s.

overboard See GO OVERBOARD.

over my dead body I will not allow you to do this. This hyperbole, often used in jocular fashion, dates from early-nineteenth-century America. H. Brighouse used it in the one-act play, *New Leisure* (1936): "Elsie Dixon doing confidential secretary! Over my dead body!" A *New Yorker* piece about evangelists described a photograph of the evangelist preacher Jerry Falwell plunging down a water slide: "He is clearly not enjoying himself. In fact, the photograph suggests that he is doing this over his own dead body" (1990).

over the hill, to be To be past one's prime. The analogy to a climber who has reached the top and is now descending has been transferred to the decline of aging since the mid-twentieth century, principally in America. Mary Roberts Rinehart used it in *The Pool* (1952): "The flawless skin goes, the lovely eyes fade, and she knows she is over the hill." However, in U.S. military slang during World War II, *going over the hill* meant going AWOL (absent without leave).

over the top, to go To surmount something. During World War I this term signified climbing over the parapet of front-line trenches to attack the enemy, and by extension this came to mean doing something dangerous or notable. After World War II the phrase took on the additional meaning of going above and beyond what had been originally planned, as in, "Her generous donation put us over the top; we've exceeded our goals." And finally, in the later 1900s, the phrase took on yet another meaning, to go too far or beyond reasonable limits, as in, "Making the entire chorus wear flesh-colored body suits—that's going over the top." With all these usages one must rely on the context to figure out which sense is meant.

own man/person, to be one's To be in charge of one's own affairs and actions. This term is very old indeed and may be obsolescent. Chaucer, who often portrayed strong women, used it (*Troilus and Criseyde,* c. 1374): "I am myn own woman wel at ese." A modern equivalent is to DO ONE'S OWN THING.

own medicine, a dose/taste of one's Repayment in kind; TIT FOR TAT. Although the idea is hardly new, the medicinal metaphor dates only from the late nineteenth century. V. Perdue used it in *The Singing Clock* (1941): "It was only fair for them to get a taste of their own medicine."

own up (to), to To admit something, to confess. Dating from the mid-1800s, this expression seems to use *own* in the sense of possessing responsibility for something. "On being arrested he owned up to his crime," appeared in the *Boston Journal* (May 23, 1890).

own worst enemy, to be one's To be the major source of one's own difficulties. The Greek philosopher Anacharsis (c. 550 B.C.) already was stating this idea: "What is man's chief enemy? Each is his own." Cicero said it of Julius Caesar (*Ad Atticum,* 49 B.C.). In more recent times, cartoonist Walt Kelly expressed the same thought through his main character, Pogo: "We have met the enemy, and they is us."

pack a wallop/punch, to To exert formidable power. In modern English *to wallop* means to thrash, and in noun form, a heavy blow, but originally the verb meant to boil with a noisy, bubbling sound, and the noun also was slang for ale. Glyndebourne, site of a summer opera festival in England, perpetuates the last meaning in the name of its restaurant, Nether Wallop (Lower Ale). The verb *pack* in this expression means "to deliver." The term dates from the early twentieth century. Eugene O'Neill used it literally in his play *The Hairy Ape* (1922): "He packa da wallop, I tella you." Figuratively it appears in such locutions as, "The candidate's speech really packed a punch."

packed in like sardines Close together, crowded. Canned sardines are jammed together as tightly as practically any such object. The condition was transferred to human crowds by the late nineteenth century. Spike Milligan played with it in his poem "Sardines" (*A Book of Milliganimals,* 1968): "A baby Sardine saw her first submarine, She was scared and watched through a peephole, 'O come, come, come, come,' said the Sardine's mum, 'It's only a tin full of people.'"

pack it in, to To give up; to stop trying. This term originated in the early twentieth century, and during World War I became military slang for dying. It alludes to packing one's bags prior to departure. A definition appeared in *Soldier and Sailor Words* (1925): "To stop. To give up. To finish. To die."

pack of lies, a An elaborate fabrication. This phrase uses *pack* in the sense of a large collection of abstract objects, and, as it has been since Shakespeare's time, in a disparaging sense. Thomas Jefferson used it in a letter of 1763: "Would you rather that I should write you a pack of lies?" A closely related expression is *a tissue of lies.* It uses *tissue* in the figurative sense of a woven fabric—that is, an intricate intertwining of separate elements, similarly abstract.

paddle one's own canoe, to To be independent and self-reliant. The analogy to steering one's boat is very old indeed; Euripides drew it in his play *Cyclops* (c. 440 B.C.). Canoes being largely a Western Hemisphere conveyance, this particular version of the term is American in origin. It dates from about 1800. An early appearance in print occurs in Frederick Marryat's

Settlers in Canada (1840). A few years later *Harper's Monthly* (May 1854) published the following ditty: "Voyager upon life's sea, to yourself be true, And whate'er your lot may be, paddle your own canoe." It became a popular music-hall song.

paid See PAY.

paid one's dues Fulfilled one's obligations; acquired experience the hard way. This mid-twentieth-century bit of American slang was adopted by jazz musicians, although it did not originate with them. It transfers the cost of being a paid-up member to the cost of gaining expertise in some field. Nat Hentoff defined the term in *Jazz Life* (1962): "'Paying dues' is the jazz musician's term for the years of learning and searching for an individual sound and style while the pay is small and irregular." However, the expression was already in print in a nonmusical context by 1943.

pain in the neck, a A nuisance. This term replaced the earlier *pain in the stomach* about the turn of the twentieth century; both are euphemisms for a pain in the posterior—*pain in the butt, pain in the ass. Rolling Stone* (April 7, 1977) had it: "It was an increasing pain in the ass to do the same material each night."

paint the town red, to To indulge in convivial carousing, making the rounds of bars, clubs, and similar places of entertainment. Originating in America in the late nineteenth century, the term appeared in the *Boston Journal* in 1884: "Whenever there was any excitement or anybody got particularly loud, they always said somebody was 'painting the town red.'"

palm off, to To pass off fraudulently. The term comes from the practice of concealing in one's palm what one pretends to dispose of in some other way. At first (seventeenth century) it was put as to palm *on* or *upon.* Charles Lamb, in one of his *Elia* essays (1822), used the modern version: "Have you not tried to palm off a yesterday's pun?"

pan out, to To succeed. The term alludes to the pan used by prospectors to wash gold from the gravel of streams; what remained in the pan was the ore. The term was transferred to other kinds of success in the late nineteenth century. Bret Harte used it in *Drift from Two Shores* (1879): "That depends pretty much on how things pan out."

paper over (the cracks), to To patch up; to repair in a makeshift way. The term alludes to paperhanging—that is, covering cracks in the walls with wallpaper. It allegedly was used by Otto von Bismarck in 1865 to describe the outcome of the Convention of Gastein, where, after Denmark's defeat, it was agreed that Austria would administer the Danish province of Holstein and Prussia would govern Denmark itself. An English translation of 1910 quoted Bismarck as saying it "papered over the cracks." The expression has been so used ever since.

pardon/excuse my French Please excuse the strong language. Exactly why *French* should mean "bad language" is not known, but this usage dates from the late 1800s. Eric Partridge speculated that the phrase was picked up by British soldiers in France during World War I and was first recorded during this period. However, given that language such as the *F-word* has become commonplace in popular entertainment and public life, this cliché is probably obsolescent, if not obsolete. Also see YOU SHOULD EXCUSE THE EXPRESSION.

par for the course Just about average or typical. The term comes from golf, where *par* means the number of strokes set as a standard for a particular hole or for the entire course, a score not attained by the majority of players. The term was transferred to other activities in the 1920s, but often with a mildly derogatory or deprecatory connotation, as in "He's nearly half an hour late; that's just about par for the course." To be *up to par* also means "to meet a standard or norm," while *below par* means "less than satisfactory," and by extension in poor spirits or health. Thus C. E. Montague (1867–1928) wrote (*Fiery Particles*), "I was born below par to the extent of two whiskies."

part and parcel An essential portion or element. This expression originally was a legal term and was so used from the sixteenth century on, principally for clauses of a law and for parts of a landholding. Alliterative and tautological, it began to be used figuratively from about 1800 on. Patrick E. Dove wrote, "The moral law of the conscience is part and parcel of man himself" (*Logic of the Christian Faith,* 1856).

parting of the ways, a A point of decision between two alternatives. This term stems from the Bible (Ezekiel 21:21): "For the king of Babylon stood at the parting of the way, at the head of the two ways," when he had to decide whether or not to attack Jerusalem. It continues to be so used. Moreover, when applied to two or more persons or groups, it implies that they will choose different paths or courses of action.

parting shot, a A final insult hurled as one is leaving, or the last word in an argument. Most authorities agree that this term is a distortion of *Parthian shot,* alluding to the ancient Parthians (first century B.C.), renowned archers and horsemen, who would turn in flight to discharge arrows at the pursuing enemy. There is no firm evidence for this etymology, but it seems reasonable. John Galsworthy used the term in *A Man of Property* (1906): "He could not resist a parting shot, 'H'mmm! All flourishing at home? Any little Soameses yet?'"

party girl A woman who is known to enjoy cocktail parties, dances, and similar social activities. Dating from the first half of the 1900s, the term sometimes, but not always, implies she is involved in sexual adventures, either for pay (as a prostitute) or not. Anthony West actually voiced the ambiguity, "He had never thought of asking himself what she was, inside of the hard shell of her disguise as the party girl who would go the limit for fun" (*The Trend Is Up,* 1960). A nongendered later version is *party animal.*

party line, the The official policy of a government, corporation, or organization. Although the term was used in the nineteenth century for the official policy of a political party—it was coined in the United States in the 1830s—it came into more general use in the mid-twentieth century, when it was applied particularly to the rigid dicta of the Communist Party in the Soviet Union and Eastern Europe, as well as to numerous other kinds of organization. Milovan Djilas, a Yugoslav dissident, is quoted as saying, "The Party line is that there is no Party line" (by Fitzroy Maclean, *The Heretic,* 1957). Nowadays the term is used much more loosely, as in, "The college's party line includes affirmative action in the admissions process."

pass muster, to To meet a required standard. This term originated in the military and once meant to undergo review without censure. George Gascoigne used it figuratively in 1575: "The latter verse is neither true nor pleasant, and the first verse may pass the musters" (*The Making of Verse*). It was a cliché by the time Jonathan Swift included it in *Polite Conversation* (1738), and it remains current.

pass the buck, to To evade responsibility by shifting it elsewhere. The term comes from nineteenth-century America, where in poker games a piece of buckshot or a knife with a buckhorn handle was passed around to indicate which player was to be the next dealer. By 1900 or so the term began to be used in the present sense of shifting responsibility. In 1949 President Harry S. Truman put a sign on his Oval Office desk saying, "The buck stops here," thereby acknowledging that he would accept ultimate responsibility for all policies and actions.

pass the hat, to To take up a collection; to ask for contributions. Presumably this term has a very literal origin: hats were and occasionally still are passed around a gathering where those present are asked to put in some money; the practice probably originated with street minstrels. In Britain it was, from the mid-nineteenth century, often put as *send round the hat* or *go round with the hat.* James Russell Lowell wrote: "Passing round the hat in Europe and America" (*Among My Books,* 1870).

pass the time of day, to To exchange greetings, pleasantries, or chat; engage in small talk. The redoubtable Ebenezer Brewer thought this turn of phrase came from the practice of greeting someone with a remark appropriate to the time of day, such as "Good afternoon." Whether or not this is true, the term dates from the first half of the nineteenth century and remains current.

past history Bygone days. This cliché, widely used since the mid-nineteenth century, is a redundancy. History *is* the past; it can never be future or current. Nor does the adjective *past* really serve to emphasize. Nevertheless, the term was and continues to be used. John Ruskin used it in *Praeterita* (1886), "I was stupidly and heartlessly careless of the past history of my family," as did James Grant in *History of the Burgh and Parish Schools of Scotland* (1876): "Mr. Innes . . . always entered enthusiastically into any proposal calculated to elucidate the past history of his native country." It is heard less often today.

patience of Job, the Long-suffering and forbearing. In the Old Testament Book of Job, the protagonist is the personification of both poverty and patience, subjected to numerous trials. His poverty has been referred to from time to time, but not nearly so frequently as his patience. Shakespeare used both in *Henry IV, Part 2* (1.2): "I am as poor as Job, my lord, but not so patient." And Jonathan Swift put it in rhyme (*The Beasts' Confession,* 1732): "While others of the learned Robe would break the patience of a Job."

patter of little feet, the The presence of small children. This now usually ironic or satiric reference to the presence or imminent arrival of offspring was originally a bit of Victorian sentimentalism, as in Lord Ronald Sutherland-Gower's *Reminiscences* (1883): "The patter of little feet, and the unconscious joyousness of children."

pave the way, to To prepare for something; to lead up to. Paving a road makes it easier to traverse, and this metaphor for smoothing one's course dates from before 1585. James Hogg's *Tales and Sketches* (c. 1817) stated: "One lie always paved the way for another."

pay as you go Paying for goods and services at the time of purchase. This notion is becoming increasingly rare in the age of the credit card, with commercial exhortations to *Buy now and pay later* (which may become a cliché). The term arose in the first half of the nineteenth century and made it into H. G. Bohn's *Handbook of Proverbs* (1855): "Pay as you go and keep from small score."

pay dirt, to hit/strike To find something very valuable; to profit hugely. The term comes from mining, where it literally refers to finding soil (dirt) that contains gold, silver, or some other precious ore. By the late nineteenth century it had been transferred to other lucrative discoveries and financial success. The term originated in mid-nineteenth-century America, probably during the Gold Rush.

pay in someone's own coin, to To repay in kind; take revenge. This term presumably once meant that repayment of a loan would be in exactly the same currency as had been lent. The term dates from Roman times (Plautus and Pliny were among the writers who used it) and was being used figuratively by the sixteenth century. "I did but pay him in's own coin," wrote George Chapman in his play *The Widdowes Teares* (1612).

pay the piper, to To bear the cost. This term refers to the musician who provides entertainment and the host's obligation to pay him or her. "Always those that dance must pay the musicke" is an early version of the current term used by John Taylor (*Taylor's Feast,* 1638). A late nineteenth-century addition was that he who does pay should *call the tune*—that is, the person who bears the cost may choose just what he or she is paying for. "I am going to pay the piper and call the tune," wrote Shaw (*Major Barbara,* 1905).

pay the price, to To obtain one thing by sacrificing another, more valuable one. The idea is old, but this expression of it dates only from the late nineteenth century. President Woodrow Wilson used it in a speech in 1916: "There is a price which is too great to pay for peace, and that price can be put in one word: One cannot pay the price of self-respect."

pay through the nose, to To be charged an enormous price. The origin of this expression has been lost. One writer suggests it may come from the Danish nose tax, imposed in Ireland in the ninth century and so called because delinquent taxpayers were punished by having their noses slit. Another believes it may be connected with the old British slang word *rhino,* for money or cash. In any event, the term has been used for exorbitant payments since the seventeenth century.

pay(s) your money and take(s) your choice, you It's your decision as long as you're willing to pay the price. This term has been traced to the mid-nineteenth century, when it first appeared in print in the English humor magazine *Punch.* It also appeared in a late nineteenth-century peep-show rhyme cited in the *Oxford Dictionary of Quotations:* "Whichever you please, my little dears: You pays your money and you takes your choice, You pays your money and what you sees Is a cow or a donkey just as you pleases."

PDQ Acronym for "pretty damn quick," indicating something that has occurred, or will or should occur, with considerable speed. This cliché dates from the late nineteenth century. The earliest citation listed by the *OED* is dated c. 1875, when B. Woolf, in the play *The Mighty Dollar,* had a character say, "That's right, you'd better step P.D.Q., pretty damn quick." The synonym *ASAP,* the acronym for "as soon as possible," has been used in a variety of contexts since the mid-1900s. For example, in a help wanted ad, "Housekeeper wanted ASAP, " or in a business memorandum, "Call him ASAP; he'll be glad to talk to you."

peace of mind Freedom from worry, a sense of calm. Although the idea of mental peace is much older, this expression dates from the first half of the eighteenth century. Alexander Pope, possibly its originator, used it in a letter of 1737: "He stuck to poverty with peace of mind."

pearl of great price, a Anything of enormous value. The term comes from the New Testament (Matthew 13:45–46), in which the kingdom of heaven is so described. The doctrinal book of the Mormons (members of the Church of Jesus Christ of Latter-day Saints) is called the Pearl of Great Price.

pearls of wisdom Brilliant sayings or precepts. This phrase, which dates from the late 1800s, is often used sarcastically. The *Daily Chronicle* had it on December 12, 1907: "The gramophonist will redistribute the pearls of wisdom which have fallen from the lips of great Unionist statesmen to crowds of admiring villagers."

pecking order The hierarchy of authority in a group. The term was invented by biologists in the 1920s to characterize the behavior of hens, who established their barnyard authority by one bird pecking another of lower status. It was transferred to human behavior in the mid-1900s. Lawrence Durrell maintained, "There is a pecking order among diplomats as there is among poultry" (*Justine,* 1957).

pen is mightier than the sword, the Writing is more powerful and effective than fighting. This adage appeared as a proverb in 1571 ("No more sword to be feared than the learned pen") and then took a slightly different form in Robert Burton's *The Anatomy of Melancholy* (1621): "The pen is worse than the sword." It has quite naturally appealed to writers ever since. *Time* magazine (1990) used "The Pen Is Mightier" as a headline for a piece announcing that Poland had a journalist as its new prime minister, Czechoslovakia a playwright as president, and Hungary an English translator as president.

penny-ante game, a A low-level enterprise. This term comes from poker, where *ante,* Latin for "before," signifies the chips placed on the table before betting begins. In a penny-ante game, a chip is worth only one cent, or a penny, the lowest possible stake. Like many other poker terms, by the mid-1800s this one was transferred to unrelated enterprises to signify "small-time" or "unimportant." Thus, the *Negro Digest* (August 1946) stated, "Compared to the man Bilbo, 63-year-old John Ruskin is strictly penny ante and colorless," and M. Maguire in *Scratchproof* (1976), "I'm not a penny-ante hood."

penny for your thoughts, a What are you thinking about? This expression was actually first stated early in the sixteenth century and was included in John Heywood's 1546 proverb collection. A penny no longer is worth much, but the expression, much repeated over the years, survives nevertheless.

penny wise and pound foolish Penurious about small expenses and extravagant with large ones. That such a course is to be deplored was already made clear in the sixteenth century and was soon transferred to the foolishness of being fastidious about unimportant matters and careless about important ones. In *The Spectator* of 1712 Joseph Addison wrote, "I think a Woman who will give up herself to a Man in marriage, where there is the least Room for such an Apprehension . . . may very properly be accused . . . of being Penny Wise and Pound foolish."

people who live in glass houses shouldn't throw stones Those who themselves are open to criticism or vulnerable to attack should not attack others. This proverb dates from the time of Chaucer, who used a version of it in *Troilus and Criseyde* (c. 1374). George Herbert wrote: "Whose house is of glass, From cast of stones must not throw stones at another" (*Jacula Prudentum,* 1640). See also POT CALLING THE KETTLE BLACK.

perish the thought May this never happen, may this never be true. This cliché, an older equivalent of BITE YOUR TONGUE, intends to suppress the very idea of something rather than just its utterance. An early recorded use occurred in Colley Cibber's 1700 version of Shakespeare's *Richard III,* in which a character says "Perish the thought!" (5:5). See also GOD/HEAVEN FORBID.

persona non grata An undesirable individual; a person out of favor. The term *persona grata* is Latin for "an acceptable person" and was used to describe diplomats acceptable to the government to which they were accredited. When such a person was, for some reason, no longer acceptable, he or she became persona *non* grata and would have to be recalled. From the late nineteenth century on, however, the term was also used more loosely for someone who had gotten in trouble or simply was disliked. The *OED* cites a 1958 issue of the *Oxford Mail:* "The BMC management should have known that the introduction of two or three people who are persona non grata with the other 350 men in the shop would create difficulty."

pet peeve, one's One's favorite gripe, a recurring source of annoyance. The noun *peeve* is what linguists call a back formation from the adjective *peevish,* but its ultimate derivation, as well as that of *pet,* is apparently unknown. The pairing of the two, an Americanism, dates from the early 1900s.

Philadelphia lawyer An extremely shrewd attorney. This term dates from the eighteenth century. In 1734 John Peter Zenger, a printer, was charged with libel for printing an exposure of a corrupt New York governor, William Cosby. Zenger did not write the article, but his print shop could be attached for damages, whereas the writer was poor. Andrew Hamilton of Philadelphia came out of retirement to defend the action, and to everyone's surprise, his eloquent argument for freedom of the press not only won Zenger acquittal but established a precedent in American law, that a true statement was not libel. As the story proliferated, however, Hamilton was made out to be a legal trickster who collected a large fee (even though he had argued honestly and charged no fee at all), whence the current definition of a Philadelphia lawyer. The *Salem Observer* of March 13, 1824, stated, "The New England folks have a saying, that three Philadelphia lawyers are a match for the very devil himself."

pick a bone (with someone), to To engage in a dispute; to disagree or quarrel with someone. This term, alluding to two dogs fighting over a bone, dates from the sixteenth century. "I will add this, which may be a bone for you to pick on," wrote James Calfhill (*Answer to Martiall,* 1565).

pick and choose, to To select very fastidiously. This redundancy—to pick and to choose mean exactly the same thing—dates from the seventeenth century. Sir Thomas Herbert (*Travels into Africa and Asia,* 1665) stated, "He found he had the liberty to pick and choose," and the term is still current.

pick of the litter, the The best of the lot. Versions of this term have been around in various forms for a long time—from the pick of the *market* and pick of the *parish* to the pick of the *basket* (all nineteenth century) and pick of the *bunch* (twentieth century). The cliché alludes to selecting the most desirable from a litter of puppies.

pick someone's brain, to To gather information or ideas from someone who is presumably more expert or more imaginative. This analogy to picking clean a bone or carcass dates from the mid-nineteenth century. "Do you possess the art of picking other people's brains," wrote clergyman Benjamin Jowett (1817–93). For picking one's own brain, see CUDGEL ONE'S BRAINS.

picture of health, the A model of well-being. This complimentary description has been around since the late eighteenth century. Jane Austen used it in *Emma* (1815): "One hears sometimes of a child being 'the picture of health.'"

picture perfect Exactly right, especially in appearance. This term, from the twentieth century, alludes to the precise resemblance of a painting or photograph to its subject, as in "The day was picture perfect for a picnic—not a cloud in the sky." *Time* magazine used the term as the caption for a photograph of the presidential candidate Al Gore, his wife Tipper, running mate Joe Lieberman, and Lieberman's wife Hadassah, calling it "the purest moment of their campaign" (Aug. 21, 2000).

pièce de résistance The most notable or most highly prized feature of a group or series; the star attraction. Originally, from the 1790s or so, this French term always referred to a meal's greatest delicacy (an appropriate matter of concern to French palates). By the mid-nineteenth century the term had been transferred to other outstanding items, at least in English. Thackeray, in an essay (1840) about art, stated: "To supply the picture lover with the *pièces de résistance* of the feast."

piece of ass/tail An act of sexual intercourse. Both terms, dating from the early 1900s, are considered vulgar slang. A version of a 1918 song popular in the military, "Mademoiselle from Armentieres," had it: "Oh, Captain, may I have a pass? For I want to get a piece of ass."

piece of cake, it's a It is laughably simple; it's easily accomplished. This term is supposedly derived from the cakewalk, originally (mid-nineteenth century) an African-American promenading contest in which couples who devised the most intricate or appealing steps won a cake as a prize. Later the phrase came to mean a high-stepping dance with a strutting step, based on the promenade, as well as the music for such dancing. Finally, by the early twentieth century, *cakewalk* came to be slang for something stylish, pleasurable, and easy to do, and by the late 1930s it had been converted to *piece of cake.* Both *piece of cake* and *cakewalk* were British armed forces slang for an easy mission during World War II, and the former was used as the title for a television drama (1989; 1990 in America) about the Royal Air Force during that conflict. See also EASY AS PIE; DUCK SOUP.

piece of goods, a Spoken either humorously or disparagingly, a woman. Literally this phrase long meant a portion of cloth, but sometime before about 1750 it began to be applied to a human being. Thomas Gray put it negatively in a letter of 1751: "That agreeable creature . . . will visit you soon, with that dry piece of goods, his wife." But Fanny Burney was more positive: "His daughter—as droll a piece of goods as one might wish to know" (*Early Diary,* 1776). See also PIECE OF WORK.

piece of one's mind, (to give someone) a To express one's disapproval quite plainly; to give one's candid opinion. This term has been around since the sixteenth century. John Dryden used it in his play *The Maiden Queen* (1667, 2.1): "I have told her a piece of my mind already."

piece of the action, a A share, usually meaning a financial share. This term originated as U.S. show business slang and referred from the 1920s on to investing in a production and thereby sharing in the profits. From the 1960s on it was transferred to other endeavors as well, as in Emma Lathen's mystery *Murder Without Icing* (1972): "What's it got to do with her if you sell your piece of the action?"

piece of work, a An obnoxious individual. Originally this expression simply referred to something that had been created, and often in an admiring fashion. Shakespeare so used it in *Hamlet* (2.2), "What a piece of work is a man! . . . the Paragon of animals." In the first half of the 1900s the term began to be used sarcastically and contemptuously, as in, "Lulu finally had to take her out of the room. Piece of work she is" (David Baldacci, *Hour Game*, 2004).

pie in the sky The promise of the good life in a future that never arrives. The term comes from a rallying song of the International Workers of the World, or Wobblies, "The Preacher and the Slave" (1911), that may have been written by their martyred organizer, Joe Hill (he was killed by the police). It went, "You will eat, bye and bye, in the glorious land above the sky! Work and pray, live on hay, you'll get pie in the sky when you die." The Wobblies, of course, wanted their "pie" in the form of decent wages and working conditions, in this life. This sentiment was echoed by boxing champion Muhammad Ali, who was quoted as saying, "You don't want no pie in the sky when you die, you want something here on the ground while you're still around" (1978).

pig in a poke, to buy a To purchase something sight unseen and risk disappointment. The term comes from the ancient dishonest practice of putting a worthless cat in a bag (poke) in place of a young suckling pig, an expensive delicacy. The term was proverbial by the time John Heywood collected his proverbs (1546) and has been used ever since. See also LET THE CAT OUT OF THE BAG.

pigs in clover See IN CLOVER.

pillar of society, a A chief supporter of one's community, social group, or other institution. The earliest example of being such a pillar dates from the early fourteenth century and involves a *pillar of the church,* which Eric Partridge deemed a particularly objectionable cliché by 1800 or so. Shakespeare used a slightly different locution in *The Merchant of Venice;* at the trial Shylock says, "I charge you by the law, whereof you are a well-deserving pillar," presumably hoping that the judge will respond favorably to this compliment. From the late nineteenth century on, *pillar of society* was often used sarcastically or pejoratively, the target generally being both the individual and the society being upheld. Ibsen so used it in his play, translated as *Pillars of Society* (1877), and his example was followed by Shaw and others. Still another variant, *pillar of the community,* may be used either ironically or straightforwardly.

pillow talk Exchanging information, often of a privileged nature, in bed. Dating from the first half of the 1900s, the term was the title of a romantic comedy motion picture (1959) starring Rock Hudson and Doris Day. A *New York Times* article had it, "Mrs. Ford makes it plain she gets her views across to Mr.[President] Ford in what she calls 'pillow talk'" (Aug. 4, 1975).

pinch pennies, to To be miserly. To be a *pinchpenny* has meant to be a miser since about 1412, the word thus being almost as old as the modern English language. The verb form in the cliché is considerably newer but remains current. Elliott Paul used it in his *Narrow Street* (1942): "Monsieur Saul . . . complaining and pinching pennies as he made his purchases."

pin money An allowance set aside for personal expenditures. The term comes from the early sixteenth century, when metal pins were very expensive. Indeed, a will recorded at York in 1542 listed a bequest: "I give my said doughter Margarett my lease of the parsonage of Kirkdall Churche . . . to by her pinnes withal." The term stuck long after pins became a very minor budget item, and was extremely common until the mid-twentieth century. It is heard less often today.

pin one's hopes on, to To attach one's aspirations for success to a particular event, individual, or the like. This term began in the sixteenth century as *pin one's faith on another's sleeve* and appeared in this form in John Ray's 1678 proverb collection. Ebenezer Brewer believed it came from the feudal practice of troops wearing their leader's badge on their sleeves. Since badges and loyalties sometimes changed, people became wary of judging where one stood from such a badge and said they would *not* pin their faith on someone's sleeve. By the nineteenth century, however, hopes were replacing faith (at least in this term) and sleeves were lost altogether.

pinpoint accuracy Extreme exactness. This somewhat hyperbolic term arose toward the end of World War II, when it was used first to describe extremely precise bombing of specific targets. Obviously a bomb could not really hit the point of a pin, but the description held. Later it was extended to other weaponry, and finally came into generalized use.

pipe down, (to) (To) be quiet. This term comes from the navy, where the boatswain's signal for "All hands turn in" was sometimes made on a whistle or pipe. By 1900 *Dialect Notes* included a definition ("to stop talking"). Laurence Stallings and Maxwell Anderson used both forms, "Pipe down!" and "to pipe down," in their play *What Price Glory?* (1926).

pissed off Furious, very irritated. This rude slangy expression dates from the mid-1900s and probably originated during World War II. Norman Mailer used it in his war novel, *The Naked and the Dead* (1948), "I bet you even look pissed off when you're with your wife."

pitched battle, a An intense fight. Originally a pitched battle meant a battle that had been planned beforehand, with the ground "pitched on," that is, chosen, and the opposing sides lined up in orderly fashion. The term was used to contrast it with a skirmish or chance encounter, and dates from about 1600. In time, however, it came to be used more loosely for any intense fight in which the combatants are fiercely engaged.

place for everything (and everything in its place), a An old maxim for neatness. The earliest citation for it is a naval novel of 1842, but it continues to be used, both in the sense of tidiness and by extension, appropriateness. The second, more figurative sense is meant in P. Dickinson's *Skin Deep* (1968), "Do you run your whole life like that? . . . A place for everything and everything in its place, and all in easy reach."

place in the sun A highly favored position. The term appears to have been originated by the French philosopher Blaise Pascal, who wrote (c. 1660), "There's my place in the sun: behold the image and beginning of the entire earth's usurpation." It did not, however, become widely known until it was used around the turn of the twentieth century concerning Germany's position in the world, at first by Bernhard von Bülow (1897) and later, several times, by Emperor William II, as a justification for his country's territorial ambitions. Subsequently, the term came to be used in somewhat more benign fashion to mean simply the glow of public recognition and achievement. As the title of the 1951 film *A Place in the Sun,* about the idle rich and dubious morals, the term was used ironically.

plain as day/the nose on your face As obvious as can be. The earliest similes for patently obvious were *plain as a packstaff* or *pikestaff* (that is, the staff on which a peddler or hobo carried his bundles), used from the fifteenth century, and *plain as the nose on your face,* from the sixteenth century. The former is obsolescent, at least in America; the latter is still very current, heard even more than *plain as day,* a nineteenth-century locution.

plain sailing Perfectly straightforward; an easy and unobstructed course. The term comes from navigation, where it means sailing in waters that are free of hazards, particularly rocks or other obstructions. Used since the nineteenth century, it may have come from the earlier navigational term *plane sailing,* the art of determining a ship's position without reference to the fact that the earth is round, and therefore sailing on a plane (flat surface), which works, but only for a short distance. *Plain sailing* was transferred to other pursuits in the early nineteenth century. Shaw used it in his preface to *Androcles and the Lion* (1916): "Without the proper clues the gospels are . . . incredible. . . . But with the clues they are fairly plain sailing." A synonymous term is *smooth sailing,* used figuratively since the first half of the 1800s. Edward Bulwer Lytton had it in *Night and Morning* (1841), "'Oh, then it's all smooth sailing,' replied the other." See also HARD/TOUGH SLEDDING.

plain vanilla Lacking embellishment or fancy features, unadorned; by extension, plain and simple. This item, dating from the second half of the 1900s, transfers the simplicity of a plain vanilla cake to other concerns, ranging from stock options to computer software, legal contracts, and so on. For example, "She bought the cheapest car she could find, a plain vanilla model." See also LESS IS MORE.

plate, to have a lot/enough on one's To have more than enough to worry about or cope with. This term originated in the 1920s and transferred the image of an overcrowded dinner plate to a very full agenda. R. Simons used it in *Houseboat Killing* (1959): "I'll leave you at it. I've got plenty on my plate at the moment." The synonymous *my plate is full* (or *to have a full plate*) date from the same period.

play ball with, to To cooperate. The term apparently comes from baseball around the turn of the twentieth century. In baseball today, *play ball* simply means to start or continue playing the game. The *with* confers the idea of a team or cooperative effort. C. Terrett used the metaphor in *Only Saps Work* (1930): "The police are too dumb . . . to play ball with the hold-up mob."

play both ends against the middle, to To maneuver two opponents so as to benefit oneself; also, to hedge against a risk. This expression comes from faro, an extremely popular gambling game in nineteenth-century

America. Played honestly, it is the fairest of the games that pit players against a bank, because there is virtually no percentage in favor of the bank (dealer). (For this reason faro has never been permitted at Monte Carlo.) However, numerous ways of cheating were developed. One such method involved marking the cards by trimming the sides and ends of certain cards in each suit by a tiny amount, unnoticeable to the ordinary player but obvious to the experienced gambler, who could then tell where the cards lay in the pack and stack it as desired. When such cards, called "strippers," were cut convex or concave, it was called "both ends against the middle." R. Maury used the expression figuratively in *Wars of the Godly* (1928): "Bennett played both ends of the religious fight against the middle."

play cat and mouse See CAT AND MOUSE.

play fast and loose, to To trifle with someone; to be unreliable and inconsistent. Several writers believe that this term, which dates from the sixteenth century, came from a cheating game called "fast and loose" that was played at fairs. A belt or strap was doubled and rolled up with the loop at the edge of a table. The customer had to catch the loop with a stick or skewer while the belt was unrolled, but it was so done that the feat was impossible. Shakespeare used the term figuratively in a number of plays, including *Antony and Cleopatra* (4.12): "Like a right gipsy, hath, at fast and loose, beguiled me to the very heart of loss." Over the centuries, writers continued to use it for trifling with someone's affections, as in Thackeray's *Lovel the Widower* (1860): "She had played fast and loose with me."

play hardball Behave aggressively and competitively, act ruthlessly. The term comes from baseball, where it is used to distinguish the normal ball from the somewhat larger and softer ball used in softball. It began to be used figuratively in the 1970s. A *New York Times* article about Senate majority leader Bill Frist, pointing out that he needs to enlist support from Democrats, quoted him saying, "I can play hardball as well as anybody."

play it by ear, to To improvise; to act as the situation requires, without advance planning. This term for playing instrumental music without reading the notes from a score, but simply going by the sound, dates from the seventeenth century. It was not transferred to other kinds of improvisation until the mid-twentieth century.

play musical chairs, to To swap jobs, prospects, or decisions in a rapid, confusing fashion. The term comes from a children's game, also called "going to Jerusalem," in which the players march to music around a row of chairs where every other chair faces in the opposite direction. When the music stops, the players must sit down, but, there being one fewer chair than the number of players, one player cannot and is eliminated (along with one more chair). The name of the game was transferred to job changes within a corporation or other organization in the early twentieth century. Britain's former prime minister, Sir Harold Wilson, played on it in his book, *The Governance of Britain* (1976): "Hence the practised performances of latter-day politicians in the game of musical daggers: never be left holding the dagger when the music stops."

play one's cards close to one's chest, to To be secretive. The analogy to holding one's hand so that no one can see what cards are in it has been used since the mid-twentieth century. Agatha Christie had it in *The Pale Horse* (1961): "I couldn't afford to give hints. You have to play these things close to your chest."

play one's cards right/well, to To make the most advantageous use of one's opportunities. Card-playing was popular in England from the mid-sixteenth century on, and terms from card games soon began to be transferred to other activities. This one appeared in print in Samuel Foote's *The Englishman in Paris* (1753): "If Lucinda plays her cards well, we have not much to fear." Whist, the antecedent of modern bridge, involves, with each hand dealt and bid, a suit that is designated as "trumps" (unless no-trumps is bid). For that hand, trump cards outrank all others. From this we have *to play a trump card,* meaning to make a winning move. Charles Lamb, who wrote extensively about whist between 1820 and 1829 (for *London Magazine*), was among the first to transfer *trumps* to mean any winning advantage: "Martin, if dirt were trumps, what hands you would hold!"

play possum, to To pretend ignorance; to feign sleep or death. This term comes from the fact that opossums fall into a kind of coma when they are caught, appearing to be dead. Whether the animal is genuinely paralyzed by fear or is smart enough to dissemble has never been determined. The term originated in the United States in the early 1820s. An early use was Adiel Sherwood's in *A Gazetteer of the State of Georgia* (1829): "He is playing 'possum with you."

play second fiddle, to To play a subsidiary role to someone, particularly to one's immediate superior. While musicians might argue that in orchestras and chamber ensembles the part of second violin is just as important as that of first violin, this term, when transferred to other enterprises, definitely denigrates the second, at least in relation to the first. It has been so used since about 1800. B. H. Malkin had it in his translation of *Gil Blas* (1809): "I am quite at your service to play second fiddle in all your laudable enterprises."

play the field, to To avoid committing oneself exclusively to one cause, person, and so on; specifically, to court or date more than one person at a time. This term originated in British horse-racing during the nineteenth century, where it meant to bet on every horse in a race except the favorite. It was transferred to other kinds of "risk-spreading" in the first half of the twentieth century. In 1966 a headline in the *New Republic* read, "Japan Plays the Field—Peace and Trade with Everyone."

play the game, to To behave fairly and honorably; also, to go along with a particular set of rules. The first meaning of this term was already being applied in Chaucer's time, but it did not come into wide use until the late nineteenth century. Rudyard Kipling, that quintessential Victorian, used it (*The Maltese Cat,* 1898), "Play the game, don't talk." This usage, however, is obsolescent, at least in America. Another version of the term appears in the poem "Alumnus Football" by the American sportswriter Grantland Rice (1880–1954), which itself gave rise to a slightly different cliché: "For when the One Great Scorer comes to write against your name, He marks—not that you won or lost—but *how you played the game.*"

In contrast, the very similar *to play games,* or *playing games,* means to act evasively or deceitfully, as in: "Her ex-husband is playing games about child-support payment."

play the heavy, to To take the role of villain; by extension, to take the blame for meanness, cruelty, and other undesirable behavior. The adjective *heavy* was used to describe the villain's part in theater from about 1800 on, and by 1900 *heavy* was being used as a noun for such a role. Only in the mid-twentieth century was it extended to offstage events, as in J. D. Salinger's *Franny and Zooey* (1962): "I'm sick to death of being the heavy in everyone's life."

play the race card Also, *pull the race card.* Invoking race, in particular bias for or against race, in order to achieve an end. The term dates from the late 1900s and alludes to card games, that is, playing a particular card to gain an advantage, trounce an opponent, or the like. For example, when President George H.W. Bush nominated an African American, Clarence Thomas, to the Supreme Court, some who considered Thomas poorly qualified accused Bush of playing the race card, nominating a man unlikely to be rejected lest one be accused of racism. The term is on its way to becoming a cliché.

play to the gallery, to To appeal to the audience for maximum applause or effect. In the British theater the gallery holds the cheapest seats, and by extension, it was assumed that the audience there was the least sophisticated, the lowest common denominator. To court popularity from such patrons was considered demeaning. Rudyard Kipling used the term: "The instant we begin to think about success and the effect of our work—to play with one eye on the gallery—we lose power and touch and everything else" (*The Light That Failed,* 1890). See also GRANDSTAND PLAY.

play with fire, to To court danger. This metaphor has been around for hundreds of years. Poet Henry Vaughan put it this way in 1655 *(The Garland)*: "I played with fire, did counsell spurn . . . But never thought that fire would burn."

pleased as Punch Delighted. In the Punch-and-Judy shows of old, the character Punch is always enormously satisfied with the success of his evil deeds. The simile was in common use for any kind of extreme satisfaction by the mid-nineteenth century. Dickens used it in *Hard Times* (1854): "When Sissy got into the school . . . her father was pleased as Punch."

plot thickens, the The situation is becoming increasingly complex. Originally the term was used to describe the plot of a play that was becoming byzantine in its complexity; it was so used by George Villiers in his 1672 comedy *The Rehearsal* (3.2). It was repeated by numerous writers and became particularly popular in mystery novels, from Arthur Conan Doyle's *A Study in Scarlet* (1887) on. Today it is often used sarcastically or ironically of some situation that is needlessly complex but scarcely meets the description of a sinister plot.

plumb the depths, to Get to the bottom of something. This term has been used literally since the first half of the 1500s for measuring the depth of a body of water, using a line weighted with a lead ball, or *plumb.* Its figurative use came a few decades later and has survived the death of the literal meaning, which gave way to more sophisticated means of measuring. E. W. Gregory used it in *The Furniture Collector* (1916): ". . . engaged in trying to plumb the depths of duplicity to which dealers can descend in faking old furniture."

point of no return, the A critical point that, if passed, allows for no reversal of direction or decision. This term comes from aviation, where it means the point in a flight beyond which there would no longer be fuel enough to return to the starting place. It originated among aviators during World War II. John P. Marquand used it as the title of a novel (1949).

poison pen A writer of a letter, usually anonymous, that is malicious and, sometimes libelous. It may attack either the recipient or a third party. The term, with its companion *poison-pen letter,* dates from the early 1900s. The poison is figurative, describing the scurrilous nature of the words. David Lodge used it in *Changing Places* (1975), "I've had what I believe is called a poison-pen letter from Euphoria, an anonymous letter."

poke fun at, to To mock or ridicule, to tease. *Poke* here means "to thrust," and the *fun* is at the victim's expense. This term has been around since 1835 or so. The *OED* cites Thomas Hood's *Up the Rhine* (1840): "The American . . . in a dry way began to poke his fun at the unfortunate traveler," a statement that leaves no doubt about who is having the "fun."

poke one's nose into, to To interfere, to meddle. This term began as *thrust* one's nose into someone's affairs, back in the sixteenth century. The analogy presumably is to a dog or other animal nosing about. Samuel Johnson used it in his *Dictionary* under "Nose" (1755): "To thrust one's Nose into the affairs of others, to be meddling with other people's matters." In America at some point *poke* was substituted.

poker face, a Total lack of expression; deadpan. This term comes from gambling, where the astute player tries not to betray the quality of his or her hand by remaining expressionless. Originating in the late nineteenth century, the term was transferred to other areas in which individuals tried hard not to betray their thoughts. C. E. Mulford used it in his western novel, *Rustler's Valley* (1924): "He glanced around the circle and found poker faces."

politically correct Avoidance of speaking or behaving in a way that would offend anyone's sensibilities concerning race, gender, sexual orientation, socioeconomic levels, or politics. Surprisingly, this cliché of the latter twentieth century, well known enough to be sometimes abbreviated as *P.C.*, was used in 1793 by J. Wilson in the U.S. House of Representatives: "'The United States,' instead of the 'People of the United States,' is the toast given. This is not politically correct" (cited by the *OED*). Presumably Mr. Wilson here was referring to precision in political language. The current meaning of the phrase did not surface until the mid-1900s and was a cliché by the 1990s.

poor as a churchmouse Singularly impecunious. This simile dates from the seventeenth century and its original analogy has been lost. Most authorities speculate that since a church usually has no place for food storage, such as a mouse might invade, mice would fare very poorly in churches. Indeed, James Howell's 1659 proverb collection states it as *hungry* as a churchmouse. The current cliché has outlived the even older and once more common *poor as Job* (who in the Bible was deprived of all his possessions by Satan), *poor as*

Lazarus, and *poor as Job's turkey* (which, according to one of Thomas Haliburton's Sam Slick tales, had only a single feather).

pop the question, to To propose marriage. The transfer of *pop,* meaning "to explode," to the idea of blurting out a proposal, seems like a slangy modernism but actually dates from the eighteenth century. Samuel Richardson used it in his novel *Sir Charles Grandison* (1753): "Afraid he would now, and now and now, pop the question; which he had not the courage to put."

possession is nine points of the law To hold or control something gives one a greater advantage than simply claiming ownership or control. This term dates from the late sixteenth century. An early appearance in print was in T. Draxe's *Bibliotheca Scholastica* (1616): "Possession is nine points in the Law." Later references sometimes put it at eleven points, but nine is what has survived. The nine points in question are: (1) a good purse (much money); (2) a good deal of patience; (3) a good cause; (4) a good lawyer; (5) good counsel; (6) good witnesses; (7) a good jury; (8) a good judge; and (9) good luck. With these advantages one is apt to win one's case. Today, however, the term is used more in the sense of squatter's rights—that is, "I have it; just try and take it away from me"—than in any strict legal sense.

post haste As quickly as possible. According to Ebenezer Brewer, in sixteenth-century England postal messengers galloping into an inn yard would cry "Post haste!" which gave them priority in selecting the horses available for their journey. Hall's *Chronicles* of c. 1548 stated, "The Duke of Somerset, with John, erle of Oxenford, wer in all post haste flying toward Scotlande." Shakespeare used the expression in numerous plays, and despite its archaic sound and the dubious speed of present-day postal service, it remains current on both sides of the Atlantic. It is also written as one word, *posthaste.*

pot calling the kettle black, the Accusing a person of faults one has oneself. The term dates from times when most cooking was done over open hearths, where the smoke tended to blacken any kind of utensil being used. The earliest references to this saying in print date from the early seventeenth century. Among the blunter versions is John Clarke's of 1639: "The pot calls the pan burnt-arse." A modern and more straightforward equivalent is *Look who's talking,* which William Safire believes is derived from the Yiddish *kuk nor ver s'ret.* In Britain, put as *listen who's talking,* it dates from the second half of the twentieth century.

pot to pee/piss in, not have a Be extremely poor. This slangy Americanism, as in "The stock market crash wiped him out—now he hasn't a pot to pee in," dates from about 1900. The pot in question is a chamber pot.

pound of flesh, a One's exact dues; the precise amount owed, no matter what. The term comes from the famous trial scene of Shakespeare's *The Merchant of Venice* (4.1), in which the moneylender Shylock demands that the pound of flesh that was promised him in payment for lending Antonio money be handed over. He is, of course, foiled by Portia, who says he may have his pound of flesh but it may not include an ounce of blood (since no blood is due him). Ever since, this expression has been used as a metaphor for exacting payment, usually in a vengeful way.

pour oil on troubled waters, to To soothe a turbulent situation; to calm down angry persons. This term refers to an ancient practice of pouring oil on ocean waves to decrease their violence. It was mentioned in Bede's *Ecclesiastical History* (A.D. 731), which tells of an Irish monk giving a priest holy oil to pour on the sea during a storm. The term was eventually transferred to smoothing over matters of any kind. "Disraeli poured oil and calmed the waters," reported W. B. Baring, writing about the British statesman (*Croker Papers,* 1847).

power behind the throne, the An individual with so much influence on a king, president, or other nominal leader that he or she is the de facto leader. The idea, although certainly much older, was first expressed in this way by William Pitt in a 1770 speech: "There is something behind the throne greater than the King himself." Among the numerous historical examples are the Russian monk Rasputin, who had enormous sway over his country's last czar, and First Lady Nancy Reagan, who was believed to have similar influence on President Ronald Reagan. See also GRAY EMINENCE.

powers that be, the Those in authority. This term comes from the Bible: "The powers that be are ordained of God," from Paul's Epistle to the Romans (13:1), asserts that all power of any kind comes from God alone. Centuries later the term was reasserted by Pope Leo XIII (*Immortale Dei,* 1885): "All public power proceeds from God." Today the term is used more loosely for any temporal authorities.

practice makes perfect The more one does something, the better at it one becomes. This ancient proverb began as *use makes perfect.* In English it dates from the fifteenth century but probably was a version of a much older Latin proverb. It exists in many languages, so presumably most people agree. Ralph Waldo Emerson almost did: "Practice is nine-tenths," he wrote (*Conduct of Life: Power,* 1860). An English writer in the *Spectator* of May 10, 1902, differed: "Practice never makes perfect. It improves up to a point."

practice what you preach Do as you would have others do. The idea is an ancient one, expressed in somewhat different form in the Bible (Matthew

23:3): "They say and do not" (King James version; the Revised Standard version changed it to "they preach but do not practice"). Repeated often over the centuries, it appears in Dickens's *Old Curiosity Shop* (1840): "Divines do not always practice what they preach." See also DO AS I SAY.

praise to the skies, to To commend lavishly; by extension, excessively. Earlier versions of this expression include *laud* and *extol* to the skies/heavens/stars, as in Sir Thomas More's "They praysed him farre above the Starres" (*The History of Kyng Richard the Third,* 1513). See also SKY'S THE LIMIT.

precious few Hardly any. The use of *precious* for "very" or "extremely" dates from the first half of the nineteenth century, and so does its pairing with "few." For some reason it is never paired with any other adjective; one never hears of "precious many." A. Gray used it in a letter of 1839, "While on the Continent I have received precious few letters," and Neville Chamberlain used it in a speech to the House of Commons (August 26, 1886): "Precious few of them have declared in favour of the bill."

press the flesh, to To shake hands, to make physical contact in greeting someone. This humorous bit of American slang dates from the 1920s. It was first used, and still often is, of politicians who are greeting as many potential voters as possible in an effort to secure their votes.

pretty as a picture Singularly attractive. The *picture* in question means a work of art, and the expression dates from Victorian times, when, one might speculate, paintings often were "prettier" than today. Mark Twain used a version of it: "He was pretty enough to frame." (*A Connecticut Yankee in King Arthur's Court,* 1889). Although *Dialect Notes* in 1909 noted that the term was often used of a piece of fruit, which presumably was good-looking enough to paint, it was and still is more often applied to human beings.

pretty penny See COST AN ARM AND A LEG.

price is right, the A good value; very reasonable. This term is often used humorously to describe something that is free of charge but not especially desirable or praiseworthy in other respects. "'It may look like Salvation Army modern, but the price was right,' laughed Mary" (Dean Sherwood, *Glass Houses,* 1979).

prick up one's ears, to To listen attentively. This term, which alludes to horses holding up their ears at a sudden noise, dates from the sixteenth century. Shakespeare used it in *The Tempest* (4.1): "Like unback'd colts, they prick'd their ears."

pride and joy, one's A prized possession. This term comes from a poem by Sir Walter Scott, "Rokeby" (1813), in which he described children as "a mother's pride, a father's joy." It was subsequently broadened to include any accomplishment or possession.

prime of life, the The best years of one's life, at the peak of one's powers. The idea that there should be a particular time of flourishing is an ancient one. Plato in *The Republic* defined it as a period of about twenty years in a woman's life and thirty in a man's. Poets, among them Robert Herrick and John Milton, generally equated one's youth with one's prime. However, the eccentric schoolteacher-heroine of Muriel Spark's novel *The Prime of Miss Jean Brodie* (and the 1969 motion picture based on it) declared the years of her rapidly advancing middle age to be her prime.

prime the pump, to To help something to succeed, as by contributing money to a cause. This Americanism dates from the nineteenth century and literally means to pour liquid into a pump so as to expel any air and make it operate. During the years of the Great Depression the phrase began to be used figuratively, at first for government measures to stimulate the lagging economy. In time it began to be used in a far more general fashion, as T. Sharpe did in *The Great Pursuit* (1977), "Significance is all . . . prime the pump with meaningful hogwash."

primrose path, the The way of easy self-indulgence. Shakespeare used this term in two ways—as a path of pleasure ("the primrose path of dalliance," *Hamlet,* 1.3) and as an easy but dangerous course of action ("the primrose way to the everlasting bonfire," *Macbeth,* 2.1). The former meaning survives in the current cliché. See also GARDEN PATH.

promised land, the A place or time of ultimate happiness; paradise or heaven. The term comes from the Bible, in which God promises the land of Canaan to Abraham, Isaac, Jacob, and their descendants (Genesis 12:7). Later, the name became attached to the Holy Land ("The land of repromission, that men calles the Holy Land," Sir John Maundeville, *Travels,* c. 1400), and still later it was extended to any place viewed as wonderful ("To all these exiled sects America was the land of promise," William Hepworth Dixon, *William Penn,* 1851) as well as to heaven. In modern times Israel is often called the promised land for Jews.

proof of the pudding is in the eating, the Performance is the only valid test. This proverbial expression of quality control dates from about 1600, appearing in print in William Camden's *Remains Concerning Britain* (1605). It has been repeated many times over the centuries, particularly by British writers (including George Bernard Shaw and W. Somerset

Maugham), for whom pudding is more of a basic dish than it is to Americans (it originally meant a kind of sausage, and later any food inside a crust); the *Economist* entitled a survey of the advertising industry "Proof of the Pudding" (June 1990). The term, generally shortened to "proof of the pudding," survives on this side of the Atlantic as well.

proud as a peacock Having an exceedingly high opinion of oneself—one's dignity or one's importance. The comparison to a peacock, believed to allude to its strutting gait, dates from the thirteenth century. Chaucer used the simile several times, and it has often been repeated. "The self-applauding bird the peacock" is how William Cowper described it (*Truth,* 1781).

pull a fast one, to To execute an unfair trick. This slangy Americanism dates from about 1920. A. Gilbert was one of many popular novelists to use it (*Death Against the Clock,* 1958): "Mad to think they can pull a fast one."

pull a rabbit out of a hat, to To come up with a surprise, usually a pleasant one. The term comes from the magician's trick of pulling a live rabbit out of a seemingly empty hat. While the trick is old, the term was being transferred to other surprises only from the 1930s on. D. Sannon used it in *Death by Inches* (1965): "Well, you pulled the rabbit out of the hat."

pull no punches, to To be perfectly blunt; to act without restraint. The term comes from boxing, where to *pull a punch* means to deliver a blow that is intentionally ineffective, that is, to hold back deliberately. In the 1930s it was being transferred to other activities, as in Harold L. Ickes's *Secret Diary* (1937): "He talked about the judiciary and he didn't pull his punches at any time."

pull oneself together, to To regain command of oneself. The image conveyed by this term is of someone who has "fallen apart" and must be put back together bit by bit. A related term is to *pull oneself up by the bootstraps,* meaning to improve one's lot by making a singular effort. The analogy here is to pulling on long boots by means of the straps or loops attached to them at the top, which requires a considerable effort. This term dates from the turn of the twentieth century (although bootstraps by then were far from commonplace). The metaphor gained currency in the late 1950s and early 1960s through Operation Bootstrap, a U.S. policy designed to help Puerto Rico gain economic viability by providing "bootstraps" (in the form of American mainland industry establishing factories there) whereby the island could "pull itself up."

pull one's (own) weight, to To do one's share of the work. This term comes from rowing, where each member of a crew must pull on an oar at least hard enough to propel his or her own weight. The term was used figuratively from about 1900 on. In a 1902 speech, Theodore Roosevelt said, "The first requisite of a good citizen . . . is that he shall be able and willing to pull his weight."

pull out all the stops, to To do one's utmost; to use all of one's resources. This term comes from organ-playing. To pull out all the organ stops means to bring into play each rank of pipes, thus providing the fullest possible sound. The term was transferred to other activities in the latter half of the nineteenth century. Matthew Arnold alluded to it in *Essays in Criticism* (1865): "How unpopular a task one is undertaking when one tries to pull out a few more stops in that . . . somewhat narrow-toned organ, the modern Englishman." A more recent synonymous phrase is *put the pedal to the metal.* A term from auto racing coined in the 1970s, it refers to the fact that in racing cars the floor under the gas pedal is naked metal. When the driver pressed the pedal down to the metal, he or she was giving the engine the most gas possible. It may become a cliché.

pull rank, to To use one's superior rank or position unfairly, to obtain a special privilege, force obedience, or the like. The term comes from the military in the first half of the 1900s and continues to be used in the armed forces. However, it has also been extended to civilian life. Helen MacInnes had it in *Agent in Place* (1976): "'What if he refuses to go with them?' 'They'll be senior men, they'll pull rank.'"

pull someone's leg, to To tease or fool someone; to trick someone in a humorous way. This term for a time was thought to allude to the gruesome practice of pulling on the legs of a person who was being hanged in order to shorten his or her agony. In fact, however, the current meaning of the cliché dates only from the late nineteenth century, long after hanging was accomplished in more humane fashion (by means of a long drop). Most authorities now believe it alludes to tricking a person by tripping them, using a cane or foot or other object that, in effect, holds back one of their legs so that they fall. Current in England in the late nineteenth century, it had crossed the Atlantic by 1910, when O. Henry wrote, "You can't pull my leg," in his story *A Little Local Color.*

pull strings, to To exert behind-the-scenes influence. The term comes from puppetry: puppets or marionettes are manipulated by means of strings or wires held by the puppetmaster. It was transferred to politics by 1860, when Bishop William Stubbs wrote (*Lectures on the Study of History*), "A king who pulled the strings of government."

pull the chestnuts out of the fire, to To do someone else's dirty work. This term comes from an ancient fable in which a monkey, not wishing to burn its own fingers, persuades a cat to retrieve chestnuts that had fallen into the fire (whence also CAT'S PAW, for being made a dupe). Recounted in numerous early collections of fables (by La Fontaine, 1678, and Sir Roger L'Estrange, 1692, among others), it was transferred to any kind of dirty work by the eighteenth century.

pull the rug out from under (someone), to To upset someone's plans or activities; to remove someone's supports. The image is undeniably clear, but a more common practice, it would seem, would be the schoolboy trick of pulling a chair away from someone who is about to sit down. It is *rug,* however, that became part of a common turn of phrase, originating in the mid-twentieth century. *Time* used it in an article about labor and the economy in 1946: "Strikes, for instance, would pull the rug out from under the best of prospects."

pull the wool over someone's eyes, to To hoodwink or deceive someone. This term comes from—and long survives—the custom of wearing a wig (except in the British legal system, where judges and barristers still do so). One writer suggests that it alludes to the slippage of the wig of a judge, who is temporarily blinded by a clever lawyer. In any event, it was used figuratively in a quite general way from the early nineteenth century on, on both sides of the Atlantic. "He ain't so big a fool as to have the wool drawn over his eyes in that way," wrote Frances M. Whitcher (*The Widow Bedott Papers,* 1856).

pull up stakes, to To leave one's residence, job, or country; to move on. This Americanism dates at least from the nineteenth century and may be older. It appeared in print in 1830 in *Massachusetts Spy:* "Our emigrants pulled up stakes and returned post haste to . . . Springfield." The stakes presumably were posts marking property boundaries.

punch drunk Confused, dazed. This term comes from boxing, where it is applied to boxers who have sustained brain damage from repeatedly being hit in the head. As a result they may have tremors of the hands, a stumbling gait, hesitant speech, and similar signs of cerebral damage. The term was first so used about 1915 and soon afterward began to be applied to any person who seems dazed or confused owing to lack of sleep, disorientation, or other circumstances.

puppy love A youthful infatuation, with the implication that it will not last. It is nearly always spoken of disparagingly, as by W. A. Carruthers (*A Kentuckian in New York,* 1834): "Oh! it is nothing more than puppy love!"

pure and simple Plainly so, without amplification or dilution. This pairing is almost but not quite redundant; it dates from the nineteenth century.

Oscar Wilde played on it in *The Importance of Being Earnest* (1895): "The truth is rarely pure and never simple."

pure as the driven snow Morally pure, physically chaste. The simile dates from Shakespeare's time, although *driven,* meaning carried along by the wind into drifts, was sometimes omitted. In *Hamlet* (3.1) he had it, "Be thou as chaste as ice, as pure as snow." It was a cliché by the time H. W. Thompson wrote (*Body, Boots and Britches,* 1940), "She was pure as the snow, but she drifted."

purple prose Exceedingly florid, oversentimental writing. This term began life as *purple patches* in the Latin poet Horace's *De Arte Poetica* (c. 20 B.C.): "Often on a work of grave purpose and high promise is tacked a purple patch or two to give an effect of color."

push comes to shove, if/when If/when matters become serious; when the situation is crucial; IF WORST COMES TO WORST. This term, with its further implication that action should back up words, appears to have originated in African-American English around the middle of the twentieth century. Murtagh and Harris used it in *Cast the First Stone* (1958): "Some judges talk nice and polite. . . . Then, when push comes to shove, they say, 'Six months.'"

push the envelope Go to extremes, go beyond accepted limits. This term comes from flight testing in the 1960s, where *envelope* signifies the limits of safe performance, and pushing it means to fly an aircraft faster or higher or dive more steeply than had ever been attempted in order to see what it could do. By the 1980s the expression was used figuratively, and so widely that it has become a cliché. Opera singer Renée Fleming used it in *The Inner Voice* (2004): "You want to go out there, push the envelope, and do something you've never done before."

push the panic button, to To overreact to a supposed emergency. This term originated during World War II, when B-17 and B-24 bombers had a bell-warning system so that the crew could bail out when the plane was badly hit. Occasionally this button would be pushed by mistake and the crew would bail out unnecessarily, even though the plane was virtually undamaged. By extension, the term came to mean acting in needless haste. In the 1950s it gained currency—and a more sinister meaning—when it also referred to releasing a nuclear warhead by pushing a button.

push up daisies, to Be dead and buried. The phrase was first recorded in 1918, in one of Wilfred Owen's poems about World War I, and alludes to flowers growing over a soldier's grave in France. It soon passed into the civilian vocabulary, where it continues to refer to being dead. Georgette

Heyer had it in *Blunt Instrument* (1938): "'Where is the wife now?'. . . 'Pushing up daisies . . . . died a couple of years ago.'"

put a good/bold face on something, to To make the best of things. This term has been around since the fourteenth century, and the practice itself, of pretending things are better than they are, is no doubt much older. "Set a good face on a bad matter," wrote Humphrey Gifford (*A Posie of Gilloflowers,* 1580).

put all one's eggs in one basket To risk all one's resources in a single venture. One might think this proverb was very old indeed, but the same idea used to be put as *trusting all one's goods to one ship,* which antedates it by many centuries. "Putting all one's eggs in the same basket," thereby incurring the risk that the basket will be dropped and all the eggs will break, was first stated only in 1710, in Samuel Palmer's *Moral Essays on Proverbs.* Mark Twain contradicted the idea in *Pudd'nhead Wilson* (1894): "The fool saith, 'Put not all thy eggs in one basket'—which is but a manner of saying, 'Scatter your money and your attention'; but the wise man saith, 'Put all your eggs in one basket, and WATCH THAT BASKET.'"

put in a good word for someone/something, to To serve as advocate for someone or something; to put someone or something in the best possible light. *Good word* has meant "a favorable or laudatory comment" since about 1205. This cliché was put as *speak a good word for* someone from 1540.

put on airs, to To assume a superior manner or appearance to which one has no real claim. *Airs* here means a manner of superiority. The term appeared in print from about 1700. Joseph Addison used it in his travel account of Italy (1704): "Which easily discovers the Airs they give themselves."

put one's best foot forward, to To try to make the best possible impression. There is something inherently puzzling about this expression, which dates from the sixteenth century. What exactly is one's "best foot," and why should it signify putting on a good show? Shakespeare made it the *better foot* (in *Titus Andronicus* and *King John*), and Sir Thomas Overby wrote, in 1613 (*Characters: A footeman*), "His legs are not matches, for he is still setting the best foot forward." One writer suggests that "best foot" always meant "right foot," the left being considered unlucky. Whatever the explanation, the metaphor is still current.

put one's faith in See PIN ONE'S HOPES ON.

put one's foot down, to To take a firm position. The analogy presumably is to setting one or both feet in a fixed position, representing a firm stand.

Although versions of this term (usually with *set* one's foot down) exist from the sixteenth century on, it became current only in the nineteenth century. The *OED* cites James Payn's *The Luck of the Darrells* (1886): "She put her foot down . . . upon the least symptoms of an unpleasantry."

put one's foot in it/one's mouth, to To make a (verbal) blunder. This term dates from the early eighteenth century and presumably was analogous to stepping where one should not. Jonathan Swift used it in *Polite Conversation* (1738), "The bishop has put his foot in it," and a century later the term was defined in a book on slang (1823). Putting one's foot *in one's mouth* is of more recent provenance; it merited a definition in P. W. Joyce's *English As We Speak It* (1910): "To a person who habitually uses unfortunate blundering expressions: 'You never open your mouth but you put your foot in it.'" Today it is sometimes referred to as FOOT-IN-MOUTH DISEASE.

put one's money where one's mouth is, to Back up your stated position with action. This term, according to Eric Partridge's informants, was current in the United States from at least 1930 and caught on in Britain and other English-speaking countries shortly after World War II. In 1975 the British government used it as an advertising slogan to persuade people to invest their savings in the National Savings Bank Accounts Department. See also PUT UP OR SHUT UP.

put one's oar in, to To insert one's opinion; to interfere in someone else's business. This term, with its analogy to contributing one's efforts to rowing a boat, dates from the late sixteenth century. Charles Coffey used it in his play *The Devil to Pay* (1731): "I will govern my own house without your putting in an oar" (1:2).

put one's shoulder to the wheel See SHOULDER TO THE WHEEL.

put on hold/ice/the back burner, to To postpone, delay, keep in reserve. The oldest of these nearly synonymous terms is to put something *on ice,* the transfer from food storage (on ice blocks) to anything kept in reserve occurring in the late nineteenth century. Chefs put food that is either finished or cooks more quickly than the rest of a meal on a back burner of the range. By about 1930, this term was transferred to temporarily shelving any item or project or plan, originally in the United States, and came into general use about thirty years later. To put *on hold* also dates from the mid-twentieth century. It began to be used for the temporary interruption or suspension of a space launch and/or a telephone conversation. It was commonplace in both activities by about 1960 and was rapidly transferred to other kinds of delay, although its literal application—interrupting a telephone connection to wait for its resumption—is still current, along with the irritations generated by call waiting. See also YOUR CALL IS IMPORTANT.

put on one's thinking cap, to To take time to reflect or ponder. This term, which at first was stated as one's *considering cap,* dates from the early seventeenth century. "Now I'll put on my considering cap," wrote John Fletcher in his play *The Loyal Subject* (1618). It only became a thinking cap in the late nineteenth century.

put on the dog, to To put on a showy display. The term originated in America around the time of the Civil War, but its ultimate origin has been lost. At least one writer believes it came from the custom of the newly wealthy to display their prosperity by keeping extravagantly pampered pets. In any event, Lyman H. Bagg catalogued it as college slang in his *Four Years at Yale* (c. 1869), in which he wrote, "To put on the dog is to make a flashy display, to cut a swell."

put on the spot See ON THE SPOT.

put out to grass/pasture, to be To be retired from active duty; to rusticate. This term, which refers to animals that are turned out to a meadow or range, particularly a horse that is too old to work, was transferred to human beings as early as the sixteenth century. John Heywood used it in his 1546 proverb collection: "He turnde hir out at doores to grasse on the playne."

put someone in the picture, to To inform someone; to include someone as an active participant. To be in the picture has meant to be involved in a particular situation since about 1900. "I feel that I am in the picture, when I wear black during Lent," wrote Clara Morris (*Stage Confidences,* 1902).

put someone's nose out of joint See NOSE OUT OF JOINT.

put that in your pipe and smoke it Take that and think about it; digest that if you can. This term alludes to the frequent appearance of pipe smokers as thoughtful and/or contemplative. The term has been current since the early nineteenth century. R. H. Barham used it in *The Lay of St. Odille* (1840): "For this you've my word, and I never yet broke it. So put that in your pipe, my Lord Otto, and smoke it."

put through one's paces To be thoroughly tested. The allusion here is to a horse being tried out by a possible buyer. Used literally in the mid-eighteenth century, it was transferred to human beings a century later. B. Taylor had it in *Faust* (1871): "I see she means to put him through his paces." See also THROUGH THE MILL.

put two and two together, to To draw conclusions from the data available. This analogy to simple arithmetic suggests that the facts lead to a simple and obvious deduction. The term dates from the nineteenth century. Thackeray used it in *The Newcomes* (1855): "Putting two and two together, as the saying is, it was not difficult for me to guess who the expected Marquis was."

put up or shut up Back up your argument or keep quiet. This term, seemingly modern slang, actually dates from the nineteenth century. It may come from gambling, serving as a request to a player either to ante up or to withdraw. Or it may come from putting up one's fists to fight. Mark Twain used it in *A Connecticut Yankee in King Arthur's Court* (1889): "This was a plain case of 'put up or shut up.'" By then the phrase was so well known that it was sometimes abbreviated. Fred H. Hart had defined it in his *Sazerac Lying Club: A Nevada Book* (1878), "'P.U. or S.U.' means *put up or shut up,* doesn't it?"

put words into someone's mouth, to To tell or strongly suggest what someone should say. This term is in the Old Testament: "So Joab put the words in her mouth" (2 Samuel 14:3). For a corollary to this cliché, see WORDS RIGHT OUT OF SOMEONE'S MOUTH.

Pyrrhic victory A victory that is worse for the winners than the losers. The term refers to the victory of King Pyrrhus of Epirus over the Romans at Asculum in 279 B.C. In this first major battle between the Greeks and the Romans, Pyrrhus lost his best officers and many of his troops. Ever since the term Pyrrhic victory has meant a victory so costly that it counts as a defeat.

Q

quake/shake like a leaf, to To tremble with fear. This simile occurs in several very early French fables (thirteenth century) and was amplified by Chaucer in the fourteenth century to *quake like an aspen leaf* (*Troilus and Criseyde, Canterbury Tales,* and elsewhere). It was repeated by numerous writers over the centuries, from Shakespeare to A. A. Milne. There is good reason for the comparison to aspens in particular. The aspens, along with poplars, have flattened leaf stalks that cause their pendulous leaves to quiver in the slightest breeze.

quantum leap A sudden, spectacular advance. The term comes from nuclear physics, where a quantum leap is an abrupt transition from one energy state to another within the submicroscopic atom. William Safire pointed out that while scientists emphasize the suddenness and discontinuity of such a change, the figurative term emphasizes the size of the advance. The term was used in physics from about 1950 and began to be transferred (at first in the form of quantum *jump*) to other events about 1955.

queer as a three-dollar bill Phoney. The adjective *queer* means not only strange and, in modern slang, homosexual, but it also long meant counterfeit. Although this last meaning has not survived, the cliché here preserves it. There has never actually been a three-dollar bill. The expression dates from the late nineteenth century, although *queer* for "counterfeit" dates back as far as 1740.

quick and the dead, the The living and the dead. The word *quick* for "living" was used as far back as King Alfred's time (*cwicum* in Middle English, c. A.D. 897) but is rarely used in this meaning nowadays, except in this cliché and in CUT TO THE QUICK. Amélie Rives used it as the title of her novel *The Quick or the Dead* (1888). A few decades later Britain's Lord Dewar is quoted as saying, "There are two classes of pedestrians in these days of reckless motor traffic: the quick and the dead" (in George Robey, *Looking Back on Life,* 1933).

quick as a wink/bunny Very rapid(ly). The earliest such simile is *quick as a bee,* which found a place in John Heywood's *Proverbs* (1546). It was followed by *quick as thought,* appearing in Thomas Shelton's 1620 translation of Cervantes's *Don Quixote* and in Samuel Richardson's *Clarissa* (1748), among other sources. Also common in the eighteenth century was *quick as lightning,* with a nineteenth-century American variant, *quick as greased lightning.* None but the last is heard much anymore, but *quick as a wink,* referring to the blink of an eye and appearing in one of Thomas Haliburton's Sam Slick stories (1843), is current, as are *quick as a flash,* presumably referring to lightning as well, and *quick as a bunny* (or *rabbit*), which dates from the late nineteenth century. See also LIKE THE WIND; LIKE GREASED LIGHTNING.

quick on the draw/trigger Fast to act or react. The term comes from the gunslingers of the American West and was transferred to other kinds of quick reaction in the first half of the twentieth century. The literal meaning of *quick on the trigger* is a century older, appearing in a letter of 1808: "I trust that all your Aids will be quick on the trigger" (M. L. Weems, in E. E. F. Skeel, *M. L. Weems: Works and Ways*).

quid pro quo Tit for tat; in law, a consideration (payment). These Latin words, literally meaning "this for that," have been used in this way since Shakespeare's time. Indeed, he used it in *Henry VI, Part 1,* when Margaret tells the Earl of Suffolk, "I cry you mercy, 'tis but quid pro quo" (5.3).

quiet as a mouse Hushed, subdued. This simile dates from the sixteenth century and presumably refers to the behavior of a mouse that stops dead in its tracks at the approach of a cat and remains as quiet as possible, hoping to avoid notice. Also put as *still as a mouse,* it has been repeated again and again, outliving the still older (fourteenth century) *quiet as a lamb.*

r

rack and ruin, gone to Dilapidated and decayed. These words originally meant utter destruction and financial ruin, rack here being a variant of *wreck.* (it was sometimes spelled *wrack,* showing the close association). The term, from the sixteenth century, no doubt owes its long life in part to alliteration. Today it is most often used of inanimate objects, such as a building or a business. In 1782 Elizabeth Blower doubled up on clichés, writing, "Everything would soon go to sixes and sevens, and rack and ruin" (*George Bateman*).

rack one's brain, to To strain to remember something or discover a solution. The *rack* here is the medieval instrument of torture on which the victim's body was stretched until it broke. The idea is old; "we break our brains for naught" comes from 1530. The word "rack" came into use about 150 years later.

rags to riches, from From poverty to wealth through one's own efforts; the self-made man or woman. This phrase was the theme of the 130 or so extremely popular novels of Horatio Alger (1834–99), whose heroes always rose from their lowly position by virtue of hard work, thrift, and pluck to win great wealth and happiness. R. de Toledano used it in *Frontiers of Jazz,* writing of the clarinetist Benny Goodman, "Goodman was the first real rags-to-riches success in the swing-jazz field."

ragtag and bobtail Low-life, riffraff. This expression dates back to the seventeenth century, when *ragtag* meant a ragged lot of people and *bobtail* a horse whose tail had been cut short ("bobbed") and was considered valueless. Samuel Pepys in his *Diary* turned it about a bit: "The dining-room was full of tag rag and bobtail, dancing, singing, and drinking" (1658–59). The expression is not heard much any longer, however, at least not in the United States.

raining cats and dogs, it's A heavy downpour. The origin of this expression, which has been around since at least 1700, has been lost. Among the theories are that a raging storm is analogous to fighting cats and dogs; that in North European myth cats supposedly influence weather and dogs symbolize wind; and, currently considered the most likely one, that with the primitive drainage systems in use in the seventeenth century, a heavy rainstorm would cause gutters to overflow with a torrent of debris that included garbage, sewage, and dead animals. Among the earliest appearances in print is a note by Jonathan Swift in 1738: "I know Sir John will go, though he was sure it would rain cats and dogs."

rain on someone's parade, to To spoil someone's plans or celebration. This term, which calls up a vivid image of a downpour spoiling elaborate floats and dampening spirits, has been around since about 1900. Sheila Rule, reporting on a plan to replace Britain's House of Lords with an elected second chamber, wrote, "But the opposition Labor Party, which has long sought to rain on the Lords' political parade, is once again aiming at those men and women" (*New York Times,* 1990).

rain or shine No matter what happens. This transfer of dubious weather to any uncertain conditions always implies that an activity or event will be carried out, no matter what the circumstances. It was in print by 1905, when Horace A. Vachell wrote (*Hill*), "With me you're first, rain or shine."

raise Cain, to To make a disturbance. This nineteenth-century Americanism alludes to the wicked biblical Cain, who killed his brother Abel (Genesis 4:5). Raising Cain is equivalent to "raising the devil." The earliest appearances of this expression in print date from the 1840s, but by the second half of the nineteenth century it had crossed the Atlantic and was used by Robert Louis Stevenson in *Treasure Island* ("I'm a man that has lived rough, and I'll raise Cain") and Rudyard Kipling in *The Ballad of the Bolivar* ("Seven men from all the world back to Docks again, / Rolling down the Ratcliffe Road, drunk and raising Cain"). A more straightforward synonym is *to raise hell,* an Americanism that dates from the late 1800s and gave rise to the slogan, "Kansas should raise less corn and more hell." Yet another Americanism from the same period is *to raise a ruckus,* the noun *ruckus* possibly derived from *rumpus.*

raise one's hackles, to To arouse one's anger. The hackles are the hair on the back of an animal's neck that sticks straight up with excitement, fear, or other strong emotion. "With the hackles up," meaning on the point of fighting, was transferred to humans in the late nineteenth century. "I almost saw the hackles of a good old squire rise," wrote Edward Pennell-Elmhirst (*The Cream of Leicestershire,* 1883).

raise the roof, to To express violent anger. The image conveyed is one of jumping so high with rage that the very roof is lifted up. Originating in mid-nineteenth-century America, the expression appeared in M. J. Holmes's *Cousin Maude* (1860), in African-American dialect: "Ole master'll raise de ruff, case he put 'em away to sell." See also HIT THE CEILING.

rake over the coals See HAUL OVER THE COALS.

rally 'round the flag Support a candidate, cause, or country. The phrase was ascribed to General Andrew Jackson at the battle of New Orleans but soon came to be used in American politics for supporting a campaign. It entered the vocabulary once and for all with George F. Root's Civil War song "The Battle Cry of Freedom": "Rally 'round the flag, boys, Rally once again, Shouting the battle-cry of freedom."

rank and file, the The general population; followers rather than leaders. This term comes from the military, where it means soldiers and noncommissioned officers as opposed to officers. Both words actually refer to specific lineups, a *rank* meaning men aligned side by side and a *file* men standing behind one another. It is the soldiers and noncommissioned who line up in this way, with the officers standing in front or to the side. The military expression dates from the sixteenth century. In the late eighteenth century it began to be applied figuratively to the general membership of a large group or the individuals in a series. Robert Burns did so in *First Epistle to Davie* (1784): "The words come skelpan, rank and file."

rant and rave, to To speak wildly and angrily about some circumstance or issue. This expression was first recorded as *rave and rant,* or literally, "raived and ranted," in James MacManus's *The Bend of the Road* (1898). The turnaround came soon thereafter and the term always appears in this form today. David Leavitt used it in *Family Dancing* (1984), "It's easy for you to just stand there and rant and rave."

rare bird, a An unusual phenomenon or person. The term is a translation from Juvenal's *Satires* (c. A.D. 120), in which, speaking of chastity, he writes, *"Rara avis in terris nigroque simillima cygno"* (A bird as rare upon the earth as a black swan). The term was soon being applied to other rare phenomena, often as sarcastically as Juvenal had used it, as, for example, for "an honest lawyer" (John Wesley, *Journal,* 1764).

raring to go Extremely eager to get started. This American locution of the late nineteenth century uses *raring* for *rearing,* the verb still used for what a lively horse does when it stands on its hind legs and is clearly eager to get moving. A colloquialism of the twentieth century, it appeared in F. N. Hart's *The Bellamy Trial* (1927): "Both sides are rarin' to go."

rat race, a A relentless competition or struggle to advance oneself, or even to keep up. A twentieth-century expression transferring the rodent's struggle for survival, it originated in America. It appears in Christopher Morley's *Kitty Foyle* (1939): "Their own private life gets to be a rat race."

rats abandon a sinking ship Smart (and disloyal) individuals will desert a failing enterprise before it is too late. This observation was made long ago about rats, which would remain on board devouring a ship's stores in the hold until the ship foundered in a storm or ran aground; then they would disappear so as not to be drowned. The transfer to human desertion was made before 1600; in some cases it was a ship they abandoned, in others a house about to collapse. "It is the Wisdome of Rats that will be sure to leave a House somewhat before its fall," wrote Francis Bacon (*Essays,* 1597).

raw deal, a Harsh or unfair treatment. The *raw* in this expression, which originated in America, means "crude." In 1912 a Canadian dictionary defined the term as "a swindle," a meaning not much invoked today. E. C. Bentley used the expression in *Those Days* (1940): "If it was what is known nowadays as a raw deal, they did not mind."

razor's edge, on the In a critical or dangerous predicament. This analogy dates from Homer's time (*Iliad,* c. 850 B.C.): "To all it stands on a razor's edge, either woeful ruin or life for the Achaeans." W. Somerset Maugham used it as the title of a philosophical novel (*The Razor's Edge,* 1944) exploring the meaning of life. Alan White used it in *The Long Silence* (1976): "He was living on a razor's edge. Sooner or later, the Germans were going to begin to suspect."

read between the lines, to To deduce hidden meanings from what is actually said and written. The term comes from cryptography, in which one kind of code actually presents a message on every second line, with a quite different sense imparted if one reads the intervening lines as well. The term began to be used figuratively in the mid-nineteenth century. James Martineau wrote (*Essays Philosophical and Theological,* 1866), "No writer was ever more read between the lines."

read my lips Listen to what I'm saying because I really mean it. This expression actually has no relation to the lip-reading done by deaf persons who try to make out what is being said from the movement of a person's mouth. It dates from the mid-1900s. In 1978 it was used as the title of an album of songs by British actor and singer Tim Curry, who in turn picked up the phrase from an Italian-American recording engineer. But it was popularized by George H.W. Bush in his acceptance speech for the 1988 Republican presidential nomination: "Congress will push me to raise taxes. . . . And I'll say to them, 'Read my lips. No new taxes.'" It continued to be widely used in politics, sports, and indeed any venue where someone wanted to make an emphatic statement. It is well on its way to clichédom.

read someone like an open book, to To discern someone's thoughts with great accuracy. The analogy of a guileless person to an open book was made by Shakespeare. "Read o'er the volume of young Paris' face," he wrote in *Romeo and Juliet* (1.3), and again, "O, like a book of sport thou'lt read me o'er," in *Troilus and Cressida* (4.5). A closely related turn of phrase is to *read someone's mind,* which dates from the late nineteenth century.

read the riot act, to To issue a severe reprimand. The term comes from a British law, the Riot Act of 1714, which required literally reading aloud a proclamation in order to disperse a crowd (defined as a gathering of twelve or more persons). The proclamation stated, "Our Sovereign Lord the King chargeth and commandeth all persons being assembled immediately to disperse themselves and peaceably to depart to their habitations." Whoever did not obey within an hour was guilty of a felony punishable by law. By the mid-nineteenth century reading the riot act was used figuratively for a vigorous scolding, as Dickens used it in *Barnaby Rudge* (1840): "The Riot Act was read."

ready, willing, and able Completely prepared and eager to do something. This term, from the first half of the twentieth century, sounds like the reply of an overeager military recruit. Most likely its rhythmic appeal is what made it survive. For example, "Have you learned all your lines so you can go on?—Ready, willing, and able."

really and truly Genuinely, undoubtedly. This redundancy (*really* and *truly* mean the same thing, but the repetition makes for emphasis) dates from the eighteenth century. The *OED* holds it is a North American children's locution, but nearly all of its citations, ranging from Henry Fielding (1742) to the present, are from adult books. Thomas Macaulay used it in his *The History of England* (1849), "The king is really and truly a Catholic."

real McCoy, the The genuine article. This term probably originated in late nineteenth-century America, when a young boxer named Norman Selby changed his name to Kid McCoy and began a spectacularly successful career in the ring. For years he averaged a fight a month, winning most of them by knockouts. Hoping to capitalize on his success, numerous other boxers adopted the name Kid McCoy, but on March 24, 1899, the real Kid, in a now legendary bout, finished off Joe Choynski in the twentieth round. The next day's headlines in the *San Francisco Examiner* proclaimed, "Now you've seen the real McCoy," and that description stuck. In real life McCoy was actually a con artist and criminal. But in 1904 the *New York Evening World* said, "Notwithstanding the hullabaloo of his life and the mischief of his legend, McCoy with his wondrous speed and guile may be the first, greatest gentleman of this fresh age" (quoted in a review of a novel based on McCoy's life, *New York*

Times, June 6, 2002). Although this etymology is more or less verifiable, there are several other theories as to the term's origin. Chief among them is that a Scotch whiskey made by the MacKay company was called the real Mackay or McCoy.

red as a beet Flushed from embarrassment, sunburn, physical effort, or some other cause. Although many of the similes involving red are very flattering, notably lips as red as a cherry or cheeks as red as an apple, being red as a beet is not: for example, "After six hours over a hot stove, Jane was red as a beet." Neither is *red as a lobster,* as in "A day at the beach left Bill as red as a lobster."

red-carpet treatment, the Lavish hospitality; a royal welcome. This term comes from the practice of rolling out a carpet for a particularly esteemed visitor to walk on. Although similar practices surely were common from the earliest days of welcoming royalty, the term *red carpet* dates only from the early twentieth century. The *OED* cites a news story in the *Daily Mail* (1960) about honoring the two-millionth passenger to leave London via TWA jet: "There was a hitch when Mr. Mueller arrived. He is just two years and four months old. The red-carpet treatment went to his mother."

red cent, not worth/don't have a Worthless; bankrupt or broke. The cent has long been the lowest denomination of American coin, and "red" refers to the fact that it used to be made of copper. The expression dates from the early nineteenth century. J. S. Jones used it in *People's Lawyer* (c. 1839): "It would not have cost you a red cent."

red flag/rag to a bull, like a Inflammatory, infuriating. This simile is based on the ancient belief that bulls react more strongly to a piece of red cloth waved before them than to anything else. In bullfighting the matador's cape, which he manipulates so as to maneuver the bull's movements, is usually lined in red. However, it has been fairly well established that it is the cape's movements that incite the bull; the red color simply makes it more visible to the spectators. Nevertheless, as early as the sixteenth century the belief that red incites bulls was recorded by John Lyly (*Euphues and his England,* 1580), who wrote, "He that commeth before an Elephant will not wear bright colours, nor he that commeth to a Bul red."

red herring A diversionary tactic; a false or deliberately misleading trail. This expression comes from the use of strong-smelling smoked herrings as a lure to train hunting dogs to follow a scent. They also could be used to throw dogs *off* the scent, and it was this characteristic that was transferred to the metaphoric use of red herring. "Diverted from their own affairs by the red herring of foreign politics so adroitly drawn across the trail," wrote W. F. Butler (*Life of Napier,* 1890).

red-letter day, a A special occasion. The term comes from the practice of printing feast days and other special holy days in red on ecclesiastical calendars, from the fifteenth century on. Charles Lamb used the expression in describing Oxford during the long vacation: "The red-letter days now become, to all intents and purposes, dead-letter days" (*Essays of Elia,* 1823).

reinvent the wheel, to To belabor the obvious; to start again from the beginning when there is no need to. This Americanism dates from the second half of the twentieth century and most likely originated in business or industry. "'The new compiler here is no different from the old one,' said a Defense Department spokesman. 'Let's not reinvent the wheel'" (*Boston Herald,* 1984).

rest in peace Let it be; leave it alone. This term is a translation and an extension of the Latin *Requiescat in pace* and its abbreviation, R.I.P., often found on tombstones. Charles Kingsley used it figuratively (*Westward Ho,* 1855): "Into her merits or demerits I do not enter deeply here. Let her rest in peace."

rest is history, the You know the end of this story, so I need not go into details. Often used for a biographical or autobiographical account, this phrase dates from the second half of the 1900s. Nigel Rees cites a play on it by Alan Bennett (*Oxford Today,* 1988), describing his career change from an Oxford history professor to a Broadway revue artist: "The rest, one might say pompously, is history. Except that in my case the opposite was true."

rest on one's laurels, to To be satisfied with one's achievement, by implication enough so as not to expend further effort. The term, dating from the mid-nineteenth century, alludes to the wreaths of laurel leaves used to crown the winner of athletic contests in ancient Greek and Roman times; the laurel today remains a symbol of victory. Emanuel Deutsch wrote, "Let them rest on their laurels for a while" (*Literary Remains,* 1874).

revenge is sweet Retaliation is wonderfully satisfying. Occasionally put as *vengeance is sweet,* this observation was made by the ancients, from Homer in the *Iliad* to Juvenal in his *Satires.* In English it was voiced by Ben Jonson, Shakespeare, Richard Brinsley Sheridan, and countless others. Here is a misogynist version by Byron (*Don Juan,* 1819–24): "Sweet is revenge—especially to women."

rich as Croesus Very wealthy indeed. This term alludes to the legendary Croesus, the last King of Lydia and proverbially the wealthiest man on earth.

The simile has been used in English since the sixteenth century. "An I get a patent for it, I shall be as rich as Croesus," wrote Thomas Dilke (*Lover's Luck,* 1696).

ride for a fall, to To behave recklessly and heedlessly. The analogy to the daredevil rider has been around since the late nineteenth century. J. D. Salinger used it in *The Catcher in the Rye* (1951): "I have a feeling that you're riding for some kind of a terrible, terrible fall."

ride hell (bent) for leather, to To move as fast as possible. *Hell* in this expression dates from the nineteenth century and simply implies very fast (as in "to go like hell"); the origin of *leather,* however, is no longer known. The most common citation is Rudyard Kipling's poem "Shillin' a Day" (1892): "When we rode Hell-for-leather, Both squadrons together." The variant, *hell-bent,* means stubbornly determined (or "bent on going to hell") as well as very fast, and is an early nineteenth-century Americanism. Sue MacVeigh used it in her 1940 murder mystery, *Streamlined Murder:* "It was going hell-bent for election."

ride herd on, to To control, boss. This phrase originally meant to control or guard a herd of cattle by riding on its perimeter. Its figurative use dates from the late nineteenth century, and it remains current. The mystery novelist Ed McBain used it in *Long Time No See* (1977): "Two men who should be taking care of people getting robbed or mugged, go to waste our time instead of riding herd on a bunch of street hoodlums."

ride off into the sunset, to A more or less happy ending or resolution. This cliché was originally a visual one—the classic final scene of the western films so popular from the 1930s on, in which the cowboy hero, having vanquished the evildoers, literally rides off into the sunset. It was transferred to other happy endings, usually with some irony, in the mid-twentieth century. "I didn't even bother getting mad at your crack about me going off into the sunset," wrote William Goldman (*Magic,* 1967).

ride one's hobbyhorse, to To dwell on one's favorite theory or project. The term alludes to the popular children's toy, a stick mounted with a horse's head on which youngsters "ride." It was transferred to pet schemes and ideas by the early seventeenth century. "Almost every person hath some hobby horse or other wherein he prides himself," wrote Sir Matthew Hale in 1676. See also AX TO GRIND.

ride roughshod over, to To act without consideration for another's feelings or interests. The term comes from the seventeenth-century practice of arming cavalry horses with horseshoes mounted with projecting nails or points. This not only gave the horses better footing on slippery terrain but also served as a weapon against fallen enemy troops. Within the next hundred years or so the term was transferred to domineering behavior, overriding others without regard or respect. An 1861 issue of the *Saturday Review* stated, "We have ridden roughshod over neutrals in our time."

ridiculous to the sublime, from the There is surprisingly little difference between the wonderful and the extremely silly. The expression linking "ridiculous" and "sublime" originated with Tom Paine in *The Age of Reason* (1794): "The sublime and the ridiculous are often so nearly related that it is difficult to class them separately. One step above the sublime makes the ridiculous, and one step above the ridiculous makes the sublime again." Napoleon, who admired Paine, repeated it in French about 1812; his version was translated as "From the sublime to the ridiculous there is only one step." The two qualities have been paired in this way ever since.

right as rain In good shape, correct. This simile does not make a great deal of sense, even in rainy Great Britain, where it originated, but it has survived *right as a trivet* (because a trivet is a tripod and therefore stands firm), *as a glove, my leg,* and numerous others. Perhaps the "right as" here originally signified "dependable as." In any event, the term has been around since the late nineteenth century.

right away Immediately, at once. This cliché, which dates from the early nineteenth century, uses *right* as an intensifier, a usage dating from about 1200, and *away* in the sense of "at once," a usage dating from the early 1600s. The term is an Americanism, the British equivalent being *straightaway.* William Safire points out that Dickens noticed it while visiting America in 1842, saying "I saw now that 'Right away' and 'Directly' were one and the same thing" (*American Notes,* Chapter II).

right off the bat Spontaneously, immediately, without forethought. This term comes from baseball and presumably alludes to something being done as quickly as a ball leaves the bat after being hit. Dating from the late nineteenth century, it began life as *hot from the bat.* A *New Yorker* article from 1955 stated: "You can tell right off the bat that they're wicked."

right on! Keep going; you're on the right track/doing well. This term dates from the early twentieth century, and there is some dispute over its origin. Several sources trace it to the 1920s in African-American speech; another holds it is an American version of the British *Bang on!* used by airmen during World War II, or possibly a shortening of *Right on target.* Still another holds it is a shortening of *Right on cue,* a reference to uttering the correct lines in a play. In any event, it became widely used in the 1950s and

1960s. Kate Millett had it in *Flying* (1974): "Right on, Vita, so you must have waged your woman's war for years."

right/wrong place at the right time, to be in the To be where one can/cannot take advantage of an opportunity. The adjective *right* in this phrase, which dates from the second half of the nineteenth century, is used in the sense of "fitting" or "appropriate." It is often used with reference to logistics, as H.W.V. Stuart did in *Egypt after the War* (1883): "Her Commander's knack of being in the right place at the right time." Other versions are *to be in the right place at the wrong time,* indicating one's timing is bad for taking advantage of something, and *the wrong place at the wrong time,* for when one is hopelessly out of luck.

right scent See WRONG SCENT.

right tack/track, to take/on the To take or be on the correct course of action or reasoning. The first expression refers to the tack of a sailing ship—that is, its course when it is tacking (steering in zigzag fashion when sailing to windward). The word "tack" was being transferred to a course of action by 1675. The second term, which dates from about 1880, alludes to the direction of a path. Both have antonyms—on the wrong tack or track—denoting a mistaken course of action or reasoning.

right up one's alley, to be To be in one's particular specialty or to one's precise taste. The word *alley* has long been used for one's special province; Francis Bacon so used it in his essay *Of Cunning* (1612): "Such men . . . are good but in their own Alley." *Up one's alley,* however, is a twentieth-century turn of phrase. Margaret Carpenter used it in her novel *Experiment Perilous* (1943): "It isn't up my alley at all." See also NOT MY CUP OF TEA.

ring down the curtain (on), to To bring something to a conclusion. In the nineteenth-century theater a bell rung backstage was often used as a signal to lower the curtain, signifying the end of a scene or act. Thackeray recorded it thus (*The End of the Play*): "The play is done, the curtain drops, slow falling to the prompter's bell." It was transferred to other kinds of ending by the early twentieth century.

ring of truth, the It sounds genuine. This term alludes to the practice of judging a genuine coin by its "ring" or sound, which dates from the days when coins had intrinsic value because they were made of precious metals. Frederick W. Robinson used it in a sermon in 1850: "Truth, so to speak, has a certain ring by which it may be known."

rings a bell, that That seems familiar or calls something to mind. This expression alludes to a memory being summoned in the same way as the bell of a telephone or door summons one to answer. Dating from the early twentieth century, the term appeared in Nicholas Monsarrat's *This Is a Schoolroom* (1939): "The things we talked about . . . rang no bell."

ring the changes, to To try every possible variation in doing or saying something. The term refers to the ancient English art of change-ringing, in which a series of tuned church bells are rung in as many different sequences as possible. Depending on the number of bells, a great many changes are possible—for example, 720 with six bells. The term was transferred to other kinds of variation by the early seventeenth century, as in T. Adams's *Devil's Banquet* (1614): "Some ring the changes of opinions." In the late eighteenth century the term also was used for a swindle in which something inferior was substituted for an article of quality; this usage is obsolete.

ripe old age Advanced in years, quite old. This expression is itself of a ripe old age—it dates from the second half of the fourteenth century—and is generally used in a positive, admiring sense. W. Somerset Maugham used it in *Creatures of Circumstance* (1947): ". . . a little house in the country where he could potter about till death claimed him at a ripe old age."

rise and shine Time to wake up. This term originated as a military order in the late nineteenth century. *Shine* presumably refers to acting lively even though one wants nothing more than to stay in bed. Rudyard Kipling used it figuratively in *Diversity of Creatures* (1917): "A high sun over Asia shouting: 'Rise and shine!'"

risen from/through the ranks A self-made man or woman; those who have worked their way to the top. Originally this term described an officer who had worked his way up from the rank of private, a rare achievement. John Ruskin used it figuratively in an 1853 letter: "Mr. Beveridge . . . rose from the ranks—as Jephson did." See also RAGS TO RICHES; RANK AND FILE.

rising tide, a A strong trend. The ocean's tides have been transferred to the flow of events and feelings since Shakespeare's day. Indeed, Shakespeare wrote, "There is a tide in the affairs of men, which, taken at the flood, leads on to fortune" (*Julius Caesar,* 4.3). A strong upward trend, as signified by the cliché, may refer to public support, as in Benjamin Jewett's statement (*The Dialogues of Plato,* 1875), "He would stem the rising tide of revolution."

risk life and limb, to To take a serious chance; to jeopardize one's life. This extravagant hyperbole for courting danger has been around since the seventeenth century, even though strictly speaking it makes little sense (life, after all, comprises one's limbs as well). "The Turk meddles not with life and limb," wrote James Howell in a letter (1623), and Thomas Burton's diary entry of 1658 states, "They venture life and member."

rob Peter to pay Paul, to To take funds from one source in order to pay another; to shift a debt. According to legend, the abbey church of St. Peter's, in Westminster, was made into a cathedral in 1540, but ten years later it was joined to the diocese of London and many of its estates were appropriated to pay for the repairs of St. Paul's Cathedral; hence St. Peter was "robbed" for the sake of St. Paul. Appealing as this source for the cliché may be, the expression actually was first used by John Wycliffe about 1340, when he wrote, "How should God approve that you rob Peter and give this robbery to Paul in the name of Christ?" In the mid-1950s George J. Hecht, founder and publisher of *Parents Magazine,* went to Washington to lobby—in the morning for lower postal rates for magazine publishers, and in the afternoon for larger appropriations to the Children's Bureau, whereupon he was accused of trying to rob both Peter and Paul.

rocket scientist, you don't have to be a This problem or idea is not that difficult to understand. This hyperbolic colloquialism dates from the mid-twentieth century, as does its synonym, *you don't have to be a brain surgeon.* Clearly they imply that these professions require unusual intellectual acumen. Reporting on an economic forum, the *Boston Globe* quoted former President Bill Clinton, "You want to save 4 million lives? Give them the medicine. It's not rocket science" (Jan. 28, 2005). Also, "And then he got murdered. Doesn't take a rocket scientist to figure there's a lot more to it than I thought" (David Baldacci, *Hour Gam,* 2004). See also NO-BRAINER.

rock of ages An unfailing source of strength. The term was originally a religious one, a translation from the Hebrew in the Bible (Isaiah 26:4), which the King James version has as "everlasting strength." It later was variously defined as God, religious faith, and salvation. The term became widely known through a hymn of that name published in *Gospel Magazine* in 1775. Its author, Augustus Montague Toplady, was addressing Jesus when he wrote "Rock of Ages, cleft for me, let me hide myself in Thee." Subsequently, the term was sometimes used more lightly to describe any highly reliable source of support.

rocks in one's head, to have To say or do something crazy, ridiculous, or stupid. This slangy expression, often used in a not very polite response to a bizarre statement or action, dates from about 1940. Presumably it accuses the person of having rocks instead of brains, as in "Drive all of two blocks to get the paper? Do you have rocks in your head?"

rock the boat, to To disturb a stable situation. The analogy here is to capsizing a small craft, such as a canoe, by moving about carelessly. Current on both sides of the Atlantic since the 1920s, it became the title of a song, "Sit Down, You're Rockin' the Boat," in the popular musical comedy *Guys and Dolls* (1950) by Frank Loesser. The song, performed on Broadway by Stubby Kaye in the role of Nicely-Nicely, was a consistent showstopper and did much to popularize the term.

rogues gallery Originally, a portrayal of a group of disreputable individuals, such as wanted criminals, but later used humorously for any group photograph. The term, also spelled *rogue's gallery,* originated in the mid-1800s for a collection of criminals' portraits. A century later it was used more lightly, as in "Bob Dylan, Arthur Lee, Keith Richard, Bob Marley—the rogue's gallery of rebel input that forms the hard stuff at the centre of rock" (Kathy McKnight and John Tobler *Bob Marley: The Roots of Reggae,* 1977).

role model An individual whose behavior serves as an exemplar to others. This expression, dating from the second half of the 1900s, alludes to acting out parts in a theatrical production. It appeared in the *New York Times Magazine* (June 26, 1977): "If the teacher was a 'role model' parents were obviously unaware of it."

rolling stone gathers no moss, a Someone who keeps moving and changing will not settle down and progress. This ancient proverb, first stated in this form by Erasmus in *Adagia* (1523), appears in numerous languages. For the first three hundred years or so it was nearly always voiced as a kind of reprimand to those who would not settle down and make good. By the mid-nineteenth century, however, the validity of this sentiment was being questioned. In Edward B. Ramsay's *Reminiscences of Scottish Life* (1858) a character replied to this adage, "Ay, but can ye tell me what guid the fog [moss] does to the stane?" Shaw later wrote (Preface to *Misalliance,* 1914), "We keep repeating the silly proverb that rolling stones gather no moss, as if moss were a desirable parasite." Today we may call the inveterate traveler, job-changer, or mover "a rolling stone." The term gained further currency in the 1960s with a very popular British rock group that called itself the Rolling Stones and a popular song by Bob Dylan, "Like a Rolling Stone" (1965).

roll with the punches, to To adapt to adversity. The term comes from boxing, in which a contestant shifts his body to the side so as to deflect the full force of the opponent's blow. By the mid-twentieth century it had become a metaphor for dealing with difficult circumstances, as in H. Kurnitz's *Invasion of Privacy* (1956): "He had mastered the tack of rolling with the punches, rendering himself invisible when a crisis darkened the skies."

Rome was not built in a day Be patient; major achievements take time. This expression was already a proverb in the late twelfth century, and then appeared in two famous English proverb collections of the sixteenth century, Richard Taverner's (1539) and John Heywood's (1546). The saying is still current.

root of the matter, the The essence of something; the true basis or cause. This term appears in the Bible (Job 19:28): "Why persecute him, seeing the root of the matter is found in me?" It is still used as a metaphor for the ultimate cause.

rose by any other name, a The name does not reflect the basic qualities of something or someone. The cliché is a direct quotation from Shakespeare's *Romeo and Juliet* (2:2), in which Juliet says, "What's in a name? that which we call a rose by any other name would smell as sweet; so Romeo would, were he not Romeo called." Today it is often used jokingly, as it was by Clyde Jinks in 1901 (*Captain Jinks*): "A cabbage by any other name would swell as sweet."

rose-colored glasses, to look/see through To view events and people very positively, seeing only their good points; unmitigated optimism. This term began to be used figuratively by the 1850s. "I was young . . . and I saw everything through rose-coloured spectacles," wrote Princess Pauline Metternich (*Days That Are No More,* 1921). A twentieth-century synonym is *to see the glass half full,* to see the favorable aspect of circumstances, to look on the bright side. The antonym, *to see the glass half empty,* is also current. "This . . . group . . . looks at a reservoir that is half full and doomfully declares that it's half empty" *(New York Times,* 1981).

rotten apple spoils the barrel, a One bad individual can spoil an entire group. The idea was stated as long ago as the fourteenth century (in a Latin proverb sometimes translated as "the rotten apple injures its neighbors"), long before the mechanism of spreading mold or other plant disease was understood. Benjamin Franklin repeated the sentiment in *Poor Richard's Almanack* (1736): "The rotten apple spoils his companion."

rough and ready Crude but vigorous and ready for action. This Americanism dates from the early nineteenth century. In print it first appeared in a collection of *Diaries and Letters* (1810) by F. J. Jackson: "A more rough and ready state of things than we had before been accustomed to." In the 1840s it became the nickname for General Zachary Taylor, "Old Rough and Ready," hero of the Mexican War (1846–48) and later the twelfth president of the United States. By then the term was used in England as well; it appears in Robert Browning's "Bishop Blougram's Apology" (1855): "You, for example, clever to a fault, The rough and ready man who write apace, Read somewhat seldomer, think perhaps even less."

rough and tumble Violent and disorderly action; a fight without rules. This early nineteenth-century Americanism may have originated in boxing—at least it was so defined by John Bartlett in 1859, although his work antedated the Queensberry rules of the ring by some years, and most boxing was of the rough-and-tumble variety. Nevertheless, the term was generally applied only to physical fights of various kinds until the second half of the century, when it began to be used more figuratively. Oliver Wendell Holmes (*The Poet at the Breakfast-Table,* 1872) wrote "That circle of rough-and-tumble political life."

rough diamond See DIAMOND IN THE ROUGH.

round peg in a square hole, a A misfit, one not suited for the job or position at hand. This graphic image was being transferred to individuals unsuited for various tasks by 1800 or so. Occasionally it was (and still is) put the other way, *a square peg in a round hole.* Historian Albany Fonblanque used both (*England under Seven Administrations,* 1836): "Sir Robert Peel was a smooth round peg in a sharp-cornered square hole, and Lord Lyndhurst is a rectangular square-cut peg in a smooth round hole."

rub elbows with, to To associate unexpectedly closely with. This term originated in Britain as *rub shoulders with,* which is still the more common locution there. Thackeray used it in his Book of Snobs (1848): "She had rubbed shoulders with the great." *Elbows* are preferred in America, as in Upton Sinclair's muckraking novel, *The Jungle* (1906): "Young white girls from the country rubbing elbows with big buck Negroes with daggers in their boots."

rub it in, to To stress something unpleasant or annoying in a teasing way; to ADD INSULT TO INJURY. The *it* in this expression may well be the salt that is in the much older related term, to *rub salt into a wound,* which dates from late medieval times (or earlier) and is still current. *Rubbing it in* originated in America; T. A. Burke used it in 1851 (*Polly Peaseblossom's Wedding*): "When it comes to rubbin' it in, I always . . . roars up." Also related is the cliché *to rub one's nose in it,* meaning to remind one of a humiliating error or experience. "I've said I'm sorry . . . Don't rub my nose in it," wrote P. Hubbard (*Flush as May,* 1963). It alludes to rubbing a dog's nose in a mess it has made.

rub the wrong way, to To annoy. This expression transfers rubbing a cat's fur in the wrong direction to irritating a human being. (See also AGAINST THE GRAIN.) The British locution is to rub someone *up* the wrong way and dates from the mid-nineteenth century. "Don't rub her prejudices up the wrong way," wrote H. Aïdé (*Carr of Carrlyou,* 1862).

ruffle someone's feathers, to To irritate someone. The transfer of stiffened, upright feathers from angry birds to human beings took place around 1800. "The Dean ruffled his plumage and said, with some asperity . . . ," wrote Frederic W. Farrar (*Julian Home,* 1859).

rule of thumb A rough measure or method, without precise mathematical or scientific basis. This term, which probably alluded to using one's thumb as an approximate measuring device, has been around since the seventeenth century and made it into James Kelly's collection of Scottish proverbs (1721): "No rule so good as rule of thumb, if it hit. But it seldome hits!" Some individuals have pointed to the "rule" proposed in 1782 by an English judge, Francis Buller, who proclaimed that men had the right to beat their wives provided that the stick used was no thicker than the husband's thumb. Misinterpretation linked it to the cliché, which is about a century older and today is never used in this context.

rule the roost, to To be the boss. This term originated as rule the *roast* in the fifteenth century. Possibly it even then referred to the rooster, who decides which hen should roost near him. On the other hand, Thomas Heywood, in his *History of Women* (c. 1630), stated, "Her that ruled the roast in the kitchen," so perhaps it did mean whoever held sway over the kitchen, the heart of a household. Shakespeare used it more broadly, however. In *Henry VI, Part 2* (1.1) he refers to "the new-made duke that rules the roast." In any event, it has been used for bossing anything from a family to an entire nation.

rule with an iron hand/rod, to Stern or tyrannical rule. This term comes from Tyndall's translation of the Bible (1526): "And he shall rule them with a rodde of yron." It was later transferred to any kind of stern domination, either serious or ironic. For the latter, Anthony Trollope used it in *Barchester Towers* (1857): "In matters domestic she . . . ruled with a rod of iron." See also IRON HAND (IN A VELVET GLOVE).

run amok, to To go crazy; to behave in a wild, frenzied manner. This term is based on the Malay word *amok,* meaning "a state of frenzy." In England, however, it was at first spelled *amuck,* as in Andrew Marvell's account (*The Rehearsal Transposed,* 1672): "Like a raging Indian . . . he runs a mucke (as they cal it there) stabbing every man he meets."

run around in circles, to To proceed indecisively or aimlessly; a fruitless endeavor. This American colloquialism dates from the first half of the twentieth century. Patricia Wentworth wrote (*Pursuit of a Parcel,* 1942), "He had been rushing around in circles." See also GO AROUND IN CIRCLES.

run a tight ship, to To direct a well-managed operation or strictly disciplined organization. This expression, dating from the second half of the twentieth century, alludes to a vessel whose ropes are taut (tight) and seams well caulked, indicating that it is well managed. The *Saturday Review of Literature* (June 24, 1972) stated: "The two student judges . . . ran a tight ship. Firm commands—'There will be no knitting in my courtroom.'"

run circles/rings around, to To defeat decisively in a contest; to outdo. The implication here is that a runner moving in circles can still beat another running in a straight line. The term began to appear in print in the 1890s. "He could run rings round us in everything," wrote G. Parker in the *Westminster Gazette* (1894).

run for one's money, (give) a A close contest or strong challenge; to give a good return for one's expense. This term may come from the racetrack, where it is used to describe deriving pleasurable excitement from a horse race even if one does not win all one's bets. The term appeared in a dictionary of slang in 1874 and has been used ever since. "They have had what is called in some circles a good run for their money," reported the *Pall Mall Gazette* in 1889.

run in the blood/family, to To be characteristic of a family or peculiar to a nation, ethnic group, or other group. Richard Brinsley Sheridan used this expression in 1777 in *The School for Scandal* (3.3): "Learning that had run in the family like an heirloom!"

run its course, to To continue to the end; until it runs out. The word *course,* the ground on which a race is run, was used figuratively for the continuous process of time, events, or an action from the sixteenth century on. "The yeare hath runne his course," wrote Abraham Fleming (*A Panoplie of Epistles,* 1576).

run it up the flagpole (and see who salutes), let's Let's try this out and see what the reaction is. This cliché, alluding to raising an actual flag up a mast or flagpole, is one of a number of phrases coined in the mid-1900s in the Madison Avenue advertising industry for trying out ads, campaigns, slogans, and the like. Another is THAT'S HOW THE COOKIE CRUMBLES. The *New Statesman* so identified it on March 25, 1966: "The decision was made—in the admen's jargon that comes naturally to Tory strategists—to run it up the flagpole and see if anyone saluted." It may be dying out.

run like clockwork, to To operate with extreme regularity. The transfer from a clock mechanism to other areas dates from the late seventeenth century. "The king's last years passed as regularly as clockwork," wrote Hugh Walpole (*Reminiscences,* 1789).

running battle An ongoing fight. The term originated in naval warfare in the late 1600s, when it signified a battle carried on while a vessel was retreating (running away). Later it was transferred and used figuratively, as in one of comedian Groucho Marx's letters (1967) in which he wrote of a running battle with Warner Brothers. See also the quotation under AT SWORDS' POINTS.

running on empty At the end of one's resources. This twentieth-century Americanism alludes to an automobile about to run out of gas, with the gauge indicating that the tank is empty. The expression gained currency with Jackson Browne's popular song "Runnin' on Empty" (1978).

run off at the mouth, to To talk incessantly. The image conveyed is that of a river of words flowing ceaselessly from someone's mouth, a case of logorrhea (verbal diarrhea). An American slang term dating from about 1900, it was defined in a 1909 issue of *Dialect Notes.* "I'm a pig coming over here and running off at the mouth," wrote Alison Lurie (*Love and Friendship,* 1962).

run of the mill An ordinary, uneventful sequence of events. The *run* in this term refers to a mill's average output, before it has been graded or sorted. Also stated as *run of the mine* or the *kiln,* these terms come from the late nineteenth century. They began to be used figuratively in the twentieth century, as in "A darned sight better-looking than the run of the mill wives" (*Hearst's International,* 1930). It is also written run-of-the-mill.

run one's head against (into) a brick/stone wall, to To make vain efforts against insurmountable difficulties. This expression, with its vivid image of futility, dates from the sixteenth century, when John Lyly (or some other author) wrote, "Thou shalt . . . have thy head runne against a stone wall" (1589). Other equally hard objects, like doors, were cited in similar fashion. By 1887, however, it was "If we run our heads against walls we're safe to hurt ourselves" (M. Sergeant, *Jacobi's Wife,* 1.1).

run out of steam, to To become weary; to exhaust one's energy. Although steam engines were a nineteenth-century invention, this term comes from the mid-twentieth century. Dick Francis used it in *Slayride* (1973): "When I'd run out of steam, they would begin to nod."

run riot, to To act without restraint or control; to overrun, to grow unrestrainedly. The earliest use of this term dates from the early sixteenth century and appears in a book on farming, John Fitzherbert's *The Boke of Husbandry* (1523): "Breake thy tenure, and ren ryot at large." It is the primary meaning of *riot*—unruliness and disorder—that was being transferred here and has been so used ever since. "Ye suffer your Tongues to run ryot," wrote Bishop Joseph Hall *(Works,* 1656).

run that by me again Please repeat what you just said. This colloquialism became popular in the 1960s, when television shows were repeated ("re-run") and instant replays were developed in sportscasts. It soon came into more general use as a request for a repetition.

run the gamut, to To extend over the entire range. The word *gamut* comes from Guido of Arezzo's scale, a contraction of *gamma,* representing the lowest note of the medieval scale, G, and *ut,* the first note in any given scale (later called *do*). Acid-tongued Dorothy Parker was quoted as saying of actress Katharine Hepburn's stage performance in *The Lake* (1933), "She runs the gamut of emotions from A to B"—that is, a very limited range of emotions.

run the gauntlet, to To be exposed to a course of danger, trying conditions, or criticism. The term originated in the seventeenth century, when the Germans adopted this military punishment from the Swedes. It consisted of stripping a man to the waist and making him run between two rows of soldiers, who struck him with sticks or knotted cords. The passage he ran was *gatloppe* in Swedish and *gantloppe* or *gantlope* in German. It was adopted as a civilian punishment in the American colonies and was spelled *gantlet* or *gauntlet.* "They have run the gauntlet of the years," wrote Oliver Wendell Holmes (*The Autocrat of the Breakfast-Table,* 1858).

run the show, to To take charge. Originating in the mid-nineteenth-century theater, this term was transferred to being responsible for any kind of enterprise. John Braine used it in *Room at the Top* (1957): "The accountants and the engineers run the show no matter who's in charge." See also CALL THE SHOTS.

run to earth, to To find. The term comes from hunting, when the hounds run their quarry to its "earth" or "lair." This meaning of "earth" survives only in the cliché, which had been transferred to tracking down just about anything or anyone by the mid-nineteenth century. The *OED* cites an 1888 issue of *The Spectator:* "All the men who helped to run to earth the various members of the Ruthven family."

run to seed, to To become old and decrepit. Plants that are allowed to set seed after flowering either become bitter to the taste (lettuce) or will not bloom as well the following year (daffodils, tulips). Henry Fielding used the term figuratively in an essay of 1740: "For Virtue itself by growing too exuberant and . . . by running to seed changes its very nature."

run with the hare, hunt with the hounds, to To stay in favor with two opponents; to take both sides at the same time. This expression, with its analogy to being both hunted and hunter, dates from the fifteenth century and appeared in Heywood's 1546 proverb collection. John Lyly used it in *Euphues* (1580): "Whatsoeuer I speake to men, the same also I speake to women, I meane not to run with the Hare and holde with the Hounde." The meaning is quite different from a similar-sounding cliché, *to run with the pack,* which means to take the same side as the majority. However, both these terms may be dying out in America.

Russian roulette, to play To engage in a potentially fatal undertaking. The term refers to a game popularized by Russian officers at the czar's court in which each player in turn, using a revolver that contains just one bullet, spins the cylinder, aims at his own head, and pulls the trigger. With a six-chamber cylinder, there is one chance in six that he will kill himself. The term was transferred to other highly risky undertakings in the first half of the twentieth century. "Abusive parents are often the scarred survivors of generations of Russian roulette," stated an article in the medical journal the *Lancet* (1976).

sack, to get/give the To be fired or dismissed from work; to fire someone. This slangy expression dates from the seventeenth century or even earlier, probably originating in France. In those days workmen provided their own tools and carried them in a bag—*sac* in French—which they took away with them upon leaving. The term appears in Randle Cotgrave's dictionary of 1611, under *sac* ("*On luy a donné son sac*—said of a servant whom his master hath put away"), and a similar term was used in Dutch as well. A newer synonym is *to get/give the ax,* which dates from the second half of the 1800s and alludes to the executioner's ax. Both expressions also have been reduced to verbs meaning "to fire": *to sack someone* ("I got sacked this morning"), or *to ax someone/something* ("The board axed the proposal for a new school building").

sackcloth and ashes, to be in To be penitent or contrite; in a state of repentance. This term alludes to the ancient Hebrew custom of donning a coarse, dark cloth from which sacks were made and dusting oneself with ashes to signify one's humility before God. It is mentioned in the Bible: "And I set my face unto the Lord God, to seek by prayer and supplications, with fasting, and sackcloth, and ashes" (Daniel 9:3). The term may be obsolescent.

sacred cow A person, group, or institution considered exempt from questioning or criticism. The term alludes to the Hindu view of cows, which are considered symbolic of God's generosity to humanity. The British coined the term in India in the late nineteenth century, and it began to be used metaphorically by 1900 or so. Margaret Mitchell used it in *Gone With the Wind* (1936): "I think of my brother, living among the sacred cows of Charleston, and most reverent towards them."

sadder and/but wiser Enlightened by an unfortunate experience; learning from one's mistakes. The pairing of these two thoughts appears in the concluding stanza of Coleridge's "The Rime of the Ancient Mariner" (1798): "He went like one that hath been stunned,/And is of sense forlorn:/A sadder and a wiser man,/He rose the morrow morn."

sad sack, a A pathetically inept individual. The term comes from a cartoon character named Sad Sack, invented by Sgt. George Baker and very popular during World War II. Baker's representation of a limp-looking soldier in ill-fitting, loose-hanging uniform, who tried to do his best but was neither smart nor lucky and consequently failed at whatever he undertook, caught on, and the name was transferred to the inept in civilian life.

sad state of affairs, a An unhappy condition, unfortunate circumstances. The use of *state of affairs* to describe events or circumstances originated as the more ambiguous *state of things,* which was first recorded in 1555. *Affairs* began to be used about two centuries later. R. L. Green played on it in *The Land of Lord High Tiger:* "Sad affairs of State! Sad state of affairs! Affairs of a sad state." It is sometimes put as *sorry state of affairs.*

safe and sound Out of danger and unharmed. This alliterative description dates from at least 1300, when it appeared in a Middle English treatise, *Cursor Mundi,* by an unknown author, and has been repeated ever since. Shakespeare (*A Comedy of Errors*) and Byron (*Don Juan*) are among the many poets undeterred by its sound, which must have been hackneyed by 1600.

safe haven A sanctuary. This term is redundant, since *haven* means "a safe place." It is quite old, the earliest citation in the *OED* being from 1581. *Haven* also was for a time used as a verb, meaning "to shelter," as in Robert Southey's poem of 1795, "Safe haven'd from the sea." The *Times* of London (Aug. 15, 1865) had the current usage: "One safe haven where no nicotine perfume intrudes . . ."

sail close to (near) the wind, to To come close to breaking a law or approaching impropriety. The analogy to sailing dangerously close to the wind began to be made in the nineteenth century. Coleridge's son Hartley, in a critical edition of the plays of Massinger and Ford (1840), used it: "Her language sails a little too near the wind." It is heard less often today.

sail under false colors, to To behave deceptively; to misrepresent oneself deliberately. The term comes from maritime piracy, rampant from ancient times until about 1825 in Atlantic and Mediterranean waters and still existing in parts of the Pacific. In order to deceive their prey, pirates would run a "friendly flag"—that is, "false colors"—to lure their victims close enough so that they could easily be captured. The term began to be used figuratively in the late seventeenth century. Robert Louis Stevenson used it in *St. Ives* (1897): "I had so much wisdom as to sail under false colours in this foolish jaunt of mine."

salad days, one's Inexperienced youth, when one is still very green (i.e., unripe). The term comes from Shakespeare, who probably coined it: "My salad days, when I was green in judgement: cold in blood" (*Antony and Cleopatra,* 1.5).

salt away, to To put aside funds for future use. Treating fish or meat with salt is an ancient way of preserving it, antedating modern refrigeration by centuries. In the nineteenth century the term, also put as *to salt down,* began to be used figuratively for saving money. "No one to hinder you from salting away as many millions as you can carry off!" wrote R. W. Chambers (*Maids of Paradise,* 1902). Also see SAVE FOR A RAINY DAY.

salt of the earth, the An individual or group of people considered to be the best or noblest of the kind. Salt has long been considered a valuable commodity, and this metaphor dates from biblical times. According to the Gospel of Matthew (5:13), Jesus told those who were persecuted for their loyalty to him, "Ye are the salt of the earth." The term has been so used ever since.

same difference No difference whatever, the same thing. This colloquialism dates from about 1940. Usually spoken with a bit of a shrug, it appears in such contexts as "He worked for them four years, or was it five? Same difference."

same old rigmarole, the An elaborate traditional procedure; nonsensical talk. The word *rigmarole* is believed to be a corruption of *ragman roll,* a name given in the thirteenth century to the "rolls" of homage and fealty given by the clergy and barons to the king. The rolls looked ragged because numerous seals were attached to them. The portmanteau word began to appear in print in the early 1700s and was mainly applied to a rambling, disconnected discourse. Byron (*Don Juan,* 1818) wrote, "His speech was a fine sample, on the whole, of rhetoric, which the learn'd call *rigmarole,*" and George Meredith wrote in *Richard Feverel* (1859), "You never heard such a rigmarole." In the twentieth century the term was increasingly used for a tiresomely elaborate procedure, such as an exceptionally complicated graduation ceremony, with "same old" indicating that one would have to undergo it yet again.

A newer synonym is *the same old song and dance,* meaning an overfamiliar, hackneyed routine. *Maclean's Magazine* of November 19, 1979, stated: "For singing-telegram junkies bored by the same old song and dance, Cookie climbs into a furry suit to deliver Gorillagrams." Still newer is the slangy *same old, same old,* a description of anything that has been repeated too often. For example, "When John asked her about her vacation, she said 'Same old, same old; we've been going to the beach for twenty years.'"

sauce for the goose is sauce for the gander, what's What's good for one is good for the other; it applies to both (especially, male and female, or husband and wife). John Ray included this expression in his 1678 proverb collection and termed it "a woman's Proverb." An early assertion of sexual equity, it has since been applied both in instances of male and female and in more general terms. The former is meant in Lawrence Block's novel *A Stab in* *the Dark* (1981): "I knew she had accused her husband of infidelity, so I thought she might be getting a bit of sauce for the goose."

saved by the bell A last-minute reprieve. The bell referred to is the one rung at the end of a round of boxing, and it "saves" the boxer who has been knocked down if it rings before he has been counted "out." Transferring the term to other kinds of fortunate intervention dates from the mid-twentieth century. "'Then I don't know it,' I told him, saved by the bell," wrote Alan Sillitoe (*The Loneliness of the Long-Distance Runner,* 1959).

save face, to To avoid embarrassment; to redeem one's dignity. The *face* here means outward appearances, the face that one presents to the world. The concept itself is often regarded as quintessentially Asian but actually is far more widespread, and perhaps it always has been. A typical example of saving face might be to resign before one is fired. The term has been around since about 1900. W. Somerset Maugham used it in his first important novel, *Of Human Bondage* (1915): "To save his face he began making suggestions for altering it."

save for a rainy day, to To put something aside for a future time of need. To keep something for future use is a very old concept indeed; to call hard times a "rainy day" dates from the sixteenth century. Nicholas Breton used it in 1582 (Works): "Wise men say keepe somewhat till a rainy day." Alternative locutions include to *lay up* for a rainy day (John Clarke, 1639), *laying by against* a rainy day (Samuel Pepys, 1666), and *putting something by* for a rainy day. Ring Lardner (*Anniversary,* 1926) used it ironically: "Louis was saving for a rainy day, and his wife had long ago given up praying for rain." See also SALT AWAY.

save one's skin, to To save one's life. The skin in question is usually one's own, and it is hard to imagine life going on without it. The term has been around since Roman times. In English it was in print by 1642: "Æquivocating with our conscience . . . for the saving of our owne skin" (Daniel Rogers, *Naaman the Syrian*).

save your breath Don't bother to tell me about it. The image of expending one's breath to utter what no one wants to hear dates from the sixteenth century. In early English parlance it often was to *keep* one's breath (or wind) to cool one's pottage/porridge/broth (by blowing on it). Jonathan Swift (*Polite Conversation,* 1738) wrote, "Pray keep your breath to cool your porridge." Today the food-cooling phrase is obsolete, but the first portion survives as a cliché. See also WASTE ONE'S BREATH.

saving grace, a A single redeeming quality, usually cited as compensating for other, negative characteristics. The term, which alludes to the theological concept of salvation from eternal damnation, was used literally from the late sixteenth century on. It began to be transferred to matters of somewhat lighter import in the late nineteenth century. J. B. Priestley so used it (*Self-Selected Essays,* 1932): "Here, in its plain lack of ideas, is the saving grace of this dull company."

say uncle, to To concede defeat. Also put as *cry uncle,* it is the schoolyard equivalent of "say when you've had enough of this battle." The term is an Americanism dating from about 1900, and its original meaning (if any) has been lost. It began to be used figuratively in the mid-twentieth century, as in Budd Schulberg's *What Makes Sammy Run?* (1941): "Okay, I said, I'll cry uncle."

say what? Did I hear you correctly? Is that true? This slangy expression, with the emphasis on *what,* dates from the second half of the twentieth century. Eric Partridge believed it originated in the "ghetto" but did not specify further.

scarce as hen's teeth Singularly rare. Also put as *scarcer than hen's teeth,* this allusion to nonexistent dentition is an Americanism of the nineteenth century. It appeared in James Gilmore's *My Southern Friends* (1863): "Horses are scarcer than hen's teeth around here."

scared silly/stiff/to death, to be To be extremely frightened; panic-stricken. The earliest version of such hyperbolic expressions seems to have been to be scared or frightened *out of one's wits,* which appeared in print in 1697: "Distracted and frighted out of his wits" (Bishop Simon Patrick, *Commentary*). Later it was frightened or scared *out of one's seven senses* (used by Jonathan Swift and Sir Walter Scott), still later replaced by *silly,* with the same meaning. *Stiff* alludes to paralysis by fright, *death* to dying of terror. A mid-twentieth-century equivalent is *to scare the pants off someone* (Ogden Nash, and others). Also see SHAKE IN ONE'S SHOES.

schoolgirl complexion, a Beautiful skin and coloring, without lines, wrinkles, or other signs of aging. This term owes its origin to the advertising campaigns for Palmolive soap, an American product. Allegedly the soap would give or preserve "that schoolgirl complexion," a slogan used from about 1923 through the 1930s. An earlier version was *peach-bloom complexion,* used by Emerson in an 1860 essay (*Conduct of Life: Beauty*) and surviving in a still current term, *peaches-and-cream complexion.*

school of hard knocks Learning from experience, including or especially from one's mistakes. This term comes from the nineteenth century, when advanced education was for the privileged few but many rose through the ranks of industry to considerable achievement. J. A. Froude used it in writing about politics: "The school of hard knocks. Experience teaches slowly, and at the cost of mistakes" (*Short Studies on Great Subjects: Party Politics,* 1850). It was more often heard from successful businessmen who had relatively little formal schooling and proclaimed quite proudly that theirs had been the "school of hard knocks." In the 1940s and 1950s Ray Herrick, a Michigan businessman who had only a grade-school education and created a million-dollar business, would proudly announce that his alma mater was "H.N., the school of 'hard nocks.'"

scout's honor See under CROSS MY HEART.

scratch the surface, to To perform a task or investigate something superficially. This term comes from agriculture, where merely scratching the surface of the earth does not adequately prepare the soil for planting. It was transferred to other activities by the early 1900s. "You haven't seen anything. They didn't scratch the surface here," wrote Lillian Hellman (*Days to Come,* 1936).

scream bloody/blue murder, to To shout loudly in pain, fear, or anger. The second term appears to have originated as a play on the French expletive *morbleu* (*mort bleu* translates as "blue murder"). The Hotten *Dictionary of Slang* (1859) defined it as a desperate or alarming cry. The term was used by Dion Boucicault about 1874: "They were standing by and trying to screech blue murder" (quoted in M. R. Booth, *English Plays of the Nineteenth Century;* cited by *OED*). It is heard less often, at least in America, than the more graphic *bloody murder,* dating from the first half of the 1900s. For example, "The one-year-old who has yelled bloody murder during his physical . . ." (B. Spock, *Problems of Parents,* 1962).

screw loose, to have a To be eccentric or peculiar. To think or act crazily. This term likens a malfunctioning machine or tool, in which a screw needs to be tightened, to a disordered human mind. It originated early in the nineteenth century. "A genius with a screw loose, as we used to say," wrote Edward Fitzgerald in 1833 (*Letters*).

screw up, to To botch, to make a mess of; to make an error. This slangy expression, which some think is a euphemism for the much ruder *to fuck up,* dates from the 1940s, the period of World War II, and may well have originated in the armed forces. Indeed, the army magazine *Yank* had it on December 23, 1942, "You screw up on the drill field! You goof off at inspection." For a synonym from about the same period, see LOUSE UP.

Scylla and Charybdis See BETWEEN SCYLLA AND CHARYBDIS.

sea change, a A radical change, a transformation. Shakespeare coined this cliché in *The Tempest* (1.2): "Nothing of him that doth fade, But doth suffer a sea change Into something rich and strange." Nearly four centuries later, J. A. Jance used it in *Devil's Claw* (2000): "For the very first time . . . she had called her future son-in-law Butch instead of Frederick. It indicated a sea change in her mother's attitude, and that was pretty damned wonderful, too."

sea legs, to get one's To adjust to a new situation. A sailor is said to get his sea legs when he is able to walk steadily despite the rolling and pitching of the vessel. The term was transferred to other kinds of learning experience by 1895, when David Lloyd George used it in a letter: "I have got my sea legs in the House. They now listen to me with deference."

seamy side, the The unsavory or worst aspect. This expression alludes to the wrong side of a garment or other fabric, in which the stitched seams show. It was first transferred by Shakespeare, "He turn'd your wit the seamy side without" (*Othello,* 4.2), and has been used ever since to describe the unfavorable side of things.

seat of one's/the pants, by the Using experience, guesswork, or instinct rather than some calculated or scientific method. The term originated among World War II aviators, who so described flying when instruments were not working and/or weather interfered with visibility. It was transferred to other activities in subsequent decades. M. Walker used it in *The National Front* (1977): "Mussolini had governed by the seat of his pants."

second nature A deeply ingrained habit that makes one behave as if by instinct. This concept is very old—"Custom is second nature" is how it was put by Plutarch, Montaigne, and other early writers—but appeared in English at first only in translations of this proverb. The modern usage dates from the early 1900s. In *The Confidential Clerk* (1954) T. S. Eliot wrote "I do feel more at ease . . . behind a desk. It's second nature."

second to none Outstanding, the best. The idea is older, but the exact expression appeared first in Shakespeare's *The Comedy of Errors* (5.1), in Angelo's description of Antipholus of Syracuse: "Of credit infinite, highly beloved, second to none that lives here." It remains current.

second wind, to get one's To proceed with renewed vigor after a lapse. The allusion here is to athletes who, after initial breathlessness, warm up and resume their regular breathing. In the early twentieth century this phenomenon was transferred to other kinds of undertaking in which, after an initial flagging of energy, one is able to continue with fresh vigor. Josephine Tey used it in *The Franchise Affair* (1946): "Perhaps it was the presence of an ally . . . or perhaps she had just got her second wind."

secret weapon A clandestine item or mode of attack unknown to the enemy. The term came into wide use during World War II, when it was rumored that Hitler was going to launch a powerful secret weapon against Great Britain. Subsequently the term was applied to pilotless planes, robot bombs, rockets, and nuclear bombs. Thereafter it entered the civilian vocabulary, where it is used in sports ("Bill's second serve, stronger than the first, is his secret weapon") and numerous other activities. Edith Simon had it in *The Past Masters* (1953): "See the candid camera at work, that misnamed secret weapon."

see eye to eye, to To agree completely. This allusion to seeing things in the same way first occurred in the Bible, when the prophet Isaiah predicts that, when the Lord is recognized as the one true God, "Thy watchmen shall lift up the voice; with the voice together shall they sing: for they shall see eye to eye" (Isaiah 52:8). Some two thousand years later came the phrase *eyeball to eyeball,* meaning face-to-face. It originated during the Korean War, where it meant face-to-face with the enemy.

seeing is believing Only concrete proof is convincing. The idea dates from ancient Greek times, and the expression appears in numerous proverb collections from 1639 on, in English and many other languages. Some writers disagree. Jesus told his doubting disciple, Thomas, that it was more blessed to believe *without* seeing (John 20:29). Also, "Seeing is believing, says the proverb . . . though, of all our senses, the eyes are the most easily deceived" (Hare, *Guesses at Truth,* c. 1848), and, "Seeing is deceiving. It's eating that's believing" (James Thurber, *Further Fables for Our Time,* 1956).

seek and ye shall find If you want something, look for it. This pragmatic advice dates from ancient Greek times and appears in ancient Roman and Chinese sources as well. It crops up in the Bible: "Ask and it shall be given you; seek, and ye shall find; knock and it shall be opened unto you" (Matthew 7:7–8). Despite the archaic *ye,* it is still current.

see light at the end of a tunnel See LIGHT AT THE END OF A TUNNEL.

seen better days, to have To have declined, to have become less prosperous, more worn, and the like. This term was first used by Shakespeare to describe a decline of fortune; Timon's steward, Flavius, says to his servants, "Let's shake our heads, and say, as 'twere a knell unto our master's fortunes, 'We have seen better days'" (*Timon of Athens,* 4.2). Sir Walter Scott used it to describe aging (*The Lay of the Last Minstrel,* 1805): "His wither'd cheek and tresses grey seem'd to have known a better day." We still use it to describe, for example, a piece of worn-out furniture ("This couch has seen better days").

seen one, seen them all, if/when you've They are all the same. This world-weary assertion was being made by the early nineteenth century. Mark Twain used it in *Innocents Abroad* (1869), "To me it seemed that when I had seen one of these martyrs I had seen them all." See also BEEN THERE, DONE THAT.

see red, to To give way to extreme anger. Some writers believe that this term, which dates from the late nineteenth or early twentieth century, alludes to the red cape waved by the matador to anger a bull. However, there is no real verification for this hypothesis, and the expression more likely reflects the long-standing association of the color red with blood, heat, and fire, in turn associated with anger. Agatha Christie used it in *Death on the Nile* (1937): "Why? Because she thinks I'm not her social equal! Pah—doesn't that make you see red?"

see the light, to To become converted to a new belief, to understand. Originally this term referred exclusively to religious conversion, but by the early nineteenth century it had begun to be used more generally: "He was opposed to a revival of navigation on the Missouri, but now he has seen the light and says he's for it" (*Kansas City Times and Star,* 1889). See also LIGHT AT THE END OF A TUNNEL.

see through someone/something, to To penetrate to the true nature; to overcome deception. This locution dates from the sixteenth century, and the idea is no doubt much older still. "He saw through him, both within and without," wrote Edward Hall (*Chronicles,* c. 1548). Ben Jonson amplified it with another metaphor (*Cynthia's Revels,* 1599, 5.4): "He is a mere peece of glasse, I see through him."

see you later Goodbye. This somewhat loose phrase—one need not necessarily intend to see a person in the future—dates from the latter part of the nineteenth century and has been widely adopted as a farewell. Children play on it with the rhyming *See you later, alligator,* sometimes adding on *in a while, crocodile.* These rhyming plays were popularized in a song, "See You Later, Alligator," by R. C. Guidry, sung in the film *Rock around the Clock* (1956). The telephone equivalent, used to end a conversation, is *Talk to you later,* a more recent phrase that is similarly widespread.

seize the hour/day Take advantage of the moment, enjoy the here and now. This phrase is a translation of the ancient Roman adage *Carpe diem,* first stated by Horace in one of his *Odes* (c. 23 B.C.). Actually, the full statement added *quam minimum credula postero,* trust the future as little as possible.

self-made man, a A man who has become rich and influential through his own actions, without the help of inherited wealth, powerful friends, or similar assistance. This term originated earlier but came into wide use from the nineteenth century on, when the phenomenon itself became more common. Two twentieth-century writers are among those who used it ironically. "A self-made man is one who believes in luck and sends his son to Oxford," wrote the novelist Christina Stead (*House of All Nations,* 1938); and E. B. White (*One Man's Meat,* 1944) wrote, "Luck is not something you can mention in the presence of self-made men."

sell down the river, to To betray. This term arose in the mid-nineteenth-century United States and referred to selling slaves down the Mississippi River, where they would almost certainly be worked to death in the cotton fields. The term was used in its literal sense by Harriet Beecher Stowe in her best-selling novel *Uncle Tom's Cabin,* but by the late nineteenth century it was being used figuratively. P. G. Wodehouse used it in *Small Bachelor* (1927): "When Sigisbee Waddington married for the second time, he to all intents and purposes sold himself down the river."

sell like hot cakes, to To be a great commercial success. *Hot cakes,* an American name for griddle cakes or pancakes since the late seventeenth century—William Penn wrote of "hot cakes and new corn" in 1683—are an extremely popular item at church sales, fairs, and similar events where food stands play an important role. Consequently, they tend to sell out as quickly as they are cooked. By the mid-nineteenth century the term had been transferred to any item that was selling extremely well. Just before the outbreak of the Civil War, O. J. Victor wrote (*Southern Rebellion,* 1860), "Revolvers and patent fire-arms are selling like hot cakes."

sell someone a bill of goods, to To cheat or defraud someone. A "bill of goods," in commercial language, is a quantity or consignment of merchandise. Selling it here means persuading someone to accept something undesirable. The term dates from the early twentieth century. The playwright Eugene O'Neill used it in *Marco Millions* (1924), "Selling a big bill of goods hereabouts, I'll wager, you old rascals?" Or, in the Toronto *Globe and Mail* (Feb. 17, 1968), "There was no production bonus . . . we were sold a bill of goods."

send packing, to To dismiss summarily. The term has been around since the sixteenth century. Robert Browning used it in "The Pied Piper of Hamelin" (1842): "Sure as fate, we'll send you packing."

senior moment A temporary lapse of memory, a kind of forgetfulness experienced increasingly as one ages. The term dates from the second half of the 1900s and has become so popular that a game for improving one's mental acuity is named "Senior Moment." Paul Krugman's review of a book about the United States's aging population and the economic outlook was entitled *America's Senior Moment (New York Review of Books,* March 10, 2005).

separate but equal The doctrine that similar facilities for different groups justifies separating them from one another. This phrase became widely known through a Supreme Court decision of 1896 in the case of *Plessy v. Ferguson.* Justice Henry B. Brown, speaking for the majority of the court, found that "separate but equal accommodations" for African Americans and whites satisfied the Fourteenth Amendment, which had been invoked by the plaintiff. The doctrine, which marked the low point of American race relations following the Civil War, was reversed in 1954 in several decisions by the Supreme Court, at that time led by Chief Justice Earl Warren. The most important of these decisions held that "separate but equal" has no place in public education, and that so-called separate but equal facilities are inherently unequal. Despite its close associations with the civil rights movement, the phrase was invoked in other contexts as well, such as gender discrimination ("Girls can't play on the baseball team but they have their own softball team—separate but equal").

separate the men from the boys, to To distinguish those who are mature and competent from those who are young and green. This term, always used figuratively, was popular in business and politics from the 1930s on, often put as "This emergency will separate the men from the boys"—that is, will show who is able to deal with it effectively. The mystery writer A. A. Fair used it in *Beware* (1956): "This is the kind of stuff that separates the men from the boys."

separate the sheep from the goats, to To sort the good from the bad, the superior from the inferior. This term comes from the Bible, in which Jesus seems to make an analogy between sheep and goats and those who would sit at God's right hand and left hand (Matthew 25:32). In the fourteenth century John Wycliffe was more explicit, stating, "Schepe that schal be savid schal be on hys rigt honde [sheep that shall be saved shall be on his right hand]." The term has been so used ever since.

separate the wheat from the chaff, to To sort the valuable from the worthless. The analogy here is to the age-old practice of winnowing grain, formerly done by hand and now mechanized. The term persists nevertheless. G. B. McCutcheon used it in *Anderson Crow* (1920): "They separated the wheat from the chaff."

set See under PUT.

set great store by, to To value highly. This phrase uses *store* in the sense of something precious, a usage dating from Chaucer's time but now obsolete except here. It has also been put as *set little* or *no store by,* meaning to value scarcely or not at all. Laurence Sterne used it in *Sentimental Journey* (1768), writing about a starling: "The bird had little or no store set by him."

set on a pedestal, to To idealize; to glorify. This term alludes to the custom of worshiping the figures of saints and other notable individuals, which are literally placed on pedestals. It was used more generally from the mid-nineteenth century on. James Joyce had it in *Ulysses* (1922), "They discovered . . . that their idol had feet of clay, after putting him upon a pedestal." See also FEET OF CLAY.

set one's cap for, to To pursue someone as a potential mate. This term dates from the eighteenth century, and although at least one writer believes it refers to ladies choosing their most becoming headgear in order to attract gentlemen, it was originally applied to both sexes. By the early nineteenth century, however, it was used mostly for females chasing males, as in Byron's *Don Juan* of 1832 ("Some who once set their caps at cautious dukes") and Thackeray's *Vanity Fair* of 1848 ("Have a care, Joe; that girl is setting her cap at you"). Shirlee Emmons's biography of Lauritz Melchior (*Tristanissimo,* 1990) says Melchior's children believed "that Kleinchen deliberately set her cap for this young man who lived alone and far from his family."

set one's heart at rest, to To stop worrying; to dismiss one's anxiety. This expression was used by Shakespeare in *A Midsummer Night's Dream* ("Set your heart at rest," 2.1) and appeared in John Ray's 1670 proverb collection.

set one's heart on, to To have an earnest desire for; to determine to obtain something. The heart has long been equated with one's innermost being, and to "set" it on something means to fix it in that direction. This term dates from the fourteenth century. It appears in the Bible: "If riches increase, set not your heart upon them" (Psalms 62:10). This passage is repeated in the Book of Common Prayer.

set one's sights on, to To select as one's goal. The *sights* in this expression are a device such as a pair of knobs or notches placed on a firearm to help one take aim. The figurative use dates from the mid-twentieth century and also appears in such phrases as *to raise one's sights,* meaning to aim higher, or *to lower one's sights,* meaning to be somewhat less ambitious. The *Economist* used it on December 9, 1950, "The United States must now raise its sights, in terms of both manpower and production."

set one's teeth on edge, to To irritate or annoy intensely. This image evokes the intense shuddering feeling that comes from biting on a piece of tinfoil or hearing a fingernail scratch on a chalkboard. It appears in several books of the Bible (Jeremiah 31:29; Ezekiel 18:2) and, graphically, in Shakespeare's *Henry VI, Part 1:* "I had rather hear a brazen canstick turn'd, Or a dry wheel grate on the axle-tree, And that would set my teeth nothing on edge, Nothing so much as mincing poetry."

settle old scores, to To avenge an injury; to get even. This term alludes to settling up accounts or paying a bill, known as a "score" in seventeenth-century England. Earlier versions of this expression were to *cut* old scores and to *quit* old scores. In the eighteenth century it was also put as to *pay off* or *rub out* old scores.

settle someone's hash, to To subdue; to get rid of someone or something. The "hash" in question is the mess that has been made of things. The term has been around since at least 1800. "We therefore mean to make a dash/To settle fighting Europe's hash," wrote T. G. Fessenden (*Pills Political,* 1809). Settling someone's hash is not quite the same as *making mincemeat of someone,* despite the superficial similarity (both involve chopped meat). The latter implies complete demolition, i.e., chopping up.

seventh heaven, to be in To be in a state of bliss. Both the Moslems and the ancient Jews recognized seven heavens, corresponding to the seven planets, the highest of which was the abode of God and the top-ranking angels. By the nineteenth century the term had been extended to mean a blissful state, without any religious or otherworldly connotation. Thus Sir Walter Scott wrote (*St. Ronan's Well,* 1824): "He looked upon himself as approaching to the seventh heaven."

seven-year itch A yearning for change, specifically a change of sexual partner after seven years of marriage. This expression gained currency through George Axelrod's play *The Seven-Year Itch* (1952), later made into a movie starring Marilyn Monroe (1955). Originally the phrase was used for various skin conditions. One such use was for poison ivy, in the belief that the rash would recur every year for seven years. Also, centuries ago *itch* was a slang word for "sexual desire." Today, the expression invariably refers to the wish for a new sexual partner and, for some reason, tends to be applied only to men. Thus Patricia Moyes wrote, "There's something called the seven-year itch . . . middle-aged men quite suddenly cutting loose" (*Angel of Death,* 1980).

shadow of one's (former/old) self, a Reduced or diminished, in vigor or size by age, illness, or fatigue, or in wealth or power. This term was a hyperbole for being emaciated as long ago as the sixteenth century. Later it was used for other kinds of reduced circumstances, as by Sir Walter Scott in *Guy Mannering* (1815): "He appeared to wither into the shadow of himself."

shake a leg Hurry up. In the first half of the nineteenth century this colloquialism meant to dance, a usage that is just about obsolete. The current meaning dates from about 1900.

shake in one's shoes/boots, to To be in a state of terror or extreme nervousness. This vivid image of trembling with fear has been around since about 1800. William Cobbett is recorded as having said it (*Political Register*, 1818): "This is quite enough to make Corruption and all her tribe shake in their shoes." See also SCARED SILLY.

shake like a leaf See QUAKE LIKE A LEAF.

shake the dust from one's feet, to To leave in a hurry, especially from a disagreeable situation; to depart forever. This term appears in several places in the Bible, in which Jesus is quoted as telling his disciples, "And whosoever shall not receive you, nor hear your words, when ye depart out of that house or city, shake off the dust of your feet" (Matthew 10:14; repeated in Mark 6:11; Luke 9:5). It remains current.

shake with laughter, to To be convulsed with amusement. This sort of shaking is much more violent than trembling with fear or cold, causing one to "hold one's sides," i.e., to double over. John Milton used the image in *L'Allegro* (c. 1635): "Laughter holding both his sides." See also SPLIT ONE'S SIDES.

shank of the evening Twilight, dusk. This expression uses *shank* in the sense of "latter part of" or "end of," a usage rare except in this phrase. The earliest citation in the *OED* is from 1828. P. G. Wodehouse used it in *Pearls, Girls, and Monty Bodkin* (1972), "'It's very late.'—'Shank of the evening.'"

shank's mare On foot, walking. This quaint expression dates from the second half of the eighteenth century, the *shank* here alluding to the leg. Also put as *to ride shank's mare,* it continues to be used, although it may be heard less often. The *Cleveland Plain Dealer* had it (Oct. 26, 1974): "The people who came to the Barons-Rangers game that night long ago came by streetcar and bus and by shank's mare as well as by auto."

shape up or ship out Behave yourself or leave. This term originated in the American armed forces during World War II, when it literally meant, behave like a soldier (sailor, marine) or be sent overseas to a combat zone. After the war the saying was extended to any situation calling for improved performance, as, for example, a warning to an employee to do better or be fired.

share and share alike, to To apportion exactly equally. This term originated in the sixteenth century and was applied to apportioning spoils, paying for a joint venture, and similar situations. It no doubt survived because of its rhythmic repetitive quality.

sharp as a tack Singularly keen or cutting; also, mentally acute. This simile has largely supplanted the earlier sharp as a *razor, needle, vinegar,* and *thorn,* the last dating from the fifteenth century and appearing in John Ray's 1670 proverb collection. The current cliché dates from the late nineteenth or early twentieth century and appeared in a 1912 issue of *Dialect Notes:* "They won't fool him; he's sharp as tacks."

shed light on, to To explain or clarify. This term was used literally, in the sense of illuminating something, from the fourteenth century. In the fifteenth century *light* came to be used figuratively for "understanding." George J. Adler used the expression in his translation of *Fauriel's History of Provençal Poetry* (1860): "On these antecedents that I shall first endeavor to shed some light."

shell game A means of deceiving or cheating by moving things from one place to another so as to conceal one's actions. The term, dating from the late 1800s, comes from an old carnival game in which three shells are moved quickly around and a person bets under which of them a small ball or pea has been placed. Thomas C. Palmer, Jr. used it in the *Boston Globe* of April 12, 2000: ". . . the nation's biggest public works project could not survive the revelations that the Big Dig was badly over budget—and that the truth had been kept from the public with an elaborate shell game."

ship of state The nation. This metaphor was used by ancient Greek poets (Aeschylus, *Seven Against Thebes;* Sophocles, *Antigone*) and numerous others, so that by 1714 Jonathan Swift was writing (*Imitations of Horace*), "The Metaphor be worn and stale Betwixt a State, and Vessel under Sail." It nevertheless is still used, although less often today, generally in conjunction with the idea of steering or guiding the ship (i.e., nation) by means of diplomacy or domestic policy. William Safire pointed out that in 1941 President Franklin D. Roosevelt sent British Prime Minister Winston Churchill a poem to encourage Britain in the war against Nazi Germany: "Thou, too, sail on, O Ship of State! Sail on, O union, strong and great! Humanity with all its fears, With all the hopes of future years, Is hanging breathless on thy fate" (Henry Wadsworth Longfellow, "The Building of the Ship," 1849).

ships that pass in the night Persons who meet briefly, in passing, but have little or nothing to do with one another. This expression comes from a poem by Henry Wadsworth Longfellow that was published in 1873 in *Tales of a Wayside Inn* as "The Theologian's Tale": "Ships that pass in the night and speak each other in passing, Only a signal shown and a distant voice in the darkness; So on the ocean of life we pass and speak one another, Only a look and a voice; then darkness again and a silence."

ship to come in, wait for one's Wait for one's fortune to be made. Also put as *when my ship comes in,* both expressions allude to the sixteenth-century merchant ship returning home, laden with rich cargo and thus enriching the owners. Shakespeare referred to such ships in *The Merchant of Venice.* The terms began to be used figuratively during the 1800s and long survived the decline of merchant shipping, but they are heard less often today and may be dying out. "Perhaps we may manage it some time. When our ship comes in," wrote Miss Mulock (*John Halifax,* 1857). Erskine Caldwell also used it several times in *God's Little Acre* (1933), as in, "I'll know doggone well [when] my ship has come in."

shit hits the fan, (when) the There'll be a violent reckoning, big trouble. This vulgar slangy term dates from about 1930. Some believe it alludes to feces being thrown about by a revolving fan. Morris West wrote, "We'll have it back on the wires in time for the Monday editions . . . Then the shit hits the fan. It might be wise if you went away" (*Harlequin,* 1974; cited by Eric Partridge).

shit or get off the pot See FISH OR CUT BAIT.

shoe is on the other foot, the Circumstances have changed, and you and I have changed places. This saying began life as *the boot is on the other leg,* appearing in print in the mid-nineteenth century. Putting the left shoe on the right foot would, of course, entail considerable discomfort, a meaning retained in the metaphor, which implies "See how you like being in my place." Winston Churchill used it in *My African Journal* (1908): "Here . . . the boot is on the other leg, and Civilization is ashamed of her arrangements in the presence of a savage."

shoo-in A sure winner. This term comes from horse racing. The verb "to shoo" has long meant to drive or urge on. In the early 1900s corrupt jockeys would select a long shot to beat the faster horses, which would then be "shooed in" by the others. Turned into a noun, the expression now is used for a team, a political candidate, or other competitor, without any connotation of malfeasance.

shoot down, to To refute an argument completely; to debunk or expose as false. The term comes from aerial warfare in World War I and is also put as "shoot down in flames." During World War II it began to be used figuratively as well. J. B. Hilton used it in *Playground of Death* (1981): "Please shoot me down in flames if you think I'm making a bloody fool of myself."

shooting fish in a barrel See LIKE SHOOTING FISH IN A BARREL.

shoot one's bolt, to To have tried one's utmost; to have spent all of one's resources. This term comes from medieval archery and was a well-known proverb by the early thirteenth century: "A fool's bolt is soon shot." The bolt was a short, heavy, blunt-headed arrow fired with a crossbow, and the archer who used up all his bolts at once, leaving him with none, was regarded as a fool. The modern (twentieth-century) counterpart is *to shoot one's wad.* This term comes from gambling, the "wad" in question being a roll of bank notes, but it has likewise been extended to mean spending all of one's resources. Bernard Malamud used the expression (*Tenants,* 1971): "I want to be thought of as a going concern, not a freak who had published a good first novel and shot his wad."

shoot oneself in the foot, to To hurt one's own cause by mistake. This expression calls up the image of someone holding a firearm pointed down and accidentally discharging it. Although the effect is the same, it must be distinguished from injuring oneself intentionally in order to avoid military service (or to be sent home from the front).

shoot the bull, to To express one's opinions on a variety of matters, whether or not one knows a great deal about them. *Bull* here appears to be a shortening of *bullshit,* which has meant nonsense, lies, or exaggeration since the early 1900s. A gathering for shooting the bull is called a *bull session* and traditionally consists entirely of males. Yet another euphemism for shooting the bull is *shooting the breeze,* which calls up the image of the hot air expended in this kind of a gossip session. *To shoot one's mouth off,* on the other hand, means both to talk indiscreetly or tactlessly and to exaggerate.

shoot the moon Leave without paying one's bill; also, GO FOR BROKE in card playing. The first usage dates from the first half of the 1800s and alludes to leaving in the dark of night (by moonlight). Richard Wheland had it in *Robert Capa* (1985), "They would occupy a hotel room for a few weeks, until they had stretched to the limit their excuses for not paying, then 'shoot the moon' and move on to new quarters." The second usage alludes to the card game of hearts, in which players lose points for every heart they hold at the end of the game. But in one version, a player dealt the right cards can "shoot the moon," that is, try to take all the hearts for a bonus. Here the phrase means to risk everything for the ultimate prize.

shoot the works, to To make an all-out effort. This twentieth-century Americanism uses *works* in the sense of "everything." "Within an hour he hoped to shoot the works," wrote Lawrence Treat in his 1943 mystery, *O as in Omen*. See also SHOOT ONE'S BOLT.

short and sweet Satisfyingly brief. Richard Taverner quoted this term as an English proverb back in 1539, and it has been repeated ever since, occasionally with some additions ("Better short and sweet than long and lax," James Kelly, *Scottish Proverbs,* 1721; "Short and sweet like an ass's gallop," F. K. Purdon, *The Folk of Furry Farm,* 1914).

short end of the stick, to get/have the To lose out; to get less than one is entitled to. Exactly what kind of stick is being referred to is no longer known, but possibly it is one used in fighting or in a tug-of-war, in which the person holding the longer end has the advantage. "He having gotten (as we say) the better end of the staffs, did wrest our wills at his pleasure," wrote Thomas Jackson in 1626 (*Commentaries upon the Apostles Creed*). Around the turn of the twentieth century in America, "the short end" of anything came to mean the inferior part, and soon this was combined with "stick" to yield the current cliché. See also WRONG END OF THE STICK.

short shrift, to get/give To spend little time on. The term comes from the days when confessing to a priest was a virtually universal practice. *Shrift* meant not only the confession but also the penance or absolution given by the priest following confession. In Shakespeare's *Richard III,* Ratclif, ordered by Gloucester (later Richard III) to have Hastings beheaded, says to him, "Come, come, dispatch; the duke would be at dinner: make a short shrift, he longs to see your head." It began to be used more loosely in succeeding centuries, as in the quotation under LOOK DAGGERS AT.

shot in the arm, a A stimulus; something that revives a person's enthusiasm, energy, or confidence. Presumably this twentieth-century term alludes to a stimulant administered by hypodermic needle. (A similar nineteenth-century Americanism was *to be shot in the neck,* which meant to be intoxicated.) By the 1920s, however, it was used figuratively, as in, "All afternoon he . . . gurgled over his ability to 'give the Boy a real shot in the arm tonight'" (Sinclair Lewis, *Babbitt,* 1922).

shot in the dark, a A wild guess. Shooting without being able to see is taking a LONG SHOT, at best. The term has been around since the late nineteenth century. It is the title of a hilarious 1964 film starring Peter Sellers as a bumbling detective, Inspector Clouseau, who is convinced that a beautiful woman (played by Elke Sommer) is innocent of murder despite all evidence to the contrary. Graham Greene used the expression in *The Third Man* (1950): "It was a shot in the dark, but already he had this firm instinctive sense that there was something wrong."

shot one's bolt See SHOOT ONE'S BOLT.

shot to hell Hopelessly ruined; completely worn out. This term once meant literally destroyed by gunfire, but by the late nineteenth century it was clearly figurative. Ernest Hemingway used it in the short story *Fiesta* (1926): "That meant San Sebastian all shot to hell."

shoulder to the wheel, to put/set one's To make a determined effort, to work hard. This allusion to pushing a bogged-down cart dates from the early seventeenth century. Robert Burton used it in *The Anatomy of Melancholy* (1621): "Like him in Aesop . . . he whipt his horses withal, and put his shoulder to the wheel." Only in the eighteenth century was it extended to any kind of hard work, as in Madame d'Arblay's diary entry (June 1792): "We must all put our shoulders to the wheel."

shout from the housetops/rooftops, to To publicize something. Obviously antedating electronic communication, this term echoes a slightly different one in the Bible, where Jesus exhorts his disciples to spread the word of God: "Therefore whatsoever ye have spoken in darkness shall be heard in the light; and that which ye have spoken in the ear in closets shall be proclaimed upon the housetops" (Luke 12:3).

show must go on, the The proceedings must continue, no matter what catastrophe has occurred. This term is a theatrical credo dating from the nineteenth century, although the idea is much older (Shakespeare used it in *Henry IV, Part 1,* 2.4: "Play out the play"). In the twentieth century it began to be transferred to other activities. Thus, E. Holding wrote: "The hotel business is like the theatre. No matter what happens, the show must go on" (*Speak of the Devil,* 1941).

show one's face, to To appear, to be present. This expression generally implies that one is appearing, despite being embarrassed about something, or that one is afraid to appear for some reason. Thus Samuel Richardson used it in the early novel *Clarissa* (1748), "I should be ashamed to show my face in public." It continues to be used in just this way.

show one's hand, to To reveal one's true motives or intentions. This term, like laying one's CARDS ON THE TABLE, comes from card-playing.

Edmund Campion used a version of it in 1581: "I would I might be suffered to shewe my cardes" (*Conferences Held in the Tower of London with Ed. Campion, Jesuit,* cited by *OED*). A variant is *to tip one's hand,* of the same provenance. *The Economist* used it on November 17, 1979: "Mr Hunt will not tip his hand on the price at which he will buy more bullion."

show one's true colors, to To reveal oneself frankly; to admit one's genuine opinions or character. This term, the converse of SAIL UNDER FALSE COLORS, similarly alludes to the practice of deceiving the enemy by flying a friendly flag. However, it also was applied to cosmetics used to conceal or enhance a complexion. Thus Thomas Dekker wrote (*A Description of a Lady by Her Lover,* c. 1632), "The reason why fond women love to buy Adulterate complexion: here 'tis read,—False colours last after the true be dead." The metaphor was used for one's genuine character by numerous writers, Dickens among them: "He didn't venture to come out in his true colours" (*The Old Curiosity Shop,* 1840).

shrinking violet, a A very shy individual. Why the violet, a small but common shade-loving perennial, should be chosen to designate shyness is unclear. On the contrary, violets can boldly take over patches of ground, and gardeners may even find them difficult to eradicate from unwanted spaces. Nevertheless, the phrase has been used since the early 1900s. *The Listener* stated (July 22, 1976), "Frayn has not forgotten the underdog. . . . The shrinking violet . . . is the most dangerous plant in the glades of privilege."

shut the stable door See LOCK THE BARN DOOR.

sick and tired Disgusted, completely weary of. This expression, also put as *sick* or *tired to death,* suggests one is fed up to the point of illness or death. J. Hector St. John de Crevecoeur used it in *Sketches of 18th-Century America* (1783): "I am quite sick and tired of these pretended conscientious non-fighting mortals."

sick as a dog, to be To feel very ill, particularly to feel nauseated. Despite being touted as man's best friend, dogs are often maligned. This proverbial simile dates from the sixteenth century or earlier and is still current. Occasionally it has appeared with *sick* meaning "tired of," as by David Garrick (*Neck or Nothing,* 1766, 1:1): "I am sick as a dog of being a valet."

sick at heart Deeply depressed and unhappy. This term equates emotional misery with physical illness of the heart, the seat of emotions. It has been used since at least the sixteenth century, and appears both in this guise and as the adjective *heartsick* (John Skolton used it in *Magnyfycence,* 1526, "Yet I am not harte seke").

sigh of relief, (heave) a Whew; an expulsion of breath indicating that one is out of a tight spot. Sighing with longing, pain, grief, and numerous similar emotions is common in the English language—especially in poetry—from the earliest days. The word "sigh" comes from Middle English and Old English words meaning exactly the same thing (to expel breath). Heaving a sigh to express intense emotion, especially amatory longing or grief, was current from about 1700 on.

sight for sore eyes, a The unexpected appearance of someone or something one is very glad to see. The implications is that it will heal ailing eyes, obviously not to be taken literally. Jonathan Swift used it in *Polite Conversation* (1738): "The sight of you is good for sore eyes."

sight unseen Without previous examination; taken on faith. This term, which implies accepting something without verification, dates from the late nineteenth century. The 1898 *Yearbook of the United States Department of Agriculture* stated, "The intelligent farmer of today has got beyond buying 'sight unseen' when it comes to fertilizer."

signed, sealed, and delivered Satisfactorily completed. This nineteenth-century term originally described a legal document, specifically a deed, which in order to be valid had to be signed, sealed with a wax seal, and delivered to the new owner. Sir Walter Scott so used it in *Rob Roy* (1818): "How does Farmer Rutledge? . . . I hope you found him able to sign, seal and deliver." In the twentieth century the expression began to be used more loosely.

sign of the times, a Typical of a particular period, notably the present. This term appears in the Bible. When the Pharisees asked Jesus to show them a sign from heaven, he replied, "O ye hypocrites, ye can discern the face of the sky; but can ye not discern the signs of the times?" (Matthew 16:3). Many centuries later, historian Arnold J. Toynbee wrote (*The World and the West,* 1953), "The people who have read the signs of the times and have taken action . . . are the obscure missionaries of half-a-dozen Oriental religions."

sign on the dotted line, to To indicate one's full acceptance of terms being offered. The dotted line in question is often used on official documents to indicate the place for one's signature. The term dates from the early 1900s. P. G. Wodehouse used it in (*Indiscretions of Archie*, 1921): "He sang a few bars from 'Rigoletto,' and signed on the dotted line."

silence is golden To keep quiet is a great virtue. This expression is the second half of an old proverb: "Speech is silvern and silence is golden." It began to be much repeated in the nineteenth century. Thomas Carlyle referred to it as a Swiss proverb in *Sartor Resartus* (1831). A number of variants came later, among them Ogden Nash's "Silence is golden, but sometimes invisibility is golder" (*I Never Even Suggested It,* 1938).

silver bullet A highly accurate projectile of death or destruction. Sir Walter Scott may have been the first to use the idea of a literal silver bullet in *Lockhart* (1808), "I have only hopes that he will be shot with a silver bullet." The term caught on in the first half of the 1900s because the popular western hero of the radio program, *The Lone Ranger,* used a silver bullet. During the Korean War an antiaircraft shell that hit precisely on target was called "silver bullet." By the late 1900s the term also was being used figuratively, as in, "We're hoping our new software will be the silver bullet to put the company on the map."

silver lining See EVERY CLOUD HAS A SILVER LINING.

silver-tongued orator An eloquent and persuasive speaker. This term has been around since the sixteenth century, when it was applied to the preacher Henry Smith (c. 1550–91) and to Joshua Sylvester (1563–1618), a translator. Silver has long been equated with something fast-flowing and dazzlingly bright, and thus is a natural metaphor for eloquent speech. The best-known recipient of the epithet "silver-tongued orator" was William Jennings Bryan (1860–1925), who not only was a wonderful speaker but advocated the free coinage of silver; he won the Democratic presidential nomination in 1896 as a result of a speech in which he said, "You shall not crucify mankind upon a cross of gold."

simon pure The real thing, the genuine article. This expression comes from the name of a character in an early eighteenth-century play, Susannah Centilivre's *A Bold Stroke for a Wife* (1710). In it, Simon Pure, a Quaker, is the victim of an impersonation by Colonel Feignwell. However, the Quaker turns up in time and proves that he is "the real Simon Pure" (5:1).

simple Simon A foolish, gullible person; a simpleton. This expression comes from the well-known nursery rhyme "Simple Simon met a pieman going to the fair," in turn a rhymed version of a tale from an eighteenth-century chapbook. By 1785 Grose's dictionary defined the term as "a natural, a silly fellow." James Joyce used it in *Ulysses* (1922): "I looked so simple in the cradle they christened me simple Simon." However, it is probably obsolescent.

since the beginning of time As long as anyone can remember. This hyperbolic phrase, also put as *from the beginning of time*, dates from the 1600s.

The *Daily Telegraph* had it on January 19, 1978: "Best of all is Mr. Ward's pithy dismissal of the sort of supernatural pseudery that has enthralled the credulous since the beginning of time." See also FROM TIME IMMEMORIAL.

sing another tune See CHANGE ONE'S TUNE.

sing for one's supper Work in order to be paid. This metaphor, alluding to the wandering minstrels who performed in English taverns and were paid with a meal, also appears in the familiar nursery rhyme, "Little Tommy Tucker sings for his supper, What shall we give him? White bread and butter," published in *Tommy Thumb's Pretty Song Book* (c. 1744). The expression is older still, appearing in Beaumont and Fletcher's play *The Knight of the Burning Pestle* (1609, 2:2): "Let him stay at home and sing for his supper."

sinking feeling, a A sense of distress, often perceived in one's midsection. This term, which dates from the late nineteenth century, alludes to feeling hungry, frightened, or discouraged. About 1920 an advertising slogan for Bovril, a brand of beef extract touted as a restorative, was, "Bovril prevents that sinking feeling."

sink one's teeth into, to To become fully engaged or engrossed in something. The analogy in this term, which began to be used figuratively only in the early twentieth century, is to the animal that bites deeply and vigorously into food. Dorothy Sayers used it in *Gaudy Night* (1935), describing a scholarly effort: "If one could work . . . getting one's teeth into something dull and durable."

sink or swim Succumb or survive; by extension, no matter what. This term alludes to the ancient practice of throwing a convicted witch (sometimes weighted down) into deep water. In case of sinking, the person drowned; in case of swimming, the person was considered in league with the devil and therefore was executed. Hence the outcome was the same. The term, which began life as *float or sink,* was already used by Chaucer in the fourteenth century. Shakespeare's Hotspur said, "Or sink or swim" (*Henry IV, Part 1,* 1.3), and across the Atlantic, John Adams said, "Swim or sink, live or die, survive or perish with my country was my unalterable determination" (in a conversation with Jonathan Sewall, 1774).

sink through the floor, to To be extremely embarrassed. This hyperbolic expression, indicating that one wishes one could actually disappear by sinking through the floor, dates from about 1900. L. M. Montgomery used it in her popular novel *Anne of Green Gables* (1908): "She thought she would sink through the floor when she saw you come in all rigged out like that."

sit on one's ass Be extremely lazy, do as little as possible or nothing at all. This is a ruder version of *sit on one's hands,* which dates from the early 1900s and is not heard much any more. The somewhat newer expression appears in numerous contexts, as, for example, "This new president is much nicer than his predecessor, but so far he's just sitting on his ass and collecting his stipend." Sometimes "butt" is substituted for "ass."

sit on the fence See ON THE FENCE.

sit tight, to To take no action; to bide one's time. This term is said to come from poker, where a player who does not want either to continue betting or to throw in his or her cards is said "to sit tight." However, it may come from the much earlier locution, *to sit close,* which similarly alludes to sitting still with one's knees close together, in effect in a waiting attitude. "He sits close and keeps his own," wrote Sir Thomas Herbert (*Travaile into Afrique,* 1634). "They would sit tight and strike out hard," wrote Sir Robert Baden-Powell (*The Matabele Campaign,* 1896).

sitting duck, a An easy target. This expression clearly alludes to the ease with which a hunter can shoot a duck that is sitting still, in contrast to one in flight. It was transferred to other enterprises in the first half of the twentieth century.

sitting pretty In an advantageous position. This colloquial Americanism dates from the early 1900s. A popular song of the period was "I'm Sitting Pretty in a Pretty Little City" (1923), by Lou Davis, Henry Santly, and Abel Baer.

sit up and take notice, to (make someone) To (make someone) pay attention; to astonish or startle someone. This late nineteenth-century expression calls up the image of a dog sitting up, wide awake and completely alert. O. Henry used it in his story *The Enchanted Profile* (1909): "Sit up and take notice—a dispossess notice if there's no other kind."

six degrees of separation The idea that everyone on earth may be linked to anyone else through a chain of connections. This newer phrase for IT'S A SMALL WORLD was the title of a play and the movie based on it (1993) by John Guare. The term is becoming a cliché.

sixes and sevens See AT SIXES AND SEVENS.

six feet under Dead and buried. The traditional depth of a grave is approximately the length of the coffin. This expression, while making good arithmetical sense, came into use only in the mid-twentieth century. J. Gerson used it in *The Omega Factor* (1979): "We make sure the dead are stiff and cold and six feet under."

six of one and half a dozen of the other It's all the same; there's no difference between them. This term dates from the early nineteenth century. Dickens used it in *Bleak House* (1852): "Mostly they come for skill—or idlenesss. Six of one, and half-a-dozen of the other."

sixth sense, a Intuitive knowledge. The term alludes to a sense in addition to those of sight, hearing, smell, taste, and touch, and dates from about 1800. "In Germany it has of late been attempted to be shown that every man is possessed of a sixth sense," wrote J. M. Good (*The Study of Medicine,* 1829). Although today we also call it "extrasensory perception" (or ESP), the expression *sixth sense* is still heard.

sixty-four-thousand-dollar question, the The hardest question of all; the crucial question. This term comes from the name of a popular television quiz show of the 1950s in which $64,000 was the top prize. It in turn may have been an inflation of the earlier *sixty-four dollar question,* named for the top prize on a CBS radio quiz show *Take It or Leave It,* which ran throughout the 1940s. This cliché may soon join its forerunner in obsolescence.

skeleton in the closet, the A shameful secret. This term likens a family secret to a murder victim hidden away in a closet or cupboard. If it ever was based on such an incident, the history has been lost. In any event, the metaphor became current in the early nineteenth century. Thackeray used it in several novels, as did Dickens, George Meredith, and other nineteenth-century British writers, and it remains current.

skid row, on Destitute, down-and-out. The term comes from the American lumber industry, where it first signified a skidway down which felled logs were slid. In time the part of a town frequented by loggers, which abounded in taverns and brothels, was called Skid Road. In the mid-twentieth century it again became "skid row" and was applied to any area of cheap barrooms and rundown hotels frequented by vagrants and alcoholics.

skin a cat See MORE THAN ONE WAY TO SKIN A CAT.

skin and bones, (nothing but) Emaciated; painfully thin. This hyperbole has been around since the time of the ancient Greeks and Romans; Theocritus, Plautus, and Vergil are among the ancient writers who used it. An unknown fifteenth-century writer stated, "Now . . . Me is lefts But skyn and boon" (*Hymns to the Virgin and Child,* c. 1430).

skin of one's teeth See BY THE SKIN OF ONE'S TEETH.

sky's the limit, the As much as one wishes; an infinite or unlimited amount. Although the idea was expressed centuries earlier, the precise wording here dates only from the twentieth century. One writer believes it originated in gambling and referred to there being no limit to the size of a bet (in poker the limit is the maximum amount by which a player may increase a previous bet). The term has been more generally applied since the 1920s.

slam dunk A very forceful move. This term comes from basketball, where it denotes a strong and often dramatic shot in which the player leaps up and thrusts the ball into the basket from above. Both term and technique date from the 1960s, and by the 1980s the term was being used in business, politics, and other areas, both as a noun and as a verb (*to slam dunk*). The *Boston Globe* has used it in both forms: "'I fear they assume this election will be a slam dunk,' Rollins said" (July 24, 1991), and "I found that very energizing. . . . There was a real opportunity to slam dunk that one" (May 5, 1992). It is well on its way to cliché status.

sleep like a log/top, to To sleep very soundly. The earliest simile of this kind, now obsolete, is to sleep like a *swine* (*pig/hog*), which dates from Chaucer's time. "I shall sleep like a top," wrote Sir William Davenant in *Rivals* (1668), no doubt referring to a spinning top that, when spinning fast, is so steady and quiet that it seems not to move at all. This simile persists, particularly in Britain. To sleep like a log is more often heard in America, although it has English forebears back as far as the sixteenth century. An older cliché is *to sleep the sleep of the just,* meaning to sleep soundly, presumably because one has a clear conscience. Its original source is a 1695 translation of a passage from the French dramatist Jean-Baptiste Racine's *Summary of the History of Port-Royal.*

sleep on something, to To postpone a decision until the next day. Both the idea and the expression are very old. The *State Papers of Henry VIII* (1519) by an unknown compiler stated, "His Grace . . . sayd thatt he wold slepe and drem upon the matter."

slender reed, a A weak and unreliable support. This metaphor dates from biblical times, appearing in both Old and New Testaments. In the former, in the books of Isaiah and 2 Kings, it was applied to Egypt, which was variously described as a "broken" or "bruised" reed, not to be trusted if the Assyrians made war on the Hebrews. The term persisted into the mid-twentieth century but is heard less often today.

slice of life A realistic portrayal of people or events typical of everyday life. The term originated as a translation of the French *tranche de la vie,* applied to French naturalist writings in the late 1800s. It was quickly taken into English and applied to plays, paintings, and other artistic works. The *Daily Telegraph* had it (Feb. 19, 1981): "Yet another indigestible slice of life about 'a warm, winning, and wise and wonderful Jewish family.'"

slice the pie, to To share the profits. This metaphor has largely replaced the early-twentieth-century *slice of the melon,* but exists side by side with the more literal PIECE OF THE ACTION. It comes from nineteenth-century America. T. N. Page used a version in *Red Rock* (1898): "Does he want to keep all the pie for himself?" And the *Boston Sunday Herald* (1967): "An appellate court victory . . . cut Weymouth's total property valuation . . . to give the town a bigger slice of the sales tax pie." A related term, *no matter how you slice it,* is a twentieth-century Americanism meaning "no matter how you look at it." Carl Sandburg used it in *The People, Yes* (1936): "No matter how thick or how thin you slice it it's still baloney."

slim pickings Little left to profit from; a small reward, scarcely worth the effort. This term, alluding to animals devouring a carcass of prey or carrion, has been around since at least the seventeenth century, and the idea is much older yet. John Milton used it in *Smectymnus* (1642): "The Vulturs had then but small pickings."

slippery as an eel Hard to grasp; elusive, and, by extension, deceitful. The eel's long slender body, with only minute scales deeply embedded in the skin, looks totally smooth and is very slippery when wet. These characteristics gave rise to the simile, which dates from the fourteenth century and is still used today. (See the quotation in SLIP THROUGH ONE'S FINGERS.)

slippery slope, a A dangerous path or situation leading to disaster. Alluding to a path down which one could slide to a bad fall, this figure of speech dates from the mid-1900s. The *Daily Telegraph* of January 6, 1964 stated, "While Western feet thus approach what some fear may be a slippery slope towards recognition of the East, Ulbricht's ground seems as firm as ever it was." In a *New Yorker* piece about writers chronicling Sherlock Holmes, one of them is quoted as saying, "I've now done...more than fifteen hundred pages and I've only gotten up to 1950. It's been a slippery slope into madness and obsession" (Dec. 13, 2004).

slip through one's fingers, to let To fail to seize an opportunity. This metaphor has been around since the seventeenth century. Beaumont and Fletcher used it in *The Prophetess* (1622, 3.2): "Hold her fast, She'll slip thorow your fingers like an Eel else."

slow as (slower than) molasses (in January) Extremely dilatory. This simile is American in origin, dates from the mid- or late nineteenth century, and is a vivid one for anyone who has ever tried to pour cold molasses from one container into another. "He's slower than molasses," wrote J. W. McAndrews (*Monologue,* c. 1880).

slow but sure Plodding but reliable. This proverbial term dates from the early seventeenth century, and the idea is as old as Aesop's fable about the tortoise and the hare. "This snail's slow but sure," wrote John Marston in his 1606 play *The Fawn* (3:1).

small beer/small potatoes Something trivial or unimportant. Literally, "small beer" is the British name for beer of low alcohol content, today more often called "light beer." As a metaphor it was already being used in Shakespeare's time, and Shakespeare himself used it in several plays (*Henry IV, Part 2; Othello*). It is heard more in Britain than in America, where *small potatoes,* likening a poor crop to something of little worth or importance, dates from the early nineteenth century. David Crockett used it in *Exploits and Adventures in Texas* (1836): "This is what I call small potatoes and few of a hill." More picturesquely, D. G. Paige wrote, "Political foes are such very small potatoes that they will hardly pay for skinning" (*Dow's Patent Sermons,* c. 1849).

smart aleck, a A cocky individual who thinks he or she knows everything and is not shy about saying so. The origin of this term, an American colloquialism from the 1860s, has been lost; no one knows who that first Aleck (or Alexander) was. The adjective *smart* in the sense of "impudent" is much older (fifteenth century) but has died out except in this expression. Budd Schulberg used it in *What Makes Sammy Run?* (1941): "He's a smart aleck. I can see already he thinks he knows more than I do."

smart as a whip Very clever, highly intelligent. The sharp crack of a whip has been a metaphor for mental quickness since the mid-nineteenth century in America. "He was as smart as a whip," wrote B. F. Taylor (*World on Wheels,* 1874), one of the early appearances of this expression in print. Several writers, among them Harriet Beecher Stowe and Erle Stanley Gardner, have used *smart as a steel trap*, presumably alluding to its rapidly closing on some hapless creature, but it has not replaced the older simile.

smart set The fashionable socially elite. A late-nineteenth-century term on both sides of the Atlantic, it was sometimes used more for the flashy nouveau riche, as by Ward McAllister: "Behind what I call the 'smart set' in society, there always stood the old, solid, substantial, respected people" (*Society As I Have Found It,* 1890). In the mid-1900s it was largely replaced by JET SET, and then by BEAUTIFUL PEOPLE.

smell a rat, to To suspect that something is wrong. Presumably this term, which is very old indeed, alludes to a cat sniffing out a rat. John Skelton used it in *The Image of Hypocrisy* (c. 1550): "Yf they smell a ratt, they grisely chide and chant."

smell fishy, to To be suspect. This term, which refers to the fact that fresh fish do not smell but stale or rotten ones do, has been around since the early nineteenth century. J. G. Holland explained it explicitly (*Everyday Topics,* 1876): "Fish is good, but fishy is always bad." The metaphor turns up in James Payn's *Confidential Agent* (1880): "His French is very fishy."

smelling like roses See COME UP SMELLING LIKE ROSES.

smell to high heaven, to To stink; to be thoroughly contemptible, dishonest, or in very bad repute. *Heaven* in this term alludes to a great distance; if something that far away can be smelled, it must smell very strong indeed. Shakespeare may have originated the metaphor. "O! my offence is rank, it smells to heaven," says the King in *Hamlet* (3.3), "It hath the primal eldest curse on't; A brother's murder!"

smoke like a chimney, to To smoke tobacco (cigarettes, cigars, and so on) to excess. Generally stated as a criticism of the smoker, this term, which likens the habit to smoke pouring out of a chimney, has become a cliché owing to increasing disapproval of the tobacco habit. C. Parker used it in *The Body on the Beach* (1989), "'I thought she'd given it up.'—'What, Mary? She smokes like a chimney.'"

smoke someone/something out, to To drive someone/something into the open. The term alludes to the practice of driving a person or animal out of hiding by starting a fire, so that the smoke will force them out. The term has been used figuratively since the early twentieth century. "Speculators were 'smoked out' by a Congressional inquiry" appeared in the *New York Times* (1948).

smoking gun Definite evidence of illegal or criminal activity. The term alludes to smoke emitted by a revolver or other kind of gun that has been fired, but it is also used more broadly for other kinds of malfeasance. For example, *Time* (Sept. 19, 1977) had it, "In fact there may be no 'smoking gun'—no incontrovertible black-and-white evidence of wrongdoing by Lance." The *New York Times* (Oct. 3, 2004) quoted National Security Adviser Condoleeza Rice, talking on CNN about aluminum tubes in Iraq suspected to be used for nuclear weapons, "We don't want the smoking gun to be a mushroom cloud."

smooth as silk Slippery; easily negotiated. The smoothness of this fine fabric was transferred to mean general freedom from hindrances by 1900. O. Henry used the simile in his 1910 story *The Dream:* "Everything goes as smooth as silk."

smooth sailing See PLAIN SAILING.

snail's pace See AT A SNAIL'S PACE.

snake in one's bosom See VIPER IN ONE'S BOSOM.

snake in the grass An underhanded, stealthily treacherous individual. The metaphor was already used by the Roman poet Virgil in his *Eclogues* (37 B.C.) as well as by the Italian poet Dante in the *Inferno* of *The Divine Comedy* ("Hidden like a snake in the grass"). Snakes have been feared and hated for centuries, and the metaphor has remained both vivid and current. It appears equally often on both sides of the Atlantic. Mark Twain used it in *Tom Sawyer* (1876), "A guileful snake in the grass," to describe how the boys in Sunday school viewed the hero, who had duped them out of enough "tickets" to win a Bible.

snake oil Quack medicine, a useless remedy. This term was first used in the early 1900s about salesmen of quack medicines who claimed "snake oil" or some other bizarre potion would cure a variety of ailments. Eugene O'Neill used it in this sense in his play *The Iceman Cometh* (1946): "I'll bet he's standing on a street corner in hell right now, making suckers of the damned, telling them there's nothing like snake oil for a bad burn." Later the term was extended to mean a worthless remedy for any kind of problem, as in "Advertisers who try to lubricate the wheels of our economy with snake oil" (*Washington Post,* May 10, 1961).

snowball's chance in hell, no more than/not a No chance at all. The hell in question, of course, is the fabulously hot place of tradition. This term appears to have replaced the earlier *no more chance than a cat in hell without claws,* an eighteenth-century locution that, according to Grose's *Dictionary,* was applied to a person quarreling with or fighting against a much stronger opponent. The current cliché comes from late nineteenth-century America; in Britain and other English-speaking countries it is sometimes put as a *snowflake's* chance in hell.

snow job Exaggerated flattery used to cover up some real issue. The term is probably derived from the figurative expression, to be *snowed under,* meaning to be overwhelmed. It originated among GIs during World War II to describe, for example, presenting a superior officer with an elaborate fiction to excuse some misdemeanor.

snug as a bug in a rug Singularly comfortable; well entrenched. The expression, which alludes, presumably, to the clothes-moth larva happily feeding inside a rolled-up carpet, dates from 1769 (*Stratford Jubilee,* unknown author) and, probably owing to its rhyme, has remained current. Benjamin Franklin used it in a letter to Miss Georgiana Shipley (1772): "Here Skugg lies snug As a bug in a rug."

soaked to the skin Wet through. Actually, this term began life as *wet to the skin,* and Cotgrave's *Dictionary* of 1611 stated it as "Wet through, or (as we say) to the skinne." It implies that this condition was not sought out. The current cliché has alliterative appeal and so is the more common version, at least in America.

sober as a judge In full possession of one's faculties; not at all intoxicated. The equation of judges and sobriety was made long ago. An early appearance in print is in *Terence Made English* (1694) by an unknown author: "I thought myself sober as a judge." It remains current on both sides of the Atlantic.

sob story An oversentimental tale; a tearjerker. This expression from the early twentieth century presumably represents a reaction to Victorian sentimentality. C. E. Montague used it in *Fiery Particles* (1923): "Thomas Curtayne, the greatest of Irishmen, was to be buried in homely state. . . . Here was a sob story." A roughly contemporary term is *sob sister,* a woman reporter who writes stories full of sentimental pathos. This expression, however, is obsolescent.

sock it to them Give them all you've got; strike the final blow. This expression dates from Mark Twain's day, and indeed he used it in *A Connecticut Yankee in King Arthur's Court* (1889). The Yankee (narrator) is describing an argument over comparative prices and salary and says, "I prepared, now, to sock it to him. I said: 'Look here, dear friend, what's become of your high wages you were bragging about?'" Although old, the term did not gain wide currency until the 1960s, when a version of it appeared on a popular television show, *Rowan and Martin's Laugh-In.* Put as *sock it to me!,* it apparently came from jazz slang and meant "liven things up." The speaker then encountered a bucket of water over the head, a blow, or some similar attack. Incidentally, the colloquial verb *to sock,* meaning to strike, dates from about 1700, and its ultimate origin has been lost.

so far, so good Everything's all right up to this point. It is hard to say why this old proverb, listed in James Kelly's *Scottish Proverbs* (1721), should have survived. The implication always is that something might go wrong, but nothing has done so yet.

soft soap Flattery. The analogy here is to a slithery, unctuous substance (which describes soft soap), and it has been drawn since the first half of the nineteenth century. "To see them flattering and soft soaping me all over," wrote John Neal (*John Beedle's Sleigh Ride,* c. 1840). A contemporary synonym, now obsolete, was *soft sawder,* a substance used for soldering. It was still used in the 1940s but is seldom heard today.

soft touch, a A person who is easily imposed upon, especially to give or lend money. A twentieth-century expression that gained currency during the Great Depression, it appeared in John O'Hara's *Pal Joey* (1940): "You get the reputation of being a soft touch."

soft underbelly The weakest, most vulnerable part of an organization, nation, or other body. The most probably source of the expression is a reference to animals like porcupines, which are well protected on their backs but not on their bellies. It was first used figuratively during World War II, when Sir Winston Churchill described the Allied invasion of Italy as an attack on the soft underbelly of the Axis. It later was extended to various vulnerabilities, as in "She was . . . sticking her knife . . . into the soft underbelly of capitalism" (John Campbell Crosby, *Snake,* 1977).

S.O.L. Acronym for *shit out of luck,* sometimes put more politely as "soldier out of luck" or "strictly out of luck." The term appears to date from World War I. Paul Dickson cites Mark Sullivan, a chronicler of that conflict, who said it was an expression used of a soldier who was late for mess or had been given thirty days' confinement to the post for being caught shooting craps. The term later entered the civilian vocabulary and has become a cliché.

so long Good-bye. This colloquial usage has been around since the first half of the 1800s and its origin is puzzling. "Long" may be short for "a long time," but there is no such implication in the phrase. The American radio newscaster Lowell Thomas, active from 1930 to the mid-1970s, had a standard sign-off, "So long . . . until tomorrow." Today the phrase is heard less often than a newer form of good-bye with an equally puzzling allusion, TAKE CARE.

something else, he/she/it is Someone or something is extraordinary, in a positive sense. It does not mean "something different" but is a slangy elaboration of the simpler "isn't that something." It is usually said admiringly, as in "Kayla Cole is something else" (James Patterson, *London Bridges,* 2004).

something is rotten in the state of Denmark Something is seriously amiss; there is a smell of corruption. This expression is a direct quotation from Shakespeare's *Hamlet* (4.1). Eric Partridge suggested that *rotten* was originally an analogy to cheese, for which Denmark has long been famous, and that possibly the expression was a catchphrase even when Shakespeare used it.

so near and yet so far Nearby but still unattainable. This term appeared in the Roman writer Martial's *Epigrams* (c. A.D. 85) but apparently did not enter the English language for some time. Tennyson used it in "In Memoriam" (1850): "He seems so near and yet so far."

song and dance, (to give someone) a (To make) an unnecessary fuss; also, a misleading story or statement, nonsense. In the first sense this term dates from mid-nineteenth-century England, where it is usually put as *nothing to make a song (and dance) about,* meaning this is an unimportant matter. The second sense originated in America in the second half of the nineteenth century. Brander Matthews used it in *A Confident Tomorrow* (1900): "It ain't a song and dance I'm giving you either." *The same old song and dance,* on the other hand, refers to an overfamiliar, hackneyed routine, whether or not that happens to be an old familiar lie or excuse. See also SAME OLD RIGMAROLE.

son of a gun A rogue or scoundrel. Some etymologists believe that this term, which originated about 1700, once meant the illegitimate son of a soldier (gun). Others, however, believe it simply was a euphemism for *son of a bitch* that appealed because of its rhyme. Still another theory, recorded in Smyth's *Sailor's Word-Book* (1867), is that it was originally applied to boys who were born at sea, in the days when women were permitted to accompany their sailor husbands, and alluded to a child being "cradled under the breast of a gun."

sooner or later At some future time or other; eventually. This expression dates from the sixteenth century and has long been a cliché. Joseph Addison used it in *The Spectator* in 1712: "The dying Man is one whom, sooner or later, we shall certainly resemble."

so to speak Put in this way; in a manner of speaking. This phrase once meant "in the vernacular" or "in dialect," and was used by artistocrats in the early 1800s as an apology for stooping to use lower-class language. However, Henry Wadsworth Longfellow used it to apologize for high-flown language: "I occupied the same chamber that you did in former times, for it seemed to be the very highest point of the dwelling, the apogee, so to speak" (letter of March 2, 1824).

sound as a bell In excellent condition. Although this simile no doubt rests on the assumption that a cracked bell is useless, it may have outlived many others—among them sound as a *top, roach, dollar,* and *the Bank of England*—because of the pun it embodies. In any event, it has been around since at least 1565, when Thomas Newton, the translator of *Touchstone of Complexions,* wrote, "They be people commonly healthy, and as sound as a Bell."

sour grapes Disparaging what one cannot but would like to have. This term comes from the punch line of one of Aesop's most famous fables, delivered by the fox when she finds she cannot reach some grapes on a very high vine. It has been used ever since to describe putting down what one can't attain.

sow one's wild oats See WILD OATS.

spanking new Brand-new, completely novel. This phrase uses *spanking* in the sense of "very" or "exceedingly," a usage dating from the late 1800s. Its origin is unknown, for it has nothing to do with the act of beating or slapping. F. Scott Fitzgerald used it in *The Great Gatsby* (1925), "The house . . . was a colossal affair . . . spanking new under a thin beard of raw ivy."

spare the rod and spoil the child Discipline makes for a good upbringing. This warning appears in the Bible ("He that spareth his rod hateth his son: but he that loveth him chasteneth him betimes," Proverbs 13:24), and is repeated in numerous subsequent proverb collections. Although today we frown on corporal punishment, the term persists, the rod now usually signifying discipline in a looser sense. Stanley Walker, who delighted in mixing metaphors and clichés, wrote: "He never spared the rod or spoiled the broth" (*The Uncanny Knacks of Mr. Doherty,* 1941).

speak for yourself Take your own part, not someone else's; also, that's your opinion, not necessarily mine. In the first meaning, this term dates from the nineteenth century and was popularized by Henry Wadsworth Longfellow in "The Courtship of Miles Standish" (1858), recounting the wooing of Priscilla Carpenter by John Alden for Captain Standish. Priscilla "said, in a tremulous voice, 'Why don't you speak for yourself, John?'" With or without *John,* the term has been so used ever since. Also, since at least the early eighteenth century, the expression has signified implicit disagreement. Jonathan Swift used it in *Polite Conversation* (1738): "Pray, sir, speak for yourself."

speak of the devil Now that one mentions that person, he or she turns up. This old proverbial saying is, as John Ciardi pointed out, a leftover from the ancient superstitious belief that pronouncing the devil's name will cause him to appear. Indeed, the full saying is, *Speak of the devil and he's sure to appear.* For primitive peoples, one's name was an essential part of one's being, and to speak a name gave one some power over the person named. The roots of the cliché have been largely forgotten, and today it is most often voiced simply when a person one has been talking about unexpectedly appears on the scene.

speak one's mind, to To say what one thinks. The idea of putting the mind's contents in words is probably ancient, but the expression is first seen in Shakespeare's works, as, "Give me leave to speak my mind" (*As You Like It,* 2.7). A synonym is *to speak one's piece,* which transfers *piece* in the sense of a recited passage to the expression of an opinion. It dates from the mid-1800s; C. F. Browne wrote in *A. Ward: His Travels* (1865), "I have spoken my piece about the Ariel." From the same period we have yet another equivalent, *to have one's say.* George Meredith used it in *Richard Feverel* (1859): "Lobourne had its say on the subject."

speak softly and carry a big stick Back up what you say with a show of strength. This term is a quotation from a speech by President Theodore Roosevelt on September 2, 1901, in which he said the country must keep on training a highly efficient navy in order to back up the Monroe Doctrine. It was often repeated and is by no means obsolete. Opera singer Renée Fleming referred to it in *The Inner Voice* (2004, describing her manager: "He is thoughtful, has enormous integrity, is highly respected, and speaks softly but carries...well, you know."

speak the same language, to To understand one another perfectly. Figuratively, this term dates from the late nineteenth century. Joseph Conrad used it in *Victory* (1915): "You seem to be a morbid, senseless sort of bandit. We don't speak the same language." See also ON THE SAME PAGE.

speak volumes, to To say a great deal about something, to be very expressive on a subject. In this hyperbolic phrase, what is being said is likened to an entire book. It dates from about 1800 and continues to be current. M. Wilmot used it in a letter of May 3, 1803, "A sentimental story that speaks Volumes in favour of the Count and his Daughter."

spick and span Neat and clean. This term is made up of two now obsolete words, *spick,* meaning a spike or nail, and *span,* meaning a wood chip. In the days of sailing ships, a spick and span ship was one in which every spike or nail and every (wooden) chip was new. The alliterative pairing of the two is very old indeed, although originally the expression meant "brand-new." It appeared in Sir Thomas North's translation of Plutarch's *Lives* (1579): "They were all in goodly gilt armours, and brave purple cassocks upon them, spicke, and spanne newe."

spill the beans, to To give away a secret. This slangy Americanism combines two earlier meanings: of *spill,* meaning to talk, and of *beans,* meaning information. Although these date from the sixteenth and thirteenth centuries respectively, the cliché has been around only since the 1920s or so. It is particularly common in detective stories and novels, in which the opportunity for revealing important secrets is a common occurrence.

spirit is willing but the flesh is weak, the I would like to do this but I don't have the willpower or strength. This term comes from the Bible. Jesus, counseling his disciples at the Last Supper, said, "Watch and pray, that ye enter not into temptation: the spirit indeed is willing, but the flesh is weak" (Matthew 26:41). John Lyly was more specific (*Euphues,* 1579): "The delights of ye flesh are preferred before the holynesse of the spirite." Today the term often is a rueful admission of physical weakness, much like *I would if I could but I can't* (also based on ancient proverbs).

spit and polish Great care for a spotless and smart appearance. The term originated in the armed services, where spit might literally be used for a hasty cleaning for an unexpected inspection. The term also came to mean more attention to appearances than to actual working order or efficiency, so that by World War I, "Spit and polish! We're winning the war," was a sarcastic expression applied by those in the front lines to the concerns of career officers sitting behind desks in the war office.

spitting image, the An exact resemblance, usually said of parent and child or other close relatives. This term comes from the earlier *spit and image,* which, since *spit* meant "likeness," was redundant. Nevertheless, it was widely used from the late nineteenth century on, and by the mid-twentieth century, probably through mispronunciation or misspelling, was converted to the current cliché.

split hairs, to To make petty, unnecessarily fine distinctions. The analogy between splitting so fine a material as a hair and making fine distinctions was drawn by Shakespeare's time. "I'll cavil on the ninth part of a hair," he wrote (*Henry IV, Part 1,* 3.1). It was probably already a cliché by the time Douglas Jerrold wrote (*The Chronicles of Clovernook,* 1846), "His keen logic would split hairs as a bill-hook would split logs."

split one's sides, to To laugh uproariously. This hyperbole dates from the seventeenth century. Thomas Brown used it in *Saints in Uproar* (1687): "You'd break a man's sides with laughing." The word "split" came into use somewhat later. Dickens used it in *The Old Curiosity Shop* (1840), "He bade fair to split his sides with laughing," and Harriet Beecher Stowe in *Uncle Tom's Cabin* (1852), "I laughed fit to split." See also SHAKE WITH LAUGHTER.

spread like wildfire, to To disseminate very quickly. Wildfire here denotes a combination of inflammable materials that catch fire very fast. The analogy to less concrete matters was drawn by about 1800. Benjamin Disraeli used it in *Venetia* (1837): "The report . . . spread like wild fire through the town."

square deal, a A fair and honest arrangement. Although *square* has been used to mean "equitable" since the fourteenth century, this expression became well known only in the early twentieth century, when Theodore Roosevelt made it the platform of his presidential campaign. "If elected, I shall see to it that every man has a square deal, no less and no more," he said (Nov. 4, 1904).

square meal, a A substantial and nourishing repast. A mid-nineteenth-century Americanism, the term appears in humorist Stephen Leacock's *Literary Lapses* (1910): "Any two meals at a boarding-house are together less than two square meals."

square peg in a round hole See ROUND PEG IN A SQUARE HOLE.

squeaky wheel gets the grease, the The loudest complainer usually obtains the most attention. This allusion to a wagon wheel that needs lubrication appears in a nineteenth-century poem attributed to the American humorist Josh Billings. Entitled "The Kicker" (i.e., The Complainer), it goes, "I hate to be a kicker, I always long for peace, But the wheel that does the squeaking is the one that gets the grease." However, this idea had been similarly expressed in various early proverb collections. "He who greases his Wheels, helps his Oxen" occurs in Thomas Fuller's collection (1732), and "A wheel badly greased creaks" in Alfred Henderson's (1830).

stab in the back, a A treacherous attack. Surprisingly, this term has been used figuratively only since the early twentieth century; literally it must be as old as the word "stab" (fourteenth century). Rudyard Kipling used it in *Limits and Renewals* (1932): "He . . . stabs me in the back with his crazy schemes for betterment."

stack the deck Arrange matters in one's own favor or against one's opponent. The term, dating from the mid-1800s, originated in card playing, where it meant secretly arranging a pack of cards in a sequence that gave the dealer a winning hand. Also put as *play with a stacked deck,* it has been used figuratively both in the sense of a dishonest maneuver or simply in the sense of describing odds in one's favor. For example, a statement like "As the home team, the Patriots are playing with a stacked deck" means only that the team has a natural advantage playing on a familiar field.

stack up against, to To compare the worth or power of something. This term comes from poker and alludes to how one player's chips, representing money, compare to another's. The higher the stack in front of a player, the more money he or she has. The very similar term *to stack something against,* however, means to reduce someone or something's chance of success. Budd Schulberg used this in *What Makes Sammy Run?* (1941): "You read the papers, you know how the cards are stacked against this nut."

staff of life, the Bread; sometimes, by extension, any essential food. Understandably this term originated in the Bible ("the stay and the staff, the whole stay of bread," Isaiah 3:1). However, it was not until the eighteenth century that *the staff of life* was definitively identified with bread (prior to that it had often been *corn,* the British term for wheat). "Bread, dear brothers, is the staff of life," wrote Jonathan Swift (*A Tale of a Tub,* 1704), and so it has remained.

stage whisper A whisper intended to be heard by one and all. In the theater this term literally meant an aside—a thought spoken aloud—communicated to the audience and allegedly unheard by the other actors on stage. It dates from the mid-nineteenth century and by 1900 or so was employed figuratively. J. V. McIlwraith used it in *Kinsmen at War* (1927): "Mrs. Secord spoke in a stage whisper."

stalking horse A pretext. This term comes from the practice of hunters sometimes dismounting and, hiding behind their horses, stalking game on foot, slowly advancing until they come within shooting distance. The transfer of this practice to a means of concealing a secret plan, or, in politics, to a candidate being used to conceal the candidacy of some other person, took place in the sixteenth century. Shakespeare used it in *As You Like It* (4.3): "He uses his folly like a stalking-horse and under the presentation of that he shoots his wit." *Time* had it on Nov. 21, 1977: "She's willingly making herself a stalking horse for the ultra right." British lexicographer Nigel Rees reported that in British politics of the early 1990s, the term was applied to a member of Parliament who stands for election as party leader with no hope of winning, in order to test whether the incumbent leader is challengeable.

stand on ceremony, to To behave very formally. This term, in which *stand on* has nothing to do with rising to one's feet but rather means "to insist on," dates from the nineteenth century. It appeared in Jane Austen's *Northanger Abbey* (1798): "I never stand upon ceremony."

stand one's ground, to To hold to one's position; to refuse to give in. This expression comes from the military, where from about 1700 it was used in the sense of holding one's position. Figuratively it was used from the early nineteenth century on. J. S. Mill had it in *On Liberty* (1859): "It is not easy to see how it [individuality] can stand its ground."

stand up and be counted Show your true opinion, even if it takes courage to do so. This Americanism, which presumably refers to counting votes, dates from the turn of the twentieth century and has been used with reference to showing where one's political sympathies lie, even if one's view is very unpopular. From the mid-twentieth century on, however, it has been used more broadly for revealing any kind of conviction. Michael Innes used it in *Appleby's Answer* (1973): "A mild-mannered man. But he felt he must stand up and be counted."

star chamber An unfair, secret judicial proceeding. This term comes from a criminal court developed in England in the 1400s in which the King's Council acted as judges in certain procedures. They met in the Star Chamber of the royal palace at Westminster, believed to have been named for the gilded stars decorating its ceiling, and were notorious for their harsh decisions and punishments. This court was abolished in 1621, but its name later was transferred to similar proceedings. In the late 1990s, when Kenneth Starr was serving as independent counsel in the investigation of First Lady Hillary Rodham Clinton, some pundits played on the term, alluding to "Mr. Starr's chamber."

stark raving mad Insane. Literally this term means "completely, wildly crazy," a graphic description of manic behavior. Versions of it have appeared since the sixteenth century, including Jonathan Swift's, "There's difference between staring and stark mad" (*Polite Conversation,* 1738). More recently, Robert Barnard piled up colloquial synonyms: "'Mad as a hatter,' said Gillian Soames complacently. 'Stark raving bonkers. Up the wall. Round the twist.'" (*Death and the Chaste Apprentice,* 1989).

start from scratch, to To begin from nothing at all, without having a head start or some other advantage. This term comes from racing, where a horse or runner is said to start from scratch when starting from the usual point—that is, the line "scratched" (marked) on the course—while others may be starting ahead with a handicap. The term was transferred to other bare beginnings by the twentieth century. George Orwell used it in *Coming*

Up for Air (1939): "We'd no fishing tackle of any kind. . . . We had to start from scratch."

start off on the right foot, to To begin auspiciously. This term is a version of PUT ONE'S BEST FOOT FORWARD. Ancient superstition had it that the right foot was the best, whereas the left was unlucky. Hence early versions of this expression include "With prosperous foot approach" and "Right foot first." (See also GOT UP ON THE WRONG SIDE OF BED.) The converse of this locution is *to get off on the wrong foot.* Both became clichés in the twentieth century.

state of the art Representing or incorporating the latest advances. This expression, dating from the late 1800s, has nothing to do with the condition of the fine arts. Rather, it first applies *art* to technology, a usage still current. B. G. Bender used it in *Microminiaturism* (1962), ". . . techniques have been developed for producing chips . . . which have advanced the state of the art." However, it also is used more broadly, and often as an adjective, as in "That redecorated living room is state of the art."

status symbol A possession or privilege that is a mark of one's social standing. Dating from the mid-twentieth century, this term is often used sarcastically, in effect deriding anyone who relies on status symbols for a sense of worth. The *New York Times* used it on September 3, 2000, in an article by Geraldine Fabrikant about lawyer Johnnie L. Cochran's purchasing a private plane: "Mr. Cochran . . . is now hitting the major money leagues as well, and he has the status-symbol issue down pat."

stay the course Hold out or last to the end. This expression alludes to a horse that runs the entire course of a race. It dates from the mid-1800s and was soon transferred to other venues. The *Times* of London used it during World War I: "If we are to stay the course set before us, other sections must be prepared for greater sacrifices" (May 8, 1916).

steady as a rock Unwavering. This simile, which clearly alludes to a very large immobile rock, dates from the mid-1800s. It is used to describe either physical steadfastness or mental, behavioral stability. The former is meant by J. B. Harwood in *Lady Flavia* (1865): "The hand that held the candle was steady as a rock." The latter appears in "You can count on John to run the office; he's steady as a rock."

steal a march on someone, to To gain an unexpected or surreptitious advantage. This expression comes from medieval warfare, when a *march* meant the distance that an army could travel in a given time, usually a day. By marching at night, a force could surprise the enemy at daybreak or at least could come much closer than was anticipated, thereby gaining an advantage. By the eighteenth century the term had been transferred to peacetime enterprises. "She yesterday wanted to steal a march on poor Liddy," wrote Tobias Smollett (*Humphry Clinker,* 1771).

steal someone's thunder, to To ruin or detract from the effect of someone's accomplishment by anticipating or copying it. This term originated in the early eighteenth-century theater, and the story behind it has been told by numerous writers. John Dennis (1657–1734), a critic and playwright, had devised a "thunder machine" for his play *Appius and Virginia* (1709); it consisted of rattling a sheet of tin backstage. The play failed, but a few nights later the same effect was used in a production of *Macbeth,* which Dennis attended and which prompted him to say, "They steal my thunder!" The term was subsequently used for similar situations and remained current long after its origin had been forgotten. Almost synonymous is the much newer *to steal the show,* meaning to outshine everyone else in a performance or at some event. It dates from the first half of the 1900s. The *steal* portion of this term implies that one is taking attention away from all the others.

steer clear of, to To avoid. This term comes from its literal use in sailing in the seventeenth and eighteenth centuries (Daniel Defoe used it in *Colonel Jacque,* 1723) and was being used figuratively by the late eighteenth century. George Washington said, in his farewell address (1796), "It is our true policy to steer clear of permanent alliance with any portion of the foreign world."

stem the tide, to To stop the course of a trend, opinion, or the like. The verb *to stem,* meaning to stop or restrain, comes from the Old Norse word *stemma,* meaning "to dam." It would take an enormous dam to stop ocean tides, but the tide of public opinion, for example, can be checked or diverted. Thus Fred A. Paley wrote (*The Tragedies of Aeschylus,* 1855), "Aristophanes evidently saw the tide . . . and he vainly tried to stem it by the barrier of his ridicule."

stem to stern, from From beginning to end; entirely. In nautical terminology the *stem* is an upright at the bow (front) of a vessel and the *stern* is the back end. This counterpart of FROM HEAD TO TOE and FROM SOUP TO NUTS was quoted by the Roman writer Cicero as a Greek proverb. In English the term was used literally from about 1600 on, and figuratively soon afterward.

step/tread on someone's toes, to To insult or offend someone. The analogy between physical and emotional pain here is obvious. H. G. Bohn's *Handbook of Proverbs* (1855) stated, "Never tread on a sore toe," which no doubt would hurt still more. The precise expression appeared in Anthony

Trollope's novel *The Belton Estate* (1866): "'But you mustn't offend my father.'—'I won't tread on his toes.'"

step up to the plate Go ahead and act; don't delay. This phrase comes from baseball, where it tells the batter to step up to home plate and prepare to bat the ball. From the late 1900s on it was frequently transferred to other enterprises, especially business and politics.

sterling qualities Outstanding characteristics. The word *sterling,* long denoting a standard of value or purity for money, is believed to have come from a medieval coin that was marked with a star. It was extended to anything of sound intrinsic worth by the early nineteenth century. Washington Irving used it in *The Alhambra* (1832): "The nephew is a young man of sterling worth."

stewed to the gills Extremely drunk. The noun *gills* here has nothing to do with the breathing organs of fish, but rather was slang for a stand-up collar. Consequently *to the gills* came to mean "up to one's neck" or "completely," and in the early 1900s *stewed,* for soaked in liquor, was added.

stew in one's own juice, left to Abandoned to suffer the consequences of one's own actions. Chaucer had a version of this expression in *The Canterbury Tales* (*The Wife of Bath's Tale*): "In his own gress [grease] I made him frie for anger and for very jalousie." A closer equivalent was Henry Carey's version (*Advertisements from Parnassus,* 1656): "He could not better discover Hypocrites than by suffering them (like Oysters) to stew in their own water." The exact modern wording dates from the second half of the nineteenth century.

stick in one's craw, to To be so offensive or disagreeable that one cannot swallow it. This expression is the modern version of stick in one's *gizzard, gullet,* or *crop,* all referring to portions of an animal's digestive system. Their figurative use dates from the late seventeenth century. Jonathan Swift recorded one in *Polite Conversation* (1738): "Don't let that stick in your gizzard." Dickens used still another in a letter in 1843: "Your dedication to Peel stuck in my throat." More recently Martin Cruz Smith wrote, "Doesn't it stick in your craw that you got absolutely nowhere in the investigation?" (*Wolves Eat Dogs,* 2004).

stick in the mud, old A person who avoids anything new; an old fogy, not necessarily old in years. This expression, which presumably likens such an individual to a vehicle whose wheels are stuck in mud, has been around since about 1700. Thomas Haliburton used it in one of his Sam Slick tales (1843): "'Well,' said old Stick-in-the-mud, 'what are you arter?'"

stick one's neck out, to To take a bold risk; to ask for trouble. This early twentieth-century Americanism most likely comes from the barnyard, where a chicken extends its neck in preparation for slaughter (by decapitation). Raymond Chandler used it in *The Black Mask* (1936): "You sure stick your neck out all the time."

stick out like a sore thumb, to To be very conspicuous. This simile is extremely apt, as anyone who has ever injured a thumb will testify. One tends to hold the injured finger stiffly, and, since it opposes the rest anyhow, it tends to stand out, thereby risking more bumps and bruises. Dating from the early twentieth century, it appears in print in Erle Stanley Gardner's *The Case of the Sleepwalker's Niece* (1936): "That's the one thing in the case that stands out like a sore thumb."

stick to one's guns, to To persist, to stand firm. Originally this term was (and in Britain still is) *to stand to one's guns* and referred to a gunner's obligation to remain at his post. By the mid-eighteenth century it was being used figuratively, as by James Boswell (*Life of Johnson,* 1791): "Mrs. Thrale stood to her gun with great courage in defense of amorous ditties."

stick to the ribs To be filling and satisfying. This description of enjoying one's food dates from at least 1603: "Some one . . . hath offred her such Kindnes as sticks by her ribs a good while after" (Wilson, *The Bachelor's Banquet*). It appeared in John Ray's proverb collection of 1670 as well.

sticky wicket, (to bat on) a To deal with a difficult situation that requires good judgment. The term comes from cricket, where it refers to soft or muddy ground around a wicket, which makes it difficult for the batsman because the ball does not bounce well. Although cricket is not well known in America, the term did cross the Atlantic in the 1920s. The *National News-Letter* used it in 1952, "Mr. Churchill was batting on a very sticky wicket in Washington."

stiff as a board Rigid, inflexible. This common simile for being unbending is replacing the earlier *stiff as a poker,* probably because central heating has made fireplace implements like pokers less common household items. Stiff as a poker dates from the eighteenth century; it appeared in numerous sources, such as "Stuck up as stiff as a poker" (George Colman, Jr., *The Heir at Law,* 1797). Earlier still was *stiff as a stake* (sixteenth century), which is now obsolete.

still as a mouse See QUIET AS A MOUSE.

still small voice, a One's conscience. This term comes from the Bible, where the prophet Elijah hears his own inner voice: "And after the earthquake a fire; but the Lord was not in the fire: and after the fire a still small voice" (1 Kings 19:12). The term was used frequently thereafter by poets such as Gray, Cowper, Byron, and Tennyson, as well as by Erasmus Darwin (Charles's grandfather): "Inexorable conscience holds his court, With still, small voice the plot of guilt alarms" (*Mores Concluded,* c. 1794). It is heard less often today.

still waters run deep A silent person may be a profound thinker; also, the quiet conspirator is the most dangerous. The expression has been a proverb in English since the fifteenth century and has counterparts in ancient Rome as well as in other countries. The analogy to the deep thinker is made plain in Anthony Trollope's novel *He Knew He Was Right* (1869): "That's what I call still water. She runs deep enough . . . So quiet, but so—clever." The other meaning, with its implication of danger, is also put as "Beware of a silent dog and still water," a translation of a Latin proverb that appeared in Thomas Fuller's *Gnomologia* (1732) and later proverb collections.

stir up a hornets' nest, to To provoke a quarrel or foment trouble. The analogy appears in the Roman playwright Plautus's *Amphitruo* (c. 200 B.C.), in which Sosia tells Amphitryon not to get in trouble by quarreling with his wife. It is cited by Erasmus in his collection of adages and repeated by Rabelais in *Pantagruel.* In English it appears from the eighteenth century on and remains current.

stitch in time saves nine, a Solving a difficulty while it is small may save a great deal of trouble in the end. The analogy to mending a small rip versus sewing an entire new seam was a proverb by the eighteenth century, appearing in Thomas Fuller's 1732 collection. It has been repeated dozens of times since; Ogden Nash played with it in the title of a verse collection, *A Stitch Too Late Is My Fate* (1938).

stock in trade One's capabilities and resources. This cliché transfers the original meaning of the phrase—that is, the goods for sale kept by a dealer, or the tools kept by a workman—to more personal attributes. Thomas de Quincey used it in *Cicero* (1842): "Such charges were the standing material, the stock in trade of every orator."

stone's throw, a A short distance. Strictly speaking, of course, this measurement would depend on the size and weight of the stone and the strength of the thrower. However, the expression has been used loosely since the sixteenth century. A. Hall had it in a 1581 translation of the *Iliad:* "For who can see a stones throw of ought thing in land or plaine?"

story of my life, that's the Describing something that summarizes one's own experience. Usually said about a difficulty, setback, or disappointment of some kind, this expression is generally stated ruefully, and with either exasperation or resignation. It dates from the second half of the twentieth century. The humor magazine *Punch* used it on March 11, 1964: "It's the story of my life—looking for small watch-straps."

straight and narrow, (walk) the (Follow) the path of virtue. This term probably alludes to the biblical caution, "Strait is the gate, and narrow is the way, which leadeth unto life" (Matthew 7:14), *life* here meaning salvation. Following the straight and narrow, however, was largely a Victorian concept of rectitude, and the term became current in the nineteenth century. John Dos Passos used it in *The 42nd Parallel* (1930): "Robbins . . . said that he . . . would have to follow the straight and narrow."

straight as an arrow Without twists, bends, or turns; upright; direct. This simile, which likens the arrow's path to a straight line, dates from medieval times and appears in English sources from then on. Chaucer (*The Miller's Tale*) had another version: "Long as a mast, and upright as a bolt," a *bolt* being the short, heavy arrow used with a crossbow. George Eliot, commenting on a person's youthful appearance, wrote (*Felix Holt,* 1868), "You are as straight as an arrow still."

straight from the horse's mouth See FROM THE HORSE'S MOUTH.

straight from the shoulder Blunt, outspoken. This term comes from boxing, and was transferred from full-force action to speech in the late nineteenth century. "Give me a chap that hits out straight from the shoulder," wrote Charles Reade (*It Is Never Too Late to Mend,* 1856), still using it in its literal sense. See also STRAIGHT SHOOTER.

straight shooter, a An honest person. This slangy Americanism, dating from the second half of the 1900s, likens honest speech to the direct path of a bullet or arrow. G. M. Brown used it in *Time to Keep* (1969), "'He's the decentest skipper ever I sailed with . . . Strict but fair . . .'—'A straight shooter.'"

strange bedfellows An odd couple; a peculiar combination. Shakespeare appears to have originated the term, with his "Misery acquaints a man with strange bedfellows" (*The Tempest,* 2.2). Several centuries later, Edward Bulwer-Lytton wrote (*The Caxtons,* 1849, "Poverty has strange bedfellows." Today we often say that *politics makes strange bedfellows,* meaning that politicians form odd associations in order to win more support or votes.

straw(s) in the wind A clue or test of public opinion or some other matter; fragmentary evidence. This term draws the analogy between blowing straws that indicate the wind's direction and a test of some other issue. The idea, with slightly different wording, appears in print from the mid-seventeenth century on. "Take a straw and throw it up into the Air, you shall see by that which way the wind is," wrote John Selden (*Table-Talk: Libels,* c. 1654). A related term is *straw vote* or *straw poll*, an unofficial tally to show people's views on an issue or candidate. O. Henry made fun of the idea in *A Ruler of Men* (1907): "A straw vote only shows which way the hot air blows."

straws, to catch at/clutch/grasp/cling to See GRASP AT STRAWS.

straw that broke the camel's back See LAST STRAW.

street smarts The ability to live by one's wits. This slangy expression, dating from the second half of the 1900s, alludes to the survival skills acquired by living largely on city streets. The *New York Times* used it, "To be free, however, requires street smarts, the cunning of the survivor" (Aug. 30, 1976).

stretch one's legs, to To stand up or go for a walk in order to relieve muscular stiffness or for the exercise. This term has been around since the seventeenth century. Izaak Walton used it in *The Compleat Angler* (1653): "I have stretch'd my legs up Tottenham Hill to overtake you."

strike oil, to To make a lucky discovery or breakthrough. Originating in nineteenth-century America, this literal expression was used figuratively by the second half of the century. James Russell Lowell (*Poetical Works,* 1888) wrote: "We are a nation which has struck ile [*sic*]." A straightforward synonym is to *strike it rich,* also from mining, which alludes to finding a substantial mineral deposit.

strike while the iron is hot, to Take advantage of favorable circumstances. This metaphor from the blacksmith's forge dates back to ancient times and appears in the works of Chaucer, John Lyly, and numerous early English writers. Oliver Wendell Holmes turned it around a bit (*A Rhymed Lesson,* 1846) with his cautionary rhyme: "And with new notions—let me change the rule—Don't strike the iron till it's slightly cool." See also the synonym MAKE HAY WHILE THE SUN SHINES.

strings attached See WITH STRINGS ATTACHED.

stroke of genius, a A brilliant idea. This cliché, in which *stroke* betokens the sudden appearance of the idea, dates from the second half of the 1800s and at first was always used admiringly. Thus the *Tacoma News* of December 13, 1889, stated, "The latest nickel-in-the slot scheme is really a stroke of genius and is destined to revolutionize cheap literature in this country."

Later, however, the term was often used sarcastically, as in "You forgot the tickets? That was a stroke of genius."

strong silent type, the A man of few words but effective action; one who masks his feelings. This phrase, today nearly always used ironically, was extremely popular with women novelists of the early 1900s who used it to depict a very romantic figure. Even today, when it may be obsolescent, it is never used for a woman. Leslie Charteris had it in *The Saint and Templar* (1978): "I've always fancied myself as the strong silent type."

stubborn as a mule Singularly obstinate. No one knows why mules in particular have been singled out for this quality, but they have, for centuries. "Contrary" and "obstinate" are other adjectives used in the simile, which became current in the early 1800s and remains so. The same is meant by the adjective *mulish*.

stuffed shirt, a A pompous, self-satisfied, rigid person. Shakespeare had the idea in *Much Ado about Nothing* (1.1), "He is no less than a stuffed man," implying that this person was so full of himself that he was, in fact, quite empty. The current cliché, which dates from about 1900, calls up the image of a shirt filled with tissue paper or some other material, which then appears to have a live person in it but actually does not.

stumbling block, a An obstacle; a hindrance to progress or understanding. Originally this expression literally signified an object over which one tripped. It so appears in the Bible: "Thou shalt not curse the deaf, nor put a stumbling block before the blind" (Leviticus 19:13). In the course of time it began to be used figuratively as well, and in the twentieth century it was turned into a maxim: "Let us turn stumbling-blocks into stepping-stones" (John R. Mott, c. 1925).

stung to the quick See CUT TO THE QUICK.

sublime to the ridiculous See RIDICULOUS TO SUBLIME.

such as it is An apologetic disclaimer for something. In effect this phrase says that the item in question is not very good but is the best or only one available. Used since the 1300s, it probably originated as a translation of the Latin *talis qualis,* for "as is"—that is, unsorted, with flaws and the like. Abbreviated to *tal qual,* it was adopted in English for "as is" merchandise. The cliché, however, was used in far more general fashion, as in Shakespeare's *Richard II* (2.3): "I tender you my service, such as it, being tender, raw, and young."

suffer fools gladly, does not Refuses to put up with stupidity. This rather flip rejection of those one considers stupid comes from the King James translation of the Bible, "For ye suffer fools gladly, seeing ye yourselves are wise" (2 Corinthians 11:19). This statement, of course, is a sarcasm; Paul actually is saying that those who put up with fools (in this instance, braggarts) are themselves fools. Today the term is always used in the negative.

suffice it to say It should be enough to state the following. This phrase, indicating that what follows is all that should be said about something, dates from the seventeenth century. John Dryden used it in *St. Evremont's Miscellaneous Essays* (1692): "It suffices to say that Xanthippus becoming the manager of affairs, altered extremely the Carthaginian Army."

sugar daddy An elderly man who bestows expensive gifts on a young woman. This term, which uses *sugar* for the "sweets" of costly gifts and *daddy* to indicate the difference in the giver and recipient's ages, dates from the first half of the 1900s. The London *Times* spelled it out: "Norma Levy, a prostitute, had a sugar daddy called Bunny who paid her rent and gave her a Mercedes car" (Sept. 20, 1973).

sum and substance The total essence of a matter. The *sum* in this cliché is not really necessary—*substance* covers the meaning quite well—but the appealing alliteration is probably what helped it survive. Shakespeare used it in *Two Gentlemen of Verona* (4.1), "My riches are these poor habiliments Of which, if you should disfurnish me, you take the sum and substance that I have."

Sunday best See BEST BIB AND TUCKER.

sun is over the yardarm, when the A time permissible for cocktails or some other alcoholic drink. *Yardarm* means either end of the outer portions of a square sail, and presumably this term alludes to the cocktail hour on a pleasure yacht, after the sun has begun to sink. It is used more in Britain than in America, where in fact it is dying out. Rudyard Kipling had it in *From Sea to Sea* (1899): "The American does not drink at meals as a sensible man should. Also, he has no decent notions about the sun being over the yardarm or below the horizon."

sure as shooting Dead certain. This nineteenth-century Americanism may be a descendant of the older simile, *sure as a gun,* which dates from the mid-seventeenth century and appears in the works of Samuel Butler, John Dryden, William Congreve, and George Meredith, among others. According to S. A. Hammett (*A Stray Yankee in Texas,* 1853), American southerners drew the comparison from their much-loved rifles and rendered the alliterative cliché.

sure thing, a An absolute certainty. This cliché dates from the first half of the nineteenth century and originally alluded to a bet one could not lose.

Appropriately, Jane Smiley used it in her racetrack novel, *Horse Heaven* (2000): "'Curtis, you've been around the racetrack for twenty-five years or more. Don't you know that the only sure thing is that a sure thing is never a sure thing?'" Without the article, *sure thing* also is a reply that means "Yes," or "Certainly." This usage dates from the late 1800s.

survival of the fittest In the long run the strongest succeed. This phrase was originated by Herbert Spencer (*Principles of Biology,* 1864) in describing Charles Darwin's theory of natural selection. It later was broadened to describe, for example, the success of a well-run corporation compared to failing businesses. The poet Sarah N. Cleghorn, however, pointed out (*The Survival of the Fittest,* 1917), "'The unfit die—the fit both live and thrive.' Alas, who say so? They who do survive."

suspense is killing me See THE SUSPENSE IS KILLING ME.

swallow one's pride, to To humble oneself when circumstances demand it. The verb *to swallow* has been used in the meaning of putting up with unpleasantness since about 1600. The original locution was to swallow one's *spittle,* which denoted suppressing anger or some other strong emotion. It appeared in the Bible, "How long wilt thou not depart from me, nor let me alone till I swallow down my spittle?" (Job 7:19).

swan song A farewell appearance or accomplishment; an artist's last work. This term rests on the ancient belief that swans are mute (most species tend to remain silent in captivity) but burst into song just before they die. The myth has been around since ancient Greek times and was mentioned often by the Elizabethans, especially Shakespeare. Among the most beautiful madrigals of this period is Orlando Gibbons's "The Silver Swan": "Who living had no note, When death approach'd unlock'd her silent throat."

swear like a trooper, to To spew forth profanity and/or obscenity. The troopers in question were the cavalry, who probably were no more apt to swear than other military men. Nevertheless, they were singled out from the early eighteenth century on, beginning with the unknown author of *The Devil to Pay at St. James's* (1727).

swear on a stack of Bibles, to To make a solemn oath. Traditionally a solemn declaration or affirmation was pronounced as being *by* some sacred being or object. This practice is perpetuated in modern courtrooms by swearing in witnesses, a procedure that involves laying their hands on a Bible and pronouncing "Do you swear to tell the truth, the whole truth, and nothing but the truth?" Swearing on an entire stack of Bibles thus is construed as carrying considerably more weight than swearing on just one book. An

American colloquialism from the mid-nineteenth century, it was used by Billie Holiday in her 1956 memoir, *Lady Sings the Blues:* "Mom . . . swore on a stack of Bibles I was eighteen."

sweat blood, to To exert oneself to the utmost; also, to experience extreme worry or fright. Both usages of this slangy expression date from the late 1800s. Earlier, *to sweat blood* also could mean to spend money; John Dryden, among others, used it in this way in the 1600s, but this usage is obsolete. The modern meanings appear in G. S. Porter's *Harvester* (1911), "He just sweat blood to pacify her, but her couldn't make it," and in D. H. Lawrence's *Memoirs of the Foreign Legion* (1924), "I sweat blood any time somebody comes through the door." A synonym for *sweat blood* in the sense of "working hard" is *to sweat one's guts out,* which George Orwell used in *The Road to Wigan Pier* (1937): "It makes one sick to see half a dozen men sweating their guts out to a dig a trench." A synonym for experiencing fright or anxiety is *to sweat bullets,* alluding to drops of sweat the size of bullets. This hyperbole dates from the mid-1900s.

sweep off one's feet, to To overwhelm; to carry away with enthusiasm. This metaphor suggests knocking a person down, or at least sideways, in the process of making an impression. The term, also put as to *carry* someone off his feet, dates from the nineteenth century. Clarence Day used it in *The Crow's Nest* (1921): "You can't sweep other people off their feet if you can't be swept off your own."

sweep (something) under the rug, to To conceal something. This allusion to hiding household dust or debris by sweeping it under a rug or carpet was used figuratively only from the mid-twentieth century. It appeared in the *Boston Globe* in 1979: "Attempts to sweep the Chappaquidick scandal under the rug have not succeeded."

sweetness and light Saccharine goodness and cheerfulness. Originally this term was used in all seriousness by Jonathan Swift (*Battle of the Books,* 1697) for the two products of bees, honey and wax (for candles), and by Matthew Arnold (*Culture and Anarchy,* 1869) for beauty and intelligence. It was the latter that led to its widespread adoption. Today, however, it is always used ironically, as in, "'This one's on Thames House.' 'That's very generous of them,' said Goss drily. 'You know us. Sweetness and light'" (Stella Rimington, *At Risk,* 2004).

sweet tooth, (to have) a A love for sugary foods. This seemingly modern expression goes back to the sixteenth century, although it did not always refer exclusively to carbohydrate goodies. "Thou hast . . . a sweet tooth in thy head, a liquorish appetite to delicate meats and intoxicating wines," wrote Thomas Adams in a sermon of 1629.

swelled head, to have a To be conceited. The image conveyed is that of having one's self-importance augment one's head size. The term dates from the nineteenth century. J. J. Cooper used it with appropriate disgust (*Simon Suggs' Adventures,* 1845): "They're all a pack of d——d swell-heads."

swim with the tide, to To go along with the majority. The idea appears in Confucius's *Analects* (c. 500 B.C.): "Swim with the tide, so as not to offend others." Conversely, *to swim against the tide* means to buck public opinion, or hold out against the majority. Both expressions clearly imply that the one course of action is much easier than the other.

sword of Damocles Impending danger or doom. The term comes from the same Greek legend about Damocles that gave us HANG BY A THREAD. Although the story illustrates the insecurity of power and high position, in later applications the term was used to signify any kind of impending misfortune.

swords into ploughshares Make peace, not war. This expression comes from the Bible, when the prophet Isaiah has a vision in which people "shall beat their swords into ploughshares, and their spears into pruning-hooks" (Isaiah 2:4). O. Henry played on this cliché (*The Moment of Victory,* 1909): "His bayonet beaten into a cheese slicer." Opponents of the Vietnam War in the 1960s abandoned it altogether and invented the slogan, *Make love, not war.*

take aback, to To surprise or discomfit. This term originally was nautical, describing sails that press against the mast and therefore suddenly impede a vessel's progress. It was used figuratively from the early nineteenth century on. Dickens used it in his *American Notes* (1842): "I don't think I was ever so taken aback in all my life." It is heard less often today but has not died out.

take a backseat, to To occupy an inferior or relatively obscure position. Equating the backseat of a vehicle with inferiority dates from mid-nineteenth century America. Max Beerbohm used the figure of speech in *Around Theatres* (1902): "He brought on a circus procession . . . and Oxford had to take a back seat."

take a bath, to To experience a major financial loss; also, to fail miserably. This slangy cliché dates from the first half of the twentieth century and originated in gambling. It transfers cleaning oneself in a tub to being cleaned out (see TAKE TO THE CLEANERS). It appeared in *Business Week* on October 27, 1975: "Our profits won't make up for the bath we took last fall and winter." In the alternative sense, the University of Tennessee's newspaper, the *Daily Beacon,* stated, "As . . . Sen. Robert Dole put it, the GOP 'took a bath' in elections for the U.S. House" (Nov. 4, 1982).

take a dim view of, to To disapprove. Today *dim* is only rarely used in the sense of "unfavorable," as it is here. This metaphor dates from the mid-twentieth century. H. Grieve used it in *Something in Country Air* (1947): "Mr. Everard took a dim view of his youngest niece."

take a leaf out of someone's book, to To imitate someone; to follow someone's example. Literally, this expression alludes to either vandalism (tearing a page from a book) or plagiarism (copying someone else's work). The figurative use of the term, which dates from about 1800, is much less nefarious. B. H. Malkin used it in his translation of *Gil Blas* (1809), "I took a leaf out of their book," meaning simply, "I imitated them," or "I followed their example."

take a leak, to To urinate. This rather vulgar slangy term dates from the early twentieth century. A verse of the popular World War I song "Mademoiselle from Armentières" (1918; author of words and music not known) had it, "The proper place to take a leak/Is right on the corner of the main street."

take a powder, to To leave quickly. The origin of this expression is obscure, even though it is relatively recent (twentieth century). Since about 1600 *a powder* has meant "a hurry," possibly derived from the speed of gunpowder. "Ile sett you in with a powder," that is, with a rush, appears in a play, *Club Law* (c. 1600), by an unknown writer. This meaning persisted well into the nineteenth century, mainly in Britain. In the 1920s, however, in popular literature, characters departing in haste were said to *take a runout powder.* P. G. Wodehouse used it in *Money in the Bank* (1942), "And have him take a runout powder? Be yourself, lady." One writer has suggested this might refer to a laxative, but that interpretation seems unlikely. Moreover, the French have a similar expression, *Prendre la poudre d'escampette,* "To take the scampering powder," or, in more idiomatic terms, "to bolt."

take a rain check, to To accept a postponement. This term comes from the practice of issuing rain checks with tickets to ball games; if the game is rained out, the rain check entitles the ticketholder to see a subsequent game. Rain checks began to be issued for baseball games in the 1880s, and in time the term was extended to other kinds of postponement. Len Deighton used it in *Twinkle, Twinkle Little Spy* (1976): "'Let me take a rain check.'—'On a love affair?' I said."

take a shine to, to To develop a liking for something or someone. The origin of this nineteenth-century American colloquialism, first appearing in print in 1839, has been lost. Nevertheless, it remains current, mostly in America. L. Meynell used it in *Papersnake* (1978): "He took a shine to you."

take at face value, to To accept something or someone at its apparent worth. The transfer of face value from monetary currency to other matters took place in the nineteenth century. "He must take advertisements of publishers at their face value and regard them as what they claim to be," wrote J. L. Whitney (*The Literary World,* 1883).

take (someone) at his/her word, to To believe someone, to regard someone as trustworthy. This locution dates from the sixteenth century, appearing in such sources as Miles Coverdale's translation of the Bible (1535) and several of Shakespeare's plays (e.g., "I take thee at thy word," *Romeo and Juliet,* 2.2). It also is part of an amusing proverb quoted in David Ferguson's *Scottish Proverbs* (1595) and numerous later collections: "Take a man by his word, and a cow by her horne."

take by storm, to To become quickly famous or popular. The term originally came from the military, where *to storm* meant to lay siege to a fortified position. By the late nineteenth century, however, the term had been extended to mean winning renown or popular acclaim. Thus Augustus Jessop wrote (*The Coming of the Friars,* 1889), "The Franciscans . . . were taking the world by storm."

take care Good-bye. This contemporary of HAVE A NICE DAY and NO PROBLEM became current in the late 1960s or early 1970s and has spread like the proverbial wildfire. It appears both orally and in written form, replacing *Sincerely,* or *Love* in signing off informal correspondence. It does not, however, mean "be careful," but rather appears to be a shortening of "take (good) care of yourself."

take (someone) down a peg, to To deflate or humble someone. This term alludes to lowering a ship's colors, which were maneuvered by means of pegs. The higher the colors were flown, the greater the honor. The term was already being transferred by 1664, when Samuel Butler wrote (*Hudibras*), "Trepanned your party with intrigue, And took your grandees down a peg." John Ray's *Proverbs* (1678) defined it as "to remind upstarts of their former condition." It is still widely used.

take (someone) for a ride, to To play a joke on someone; also, to murder someone. As a euphemism for murder, this term was American underworld slang that became popular with mystery novelists of the 1930s and 1940s. Thus, Eric Ambler wrote (*Journey into Fear,* 1940), "He was to be 'taken for a ride.'" In the meaning of playing a trick or deceiving someone, the term is slightly older, being so defined in *Dialect Notes* in 1925. J. P. McEvoy used this version in *Hollywood Girl* (1929): "She certainly took him for a ride."

take into one's head, to To conceive an idea. This vivid image of putting an idea inside one's head was already known about 1700. Joseph Addison used the expression (*The Spectator,* 1711): "When every Body takes it in his Head to make as many Fools as he can."

take into one's own hands, to To assume responsibility or management. This term was first used with respect to *taking the law into one's own hands*—that is, replacing the established authority with one's own. Thomas Dekker used it in *The Seven Deadly Sinnes of London* (1606): "They . . . take the law into their owne hands." The expression still is used in this way and usually implies disapproval.

take it from me, (you can) Accept it on my say-so. This very modern-sounding phrase actually was in use in the seventeenth century. Thomas Wentworth, the Earl of Stratford, used it in a letter (c. 1641) to King Charles I: "He is young, but, take it from me, a very staid head."

take it in stride, to To accept circumstances as they are; to deal calmly with a setback, sudden popularity, or any other occurrence. This expression calls up the image of a horse clearing a hurdle without checking its gallop. It began to be used figuratively about 1900, as by Edith Wharton (*The House of Mirth,* 1905): "I'd want something that would look more easy and natural, more as if I took it in my stride." A similar locution is *take it as it comes*—that is, accept whatever happens. W. S. Gilbert used it as an admirable philosophy in *The Gondoliers* (1889, "Life's Tangled Skein," Act I): "Life's a pleasant institution, / Let us take it as it comes!"

take it lying down, to To submit to insult or oppression without resistance. The image conveyed by this expression is that of a cowed animal, which accepts its unhappy fate instead of jumping up in protest. This metaphor appeared first in the late nineteenth century and is most often put negatively. It was so used by Shaw in *Androcles and the Lion* (1914): "I should feel ashamed if I let myself be struck like that, and took it lying down."

take it or leave it Accept or reject it, but make a decision, for this offer is final. This expression dates from the fourteenth century, and several versions appear in Shakespeare's plays. The precise modern wording and sense are in Thomas Killigrew's play *Thomaso* (1664, 1:4): "That is the price . . . take it or leave it." A modern variant is *I can take it (him/her) or leave it (him/her),* meaning I don't feel strongly one way or the other.

take no prisoners Behave with utter ruthlessness. The term refers to the harsh military policy of killing the enemy rather than capturing them and taking prisoners. In the late 1900s it began to be transferred to other contexts as in, "As for a tax increase, our candidate is totally committed; he'll take no prisoners on this issue." It may be turning into a cliché.

take off one's hat to, to To express admiration; a form of applause. Doffing one's hat was long a mark of deference or respect, and to some extent it still is, even now that hats are no longer standard attire. The figurative use of the term dates from the mid-nineteenth century. In 1886 *Harper's Magazine* stated, "We should take off our hats to them and wish them godspeed."

take one's breath away, to To astound. This expression is pure hyperbole: one is so flabbergasted that one stops breathing. (The same idea is conveyed in the adjective *breathtaking.*) In the mid-nineteenth century Robert Browning used the term in *Dramatis Personae* (1864): "He never saw . . . what was able to take his breath away."

take one's name in vain, to To mention a person casually and disrespectfully. This expression, today always used jocularly, comes from the biblical commandment against blasphemy: "Thou shalt not take the name of the

Lord thy God in vain" (Exodus 20:7). It was already used more lightly in the eighteenth century, when Jonathan Swift included it in *Polite Conversation* (1738): "Who's that takes my name in vain?"

take pains, to To make a laborious effort; to take assiduous care. The use of *pains* for "troubles" dates from Shakespeare's time and survives mainly in this cliché (and in the adjective *painstaking*). "Yet much he praised the pains he took, And well those pains did pay," wrote Sir Walter Scott (*Marmion,* 1808).

take root, to To become firmly established. Likening the establishment of an idea, program, or similar abstraction to a botanical rooting is very old indeed. It appears in the Bible, where the psalmist says God has brought a vine (i.e., the Jewish people) out of Egypt and planted it, "and didst cause it to take deep root, and it filled the land" (Psalm 80:9). Leon Trotsky allegedly said, "We only die when we fail to take root in others" (quoted in Trevor Griffiths' play, *The Party*).

take the bit between the teeth, to To be stubbornly self-willed; to push aside restraints and go one's own way. The analogy here, to a horse that catches the bit in its teeth so that the rider or driver has no control over it, dates from the sixteenth century. John Lyly used it in his *Pappe with an Hatchet* (c. 1589): "But if like a resty iade [restive jade, or nag] thou wilt take the bit in thy mouth, and then run over hedge and ditch, thou shalt be broken as Prosper broke his horses." The expression is used less often today and may be obsolescent.

take the bitter with the sweet One must accept the bad along with the good. "For how might ever sweetness have be knowe to him that never tasted bitternesse?" asked Chaucer in *Troilus and Criseyde.* Poets have connected *bitter* and *sweet* ever since, and the concept also made its way into several collections of proverbs. See also the synonymous TAKE THE ROUGH WITH THE SMOOTH.

take the bull by the horns, to To meet a difficulty head-on. The analogy to a matador who actually seizes a bull by the horns in order to wrestle it to the ground seems a little far-fetched but is often cited. A more likely origin is the barnyard, where a safely tethered bull could indeed be so grasped. The transfer to meeting other kinds of difficulty had taken place by 1800 or so. "It would never do to take the bull by the horns in that manner," warned John Galt (*The Provost,* 1822).

take the cake, to To win; to top them all. This reference to a cake as a prize today is often used ironically, as in O. Henry's "You Yankees assuredly take the cake for assurance" (*Helping the Other Fellow,* 1908). Apparently this was not always so, for the ancient Greeks awarded a cake to the person who best stayed awake during an all-night party. However, they then transferred the expression to any kind of prize-winning feat; the playwright Aristophanes wrote, "In all craftiness we take the cake" (the *Thesmophoriazusae,* translated as *The Women at Demeter's Festival,* 411 B.C.). The term was revived in late-nineteenth-century America, and many etymologists believe that, rather than referring to the ancient practice, it alluded to the then popular African-American contest called the "cake walk," in which couples walked around and around a cake that was then awarded to the couple judged to be the most graceful. See also PIECE OF CAKE.

take the heat, to To be blamed or censured severely. This colloquial term, from the first half of the 1900s, uses *heat* in the sense of severe pressure. R. Boyer used it in *The Dark Ship* (1947), "One guy, Stack, is takin' all the heat."

take the law into one's own hands See TAKE INTO ONE'S OWN HANDS.

take the load off one's feet Sit down. Also put as *take a load off,* this colloquial saying dates from about 1940. Both versions, often preceded by *sit down and,* are generally stated as imperatives.

take the money and run Be satisfied with what you have achieved or won, and don't try for more. This mid-twentieth-century saying was used as the title of Woody Allen's hilarious 1968 film about a compulsive thief. The original allusion is lost, but other than referring to theft, it might well allude to one's winnings at gambling.

take the rough with the smooth, to Accept the bad with as much equanimity as the good. This adage dates from the fifteenth century. The unknown author of the *Tale of Beryn* (c. 1400) stated it as "Take your part as it comyth, of roughe and eke of smooth." See also TAKE THE BITTER WITH THE SWEET.

take the wind out of someone's sails, to To put someone at a disadvantage; to stop someone, literally or figuratively. This term, which alludes to impeding a sailing vessel by sailing to windward of it and thereby robbing it of the wind, was used literally until about 1800. Sir Walter Scott used it figuratively in *The Fortunes of Nigel* (1822): "He would take the wind out of the sail of every gallant."

take the words out of someone's mouth See WORDS RIGHT OUT OF ONE'S MOUTH.

take to heart, to To be deeply moved or affected; to grieve over; to concern oneself seriously with. This expression was already being used in the sixteenth century and is by no means dated. Anthony Trollope used it in *The Belton Estate* (1865): "She had no idea when she was refusing him that he would take it to heart as he had done."

take to it like a duck to water, to To find a special affinity for it; to try something and like it. This rather obvious simile dates only from the late nineteenth century. Sir John Astley used it in his memoirs (*Fifty Years of My Life,* 1894): "I always took to shooting like a duck to water."

take to one's heels, to To flee. Clearly this term does not refer to running *on* one's heels, which would not make for a particularly rapid escape. Rather, the heels are all one sees of a person who turns tail (see also TURN TAIL). Thus Shakespeare wrote: "Darest thou . . . play the coward . . . and show it a fair pair of heels and run from it?" (*Henry IV, Part 1*, 2.4). John Ray recorded "show them a fair pair of heels" in his 1678 proverb collection, but in the nineteenth century it became a *clean* pair of heels (with Sir Walter Scott and Robert Louis Stevenson, among others). The current cliché dates from the nineteenth century as well. Henry Thomas Riley (1816–78) used it in his translation of Terence's play *Eunuchus:* "I took to my heels as fast as I could."

take to task, to To reprimand; to blame or censure. This term was used from the mid-eighteenth century to mean either assigning or challenging someone to a task. In its present meaning it has been current only since the late nineteenth century. Sir Arthur Conan Doyle used it in *Captain Polestar* (1890): "My employer took me severely to task." It sounds a bit stilted now and may be dying out.

take to the cleaners, to To dupe or defraud; to wipe out financially. This term may have been derived from the older *to be cleaned out,* which dates from the early nineteenth century and has precisely the same meaning. The current cliché is American slang dating from the mid-twentieth century, when commercial dry-cleaning establishments became commonplace, but it probably originated, like the older term, among gamblers. H. MacLennan used it in *Precipice* (1949): "He had taken Carl to the cleaners this time."

take umbrage, to To feel slighted; to take offense. The word "umbrage," which comes from the Latin *umbra,* meaning "shade" or "shadow," is rarely heard today except in this expression. Presumably the analogy here is to the shade or shadow of displeasure. A 1934 interview with Alan Dent used it with a play on words: "*Interviewer:* Can ghosts be angry?—*Dent:* What else is there to do in the shades except take umbrage?" (quoted in James Agate, *Ego,* March 11, 1934; cited in *Penguin Dictionary of Modern Quotations*).

take under one's wing See UNDER ONE'S WING.

take up the gauntlet See THROW DOWN THE GAUNTLET.

talk of the devil See SPEAK OF THE DEVIL.

talk of the town, the The latest gossip, a widespread rumor. This term appears in at least two Latin sources, Horace's *Satires* and Ovid's *Amores* ("You do not know it, but you are the talk of the town"). Samuel Pepys used the expression in his *Diary* (Sept. 2, 1661): "Though he be a fool, yet he keeps much company, and will tell all he sees or hears, so a man may understand what the common talk of the town is." Since its earliest publication, in 1925, the *New Yorker* magazine has carried a department called "Talk of the Town," at one time written entirely by James Thurber, and consisting of short articles of current interest.

talk one's head off, to To be extremely loquacious. This hyperbole, also put as *to talk someone's head* or *someone's ear* off, implies that the boredom of relentless loquacity is making either the speaker's or the listener's head fall off. These expressions have largely replaced the earlier *talk the hind leg off a horse/donkey/dog,* current from the mid-nineteenth to the mid-twentieth century. G. and S. Lorimer point out, in *The Heart Specialist* (1935), "An American will talk your ear off about his sport with a little encouragement." Yet another is *talk the ear off a brass monkey.* See also LIKE GREASED LIGHTNING.

talk the talk, walk the walk Speak or behave appropriately to some image. Although the first part of this term appears to have originated in the late 1800s—George Meredith used it c. 1887 in *Marian,* "She can talk the talk of men. And touch with thrilling fingers"— it did not become current until the second half of the 1900s. A *New York Times* headline for an article about an organization facing a sex discrimination suit even though it advised the Labor Department on this very subject, read, "Does RAND Walk the Talk on Labor Policy" (Sept. 5, 2004). In *The Inner Voice* (2004) by opera singer Renée Fleming, she wrote: "Musetta, of course, is a legendary coquette, and I was a famously shy girl from upstate. Even if I could learn how to talk the talk, I was hopeless when it came to walking the walk."

talk through one's hat, to To talk nonsense; to pontificate about something one knows little or nothing about. This late nineteenth-century expression calls up an image that makes no sense whatever. Theodore Pratt (*Thunder Mountain,* 1944) added a little meaning to it, writing, "You're talking through your hat, and your hat is full of holes."

talk turkey, to To get to the point, speak plainly. This expression has been ascribed to an apocryphal tale about a white man and an Indian hunting and then dividing the spoils. When the white man suggested, "Either I'll take the turkey and you the buzzard, or you take the buzzard and I the turkey," the Indian replied, "Now talk turkey to me." Whatever the true origin, the term was around by the time Thomas C. Haliburton edited *Traits of American Humor* (c. 1840), which stated, "I was plagy apt to talk turkey."

tall, dark, and handsome Supposedly what a woman wants in a man's appearance. This standard description of the romantic hero found in women's fiction of the first half of the 1900s was given further currency by the 1941 film, *Tall, Dark, and Handsome.* It starred dark-haired, good-looking Cesar Romero as an underworld boss who is really a softie at heart. See also STRONG SILENT TYPE.

tan someone's hide, to To give someone a beating. This term, in which the human skin is referred to as a hide (as it was from about the seventeenth century), may be on its way out, viewed with the same disfavor now accorded to SPARE THE ROD. Nevertheless, during the years when corporal punishment was considered a normal procedure, it became a cliché. (Incidentally, the tanning process, in which animal hide is converted into leather, does not involve beating but rather a soaking in chemicals.) The expression dates from the seventeenth century. Charles Coffey used it in *The Devil to Pay* (1731): "Come and spin . . . or I'll tan your hide for you."

tarred with the same brush, to be Characterized by the same faults or bad qualities. This expression probably comes from sheepherding, where it was long the practice to treat a sheep's sores by applying a brush dipped in tar. Since presumably all the sheep in one flock would be treated in this way, the term was transferred to humans sharing the same qualities. The figurative use dates from the early nineteenth century. In print Sir Walter Scott used it in several novels. John Ciardi, however, believed it came from the practice of sailors working with tar brushes (for caulking), and, being in cramped quarters, often tarring one another. This origin seems less likely.

tea and sympathy See under TLC.

teach an old dog new tricks, one can't/it's hard to The elderly cannot or will not change their ways. This saying dates from the sixteenth century, at first appearing with a literal meaning in a book of *Husbandry* (1523) and then in John Heywood's 1546 proverb collection. It is still current.

tear one's hair, to To show extreme anger, frustration, or grief. In ancient times it was customary to show grief by literally pulling at one's hair. The practice was referred to by Homer in the *Iliad,* with reference to Agamemnon, and appears in other ancient writings. Shakespeare used it in *Troilus and Cressida* (4.2), "Tear my bright hair, and scratch my praised cheeks," and Thackeray in *The Rose and the Ring* (1855), "Tearing her hair, crying and bemoaning herself." Today we are more apt to use it for anger or vexation, and entirely figuratively.

tell it like it is, to To tell the truth even though it is unpleasant. Linguistics professor Margaret G. Lee lists this among the verbal expressions borrowed from African-American English (*American Speech,* winter 1999). It undoubtedly gained currency as the title of a number-one rhythm and blues hit of 1967, and has become a standard and somewhat overused colloquialism. Jane Smiley played on it in *Horse Heaven* (2000): "He wasn't a funny guy like Baffert, but they always said he 'is peppery and straightforward,' 'pulls no punches,' 'tells it like it is.'" See also PULL NO PUNCHES; UNVARNISHED TRUTH.

tell tales out of school, to To reveal secrets; to talk out of turn. The earliest appearance of this expression in print occurred in William Tindale's *The Practyse of Prelates* (1530): "What cometh once in may never out, for fear of telling tales out of school." Presumably it first applied to children gossiping about what they heard at school, but it soon was used figuratively. It is now on the verge of obsolescence. However, just plain *to tell tales,* meaning to lie, survives.

tell that/it to the Marines Try fooling some more gullible person, because I won't fall for that story. This term originated about 1800 in Britain, when sailors had nothing but contempt for marines, whom they regarded as gullible greenhorns. Byron used the expression in *The Island* (1823): "That will do for the Marines but sailors won't believe it," remarking that this was already an old saying.

tempest in a teapot, a A storm over a trifle; MUCH ADO ABOUT NOTHING. This expression has appeared in slightly varying forms for hundreds of years—*a storm in a cream bowl* (1678 letter from the duke of Ormond to the earl of Arlington), *a tempest in a glass of water* (the grand duke Paul of Russia, c. 1790), *a storm in a hand-wash basin* (Lord Thurlow, c. 1830), and, throughout much of the nineteenth century, *a storm in a teacup* (still preferred in Britain). In the twentieth century it changed to its present form, at least in America.

tempt fate, to To expose to danger, to risk something. This expression dates from about 1700, when it replaced the earlier *to tempt fortune.* It appeared in John Dryden's translation of one of the satires of *Juvenal* (1693): "Thy Perjur'd Friend will quickly tempt his Fate."

tender loving care See TLC.

test of time, stood the/passed the Proved to be of lasting value. Although the idea is undoubtedly older, this expression appears to date only from 1800 or so. Washington Irving used it in his *Sketch Book* (1820): "They have borne the test of time."

test the water (waters), to To try something out. This expression, which alludes either to testing the purity of water in a well or to putting one's hand or foot into water to test its temperature, dates from the late 1800s. Diana Ramsay used it in *A Little Murder Music* (1970), "'If you're attempting to establish a motive. . . .'—'I'm just testing the water,' Meredith said."

T.G.I.F. Acronym for *thank God it's Friday,* indicating one is glad to reach the last day of the traditional five-day workweek. Eric Partridge suggested that this semi-humorous cliché may have originated among schoolteachers, but by the mid-1900s it had been taken over by anyone who worked a five-day week. From about 1991 to 2000 the *Boston Globe* business section ran a weekly Friday column entitled "T.G.I.F.," written by Alex Beam. New Hampshire's *Manchester Union-Leader* also has one, and probably countless other newspapers as well. At one point, Beam said, he also wrote a column called "T.G.I.W.," which ran on Wednesdays, but so many readers were baffled by this acronym that it was discontinued. T.G.I.F., on the other hand, definitely qualifies as a cliché.

thank God for small favors Be grateful for a minor advantage or gain. Generally this catchphrase is invoked without any religious significance, but rather as an expression of relief that something has gone well, or at least better than expected. An alternate version is *give thanks for small blessings.*

thank God it's Friday See T.G.I.F.

thank one's lucky stars, to To be grateful for good fortune. In ancient and medieval times, the stars were believed to have a powerful influence over the lives and destinies of human beings. Thanking them for good fortune, therefore, was a bit of superstitious politeness. Ben Jonson used the term "I thank my Starres for it" in his play, *Every Man Out of His Humour* (1599). The modern variant came into use during the last century and is more an expression of general relief at emerging unscathed from some dilemma than of belief in celestial influence.

thanks but no thanks It's nice of you/them to offer, but I/we don't want it. This phrase, dating from the late 1900s, may be put either seriously or ironically. The former usage appeared in the *New York Times* on the op-ed page on December 5, 1997: "Paul R. Gross properly laments the 'thanks but no thanks' attitude of the California commission." The latter attitude is seen in, "She offered to trade seats at the opera, hers being in the last row at the top of the balcony—thanks but no thanks!"

that ain't hay That's a lot; also, that's important. This American colloquialism, with its ungrammatical "ain't" for "isn't," dates from the first half of the 1900s and at first was used mainly to describe a large amount of money. It was used in this sense in the motion picture *The Killers* (1946), where a character says, "I'm out ten G's and that ain't hay for me these days." But it was also extended to other matters. Thus, a 1994 television serial, *Sally Jessy Raphaël*, had it: "Seven husbands! That ain't hay!"

that does it That accomplishes it, that completes it. This synonym of *that does the trick* (see DO THE TRICK) is quite a bit newer and simpler, *it* having been substituted for *the trick*. It also has more of a ring of finality than the older locution, as in "The last coat of paint is on; that does it."

that dog won't hunt This idea or excuse won't work. This folksy expression originated in the American South, where dogs are commonly used to hunt raccoons and other wild animals. Also put as *that old dog won't hunt,* it originated in the late 1800s.

that goes without saying See GOES WITHOUT SAYING.

that'll be the day That is very unlikely to occur. Also put as *that will be the day,* this phrase, stated with an emphasis on *that,* dates from the early 1900s, and quickly spread throughout the English-speaking world. Eric Partridge pointed out it was so popular in South Africa that it even spawned an Afrikaans equivalent, *dit sal die dag wees.* A 1957 song by Buddy Holly was entitled "That'll be the Day," and the phrase also was used as the title of a 1973 British film.

that's how (the way) the ball bounces/cookie crumbles This is the way things have turned out and nothing can be done about it; that's fate. These expressions became current in America in the mid-twentieth century and quickly spread to the rest of the English-speaking world. Both are enhanced by alliteration, and neither has a totally clear meaning. The bounce of a ball on an uneven surface can affect the outcome of a game, and a cookie disintegrating into crumbs is difficult to consume neatly. Edward Albee used the latter in his play, *The Zoo Story* (1960): "'Well . . . naturally every man wants a son, but . . .'—'But that's the way the cookie crumbles?'"

that's that That's all; that finishes it. This expression may have begun life as *that's for that;* James Kelly's *Scottish Proverbs* (1721) stated, "That's for that. . . . Spoken when a thing fits nicely what it was design'd for." The present-day locution dates from the early twentieth century, and there are several variants: *and that is that; and that's that; well, that's that.* All of them became current in the middle of the century.

that's the ticket That's exactly right; that's what is wanted. There is considerable dispute about the origin of this colloquial term, which has been around since the early nineteenth century. One theory holds that it is a corruption of the French *C'est l'etiquette,* meaning "It's the proper course to pursue." Another holds it comes from the custom of nineteenth-century charities issuing tickets to the poor for obtaining soup, coal, and other necessities. That might explain its use in an early British reference, W. N. Glascock's *Sketch-Book* (1834), cited by Eric Partridge. An early American reference, in Thomas Haliburton's Sam Slick tale *The Clockmaker* (1838), would not fit, however. Possibly, it has been suggested, the term refers to a political ticket. Or perhaps it means a winning ticket in a lottery. Also put as *just the ticket,* it has by now reached cliché status.

the bigger they come/are, the harder they fall The mighty are brought lower than the lowly. Although the concept is as old as anyone who has faced a more powerful opponent, the saying is attributed to several turn-of-the-twentieth-century boxers who were facing such odds. One was Robert Fitzsimmons, who allegedly said it in 1902 before losing to James J. Jeffries, a much heavier man than he. Another was James J. Corbett, who had to fight Fitzsimmons, much taller than he, in 1897. According to Eric Partridge, the expression caught on as a term of defiance against one's superiors in the British armed forces of World War I. Several variants have sprung up, among them *the taller they are, the further/farther they fall;* and *the harder you fall, the higher you bounce.*

the big picture The overall or long-range view of a situation. This phrase, which implies that details will be omitted in favor of presenting a BIRD'S-EYE VIEW, dates from the second half of the twentieth century. Originally American, it was used by *Time* magazine (Sept. 19, 1977): "The Bunyanesque extrovert who cheerfully mangled facts in his haste to paint the big picture." In Britain the term was used from the first half of the 1900s to describe the feature film in a movie presentation. However, British usage now is the same as the American. Stella Rimington's 2004 thriller, *At Risk* had it: "Clyde, might I propose that, if they've got the time, we show our guests around? Give them the big picture?"

the feeling is mutual You and I feel the same way. Strictly speaking, *mutual* means "reciprocal." When Jack says, "I can't stand your affected accent," and Jill replies, "The feeling is mutual," Jill is saying that she feels the same way about Jack's accent. Nevertheless, in the course of the twentieth century, when this expression became a cliché, it was—and still is—often misused, in that it is used to describe a common or shared feeling about something or someone else. For example, when Jill says, "I think the president is marvelous" and Jack says, "The feeling is mutual," he really means he thinks the same as she, but no reciprocity is involved. (This misuse has an honorable ancestry; Dickens made the same mistake in the title of his novel *Our Mutual Friend.*) See also MUTUAL ADMIRATION SOCIETY.

the hard way The most difficult method or path. This term comes from the game of craps, where it means making two dice come up with a pair of equal numbers totaling the point. For example, if eight is the point to be made, *the hard way* calls for rolling two fours; neither five-three nor six-two will do. Since the chances of rolling two fours are much less than the other combinations, this way is "hard." The term then was extended to such phrases as "learn something the hard way," meaning to learn through bitter experience, and "come up the hard way," meaning to rise by one's own efforts.

the king is dead, long live the king! A rapid succession of power has taken place. Allegedly this expression was used in France on the death of Charles VII in 1461, Louis XIV in 1715, and Louis XVIII in 1824. This allusion to the concept of royal succession, far less important in the present day, is now more often applied to other bastions of power—chief executives of large corporations, leaders of political parties, and the like.

then and there At that particular time and place, on the spot. This fifteenth-century phrase has probably survived owing to its pleasing alliteration. It is often used as a synonym for "immediately," as in "The doctor stitched her up then and there." For a time it also was put as *there and then,* but this usage is far less common and consequently does not qualify as a cliché.

the pits, (it's) It can't get any worse than this; wholly objectionable. Originating in America in the second half of the twentieth century, this expression is nonetheless mysterious in origin. Some speculate that it originally meant the coal pits, an unpleasant place for miners; some think it alludes to armpits, traditionally a smelly place. The American humorist Erma Bombeck played on it in the title of her book *If Life Is Just a Bowl of Cherries, What Am I Doing in the Pits?* (1978). And Robert Barnard (*Death and the Chaste Apprentice,* 1989) has a character say, "I think anyone would have been a letdown. But Capper she thought the absolute pits."

there but for the grace of God go I I could be in that miserable situation myself. Many writers have attributed this expression to John Bradford, who uttered it on seeing some criminals being led to their execution about 1553. However, it also has been attributed to John Wesley, John Bunyan, and several other important religious leaders. In fact, Bradford himself was executed two years later as a heretic (he was a Protestant in then Roman Catholic England). The expression today is used upon seeing such minor mishaps as a flat tire, as well as for more serious disasters.

thereby hangs a tale That reminds the speaker of another anecdote. This punning expression was not original with Shakespeare, but he used it in at least four plays (*The Taming of the Shrew, As You Like It, The Merry Wives of Windsor, Othello*), helping it to become a cliché. "A tale that thereby hangs drops easily off the gossip's tongue" appeared in *Meditations in Wall Street* (1940).

there's no business like show business The theater and those who work in it belong to a special sphere. This rhyming expression was the title of a song by Irving Berlin (in *Annie Get Your Gun,* 1946) and has virtually attained cliché status. See also SHOW MUST GO ON.

there's no flies on him/her This person is very sharp and shrewd. The expression refers to the fact that he or she doesn't stand still long enough for flies to land. A late nineteenth-century Americanism, it appeared in Eugene Field's poem "Jest 'fore Christmas" (1892): "Most all the time, the whole year round, there ain't no flies on me." It also was in the title of a Salvation Army song (1900), "There Are No Flies on Jesus" ("There may be flies on you and me, / But there are no flies on Jesus"). More recently, Robert Barnard used it (*Death and the Chaste Apprentice,* 1989): "'Oh, I've ideas all right. There's no flies on me, you know. I'll get to the bottom of it.'"

there's no fool like an old fool Foolishness does not abate with age. This observation was already a proverb when John Heywood amassed his 1546 proverb collection. It has been repeated ever since.

there's no place like home One is most comfortable in one's own surroundings. This phrase is a quotation from the song "Home, Sweet Home" (1823), words by John Howard Payne and music by Sir Henry Rowley Bishop, from the opera *Clari,* introduced at London's Covent Garden. The song, sung at the end of the first act, brought down the house (see BRING DOWN THE HOUSE) and quickly became popular throughout the English-speaking world. It was used as an encore by two of the most famous singers of their time, Jenny Lind and Adelina Patti. The text alluded to is "'Mid pleasures and palaces though we may roam, / Be it ever so humble, there's no place like home." Allegedly expressing Payne's own homesickness, the phrase echoes a sixteenth-century proverb listed by John Heywood in 1546 ("Home is homely, though it be poore in syght") and repeated by John Ray in 1670 ("Home is home though it be never so homely").

there's no two ways about it See NO TWO WAYS ABOUT IT.

there's something in the wind Something unknown or unexpected is about to happen. This expression dates from the early sixteenth century. R. Edwards used it in *Damon and Pithias* (c. 1566), "There is sumwhat in the winde," as did John Dryden in *The Spanish Friar* (1681), "There's something in the wind, I'm sure."

there's the rub There's the drawback; that's the impediment. This term may come from the ancient game of bowls, in which *rub* meant some uneveness in the ground that hindered or diverted the free movement of the bowl. It was transferred to other kinds of hindrance by the late sixteenth century, but the term really gained widespread currency through Shakespeare's use of it in Hamlet's soliloquy: "To sleep; perchance to dream: ay there's the rub: for in that sleep of death what dreams may come" (*Hamlet,* 3.1).

there you go A phrase with multiple meanings: you're right, you've done well, here is what you ordered or asked for, here is your answer, and the like. This meaningless (or multiple-meaning) locution dates from the first half of the 1800s. It acquired yet another meaning when Ronald Reagan said, "*There you go again*" in a debate with Jimmy Carter during the 1980 presidential campaign. Reagan here meant, "You're wrong again," denying Carter's repeated charge that Reagan was a warmonger. This usage, as a dismissal suggesting someone repeatedly says something wrong or misleading, has remained current.

the royal we The first person plural used by a person with supreme authority, or, in modern times, sometimes to preserve anonymity. Supposedly, the first king to use *we* in this way was Richard I in the Charter to Winchester (1190). "We are not amused" is a rebuke often attributed to straitlaced Queen Victoria. In the twentieth century, magazines and newspapers frequently use *the editorial we* to express an opinion that may in fact be shared by no one but the writer. Lisa Alther expressed an opinion about that in her novel *Kinflicks* (1979): "She had learnt . . . that it was impossible to discuss issues civilly with a person who insisted on referring to himself as 'we.'"

the suspense is killing me I can't wait to learn the outcome. This hyperbole of impatience is a twentieth-century expression of an age-old idea. "Suspense in news is torture, speak them out," wrote John Milton (*Samson Agonistes,* 1671). Jonathan Swift claimed, "It is a miserable thing to live in suspense; it is the life of a spider" (*Thoughts on Various Subjects,* 1714), and

F. E. Smedley wrote, "Suspense, that toothache of the mind" (*Frank Fairlegh,* 1850).

the time of one's life An occasion of outstanding enjoyment. This term, a colloquial Americanism of the late nineteenth century, gained currency throughout the English-speaking world in the twentieth century. William Saroyan used it as the title of his 1939 play, *The Time of Your Life.*

thick and fast Quickly crowding; in such rapid succession that they run together. This term began life in the sixteenth century as *thick and threefold* ("Thicke and threefold trends will flocke," Timothy Kendall, *Epigrammes,* 1577). The change to "thick and fast" occurred about 1700 and definitively replaced the older term. Lewis Carroll, in his poem about the walrus and the carpenter (*Through the Looking Glass,* 1872), wrote about the oysters, "And thick and fast they came at last, / And more, and more, and more—." See also FAST AND FURIOUS.

thick as thieves On intimate terms; very good friends. The use of *thick* for "intimate" survives mainly in this cliché, which no doubt owes its popularity to alliteration. It was already proverbial, according to Theodore E. Hook, in 1833 (*The Parson's Daughter*): "She and my wife are as thick as thieves, as the proverb goes."

thick skin, to have a To be insensitive to shame, reproof, slander, or criticism. The transfer of a tough epidermis to mental toughness is ancient, appearing in the writings of the Roman orator Cicero, among others. Carlyle wrote in *Frederick the Great* (1858), "Voltaire was a fool not to have thicker skin." The opposite is meant by having a *thin skin*—that is, being hypersensitive to reproof or criticism, or being easily hurt. This usage dates from the late 1600s.

thin edge of the wedge, the An unimportant action that is the start of a major development, often an undesirable one. This expression alludes to the pointed metal wedge inserted into a log for splitting wood. The expression began to be used figuratively in the nineteenth century. Anthony Trollope used it several times in *Dr. Thorne* (1858), and it was commonplace by the end of the century. Richard Blackmore had it in *The Remarkable History of Sir Thomas Upmore* (1884): "My father kept calling him . . . the thin edge of the wedge, and telling dear mother . . . not to let him in."

thing of beauty (is a joy forever), a True loveliness (is a lasting quality). The complete thought is a line from John Keats's great poem, "Endymion" (1818), and continues, "Its loveliness increases; it will never pass into nothingness." The thought is hardly original, but the expression caught on. In the twentieth century it began to be shortened and used simply to describe something lovely, often ironically. Eric Partridge mentioned a play on it made by "flappers," fashionable young women of the post–World War I era: "A thing of beauty is a boy forever." Today one is apt to say it of, for example, an elaborately decorated cake.

think nothing of it You're welcome; it's no big deal. This airy dismissal of thanks came into wide use around 1940 on both sides of the Atlantic. It survives, though it is rapidly being replaced by NO PROBLEM. An early appearance in print was in Terence Rattigan's play *The Sleeping Prince* (1948), in which Mary responds to "I shall not soon forget your kindness" with "Think nothing of it."

think positive Concentrate on the bright side, on what is constructive and good; ignore the negative aspect. This exhortation comes from Norman Vincent Peale's inspirational best-seller, *The Power of Positive Thinking* (1953). Although the idea had been developed by numerous psychologists of the early twentieth century, the term itself became current after the publication of Dr. Peale's book.

think twice, to To consider carefully before speaking or acting. It is an old idea, but this particular expression of it did not become widely used until the late nineteenth century. In his poem "Think Twice" (c. 1885), Eugene F. Ware wrote, "Results are often grevious When people get too previous; 'Think twice' is good advice."

third degree, to give/get the To give or be subjected to intensive questioning and/or rough treatment. In Freemasonry, the third and highest degree is that of master mason, attained after a stiff examination, and several writers speculate that this may be the source of the late nineteenth-century expression for an inquisition. Today the term is used both for the sometimes brutal tactics of the police and other authorities to make a prisoner tell the truth or reveal secrets, and more lightly for questioning about less important matters, as in "Jane gave Martha the third degree about her good-looking new boss."

thirty pieces of silver The symbol of treason. This term comes from the Bible, where Judas's price for betraying Jesus was thirty pieces of silver (Matthew 26:15). It has symbolized betrayal ever since.

this, too, shall/will pass These troubles are temporary; be patient and things will work out. This term originally was used in a very serious way about the fleeting nature of human life, words, and endeavors. It was so used in the biblical Apocrypha (c. 100 B.C.), as well as later philosophical writings. The current cliché is a more lighthearted expression of forbearance.

thorn in the flesh/one's side, a A source of constant irritation. This expression appears in several books of the Bible; in the Book of Judges (2:3) it refers to enemies who "shall be as thorns in your sides," and in the New Testament Paul refers to his infirmities as "given to me a thorn in the flesh" (2 Corinthians 12:7). The term remains current.

threat or a promise, is that a Are you giving me bad news or good? According to lexicographer Eric Partridge, this was the soldier's answer to the vulgar phrase, "Fuck you!" and dates from World War I or even earlier. In civilian language it came to be applied other than sexually, whenever a doubtful proposition was made. Partridge quoted Julian Symons's *A Three Pipe Problem* (1975): "'Goodbye, I advise you to keep out of my way.' . . . She smelt of cigarette smoke and gin. 'Next time, Mr. Holmes? Is that a threat or a promise?'"

three-ring circus, a An occasion of utter confusion. This late nineteenth-century Americanism alludes to a circus in which three rings or arenas are featuring performances at the same time. Possibly invented by P. T. Barnum, the epitome of American show business entrepreneurs, the term was transferred to other extravagant events and disorderly situations by about 1900. Rudyard Kipling used it in *A Diversity of Creatures* (1914): "I can see lots of things from here. It's like a three-ring circus!"

three R's, the Basic education. This term may have been coined by Sir William Curtis (1752–1829). According to several sources, this illiterate alderman, who became Lord Mayor of London, presented a toast to the three R's: Reading, Riting, and Rithmetic. Whether or not this tale is true, the term was picked up by others and became current in the early nineteenth century.

three's a crowd See TWO'S COMPANY.

three sheets in/to the wind Drunk. The term comes from sailing ships and refers to the sheet, or rope, that controls the sail. If a sheet is allowed to flap freely in the wind, the sail also flaps about and the vessel proceeds on a tottering course, like that of an intoxicated person. The more sheets are loose, the shakier the course. Dickens used the expression figuratively in *Dombey and Son* (1848): "Captain Cuttle, looking . . . at Bunsby more attentively, perceived that he was three sheets in the wind, or in plain words, drunk." The expression may be obsolescent today, at least in America.

through and through Thoroughly, wholly, repeatedly. This expression, which at first meant literally penetrated, dates from about 1500. Hugh Walpole used it in *The Fortress* (1932): "The mist immediately surrounding him was . . . so wetting that he was already soaked through and through."

through the mill, to go/to be put To undergo hardship or rough treatment. The analogy here is to being ground down like grain. The figurative use of the term dates from the nineteenth century. "We've all passed through that mill," wrote Rolf Bolderwood (*A Colonial Reformer,* 1890).

through thick and thin Despite all difficulties; overcoming all obstacles. This term, which today is often used together with the idea of continuing to support another person despite all difficulties, appeared in Chaucer's *Canterbury Tales.* The analogy is to penetrating difficult terrain, such as a forest consisting of thick growth as well as sparse vegetation. It was made clear by Edmund Spenser in *The Faerie Queene* (1590): "His tyreling Jade he fiersly forth did push. Through thicke and thin, both over banck and bushe."

throw down the gauntlet, to To issue a challenge. Conversely, *to take up the gauntlet* means to accept a challenge. These terms date from the time of knighthood, when the gauntlet, a glove of mail or plate used to protect the hand, was part of the standard armor. Throwing it down was a challenge to combat, as chronicled by Edward Hall in the sixteenth century. "I cast them my Gauntlet, take it up who dares," wrote Thomas Nashe (*Pasquil's Apologie,* 1590). By the eighteenth century both terms had been extended to any kind of challenge, as in *Theodric* by Thomas Campbell (1777–1844): "Her towns, where civic independence flings The gauntlet down to senates, courts, and kings." See also RUN THE GAUNTLET.

throw dust in someone's eyes, to To mislead someone. This term, already known in ancient Roman times, comes from the practice of soldiers confounding the enemy by literally throwing dust or sand in the air, creating a primitive kind of smoke screen. Used by Mohammed's armies as well as many other early peoples, the practice was referred to by Erasmus (*Adagia,* 1523), who called it "A useful stratagem." By Benjamin Franklin's time the term was being used figuratively. "It required a long discourse to throw dust in the eyes of common sense," he wrote (*Works,* 1767).

throw good money after bad, to To continue wasting resources on a hopeless project. Although the idea is much older, the expression appeared only in the nineteenth century. "If they would . . . start free, instead of sending good money after bad—how much happier would be this world of ours!" wrote James Payn (*The Canon's Ward,* 1884).

throw in the sponge/towel, to To acknowledge defeat; to give up. J. C. Hotten's *Slang Dictionary* of 1860 explained that this term comes from prizefighting, where throwing up the sponge used to clean the contender's face was a signal that the "mill," or round, was concluded. However, Hotten got it wrong; the sponge (or later, towel) more often was thrown up as a signal of defeat, and it is in this sense that the expression was transferred to other enterprises. "If ever you are tempted to say . . . 'I am beaten and I throw up the sponge,' remember Paul's wise exhortation," wrote Alexander Maclaren (*Philippians,* 1909). Later *up* was changed to *in,* at least in North America.

throw light on See SHED LIGHT ON.

throw one's weight around, to To use one's wealth or standing to manipulate others; to act officiously. This expression dates from the early twentieth century and uses *weight* in the sense of "authority." John P. Marquand had it in *H. M. Pulham, Esquire* (1941): "Bo-jo was a bastard, a big bastard. Perhaps he meant that Bo-jo sometimes threw his weight around."

throw out the baby with the bathwater, to/don't To discard the good along with the bad. The source of this expression may be a German proverb, *Das Kind mit dem Bade ausschütten* (Pouring the baby out with the bath), and its vivid image of upending a small tub clearly caught on. It appeared in English in 1853, possibly as a translation from the German by Thomas Carlyle, and was favored by George Bernard Shaw, who used it in several books, including *Parents and Children* (1914): "We are apt to make the usual blunder of emptying the baby out with the bath."

throw the book at, to To scold or punish severely. The term comes from a legal one meaning to sentence an offender to the maximum penalties allowed, the *book* meaning the entire roster of laws and penalties applicable to the particular crime. The legal metaphor was in use in the early twentieth century, and by the middle of the century it was broadened to include reproaches and nonlegal remedies. Joseph Heller's wonderful satire on military mores, *Catch-22* (1961), stated, "He was formally charged with breaking ranks while in formation, felonious assault, indiscriminate behavior, mopery, high treason, provoking . . . In short, they threw the book at him."

throw to the winds, to To cast away or reject something. This phrase has been so used since the mid-1600s, alluding to the fact that the winds will blow away a trait or feeling. Thus *to throw caution to the winds* means to act boldly, *to throw modesty to the winds* means to abandon reserve or demureness, and so on. In *At Bay* (1885), Mrs. Alexander wrote, "You must throw fear to the winds."

throw to the wolves, to To abandon or deliver something or someone to a terrible fate. This term comes from Aesop's fable about a nurse who threatens to throw her charge to the wolves unless the child behaves better. She never intends to carry out her threat, so the wolf waits in vain for its prey. It is the idea of sacrificing someone that survived in the cliché, as, for example, in Clarissa Cushman's mystery *I Wanted to Murder* (1941): "She was his wife. He couldn't throw her to the wolves."

throw up one's hands, to To express despair, frustration, or exasperation. Although this gesture must be very old indeed, the expression appeared in print only from the late nineteenth century. George M. Fenn used it in *The Double Knot* (1890): "The woman threw up her hands and reeled."

tickled pink/to death, to be To be extremely pleased; to be overcome with amusement or delight. Both versions rest on the fact that tickling causes laughing, an expression of pleasure. The older is to be tickled to death, which dates from about 1800. Paulding used it in his play *The Bucktails* (1815, 4.2): "Stab me, but do not tickle me to death in sport." Tickling someone pink means they turn pink with the blush of either pleasure or suppressed laughter. P. G. Wodehouse wrote (*Nothing Serious,* 1950), "Your view, then, is that he is tickled pink to be freed from his obligations?" Both expressions have largely supplanted *to tickle one's fancy,* meaning to divert or please or amuse and in use since the eighteenth century. John Doran had it in *The History of Court Fools* (1858): "The joke . . . tickled the fancy of the Tirynthians."

tie the knot, to To get married. This expression dates from the sixteenth century, or rather, is an abbreviation of one used then. It originally was *to tie a knot with one's tongue that one cannot untie with one's teeth,* and so appeared in several earlier printed sources as well as in John Ray's 1670 proverb collection. The analogy is clear: the bonds of marriage are viewed as a knot, which, were it of string or cord, could be undone with the teeth—in other words, an early mixed metaphor. Although the full saying still appears in *Rustic Speech,* a collection by E. M. Wright published in 1913, all but "tie the knot" had long been dropped and survives as the current cliché, although in this age of relatively common and simple divorces it may be obsolescent.

tiger by the tail, to have a To take on something that turns out to be too formidable or difficult. This term, with its vivid image of manually catching a wild beast that rewards one with violent thrashing about (or worse), replaced the earlier *catch a Tartar,* used from 1663 to the late nineteenth century. Emma Lathen wrote, in *Murder Without Icing* (1972), "The Sloan Guaranty Trust . . . might well have a tiger by the tail," alluding to an impossible investment.

tight as a drum Close-fitting and taut. The analogy is to the skin of the drumhead, which is tightly stretched so that when it is struck the drum sounds as it should. This term was transferred in the nineteenth century to anything stretched taut; Thomas Hughes (*Tom Brown's School Days,* 1857) described his hero as having eaten so much that "his little skin is as tight as a drum." In succeeding years, however, the analogy itself was sometimes to a drum-shaped container for liquids, such as an oil drum, which of course must be well sealed to prevent leakage. Hence the expression "tight as a drum" also became synonymous with "watertight," as in "The shelter they rigged up was as tight as a drum."

tight as a tick Intoxicated. Presumably the analogy here is to a tick engorged with blood (since ticks feed on warm-blooded animals). *Tight* has long been a colloquial term for "drunk," and "tight as a tick," an Americanism enhanced by alliteration, dates from the mid-nineteenth century. Anthony Price combined two synonymous clichés in *Soldier No More* (1981): "He was drunk as a lord . . . tight as a tick."

tighten one's belt, to To be more frugal; to undergo adversity with patience. The analogy here is to tightening one's belt after losing weight from going hungry. *The London Observer* of 1927 described "A traveling troupe who quoted Corneille while tightening their belts."

till hell freezes over Forever, endlessly. This hyperbole, like NOT A HOPE IN HELL, dates from the early twentieth century, first appearing in print about 1919. F. Scott Fitzgerald reportedly liked ending a letter with, "Yours till hell freezes over," and A. A. Fair used it in *Stop at the Red Light* (1962): "They'll investigate until hell freezes over." During the Cuban missile crisis of 1962, U.S. ambassador to the United Nations, Adlai Stevenson, asked the Soviet ambassador if his country had placed missiles in Cuba and said, ". . . I am prepared to wait for my answer until hell freezes over" (Oct. 25, 1962). The negative version, *not till hell freezes over,* means, of course, "never."

till the cows come home See NOT UNTIL THE COWS COME HOME.

tilt at windmills, to To pursue a fruitless course or attack nonexistent enemies. This expression comes from Cervantes's famous hero, Don Quixote, who rides with his lance at full tilt (poised to attack) upon a row of windmills, which he mistakes for evil giants (*Don Quixote,* Part 1, chapter 8; 1605). The image has caught the imagination of subsequent writers to the present day.

time and tide wait for no man Stop procrastinating; do it now. This old proverb is usually interpreted to mean that the course of neither time nor the seas' tides can be halted or delayed, so you'd better get on with what you're supposed to do. An early version (1592) stated, "Tyde nor time tarrieth no man." Later it was "Time and tide for no man stay." Sir Walter Scott was fond of the present locution, using it several times. There are versions in German and French as well.

time and time again Repeatedly, often. This version of the earlier *time and again,* or *again and again,* dates from the late nineteenth century. Evelyn Waugh used it in *The Ordeal of Gilbert Pinfold* (1957): ". . . envying painters who are allowed to return to the same theme time and time again."

time flies Time moves swiftly onward. Time was said to *fly* or *flee* by numerous ancients, especially the Romans, for whom *Tempus fugit* (translated as "time flies," although it also means "flees") was a well-known proverb. Chaucer wrote, "For though we sleep or wake, or rome, or ryde, Ay fleeth the tyme, it nil no man abyde" (*The Clerk's Tale*). Occasionally the term was amplified, such as "Time flies as swiftly as an arrow" (in Ken Hoshino's translation of Kaibaka Ekken's *Ten Kun,* 1710). Today we sometimes say, *how time flies,* occasionally amplified (either seriously or satirically) with *when you're having fun.*

time is money One's time is a precious commodity. The sentiment for this phrase dates from ancient times, but the exact wording is most often attributed to Benjamin Franklin in his *Advice to a Young Tradesman* (1748): "Remember that time is money." Charles Dickens elaborated on it in *Nicholas Nickleby* (1839): "Time is money . . . And very good money too to those who reckon interest by it."

time is ripe, the This is a suitable occasion or moment for a particular event. Time here is likened to fruit that has ripened and is ready to pick or eat. The term was already known in Shakespeare's time. He used it in *Henry IV, Part 1*: "I by letters shall direct your course. When time is ripe, which will be suddenly, I'll steal to Glendower and Lord Mortimer" (1.3).

time of day See GIVE (SOMEONE) THE TIME OF DAY.

time on one's hands, (to have) To be idle or bored; not have enough to do. This expression dates from the late seventeenth century and was in print by 1700. "My time lies heavy on my hands" appears in George Farquar's 1703 play *The Inconstant* (5.3). See also TIME TO KILL.

time out of mind See under FROM TIME IMMEMORIAL.

times are out of joint, the This is a disrupted or confused state of affairs; things are in disarray. This expression comes from Shakespeare's *Hamlet.* When the hero has just learned that he is to avenge his father's murder by his uncle, he says, "The time is out of joint: O cursed spite That ever I was born to set it right" (1.5). The poet's allusion to a dislocated bony joint was taken up by others, but it may now be obsolescent.

time to kill Spare time which one must somehow occupy. The word *kill* here implies wasting or using time frivolously, and indeed this is the implication in Vanbrugh and Cibber's play *The Provok'd Husband* (1728): "What think you, if we three sat soberly down to kill an hour at ombre [a card game]?" Ugo Betti (*The Fugitive,* 1953) took a more sober and critical view: "Killing time is the chief end of our society."

time warp A distortion of space/time causing a person to remain stationary or travel back and forth in time. Originating in the mid-1900s in science fiction, the term soon was used about people or things who seemed to be caught in a particular stage of the past. Thus, *Modern Railways* used it in February 1986: "The collapse of the Advanced Passenger Train project has left InterCity services on the West Coast main line in a 1970 'time warp.'"

time will tell Wait and see. This cautionary adage was already in print in 1539 in R. Taverner's translation of Erasmus: "Tyme discloseth all thynges." It was certainly a cliché by the time E. H. Porter used it in *Pollyanna* (1913): "The doctor had looked very grave . . . and had said time alone could tell."

tip of the iceberg, (only) the A small and superficial manifestation of a much larger (and often worse) situation. Icebergs are large, floating masses of ice detached from a glacier and carried out to sea; the bulk of their mass is below the water's surface. This metaphor dates from the mid-twentieth century. Michael Gilbert used it in *The Etruscan Net* (1969): "I think, to employ a well-known metaphor, that all we can see at the moment is the tip of the iceberg."

tip/turn the scales, to To change the balance slightly so as to favor one side. The idea was expressed as long ago as Aristotle's *Politics* (c. 340 B.C.), in which he wrote "The addition of the middle class turns the scale and prevents either of the extremes from being dominant" (Benjamin Jowett translation, c. 1875). Jowett's wording may have been influenced by William Wordsworth's "Ode" (1815): "Thy presence turns the scale of doubtful fight, / Tremendous God of battles, Lord of Hosts!"

tissue of lies See PACK OF LIES.

tit for tat Payment in kind; precise retaliation. Most authorities believe this expression was a corruption of *tip for tap,* meaning "a blow for a blow." It was already in its current form in the sixteenth century. John Heywood's *Proverbs* (1546) stated, "Sens tyt for tat (quoth I) on euen hand is set, Set the hares head against the goose ieblet," and in his *Spider and Flie* (1556), "That is tit for tat in this altricacion."

TLC Acronym for *tender loving care.* In modern times this phrase is believed to have originated in a hospital or other sick-care setting, where it alludes to kind and solicitous treatment by nurses. From the mid-1900s on it caught on in a more general way, particularly among songwriters, according to wordsmith Nigel Rees, who found nearly a dozen songs with this title written between 1960 and 1983. Today the term, both spelled out and abbreviated, is applied to kind or gentle treatment for almost anything—a pet, person, plant, automobile, and so on. It has just about replaced the almost synonymous *tea and sympathy,* meaning special kindness shown to someone who is upset. This term was always most common in Britain, where a cup of tea is standard treatment in such situations. It gained currency as the title of a play by Robert Anderson and a motion picture based on it (1956) about a prep school boy's affair with a teacher's wife, but it has largely died out, at least in America.

to a fault Excessively so. This locution, which is always applied to a quality that is inherently good but may not be so in excess—for example, "generous to a fault"—dates from the nineteenth century. The *fault* in question, of course, is that of excess. Robert Browning used it in *The Ring and the Book* (1868), "Faultless to a fault"—that is, too perfect. A similar phrase is *to a fare-the-well,* but it implies perfection and not necessarily excess. For example, "The table was decorated to a fare-the-well; nothing was lacking." See also TOO MUCH OF A GOOD THING.

to a T Exactly so; a perfect fit. Some writers believe this expression, which dates from the late seventeenth century, alludes to the T-square, used by draftsmen for accurate drawing. Others lean toward the idea that it comes from crossing one's t's (see DOT THE I'S AND CROSS THE T'S). An early appearance in print is in George Farquar's play *Love in a Bottle* (1699, 4.3): "He answered the description . . . to a T, sir."

to beat the band Outstandingly, surpassing all others. One writer believes this term comes from the idea of making more noise than a loud band, and the *OED* concurs, saying it means literally to drown out the band. It originated in late-nineteenth-century Britain and soon traveled to the United States, Canada, and other English-speaking lands. "I was driving lickety-split to beat the band," boasted C. M. Flandrau (*Harvard Episodes,* 1897).

to each his own Every person has his or her own preferences. This phrase, appearing in slightly different versions since the 1500s, is most often a remark that someone has a right to different preferences from one's own. See also NO ACCOUNTING FOR TASTES.

toe the line/mark, to To meet a particular standard; to conform strictly to a rule. The term comes from track, when the runners in a race line up with their toes placed on the starting line or mark. It began to be used figuratively in the early nineteenth century. The *OED* cites "He began to think it was high time to toe the mark," from *The Diverting History of John Bull and Brother Jonathan* (1813) by "H. Bull-Us."

to hell and gone A long way off; forever. This term dates from the first half of the twentieth century. Margaret Millar used it in her *Soft Talkers* (1957): "I can contradict myself to hell and gone if I feel like it." From the mid-1800s, this term also was used for "utter ruin," as in "The stock market's blown him to hell and gone." This usage appears to be obsolete.

tomorrow is another day You've done enough for one day so leave the rest until tomorrow; also, you may have lost today but you may win the next time. The first meaning, similar to ROME WAS NOT BUILT IN A DAY, dates at least from the sixteenth century, when it was sometimes put as *tomorrow is a new day* (by Lyly and others; quoted by Jonathan Swift in 1738). The exact current wording dates from the early nineteenth century, and the second meaning of that same expression from the early twentieth century. "Tomorrow's another day," wrote Paul Green (*The Field God,* 1927), and less ambiguously, Barbara Pym in *A Few Green Leaves* (1980), "He would probably have . . . missed his opportunity. Still, tomorrow was another day." In the motion picture *Gone With the Wind* (1939), Scarlett O'Hara's concluding line, after losing Tara and Rhett Butler, is, "After all, tomorrow is another day."

tongue in cheek, with To speak ironically or mockingly; slyly insincere. Presumably this term originally referred to the mocking facial expression resulting from poking one's tongue in one's cheek. It dates from the first half of the nineteenth century. H. McLeave used it in *Borderline Case* (1979): "'Only for those people who have something sinister to hide,' he said, tongue-in-cheek."

too big for one's britches (breeches) Conceited, self-important. This expression, alluding to becoming so swelled with self-importance as to burst out of one's clothes, sounds ancient but dates only from about 1900, as does the closely related *too big for one's boots.* The latter appeared in Sir Henry Maxwell's *Life of W. H. Smith* (1894): "Sometimes a young man, 'too big for his boots,' would sniff at being put in charge of a railway bookstall." And H. G. Wells (*Kipp, The Story of a Simple Soul,* 1905) wrote, "He's getting too big for 'is britches."

too close for comfort/to home See CLOSE CALL/SHAVE.

too close to call It is impossible to guess who is the winner. This term comes from CLOSE CALL, which since the late 1800s has meant a narrow escape. The current phrase seems to have originated in the 1960s in political broadcasting, according to William Safire, when it began to be used in reporting election results. In a situation where all the votes had been reported but there was no certain winner, the election was said to be too close to call. Since then the phrase has also been used of certain sports decisions, such as line calls in tennis (was the ball in or out?), penalty plays in basketball, and the like.

too good to be true Exaggeratedly optimistic; seeming so wonderful that something must be wrong with it. This cautious view is undoubtedly even older than its first expression in English, in the sixteenth century. Nevertheless, it has been repeated in the same form ever since, with only such slight variations as Mark Twain's, "It's too good for true, honey, it's too good for true" (*Huckleberry Finn,* 1884). Shaw played on the expression in the title of his 1932 play *Too True to Be Good.* See also TOO MUCH OF A GOOD THING.

too little too late An insufficient remedy applied too late to work. It is probably safe to speculate that this term originated in the military and was first applied to reinforcements that were insufficient in number and arrived too late to ensure victory or avoid defeat. Certainly the historian Allan Nevins used it with that in mind when writing about Nazi Germany in May 1935 (*Germany Disturbs the Peace*): "The former allies have blundered in the past by offering Germany too little, and offering even that too late, until finally Nazi Germany has become a menace to all mankind."

too many chiefs and not enough Indians Too many bosses and not enough workers. This expression, also stated more hyperbolically as *all chiefs and no Indians,* originated in the first half of the 1900s. Although the term refers to native American tribal organization, it is not considered offensive.

too many cooks spoil the broth Too many individuals involved in a decision or project reduce its chances of success. The analogy to each cook adding a bit of this or that to the soup was drawn so long ago that in 1575 George Gascoigne already was referring to the expression as a proverb. There are many variants, such as *too many generals lose the battle* and *too many commanders (or steersmen) sink the ship,* but *too many cooks* is the principal survivor of this long-standing cliché.

too many irons in the fire See IRONS IN THE FIRE.

too much of a good thing A large quantity of something good can be excessive. This celebration of moderation dates from the sixteenth century, although the idea is much older yet. Shakespeare was one of the first to use the precise expression in writing ("Why then, can one desire too much of a good thing?" *As You Like It,* 4:1), and over the centuries it has been greatly overworked. See also TO A FAULT.

to one's heart's content See HEART'S CONTENT.

tooth and nail, fight/with Fight vigorously, with all one's resources. The analogy to biting and scratching was drawn by the sixteenth century and has been used ever since for fierce contention or, by extension, effort. Dickens used it in *David Copperfield* (1850): "I go at it tooth and nail."

top banana/dog The main leader of an organization or undertaking, the chief. *Top banana* comes from vaudeville, where the term denoted the starring comedian. Possibly it originally alluded to an individual who used bananas in his or her act. The 1954 film *Top Banana,* starring Phil Silvers, features a television comic and uses a great many vaudeville jokes. (A related term is *second banana,* for a supporting comedian, usually the straight man. However, it has not been as widely extended to other venues and cannot be considered a cliché.) *Top dog* came from sports in the late 1800s and alluded to the dog who wins in a dogfight (emerges on top); it was quickly extended to the winner or favorite in other competitions, and eventually simply to the principal leader.

top brass, the The highest-ranking officials or executives in an organization. The expression is generally thought to come from the late-nineteenth-century British army, when senior officers had gold oak leaves decorating the brim of their caps. John Ciardi, however, proposed another etymology, from the cocked hat worn by French officers in Napoleon's time, which was folded and carried under the arm (in French, *chapeaux à bras*) while indoors; Ciardi believed the British changed *bras* to *brass,* and referred to officers as *brass hats.* By World War II both that term and top brass were in common use and afterward were transferred to peacetime officialdom as well. Thus, "The top police brass spreads out a hot carpet for the local cops" (*Philadelphia Bulletin,* 1949).

top drawer Of the highest quality or rank. The term alludes to the uppermost drawer of a bureau or dresser, where jewelry and other valuables often are kept. It was transferred to mean high social standing or first quality about 1900. It is the former that Ngaio Marsh referred to in *Colour Scheme* (1943): "He's not out of the top drawer, of course." The cliché may now be obsolescent.

toss and turn, to To move about restlessly while in bed. If this alliterative expression were older, it would be redundant, since *to toss* once also meant to turn over and over. However, it did not surface until the late 1800s, and it is always used for this behavior while one is in bed. J. R. R. Tolkien used it in

The Fellowship of the Ring (1954), "He lay tossing and turning and listening fearfully to the stealthy night-noises."

to the hilt See UP TO THE HILT.

to the manner/manor born Used to elegance and luxury. This term originated with Shakespeare, who in *Hamlet* (1.4) wrote, "Though I am native here, And to the manner born,—it is a custom more honour'd in the breach than the observance." Although Hamlet was discussing his father's corpse waking and carousing, so that *manner* here simply means "way of doing things," it later was often corrupted to *manor,* meaning the home of the well-to-do, and so the expression came to mean high-born and therefore accustomed to the best of everything. O. Henry played with it in *The Venturers* (1910): "He ordered dinner with the calm deliberation of one who was to the menu born." A delightful British television comedy series of the 1970s may have helped preserve the cliché with its title *To the Manor Born,* but it may be dying out nevertheless.

to the nth degree To the utmost possible. In mathematics *to the nth* has meant "to any required power" since the eighteenth century, and it soon came to be used figuratively as meaning "to any extent" or "to the utmost." Thus Francis E. Smedley wrote (*Lewis Arundel,* 1852), "Minerva was great . . . starched to the nth."

to the quick See CUT TO THE QUICK.

to the victor belong the spoils Winner gets all. The Roman historians frequently mentioned *spolia optima*—very best spoils—which actually referred to the personal spoils of the enemy's general when slain by the opposing commander. The current cliché became popular long after that and was frequently used in connection with the spoils system in American politics (whereby the winning party gives desirable posts to its supporters) by Senators William Marcy (1832), Huey Long (1934), and others. Justice William J. Brennan used it in writing the 1990 U.S. Supreme Court decision against political patronage: "To the victor belong only those spoils that may be constitutionally obtained" (*Rutan v. Republican Party of Illinois,* 88-1872).

to think outside the box To do something daring or unprecedented; to ignore a conventional path or method and devise a new one. This term, dating from the second half of the 1900s, is applied to just about any kind of innovation but seems particularly apt for scientific research. For example, "The researchers who concentrated on finding a cancer drug that cuts off a tumor's blood supply were really thinking outside the box."

touch and go Risky, precarious. This term, which originated in the early nineteenth century, appears to allude to a vehicle barely escaping collision—for example, a ship rubbing against the bottom with its keel but still able to move, or a cart's wheel dragging against another without harm. An early figurative use in print occurred in a letter written by Ralph Wardlaw (1815): "'Twas touch and go—but I got my seat."

tough act to follow See HARD ACT TO FOLLOW.

tough nut to crack, a A difficult problem; a hard person to deal with. This early analogy, also put as *a hard nut to crack,* was first drawn in the early eighteenth century. Benjamin Franklin used it in a letter in 1745: "Fortified towns are hard nuts to crack; and your teeth have not been accustomed to it." A similar term from a somewhat later era is *tough customer,* likewise meaning a person difficult to deal with. Dickens used it in *Barnaby Rudge* (1841): "Rather a tough customer in argument, Joe, if anybody was to try and tackle him."

tough/hard/long row to hoe, a A difficult course to follow; hard work to accomplish. This metaphor comes from nineteenth-century America, when most people lived in rural areas and cultivated at least some land. David Crockett used it in his *Tour to the North and Down East* (1835): "I never opposed Andrew Jackson for the sake of popularity. I knew it was a hard row to hoe; but I stood up to the rack."

towering rage, in a Extremely angry. *Towering* has been used in the sense of rising to a pitch of violence or intensity since Shakespeare's time. Shakespeare wrote, "The brauery of his griefe did put me into a towring passion" (*Hamlet,* 5.2). The precise modern locution appeared in William Black's *Green Pastures and Piccadilly* (1877), "He came down in a towering rage." It may now be obsolescent.

tower of strength A reliable, supportive person, dependable especially in time of trouble. In the Bible this image is often reserved for God or, later, for religious faith. In the nineteenth century Tennyson used it for the duke of Wellington: "O fall'n at length that tower of strength" ("Ode on the Death of the Duke of Wellington," 1852). It remains current.

track record The sum of a person's performance or achievements in a given line. The term comes from horse racing, where it is defined as the best time a horse ever made over a given distance on a particular track. It was transferred to human endeavor about 1950. "[Billy] Wilder has had a series of extremely successful pictures. . . . We were betting on his track record that this one would be, too" (*Life,* 1965).

train of thought A succession of connected ideas; a process of reasoning. This term appeared in Thomas Hobbes's *Leviathan* (1651), and indeed Hobbes may have coined it. He defined it there as "that succession of one thought to another, which is called, to distinguish it from discourse in words, mental discourse." It is still so used.

trials and tribulations Troubles and afflictions. This cliché, from the late nineteenth century, is actually redundant, for *trial* here means "trouble" or "misfortune," as, in effect, does *tribulation.* It is a case of repetition for emphasis, as well as alliteration, and today is used more lightly than in the past. For example, "Jane told me about the trials and tribulations of her trip—flight cancellations, lost baggage, and a horrid hotel."

tried and true Tested and proven effective. Although this term has the archaic sound of a medieval contest, it dates only from the twentieth century. William Faulkner used it in *A Fable* (1954): "His enslavement . . . from which he will emancipate himself by that one ancient tried and true method."

trim one's sails, to To modify one's stand, adapting it to circumstances. Trimming a boat's sails means simply to adjust them so as to take advantage of current wind conditions. The term was transferred to human affairs by 1800 or so, but may be obsolescent today. Lytton Strachey used it in *Elizabeth and Essex* (1928): "Burghley, trimming his sails to the changing wind, thought it advisable to take the side of Essex."

trip the light fantastic, to To dance. This locution was coined by John Milton, who wrote, "Come, and trip it as ye go, On the light fantastick toe" ("L'Allegro," 1632). For some reason it caught on (although *fantastick* was not then, and never became, the name of a particular dance). James W. Blake used it in the lyrics to a very popular Gay Nineties song, "The Sidewalks of New York" (1894): "We tripped the light fantastic - On the sidewalks of New York."

Trojan, he is a/works like a/a regular A determined, energetic individual; hardworking. The term comes from Homer's description of the Trojans in the *Iliad* and Vergil's description in the *Aeneid.* In both epics they are pictured as brave patriots who work hard for their country. This view was adopted by later writers, such as Samuel Butler, who wrote (*Hudibras,* 1663), "There they say right, and like true Trojans."

true blue Staunchly loyal. This term comes from the old proverb "True blue will never stain," which appeared in James Howell's proverb collection of 1659. It referred to a blue dye that never ran, and therefore the color came to symbolize constancy, or, as John Ray described it in 1670, "one that was always the same and like himself," a man of fixed principles. In Britain it was applied to loyal members of various groups, the Presbyterians of Scotland, the Whig Party, and later the Tories (whose official color was blue) and various university varsity teams. In America in the 1900s the term referred to team loyalty but has largely died out.

trust someone as far as one could throw him, not to/I wouldn't An indication of profound mistrust. This hyperbolic metaphor dates from about 1870 and presumably alludes to an individual too heavy to pick up and toss (in other words, not a small child).

truth is stranger than fiction Facts may be more remarkable than an invented story. The phrase first appeared in Byron's *Don Juan* (1823)—"'Tis strange—but true; for truth is always strange,—stranger than fiction"—and has been repeated ever since, often with ironic variations. Mark Twain had it in *Pudd'nhead Wilson's New Calendar* (1893), "Truth is stranger than fiction—to some people, but I am measurably familiar with it." And novelist Margaret Echard wrote, "Truth is not only stranger than fiction but far more interesting" (*Before I Wake*, 1943).

truth of the matter See FACT OF THE MATTER.

truth to tell Speaking frankly and honestly. This phrase is another version of *to tell the truth* and dates from the mid-1300s. Both phrases are used to emphasize a statement, such as "Truth to tell, I hated the play." See also IF TRUTH BE TOLD.

truth will out The facts will emerge sooner or later. The idea is ancient. Shakespeare expressed it as "Truth will come to light" (*The Merchant of Venice,* 2.2), and the modern cliché was voiced by Roger North in 1740: "Early or late, Truth will out."

tunnel vision A very narrow view, inability to see beyond a limited viewpoint. The term, dating from the mid-1900s, transfers the physiological inability to see peripheral objects to a mental outlook. For example, "Preble had the ghetto mind and the tunnel vision of a committed social climber" (T. Barling, *Goodbye Piccadilly*, 1980).

turn a blind eye/deaf ear, to To overlook something deliberately. One of these expressions appears to have a specific historic origin. In 1801 Lord Horatio Nelson, second in command of the English fleet, was besieging Copenhagen. The flagship had sent up signals for the fleet to withdraw, but Nelson wanted badly to attack. He had lost the sight of one eye at Calvi, so he put the glass to his blind eye and told his lieutenant he could see no signals to withdraw. His attack forced the French to surrender, a major victory.

"Turning a deaf ear" to what one does not wish to hear is much older. Walter Hylton (*Scala Perfeccionis*) used it about 1440: "Make deef ere to hem as though thou herde hem not." Versions of the cliché are found in all of the principal proverb collections from 1546 (John Heywood) to 1721 (James Kelly). See also FALL ON DEAF EARS.

turnabout is fair play See under TURN THE TABLES.

turn back the clock See TURN THE CLOCK BACK.

turning a hair, not/without Showing no sign of agitation or distress; quite unruffled and unafraid. This expression comes from horse-racing, where a horse that is extremely sweaty shows it in the roughening of its hair. It was transferred, but only in the negative, to human sangfroid in the late nineteenth century. Still referring to its origin, Richard D. Blackmore wrote (*Dariel,* 1897), "She never turned a hair—as the sporting people say."

turn of the tide A reversal of fortune. The changing ebb and flow of the ocean's tides have been transferred to human affairs for many centuries. Shakespeare pointed out the parallel and used it metaphorically in *Julius Caesar,* in one of his most often-quoted passages: "There is a tide in the affairs of men, Which taken at the flood, leads on to fortune" (4.3). In the nineteenth century the current cliché became common. Edward Bulwer-Lytton used it in *The Last of the Barons* (1843): "This speech turned the tide."

turn one's back on, to To reject; also, to run away (from a fight). Emerson used it in the first sense in his famous Transcendentalist poem, "Brahma" (1857): "Find me, and turn thy back on heaven." Tennyson used it in the second sense in "The Revenge": "Let us bang these dogs of Seville . . . For I never turn'd my back upon Don or devil yet." The second figurative meaning is the older one, dating from about 1400; the first began to be used about 1600.

turn over a new leaf, to To make a new start; to improve one's conduct or outlook. The *leaf* in question means the page of a book, and the term dates from the sixteenth century. Sometimes "new" was omitted, as in John Heywood's *Proverbs* (1546): "Naie she will tourne the leafe." But Roger Ascham already had the modern version (*The Scholemaster,* 1570): "Except soch men thinke them selves wiser than Cicero . . . they must be content to turne a new leafe."

turn over in one's grave, (enough to make one) An idea or action that would have greatly upset the deceased. This hyperbole dates from the mid-nineteenth century. "Jefferson might turn in his grave if he knew," wrote historian James Bryce (*The American Commonwealth,* 1888). It also is put as *to roll over in one's grave,* and the *Boston Globe* quoted Leah Rabin, the widow of Israel's prime minister Yitzhak Rabin, in a headline, "Rabin spinning in his grave on Jerusalem, widow says" (Sept. 9, 2000).

turn someone's head, to To influence someone's mind-set, particularly so as to make him or her conceited. Seneca had the idea (and his translator the phrase) almost two thousand years ago (*Ad Lucilium*): "His head was turned by too great success."

turn tail, to To turn one's back on; to run away. This term, with its image of turning one's rear in flight, has been used since the sixteenth century. "Such a haggarde as would turne taile to a full fist," wrote Robert Greene (*Euphues His Censure,* 1587).

turn the clock back, to To return to an earlier way of life; to restore past conditions. This metaphor dates from the nineteenth century and generally represents a vain attempt to return to a past era. "You can't turn back the hands of the clock," wrote Erle Stanley Gardner (*The Case of the Turning Tide,* 1941).

turn the corner, to To begin to recover. *Corner* here refers to a street corner, and turning it betokens going in a new and presumably better direction. However, this expression was used in several different senses in the past. "That expression . . . He has turn'd the corner, i.e., gone away so as no more to be seen," wrote Samuel Pegge (*Anonymiana,* 1796), defining the term to be synonymous with dying. Both Dickens and Trollope used it in the sense of financial recovery. "Now he had turned the corner, he could afford [it]," wrote Trollope in *Orley Farm* (1862).

turn the other cheek, to To respond meekly to insults, provocation, or oppression. The term comes from the Bible, where Jesus exhorts his followers, "Unto him that smiteth thee on the one cheek offer also the other" (Luke 6:29). Although the term persists to the present, over the centuries it has given rise to heated arguments concerning the wisdom of such behavior. "Turning the other cheek is a kind of moral jiu-jitsu," wrote Gerald S. Lee in *Crowds* (1913), but some psychologists believe it simply encourages the aggressor and heightens hostilities.

turn the tables, to To reverse the situation between two persons or groups, especially so as to gain the upper hand. This term comes from the custom of reversing the table or board in games like chess and draughts, so that the opponents' relative positions are switched. It was being used figuratively as long ago as 1612, when George Chapman wrote (*The Widow's Tears,* 1.3), "I may turn the tables with you ere long." Another cliché with the same meaning is *turnabout is fair play,* which dates from the nineteenth century. Robert Louis Stevenson used it in one of his last works, *The Wrecker* (1892): "You had your chance then; seems to me it's mine now. Turn about's fair play."

turn turtle, to To capsize or overturn. This term comes from the helplessness of a turtle turned onto its shell-covered back, exposing its soft legs and body to danger. The metaphor, at first used for a capsized ship and later for any overturned endeavor, dates from the first half of the nineteenth century. Describing an early motor accident, the *Daily News* had it, "An engine and two trucks had turned turtle on the embankment" (July 9, 1896; cited by the *OED*).

turn up one's nose at, to To express disdain or contempt for something or someone. The term presumably alludes to the facial expression of a sneer or to the haughty tossing of one's head to express contempt. In any event, it has been around since the sixteenth century. "When you are down and out, something always turns up—and it is usually the noses of your friends," said actor Orson Welles (*New York Times,* 1962).

turn up the heat Increase or intensify some activity. The use of "turn up" for literally increasing light or heat dates from the late 1800s. This figurative usage is much newer and appears in such contexts as, for example, "This interrogation is going nowhere; we'll have to turn up the heat."

tweedledum and tweedledee Not much difference between these alternatives; same as SIX OF ONE AND HALF A DOZEN OF THE OTHER. These actually were two names invented by John Byrom, who was satirizing two quarreling schools of musicians. Byrom (and others) claimed there was not much difference between Handel and Bononcini—one's music went "tweedledum" and the other's "tweedledee"—and wrote an amusing verse to this effect for the *London Journal* (June 1725). Lewis Carroll's use of the names for two fat little men in his *Through the Looking-Glass* (1872) helped the term to survive.

twenty-four/seven Also *24/7.* Indication that something—a store, a service, a person—is available at all times (twenty-four hours a day, seven days a week). Used since the second half of the 1900s, at first for shops that never close, the term was soon applied in numerous other contexts. For example, "I'm not looking to get a knife in my chest. I've got twenty-four/seven protection on me" (David Baldacci, *Hour Game*, 2004). A theater review by Ed Siegel in the *Boston Globe* (Feb. 1, 2005) also had it: "The younger generation. What are we to do with them, with their 'whatever' attitude, their irony, and their 24/7 access to sex, drugs, rock'n'roll, and the Internet?" See also WHATEVER.

twenty-twenty hindsight, with With complete after-the-fact knowledge. This expression, usually preceding a statement like "I would have done or said such-and-such," uses the optometrist's term for perfectly normal vision. The idea that hindsight, with its superior knowledge, is better than foresight has been stated since at least the nineteenth century. "If a man had half as much foresight as he had hindsight, he'd be a lot better off," wrote Robert J. Burdette (*Hawk-eyes,* 1879). The Hollywood screenwriter Billy Wilder is quoted as having said, "Hindsight is always twenty-twenty."

twiddle one's thumbs, to To be bored; to be idle. The habit of idly turning one's thumbs about each other during a period of enforced inactivity gave rise to this cliché, which began life in the mid-nineteenth century. "You'd have all the world do nothing . . . but twiddle its thumbs," wrote Douglas Jerrold (*Mrs. Caudle's Curtain Lectures,* 1846).

twinkling of an eye, in the Very fast; QUICK AS A WINK. This reference to the speed of the blink of an eye comes from the Bible, where Paul, writing of the Last Judgment, says, ". . . we shall all be changed. In a moment, in the twinkling of an eye, at the last trump . . . the dead shall be raised incorruptible" (1 Corinthians, 15:51–52).

twist/wind around one's little finger, to To exert a strong influence or complete control (on or over someone). This hyperbole dates from the nineteenth century. J. L. Motley used it in *Rise of the Dutch Republic* (1855): "She had already turned that functionary around her finger." A more violent twentieth-century locution is *to twist someone's arm,* a form of none too gentle persuasion. However, it often is used jocularly, as in, "You twisted my arm," meaning either "You talked me into it" or "I don't need to be persuaded to do this; I'd do it anyway."

twist in the wind, be left to Be abandoned; be exposed to blame or severe criticism. This slangy term alludes to the body of a hanged man left dangling in the air, and indeed *twisted* was slang for "hanged" in the 1700s. In modern times the phrase was initially used by John Ehrlichmann in 1973, when it was applied to President Nixon's withdrawal of support for his own nominee in the face of strong opposition, who was then left to "twist in the wind." It has since been applied to similar situations, and is on its way to clichédom. Also see OUT ON A LIMB.

two cents (worth), for/put in your Of little value; an unwanted expression of opinion. Why "two cents" should signify little value when one cent would be worth even less is not known. But *two* was long ago selected in Britain (for *twopennyworth,* or *tuppence*). "I care not twopence" is in Beaumont and Fletcher's *The Coxcomb* (1610). And *two bits* (for twenty-five cents) or *two cents* was used in America during the nineteenth century. As for *putting in one's two cents,* meaning to insert one's own view, it dates from the late nineteenth century.

two heads are better than one The advice of a second person can be very useful. The idea is ancient, and the expression was already a proverb in John Heywood's 1546 collection ("For two heddis are better than one").

two's company, three's a crowd A couple is an ideal combination, which is spoiled by the addition of a third person. This celebration of duality, much used by lovers, found its way into practically all the early proverb collections, from 1546 on. One later version stated, "Two is company, three is trumpery, as the proverb says" (Edna Lyall, *Wayfaring Men,* 1897); *trumpery* means excessive frippery.

two sides of the same coin Two seemingly different things that are actually similar. In contrast to the OTHER SIDE OF THE COIN, which does betoken a different side, this cliché emphasizes similarity—for example, "A talent for music and facility in mathematics are two sides of the same coin."

two strikes against someone/something, to have The odds are already against someone or something. This term comes from baseball, where the batter is allowed three strikes (swings at the ball) before being called out (losing the turn at bat). Thus a batter with two strikes called has only one more chance to swing and connect. The term was transferred to other undertakings by the early twentieth century. Thus, "All movements for social good will . . . have two strikes on them before they start" (*New Republic,* 1938).

two strings to one's bow More than one way of reaching one's goal. This term comes from the custom of archers carrying a reserve string. It first appeared in English in the mid-fifteenth century, and by 1546 it was in John Heywood's proverb collection. In the nineteenth century a number of novelists, including Jane Austen and Anthony Trollope, used the term as a metaphor for lovers: if one love affair fails, there is always another lover to be had. The current cliché is used more generally to mean resources in reserve.

two-way street A reciprocal situation. This figure of speech applies to a roadway in which traffic can move in opposite directions. Its figurative use dates from the mid-1900s. *The Times Literary Supplement* used it on November 21, 1975, "Tolerance . . . was a two-way street; if the Germans were to learn

u

ugly as sin Hideous, either physically or spiritually. This simile appears to have replaced the earlier *ugly as the devil,* mentioned by Daniel Defoe in his *History of the Devil* (1726). The first appearance in print was in Maria Edgeworth's *Popular Tales* of 1804: "Why, she is ugly as sin!"

ugly duckling An unattractive or unpromising child who turns into a beautiful or much admired adult. The term comes from Hans Christian Andersen's fairy tale in which a baby cygnet, hatched with a brood of ducklings, is despised by both mother and siblings for its clumsiness until it grows up and becomes a beautifully graceful swan.

ulterior motive, an A hidden purpose, a secret reason for saying or doing something. The adjective *ulterior* originally meant "beyond" or "more distant," a usage taken from the Latin and dating from the mid-1600s. Less than a century later it began to be used more specifically to mean "beyond what is said or evident." It then was combined with several nouns—*ulterior intentions, ulterior designs, ulterior purpose.* Its frequent combination with *motive* is more recent.

under a cloud, to be To be under suspicion, in trouble, or out of favor. The metaphor calls up the image of sunny blue skies marred by one cloud over the head of a particular individual. Al Capp (1909–79), the cartoonist remembered best for his comic strip "L'il Abner," included in it one ill-fated character, Joe Btfsplk, who went everywhere with a black cloud hanging over his head and brought misfortune with him. The term was already being used figuratively by 1500.

under one's belt A successful past experience. The term alludes to food that has been consumed, likening it to experience that has been digested. P. G. Wodehouse used it figuratively (*Encounter,* 1954): "Just as you have got Hamlet and Macbeth under your belt."

under one's breath In a whisper or an undertone. Presumably this term is a hyperbole for something softer than breathing. It dates from the early nineteenth century. Edward Bulwer-Lytton used it in *Eugene Aram* (1832): "Hush, said Ellinor under her breath."

under one's nose, (right) In plain sight. This expression, nearly always used as a reminder that something one cannot find or see is actually right there, dates from 1600 or even earlier. John Norden used it in *The Surveyor's Dialogue* (1607): "You are but a meane observer of the course of things passing dayly under your nose."

under one's wing, to be/take someone To be protected or to protect someone. The analogy here is to a hen sheltering her chicks and was drawn as early as the thirteenth century, when it appeared in a Middle English manuscript. A little later, Stephen Hawes wrote (*The Example of Virtue,* 1510), "Under the wynge of my proteceyon All rebels brought be to subieccyon."

under someone's thumb Under a person's influence or power. Why the thumb should have been singled out as a symbol of control or power is open to speculation, but it was, and as early as the mid-eighteenth century. "Authors . . . are under the thumb of booksellers," wrote B. H. Malkin in his translation of *Gil Blas* (1809). The situation has not changed since Malkin's day, and the cliché is also very much alive.

under the table Secret and dishonest. This term alludes to money literally being passed under a table in some dishonest transaction, such as a bribe or cheating at cards. During Prohibition, there arose a variant, *under the counter,* alluding to illegal liquor sales. Later, during World War II, this same term applied to rationed or black-market items kept there by storekeepers for favored customers.

under the weather Unwell, out of sorts. This phrase is thought to allude to being under the influence of weather that causes one to feel ill. Oddly enough, several early appearances in print deny that it means genuinely ill, the sense in which it is generally used today. Thus, William Dunlap wrote (*The Memoirs of a Water Drinker,* 1836), "He seems a little under the weather, somehow; and yet he's not sick."

united we stand There is strength in union. This expression is derived from numerous similar ones pronounced by leaders in ancient Greece, Rome, and other states. The Romans said *unitate fortior,* a translation from the Greek of Periander, the tyrant of Corinth (c. 627–586 B.C.). American patriots revived the completion of the phrase, *divided we fall,* which became a kind of national slogan in the nineteenth century. However, it also was applied to entities smaller than a nation. "The prosperity of the House of Rothschild is due to the unity . . . of its members . . . a fresh example of the saying that 'union is strength'" (Edward Walford, *Tales of Great Families,* 1877). Today the cliché is often used in a semijocular fashion, as, for example, by a doubles team in tennis.

unkindest cut of all, (most) The worst insult, the ultimate in treachery. This expression was used by Shakespeare to describe the assassination of

Julius Caesar by his friends: "This was the most unkindest cut of all" (*Julius Caesar,* 3.2). It found its way into the proverb collections of James Howell, John Ray, and Thomas Fuller, which helped its long survival, although today *most,* which made it a double superlative, is usually omitted.

unmitigated gall Absolute impudence, out-and-out effrontery. The use of *gall,* which strictly speaking means the liver's secretion, or bile, and its extension to bitterness of any kind, dates from about A.D. 1000. In late nineteenth-century America, however, it began to be used in the sense of "nerve" or "brazenness." Its frequent pairing with *unmitigated,* meaning "unmodified" or "intense," occurred in the twentieth century.

unsung heroes Individuals not famous or celebrated as they deserve to be. *Unsung* alludes to the long epic poems of Homer and Virgil, which celebrated the heroes of Greece and Troy. Indeed, a version of the term, which dates from the late seventeenth century, appears in Alexander Pope's translation of Homer's *Iliad*—"Unwept, unhonour'd, uninterrid he lies!"—words picked up a century later by Sir Walter Scott in one of his most famous poems, "The Lay of the Last Minstrel" (1805): "And, doubly dying, shall go down To the vile dust, from whence he sprung, Unwept, unhonour'd, and unsung."

until hell freezes over See TILL HELL FREEZES OVER.

unvarnished truth, the The straight facts. This expression has antecedents in the writings of Aeschylus ("Simple are the words of truth"), Euripides ("Plain and unvarnished are the words of truth"), and other ancient writers. Shakespeare came close to the modern wording: "In speaking for myself . . . I will a round unvarnish'd tale deliver of my whole course of love" (*Othello,* 1.3). See also TELL IT LIKE IT IS.

unwritten law Rules accepted by custom or tradition rather than codification in a formal body of law. The idea was already expressed by Plato: "There is a written and an unwritten law. Written law is that under which we live in different cities, but that which has arisen from custom is called unwritten law" (quoted by Diogenes Laertius; in Latin, *lex no scripta*). In a famous legal case in which he succeeded in having his client, Harry Thaw, who was accused of murdering Stanford White, declared insane, Delphin Michael Delmas coined the phrase (1907), "Dementia Americana; the unwritten law."

up a/the creek (without a paddle) In deep trouble; in a tight spot. Also put more baldly as *up shit creek,* this expression is almost certainly of American vintage from the early twentieth century, but the exact origin has been lost. Joseph Heller used it in *Catch-22* (1961): "You really are up the creek, Popinjay."

up against it/the wall In trouble. This slangy Americanism of the late nineteenth century uses "it" in a general way to mean any kind of difficulty. When "the wall" is substituted, it may refer to the practice of lining criminals up against a wall, or, more likely, of having one's BACK TO THE WALL. "I saw I was up against it," wrote George Ade (*Artie,* 1896).

up and about/doing Resuming activity, especially after a rest or an illness. These terms seem to be American in origin. One appears as an exhortation in the tireless Benjamin Franklin's *Poor Richard's Almanack* (1755): "The Day is short, the Work great, the Workman lazy, the Wages high, the Master urgeth; Up, then, and be doing."

up and at 'em Get going, become active. This interjection, from the late 1800s, is a kind of wake-up call. The *at 'em*, for "at them," does not refer to any particular individuals but rather is used in the general sense of tackling some work or undertaking an activity. For example, "We only have a week to write the budget, so up and at 'em, fellows."

up a notch An increase in value, intensity, importance, or the like. This term, from the later 1900s, is often paired with a verb, as in "take" or "step" up a notch." For example, "His heavy press schedule has been stepped up a notch, his swings across the state planned to hit every available media market" (*New York Times Magazine*, Oct. 27, 1991). The converse, *down a notch,* means exactly the opposite, that is, a decrease in value, intensity, and so on. Thus, "The confrontation was dialed down a notch after Pakistan moved to arrest leaders of militant groups" (*Wall Street Journal,* Jan. 2, 2002). Both phrases use the noun "notch," meaning one of a series of nicks on a stick used as a measure, figuratively. They may be on the way to clichédom.

up a tree Stranded or cornered. This term is clearly American in origin and dates from about 1800. "I had her in my power—up a tree, as the Americans say," wrote Thackeray (*Major Gahagan,* 1838). The original allusion is to an animal, such as a raccoon, that has taken refuge from attackers by climbing a tree.

up for grabs Available for taking, implicitly by anyone. This colloquialism became popular, especially in America, from about 1950. The *OED* cites a *Boston Globe* sports item: "Right now every position [on the team] is up for grabs."

up in arms Openly rebellious; angry. Originally (sixteenth century) this expression meant literally to take up arms against an enemy. It was being used figuratively by about 1700; Jonathan Swift had it in 1704, "All the men of wit . . . were immediately up in arms."

up in the air Unsettled, undetermined. This metaphor for unsettled matters floating about like clouds, or perhaps like birds flying in the air, was occasionally put simply as *in the air.* Thomas Jefferson used it that way in 1797 (*Writings*): "I consider the future character of our Republic as in the air."

up one's alley See RIGHT UP ONE'S ALLEY.

up one's sleeve, to have something To have a hidden surprise or resource in reserve. The idea of keeping something up one's sleeve dates at least from the sixteenth century, when clothes generally had no pockets and sleeves were a usual storage place. "He had contrary Edicts from the King in his sleeve," wrote F. de L'Isle (*Legendarie,* 1577), and his meaning was probably both literal and figurative. In the nineteenth century a dishonest card shark might have an *ace up his sleeve,* an expression that came to be used figuratively in the same way.

upper crust, the An older name for HIGH SOCIETY. This term appears to have been coined by Thomas Haliburton in his Sam Slick tales. "It was none of your skim-milk parties, but superfine uppercrust," he wrote (*The Clockmaker,* 1835). By 1850 others were using the term, which alluded to the choicest part of a pie or loaf of bread. "Those families, you know, are our upper crust, not upper ten thousand" wrote James Fenimore Cooper (*Ways of the Hour,* 1850). The term is heard less often nowadays but is not quite obsolete.

upper hand, to have the To be in a dominating or controlling position. This term has been around since the fifteenth century. It comes from an ancient gambling game in which each player in turn puts one hand on a stick, beginning at the bottom, and the last one able to put his hand at the top wins. The Anglican Book of Common Prayer has it, "Up, Lord, and let not man have the upper hand" (from Miles Coverdale's translation of Psalm 9:19).

ups and downs Good times and bad; life's vicissitudes. The association of "up" with good fortune and "down" with misery occurred in ancient Greek and Latin, and the idea that life doles out both is equally old. The precise expression dates from the seventeenth century. Dickens used an unusual application in *Martin Chuzzlewit* (1843): "Fraudulent transactions have their downs as well as their ups." See also WIN SOME, LOSE SOME.

upset the applecart, to To ruin carefully laid plans. This metaphor, without the modifying "apple," dates from Roman times. Both Plautus and Lucian used "You've upset the cart" to mean "You've spoiled everything." Specifying "applecart" dates from the late eighteenth century, and the changed phrase is the one that survives. Grose's *Dictionary of the Vulgar Tongue* (1796) suggests that "applecart" stood for the human body, and that the phrase meant to throw a person down, but that interpretation was either mistaken or the particular symbolism died out.

upside the head Against one's head. This locution, originally from black English, most often appears in the context of hitting someone on the head. The use of *upside* for "alongside" or "against" dates from the 1920s, and by the 1970s *the head* had been added. William Safire cited a 1976 *New Yorker* article, "There is a further penalty of a hit upside the head for stiffing the toll collector." The phrase is rapidly becoming a cliché.

up the creek See UP A/THE CREEK.

up the wall See DRIVE UP THE WALL; UP AGAINST IT.

up to one's ears/eyes/eyebrows, to be To be completely engrossed or overwhelmed. These phrases, likening physical immersion in something to figurative engrossment, have been around a long time. Richard Barnfield used "In love up to the eares" in *The Affectionate Shepheard* (1594). Anthony Trollope had "All the Burtons are full up to their eyes with good sense" in *The Claverings* (1866), about a century after the term came into use.

up to par See under PAR FOR THE COURSE.

up to scratch, (to come/be) An adequate performance; satisfactory. The word "scratch" alludes to a line or mark used in several sports (see also START FROM SCRATCH). In early nineteenth-century boxing a rule was introduced that after a knockdown and a thirty-second wait, a fighter had eight seconds to make his way to a mark scratched in the center of the ring; if he could not do so without help, he was considered defeated. The term was used literally by William Hazlitt in an 1822 essay on boxing and began to be used figuratively about the same time. George Orwell had it in *Burmese Days* (1934): "If they won't come up to scratch you can always get hold of the ringleaders and give them a good bambooing."

up to snuff Satisfactory in performance, health, or some other respect. This term, which probably has something to do with the once popular habit of taking snuff, dates from at least 1800, but its origin has been lost. "He knows well enough the game we're after; zooks he's up to snuff," wrote John Poole in his play *Hamlet Travestie* (1811), meaning that the character was wide awake and sharp. "Up to snuff, and a pinch or two over," wrote Dickens (*Pick-*

wick Papers, 1836), meaning that something was more than satisfactory. Along with the use of snuff, the term may be dying out.

up to speed Attaining an adequate level of performance. This term, from the first half of the 1900s, originally referred to automobile racing and meant achieving full speed at the beginning of a race or after a fueling stop. In time its meaning was extended to other activities, as in "He's just a beginner at writing programs, but he'll soon be up to speed."

up to the hilt To the utmost. The hilt is the handle of a dagger or sword; when the weapon is plunged all the way into something, only the hilt stays out. The term, also put as *to the hilt,* was transferred to other kinds of extreme by the seventeenth century. "The estate was mortgaged up to the hilt," wrote James Payn (*Thicker than Water,* 1883).

V

vanish into thin air, to To disappear altogether. Exactly when it was known that the higher one goes the thinner the air (owing to less available oxygen) is not certain. Shakespeare, however, wrote of ghosts that "Melted into air, into thin air" in 1610 (*The Tempest,* 4:1). A twentieth-century version of this cliché is the *vanishing act,* said of a person who unexpectedly disappears. It comes from the magician's trick of making something disappear (hence "act"). The essayist Logan Pearsall Smith used it poignantly in *All Trivia* (1933): "I cannot forgive my friends for dying; I do not find these vanishing acts of theirs at all amusing."

variety is the spice of life Diversity keeps life interesting. This phrase comes from William Cowper's poem "The Task" (1785): "Variety is the very spice of life, That gives it all its flavour." It became so well known that numerous writers punned on it: for example, "Variety is the spice of love" (Helen Rowland, *Sayings of Mrs. Solomon,* 1913), and "Variety is the vice of wives" (Phyllis McGinley, *Much Ado about Nothing,* 1940).

various and sundry Miscellaneous, of different kinds. This phrase is actually redundant, the two adjectives having almost identical meanings. *Various* has meant "a variety of" since the 1500s; *sundry,* which is rarely heard today except in this cliché, has meant "consisting of miscellaneous items" since the late 1700s. Their pairing appears to come from inventory lists of some kind.

vengeance is sweet See REVENGE IS SWEET.

vested interest A personal stake in an existing arrangement or institution; also, in the plural (*vested interests*), those who have such a stake. In his oft-quoted essay *On Liberty* (1859), John Stuart Mill wrote, "The doctrine ascribes to all mankind a vested interest in each other's moral, intellectual, and even physical perfection."

vicious circle A series of events in which the solution of one difficulty creates another or worsens the original problem. This expression comes from the philosophical discipline of logic, where it means proving one statement by another that itself rests on the first for proof; it is also known as "circular reasoning." George du Maurier used it in *Peter Ibbetson* (1892): "The wretcheder one is, the more one smokes; and the more one smokes, the wretcheder one gets—a vicious circle."

vim and vigor Enormous vitality and energy. This alliterative phrase is actually redundant. The noun *vim* is thought to come from the Latin *vis,* meaning strength and energy, and became American slang around the mid-1800s. *Vigor,* on the other hand, has meant energetic strength since the 1300s.

viper in one's bosom, (nourish) a An ungrateful and treacherous friend; an individual whom one has helped and who returns the favor with treachery. This term comes from Aesop's fable about a peasant who brings indoors a snake dying from the cold and is fatally bitten as soon as the snake recovers. Chaucer was among the first of the many writers to use this metaphor, which also made its way into the proverb collections of John Ray (1670), James Kelly (1721), and Thomas Fuller (1732). The term is variously put as *snake* or *viper.*

vive la différence Hurray for the difference (between men and women). This jocular approval of diversity dates from the mid-twentieth century, at least for use by English-speaking individuals. The *New York Times* had it in an article on men and women jockeys in 1969: "The male riders . . . continue to bellow 'Vive la Différence.'" It also has been extended to differences other than gender, as in the *Manchester Guardian*'s seeming truism (1964), "'Vive la différence' Tories are recognizably Tories, and Socialists are demonstrably Socialists."

vote with one's feet, to To register disapproval by leaving. This slangy Americanism dates from the mid-twentieth century and, one writer speculates, may originally have referred to refugees who emigrate because they disapprove of their country's policies or way of life.

W

wages of sin, the The consequences for wickedness. The term comes from the Bible, where Paul writes to the Romans, "The wages of sin is death" (6:23). Although numerous later religious writers, including Mary Baker Eddy, echoed this sentiment, in the twentieth century the term is more often used ironically. "The wages of sin and the reward of virtue are not so different," remarked Joseph Shearing (*The Strange Case of Lucile Cléry,* 1932), and "The wages of sin is death . . . Don't trouble whether it's the real sinner who gets the wages," wrote H. C. Bailey (*The Apprehensive Dog,* 1942).

wail like a banshee, to To scream shrilly. In Irish folklore, a "banshee" is a spirit in the form of a wailing woman who appears or is heard as a sign that one member of a family will soon die. The word appeared in English (from the Gaelic *bean sidhe*) in the second half of the eighteenth century. The simile dates from the late nineteenth century.

wait and see Bide one's time and await developments. Daniel Defoe used this term in *Robinson Crusoe* (1719): "We had no remedy but to wait and see." In England it became firmly associated with Prime Minister H. H. Asquith, because it was his repeated reply to demands by the opposition that he reveal in advance, against precedent, the terms of an impending bill to the members of the House of Commons (1910). A popular song making fun of Asquith did much to perpetuate his new nickname, Old Wait and See.

wait on hand and foot, to To serve someone's every need, to attend assiduously. This expression is very old indeed; a manuscript of c. 1330 states "Sche . . . servede hem hande and fete." In *The Perfect Woman* (1955) L. P. Hartley wrote, "He has everything he wants and servants who wait on him hand and foot."

wake the dead, to Very loud. This hyperbole has been around for ages. John Woodcock Graves used it in his poem "John Peel" (c. 1820), which later became a popular folksong: "'Twas the sound of his horn called me from my bed . . . For Peel's view-hollo would waken the dead, Or a fox from his lair in the morning."

walk all over someone, to To treat someone with utter contempt. This hyperbole comes from mid-nineteenth-century America. Mark Twain used it in *Huckleberry Finn* (1884): "In the North, he lets anybody walk over him that wants to."

walking encyclopedia, a An extremely knowledgeable individual. The term likens a person to a huge amalgamation of learning. One of the earliest versions of this cliché occurred in the poem "Tears of Peace" by George Chapman (c. 1559–1634): "And let a scholar all Earth's volumes carry, He will be but a walking dictionary." In Louisa May Alcott's *Little Women* (1869) Meg speaks admiringly of a man she considers "a walking encyclopedia."

walk in the park, a Easy, without problems or difficulty. This slangy transfer of a pleasant outing to other contexts dates from the twentieth century. James Patterson used it in *London Bridges* (2004), when a character checks on the safety of his grandmother: "Everything fine there. Walk in the park, right, Nana?" The synonymous *walk on the beach* is sometimes substituted but is heard somewhat less often.

walk on air, to To feel exuberantly joyful. The expression calls up the image of floating, perhaps (originally) like an angel. John Keats, in his romantic poem "Isabella," describes two lovers, "Parting they seemed to tread upon the air, Twin roses by the zephyr blown apart only to meet again more close."

walk on eggs, to To proceed very carefully. One could not, of course, literally tread on eggs without breaking them, so the image of extreme caution is actually hyperbole. The expression dates from the late sixteenth century. Robert Burton used it in *The Anatomy of Melancholy* (1621): "Going as if he trod upon eggs."

walk on water, to To perform a miracle. This hyperbole refers to one of Jesus's miracles as recounted in the New Testament. The Gospel of Matthew states, "And in the fourth watch of the night Jesus went unto them, walking on the sea" (14:25; it is also in Mark 6:48). Sarah Graves used it in her mystery *Dead Cat Bounce* (1998): "I had been depending on George since practically the day I moved here, and while I was not convinced that he could walk on water, I thought he would probably take two or three steps before he went down."

walk tall, to To show pride and self-confidence. This twentieth-century Americanism, transferring an upright posture to a sense of pride, gained currency in the 1970s from the motion picture *Walking Tall* (1973), a film so popular that three sequels were made. It was based on a real-life legendary southern sheriff, Buford Pusser, who rid his county of gambling, prostitution, and other crime. The term was current in Britain as well. In 1970, the

Manchester Guardian had "Walk tall, sisters . . . One woman's distinction adds a tiny bit to the stature of every other woman."

walk the plank, to To be forced to die or to give up one's position. The term refers to a form of execution favored by seventeenth-century pirates. A board was placed on the ship's deck extending over the water, and the condemned was forced to walk off the end. Thomas Macaulay used it in 1844: "It would have been necessary for Howe and Nelson to make every French sailor whom they took to walk the plank."

walls have ears, the Your secret will be overheard. This warning allegedly refers to a story about Dionysius, the Greek tyrant of Syracuse (430–367 B.C.). He had an ear-shaped cave cut into a rock and so connected between palace rooms that he could hear what his prisoners said from another room. In the course of history, other palaces, including the Louvre in Paris and Hastings Castle in England, were said to have such listening posts. An early appearance of the term in print occurred in James Shirley's play *The Bird in a Cage* (1633, 1.1): "Take heed what you say. Walls have ears."

wall-to-wall Completely covering available space. This expression, from about 1930, originally referred to carpeting that covered the entire floor of a room, and it still does. However, from about 1960 it was being used figuratively, and usually hyperbolically—for example, "A respite from wall-to-wall Mozart on radios" (*The Listener,* April 19, 1973).

warhorse, a (an old) An experienced veteran; also, a reliably popular attraction. This term originated in the mid-seventeenth century, when it literally meant a battle-scarred military charger. By the nineteenth century it had been transferred to experienced officers, such as the Confederate General James Longstreet, who was nicknamed the War Horse, as well as to veterans of political and other struggles. Using the second meaning, in 1990 a *New York Times* music critic wrote, "The first half of the orchestral program consisted of warhorses."

warm and fuzzy Friendly, affectionate, amiable. Originally used to describe a textile fabric that was literally warm and fuzzy, the term began to be used figuratively by the 1930s. Lee Child used it in *Persuader* (2003), "'You still feel all warm and fuzzy about this Gorowski guy?' She nodded. 'It would be a tragedy to bust him.'"

warm heart, a Full of love, tender. This term has been around since about 1480. It was surely a cliché by the time F. Verney wrote (*Memoirs of the Verney Family,* 1904), "Her warm heart . . . made her welcome in every household." See also COLD HANDS, WARM HEART; COLD HEART.

warm the cockles of one's heart, to To gratify; to make someone feel good. This term comes from the Latin for the heart's ventricles, *cochleas cordis,* and has been used figuratively since the late seventeenth century. "This contrivance of his did inwardly rejoice the cockles of his heart," wrote John Eachard (*Observations upon the Answer to Contempt of Clergy,* 1671).

warm welcome, a An enthusiastic greeting. This term has been around since at least the mid-eighteenth century, and perhaps much longer. "Whoe'er has travell'd life's dull round, May sigh to think he still has found the warmest welcome at an inn," wrote William Shenstone (*Written at an Inn at Henley,* c. 1763). A very similar cliché, a *warm reception,* often has just the opposite meaning—that is, a greeting full of hostility.

war of nerves, a A conflict that employs psychological techniques rather than direct violence. This term, which refers to a barrage of propaganda, threats, false rumors, and sabotage calculated to undermine the enemy's morale, came into being in the mid-twentieth century. Edith Simon used it in *The Past Masters* (1953): "War of nerves . . . best thing is to take no notice."

warts and all With all one's faults, blemishes, and shortcomings. This term allegedly comes from instructions Oliver Cromwell (1599–1658) gave to Sir Peter Lely when commissioning him to paint his portrait: "But remark all these roughnesses, pimples, warts, and everything as you see me, otherwise I will never pay a farthing for it." It is still current.

wash one's dirty linen in public, to To expose one's private affairs in public, particularly any unsavory family secrets. This metaphor is a French proverb that became famous when Napoleon used it in a speech before the French Assembly upon his return from exile in Elba in 1815. It was picked up by numerous English writers, among them Trollope, who wrote (*The Last Chronicle of Barset,* 1867), "There is nothing, I think, so bad as washing one's dirty linen in public."

wash one's hands of (something), to To dismiss or renounce interest in; to turn away and refuse responsibility. The term comes from the Bible, where at Jesus's trial the Roman governor, Pontius Pilate, saw that he could not save Jesus and "washed his hands before the multitude, saying I am innocent of the blood of this just person" (Matthew 27:24). Shakespeare referred to it directly in *Richard II* (4.1): "Some of you with Pilate wash your hands." Dickens and others used it somewhat more lightly: "He had entirely washed his hands of the difficulty" (*Bleak House,* 1853).

waste not, want not Economical use of one's resources pays off. This adage was quoted—and perhaps coined—by Maria Edgeworth (*The Parent's*

Assistant, 1800), who wrote that those very words "were written over the chimneypiece . . . in his uncle's spacious kitchen." It was widely repeated throughout the nineteenth century, but has been heard less in the current throwaway society.

waste one's breath, to To talk in vain, because no one will listen. The idea that breath is something that can be saved or wasted dates from the sixteenth century (see also SAVE YOUR BREATH). Tennyson used the term in "In Memoriam" (1850): "I trust I have not wasted breath."

watched pot never boils, a Anxiety does not hasten matters. This homely piece of kitchen wisdom, whose truth is readily attested by anyone who has ever been in a hurry to cook something in boiling water, dates from the mid-nineteenth century. Clare Boothe Luce, reporting during the early years of World War II (*Europe in the Spring,* 1940), wrote, "A watched pot never boils, they say—only this one finally did."

water over the dam Over and done with; past. This term, along with the slightly older *water under the bridge,* is a metaphor for anything finished and irreversible just as water that has once flowed through a spillway or under a bridge is gone forever. Richard Sale combined both metaphors in *Passing Strange* (1942): "'That's water under the dam.'—'Bridge,' I said. 'Or water over the dam.'"

way out in left field See OUT IN LEFT FIELD.

way to a man's heart, the How to win someone's affection. This term, from the mid-nineteenth century, traditionally was completed "is through his stomach/belly," meaning that a good meal would win his affection. Edward Albee gave it a cynical twist in his 1962 play *Who's Afraid of Virginia Woolf?* (Act 2): "Until you start ploughing pertinent wives, you really aren't working. The way to a man's heart is through his wife's belly, and don't you forget it."

way to go Well done, good for you. Generally uttered as an exclamation, this expression of approval and encouragement originated in sports and in the 1960s began to be transferred to other endeavors. Emma Lathen had it in the mystery novel *Murder without Icing* (1973), "'Way to go, Billy!' 'Rah! Rah! Billy Siragusa!'"

weak as a kitten Feeble, defenseless. This proverbial simile goes one better than *weak as a cat,* dating from the early nineteenth century. Erle Stanley Gardner had "He felt as weak as a kitten" in *The Case of the Drowsy Mosquito* (1943). Other variations are O. Henry's *weak as a vegetarian cat* (*Cupid à la Carte,* 1907) and *weak as a newborn kitten.*

wear one's heart on one's sleeve, to To show one's feelings, especially amorous ones, openly. This term comes from the old custom of tying a lady's favor to her lover's sleeve, thus announcing their attachment. Shakespeare used it in *Othello* (1.1): "But I will wear my heart upon my sleeve for daws to peck at."

wear out one's welcome, to To prolong a visit more than one's host wishes. The ancients claimed that after three days guests and fish are equally stale. In the mid-nineteenth century the present locution was devised, as "an elegant rendering of the vulgar saying, 'Fish and company stink in three days'" (*Notes and Queries,* 1869).

wear the pants, to To be boss. This term was long applied to women, particularly wives, who assumed the domineering household role that was believed to belong to the husband. It dates from a time when only men wore pants or breeches and women wore skirts exclusively, at least in the Western world. Times have changed since the sixteenth century, yet although women's apparel has included both short and long pants for many decades, the phrase still means to assume authority that is properly masculine. It reflects, of course, an indelibly sexist attitude.

wear two hats (more than one hat), to To play two (or more) roles; to hold two different positions. This expression alludes to the hats of two different uniforms. The practice is ancient, and Gilbert and Sullivan made glorious fun of it in *The Mikado* in the person of Pooh-Bah, who holds practically every office in the town of Titipu. The term dates from the mid-nineteenth century. A 1972 issue of the *Village Voice* stated, "I wear two hats. Are you asking me this question as president of the Bartenders' Union or as chairman of the ABC?"

weasel word A word that takes away the meaning from a statement, just as a weasel sucks the meat from an egg. The term dates from about 1900 and was popularized by Theodore Roosevelt. In a 1916 speech criticizing President Woodrow Wilson, Roosevelt said, "You can have universal training or you can have voluntary training but when you use the word 'voluntary' to qualify the word 'universal' you are using a weasel word; it has sucked all the meaning out of 'universal.' The two words flatly contradict one another."

weather eye, to keep a To remain on guard, to watch out for trouble. In maritime language keeping a weather eye means looking toward the wind to observe weather conditions and look for squalls. The term appeared in a *Sailor's Word-Book* (Smyth, 1867) but by the end of the nineteenth century was being used figuratively for keeping any kind of careful watch. Thus Lee Thayer used it (*Murder Is Out,* 1942), "You know how to keep your weather eye lifting."

weather the storm, to To survive hard times. The term, alluding to a ship safely coming through bad weather, has been used figuratively from about 1650. Thomas Macaulay did so in *The History of England* (1849): "[They] weathered together the fiercest storms of faction."

weighed (in the balance) and found wanting Tested and proved faulty. This expression comes from the Bible, as part of Daniel's interpretation to King Belshazzar of the WRITING ON THE WALL (Daniel 5:27). It has been used ever since to mean a deficiency or failure.

weigh one's words, to To speak or write thoughtfully and prudently. *Weigh* here is used in the sense of measuring the weight, or impact, of one's words. This metaphor dates from ancient times and was already in print in the early fourteenth century. Dan Michel wrote, "[he] ne wegth his wordes ine the waye of discrecion" (*Ayenbite of Inwyt,* 1340).

well and good All right, but something else may be better yet. This expression has been around since the late seventeenth century. Robert S. Surtees used it in *Handley Cross* (1854): "If you . . . can find anything out about them, you know, well and good."

well-heeled, to be To be prosperous. This late nineteenth-century Americanism presumably refers to a well-off person who is not DOWN AT THE HEELS but is well shod. "To travel long out West, a man must be, in the local phrase, 'well heeled,'" wrote W. Beadle (*The Undeveloped West,* 1873).

well's run dry, the A plentiful source has been used up. The word "well" for an underground water source has been used figuratively since 1400. This expression appeared in Benjamin Franklin's *Poor Richard's Almanack* (1757) and may have been original with him: "When the well's dry, they know the worth of water."

wend one's way, to To go in a particular direction. The verb *to wend,* which survives mainly in this cliché, here means "to turn." (It had numerous other meanings, all now obsolete.) This term was known in the late fourteenth century, appearing in the anonymous *Cursor Mundi.* It was used for about two hundred years, was largely forgotten, and then was revived in the early nineteenth century. Numerous writers used it, including Dickens: "As she wended her way homewards" (*Nicholas Nickleby,* 1839).

wet behind the ears, (still) Immature, inexperienced. This term refers to the fact that the last place to dry on a newborn colt or calf is the indentation behind its ears. Although the observation is surely older, the term dates from the early twentieth century. J. F. Straker used it in his novel *A*

Coil of Rope (1962): "You're still wet behind the ears, darling. It's time you grew up."

wet blanket, a A person or thing that spoils the fun. This term, alluding to a device used to smother a fire, has been around since the early nineteenth century. Mrs. Anne Mathews used it in *Tea-Table Talk* (1857): "Such people may be the wet blankets of society."

wet one's whistle, to To have a drink. It is very difficult to whistle with dry lips. An old children's party game involves eating some dry crackers or bread and attempting to whistle; the first to succeed in doing so wins a prize. The term has been around since the fourteenth century. It appeared in Chaucer's *Canterbury Tales:* "So was her joly whistle wel y-wet" (*The Reeve's Tale*).

wet to the skin See SOAKED TO THE SKIN.

what do you know, (well) What a surprise. This expression, which often precedes an ironic announcement of some kind, has been around since the turn of the twentieth century. Robert Benchley used it in his "Watching a Spring Planting" (in *Love Conquers All,* 1923): "Hey, what do you know? Steve here thinks he's going to get some corn up in this soil!"

whatever In any case; anything goes; as you wish. One of the most recent additions to clichédom, this adverb is used very loosely. David Rosenfelt has it in a character's conversation with a waitress: "'. . . I can remember a time when the bananas and walnuts would have been *inside* the pancakes.' 'Whatever,' she says, demonstrating a disregard for cultural history. 'You want coffee?' 'Not until after the Olympics,' I say. 'Whatever.'" (*Bury the Lead*, 2004). Uttering "whatever" can be irksome, and even incendiary, as well as nonchalant. A *New Yorker* piece by Nick Paumgarten (July 11 and 18, 2005) reports that actor Russell Crowe, who assaulted a hotel clerk for failing to help him place a telephone call to Australia, did so after the clerk, responding to a threat, replied "Whatever." The 1995 film *Clueless,* about Beverly Hills teenagers of the 1990s, popularized the "whatever" gesture, made with holding up the thumb and forefinger of both hands to form the letter W. Perhaps the most chilling use of the word came at the court martial of Private First Class Lynndie R. England, who told the judge that when pressed to join in the abuse of Iraqi prisoners at Abu Ghraib, she responded "OK. Whatever" (quoted by James Carroll, *Boston Globe,* May 10, 2005). See also the quotation under TWENTY-FOUR/SEVEN.

what goes around comes around A person's bad deeds will earn revenge; also, what has happened before will recur. According to the linguist Margaret G. Lee (*American Speech,* winter 1999), this expression originated as an African proverb and came into general use via African-American speech. Kevin Cullen used it in an article about the failed peace-keeping efforts in Kosovo: "But what goes around always comes around in the Balkans, and today Albanians are exacting their revenge, killing Serbs" (*Boston Globe,* April 22, 2000). Jon Cleary, in *Dilemma* (1999), wrote, "When I was young, condoms were for stopping pregnancies. Then they tell me, sales fell right away when the Pill came in. Now the condom is back as armour-plating [against infection]. What goes around comes around."

what's new (with you)? What has been happening in your life? How are you? This term, now used as a conversation-starter, may have originated in "What's the news?" and dates from the early twentieth century. Robert M. Pirsig gives it broader meaning in *Zen and the Art of Motorcycle Maintenance* (1974): "'What's new?' is an interesting and broadening eternal question, but one which, if pursued exclusively, results only in an endless parade of trivia and fashion, the silt of tomorrow."

what's sauce for the goose See SAUCE FOR THE GOOSE.

what's what See KNOW WHAT'S WHAT.

what you see is what you get What's on the table or who's present is all there is. This expression, often used humorously or ironically, may have originated in Australia, according to Eric Partridge. Possibly it alludes to what a salesperson explains to a customer (as in, "No, this model doesn't have four-wheel drive—what you see is what you get"). It gained currency in the United States with *The Flip Wilson Show* in the early 1970s, in which the comedian dressed in women's clothes as the character Geraldine and declared "What you see is what you get." This writer used it on being introduced to her daughter's future in-laws, who asked about other relatives in our family. Pointing to her husband and herself, she declared, "What you see is what you get." The Australian novelist Jon Cleary used it in *Dilemma* (1999), "Yet there was no mystery to her, something else he always looked for in a woman . . . What you saw was what you got had never interested him as an attraction."

wheel and deal, to To operate or manipulate for one's own profit. According to at least one writer, a "wheeler-dealer" was a heavy bettor on the roulette wheel and cards in the American West. However, the *OED* lists its first citation as approximately 1960 and suggests it comes from an important person being "a wheel" or "big wheel." R. Dentry used it in *Encounter at Kharmel* (1971), "In other words, if we agree to shut up, you'll wheel and deal some pin money for us." The principal meaning today is to engage in scheming and shrewd bargaining.

wheel of fortune, the The agent of change in human affairs. The term refers to the goddess Fortune, traditionally represented with a wheel in her hand, which symbolizes inconstancy. The ancient Chinese and Babylonians referred to fortune's ever-turning wheel, and Chaucer used it (*The Knight's Tale*), "Thus can fortune hir wheel govern and gye, and out of joye bringe men to sorwe." A popular American television quiz show of the 1980s and 1990s bore the name *Wheel of Fortune*.

wheels within wheels Complex motives or actions that interact with one another. This seemingly modern mechanistic term comes from the Old Testament of the Bible: "Their appearance and their work was as it were a wheel in the middle of a wheel" (Ezekiel 1:16). About the middle of the eighteenth century *wheel* became plural and has so remained. "There are wheels within wheels—permutations and combinations which they never hope to unravel," wrote Francis Beeding (*Eleven Were Brave,* 1941).

when all's (is) said and done In the end, nevertheless. This cumbersome locution dates from the sixteenth century. The *OED* cites Thomas Ingelend in *The Disobedient Child* (1560): "When all is saide and all is done, Concernynge all thynges both more and lesse."

when in Rome do as the Romans do Follow the local customs. This old proverb supposedly comes from St. Ambrose's answer to St. Monica and her son, St. Augustine, who asked whether they should fast on Saturday as the Romans do, or not, according to Milanese practice. Ambrose replied, "When I am here (in Milan) I do not fast Saturday, when I am in Rome, I fast on Saturday." This Latin saying was translated into English by the fifteenth century or so and has been repeated ever since.

when my ship comes in See SHIP COMING IN.

when push comes to shove See PUSH COMES TO SHOVE.

when the balloon goes up When some activity or enterprise begins. This expression dates from World War I, when the British artillery would send up a balloon to signal gunners along the line to begin firing. In time the term was extended to any undertaking, such as the opening of a store, the time a court session begins, and so on. John Braine used it in his novel *Room at the Top* (1957): "Merely because I let you give me a beery kiss in the Props Room, you think the balloon's going up." The term may be dying out, however, at least on this side of the Atlantic.

when the cat's away (the mice will play) When the authorities are absent, people will break rules and do as they please. This proverb, which exists in numerous languages, appeared in several different forms in English in the seventeenth century. Thomas Heywood used it in *A Woman Kill'd with Kindness* (1607): "There's an old proverb—when the cat's away, the mouse may play." Today it is often shortened.

when the chips are down See CHIPS ARE DOWN.

when the going gets tough, the tough get going When there are major difficulties, capable individuals are spurred on to overcome them. This colloquialism has been ascribed to Joseph P. Kennedy, father of President John F. Kennedy. He may well have used it—J. H. Cutler said so in *Honey Fitz,* his biography of the Boston mayor, Joseph Kennedy's father-in-law—but probably did not originate it. It clearly was one of the various ways in which the ambitious father spurred on his sons, three of whom became very successful in politics.

where's the beef? Where is the substance to this issue? This expression began life as an advertising slogan for Wendy's, the third-largest American hamburger chain. In a 1984 television commercial, three elderly women are given a small hamburger on a huge bun, a competitor's product. They admire the bun, but one of them, a retired manicurist named Clara Peller, asks, "Where's the beef?" The slogan caught on, and Walter Mondale, seeking the Democratic nomination for president, used it to attack his opponents' stands and policies. The phrase echoes another, much older slang expression, *what's the beef?,* meaning what's the complaint. The use of the noun *beef* for gripe or complaint dates from the late 1800s. George V. Higgins used it in *Deke Hunter* (1976), "I agree with you . . . so what's the beef?"

where there's smoke there's fire Every rumor has some foundation; when things appear suspicious, something is wrong. The metaphor for this idea already appeared in John Heywood's *Proverbs* (1546): "There is no fyre without smoke," and indeed it is a proverb in Italian, French, German, and Spanish.

which way the wind blows, (to know) How matters stand. Wind direction has been a metaphor for the course of events since the fourteenth century. It appeared in John Heywood's *Proverbs* of 1546 and remains current. "My questions must have showed him whence the wind blew," wrote Sir Arthur Conan Doyle (*Sir Nigel,* 1906). See also STRAW IN THE WIND.

while/where there's life there's hope So long as there's a chance of success, there's hope that it will happen. This ancient saying goes back to the time of the Greeks and Romans, and presumably at first referred to very ill individuals who, it was hoped, might still recover. It soon was extended to other situations. The Roman writer Seneca reported that Telesphorus of Rhodes, who was put into a cage by the tyrant Lysimachus about 310 B.C., made this statement, adding "only the dead are hopeless." Cicero used it in *Ad Atticum* (c. 49 B.C.), "As a sick man is said to have hope as long as he has life, so did I not cease to hope so long as Pompey was in Italy." The saying entered numerous proverb collections and remains current, although sometimes it is used in a lighter context: for example, "The soufflé fell but it's still edible; while there's life there's hope."

whipping boy, a A scapegoat; one who receives the blame and/or punishment for another's mistakes or misdeeds. The term comes from the early practice of keeping a boy to be whipped in place of a prince who was to be punished. Sir William Petrie used the term figuratively in *Ancient Egypt* (1914): "With some writers . . . Manetho is the whipping-boy, who must always be flogged when anything is not understood."

whistle in the dark, to To try to call up one's courage or hopefulness in a difficult or frightening situation. The literal idea is a very old one, attested to by John Dryden in *Amphitryon* (1690): "I went darkling, and whistling to keep myself from being afraid." An unknown parodist of Benjamin Franklin's *Poor Richard's Almanack* (*Poor Richard, Jr.*, 1906) managed to combine two clichés: "Whistling to keep the courage up is all right, but the whistle should not be wet."

whistlin' Dixie, you ain't just You said a mouthful. The origin of this expression has been lost, but it is generally thought to allude to the 1860 song "Dixie," with words and music by Dan Emmett. Originally written for a minstrel show, it became famous as a Civil War marching song of the Confederacy, "Dixie" being a nickname for the South whose origin has also been lost. Allegedly General Pickett, just before he made his famous charge at Gettysburg, ordered that the song be played to bolster the morale of his troops. The saying presumably means that you're not just whistling the marching song and mouthing empty words, but instead getting down to the actual combative meaning. See also YOU SAID A MOUTHFUL.

white as a sheet Pale in the face. This simile dates from Shakespeare's time; he wrote, "And whiter than the sheets!" in *Cymbeline* (2.2). The term was repeated by Henry Fielding, Frederick Marryat, Artemus Ward, and Thomas Hardy, among many others, and remains current.

white elephant, a An unwanted possession that is hard to get rid of but too valuable to throw away. The term comes from a widely told story of an ancient Siamese custom whereby only the king could own an albino elephant, which therefore was considered sacred. When the king was displeased with a courtier, he would give him such a white elephant and wait until the high costs of feeding the beast—being sacred, it could not be killed—caused the man to be ruined. The custom became known in England in the seventeenth century, and by the nineteenth century the term had been transferred to other unwanted items. G. E. Jewsbury wrote, "His services are like so many white elephants of which nobody can make use, and yet that drain one's gratitude" (letter, 1851).

white feather, to show the To behave in a cowardly way. This term alludes to cockfighting, in which a cock with a white tail feather is deemed to be of inferior stock. It was so defined in Francis Grose's *Dictionary* (1785) and has been so used ever since. "He had certainly shown the white feather," wrote Thackeray (*Pendennis,* 1850).

white flag, hang out/show the Surrender; give up, yield. In military circles the white flag betokened surrender by 1600 or so. "A ship garnished with white flags of peace," wrote Philemon Holland in his 1600 translation of the Roman historian Livy.

white lie, a A fib told out of politeness, to spare feelings, or for a similar reason. The term is intended to distinguish between such a fib and a black lie, considered heinous dishonesty. A 1741 issue of *Gentleman's Magazine* stated, "A certain Lady of the highest Quality . . . made a judicious distinction between a white Lie and a black Lie. A white Lie is That which is not intended to injure any Body in his Fortune, Interest, or Reputation, but only to gratify a garrulous Disposition, and the Itch of amusing People by telling them wonderful Stories." However, warned William Paley in *Moral Philosophy* (1785), "White lies always introduce others of a darker complexion."

whitewash, a A glossing over of bad conduct, dishonesty, or other misdeeds. Using clean paint as a metaphor for concealing misconduct dates at least from the early eighteenth century. "The greater part of whitewashing is done with ink," wrote George D. Prentice (*Prenticeana,* 1860).

whole hog, the/to go The ultimate extent; to do something completely or thoroughly. The precise meaning and origin of this cliché have been lost. Charles Funk thought it came from a poem by William Cowper (1731–1800) that told of the Islamic prohibition against eating pork: "But for one piece they thought it hard From the whole hog to be debar'd." A more likely source is the Irish word *hog* for the British shilling, American ten-cent piece, and other coins, whereby "going the whole hog" would mean spending the entire shilling or dime at one time. On the other hand, Frederick Marryat, writing in 1836 (*Japhet*), called it an American term. It may be derived from the American colloquialism *to hog,* meaning to appropriate greedily. Whichever is true, the term is a cliché on both sides of the Atlantic.

whole new ball game/ball of wax, a An entirely changed situation. The first, an Americanism originating about 1970, applied the idea of a new sport with different rules to changed circumstances in almost any situation: for example, "If this were to happen, some official of our government would no doubt announce that we were in a 'whole new ballgame,' which would mean that none of the policies or promises made in the past were binding any longer" (*New Yorker,* 1971). It is also put as *a whole other ball game.*

The second phrase, which has exactly the same meaning, may, it has been suggested, come from a seventeenth-century English legal practice whereby land was divided among several heirs. Wax was used to cover small pieces of paper on which portions of land were identified; each was rolled into a ball, and the balls were drawn from a hat by the heirs in order of precedence (the eldest first, the youngest last). Whether or not this was the source, "the whole ball of wax" today also means all the elements of a plan, situation, or action, as well as all related elements. Thus one might say, "He sold her his house, his boat, his car—the whole ball of wax."

whole nine yards, the The entire distance; the whole thing. The source of this term has been lost, but as usual there are several etymological theories. The following were suggested by William Safire's correspondents: nine yards once constituted the entire amount put onto a bolt of cloth, and for an ornate garment the "whole nine yards" would be used; the standard large cement mixer holds nine yards of cement, and a big construction job would use up the "whole nine yards"; in the square-rigged, three-masted sailing ship of former times, each mast carried three "yards" (the spars supporting the sails), and the expression "whole nine yards" would mean that the sails were fully set.

whole shebang, the The entire structure; the whole business and everything connected with it. The precise meaning of *shebang* in this phrase has been lost. It dates from mid-nineteenth century America, when it denoted a hut or shack, which makes no sense in the current cliché. Bret Harte used it: "That don't fetch me even of [*sic*] he'd chartered the whole shebang" ("The Story of a Mine," 1877). An alliterative synonym is *the whole shooting match* (also put as *the whole shoot*). Originally this meant a shooting competition, a usage dating from the mid-1700s. The addition of *whole* and the figurative meaning are much newer, dating from the 1900s. Also see KIT AND CABOODLE.

whys and wherefores, the The underlying reasons. Although this alliterative term seems tautological, originally *why* alluded to the reason for something, and *wherefore* to how it came to be. However, *wherefore* also was, in the sixteenth century, used in the meaning of "because." Thus George Gascoigne (*Supposes,* 1566) wrote, "I have given you a wherefore for this why many times," and Samuel Butler (*Hudibras,* 1663), "Whatever Sceptic could inquire for, For ev'ry why he had a wherefore." Today, however, the term is simply a cliché for all the reasons for something.

wild and woolly (West), the The untamed, wide open western United States. The term dates from the late nineteenth century, popularized by a book title, Adair Welcker's *Tales of the "Wild and Woolly West"* (1891). A publisher's note on the book said "wild and woolly" referred to the rough sheepskin coats worn by cowboys and farmers, but Franklin P. Adams said "wild, woolly and full of flies" was a cowboy's expression for a genuine cowboy. Owen Wister's *The Virginian* (1902) stated, "I'm wild, and woolly and full of fleas," which was later picked up in the cowboy ditty, "Pecos Bill and the Wilful Coyote" (c. 1932) by W. C. White: "Oh, I'm wild and woolly and full of fleas, Ain't never been curried below the knees."

wildfire See SPREAD LIKE WILDFIRE.

wild-goose chase, a A fruitless search or senseless pursuit. Pursuing a wild goose was already transferred to other wild chases by Shakespeare's time. A popular follow-the-leader game was so called, and referred to by Shakespeare: "Nay if thy wits run the wild-goose chase, I have done" (*Romeo and Juliet,* 2:4).

wild horses couldn't drag me Nothing could persuade me. This is the current version of an older term, *wild horses couldn't draw it from me,* that is, "make me confess," which is believed to allude to a medieval torture. The cliché, which always states it in negative form, began to be used by 1834 or so. David Murray used it in *Healy* (1883): "After that wild horses could not have drawn him to an exculpation of himself."

wild oats, to sow one's To behave foolishly and indulge in excess while one is young. The term has been around since at least the late sixteenth century. It alludes to sowing inferior wild grain instead of superior cultivated grain, analogous here to sexual promiscuity, and suggests that one will eventually outgrow such foolishness. As Thomas Hughes wrote in *Tom Brown at Oxford* (1861), "A young fellow must sow his wild oats," but he then adds, "You can make nothing but a devil's maxim of it."

willy-nilly, to do something Willingly or not; anyhow, any old way. This very old term was once *will-he, nill-he, nill* being the negative of *will* (i.e., will not or won't). It was in print by the late thirteenth century and was picked up by numerous writers, including Shakespeare (in *Hamlet*).

Today it is sometimes used in the original sense—that is, this will happen, whether or not one wants it to—and also (erroneously according to the *OED* but not American dictionaries), in the meaning of sloppily or in disorganized fashion.

wind around one's finger See TWIST AROUND ONE'S FINGER.

window of opportunity, a A short time in which to accomplish something. This usage became popular during the years of the arms race between the Western and Communist powers, when it referred specifically to a chance for attacking. By about 1980 it had been extended to other narrow chances. Thus the London *Sunday Times* used it on June 16, 1985, "Regional bank bosses know that they must rush to acquire their neighbours, to make the most of their window of opportunity." It is rapidly becoming a cliché.

wine, women, and song The good life, in a dissolute fashion. The precise locution first appeared in German and in the late eighteenth century was translated (and attributed to Martin Luther, without real authority). "Who loves not women, wine, and song, remains a fool his whole life long," it went, and in 1862 Thackeray (*Adventures of Philip*) prefaced it with, "Then sing, as Martin Luther sang, as Doctor Martin Luther sang." Johann Strauss the Younger (1825–99) used it as the title of one of his famous waltzes (opus 333).

wing it, to To improvise. This aeronautical-sounding cliché comes from the nineteenth-century theater, where it originally meant to study one's part while standing in the wings because one has been called to replace an actor or actress on short notice. It soon was extended to mean improvisation of any kind. Thus *Publishers Weekly* (1971) used it to describe talk-show hosts interviewing authors whose books they had not read: "They can talk about the book, kind of winging it based on the ads."

win hands down, to To come in first by a wide margin. The term comes from racing, where jockeys ride with their hands down, relaxing their hold on the reins, when victory seems certain. The term was first used figuratively about 1900. In 1958 the London *Time* stated, "Double this speed, however, and the submarine wins hands down."

win some, lose some, (you) Accept that some ventures end in victory and others in defeat. This philosophical phrase of acceptance has numerous ancestors with the same meaning—*if I lose on the swings I'll get back on the roundabouts* was a common version in early twentieth-century Britain—but the current cliché dates only from about 1920 or so. It probably originated in gambling, possibly in betting on sports events. The London *Times* used it in

1976: "On the other hand, you . . . got your way over Mrs. Thatcher's nominee . . . you win some, you lose some." In July 1990, *Time* reported, "For a man facing the possibility of 20 years behind bars, John Mulheren was remarkably philosophical. 'You win some, you lose some,' said the fallen Wall Street arbitrager last week after a Manhattan jury found him guilty on four felony counts." See also YOU CAN'T WIN THEM ALL.

wipe the slate clean See under CLEAN SLATE.

wishful thinking Interpreting events, facts, or words as one would like them to be as opposed to what they are; also, fantasizing as actual something that is not. This term comes from Freudian psychology of about 1925, but the idea is much older. "Thy wish was father, Harry, to that thought," wrote Shakespeare (*Henry IV, Part 2,* 4.5), an expression that practically became a proverb. The current cliché was used by F. H. Brennan (*Memo to a Firing Squad,* 1943): "We're lousy with wishful thinkers."

with a grain/pinch of salt, (to take) Not to be believed entirely; to be viewed with skepticism. This term comes from the Latin *cum grano salis,* which appeared in Pliny's account of Pompey's discovery of an antidote against poison that was to be taken with a grain of salt added (*Naturalis Historia,* c. A.D. 77). The term was quickly adopted by English writers, among them John Trapp, whose *Commentary on Revelations* (1647) stated, "This is to be taken with a grain of salt."

with all due respect Although I give you appropriate consideration and deference. This polite little phrase, dating from 1800 or even earlier, always precedes a statement that either disagrees with what has been said or broaches a controversial point. Thus the *Church Times* (1978) stated, "With all due respect to your correspondents, I do not think they have answered M. J. Feaver's question."

with all my heart With all the energy and enthusiasm I can muster. This phrase has been around since the sixteenth century, and was so well known by the time Jonathan Swift assembled *Polite Conversation* (1738) that he wrote, "With all my heart and a piece of my liver." A century earlier Philip Massinger also had played with it (*The Great Duke of Florence,* 1636): "Once more to you, with a heart and a half."

with a vengeance Forcefully, extremely hard. *Vengeance* in this old expression is not the same as "revenge" (see also REVENGE IS SWEET). It was already in print in 1533, in the same meaning it has today. "Be gone quickly, or my pikestaff and I will set thee away with a vengeance," wrote George Peele (*King Edward I,* 1593).

with bated breath Holding one's breath back in expectation. *To bate* meant to restrain, but this verb is scarcely heard today except in this cliché, which itself has an archaic sound and often is used ironically. Shakespeare used it in *The Merchant of Venice* (1.3): "Shall I bend low, and in a bondsman's key, With bated breath, and whispering humbleness." A more recent colloquial locution is *don't hold your breath,* meaning "don't wait in vain."

with friends like that, who needs enemies See under ET TU, BRUTE!

within an ace of, to be Very close to, within a narrow margin of. This term refers to the ace of dice (not playing cards)—that is, the one pip on a die. Since the lowest number one can throw with a pair of dice is two (two aces), such a throw is within an ace of one. The term was transferred to other near misses by 1700 or so. Thomas Browne wrote, "I was within an ace of being talked to death" (letter, 1704), and Alexander Pope, "I was within an ace of meeting you" (letter, 1711).

with it, to be/to get To be (become) up-to-date, conversant with the latest style. This American slang expression originated during the 1920s, when *it* became associated with sex appeal (thanks to Elinor Glyn, author of a stream of popular fiction, and the movie star Clara Bow, the "It Girl"). Richard Condon used the cliché in *The Manchurian Candidate* (1959): "They are with it, Raymond. Believe me."

with one's tail between one's legs, (to go off with) With a feeling of shame or embarrassment. The expression alludes to a dog that slinks off in defeat, a usage dating from about 1400. The transfer to human beings had taken place by the 1800s. W. E. Norris used it in *Thirlby Hall* (1884), "We shall have you back here very soon . . . with your tail between your legs." The French have an identical phrase, *s'en aller la queue entre les jambes.*

without a leg to stand on See LEG TO STAND ON.

without batting an eye Betraying no surprise or emotion, remarking nothing unusual. *Batting* here is an older word for "blinking," but the term dates only from the turn of the twentieth century. O. Henry used it in *Whirligigs* (1910): "I've stood by you without batting an eye, in earthquakes, fires, and floods."

without rhyme or reason See NEITHER RHYME NOR REASON.

with strings attached With some condition or limitation. This term originated simply as "a string" in the second half of the 1800s; "attached" was added a few decades later. Sandra Brown used it in her novel *Alibi* (1999):

"His fantasy evening with the most exciting woman he had ever met not only came with strings attached, but those strings were probably going to form a noose that would ultimately hang him." The term is also used in the negative, *no strings attached,* as in "They made a huge donation to the college with no strings attached; it was to be used however it was needed."

with the gloves off Rough treatment. This term alludes to the old style of boxing, in which the combatants fought barehanded; it is the opposite of handling someone with KID GLOVES. "Marion County has been handled without gloves," wrote Adiel Sherwood in his *Gazetteer of the State of Georgia* (1827).

wolf in sheep's clothing, a An enemy masquerading as a friend. The term comes from Aesop's fable about a wolf dressing up as a shepherd (in some versions, as a sheep) and sneaking up on the flock. In the Bible, Jesus warns of "false prophets which come to you in sheep's clothing but inwardly they are ravening wolves" (Matthew 7:15). The expression has appealed to hundreds of writers. Clare Boothe Luce (*Kiss the Boys Good-bye,* 1939) used it to describe a predatory male collegian: "A wolf with a sheepskin."

wonders will never cease That is really surprising. This expression, today usually put ironically and nearly always a response to a statement about something the speaker thinks is unusual, dates from the late eighteenth century. Anthony Price used it in *Other Paths to Glory* (1974): "Wonders will never cease . . . Early Tudor, practically untouched." This saying has become so familiar that Ed McBain could abbreviate it: "Would wonders never?" (*Hark!* 2004).

won't See under WOULDN'T.

word of mouth, by Orally. This phrase dates from the sixteenth century and persists to the present, though simply "orally" would be more direct. "A little message unto hir by worde of mouth," wrote Nicholas Udall in *Ralph Roister Doister* (c. 1553), presumably differentiating it from a written message.

words fail me An expression of surprise or shock, uttered when one does not know what to say: for example, "On their wedding day, she went to have breakfast with both of her former husbands—well, words fail me!" It dates from the second half of the twentieth century.

words right out of one's mouth, to take To agree with someone completely; to anticipate what someone else is about to say. This vivid image was expressed as long ago as the sixteenth century. Richard Grafton used it in *A Chronicle at Large* (1568; published 1809): "The Pope . . . takying their wordes out of their mouthes, said . . ."

word to the wise, a This is good advice; you would do well to heed this. Several Roman writers put good advice in just this way, saying, "A word to the wise is enough" (Plautus, Terence). Ben Jonson used it in his play *The Case Is Altered* (c. 1600): "Go to, a word to the wise." A somewhat more recent equivalent, also a cliché, is *words of wisdom.*

work cut out for one, to have one's To have trouble completing a task; to face a difficult job. This term, which alludes to a pattern cut from cloth that must then be made into a garment, has been used since about 1600. Anthony Trollope used it in *Orley Farm* (1862): "Everyone knew that his work was cut out for him."

work one's fingers to the bone, to To work extremely hard. This hyperbole, with its image of working the skin and flesh off one's fingers, dates from the nineteenth century. The eighteenth century had *to work like a horse;* Jonathan Swift used this version in his *Journal to Stella* (1710): "Lord Wharton . . . is working like a horse for elections." Some nineteenth-century exaggerators stated *to work like a galley-slave.* In America that translated into *work like a nigger,* which of course is offensive in the extreme (and probably was then, too).

work one's tail off, to To work very hard. This inelegant locution dates from the first half of the twentieth century. James Farrell used it in *Studs Lonigan* (1932–35): "This idea of sweating your tail off with work." It also is put as to work one's *ass* or *butt* off. See also BREAK/BUST ONE'S ASS.

world is my oyster, the Everything is going well for me. This metaphor, alluding to the world as a place from which to extract profit, just as one takes pearls from oysters, may have been coined by Shakespeare. He used it in *The Merry Wives of Windsor* (2.2): "Why then, the world's mine oyster, Which I with Sword will open." It is heard less often today.

world of good, a An enormous benefit. *World* has been used to mean "a great deal" since the sixteenth century, but this phrase dates from the nineteenth century and was generally used in connection with something that was beneficial to one's health. "The mountain air will do him a world of good," wrote Thomas Mann in *The Magic Mountain* (translated by H. Lowe-Porter, 1927).

worm turns, the The loser becomes a winner. The expression comes from an old proverb, *tread on a worm and it will turn,* meaning that the lowliest individual will resent being treated badly. It appeared in John Heywood's 1546 proverb collection and was repeated by Shakespeare. Robert Browning used it in *Mr. Sludge* (1864): "Tread on a worm, it turns, sir! If I turn, Your fault!"

worn to a frazzle Reduced to a state of nervous exhaustion. The word *frazzle* here means a frayed edge. It originated in America and also gave rise to *to be frazzled* (be nervously exhausted). The expression appears in one of Joel Chandler Harris's Uncle Remus stories (1881): "Brer Fox dun know Brer Rabbit uv ole, en he know dat sorter game done wo' ter a frazzle."

worry wart A person who agonizes unduly, anticipating failure or disaster or other misfortune. This slangy term, also spelled *worrywart*, dates from about 1930. For example, "'So who's alarmed?' I asked. . . . 'You were, Mr. Worry-wart. You saw the Health truck outside and what did you think? Sickness'" (James Patterson, *London Bridges,* 2004). See also NERVOUS NELLIE.

worship the ground someone walks on, to To hold in reverent regard. This hyperbole for great admiration or deep romantic feeling has an archaic ring to it. Indeed, Christopher Hale wrote, in *Murder in Tow* (1943), "He worships the ground she walks on. Bill thought there should be a closed season on that cliché for about twenty years." The season remains open.

worth its/one's weight in gold Extremely valuable; singularly useful. The Roman playwright Plautus was fond of this metaphor, which also appeared in several Middle English works of the early fourteenth century. Somewhat later Henry Medwall (*A Goodly Interlude of Nature,* c. 1500) wrote, "Nay ye ar worth thy weyght of gold," thereby becoming among the first of thousands to use the expression. See also WORTH ONE'S SALT.

worth one's salt, to be To be worth one's wages; a good employee. This term alludes to the practice of paying Roman soldiers with rations of salt and other valuable and essential items, whence the Latin word *salarium* (whence the English *salary*), or "salt money." The term was picked up by numerous nineteenth-century writers. Robert Louis Stevenson used it in *Treasure Island* (1883): "It was plain from every line of his body that our new hand was worth his salt."

wouldn't give someone the time of day See GIVE THE TIME OF DAY.

wouldn't touch it with a ten-foot pole Avoid it at all costs; stay away from it. The image of keeping one's distance by means of a long pole dates from the mid-eighteenth century. It was preceded by "not to be handled (touch it) with a pair of tongs," which appeared in John Clarke's *Paroemiologia* (1639) and was repeated by numerous others, including Dickens. In the nineteenth century *barge pole* was sometimes substituted for ten-foot pole. Barges pushed with poles are seldom seen now, so ten-foot pole is what has survived.

wrack and ruin See RACK AND RUIN.

wrath of God, look/feel like the Look a mess, feel miserable. Originally *the wrath of God* literally meant the anger of the Almighty, and it appears a number of times in the New Testament. Likening it to human appearance or feelings, however, dates only from the twentieth century. W. R. Duncan used it in *The Queen's Messenger* (1982), "Are you ill? You look like the wrath of God." It has largely replaced a late nineteenth-century synonym, *to look like the wreck of the Hesperus,* which alludes to a once very popular poem of 1841, "The Wreck of the Hesperus," by Henry Wadsworth Longfellow (it describes an actual shipwreck off the New England coast).

wreak havoc Create confusion and inflict destruction. *Havoc,* which comes from the medieval word for "plunder," was once a specific command for invading troops to begin looting and killing in a conquered village. This is what Shakespeare meant by his oft-quoted "Cry 'havoc' and let slip the dogs of war" (*Julius Caesar,* 3.1). Although the word still means devastating damage, to wreak it has been transferred to less warlike activities, as in "That puppy will wreak havoc in the living room." Henry Wadsworth Longfellow in the *The Birds of Killingworth* (1863) stated, "The crow . . . crushing the beetle in his coat of mail, and crying havoc on the slug and snail."

writing on the wall, the A presentiment or prediction of disaster. The term comes from the Bible (Daniel 5:5–31). During a great feast held by King Belshazzar, a mysterious hand appears and writes some words on the wall. Daniel is called to interpret this message and tells the king it is a sign of his coming downfall. Later that night Belshazzar is killed and Darius of Persia takes over his kingdom. The term is sometimes put as *handwriting on the wall.*

wrong end of the stick, (got hold of) the Mistaken, misunderstood; a distorted version of the facts. This expression, which some believe refers to a walking stick held the wrong way, presumably means that one cannot proceed very far, either literally or figuratively, if one does not hold onto the right end. Another theory is that it alludes to a stick kept in an outhouse, and grabbing the wrong end in the dark meant one got feces on one's hands. Whatever the precise origin, it began life in the fourteenth century as the *worse end of the staff,* a wording that survived into the eighteenth century. In the nineteenth century the current wording was adopted. Shaw was fond of it, using both *wrong* and *right* end of the stick in a number of plays (*Misalliance,* 1910; *Androcles and the Lion,* 1912; *Saint Joan,* 1924). See also SHORT END OF THE STICK.

wrong scent, to be on the To follow a false trail or track. This term, which comes from hunting with hounds, was already being used figuratively in Shakespeare's time. Laurence Sterne used it in *Tristram Shandy* (1705): "Tristram found he was up on a wrong scent."

wrong side of bed See GOT UP ON THE WRONG SIDE.

wrong side of the blanket, born on the Illegitimate. This term was current in the eighteenth century and may well be obsolete. Tobias Smollett used it in *Humphry Clinker* (1771): "My mother was an honest woman. I didn't come in on the wrong side of the blanket."

wrong side of the tracks, the The undesirable side of town. This term came into being after the building of railroads, which often sharply divided a town into two districts, one prosperous and one not. (Of course, the same phenomenon had existed prior to railroad tracks.) Thus Miss Cholmondeley wrote, in *Diana Tempest* (1893), "The poor meagre home in a dingy street; the wrong side of Oxford Street."

X, Y

X marks the spot This mark shows the scene of the crime, the hiding place of a treasure, or some other special location. Although this term dates only from the nineteenth century, the use of a cross or the letter *X* as a special indicator is surely much older. The *OED*'s earliest citation is from a letter by Maria Edgeworth in 1813: "The three crosses X mark the three places where we were let in." The term often appeared in romantic pirate stories in which hidden treasure marked on a map figured, as in Robert Louis Stevenson's *Treasure Island* (1883).

yada yada yada Also, *yadda, yadda.* And so on and so on. This term describes tedious or long-winded talk, and its origin is not definitely known. Possibly it imitates the sound of a person droning on and on. It was popularized from about 1990 on in *Seinfeld,* a television sitcom, and caught on very quickly. In one episode Marcy and George are speaking: "'Are you close with your parents?'—'Well, they gave birth to me and...yada yada yada.'" Jeffrey Deaver used it in *The Vanished Man* (2003): ". . . and she's going on about this guy, yadda, yadda, yadda, and how interesting he is and she's all excited 'cause she's going to have coffee with him." It is on its way to clichédom.

year in, year out Continuing, all the time, on and on. Although versions of this thought existed long before, this wording of it dates from the nineteenth century. Louisa May Alcott used it in *Little Women* (1868): "You see the other girls having splendid times, while you grind, grind, year in and year out."

yes and no That is partly true. This equivocal reply to a question dates from the mid-nineteenth century. C. M. Young used it in *Pillars of the House:* "'Do you come from his father?'—'Well, yes and no. His father is still in Oregon.'" A teasing version, originating in the twentieth-century schoolyard, is *yes, no, maybe so,* meaning, of course, wouldn't you like to know (the answer)!

you better believe it See YOU'D BETTER BELIEVE IT.

you (can) bet your (sweet) life) Absolutely; for sure. The idea that something is so definitely true that you can wager your life on it originated in nineteenth-century America. The *San Francisco Sun Dispatch* used it in 1852: "He's around when there's money . . . bet your life on that." Other versions are *you can bet your bottom dollar,* referring to the last of a pile of them, and *you can bet your boots* (also a valuable item), both of nineteenth-century American provenance, and *you bet your (sweet) bippy,* a euphemism for *you bet your (sweet) ass,* which was "bipped" out on television programs. The last two are both mid-twentieth-century Americanisms.

you can lead a horse to water but you can't make him drink You can create favorable circumstances for a person to do something but cannot force him or her to do it. This metaphor was already being used in the twelfth century, when horses were a principal mode of transport, and appeared in John Heywood's proverb collection of 1546. Several eighteenth- and nineteenth-century writers rang changes on it, mainly by increasing the second "you" to a large number. Samuel Johnson wrote "twenty cannot make him drink" (1763); Anthony Trollope made it "a thousand" (1857). In the twentieth century, keen-witted Dorothy Parker, in a speech before the American Horticultural Society, quipped, "You can lead a whore to culture but you can't make her think."

you can't fight City Hall See CAN'T FIGHT CITY HALL.

you can't make an omelet without breaking eggs To accomplish something, you have to be willing to make sacrifices. This term is a straight translation from the French (*On ne saurait faire une omelette sans casser des oeufs*), who not only invented omelets but transferred the term to other affairs. It was translated into English in the nineteenth century. Combining two clichés, General P. Thompson said, "We are walking upon eggs, and whether we tread East or tread West, the omelet will not be made without the breaking of some" (*Audi Alt,* 1859; cited by *OED*).

you can't make a silk purse out of a sow's ear You cannot turn something inferior or bad into something of value. This proverbial warning was issued in various forms from the sixteenth century on. It clearly had no literal basis; indeed, the absurdity of trying to turn pig's ears into silk (or velvet or satin, as some variants have it) no doubt helped the saying survive.

you can't take it with you It's of temporal value; you may as well enjoy it now. This phrase dates from the early nineteenth century. Frederick Marryat used it in *Masterman Ready* (1841): "He was very fond of money; but that they said was all the better, as he could not take it away with him when he died." The expression gained even wider currency when George Kaufman and Moss Hart used it as the title for one of their great comedies (1937).

you can't teach an old dog new tricks See TEACH AN OLD DOG.

you can't win 'em all It's impossible to succeed in every undertaking. This twentieth-century Americanism slightly antedates the synonym WIN SOME,

LOSE SOME, having originated about 1940. Also a philosophic view of losing, it appears in Raymond Chandler's *The Long Goodbye* (1954): "Take it easy, Doc. You can't win 'em all." In contrast, the shorter *you can't win* is generally spoken out of frustration with defeat and originated somewhat earlier, probably about 1910.

you could have heard (hear) a pin drop See HEAR A PIN DROP.

you'd better believe it You can be absolutely sure. An Americanism of the mid-nineteenth century, it appeared in print in 1856. The *Toronto Globe and Mail* used it in 1968: "You'd better believe it . . . We've got 'em." For a similar affirmation, see TAKE IT FROM ME.

you get what you pay for Inexpensive items may be of poor quality; a bargain may not be a good buy. This economic truism dates from ancient times and is a point of contention among today's value analysts. High price does not always indicate high quality, but it is hard to convince the buyer whose bargain-bin running shoes lost their soles in the first rainstorm.

you name it Just about everything you can think of about this subject. This colloquial phrase from the mid-twentieth century indicates a list of things too extensive to enumerate: for example, "He's been a smuggler, a gun runner, a dope peddler—you name it" (Dan Lees, *Zodiac,* 1972).

you pays your money and takes your choice See PAY YOUR MONEY AND TAKE YOUR CHOICE.

your call is important to us One of the frequent maddening phrases one hears over the phone when one is put on hold and is asked to wait "for the next available agent/operator/representative." It is often augmented with "We thank you for your patience," a quality that the person on hold is generally running out of. It doesn't seem to matter whether the call concerns an order, complaint, or a question; allegedly all calls are equally important. These usages date from the late 1900s, when waiting for calls to be put through became a kind of art form. Laura Penny used it as the title of her 2005 book, *Your Call Is Important to Us: The Truth about Bullshit.*

your guess is as good as mine I don't know the answer any more than you do. This American term first appeared in print in 1939, in Irene Baird's *Waste Heritage,* but it may have originated a decade or more earlier.

yours truly I, me, myself. This phrase has been used as a closing formula for letters since the late eighteenth century. By the mid-nineteenth century it was also being used as a synonym for "I," as in George A. Sala's *The Baddington Peerage* (1860): "The verdict will be 'Guilty, my Lord,' against yours truly."

you said a mouthful What you said is absolutely true or important or relevant. This American colloquialism dates from the early 1900s. Dorothy Parker used it in *Life* (Feb. 3, 1921), "'You said a mouthful.' I confess."

you said it You are absolutely right, I couldn't agree more. This colloquial Americanism dates from the first half of the 1900s. The British mystery novelist Dorothy Sayers used it in *Murder Must Advertise* (1933): "'The idea being that . . . ?'—'You said it, chief.'" See also YOU SAID A MOUTHFUL.

you should excuse the expression Please forgive what I just said or am about to say. This polite disclaimer for uttering a profanity, obscenity, or vulgarity was adopted from Yiddish about 1930 and became common soon thereafter. See also PARDON MY FRENCH.

you've got another think coming You're completely wrong. This phrase from the first half of the twentieth century uses *think* as a noun meaning "what one thinks about something." T. Bailey used it in *Pink Camellia* (1942), "If you think you can get me out of Gaywood, you've got another think coming."

Index

In this index, all cross-references refer to main entries in the body of the book, which are printed in **boldface** and are listed alphabetically. For example, the index entry "Hoyle, according to: *see* according to Hoyle" directs the reader to look up the entry **according to Hoyle** in the book, on page 1. In some cases very long entry names may be abbreviated in the index; thus "throw out the baby with the bath water" may be shortened to "throw out the baby . . ." Numbers are alphabetized as though written out ("catch-22" as though "catch-twenty-two"), and parenthetical words are ignored in alphabetizing ("straw[s] in the wind" is alphabetized as "straw in the wind").

H

O

U

X

Y